BUSINESS ETHICS

SAGE PUBLISHING: OUR STORY

We believe in creating fresh, cutting-edge content that helps you prepare your students to make an impact in today's ever-changing business world. Founded in 1965 by 24-year-old entrepreneur Sara Miller McCune, SAGE continues its legacy of equipping instructors with the tools and resources necessary to develop the next generation of business leaders.

- We invest in the right **authors** who distill the best available research into practical applications.

- We offer intuitive **digital solutions** at student-friendly prices.

- We remain permanently independent and fiercely committed to **quality, innovation, and learning**.

BUSINESS ETHICS

Contemporary Issues and Cases

Richard A. Spinello

Boston College

Los Angeles | London | New Delhi
Singapore | Washington DC | Melbourne

FOR INFORMATION:

SAGE Publications, Inc.
2455 Teller Road
Thousand Oaks, California 91320
E-mail: order@sagepub.com

SAGE Publications Ltd.
1 Oliver's Yard
55 City Road
London EC1Y 1SP
United Kingdom

SAGE Publications India Pvt. Ltd.
B 1/I 1 Mohan Cooperative Industrial Area
Mathura Road, New Delhi 110 044
India

SAGE Publications Asia-Pacific Pte. Ltd.
18 Cross Street #10-10/11/12
China Square Central
Singapore 048423

Printed in the United States of America

ISBN: 978-1-5063-6805-4

Acquisitions Editor: Maggie Stanley
Senior Content Development Editor: Darcy Scelsi
Editorial Assistant: Alissa Nance
Production Editor: Jane Martinez
Copy Editor: Rachel Keith
Typesetter: C&M Digitals (P) Ltd.
Proofreader: Barbara Coster
Indexer: Joan Shapiro
Cover Designer: Scott Van Atta
Marketing Manager: Sarah Panella

This book is printed on acid-free paper.

19 20 21 22 23 10 9 8 7 6 5 4 3 2 1

BRIEF CONTENTS

DETAILED CONTENTS

PART III • CORPORATE VALUES AND RESPONSIBILITIES

PART IV • GLOBAL CAPITALISM, CULTURE, AND JUSTICE

PART V • GLOBALIZATION AND CORPORATE RESPONSIBILITY

LIST OF CASE STUDIES

PREFACE

Business Ethics: Contemporary Issues and Cases is designed primarily as a core textbook for courses such as Business Ethics, Corporations and Morality, Business and Society, and The Moral Aspects of Corporate Leadership. Although *Business Ethics: Contemporary Issues and Cases* is primarily a casebook, it contains some background on capitalism and the nature of the corporation along with relevant theoretical material on ethics and corporate social responsibility. It also incorporates a number of briefings on public policy and management issues that may be unfamiliar to students (such as intellectual property rights, privacy and cybersecurity, bribery laws, and employee rights). While we focus almost exclusively on contemporary moral dilemmas and calamities, some older cases are included to give students historical perspective. The last several decades are littered with infamous corporate scandals that have damaged the reputation of whole industries and even the capitalist system itself, and students should have some familiarity with a few of these legendary ethical debacles.

Historical context can also help us to appreciate current cases such as the safety crises involving the Chevy Cobalt's faulty ignition switch and the defective Takata airbag. The automotive industry briefing provides an overview of the safety woes that have bedeviled this industry for many years so students can discern problematic patterns of behavior that resurface in those incidents. Similarly, we review the history of global capitalism, which vividly reveals the limits of the multinational corporation's ability to manage social and ethical issues effectively.

The aim of this book is to deepen every student's knowledge of business ethics, corporate social responsibility, and the management of nonmarket issues through an interdisciplinary methodology based on ethical theory, management principles, business history, political philosophy, and economics. Business students should not see management instruction as isolated from other disciplines such as economics, philosophy, and history. The ultimate goal is to help educate versatile corporate and organizational managers who are capable of making sound and responsible ethical choices and defending those choices with intellectual coherence and credibility.

The book is divided along the simplest lines possible into five parts. The first section is composed of theoretical material and provides a broad context for the case studies that follow. The theme of free-market capitalism is the springboard for an exposition of the book's overarching framework, which is centered on corporate purpose, defined in terms of the common good for which the corporation is organized. From this foundation, we derive the corporation's three fundamental obligations to society: create economic value, comply with all relevant laws and regulations, and observe common ethical principles. A second framework, which captures those ethical standards in a formula, is known by the acronym DRJ (duties-rights-justice). It is based on several traditional ethical theories that are explained with as much clarity and conciseness as possible.

The next four sections turn to the case studies, which are organized around three major themes: personal values, corporate values, and multinational responsibilities. These chapters keep clearly in view the perspectives of Part I. The first set of cases in Part II involve individuals struggling with different moral dilemmas, hoping to preserve their integrity in the workplace. The issues covered here include promise-breaking, deception, fraud, lying, cheating, and whistle-blowing.

Parts III and IV look at the corporation's values and its responsibilities to different external constituencies, such as customers and shareholders, and internal constituencies, such as employees. It focuses on the challenge of integrating competitive strategy with socially responsible behavior. The cases in these sections cover a range of topics: employee privacy rights, insider trading, marketing predatory products, product safety, environmental integrity, equitable pricing, fair competition, privacy, and cybersecurity. Some of the specific cases include Hobby Lobby's claim to religious liberty, Apple's contentious fight with the FBI over privacy, Volkswagen's "Dieselgate," Takata's airbag controversy, Microsoft's anticompetitive tactics in the browser wars, the LIBOR scandal at Barclays Bank, the BP oil spill in the Gulf of Mexico, and Valeant Pharmaceuticals' pricing strategy.

Part V is dedicated to cases involving multinational companies doing business abroad. One of the defining features of the new economy is the immense volume of global expansion through foreign direct investment. But investing in different political and cultural environments poses challenges for multinational corporations. They have struggled to develop policies respecting cultural diversity without accommodating injustice. Key themes in this section are the scope of corporate political activism abroad and the extent to which a multinational enterprise should adopt the customs and moral norms of a particular culture. Cases include Firestone's decision to support the dictator Charles Taylor in order to keep its rubber plantation in Liberia, ITT's misadventure in Chile, and worker abuses at Foxconn and Pegatron, two Asian companies making Apple products.

Finally, a word or two should be said about the state of business ethics and why this field continues to be of such crucial importance. The business ethics course is by no means a novel enhancement of the management curriculum. The Harvard Graduate School of Business Administration, founded in 1908, offered its first course on social issues in business in 1915, called Social Factors in Business Enterprise. Starting in 1928, Harvard offered an elective business ethics course. Harvard was not alone in this commitment to business ethics. By 1931, a number of schools had developed formal instruction on the ethical aspects of business conduct.[1]

Arguably, these courses have taken on a new urgency because of the proliferation of recent scandals that have touched virtually every major industry. There seems no end to this corporate malfeasance. As one reporter opined, "Almost every year, it seems, some scandal envelops a Fortune 500 company and causes a new spasm of public distrust of big corporations."[2] For pragmatic reasons alone, corporations should take ethics more seriously, and ethical coursework can certainly help. Fortunately, virtually every business school offers these courses, and in most cases they are a vital component of the business core. Harvard Business School, for example, teaches Leadership and Corporate Accountability to its first-year MBA students. The London Business School has offered a required ethics course for many years. And Catholic University of America has opened the School of Business and Economics, where the entire curriculum revolves around ethical and social issues.

Some students, of course, resist an ethics requirement. However, pragmatic students who question whether or not this course is worth taking should recognize the intrinsic value of business ethics courses. Lynn Sharp Paine, professor at the Harvard Business School, has made a compelling case that "moral thinking . . . is as essential for managers of profit-making businesses as the strategic or instrumental thinking which comprises the bulk of the typical business school curriculum."[3] A rigorous ethics course based on sound classroom material helps students to ponder business in a broader context so that they can become flexible thinkers with critical skills and can perceive the subtleties embedded in most moral dilemmas.

We hope this book will contribute to such a positive classroom experience. We also hope every student enjoys and profits from this book—it should inspire you to solve problems creatively and to always think beyond the bottom line.

DIGITAL RESOURCES

The **SAGE Edge** site for *Business Ethics: Contemporary Issues and Cases* by Richard Spinello offers a robust online environment you can access anytime, anywhere, and features an impressive array of free tools and resources to keep you on the cutting edge of your learning experience.

Visit **edge.sagepub.com/spinello**.

For Students:

- Multimedia and Web Resources
- Learning Objectives
- Quizzing
- Flash Cards

For Instructors:

- Test Bank
- PowerPoints
- Instructor Manual with Case Notes

ACKNOWLEDGMENTS

I would first like to thank the Carroll School of Management (CSOM) at Boston College for its ongoing and generous support of my teaching and scholarship. This school has been committed to the teaching of business ethics and corporate social responsibility for many years, well before these subjects became so fashionable. My special gratitude extends to my colleagues, to the chairperson of the Management and Organization Department, Judy Gordon, and to Dean Andy Boynton, for creating an environment so conducive to this sort of research. A special word of thanks should also be extended to former faculty members at Boston College, such as the late Professors Ray Keyes, Walter Klein, and George Aragon, for their inspiration during my early days as a business ethics instructor. Professor Aragon's wonderful book on *Financial Ethics* was particularly instructive. I also appreciate the support of current faculty members and administrators, including Associate Dean Richard Keeley, Professor Richard Nielsen, and Professor Sandra Waddock. I also thank Professor Dan Coquillete, former dean of the Boston College Law School. The materials developed for his courses on legal ethics have been a great help to me. Finally, I thank our former dean, Dr. Jack Neuhauser, now president of St. Michael's College in Vermont, for hiring me at the Carroll School and encouraging my career as a scholar and teacher.

I am also especially grateful to the CSOM students I have taught in globalization and business ethics courses over the years for their perceptive questions and comments. Both our MBA students and our undergraduates have helped me to write better cases and also to refine several of the key ethical arguments in this book. I am indebted to my colleague Professor Sarah Cabral for her helpful insights on some of the issues involving gene patents covered in Chapter 7. Special thanks to Michael Smith for assisting me in handling some of the logistics of manuscript preparation, and to Ezabel Lynch for her invaluable help in acquiring research material for this project. And many thanks also to the Boston College librarians for helping me track down necessary but sometimes elusive material.

At SAGE, I must thank both Darcy Scelsi for her adroit editorial assistance and scrupulous attention to this text and Jane Martinez for supervising the production process. I am also grateful for the careful reading and improvements provided by the copy editor, Rachel Keith. A very special thanks to my editor, Maggie Stanley, for her invaluable advice and complete confidence in this project. I have learned a great deal from working with her and her colleagues. Thanks also to those who reviewed the book in its different stages and offered constructive feedback for improvement and enhancements:

Cherie Ann Sherman, Ramapo College of New Jersey; Rochelle Brooks, Viterbo University; Lisa M. Sticca-Conrod, Fairfield University; Laura Gow-Hogge, Eastern Oregon University; David M. Kopp, Barry University; Joni A. Koegel, Cazenovia College; Si Hyun Kim, University of La Verne; George G. Klemic, Lewis University; Travis Dalton, Columbia College; William S. Brown, Marist College; Gail O'Connor,

Massachusetts College of Liberal Arts; Troy D. Irick, Huntington University; Mark M. Alexander, Fontbonne University; Joseph Bucci, Chestnut Hill College; Robert W. Halliman, Austin Peay State University; Sumi Srinivason, Cuyahoga Community College; John Moran, Wagner College; Michael P. Leeds, Eastern Michigan University; Rashada Houston, Florida A&M University; Rikki Abzug, Ramapo College; William Patrick Leonard, Rio Grande Foundation; Eric Reitan, Oklahoma State University; Matthew Caulfield, University of Pennsylvania; Michael D. Baumtrog, Ryerson University; and Thomas Baldridge, Gallaudet University.

Finally, I also wish to thank my wife, Susan, for her continued love and support. This was a long and sometimes demanding project made possible by her patience and encouragement.

The usual caveat about errors and mistakes applies.

Richard A. Spinello
September 2018
Dedham, Massachusetts

For the Brinton family,
Helen, John, Susan, Mark, Elaine, and Jill

ABOUT THE AUTHOR

 **Richard A. Spinello** is Professor of Management Practice at the Carroll School of Management at Boston College, where he teaches courses on ethics, leadership, and globalization. He is the author of numerous articles and books on business and business ethics, including *Global Capitalism, Culture, and Ethics.*

ETHICAL DECISION-MAKING FRAMEWORK

A Decision-Making Framework

The Three Fundamental Duties of Corporations

Duty 1: Creation of Value and Wealth

- Provide goods and services that enhance and support social welfare

- Allocate resources in a way that efficiently creates and appropriates value for shareholders and other stakeholders

- Sustain a long-term competitive advantage

Duty 2: Compliance with the Law

- Implement value-added activities within the rules of the game

- Adhere to the general laws of society and specific regulations that govern a particular industry

- Honor contracts, respect valid property rights, avoid fraud, refrain from unfair competition, and comply with fiduciary obligations to shareholders and investors

Duty 3: Observance of Common Moral Norms

- Exercise principled moral reasoning

- Respect basic human rights and moral duties that protect the well-being and dignity of persons whose interests may be affected by corporate actions

- Avoid compliance with unjust laws

- Endorse extralegal duties based on principles such as honesty and transparency that ensure free and open competition

THEORIES AND PRINCIPLES

PART I

WHY CAPITALISM?

Though my heart may be left of center, I have always known that the only economic system that works is a market economy. This is the only natural economy, the only kind that makes sense, the only one that leads to prosperity, because it is the only one that reflects the nature of life itself. The essence of life is infinitely and mysteriously multiform, and therefore it cannot be contained or planned for, in its fullness and variability, by any central intelligence.

—Vaclav Havel[1]

Socialism is the name of our desire.

—Irving Howe[2]

LEARNING OBJECTIVES

Upon completion of this chapter, you should be able to:

1.1 Discuss the broad economic ecology within which corporations and managers operate.

1.2 Recognize capitalism's requirement for an institutional framework and a supportive moral culture.

1.3 Explain the critical role of managers in sustaining free-market capitalism.

Thanks to recurring waves of corporate scandals, modern corporations have been subject to withering criticism in recent years for a lack of integrity. Corporations are frequently accused of moral turpitude and indifference. Some say that the corporation is ruled by Darwinian principles in its pursuit of profit and economic progress. Journalists once referred to the titans of American business as "robber barons." Hollywood movies like *Deepwater Horizon*, *Elysium*, *Wall Street*, and *The Constant Gardener* consistently portray inhumane, callous executives. According to Hollywood, corporate America is full of these moral villains who will stop at nothing to achieve success.

This reproach of the modern corporation is often linked with strident critiques of the present structure of capitalism. Artificial barriers to competition contribute to unprecedented rent-seeking as companies pile up unreasonably high profits. Many for-profit corporations clamor for preferential treatment from government regulators along with government subsidies when they fail. This crony capitalism, with its Wall Street bailouts, rigged regulations, and excessive lobbying, seems to have displaced the more authentic entrepreneurial capitalism that Adam Smith envisioned when he wrote *The Wealth of Nations*. While some call for reforms and a retrieval of this "true" version of capitalism, others are convinced that the only way to overcome corporate malfeasance is to radically transform the whole corrupt system. Missing from the scene today are thinkers like Ayn Rand and Milton Friedman who tend to valorize capitalism for its bountiful efficiencies.

Those who impugn capitalism contend that it disproportionately benefits the wealthy and powerful and exacerbates economic inequality. Some economists base their arguments on the fact that while there have been gains from the spread of global capitalism, those gains have not been evenly distributed. The income divide has deepened in China and Latin America in the wake of economic liberalization. This growing inequality has alienated those on the bottom of the pay scale and reinforced populist perceptions that globalization benefits only the elite. Capitalism's critics underscore these inequities along with the world's persistent poverty as a sign of capitalism's ongoing malaise. Perhaps a more socialistic economy can create the social justice and equality that we "desire" and dream about.[3]

Rhetoric aside, there is certainly some merit to these observations. An increase in income inequality undermines some of capitalism's ideological appeal as a fair system that compensates for hard work and innovative solutions. Modern capitalism unfortunately promotes inefficient cronyism and special access to regulators. When this happens, there is a misallocation of corporate resources from innovation and wealth creation to political bureaucracy. Moreover, while capitalism surely has the capacity to innovate and create wealth, it is too often prone to excess. Those excesses put the whole economy at risk by causing the financial collapse of 2008. Quite simply, capitalism has a difficult time moderating itself in a relentless quest for surplus profits and material rewards.

Even Bill Gates, billionaire and founder of the capitalist icon Microsoft, now claims that he is impatient with capitalism and its inability to help resolve broad social problems. He is especially concerned that new advances in technology, health care, and education tend to help only the middle class and to bypass the poor. He joins other critics like Naomi Klein who contend that the structures of capitalism impede the resolution of society's most severe social problems, such as environmental degradation and global warming. As the 2016 U.S. presidential campaign revealed, there is a groundswell of popular sentiment for socialism or at least for radical changes to the capitalist system.

There are frequent demands for more government regulation and income redistribution. Economist Thomas Piketty, for example, has proposed a plan to "save" capitalism by imposing taxes on capital and wealth in order to create a more egalitarian society.[4]

Yet while concerns about capitalism are warranted, what economic system can take its place? The problems with abandoning the market price system or free trade have been made abundantly clear by the failure of collectivist economies like Mao's China, where the state was the principal employer of labor. Few countries would want to emulate the socialist economies of Cuba and Venezuela or the isolationism of North Korea. The resources of land, labor, and capital are guided to their best use by the constant feedback of the marketplace. Moreover, an egalitarian distribution of goods, coerced by government's heavy hand, typically holds economic freedom and property rights hostage to an unworkable utopian vision. As Friedrich Hayek has pointed out, the pursuit of equality at any cost soon becomes the well-trodden "road to serfdom."

Is there a way to achieve capitalism's high economic performance without the heavy social costs? Can capitalism coexist with noble moral sentiments as Bill Gates suggests? And, is a more humanistic vision of a free-market economy possible? The creation of such an economy actually begins with fidelity to the values embedded in capitalism itself. Liberal capitalism is predicated on a web of values that includes economic liberty, private property rights, open and fair markets, and free-market clarity. Markets can work properly only if consumers are autonomous and well informed enough to make sound economic choices. Free markets depend on consumer sovereignty to direct society's resources to their most efficient use. Consumers must be able to judge the intrinsic value of the goods they seek to purchase or they will end up wasting their money. When this happens, scarce resources are not allocated efficiently or prudently. Markets also greatly depend on trust and cooperation, and trust is achieved primarily through transparency and candor. Lying, fraud, cheating, and deception subvert free markets and cause them to fail. The moral logic of capitalism, therefore, is severely strained when there is opportunistic behavior or selfish instrumentalism that undermines free, fair, and open competition.[5]

The endurance of competitive markets is also contingent on strong institutional foundations to support those free-market values. The proper institutional and legal frameworks are essential to enforce contracts, protect valid property rights, and ensure respect for fiduciary duties. Without well-defined property rights, enforced by law, the voluntary exchange that is the essence of a market economy is impossible. In addition, capital formation depends on strong fiduciary duties safeguarded by the law. Those duties constrain the self-interest of executives who are required to be loyal to the corporation and its shareholders and avoid seeking personal gains at the corporation's expense. In addition, direct government intervention in competitive markets is sometimes necessary when there are market failures such as externalities or information deficiencies.[6]

However, these institutional foundations that enforce the rule of law and preserve key market values do not go far enough. There is also a need for a stronger ethical commitment by managers and market participants. Respect for moral duties and basic human rights serves as an additional and welcome counterweight to the calculus of economic efficiency. Paying unfair, rock-bottom wages in Bangladesh may be efficient (and legal), but such a policy is inconsistent with the rights of workers for fair wages and benefits. Hence, a humane free-market economy depends on the support of a strong moral culture that encourages sensitivity to basic human rights and the demands of justice.

Through its social and educational institutions, this culture can foster in its managers those virtues needed for markets to achieve their objectives with minimal social cost. It can also provide the moderating influences necessary to temper market excesses, and thereby inspire a confidence in capitalism that goes beyond the economic elite. Economic activity, therefore, should ideally take place within a free polity under the rule of law and within a culture that emphasizes the benefits and burdens of personal and corporate moral responsibility.[7]

These issues may seem overly theoretical and irrelevant for a book on business ethics, but that is not so. First, some scrutiny of the capitalist system allows us to see the corporation and the issue of corporate social responsibility in a broader context. Students should certainly learn how to think critically about the economic system they will inherit. They must appreciate the complex ecology within which firms compete and workers make their living. Along these lines, it is instructive to consider different types of capitalism and evaluate which ones have the capacity to stimulate innovation and preserve economic liberty. Second, managers have a definite role to play in sustaining free-market capitalism. Above all, they must not destabilize the delicate moral and legal underpinnings of that system with an unprincipled focus on their own private interests. Managers should not exploit information asymmetries, violate fiduciary duties, or erect artificial barriers to competitive markets. Engaging in these activities not only damages the market ideals of transparency and fairness; it also potentially disrupts the free market in ways that might eventually lead to its demise.[8]

The case for capitalism is certainly strong, but we cannot overlook the precariousness of the capitalist achievement. The long-term success of the free-market system depends on containing its immoderation and reducing the enormous drag of transaction costs on the economy. Managers and corporations must be morally conscientious in order to ensure a more benevolent capitalist free-enterprise system that puts Adam Smith's goal of "universal opulence" in reach of wider segments of the global population.[9]

With all this in mind, the pages ahead will concentrate on the nature of capitalism and include a review of the basic archetypes of capitalism. We then give voice to the critics of capitalism along with some of their proposals to rectify the injustice of excessive wealth accumulation. We consider the institutional foundation of capitalism along with the role of those institutions in resolving market failures. After some treatment of the need for a strong moral culture, we briefly discuss the responsibility of managers to sustain free-market capitalism through "principled entrepreneurship": creating value while acting with integrity.[10]

WHAT IS CAPITALISM?

There are two main pillars of capitalism: property rights and a free and open market.

Property Rights

At the system's core, we find strong and extensive property rights. Individuals cannot trade goods or engage in market exchanges unless the law defines private-property rights. Each person needs to know what she owns and what she can sell or transfer to others.

Experience has shown that taking responsibility for one's own property enhances the common good and leads to greater prosperity. As Aristotle observed, "Property should be as a general rule, private; for, when everyone has a distinct interest, men will not complain of one another, and they will make more progress, because everyone will be attending to his own business."[11]

The **right of ownership** is actually a bundle of rights that are usually differentiated and defined in mature legal systems. That bundle of rights includes (but is not limited to) the right to possess (through exclusive physical control or the right to exclude others from use), the right to use, the right to manage, the right to income, the right to alienate (to sell or otherwise dispose of the property), and the right to security (that is, immunity from expropriation). In summary, **property rights** are best understood as full proprietary control over tangible or intangible things. Like most rights, property rights can be reasonably restricted and limited by the state for the sake of the common good.[12]

Capitalist systems typically support this extensive spectrum of rights for each individual property owner. But liberal capitalism also recognizes a broad scope of things that can be privately owned. Unlike in communism, so-called capital goods or the goods of production can be owned and controlled by private companies or individuals. Natural resources can also be owned by private citizens and corporations. In a purely laissez-faire market economy, there would be no restrictions on the sorts of things people could possess. However, a responsible government will prohibit ownership of some things such as people, and hence it will declare slavery to be illegal. The government will also own most of its infrastructure, such as roads, bridges, and seaports, so its citizens are not denied access. But in general, the capitalist ideal seeks to maximize the rights of ownership along with the range of objects that can be owned.[13]

Free and Open Market

The second pillar of capitalism is a free and open market. A "**market**" refers to the free choice of different parties to make certain exchanges. Individuals and companies "reassign" their property rights when goods are exchanged. In a market, participants have the opportunity to affect the allocation of resources through an expression of their preferences. A competitive market will send signals to producers that reflect the preferences or values of consumers. Thus, the market is a means for deciding how goods are to be produced and distributed based on consumer demand and willingness to pay. When the local shoemaker sells an abundance of her popular products for a price her customers are willing to pay, these transactions constitute a market where both buyers and sellers express their preferences. The price captures how those shoes are valued by the buyer, and the quantity sold reflects the level of demand for these products. In competitive markets, products that generate high profits will attract more sellers and thereby channel resources into more productive uses and draw them away from less productive uses.[14]

The market mechanism will also set wages or the price for labor. Those with special skills in big demand will command higher wages than unskilled laborers. Ideally, in a commercial society, there is a formal equality of workers with jobs open to all based on talent, skills, and experience. For every commodity in a well-functioning market, including labor, the forces of supply and demand determine the market-clearing price and the efficient quantity.[15]

As Adam Smith has explained, under certain conditions market capitalism allocates resources efficiently, producing the optimal outcome that maximizes social welfare. Society is guided to this result by an "invisible hand" that directs uncoordinated individuals to supply the right amount of goods that are demanded by consumers at a competitive price. When there is elastic demand, producers are incentivized to strive for lower production and sales costs in order to increase revenues by selling higher quantities at lower prices. Each seller in the marketplace acts in accordance with her own self-interest but also ends up promoting the social good. According to Smith,

> the natural effort of every individual to better his own condition, when suffered to exert himself with freedom and security, is so powerful a principle that it is alone . . . capable of carrying on the society to wealth and prosperity. . . . Every individual endeavors as much as he can to direct . . . industry so that its produce may be of the greatest value, . . . neither intending to promote the public interest, nor know[ing] how much he is promoting it. He intends only his own gain, and he is, in this, as in many other cases, led by an *invisible hand* to promote an end that was no part of his intention. By pursuing his own interest he frequently promotes that of society more effectually than when he really intends to promote it.[16]

As markets for particular products expand, they become more efficient, since they allow for the laborers to specialize. For example, as automobile and truck markets expanded, brake specialists emerged, which could make brakes cheaper and more efficiently thanks to experience curve effects and economies of scale. As Smith explained so clearly, "Division of labor is limited by the size of the market."[17] For Smith, division of labor and specialization are the engines of economic growth.

Open competition with minimal entry barriers is another feature of a well-functioning market economy. Competition disciplines market participants. If some producers charge artificially high prices and reap big profits, competitors will enter the market with a fresh supply of products that will force down the price. If consumers are looking for product features industry incumbents are unwilling to provide, new competitors will most likely fill this need. This competitive economic structure differs from a command-and-control economy and results in the most effective coordination of individual efforts. Socialist governments are often uneasy over the chaotic and disorderly free market and its apparent lack of coordination. As a consequence, the bureaucratic state seeks to guide it in one direction or another in accordance with some comprehensive economic plan. Often this intervention is counterproductive and misguided because it fails to reflect consumer needs and preferences. But Smith believed that a dynamic free market creates its own social order that results *spontaneously* from the cooperation and competition of ordinary people.[18]

With its emphasis on free and open markets, true capitalism in the spirit of Adam Smith leverages the power of competition to serve the diverse needs of producers and consumers. It rewards those who contribute to technology improvements or more efficient output. Entrepreneurs are free to bring innovative solutions to the marketplace with the support of investors who have faith in their projects. These firms will all be rewarded for their hard work and commitment if they can prevail against the competition by creating and appropriating value, which is accomplished by boosting willingness-to-pay without incurring commensurate costs. The entire system of market capitalism promotes upward social and economic mobility for a vast number of market participants.[19]

Defenders of capitalism argue that this system is necessary not only to deliver efficiency but to preserve economic and political liberty. A free-market economy can help safeguard essential political rights from encroachment by the state. The right to private ownership of productive property along with the right to freely enter contracts constrains the powerful forces of government. The experience of the last century has shown there is no substitute for the dynamic simplicity of market forces. At the same time, as we have noted, markets cannot survive without strong institutional support, so government has a conspicuous role to play in preserving a "free" and open market. Thus, as Charles Taylor has observed, "We can't abolish the market, but nor can we organize ourselves exclusively through markets."[20]

ARCHETYPES OF CAPITALISM

There is little doubt about capitalism's capacity to create wealth and expand prosperity, but what type of capitalism is apt to yield the optimal results? It is a mistake to make assumptions about the uniformity of capitalism. In a book called *Good Capitalism, Bad Capitalism, and the Economics of Growth and Prosperity*, William Baumol and his coauthors explain that there is no standard definition of capitalism and no ideal form of economic organization. Rather, they contend that there are several types of capitalism that are qualitatively different. Some capitalist economies are heavily regulated and approximate the visible hand of socialism, while others are firmly committed to more libertarian principles. Accordingly, they classify economies of capitalist countries into four different categories: state-guided capitalism; oligarchic capitalism; big-firm capitalism; and entrepreneurial capitalism.

While these models are quite distinctive, they share in common the recognition of private-property rights, including the right to own capital goods and the means of production, and this sets them apart from socialism. Also, in all these versions of capitalism, a preponderance of productive assets are in the hands of the private sector. Economies change over time and can evolve from one type of capitalism to another. An economy can be a mix of these different archetypal approaches to organizing a capitalist economy. There are some "precapitalist" economies that do not fit easily into any of these four prototypes. These economies will usually be found in very poor countries with primitive government institutions.[21]

State-Guided Capitalism

The first capitalist prototype is **state-guided capitalism**, which attempts to link the powers of the state with the powers of the free market. Governments assist the markets in selecting the economy's "winners," and they also direct the country's "economic traffic." They determine which firms and industries are especially promising and so deserve investment or special protection from outside competition. Sometimes the state exercises direct control by owning a majority share in the targeted companies. The Russian government, for example, has a 35% ownership stake in the country's natural gas monopoly, Gazprom. The state can support favored firms by means of tax breaks, subsidies, government contracts, and other mechanisms. But the state also relies on familiar capitalist tools for capital formation, such as listing state-owned companies on the stock market.[22]

Examples of state-guided capitalism include many of the countries in Southeast Asia and Latin America and, of course, China. In China, four state-owned banks dominate the financial system. State-guided capitalism also claims some of the global economy's most powerful companies, such as Russia's Gazprom, Brazil's Petrobras, China Mobile, and Saudi Basic Industries Corporation. Companies in state capitalist systems typically achieve success not through innovation and true entrepreneurship but by importing foreign technology and combining it with their own low-cost labor. State-guided capitalism can overlap with big-firm capitalism when there are many globally efficient national champions.

In recent years, state-guided capitalism has emerged as an ideological rival to liberal capitalism and perhaps even a modest surrogate for collectivism and central planning. State-guided capitalism tends to be skeptical about global trade and investment, and the result has been a shift toward "gated globalization." However, for the most part, state capitalists like Russia and China adhere to the rules of the global system and avoid most of the hazards of state-sponsored growth. State capitalism, however, has been a disappointment. Despite the merits of this system, which tends to limit economic inequities, state capitalism has so far been unable to deliver sustainable growth.[23]

Oligarchic Capitalism

Oligarchic capitalism is easily confused with state-guided capitalism, because in both cases the state is conspicuously involved in governing the economy. But government policies in the former system are oriented toward the promotion of the vested interests of a small segment of the population, such as the family and cohorts of the ruling autocratic dictator. The goals of economic growth or consumer welfare are far subordinate to the goal of wealth acquisition for the privileged few. Leaders in these economies seek growth only as a "peripheral" objective to placate the populace and prevent revolution. Most oligarchic economies exhibit extreme inequities in the distribution of wealth, which is usually found only in the hands of the political elite. They are plagued by cronyism, pervasive corruption, and intolerance of internal dissent. Moreover, within this economic culture, there tends to be considerable "informal activity," such as construction without permits along with an unofficial and chaotic system of property rights.[24]

Some African countries, such as Nigeria, Equatorial Guinea, and Angola, which suffer from the "resource curse" of superabundant oil, clearly resemble oligarchic capitalism. These regimes become easily addicted to the rents generated by oil, which are not shared with the general population. Between 1965 and 2000, the Nigerian government received $350 billion from the sale of oil. Yet while rulers and their cronies in this resource-dependent country live in great luxury, the vast majority of its citizens have remained in a condition of abject poverty.[25] At the same time, the sale of these natural resources raises the value of the currency and makes the country's other goods too expensive on world markets. Oligarchic systems built on natural resources like oil are usually controlled by autocratic leaders who invest heavily in military forces in order to preserve their political power and protect their vast wealth.

Big-Firm Capitalism

The third archetype is **big-firm capitalism**. In this case, the economy has a substantial proportion of very large corporations whose ownership is typically dispersed among institutional investors representing millions of small shareholders. These firms are run by elite professional managers who act as trustees of these principal investors. This sort of oligopolistic capitalism is found predominantly in the mature economies of Western Europe, the United States, and Japan.

The companies that operate in this environment pursue a classical business strategy: be big and create sustainable competitive advantage. Size, which creates economies of scale and scope, is a self-reinforcing benefit that protects these firms from new competitors. FedEx and UPS, for example, maintain their leadership in the express-mail industry because competitors would need to make huge cash investments to replicate their scale.[26] Platforms like Google, eBay, and Facebook also depend on the advantages of scale as they seek dominance in networked markets. Many of these companies that prosper under "big-firm capitalism" generate economic rents by harvesting well-established consumer brands. They strive to keep costs low, and they usually concentrate only on incremental innovations. Entrepreneurs in these firms dwell on the margins and usually do not provide the economic energies that fuel growth and profits.

Big firms, including conglomerates like General Electric, discount retailers like Walmart, and traditional manufacturers like General Motors, have become masters of efficiency. They cultivate close supplier relationships and consistently focus on cost controls and productivity gains. Others, like Microsoft and Intel, have exploited network effects in order to achieve winner-take-all status by locking in their customer base. On occasion, big firms (like Apple Inc.) can act like entrepreneurs, but most of them are ill suited to orchestrate major, disruptive innovations that change the way they do business.[27]

Some economists, including Joseph Schumpeter and John Kenneth Galbraith, have expressed reservations about an economic system dominated by too many large and powerful companies. Galbraith believed that the interaction of countervailing powers like trade unions (which negotiate the price of labor) and oligopolistic buyers disrupted the market and diminished competition. In the long run, the ineffectual state could easily become the servant of large corporations as regulators become "captured" by these potent economic entities. In addition, any of these massive corporations would go to almost any lengths to protect its economic rents, "which assures its autonomy and hence its survival."[28]

Entrepreneurial Capitalism

The last of the four archetypes is **entrepreneurial capitalism**. Under such a system, firms are far more visionary than in big-firm capitalism. Firms strive not to be big but to be first as they seek to "create" the future with some degree of predictability. The visionary firm thrives on a "blue ocean" approach: generate an exciting new product idea, a new business model, or even a whole new market, and occupy the center until rivals catch up.[29]

These innovations would not exist without highly motivated and talented entrepreneurs who perceive an opportunity to sell a bold new product or service that often disrupts or reshapes an entire industry. Consider the great entrepreneurial skill and foresight of someone like Apple's Steve Jobs, who conceived and designed the iPod, the iPhone, and the iPad. According to Jobs, the iPhone essentially "reinvented" the telecommunications industry. Or consider the extraordinary saga of Jeff Bezos, who was a pioneer in e-commerce and online retailing. His innovative company, Amazon, continues to radically restructure the whole retail industry. Of course, Amazon is also an example of big-firm capitalism, as Bezos delivers on his grand vision to dominate global retail along with the supporting infrastructure that other consumer businesses will need to access.[30]

With rare exceptions, such entrepreneurs have been found in capitalist economies (instead of socialist ones) where the innovator is amply rewarded for his or her efforts. Collectivism provides little or no incentives for entrepreneurs to take the risks necessary to challenge entrenched nationalist enterprises. Thanks to their communist heritage, many East European countries have a disappointing track record in turning start-ups into viable enterprises. In Poland, for example, a high fear of failure makes aspiring entrepreneurs unwilling to take the risks associated with starting and building new business ventures. Entrepreneurs must also combat low social status and other negative perceptions, which are not likely to motivate talented people to start new businesses. As a result, there are no Polish products that are internationally successful or well known in global markets. As the founder of Kozminski University once inquired, "Why is there no Polish Apple or Google?"[31]

Comparing the Archetypes

The U.S. economy is a special synthesis of entrepreneurial and big-firm capitalism. Entrepreneurs prosper in this dynamic environment where change and innovation quite often disrupt entrenched industries and established technologies. Economies cannot survive without entrepreneurs whose radical innovations fuel new waves of economic growth. But bigness still counts: size and scale are necessary to efficiently produce the most successful innovations discovered by entrepreneurs. These companies find ways to scale up their innovations at low cost and thereby prevail over the competition. Unlike state capitalism, the U.S. system exemplifies liberal capitalism with its commitment to property rights (including liberal intellectual property rights) and minimal state involvement.[32]

Baumol and his coauthors regard entrepreneurial and big-firm capitalism positively. In their view, these are forms of "good capitalism" because they promote innovation and efficiency. However, they are far less sanguine about state-guided capitalism, which is especially prone to cronyism and corruption. Politicians have far more power in this system than they do under liberal capitalism. The system is often rife with conflicts of interest. The state, for example, must regulate companies that it also operates. Can distracted politicians provide the necessary oversight of state-run businesses? On the other hand, state capitalism has been successful in building infrastructure. China, for example, has successfully engineered many world-class projects, such as Three Gorges Dam and its high-speed rail system. It has also been successful in producing many "national champions," corporations like Lenovo and Geely that compete effectively in global markets.[33]

However, there is a growing body of evidence that guidance and direction by the state are not the optimal path to economic growth. State-owned enterprises have underperformed in almost every country. Their share of global market capitalization shrank from its peak of 22% in 2007 to 13% in 2014. The woes of giant state-owned companies like Gazprom are well documented. The Russian government once boasted that Gazprom would be the first firm to be worth $1 trillion, but its worth in 2016 was only $73 billion. In China, investors have shunned the state-owned enterprise, China Mobile, in favor of private enterprises like Xiaomi.[34]

Yet despite its setbacks, state capitalism seems to be expanding while entrepreneurial capitalism is contracting. Through major corporate acquisitions by companies operating within state capitalist systems, the role of the state in the global economy is steadily expanding. Pure socialism has been vanquished, but state capitalism may be destined to take its place. As the *Economist* points out, the "defining battle" of the 21st century will not be between capitalism and socialism but between these different versions of capitalism.[35]

CAPITALISM AND ITS CRITICS

Some opponents of capitalism do not differentiate between "good" and "bad" versions of capitalism but favor an alternate system that resembles the centrally planned economies of the past. They prefer to see an expanded role for the state as the primary owner of income-producing assets. A chief complaint of market capitalism is the reliance on enlightened self-interest as the organizing principle for the economy. Self-interest can lead to an extreme "market ethic" of avarice as the prevailing motivating force of economic life. Second, capitalist efficiency and innovation are achieved at the high cost of inequalities in income and wealth. These inequalities are an inevitable result of the private ownership of all forms of capital along with market-determined wages and salaries. In this section, we elaborate on this general critique against capitalism and then concentrate on the specific problem of income inequality.[36]

Capitalist Excesses

Critics of capitalism say that the liberal market economy is impersonal and morally indifferent to everything but the end result. Efficiency is the preeminent value. The factors of production, including labor, become instrumentalized toward the objective of generating profits. For the most part, the market is single-minded in its dealings, and this is precisely why it is so productive and effective. It is blind to all other nonmarket dynamics, including race, religion, and social class. Since the market is impersonal and faceless, it can lead to great miseries and impose burdensome costs on innocent bystanders. It usually responds with alacrity and efficiency to general market forces, but not to social or moral considerations. Without more internal and external constraints, the capitalist model suffers from grave moral defects. There are three specific problems that have bedeviled the system of capitalism for a long time.[37]

First, markets and market participants are prone to excess. The self-interest praised by Smith as the cornerstone of free markets sometimes slides into selfish and even predatory egoism. Thus, one of the principal criticisms of capitalism is its inability to moderate itself when necessary for the sake of the common good or public welfare. These excesses create accumulations of wealth and intolerable inequities for society. During the housing boom of the last decade fueled by subprime mortgages, prosperous Wall Street bankers seized on unorthodox financial mechanisms to bet against that boom and amass huge profits and bonuses. They had little concern for the social ramifications of their actions. This culture of greed and secrecy on Wall Street inspired actions that constituted a mortal threat to the whole economy.

Second, in addition to capitalism's immoderate proclivities, competition, the essence of the free-market dynamic, often becomes a breeding ground for unethical behavior. According to economists like Andrei Shleifer, under some circumstances, intense market competition increases opportunities for opportunistic and self-centered conduct. When competition grows and market pressures are magnified, companies are more likely to pay bribes, cut corners on product quality and safety, or infringe on the rights of employees to preserve their market position. Consider the case of Microsoft, which became a rapacious and unscrupulous competitor when its market dominance was jeopardized by a new technology paradigm offered by the upstart company Netscape. The conclusion, which cannot be ignored, is that market competition is not always salutary but can easily lead to a lack of managerial restraint.[38]

Third, the social costs associated with market liberalism are disproportionate to its benefits. Most foes of capitalism concede that the system survives because it is capable of creating vast amounts of wealth for corporations and their owners. But they contend that the market along with the material rewards it fosters is not conducive to producing large social benefits. Free-market fundamentalists tend to exaggerate those benefits and conveniently ignore or rationalize the market's corrosive effects on society. As evidence, capitalism's adversaries cite how Walmart has destroyed so many small businesses and how many apparel and information technology companies have ruthlessly exploited workers in developing countries in their quest to find locations with the lowest possible wage structure. There is also a long list of multinational companies such as BP and Royal Dutch Shell that have misused environmental resources and failed to manage environmental externalities. As a result, the social costs of the capitalist achievement have been intolerably high for a long period. Hence, among some of capitalism's harshest foes, there is a pessimistic conviction that the exercise of economic freedom promoted by liberal capitalism will continue to yield the contamination of natural ecologies, the dissipation of communities, and even the loss of many human lives.[39]

Capitalism and Income Inequality

One of the most severe criticisms of capitalism is the claim that it grossly aggravates income inequality. Global capitalism has created a global plutocracy by making the wealthy even wealthier and by adding to their ranks. There have been some other winners besides the very rich, including the Asian poor and middle class. The biggest losers have been the lower middle class of Western countries, who have suffered lost jobs and lower wages thanks to globalization's relentless progress. Milanovic has presented convincing data that the total wealth of the hyper-wealthy (the top 1%) has more than doubled from 1987 to 2003. He has also demonstrated the dramatic negative impact of globalization on lower-class workers in Western economies.[40]

Karl Marx, author of the *Communist Manifesto*, pointed out many years ago that the capitalist system is a source of social and economic inequities in society. According to Marx's apocalyptic vision, capitalism would eventually self-destruct. As the gap between labor and capital grew to be intolerably wide, there would be a revolt of the proletariat marking the abrupt end of capitalism. It would be replaced by communism or socialism that would give priority to egalitarianism and bring to an end the huge wage disparities between laborers and the owners of capital. Some might contend that the current economic system is now veering toward a destabilizing level of inequality that confirms Marx's dire predictions.

However, the fall of communism and the Soviet Union seemed to sound the death knell for the planned economy along with Marxist economics. But despite the shriveling away of pure socialism across the globe, Karl Marx is back in fashion. The recent economic upheaval and the surprising success of 2016 presidential candidate Bernie Sanders have given new popularity to the Marxist creed. There have also been several Marxist-inspired critiques of capitalism that warrant some attention. The first is a highly popular book by Michael Hardt and Antonio Negri called *Commonwealth*. The goal of this new commonwealth is to "re-imagine" Marxism for the 21st century. According to Hardt and Negri, the time has finally come to get rid of private property, which only supports unjust social structures and excessive wealth that is undeserved by its owners. This abolition of private property will prepare the way for the "multitude," workers of all nations and backgrounds, to bring about the revolution once envisioned by Karl Marx.[41]

A subtler and more balanced critique is found in the work of Thomas Piketty. In 2013, Piketty, a French economist, wrote *Capital in the Twenty-First Century*, an intellectual phenomenon in both Europe and the United States. Echoing the themes of Thorsten Veblen's *The Leisure Class*, Piketty's dense inquiry concludes that the dynamics of private capital accumulation are leading to a dangerous concentration of wealth in very few powerful hands. At the same time, the counterbalancing forces of competition, economic growth, and technological progress have not succeeded in reducing that inequality.[42] As a result, our relatively egalitarian society is rapidly becoming more aristocratic. This trend is a threat to democracy and to the social values on which it is based. There is no doubt that Piketty's bleak message has resonated with many people. The success of this book reflects a declining confidence in the fairness and efficacy of market liberalism. Can there be a fair economic system when government fails to tame its biggest monopolies or control Internet platforms like Google that accumulate market power on the basis of scale? That lack of confidence should surely be of some concern to corporations and their executives.

Capital in the Twenty-First Century seeks to provide its readers with an objective look at the distribution of income and wealth based on facts rather than prejudice and opinion. Piketty sees some forces for convergence and equality, but far more forces for divergence and inequality. The diffusion of knowledge represents a push toward convergence, but the primary force for divergence is the low rate of economic growth. Piketty's study is premised on a central contradiction of capitalism, which we can neatly capture in the following formula,

$$r > g = I,$$

where r is the rate of return on capital, g is the rate of economic growth, and I is widening inequality.

His main argument is that "when the rate of return on capital exceeds the rate of growth or output and income, as it did in the nineteenth century, and seems quite likely to do again in the twenty-first, capitalism generates arbitrary and unsustainable inequalities."[43] It should be observed that Piketty uses *wealth* and *capital* as interchangeable terms, even though capital is a factor of production, and wealth can include assets that have value (such as artworks) but have no productive import.[44]

Piketty assumes that those whose income derives exclusively from their labor can expect their income to rise about as fast as the economy's productivity increase, which is a little less than the overall growth rate. On the other hand, those whose income comes primarily from their accumulated wealth earn r percent on their money. Moreover, these wealthy individuals are unlikely to consume more than a small percentage of that income. Thus, reasons Piketty, when the rate of return (r) on capital is higher than the economic growth rate (g), the income and accumulated wealth of the affluent will grow much faster than the income from work. Piketty demonstrates that according to the historical record, conditions will be such that $r > g$, and the end result will be a wider gap between the affluent and society's laborers or lower economic classes. Modern capitalism is an unequal society where the rich will continue to get much richer.[45]

Piketty's solution is predictable: higher taxes to correct this escalating inequity. He favors an annual progressive tax on wealth. A global tax would be optimal in order to prevent capital flight to tax havens, but a regional wealth tax in Europe or the United States is a more realistic possibility. He envisions this wealth tax with a rate schedule that would include a 2% tax on fortunes above €5 million (a euro is currently worth about $1.35).[46] These and other measures, such as higher inheritance taxes, will counteract the destabilizing forces of capital accumulation accompanied by inadequate economic growth. The tax, writes Piketty, "will make it possible to avoid an endless inegalitarian spiral while preserving competition and incentives for new instances of primitive accumulation."[47]

But is such a capital tax the most effective way to achieve this redistribution? Some economists, sympathetic with Piketty's overall analysis, are not so convinced about this. There is ample research confirming that a wealth tax may be both inefficient and counterproductive. Such a tax does not address the problem of income inequality or deal with large earned income disparities. Moreover, Piketty's drastic approach is not the only way to achieve the redistribution he is advocating.[48]

Other economists accept Piketty's analysis of the growth rate but are skeptical about the overall impact of investment returns. Returns on financial assets have declined appreciably over the past 30 years, with bond yields being at their lowest level ever. Future returns on wealth and capital are very much in doubt. Thus, while g may indeed have fallen, so will the future rate of r. These economists also contend that Piketty fails to take into account other factors that reduce the net return to investors, such as taxes and fund-management expenses.[49]

How serious a problem is the economic inequality described by Piketty? Can it threaten Western capitalism and political stability? Capitalism now dominates the entire world, even though it takes different forms. Despite its shortcomings, there is a palpable wariness about resurrecting insular collectivist economic systems. Also, the deglobalization called for by the foes of capitalism will most likely result in a regressive pattern of slower economic growth. In addition, central planning and even extreme income redistribution would unquestionably threaten economic liberty and create an expensive government bureaucracy. Can innovation ever flourish without strong market incentives? Thus, there are ideological, Marxist-inspired challenges to capitalism, but can they be translated into a realistic substitute for this highly efficient economic system that preserves economic and political freedom?[50]

Piketty's supporters might concede some of these points, but they still contend that his main message about the system's crass inequalities should not be casually discounted. Vast accumulations of wealth can have destabilizing economic and social effects. When capital reproduces itself so fast, the wealthy leverage their successes into an enduring dominance whereby the "past devours the future."[51]

GOVERNMENT INSTITUTIONS AND MARKET FAILURES

There are many convincing arguments about capitalism's flaws and excesses. However, those critics who point out that the fulcrum of market capitalism is greed (or what Smith calls self-interest) fail to acknowledge that liberal market capitalism will not reach its objectives without self-imposed limits along with external governance mechanisms. Capitalism quickly becomes dysfunctional if it operates within an institutional void. Those market values, such as transparency and fair play, that are intrinsic to capitalism's success will sometimes be disregarded by corrupt businesses. As a result, corporate behavior must be regulated so that conscientious companies are not forced to compromise their integrity by unethical competitors.

A free-market system, therefore, needs a strong institutional foundation, with an independent judiciary, a free press, and an adequate, unbiased legal framework. That legal system is essential to ensure the protection of property rights, the enforcement of contracts, and the prevention of third-party interference with market exchanges between buyer and seller. When institutional support is weak, when laws are vague or unenforced, authentic free-market capitalism is simply unsustainable. Fiduciary obligations to investors, for example, help ensure capital formation and economic expansion, while laws forbidding bribery and corruption seek to maintain a level playing field among competitors. The market cannot survive for long unless it functions within such a highly developed institutional context.[52]

Government institutions also provide a corrective to markets when markets fail and fall short of the competitive ideal. Market failure does not suggest a complete breakdown, but merely implies that the market is producing less than optimal results. When the market fails, market transactions do not fully account for the costs and benefits received by others. The results are inefficiencies in the allocation of resources that are harmful to social welfare. The competitive ideal supposes many buyers and sellers (no monopolies or oligopolies), minimal entry barriers, no differentiated goods or services, clearly assigned property rights, perfect information, and no switching costs. Since markets function efficiently only under these conditions of perfect competition, which are not always easy to satisfy in the real world, market failures are commonplace.[53]

There are four generic forms of market failures: imperfect competition, public goods, externalities, and imperfect information. Markets fail when they are dominated by one seller or a few sellers who limit competition. The market might be a natural monopoly, where the optimal number of sellers is one, or it might be more efficient to have only a few rivals operate within a given industry, especially if there are high scale economies. In other situations, firms engage in strategic behavior to constrain competition and create an oligopolistic structure where there should be a wider rivalry. But these forms of limited competition lead to waste and economic inefficiency. In the absence of competition, monopolists and oligopolists will underproduce, charge higher prices, and reap monopoly rents; without the push of competitive rivalry, there are fewer incentives for innovations and no pressure to lower prices.[54]

Government agencies play a key role in curtailing monopoly power and forbidding any strategic behaviors that serve to discourage new market entry. In the United States, for example, the Sherman Antitrust Act, enforced by the Department of Justice, prohibits abuses of monopoly power and places other restraints on interstate and foreign commerce. In 1914, an amendment to the Sherman Act established the Federal Trade Commission (FTC), a federal agency responsible for preventing unfair methods of competition. Without these vigorously enforced laws, it is unlikely that the free market could sustain a level playing field where firms in most industries compete with each other on the merits of their products and prices.[55]

A second market failure is negative externalities. These are side effects of production that impose costs involuntarily on others who are powerless to affect the decisions about that production. Markets tend to overlook environmental externalities, which leads to the underpricing and overproduction of those goods that pollute the environment. A cement company that constantly spews soot into the environment by burning its waste imposes a cost on others that is not reflected in the price of the cement nor in the amount of cement supplied. If the manufacturer had to internalize these costs, the price of cement would increase and production would decrease. Without the visible hand of government, the social cost of pollution and other negative externalities is apt to be quite excessive. The Environmental Protection Agency (EPA) regulates environmental externalities, and many companies rely on its regulatory schemes to manage the environmental impact of their operations.[56]

Informational deficiencies and inaccuracies represent another source of market failure. Efficient markets rely on the availability of clear and unbiased information. If there are information asymmetries, one party (the seller) is in a position to exploit the other party (the buyer). Asymmetric information and opaque transactions clearly impede the imperative of free-market clarity. In these situations, the seller is better informed than the potential buyers about the quality of goods he is attempting to sell. Buyers will then be forced to expend resources to confirm the quality of these goods. Sellers will also be inclined to invest considerable resources in order to convince a skeptical public about the quality of their merchandise. These activities entail transaction costs that create no value, and so the end result is an inefficient use of society's resources. Some social critics also maintain that opaque technologies such as Google's search algorithms are one of the biggest threats to the proper functioning of the capitalist system.[57]

Finally, some goods such as "public goods" cannot be adequately supplied by independent markets in sufficient quantities. These public goods exhibit two features. First, their consumption is nonrivalrous. This means that unlike private goods (such as a cake), one person's consumption of a public good (a cake recipe) does not reduce what is available for others. These goods are also nonexcludable, which means that it is difficult to exclude or fence out those who haven't paid. Public goods include information-based goods such as books, movies, and music along with the formulas for pharmaceutical products. They are all vulnerable to free riders. There is a strong temptation to imitate others' innovations or to "free ride" on their contributions. As a consequence, these goods tend to be underproduced in unregulated markets that lack some sort of protection such as patents and copyrights. Pure public goods include environmental goods such as the ocean or a forest habitat for owls. In most countries, privately owned corporations provide private goods, while the government is responsible for maintaining public goods such as clean air and unpolluted waterways. But every company is expected to do its part to conserve public goods such as a stable ecosystem. However, markets reward producers for the private goods they produce but not for the public goods they might choose to preserve.[58]

In an imperfect world, these market failures and inefficiencies are an inevitable byproduct of free-market competition. In some instances, it might be possible to wait for the market's self-correcting mechanisms to take effect. Free-market fundamentalists contend that in due time, competitive markets will dissipate their own failures and thereby bring about the most efficient use of economic resources. For example, the problem of asymmetric information in the automotive industry that might harm consumers has been largely corrected by third parties that provide objective information about vehicle costs and qualities. In general, market-based solutions are advantageous, since they are voluntary and usually less expensive than solutions imposed by government.

However, while the market itself can bring about some progress in eliminating certain imperfections and correcting externalities, government intervention will be necessary to fix most of these failures. The warrant for government intervention in situations of market failure should be twofold: (1) the failure must be serious and harmful; (2) there is a high probability that government intervention will be welfare enhancing such that its benefits will exceed the cost of intervention. Market failures are an unfortunate reality of the free-market system, and they do reduce social welfare. If governments can correct these failures in a cost-effective manner, they create value similar to the way successful private firms create value.[59]

MORAL CULTURE AND MODERN MANAGERS

Social and political institutions that oversee free markets from outside the system are a necessary but not a sufficient condition for the ultimate success of those markets. There is an overwhelming consensus that these institutions are necessary to address the defects of liberal market capitalism, such as social costs or the lack of competition. A more controversial proposition is that the market's long-term success also depends on prudent managers who follow basic moral norms for the conduct of their business. Even when there is the rule of law supported by a strong institutional framework, responsible corporate behavior is not guaranteed. And that corporate malfeasance can sometimes do damage to market capitalism and its credibility.

Without transparency, loyalty, and fairness that go beyond legal requirements, markets will struggle to function efficiently and smoothly, since trade-offs between risk and reward will be too obscure. Markets demand trust, and trust is fortified when market players abide by agreements and contracts without duplicity, gamesmanship, or the exploitation of legal loopholes. Trust breaks down when deception or clever deceit leads to compromised market outcomes or when privileged "insiders" rely on opaque complexities to generate excess rents to the detriment of other market participants. A successful economic culture, therefore, will always depend on the principles of justice and fair play rather than the primacy of self-interest.

In the long run, markets will not thrive if corporations and managers are so preoccupied with efficiency and opportunism that they become incapable of self-moderation. How many times can markets endure a financial collapse that brings the global economy to the precipice of disaster without demands for a fundamental revision of the whole economic system? But sometimes the always-evolving legal framework, which facilitates capital formation, cannot suitably restrain the reductive self-interest of market participants. The legal system could not have anticipated the dense financial mechanisms and opaque trading schemes that were instrumental in exaggerating the collapse of the housing market that led to the Great Recession of 2008. Markets need the additional restraint of moral codes and informed public opinion, which encourage ethical self-regulation. Mature moral behavior can also forestall future regulations and so limit transaction costs that can easily become a drag on the economy and a barrier to innovation.[60]

It follows, therefore, that a well-functioning market requires a strong moral culture that will reinforce those moral values that can tame the excesses of capitalism and inspire greater confidence in this economic system. A durable moral culture creates the epistemic conditions necessary for the recognition and assimilation of moral truths about the rights of others along with marketplace duties such as honesty and fair play. Cultural institutions such as church, family, and education are responsible for developing virtuous habits and correcting human vices. And the market will reflect the well-formed habits of its surrounding culture.[61]

Within such a moral environment, managers will be well attuned to the need for virtues like moderation and self-discipline that offset and mitigate the impulse of self-interest that drives the system. These virtues are not accidental to a sound economic order but essential for its ultimate success. A weak or disordered moral culture, on the other hand, will hamper the ability of managers to develop moral discipline or to think soundly about moral issues. As Aristotle explained, "To be a competent student of what is right and just, and of politics generally, one must first have received a proper upbringing in moral conduct."[62]

It also follows that every corporate manager and executive has a definite role to play in sustaining the integrity of free markets by preserving candor, responsiveness, fairness, reliability, and other key moral principles that underpin the stability of market capitalism. The market will ultimately flounder and lose the public's trust and confidence if its participants are consistently guided by selfish instrumentalism. It has been over a decade since the 2008 recession and the panic over financial markets, yet the trust in those markets and Wall Street institutions has still not been fully restored. That lack of trust inhibits the capital formation needed to drive economic growth.[63]

How can individual managers cooperate in sustaining market capitalism? Consider their economic and ethical responsibilities for the proper deployment of information. As we have emphasized, well-functioning markets always depend on equal and fair access to information. Market success should not be based on unfair information advantage but on real productivity gains and authentic innovations. The legal but opportunistic manipulation of information through strategic disclosures and omissions creates serious distortions that can affect the capacity for markets to function competitively. There is ample evidence that some corporations use their information advantage to structure market institutions to further their own private interests.[64] Former Federal Reserve chairman Alan Greenspan has opined that markets are now driven by an "unredeemably opaque" adaptation of Adam Smith's "invisible hand." This knowledge gap to which he refers is not intrinsic to markets, but deliberately fostered in order to gain the upper hand over clients and to confound regulators. Such opacity, however, endangers not only financial markets but the entire free-market culture.[65]

If managers sincerely believe in the merits of free-market capitalism, they have a duty to reinforce the operations of competitive markets rather than to deliberately undermine them. Executives on Wall Street, therefore, can help to sustain the moral and political legitimacy of market liberalism by embracing the moral principles of honesty and transparency. Those principles preclude murky accounting procedures that obscure risk. They also preclude reliance on those complex "black box" trading schemes favored by some financiers. Instead, they would require transparent financial reporting and demand that investors or customers be provided with relevant, accurate, and timely information. Markets benefit immensely when both regulators and investors can accurately assess the quality of securities and financial assets.

Thus, as summarized in Figure 1.1, open and free markets are critically important, but they are not the sole essence of authentic market capitalism as some have surmised. Markets heavily depend on the order provided by the rule of law and external institutions along with a robust moral culture that encourages "principled entrepreneurship."[66]

FIGURE 1.1 ■ Requirements of Market Capitalism

Open and Free Markets　　　Legal and Social Institutions　　　Strong Moral Culture

CONCLUSION

So what is the "big picture," and what does it mean for corporations, executives, and students of business ethics? First, the free-market economy, relying on self-interest as the key motivating force in economic life, is superior for delivering efficiency and creating wealth. But we must acknowledge the trade-off between ethics and efficiency. Efficiency comes at the cost of inequality in wealth and income, while self-interest too easily slides into greed. Yet there are certain values and restraints embedded in authentic free-market capitalism that impose limits on self-interest. Values such as transparency, consumer sovereignty, reward for contribution, and open competition are essential for the success of free markets.

Second, in an ideal world, managers would voluntarily abide by these values that sustain competitive markets. But in reality, some will always try to cheat and subvert the system. Hence, the success of market capitalism is contingent upon the rule of law along with external institutions to formulate and enforce the law. Without an independent judiciary, a free press, and government agencies to apply the principles of fair competition, the markets will not function efficiently. The state is also needed to correct the inevitable market failures that reduce social welfare. At the same time, a suitable moral culture endorses moral principles that can fill legal vacuums or policy voids and also promotes the protection of human rights. A culture that extols the values of personal responsibility, solidarity, and ordered liberty can help markets to deliver efficiency and economic growth without a high social cost.

Third, managers have a critical role to play in sustaining market capitalism. Their unprincipled behavior can undermine the critical value structure on which the market depends so heavily. A manager's actions have ramifications that go well beyond the firm and its immediate stakeholders. The cumulative effect of corporate malfeasance could damage the legitimacy of market capitalism. On the other hand, if entrepreneurs foster free-market clarity and open competition, they can contribute to the flourishing of market capitalism and the freedom from want that it is quite capable of providing.

Student Study Site

Visit **edge.sagepub.com/spinello.**

Key Terms

big-firm capitalism 10

entrepreneurial capitalism 11

market 7

oligarchic capitalism 10

property rights 7

right of ownership 7

state-guided capitalism 9

Review Questions

1. What are the characteristics of the economic environment corporations and managers are currently operating in?

2. State the need for institutional involvement in a capitalist economy.

3. Describe a manager's responsibilities in sustaining free-market capitalism.

Discussion Questions

1. Is there a way to balance high economic performance and social responsibility?

2. What are the optimal results of capitalism?

3. Do you agree that a moral culture needs to exist in a free-market economy? Defend your response.

CORPORATE MORAL AGENCY, PURPOSE, AND RESPONSIBILITIES

In both law and the culture, the corporation was considered a subordinate entity that was a gift from the people in order to serve the public good. So you have that history, and we shouldn't be misled by it, it's not as if these were the halcyon days, when all corporations served the public trust, but there's a lot to learn from that.

—Richard Grossman[1]

Did you ever expect a corporation to have a conscience, when it has no soul to be damned, and no body to be kicked?

—Edward Thurlow[2]

LEARNING OBJECTIVES

Upon completion of this chapter, you should be able to:

2.1 Explain the rationale for the corporation and its moral agency.

2.2 Appraise different perspectives on the corporation's purpose and scope of responsibilities.

2.3 Apply the basic framework for the case analyses.

A large portion of this book is dedicated to the theme of corporate responsibility, but in order to understand this concept we must first present a proper moral vision of the corporation. It is essential to explore the corporation's moral and legal status before we can fully account for its misconduct. Does the corporation itself possess a certain subjectivity or moral agency that requires it to assume the burden of moral responsibility, while it also obliges society to respect certain corporate rights? Many philosophers and legal scholars have argued that there is enough of a likeness between the person and the corporation to warrant assigning the corporation itself blame for its misdeeds. For example, the U.S. Coast Guard Bureau of Ocean Management's report held BP accountable for the Deepwater Horizon explosion and the massive oil spill in the Gulf of Mexico. According to the report, BP as a corporate person was responsible for the negligence and moral indifference that led to the loss of life and the subsequent contamination of the gulf's ecology.[3]

If we can intelligibly speak about corporate personification and corporate duties, what about rights? Does corporate personhood mean that companies should be extended some of the same rights as natural persons? The U.S. Supreme Court has been fairly generous in awarding constitutional protections. In recent Supreme Court cases such as *Citizens United* and *Hobby Lobby*, corporate claims to rights such as free speech and religious liberty have been vindicated, to the dismay of those opposed to liberty rights for corporations. Hence a second related issue for discussion is the validity of these constitutional protections for a corporate entity.[4]

Finally, what is the purpose of this corporation that seems to enjoy some of the same rights as natural persons? Does the firm exist just to make a profit and enrich its owners? Or does it have a broader purpose that includes a social agenda? Critics of corporate personhood and rights tend to possess a low vision of the corporation as nothing more than a moneymaking machine with minimal moral standards. But others argue for a higher purpose and more demanding standards. There are two theoretical views of the corporation's purpose that are presented in this chapter. The first view is known as the property model and the second is called the social entity model. We explain the arguments supporting both of these alternatives and invite you to make your own choice about the role of the corporation in modern society.

In our treatment of these three interrelated issues, we make a modest case for corporate moral agency. The corporation has a conscience and can be held accountable for its actions and policies. But if the corporation qualifies for moral agency, it follows that, like all moral agents, it also has certain obligations to society. Those core obligations, which are sometimes in conflict, fall into three broad categories: creation of wealth, compliance with the law, and observance of common moral norms. By accepting the burden of conformity to the precepts of law and morality in pursuit of its economic mission, the corporation shares in the benefits of social harmony and a well-functioning capitalist system.

THE CORPORATION AND THE TRIUMPH OF CORPORATE RIGHTS

In his famous article "The Nature of the Firm," economist Ronald Coase explains with admirable clarity why the corporation exists. Instead of incorporation, asks Coase, why not license the production and marketing of your product to others? Further, why not rely almost exclusively on temporary or contract workers who can be used on an ad hoc basis? The problem is that going to the market all the time drives up transaction costs. Finding good staffing agencies, negotiating prices, and drawing up and enforcing contracts are time-consuming and expensive. But employing permanent workers, organizing your own production, and hiring your own marketing experts solves this transaction cost problem. The firm, according to Coase, is a means of creating long-term contracts when short-term ones are too inconvenient and costly. Thus, many entrepreneurs choose to lower the transaction costs of going to market by incorporating or forming firms.[5]

A **corporation** is a group, organized for a business purpose, that has been authorized by a sovereign state to act as a single entity and is recognized as such in law. A new corporation is created through a simple process of registration. Registered corporations assume a legal identity. They can enter into contracts and own property. They are typically owned by shareholders whose liability is confined to their investment. Limited liability is one of the major attractions of incorporation. In the vast majority of cases, shareholders do not directly manage the corporation in which they have invested their capital. Instead, they elect or appoint a board of directors to control that corporation. The board hires a chief executive officer, who in turn employs a cadre of professional executives to help him or her manage corporate affairs. All of these professionals have a fiduciary obligation to act in the best interests of the owners or shareholders. According to the American Law Institute, "A corporation should have as its objective the conduct of business activities with a view of enhancing profit and shareholder gain."[6]

Thus, the corporation is analogous to a person in the eyes of the law, but how should we interpret this analogy? Does it merely mean that the corporation can enter into contractual agreements and is obliged to pay its taxes? Or does the corporation, distinct from its members, possess enough aspects of human personhood to warrant certain constitutional protections? A review of the extensive jurisprudence dealing with this issue is instructive in order to understand the rich contours of this debate.

The first seminal legal case that grapples with the corporation's peculiar status was *Trustees of Dartmouth College v. Woodward* (1819). In that decision, Chief Justice Marshall rendered a precise legal definition of the corporation: "The corporation is an artificial being, invisible, intangible, and existing only in contemplation of law. Being the mere creation of law, it possesses only those properties which the charter of its creation confers upon it, either expressly, or as incidental to its very existence."[7] The corporation exists to manage its affairs and hold property without the intricacies of transferring that property to new groups of individuals. Although the Constitution never refers to the corporation, the *Dartmouth College* decision affirms that the corporation is a distinct legal entity. According to Pollman, "The decision thus recognized the corporation itself as 'an artificial being' having constitutional rights to protect the property interests of its individual donors."[8] Corporate contracts were entitled to the same level of protection as contracts entered into by natural persons.

However, according to Marshall, this "creature of law" could possess only those characteristics that a state or federal charter conferred upon it. The corporation possessed certain properties of "individuality," but it was conceived as a "person" only for special purposes in "contemplation of law."[9] As an abstract or "fictional" entity, the corporation did not possess a moral persona. While Marshall's opinion flirts with the idea of corporate personhood, it ultimately maintained that the corporation, apart from its members, possesses no intrinsic features that warrant any moral consideration. Nonetheless, *Dartmouth College* represents the legal foundation for treating corporations as individual agents who could make contracts or own property.[10]

The first case that awarded the corporation strong constitutional protections was *Santa Clara v. Southern Pacific Railroad Co.*, which was handed down in 1886 by the U.S. Supreme Court. In this case a California railroad tax was challenged based on the railroad's assertion of its Fourteenth Amendment equal-protection rights. The court ruled in the railroad's favor as it affirmed that the Equal Protection Clause of the Fourteenth Amendment did indeed apply to the business corporation.[11] According to Margaret Blair, the *Santa Clara* case "was the first time the Court had ever ruled that corporations had constitutional rights as 'persons.'"[12] The court reasoned that corporations needed the important Fourteenth Amendment rights of equal protection and due process in order to properly safeguard the property rights of its shareholders.

Two decades later in *Hale v. Henkel* (1906), the Supreme Court ruled that a corporation is protected by the Fourth Amendment against "unreasonable searches and seizures." In that same case, however, the court ruled that a corporation could not assert Fifth Amendment protection against self-incrimination because it is not a "natural person." The court's logic behind granting Fourth Amendment protection rested on corporate personhood. The majority opinion envisioned the corporation as an independent legal actor that needed and deserved property rights such as the protection of its "papers and effects" from being unreasonably searched or seized by the government. What the corporation did not require, however, were liberty rights, including the right against self-incrimination.[13]

Despite the verdict in *Hale v. Henkel*, corporations soon won those liberty rights. The *Bellotti v. First National Bank of Boston* ruling in 1978 declared that the corporation had a limited right to free speech. The Supreme Court's 5–4 decision, written by Justice Powell, struck down a Massachusetts state law that banned corporate spending used to influence referendum elections. In its oral arguments, the Massachusetts legal team had emphasized the asymmetry between business corporations and natural persons, but those arguments largely fell on deaf ears. The Supreme Court clearly recognized corporate free speech rights as it abolished restrictions on corporate political spending on behalf of ballot initiatives. According to Justice Powell, "The speech proposed by the banks and corporations is at the heart of the First Amendment's protections."[14] The corporate "identity" of the speaker did not deprive that speaker of First Amendment protection. What is also noteworthy about this case is the court's conclusion that political expenditures by banks and other corporations must be treated as a form of political speech.

Similarly, the 1980 U.S Supreme Court case of *Central Hudson Gas & Electric Company vs. Public Service Corporation of New York* endorsed the corporation's free-speech rights. The State of New York attempted to forbid promotional advertising by utility companies, but the court ruled that the law was unconstitutional.[15] Thanks to these cases and other developments, the corporation was no longer seen through the lens of *Dartmouth* as an abstract entity with limited privileges granted by the state. The corporation now enjoyed many of the same constitutional protections as individual persons. While several of these cases acknowledged the separate personhood of the corporation as the basis for those protections, other cases relied on a different notion of the corporation as an association capable of asserting the rights of its members.[16]

More recently, in 2010, the U.S. Supreme Court reaffirmed the free-speech rights of the corporation in the *Citizens United v. Federal Elections Commission* case. In another 5–4 opinion, the court ruled that the Bipartisan Campaign Finance Reform Act (2002), which forbade corporations from making "independent expenditures" from general funds that advocated for the election or defeat of political candidates, was unconstitutional.[17] Following the precedent of *Bellotti*, the court ruled that corporations have the same right as individuals to try to influence political campaigns through advertisements. According to the five justices in the majority, the government must treat individual and corporate speakers in the same manner. It cannot limit speech based on the speaker's corporate status or wealth: "the rule that political speech cannot be limited based on a speaker's wealth is a necessary consequence of the premise that the First Amendment generally prohibits the suppression of political speech based on the speaker's identity."[18]

Four years later in *Burwell v. Hobby Lobby*, the Supreme Court also ruled that a closely held corporation (such as Hobby Lobby) had the right to exercise its religious beliefs in accordance with the First Amendment and the Religious Freedom Restoration Act (RFRA).[19] Prior to this decision, no Supreme Court ruling had ever recognized such a right for a for-profit corporation. At the core of this decision was the court's assumption that the corporation could be considered a "person" within the meaning of the RFRA. However, the Supreme Court opinion, crafted by Justice Samuel Alito, did not really treat the corporation as an independent entity, as some previous courts had done. Rather, the court based its decision on the religious beliefs of the Green family, which owned Hobby Lobby. Alito and his colleagues in the majority "pierced the corporate veil" and focused on the people who made up the corporation and concluded that this association of persons was entitled to assert religious rights. The court did not address the question of whether the religious beliefs of Hobby Lobby, the corporate entity itself, should be recognized in the law.[20]

Thus, it is fair to say that the U.S. Supreme Court has adopted a fairly liberal stance in granting rights to the corporation. There have been some exceptions, such as the *FCC v. AT&T* case, where it refused to recognize a corporation's right to personal privacy.[21] However, despite this trend in jurisprudence to recognize the corporation as a separate person or as an association of persons with certain rights, many scholars believe that these decisions are profoundly misguided. Particularly worrisome are the political ramifications for granting such broad free-speech rights to prosperous and powerful corporations.

CORPORATE MORAL AGENCY

The personification of the corporation is a contentious matter that cannot be fully resolved in these pages. Nonetheless, we must probe the related issue of **corporate moral agency** further and determine whether it can withstand more thorough scrutiny. Does the corporation have certain qualities similar to those of a person that allow us to make a convincing case for corporate moral agency? Can we hold the corporation, distinct from its members, responsible for derelictions of duty and abuses of economic power?

To address these questions, we must try to capture more precisely why the corporation is qualified to be an agent or a moral subject. A corporation is a small community or group, and, like any group, its members act collectively with a shared aim. There are multiple interactions within the group over an appreciable span of time. But far more significant is the joint purpose of the participants whose activities are coordinated for the sake of some future shared objectives. These participants will conceive themselves as a unified group and establish conventions and norms for resolving their coordination challenges and guiding their choices. They will also undoubtedly elect someone with authority who can settle internal disputes and select among various alternatives. Thus, as the group comes into existence, so too do these norms or social rules along with the presence of authority.[22]

Like a human person, therefore, the corporation has objectives, and it is governed by certain rules or norms as it makes choices to realize those objectives. And like a human person, the corporation (as a collective) acts. Furthermore, it is logical to assume that this collective action should be subject to the same moral standards as the action of an individual moral agent. Why should the same action, which is immoral for an individual, be morally valid for a group of individuals? Precisely how do groups or corporations exercise their moral agency? As Hess points out, several theories have been proposed focusing on the "shared intentions" of the group. Also, corporations rely on a number of mechanisms to guide the behavior of their members, which include different institutional decision-making structures tied to corporate policies.[23]

It is especially instructive to concentrate on the corporate mindset that shapes a corporation's culture and directs the decisions and behavior of its workers. Both ordinary persons and organizations have a mindset, and the ideas of *decision maker* and *mindset* are linked together. The **corporate mindset** flows from a firm's norms and values, along with a discrete set of factual beliefs. Every firm has certain commitments about these beliefs and values that guide its activities and determine its strategic choices. For example, a company may have certain "beliefs," perhaps shaped by past experience, about the proper steps needed to implement a new acquisition strategy. And that same company may promote specific values or attitudes such as speed, agility, and simplicity as the key to its long-term success.[24]

Henri Termeer, longtime CEO of Genzyme, the Cambridge biotech company, instilled in that organization a distinguishing mindset focused on the centrality of the patient. Thanks to Termeer's influence, the company valued the needs of the patient over the maximization of corporate profits. But the company also believed that if it took care of the patient, profits would follow. These guiding values and beliefs led to practices such as the universal provision policy, which ensured that those who could not afford expensive drugs like Cerezyme (for Gaucher disease) would be given those drugs for free. This mindset also inspired Genzyme to devote resources to neglected diseases without any compensation. Although Termeer has stepped down as CEO after the purchase of Genzyme by Sanofi-Aventis, the same mission and values continue to persist within the organization.

Thanks to this "mindset," the corporation qualifies as an agent because its commitments about factual beliefs and values constitute the equivalent of "intentional states" that steer its conduct in one direction instead of another. When manager and employee behavior is guided by the corporation's mindset, the resulting action is not the action of an individual manager but the *firm's action*.[25] In similar terms, personalist philosophers such as Karol Wojtyła (later Pope John Paul II) have discussed the collective subjectivity or the "quasi-subjectivity" of an organization or corporation. The distinctive mark of personhood is subjectivity: every person is a self-determining moral subject who intentionally defines herself through rational choices. To be sure, the person is the "proper subject" of action, and the corporation is only a subject by analogy and in a derivative way. But the organization as a "community of action" manifests a certain subjectivity because it engages in collective action guided by a set of commitments about beliefs and values.[26]

Moreover, if the corporation is an agent, it must be a moral agent. In its decision-making process, the corporation will have reasons for its choices, and some of those reasons will be morally relevant. Those reasons will reflect a corporation's commitments to certain *moral values* or principles that are integrated into the corporate mindset. As Thomas Donaldson points out, "Obviously, corporations are unable to think as humans, but they can employ reasons of a sort, . . . that is, with the proper internal structure, corporations, like humans, can be liable to give an account of their behavior where the account stipulates which moral *reasons* prompted their behavior." Thus, while the corporation is not a moral person, it qualifies as a moral agent because it acts, and sometimes its action is guided by moral commitments.[27]

In summary, the corporation's members are unified by shared intentions, collective goals, and, to some extent, by institutional structures and policies. Every corporation is committed to certain beliefs and values that constitute its mindset and direct its actions. When that mindset shapes the behavior of the firm's members, the result is a corporate action. And if the corporation can have values and beliefs pertaining to nonmoral or economic matters, it can also have moral values and beliefs. When these moral commitments are present, they too will help steer the firm's actions in a particular direction. A company, for example, might refrain from pursuing a potentially lucrative strategy because of a settled commitment to human rights and a belief that its strategic policies would violate the privacy rights of its customers. Thus, corporations, like individuals, are capable of acting on the basis of morally relevant information or principles that provide a reason for that action. And since the corporation can act on the basis of this morally relevant information, it qualifies for moral agency.[28]

Although it is a mistake to exaggerate the likeness between the corporation and the person, we can speak intelligibly about corporate conscience. The task of the chief executive officer and other managers is to form that conscience in the proper way. As Goodpaster explains, the corporation is a "macro version" or projection of ourselves as individuals. According to the principle of moral projection, it is appropriate to describe organizations by analogy with individuals and also to foster the same moral attributes in organizations that we aspire to as individuals.[29] For example, we expect both individuals and corporations to abide by a standard of honesty and candor when they communicate with others.

Arguably, once we comprehend the reasoning behind corporate moral agency, the moral logic for corporate rights becomes more intelligible. Just as the individual agent is owed certain rights that make it possible to responsibly choose actions oriented toward achieving its objectives, so too is the corporate agent entitled to at least some of those same rights. These property or liberty rights will allow the corporation to accomplish its collective goals consistent with its moral and nonmoral commitments. Moreover, the corporation's moral personality implies that it enters into relationships shaped by duties and obligations. This moral liability also requires the corporation's prerogative to assert its rights or make moral claims of its own.[30] The scope of those corporate rights is a matter of legal and philosophical debate, but this debate is another chapter that cannot be opened here.

CORPORATE PURPOSE

What does corporate personhood or moral agency imply about the modern corporation's purpose? There has been a tendency among those who reject the doctrines of corporate personhood and rights to regard the corporation as a one-dimensional entity organized for the sole purpose of pursuing profits for its owners. Justice Ginsberg's trenchant dissent in the *Hobby Lobby* case proclaimed that "corporations have no consciences, no beliefs, no feelings, no thoughts, no desires." She distinguished for-profit corporations from religious nonprofits because the former "use labor to make a profit, rather than to perpetuate the religious values shared by a community of believers."[31] According to this line of reasoning, for-profit corporations exist not to exercise rights or commit to noneconomic principles but solely to make a profit. Stripped of its personal attributes and moral agency, the corporation is destined to have a myopic focus on profitability and shareholder wealth with only minimal obligations to society.

During the rise of "big business" in the early 20th century, a corporation's purpose was commonly conceived in these very restricted terms. The predominant interpretation was that the corporation belonged to its owners or stockholders. When the Dodge brothers sued Ford Motor Company because of its policy limiting shareholder dividends, the Michigan Supreme Court ordered Ford to pay a larger dividend to its shareholders. The court also rendered a clear description of the nature and purpose of the corporation:

> There should be no confusion . . . of the duties which Mr. Ford conceives
> that he and the stockholders owe to the general public, and the duties which
> in law he and his co-directors owe to protesting minority stockholders. A
> business corporation is organized and carried on primarily for the profit of the
> stockholders. The powers of the directors are to be employed to that end.[32]

According to this widely held perspective, managers are endowed with fiduciary obligations to the corporation's shareholders, who seek to maximize their economic returns. In almost all publicly held, for-profit companies, the owners or stockholders are not the managers. Stockholders entrust managers with their financial resources, and those managers are bound by law to make sound economic and strategic decisions on the shareholders' behalf.

The Property Model

The *Dodge v. Ford Motor* case reflects the **property model** of the corporation. According to this model, the shareholders' interests have primacy in all corporate affairs because they effectively "own" the corporate assets. The rights of suppliers, customers, employees, and others are limited to their contractual or legal claims. Any assent to non-profit-maximizing behavior is to tolerate the spending of other people's money on behalf of the manager's own subjective views of the public good or social welfare. Those who adhere to the property model are skeptical of claims that corporations should be operated to accomplish some purpose other than shareholder wealth maximization.[33]

Economists such as Kenneth Arrow, Milton Friedman, and Friedrich Hayek have enthusiastically endorsed this view of shareholder primacy. There are also unmistakable echoes of the property view in the writings of more contemporary conservatives and in the editorial pages of publications such as the *Wall Street Journal*. According to the property model, corporate purpose is quite narrowly conceived, confined to advancing the interests of stockholders who have committed their capital to the firm for a long period of time. Proponents of this model contend that social welfare will be enhanced if each corporation strives to allocate its economic resources in a way that maximizes shareholder wealth. They reason that capital will flow to those proficient firms that reward their owners, and market assets will then be dedicated to their optimal use.[34]

The property model, which appears to justify a corporation's existence solely by its productive capacities, may have served society well during the early days of managerial capitalism. But some argue that the corporation has evolved into a social institution, which is capable of exercising enormous social, political, and economic power. A corporation can be a force for social good rather than just a profitable institution. Pharmaceutical companies, for example, serve humanity by offering products that improve health and the overall quality of life. Corporations also have the capacity to shape popular culture and influence consumer tastes.

The Social Entity Model

In light of these and other developments, a new model has been proposed, which is sometimes referred to as the **social entity model**. According to this concept, the corporation exists not only to create shareholder wealth but also to satisfy the needs of customers, to provide jobs for employees, and to contribute to the vitality of the local community. Corporate purpose, therefore, must be conceived in social rather than exclusively economic terms. According to Charles Handy, "The purpose of a business, in other words, is not to make a profit, full stop. It is to make a profit so that the business can do something more or better. That 'something' becomes the real justification for the business."[35] In some states, statutes have even been modified to authorize corporate boards of directors to consider the welfare of these constituencies when it exercises corporate power.[36]

Those who embrace the social entity model contend that the corporation's purpose is broader than serving the end of enriching the corporation's owners. In its strong form, the entity paradigm sees all constituencies or stakeholders, including employees, customers, communities in which corporations operate, and suppliers, as entitled to having their interests considered in corporate decision-making. These groups would no longer be viewed instrumentally, but as entitled to a much stronger voice than the property model is willing to tolerate. This type of substantive commitment to stakeholders implies that managers would be bound to *maximize stakeholder equity*. They must give the same consideration to the demands of stakeholders that they give to the economic interests of their stockholders.[37]

Limitations of the Models

Both of these simple models have limitations. The property model suffers from certain deficiencies because of its exclusive focus on the shareholder. This model relativizes the interest of its nonshareholder constituencies and subordinates them to the interests of shareholders. Even core stakeholders such as employees and suppliers are generally treated as an instrumental means to the end of higher profits. Critics of the property model observe that the goal of shareholder enrichment is too constraining to serve as an acceptable orientation for corporate strategy. For example, this model does not adequately account for the investment of employee time and energy or the impact of corporate decisions on the welfare of employee families and the local community.

On the other hand, the social entity model in its thick form tends to envision stockholders as one of several "coequal constituencies" that a CEO or board of directors may consider when making strategic decisions. But the objective of maximizing stakeholder equity is too broad, and defenders of this view fail to provide criteria for prioritizing the claims of those stakeholders.[38] In addition, we cannot lightly dismiss the fact that corporations are formed to generate economic returns for shareholders who invest large amounts of capital in risky projects. Rewarding those shareholders may not be the only mission of the corporation, but it must be given a high priority and cannot be marginalized. If the economic mission of a corporate enterprise is heavily compromised for social purposes to the detriment of shareholder wealth, its ability to raise capital will be obstructed. Without giving investors an adequate return, corporations will face huge obstacles in capital markets and they will be unable to attract funding necessary to expand their business and create new jobs. As a result, if followed to its logical conclusion, the social entity model will not enhance social welfare in the long run. Finally, other corporate constituencies such as employees are often protected against predatory corporate behavior by laws and contracts.[39]

The Modified Entity Model

Is there a way to bridge the gap between these divergent models? One approach is to preserve the fiduciary obligation of corporations to shareholders but also recognize the nonfiduciary obligations to the other stakeholders. We might call this the *modified entity model*. This model takes seriously the corporation's status as a social institution, but it recognizes a higher, fiduciary duty only to owners or stockholders. Priority, therefore, is ordinarily given to equity holders who undertake significant economic risk. However, there are morally and socially significant obligations to other constituencies, such as employees and customers, whose welfare is affected by corporate behavior. For example, corporations are morally bound to avoid predatory marketing tactics, to disclose risks to consumers, to pay a fair wage to their workers, and to respect employee rights. Corporations must also avoid unfair competition and corrupt business practices such as bribery or fraud. The corporation, therefore, has definite moral and legal obligations to individuals and groups impacted by its decisions.[40]

This third model, which we propose, conceives corporate purpose in terms of the common good of the business as a community of persons who cooperate in a set of activities to achieve the aim for which that business was created. An oil company, for example, exists to make oil products. It creates value through the exploration, drilling, and refining of crude oil, which is then transported and distributed as petroleum products to the end consumer. This business is an association that facilitates a collaborative effort by which capital, labor, and other inputs are deployed in order to provide a basic commodity that people need. [41]

Since the corporation is an association for ongoing cooperation, its purpose will be best defined by reference to its common good: *efficient economic cooperation* in the value-creation process, and *fairness* to all who voluntarily participate in that process (Figure 2.1). The common good is not the "greatest net good" of utilitarianism, but the *shared good* or welfare of those groups and individuals who comprise this community and contribute to the task of economic cooperation. All of these constituencies, including investors, managers, employees, suppliers, and outside contractors, deserve a fair reward commensurate to their contribution. Employees are entitled to fair wages and benefits for their efforts, and suppliers should earn a fair price for their inputs. The cooperation of these core stakeholder groups should not be regarded as merely instrumental to the enrichment of the company's owners. Even secondary stakeholders, such as the local or national community, are entitled to some consideration, since they serve the corporation by providing the necessary infrastructure and civil services. This obligation to the community also implies that companies should be operated sustainably with as little damage to the environment as possible.[42]

If the company is financially successful, its investors or shareholders, who provide the needed capital, deserve a reasonable rate of return on their investment. Shareholders and other stakeholders need not be in conflict. But if there are conflicting interests between these two groups, *ceteris paribus*, the interests of shareholders must take precedence, as long as stakeholders such as suppliers, customers, and employees are being treated fairly. For example, philanthropic projects for the community or other social objectives should not come at the expense of corporate profits that will diminish the reasonable return justified by owners who put their capital at risk.[43]

Since this model does not envision the corporation's end as maximization of profits, it avoids the extreme view that perceives the corporation as an amoral and impersonal tool, a moneymaking machine with no higher calling. But it also preserves the unique obligation owed to the shareholders who own the company. Fairness to those shareholders implies that to a great extent, managerial decisions are justified by anticipated economic benefits that will generate positive financial returns and enhance shareholder wealth.

FIGURE 2.1 ■ Defining Corporate Purpose

Corporate Purpose
The common good: Efficient economic cooperation and fairness to all who participate in value-added activities

Structure of Corporate Responsibilities
Pursuit of economic mission through effective allocation of resources and creation of shareholder wealth
Compliance with all legal and regulatory obligations
Respect for extralegal ethical principles

CORPORATE ACCOUNTABILITY AND ECONOMIC MISSION

With this compromise in mind, we can discern the responsibilities of the corporation according to a modified social entity model. At a minimum, all corporations have *three fundamental duties*:

1. to pursue their economic mission through the efficient allocation of resources that creates value and enhances shareholder wealth

2. to follow society's rules and laws

3. to recognize and respect human rights and other moral principles that ensure justice and social harmony

This trio of duties will direct a corporation to responsibly achieve its purpose by realizing the common or shared good of the stakeholder groups that take part in this corporate association. It underscores the binding legal and moral obligations not only toward those core stakeholder groups, who deserve fair treatment and benefits proportionate to their contributions, but toward every individual or group affected by the corporation's activity. These legal and moral principles prescribe the avoidance of harm along with fair competition in the wider community or industry to which the corporation belongs.[44]

A Decision-Making Framework

This simple model represents a decision-making structure within which executives and corporate CEOs can prudently manage their organizations and develop strategies for sustainable competitive advantage. We will rely on this overarching framework for analyzing the case studies in the chapters to follow (Figure 2.2 on page 39). As we will see played out in many of those cases, one of the most formidable challenges for managers is to reconcile the tensions that sometimes arise when trying to simultaneously follow these three obligations.

Creation of Value and Wealth

The first obligation is to allocate resources in a way that efficiently creates value in the marketplace. According to traditional economics, value is added by creating the biggest differential possible between willingness to pay for a product and the supplier opportunity cost. **Willingness to pay** is the most that consumers will pay for a product and usually corresponds to the price. Almost any activity in the value chain can influence a customer's willingness to pay. The oil company, for example, might commit to extensive downstream marketing and customer service in order to increase willingness to pay for its petroleum products. Sometimes vendors charge a price below willingness to pay to capture market share. **Supplier opportunity cost** is the least suppliers will accept for their inputs. The bigger the wedge between willingness to pay and supplier opportunity cost, the bigger the added value. Efficient corporations will strive to contain the costs of adding such value (labor cost, overhead, etc.). As a result, they will be able to capture or appropriate a healthy proportion of that value added in the form of corporate profits.[45]

If a corporation is not proficient in creating value and appropriating that value, it will struggle to survive in a competitive marketplace. The stubborn logic of corporate success suggests the need for size or economies of scale and scope to sustain a long-term competitive advantage. Some companies, however, thrive on a "blue ocean" strategy of radical innovation with little competition and a high willingness to pay. Successful corporations must also sustain their competitive advantage by effectively counteracting threats to their position. Those threats typically come from imitators or competitors that offer substitute products or services, but it can also come from powerful buyers and suppliers. The economic mission of sustainable value creation is the primary contribution the corporate enterprise makes to society.

It is a mistake, therefore, to minimize the corporation's economic mission and marketplace competence. At the same time, the corporation cannot be reduced to an impersonal wealth-generating tool. This community of persons cooperates in the production and distribution of products or the provision of services that serve the material needs of society and contribute to our social welfare. But the corporation is obliged to create value sustainably, and to do so in such a way that conforms to society's legal rules along with its ethical standards of human decency. Rights and duties must be respected in the exercise of corporate authority.

Compliance with the Law

Even free-market fundamentalists such as Milton Friedman acknowledge that the corporation's value-added activities must always be carried out within the rules of the game. While Friedman espoused the doctrine of shareholder primacy, he expected corporations to be law-abiding citizens. Those rules include the general laws of society and specific regulations that govern a particular industry. Since the corporation has a degree of moral agency or subjectivity, it is obliged to conscientiously follow society's laws, just as a person must follow those laws. Moreover, laws can help a business to achieve its common good by ensuring the fairest possible treatment for those who cooperate in its value-creating activities. Fiduciary rules, for example, prevent abuse to shareholders and others who are invested in the corporation's economic welfare. Basic legal requirements of the corporation and its managers would include honoring contracts, averting conflicts of interest, respecting property rights, avoiding fraud, and refraining from unfair competition, such as the solicitation or payment of bribes.

Laws that compel corporations to honor contracts and to compete without fraud temper pure economic rationality, with its laserlike focus on gaining market share and maximizing long-term profit. A sound economic strategy will induce the company to lock in its customers and negotiate the lowest possible costs with suppliers in order to enhance its value added. But this sort of rationality is sometimes attentive to others only in an instrumental way. No company can afford to completely ignore the interests of its stakeholders, such as suppliers or employees. But if strengthening competitive advantage seems to call for a temporary bypassing of labor contracts or the exploitation of suppliers, some companies will simply follow their poorly formed instincts and pursue these strategies. Society's laws, however, enforce contractual obligations and protect employee rights, and thereby help to constrain the egocentric pull of economic rationality.

While arm's-length contracts protect the legal interests of both parties, fiduciary principles go much further. They require duties of loyalty, candor, and care for those who serve in the capacity of a trusted party. Fiduciary law applies to corporate officers, directors, and executives who are in a fiduciary relationship to the corporation and its shareholders. A **fiduciary relationship** is in effect whenever a certain party is entrusted with property, information, or power to make decisions that entail discretionary judgments for the benefit of someone other than this trusted party. Fiduciary rules constrain the self-interest of corporate executives, who must give their undivided and unselfish loyalty to the corporation and avoid conflicts between that duty and their own self-interest. Corporate managers cannot put their own interests above those of the corporation or its owners. According to *Guth v. Loft*, "Corporate officers and directors are not permitted to use their position of trust and confidence to further their private interests."[46] These fiduciary rules are critical for the vitality of capitalism and especially for capital formation, since they assure investors that corporate managers will act on their behalf.[47]

In general, legal arrangements reflect a society's plan for the coordination of its citizens and institutions. Since law is intended for the common good, it is an appeal to human reason. This orientation to the community's common good provides the rationale for respecting the law as authoritative and obligatory. But what exactly is the nature of law? Law, according to Thomas Aquinas, is a "rule" and "measure" of action that binds us to act in the right way.[48] As a rule, the law tells us what to do, and as a measure, it provides a standard or baseline to evaluate our actions. Aquinas's view of law is echoed in more contemporary definitions. Law is described as "the command of the sovereign, expressed in the form of a rule."[49] Sovereignty is embodied in any person or collective who is entrusted with care of the community and who has been authorized to make laws on its behalf.

Therefore, law is one important measure of corporate actions and policies, and when companies fall short of observing their legal obligations for selfish motives, they do a great disservice to the community by undermining its common good. If a company is engaged in bribery or unfair competition in violation of the law, it interferes with the communal benefits associated with free-market competition. If it ignores property rights, it invites others to do the same and disrupts relationships between members of the political community. Laws are stated in universal terms, but they apply to particular situations that are "referable to the common good." John Smith's property is not itself a common good, but the integrity of property is such a good. To safeguard the integrity of property, the law must protect the property of Mr. Smith. Corporations, like all moral agents, must respect common goods, such as the integrity of property or the binding nature of contracts, and therefore obey the laws that preserve those goods.[50]

Compliance with legal standards is also consistent with a corporation's enlightened self-interest. If corporations diligently attend to their legal duties, they will avoid many abusive actions that can ultimately undermine their ability to create value in the long run. They will preserve their reputation along with the trust of the community and also do their fair share to promote and sustain a strong free-market economy.

Moral Values and Corporate Conscience

Someone may question why we need morality if there is an effective legal system that promotes the common good and protects society from the predatory behavior of corporations. According to this perspective, the corporation qualifies as a responsible moral agent if it passively but dutifully follows the laws already intended to achieve justice. Isn't ethics superfluous so long as there is a sound legal structure? Albert Carr takes this reasoning a step further and contends that "as long as a company does not transgress the rules of the game set by law, it has the legal right to shape its strategy without reference to anything but its profits."[51]

There are many reasons why law, however important and necessary, is insufficient. Law and ethics are not identical, as some assume, and do not always coincide. Moreover, the law is a reactive force that takes time to be properly formulated and implemented. Regulators must comprehend and respond to complex problems such as unsafe drugs, dangerous chemicals, and harmful financial practices. It is not easy to develop laws to effectively handle these dangers. Managers cannot assume that until the law is passed, they have no responsibilities beyond the law to address these problems.[52]

Also, law is a fallible and indeterminate means for preserving the common good and promoting justice. Often lawmakers lack adequate data or public feedback to craft laws in a satisfactory way. And in many contexts, the law will not be comprehensive enough to address market failures and imperfections in a thorough way that adequately limits or prevents harm to innocent victims. There will be deficiencies and loopholes that can be easily exploited by opportunistic corporations and individuals.

Moreover, the law has a particularly hard time keeping pace with the development of new computer and network technologies and addressing the dangers of those technologies. There are often policy voids that take time to fill as society grapples with the values it wants to advance or preserve. There are no laws, for example, that direct information technology companies such as Apple to cooperate with legal authorities seeking to unlock the strong encryption code that protects data on the smartphones of terrorists or criminals (see "Going Dark: Apple versus the FBI" in Chapter 10). These situations call for principled moral reasoning in order to fill this legal vacuum. This is a complex dilemma for Apple, which aspires to protect the privacy rights of its users. But a potent case can be made that security concerns in an age of terrorism trump those rights in certain situations. Thus, in dynamic markets, passive obedience to law is not sufficient to ensure that the corporation achieves justice and respects human rights, which are authentic grounds of obligation to others.

There is yet another reason why the law cannot account for the sum total of a corporation's noneconomic responsibility to society. Legal obligations are presumptively valid, but in some circumstances a law may be unjust, and no moral agent is under obligation to obey such a law. When Google entered China to compete with China's search engine company, Baidu, it agreed to follow China's stringent censorship laws and censor its search results. However, are China's laws restricting political speech just? Don't these laws infringe upon a person's natural right to free political expression, and if so, should Google be a party to such wrongful infringement? Companies striving to respect the rights and dignity of others as they pursue their economic goals could choose to disobey China's laws if they believe those laws unjustifiably restrict the right to free expression.

What precisely makes a law unjust? Unjust laws arise when a country's lawmakers abuse their authority or give themselves special favors through the legal process. Laws are also unjust when they distribute society's burdens unfairly or trample on the rights of others. These defective laws lack moral authority and do not bind in conscience as a just law would. A law of this sort is unreasonable, "not law without qualification but more a perversion of law." Therefore, under most circumstances they must be discounted and in some cases strongly resisted. These legal prescriptions retain the "character of law" but lack any moral validity.[53]

We find this insight expressed not only in traditional philosophy but also in the writings of modern thinkers such as Dr. Martin Luther King Jr., who called attention to the radical injustice of asserting that some people do not count or are inferior to others. Dr. King persuasively argued that the racist and discriminatory laws of the American South could not possibly be just laws. These laws, he writes, are "out of harmony with the moral law" because they degrade the human person.[54] Similar arguments were put forth about the racist anti-Semitic laws enacted in the 1930s in Nazi Germany. According to Lon Fuller, Nazi laws ignored the "inner morality of law itself" and resulted in a general debasement of the social order.[55]

Thus, the rational, conscientious corporation cannot simply assume that laws are just and automatically create an obligation of compliance. Only sound moral reasoning, sensitive to natural rights, can discern when the law is unjust and when covert or overt resistance to such an unjust law is called for.

If we conclude that legal obligations cannot exhaust a corporation's responsibility to society, how are we to express the ethical values that a corporation is also bound to follow? To some extent, how one answers this question will depend on how corporate purpose is defined. If the end of the corporation is simply to pursue profits, standards of behavior beyond what is required by law will be minimal. As Friedman suggests, those standards may include only a requirement not to engage in fraud or deception, to avoid coercion, and to avoid doing harm to others.[56]

On the other hand, if the corporation as a community of persons is a moral agent in its own right, committed to the common good understood as effective economic cooperation and *fairness* to all participants, more demanding moral standards are appropriate. But what precisely are the moral principles by which moral agents should be guided? This is a controversial issue over which philosophers and ethicists have had profound disagreements. The "do no harm" principle is a good beginning, but this standard is too general and must be further specified. A more substantive ethical approach demands that moral agents respect fundamental human rights and adhere to basic moral duties. Rights, for example, determine what is owed to a person in justice. A rights-based analysis of moral problems will consider whether a particular action or policy violates moral entitlements such as the right to privacy, the right to own property, or the right to a fair and decent wage. In addition, corporations cannot neglect their voluntary duties along with those duties owed to other persons by virtue of their rational personhood. By attending to rights and duties, corporations will not fall into the trap of regarding other peoples' activities, essential for their success, as a mere instrumental means of generating profits. Framing ethical obligations through the lens of rights and duties is the most productive way to capture a corporation's social and moral responsibilities.

In summary, while a corporation's primary mission is economic, it should pursue strategies and financial policies within the boundaries of the law and ethical norms. The chief principle that should shape managerial decisions is the common good of the business as a community of persons. That shared good can be realized by attentiveness to the legal requirements and moral norms that protect the rights of those individuals and groups who cooperate in the activities for which the business was organized and who should benefit appropriately if this enterprise is successful. Those benefits include fair wages and benefits (along with decent working conditions) for employees, fair prices for supplier inputs, quality products at fair prices for customers, and a reasonable rate of

FIGURE 2.2 ▪ **A Decision-Making Framework**

The Three Fundamental Duties of Corporations

Duty 1: Creation of Value and Wealth

- Provide goods and services that enhance and support social welfare

- Allocate resources in a way that efficiently creates and appropriates value for shareholders and other stakeholders

- Sustain a long-term competitive advantage

Duty 2: Compliance with the Law

- Implement value-added activities within the rules of the game

- Adhere to the general laws of society and specific regulations that govern a particular industry

- Honor contracts, respect valid property rights, avoid fraud, refrain from unfair competition, and comply with fiduciary obligations to shareholders and investors

Duty 3: Observance of Common Moral Norms

- Exercise principled moral reasoning

- Respect basic human rights and moral duties that protect the well-being and dignity of persons whose interests may be affected by corporate actions

- Avoid compliance with unjust laws

- Endorse extralegal duties based on principles such as honesty and transparency that ensure free and open competition

return for investors. By following this trio of obligations (creation of value and wealth, compliance with the law, and observance of common moral norms), the corporation also lives up to its role as a moral agent with both rights *and* responsibilities toward every individual or group affected by its actions (Figure 2.2). On occasion, legal boundaries will be blurry and sophisticated moral reasoning will be essential. At other times, it will not be possible to simultaneously conform with one's legal and ethical obligations if the relevant law is unjust. But justice, which always accords the other his or her rights, always takes precedence over positive laws.[57]

CONCLUSION

Martin Shkreli, an ambitious pharmaceutical executive, was once called the "most reviled person in America." Shkreli's company, Turing Pharmaceuticals, purchased a drug called Daraprim from a rival pharmaceutical firm. Daraprim has been classified as an "essential medicine" because it treats parasitic infections that can be fatal for pregnant women or people with HIV/AIDS. Shkreli immediately increased the price of Daraprim from $13.50 per tablet to $750, one of the most dramatic price increases in the pharmaceutical industry's history. Industry experts claimed this price increase could not be justified—there had been no increase in production or marketing costs and no additional research-and-development investment. The drug had been making a respectable profit at its current price and there was no competition from generics. Shkreli first said that he would lower the price in the wake of public outrage, but then changed his mind. The embattled executive was eventually removed from Turing for other reasons, but the company's reputation was irreparably damaged by this unjust price increase.

Shkreli was unrepentant, however, and wondered why people were so shocked to discover a pharmaceutical executive motivated by the prospect of bigger profits. He also reminded his critics that there was nothing illegal about the substantial price increase. When asked in a television interview if he would do anything differently, he answered, "I probably would have raised the price higher, [because] my investors expect me to maximize profits, not minimize them, or go half, or go 70%."[58]

The saga of Mr. Shkreli reminds us about the central importance of ethics and corporate responsibility. Pharmaceutical executives must not just consider economic and legal issues but also ask whether a price increase of this magnitude is fair to those who depend on this drug. In addition, if we depersonalize the corporation and see it merely as an economic tool ordered to make profits, the mentality of Mr. Shkreli begins to make perfect sense. If the corporation has no conscience, as Justice Ginsberg opined in *Hobby Lobby*, neither will some of its executives who direct its economic activities. Turing and its maligned leader acted as Ginsberg expected, that is, as a corporation without a well-formed conscience whose sole purpose is "to use labor to make a profit."[59]

How we define the corporation and its purpose will undoubtedly shape the attitudes and behavior of its executives and its workers. We can recognize a corporation's moral agency along with its rights and responsibilities, expressed in its mission, values, and general mindset. When that mission reflects a purpose higher than profit maximization and those values reflect respect for the corporation's common good, employees can be influenced to act responsibly in the corporation's name. Or we can reduce the corporate entity to a blind economic tool with no rights, no conscience, and no vision or sense of a common good. But that distorted perception of the corporation will lead to endless abuses of economic power as managers, restrained only by the letter of the law, strive to further corporate self-interest. And society is more apt to get corporate leaders like Mr. Shkreli who will not hesitate to use this economic tool for its intended purpose.[60]

Student Study Site

Visit **edge.sagepub.com/spinello.**

Key Terms

corporate mindset   28

corporate moral agency   27

corporation   25

fiduciary relationship   36

property model   30

social entity model   31

supplier opportunity
   cost   34

willingness to pay   34

Review Questions

1. What are the concepts cited in legal cases supporting the corporation as a moral agent?

2. Choose a perspective on the corporation's purpose and explain the scope of responsibilities based on this perspective.

3. Apply the decision-making framework of the three duties of a corporation to the Shkreli case presented in the conclusion to this chapter. What would you have done differently based on these duties?

Discussion Questions

1. Do you agree with the "personhood theory" of the corporation? What are the strongest arguments supporting this viewpoint? How would you answer some of Justice Ginsberg's arguments about the status of the corporation?

2. In your opinion, what is the *purpose* of the corporation in modern society, and what does it mean to be a good global citizen? Do

you agree with the property or social entity model? What are the benefits and liabilities of each approach?

3. Explain what makes a law unjust. In general, how should corporations deal with unjust laws when they do business abroad? When should they protest or violate those laws?

ETHICS AND CORPORATE SOCIAL RESPONSIBILITY

Moral judgement is not a luxury, not a perverse indulgence of the self-righteous. It is a necessity. . . . Morally as well as physically, there is only one world, and we all have to live in it.

—Mary Midgley[1]

What is most important is that management realize that it must consider the impact of every business policy and business action upon society. It has to consider whether the action is likely to promote the public good, to advance the basic beliefs of our society, to contribute to its stability, strength, and harmony.

—Peter Drucker[2]

LEARNING OBJECTIVES

Upon completion of this chapter, you should be able to:

3.1   Assimilate the basic practical frameworks for ethical deliberation and the DRJ formula for ethical reasoning.

3.2   Discuss the concept of corporate social responsibility.

In the last chapter, we presented the three basic responsibilities of the modern corporation and its managers: *to create wealth through the efficient allocation of resources*; *to follow all relevant and just laws*; and *to observe ethical principles or standards of conduct*. We also discussed the need for ethical reasoning in order to accommodate legal and policy vacuums. But what exactly is ethics? Many people have a vague notion about the meaning of ethics and often reduce ethical standards to social conventions or cultural norms. So before we discuss ethical principles such as justice, we must come to terms with this more fundamental question.

According to Aristotle, ethics is an applied science. It is a science because it entails knowledge, and it is an applied science because of its concern with the application of abstract normative principles to concrete situations. Thus, the object of ethics is both knowledge and action. The person who wants to be moral must know what is morally right and do it. Similarly, the violinist or pianist must know her music and translate that knowledge into a good performance. She aims to be a competent musician who is good at what she does. Morality is different from other areas of knowledge and action (such as music) because the aim is to be a good person, someone who knows the right choices and acts in the right way.[3]

Ethics is a practical discipline because it inspires us to evaluate our conduct by making prescriptive judgments about what ought to be done. Ethics of this type, often called **normative ethics**, is distinct from the discipline of metaethics, which is merely the study of moral discourse, the meaning of ethical terminology, and the logic underlying ethical judgments. Normative ethical inquiry, on the other hand, is a quest for the practical truth of how one's choices and actions can be good and worthwhile. Thus, the goal of normative ethics is not an appreciation of the structure of moral language but the acquisition and application of knowledge of right and wrong.

Although ethics is a science, it cannot always be as precise as mathematics or the empirical sciences. According to Aristotle, we find "that degree of precision in each kind of study which the nature of the subject at hand admits."[4] Ethical judgments usually do not conform to the standard of mathematical precision. But the fact that most specific ethical judgments do not have the same level of objectivity as scientific ones should not mean that ethics itself is purely subjective or merely a matter of convention and taste. Aristotle would certainly reject such an idea. He and other philosophers make a strong case that ethics is a rational and intelligible discipline. Specific moral judgments can and should be based on objective, defensible principles (such as "it is wrong to intentionally inflict harm on another person" or "there is an obligation in some circumstances to intervene in order to prevent serious harm to another"). Ethics can also be taught—its principles and the conclusions based on those principles can be understood, communicated, debated, and integrated with other nonmoral principles. We can objectively assess moral judgments in terms of whether they respect basic human rights, remain open to human fulfillment, and so forth.[5]

Some managers and professionals may want to rely exclusively on emotional sentiment and intuition when making tough moral choices. Others will say that convention and custom are the test of right and wrong, and hence their moral convictions will be guided solely by societal consensus. But can we always make reliable moral decisions in such an arbitrary fashion? Our moral intuitions and sentiments are sometimes unstable, while social conventions frequently represent cultural bias. Immoral customs are common, and persons can easily lose sight of what is morally reasonable with rationalizations perpetuated in language, educational institutions, and the law. What if a certain society lived by a moral code that approved bonded child labor or other forms of child abuse? In the United States, for example, slavery was once considered to be legally and socially acceptable, while racism was once codified in the laws of South Africa and Nazi Germany.[6]

Therefore, we cannot approach the vexing moral dilemmas that arise in business without some fixed principles, a set of transcultural standards of right and wrong. At the root of morality, we find two primary and self-evident precepts:

- One should not do harm to another human person

- One should love one's neighbor as oneself

According to Aquinas, these simple, practical rules capture the very meaning of morality, which demands that each person look beyond his or her own selfish interests.[7] The moral person is one who considers and assesses positively the desires, interests, needs, and concerns of others. Moreover, mutual cooperation and fellowship, essential for human flourishing, are impossible unless one turns away from narrow self-interest to a wider interest in others. However, these two primary principles proposed by Aquinas are general and need further specification. We must refer to normative ethical theory, which can supply such specification and also offer an opportunity for further reflection on the sources of moral norms.[8]

In this chapter, we will consider the most prominent normative theories that can equip us with the tools necessary for addressing the ethical conundrums that frequently arise in commercial society. A review of these key theories begins with virtue ethics, inspired by Aristotle. To avoid eclecticism, we will propose and defend a rights/duty-based ethical approach as the optimal avenue for deliberating about moral issues. Finally, the chapter assesses the scope of a corporation's obligations. Is there also a duty to go beyond observance of ethical principles and to help resolve society's problems through corporate charity?

PLATO, ARISTOTLE, AND VIRTUE ETHICS

While our principal focus is on modern philosophical frameworks, it is instructive to concentrate briefly on the antecedents of those theories in the works of Plato and Aristotle. The insights of these thinkers have become an indispensable part of the ethical heritage of Western culture.

Plato sought to rescue Greek society from the morass of moral nihilism by insisting upon the independent reality of the Good. To achieve what is good for me, I need to understand what is intrinsically good. In his passionate dialogue, the *Gorgias*, Plato deftly demonstrates that we possess a rational inclination toward those goods that fulfill and perfect us. In addition, we cannot neglect the role of practical knowledge in any comprehensive account of the human good. In that dialogue, we find Callicles arguing that the good life is all about pleasure and self-gratification: "A man who is going to live a full life must . . . gratify every fleeting desire as it comes into his heart."[9] But Socrates reminds him that some pleasures (such as overeating) can be harmful and dangerous. Moreover, if we follow Callicles's reasoning to its logical conclusion, sadistic pleasures would be classified as morally permissible. Therefore, we need knowledge to distinguish good from bad pleasures. Also, "the pleasant and the good are not the same," and therefore pleasure must be subordinate to goods such as life, health, and friendship.[10] The good life for Socrates is one of order and harmony, where practical reason with the help of the virtues directs us to those and other authentic human goods, worth pursuing for their own sake. Virtue is its own reward precisely because it helps to promote human flourishing.

Aristotle devoted a whole treatise to ethics known as the *Nicomachean Ethics*. In that work, Aristotle emphasized that every individual seeks the ultimate human good of happiness or fulfillment (*eudaimonia*), and he defined happiness as an activity of the soul in accordance with virtue (or excellence) "in a complete life." *Eudaimonia*, therefore, consists of virtuous activities of the soul. According to Aristotle, there are intellectual virtues, such as practical reasoning and wisdom, that pertain to the reasoning part of the soul, and moral virtues that pertain to its appetitive (or desiring) part. Aquinas also followed Aristotle's main doctrine on virtue. For both philosophers, the moral and intellectual virtues are interdependent. A person who is imprudent and lacks intellectual virtue cannot possess moral virtue. Similarly, there cannot be intellectual virtue without moral virtues such as moderation that make the passions docile for the guidance of reason.[11]

The art of living well greatly depends on moral virtue or excellence. Moral virtue is defined by Aristotle as the disposition or acquired habit of choosing the mean between the polar vices of excess and deficiency. The courageous individual, for example, "hits the mark" and possesses the right amount of fear to avoid the vices of rashness and cowardice. The mean is discerned by practical wisdom (*phronesis*), which tells us how we should act in a given situation. Intellectual virtues require time and experience, while the moral virtues are formed by habits. Moral virtues are not innate, but everyone has the capability to develop them, "and habit brings this ability to completion and fulfillment."[12] These virtuous habits are acquired by actions, and so actions shape character and determine future acts. It is through deliberate, courageous acts that one becomes a person of courage. Other virtues highlighted by Aristotle include temperance, generosity, self-respect, and justice. Justice prompts us to consider the needs of others in the distribution of goods.

Aristotle's virtue ethics, sometimes referred to as the classical approach, underscores practical wisdom, moral and intellectual virtue, and human flourishing. Virtue cannot be put to bad use, since the principle from which virtuous action springs is oriented to a good end discerned by reason.[13] The heart of ethics is to become better than we are and to achieve the final end of human flourishing through intelligent and prudent choices. Aristotle's ethics is grounded in the teleology of human nature ordered to its own final end or perfection. The ultimate goal is to live well as a human person, taking into account our natural tendencies, capacities, and unique features (such as rationality and freedom).[14]

Virtue ethics has enjoyed renewed interest in recent years, but these new interpretations are markedly different from Aristotelian ethics. In contrast to the classical approach, contemporary virtue ethics is not grounded in any teleology of human nature. It puts more emphasis on the moral agent along with his or her motives and intentions. Virtue ethicists like Martha Nussbaum emphasize the character of the inner moral life, its "settled patterns" of motive, emotion, and reasoning. Nussbaum further argues that "we should rely less on reason and more on non-rational sources of guidance, such as emotion and desire (if we should construe them as non-rational), and habit, and tradition."[15] Thus, in contrast to Plato, she seems to downplay the role of reason and the need for universality in ethics. We don't want to become preoccupied with isolated acts of choice but instead consider how moral choices fit into the whole course of a moral agent's life.

In summary, contemporary virtue ethics emphasizes virtues and moral character instead of duties, rights, or consequences. If someone is in need of being helped, the utilitarian will justify coming to the person's aid because it maximizes well-being. Others will claim they must act because it is their duty to follow moral rules such as "love your neighbor as yourself." But the virtue ethicist will encourage helping someone in need not because it optimizes consequences or it is a person's duty, but because it is generally consistent with the virtues of charity and benevolence.[16]

To some degree, virtue ethics can make a distinctive contribution to business ethics. Since virtuous acts are noble and exemplary, we can identify virtuous leaders within the corporation as role models for others. These individuals can make ethical behavior look more intelligible and attractive in a corporate setting. Also, since past actions mold character, the virtue ethicist considers not just whether a particular act is right or wrong but how it has been shaped or influenced by past decisions. Virtue ethics concentrates on patterns of past and present behavior so it can appreciate why a manager may have made wrong choices. GlaxoSmithKline's managers in China paid bribes to doctors and hospital officials in order to sell their pharmaceutical products, but what patterns of behavior or features of the GSK environment allowed them to feel justified about making these illegal payments?[17] Classical virtue ethics also underscores the importance of confirming good habits in the workplace by sound corporate policies so that managers can be prudent decision makers.

Despite its merits, however, virtue ethics offers insufficient direction about deciding how to act in complex circumstances where virtuous persons can disagree. Virtue ethics simply does not provide adequate guidance for prudent moral action. Should euthanasia in extreme cases be morally justified simply because it appears to be consistent with the virtue of compassion? Aren't there many other factors involved in reaching a morally reasonable judgment? In addition, there is a lack of consensus over which habits (or dispositions) are suitable virtues and which are vices. Thus, virtue ethics seems open to a challenge of subjectivism or relativism. However, insights about virtue and character can certainly inform discussion about business ethics and what it means to act well as a businessperson.

CONSEQUENCES AND UTILITARIANISM

Following Aristotle, medieval philosophers, such as Thomas Aquinas, continued to stress the importance of teleology and human nature ordered to a final end of perfection or fulfillment. His theory of natural law is centered on a common human nature and the fundamental human goods that contribute to that nature's fulfillment. But modern theories of ethics take a sharp turn away from any sort of teleological or natural-law reasoning. The most popular modern frameworks represent a distinct dichotomy between consequences and duty. The former theory of utilitarianism confines itself to the consideration of consequences, while the latter believes that moral rightness is independent of consequences. Ethical reasoning among some business leaders has tended to follow the utilitarian model, which links pragmatic rationality with goodness. Hence this theory requires careful consideration.

Unlike virtue ethics, which is focused on character, **utilitarianism** is strictly centered on the effects our actions will produce. Classic utilitarianism was developed by two British philosophers, Jeremy Bentham (1748–1832) and John Stuart Mill (1806–1873). At the time, utilitarianism was regarded as a radical philosophy opposed to more traditional moral reasoning based on natural law and natural rights. For Bentham, however, the idea of natural rights was just "nonsense on stilts." This theory has been referred to as **consequentialism** by Elizabeth Anscombe, who saw this ethical paradigm as a "shallow philosophy" because its exclusive focus on consequences was far too narrow.[18]

According to utilitarian reasoning, the right course of action is to promote happiness or the general good. The general good can be described in terms of "utility," and this principle of utility is the foundation of morality and the decisive criterion of right and wrong. Bentham argued that the highest demand of morality was to maximize happiness, which amounts to the overall balance of pleasure over pain. The right action, therefore, will maximize utility, and, for Bentham, utility is equivalent to whatever produces pleasure and reduces pain. Modern versions define *utility* in terms of net benefits and argue that an action is the right one when its consequences consist of a maximum of nonmoral goods or a minimum of nonmoral evils for all parties affected by that action. There is always a weighing of goods that underlies utilitarian reasoning. Moreover, the moral rightness of action is measured in terms of ends (or outcomes) and not by intentions or the means used to achieve those ends.[19]

Utilitarianism in all its various forms must be distinguished from ethical egoism. The egoist cares only about his or her own good. However, utilitarianism cannot be reduced to such a myopic self-centered perspective, since it considers the goods of everyone affected by a particular action or moral choice. Utilitarianism goes beyond a self-interest model of business ethics where the overriding moral calculus for corporate executives is based on corporate profits or return on investment. The conscientious executive weighs the consequences for each stakeholder group affected by a decision, not just the results for herself and her company.

With all this in mind, we can formulate the moral principle of utilitarianism as follows: *every moral agent is obliged to perform that action by which he or she can maximize net expectable utility, that is, the greatest net benefits or the lowest net costs, for all parties affected by that action.*

The consequentialist assumes that one action with better consequences is preferable to another action whose consequences are not as good. The moral value of an action, therefore, depends on the value of the causal outcome of that action. As G. E. Moore explains, "To ask what kind of action we ought to perform, or what kind of action is right, is to ask what effects such action and conduct will produce."[20]

How does consequentialism work in practice? The moral agent engages in a moral calculus or cost/benefit analysis to determine which option would optimize the consequences or yield the best possible outcome for all concerned. For example, let's assume that a senior vice president of operations who oversees the production of smartphones must consider whether to outsource jobs to a supplier in an emerging economy or continue the current policy or insourcing. Offshore outsourcing has the potential to reduce the phone's cost structure by 30%, but it will also result in high social costs, since domestic plants will be closed, workers laid off, and local communities distressed. The first option will include a high proportion of nonmoral goods: more substantial profits, better returns for shareholders, additional funds to invest in research and development (R&D), and a greater ability to attract capital. The second option will avoid the psychological and social costs associated with the layoffs that accompany outsourcing, but the company's high cost structure will make it more difficult to compete efficiently with aggressive Asian competitors who operate with low labor costs. The upright but presumptively disinterested manager must account for the concerns of all these stakeholders in her deliberations. She must weigh all of these dispersed costs and benefits and somehow choose the alternative that optimizes consequences and thereby promotes the general social welfare for those affected by this decision.

The difficulty of putting aside self-serving assumptions and personal biases to make these decisions underscores the practical problems with consequentialism. How can subjectivism be avoided in the evaluation of consequences? Are managers capable of overcoming partiality and bias when they engage in utilitarian reasoning? There are also difficulties in achieving adequate knowledge about future causal outcomes. Can a manager be sure that an action will yield the maximum possible benefits? To what extent should consequences be investigated, and how do remote consequences relate to more immediate ones? These and other questions have vexed proponents of consequentialism for a long time, and yet no satisfactory answers have been forthcoming. As Lynn Sharp Paine concludes, "For all its aura of objectivity and precision, cost-benefit analysis is highly vulnerable to distortions and biases that cloud the moral issues."[21]

While we cannot underestimate the practical difficulties associated with utilitarian reasoning, the biggest problem involves its theoretical shortcomings. Is it possible to translate these premoral goods into a single currency of value without losing something in the process? Often, cost/benefit analysis falls short because it attempts to translate costs and benefits into monetary terms, which is not always possible.[22] In addition, this pragmatic ethical paradigm represents a form of soft relativism. Utilitarian logic fails to protect the dignity of persons through the recognition and acceptance of inviolable rights. Moral agents who follow this logic are easily tempted to suspend certain rights in light of the positive consequences for doing so. It is permissible, for example, to torture a prisoner if it is evident that this act would yield the most positive results (such as the location of a group planning a terrorist attack). Or, as Michael Slote explains, "If killing an innocent person is necessary in order to avoid a large-scale catastrophe, then one may and even should perform the killing."[23]

Although utilitarianism cannot deliver the final word about an ethical solution, the general idea that "consequences matter" warrants our attention. As part of an ethical diagnosis, managers should dispassionately assess the impact of their decisions and policies on different stakeholder groups, such as their customers and employees. A pharmaceutical company, for example, must surely take into account the effects of a substantial product price increase on its customer base as well as its investors. Such an impact analysis is a sensible and reasonable starting point for ethical deliberation.

ETHICS AS DUTY

A plausible alternative to consequentialism that does not suffer from its practical difficulties or theoretical flaws is moral reasoning informed by respect for moral duties. Duties are distinct markers that help to establish the borders of acceptable behavior. Prudent leaders and executives acknowledge that there are certain moral duties essential for the proper conduct of business. Michael Sandel describes three categories of duties:

1. Particular voluntary obligations

2. Particular obligations of solidarity

3. Universal natural duties[24]

The first category, voluntary obligations, arises from our consent and includes promises and contractual agreements. If a manager signs a contract to deliver supplies to a factory by a certain date, he has an obligation to do so. Similarly, if a person voluntarily promises to repay a loan within six months, he or she is obliged to live up to this self-imposed obligation.

The second category, obligations of solidarity, constitute those duties that arise because of one's membership in particular communities such as the family, the corporation, the local town where one resides, and the country where one is a citizen. Family members, for example, have definite duties of care and loyalty to one another. Similarly, nations have certain responsibilities to care for the welfare of their citizens. While every nation has a universal duty to respect the rights of all persons, the obligation of solidarity carries more moral weight and implies special responsibilities to care for its own people. At the same time, a country's citizens are also bound by ties of loyalty.[25]

Finally, there are natural duties that are owed to others by virtue of their humanity or rational personhood. This type of universal duty is best exemplified in the moral philosophy of Immanuel Kant (1724–1804). Kant wrote two critical works on ethics: *Fundamental Principles of the Metaphysics of Morals* and *The Critique of Practical Reason*. In the first work, he underscores that moral philosophy must be predicated on the "common idea of duty." Our sense of duty sets us above the order of nature that governs other creatures. Duty is paramount, and the consequences of one's action are immaterial for assessing an action's moral worth. Duty, on the other hand, subjects us to certain demands that supersede countervailing considerations, and duty alone is the proper motivation for ethical choices. A daughter who takes care of her sick father is acting morally only if she is undertaking this action for the sake of duty. If she is taking care of him simply because she is naturally inclined to do so by love or sentiment, the action has no moral worth in Kant's eyes. She is doing the right thing but for the wrong reason, since she is not motivated by duty. This dichotomy between natural inclination and duty shadows Kant's austere moral system.[26]

But what exactly is the moral duty of rational creatures, and how is it derived? In Kant's systematic philosophy, a person's duty is simple: follow the moral law. According to Kant, "Duty is the necessity to act out of reverence for the law."[27] That moral law is determined by practical reason that discerns the law's universality and necessity by means of the categorical imperative. According to that imperative, we are obliged to "act so that the maxim of [our] will could always hold at the same time as a principle of universal law-giving."[28] Can the maxim or implied rule that expresses a specific action become a valid universal moral law? If not, that action is contradictory in some way and cannot be universalized. As a result, it is not morally valid.

For example, if a businessperson breaks a contract whenever it is in her best interest to do so, she acts according to the private maxim that contract breaking is an acceptable behavior. But can this maxim be transformed into a universal moral law? As a universal law, this particular maxim would be expressed as follows: "It is permissible for everyone to break a contract when it is in their best interests to do so." Such a law, however, is invalid, since it entails both a pragmatic and a logical contradiction. There is a pragmatic (or practical) contradiction, because the maxim is self-defeating if it is universalized. If everyone broke contracts, no one would be trusted when they entered into a contractual arrangement, and hence contracts would be abolished. And if anyone acts on a principle that would be impossible for everyone else to follow, that individual's action is wrong.[29] According to Korsgaard, "Your action would become ineffectual for the achievement of your purpose if everyone [tried to] use it for that purpose."[30]

Universal contract breaking also implies a logical contradiction or impossibility (like a square circle). For Kant, if a maxim (such as "contract breaking is morally acceptable") cannot even be conceived as a universal law, it is contrary to our strict or perfect duty. A universalized broken contract is certainly a conceptual absurdity, because there would be no such thing as a binding contract in a world where such a maxim had been universalized. Therefore, a world of universal contract breaking is logically inconceivable. Thus, in view of the contradictions involved in universalizing contract breaking, we have a perfect duty to abide by the contracts we make. Kant differentiates between perfect and imperfect duties. If a maxim can be conceived as a universal law but cannot be willed without contradiction, it is an imperfect duty.[31]

Kant's categorical imperative is the ultimate criterion for distinguishing right actions from wrong ones. The categorical imperative functions as a guide, a "moral compass" that gives us a reliable way of determining a correct and consistent course of action. It can be conceived as a principle of justice or fair play. The essence of fairness is avoiding partiality and not making an exception for oneself. In Kant's words, the transgression of duty implies that we make such an exception because "we do not actually will that our maxim should become a universal law."[32] The categorical imperative inspires us to answer a simple question: "What if everybody did what you did?"

Kant also offers a second version of his categorical imperative: "Act so that you treat humanity, whether in your own person or in that of another, always as an end and never as a means only."[33] Each person must be respected as an end, affirmed for his or her own sake, and never used only as an instrumental means for something else. This obligation flows from the person's rationality and autonomy. This is why human persons, whose rational capacities enable them to project their own ends along with the means to achieve those ends, should never be coerced or deceived. Rational nature is the unconditional value which bestows on each person his or her dignity. Kant's categorical imperative stipulates that since persons have the dignity of reason and autonomy, they are ends in themselves, and this moral status sets them apart from nonpersonal being. According to Kant, "Concerning man (and thus every rational being in the world) as a moral being one cannot ask further, for what end does he exist? His existence has the highest purpose in itself."[34]

Kant's moral system deserves praise for its anticipation of philosophies like personalism that vindicate personal freedom and draw attention to the immeasurable dignity of the human person. However, Kantian morality is riddled with conceptual difficulties. Perhaps the most serious problem with Kant's moral philosophy is its rigidity: the absolute norms derived from the categorical imperative allow for no exceptions. There may be occasions when it is necessary to break a contract or a promise, yet I am still forbidden to do so since the maxim cannot be validly universalized. Consider a scenario where my neighbor gives me his gun for safekeeping with the promise that I give it back to him when he returns from a long trip. Should I keep that promise even if he comes to me looking for his gun and tells me that he wants it in order to shoot his boss?

In addition, philosophers as far back as Hegel have also criticized Kant's formalism for separating the moral obligation from its object and for its "emptiness" or lack of content. Morality is reduced to the formula of the categorical imperative, and there is nothing else, such as an account of the good. But there *is* a content to Kantian moral philosophy that is implicit in the categorical imperative. The second formulation of that imperative, "Act so that you treat humanity, whether in your own person or in that of another, always as an end and never as a means only," commands us to treat our fellow human beings with respect because of their dignity as free, rational beings. Thus, the dignity of the other as an end is the unconditioned principle and the real "content" of Kantian morality.

How might we sum up the practical implications of this duty-based view of morality? All three forms of duty or moral obligation arise in a business context, and some are formalized in the laws that govern corporations and other associations. Table 3.1 contains a summary of general moral obligations that entail more specific duties especially relevant to managers and executives.[35]

TABLE 3.1 ■ General Principles and Duties	
General Obligations	**Specific Moral/Legal Duties**
Fiduciary Requirements	Loyalty of executives to the corporation and its shareholders; sustain company's economic welfare and allocate corporate resources prudently; proper risk management; disclose all conflicts of interest
Acknowledge Dignity of All Persons	Safeguard health and safety of all employees; ensure that products are safe and reliable and do not endanger customer health; avoid deprivation of basic human rights and protect rights from being deprived; refrain from coercion and deception that undermine a person's autonomy
Respect for Property Rights	Honor valid property claims of stakeholders and others, including intellectual property; deploy company property conscientiously; safeguard company assets; do not acquire proprietary information of competitors through dishonest means
Transparency and Honesty	Be accurate, truthful, and open; disclose relevant information to consumers, including product risks; avoid fraud, deception, misrepresentation, and unnecessary opaqueness
Fairness and Fair Play	Compete on merit and avoid all forms of devious or subversive competition; treat suppliers and partners equitably; offer just and reasonable compensation to managers and employees; protect against discrimination or arbitrary treatment of employees and other stakeholders
Civic and Social Responsibilities	Cooperate with public authorities in dealing with public health or safety issues; obey laws and regulations such as environmental and tax laws; correct and compensate for damage to environment or community; avoid forms of free riding that impair social welfare

NATURAL RIGHTS

Another avenue of ethical reasoning is based on a consideration of natural rights. Rights too are distinctive markers that set boundaries of permissible conduct. Natural rights are not subjective, and they are not derived from some sort of social contract between individuals and their respective governments. Rather, natural rights are what people possess by virtue of their humanity or personhood. These rights are universal and exist independently of any recognition in local custom or of the legal systems of particular countries. They may have no effect unless they become codified in law, but they do not depend on legalization for their validity. Rights of this sort are moral guarantees of liberties, benefits, and protections that ensure a person's dignity.[36]

A rights-based orientation to ethics is disfavored by some who see rights as atomistic and individual. Those who assert their individual rights, critics claim, look past the common good or the needs of the community. Such a viewpoint, however, is easily refuted. Rights are intricately tied to the promotion of solidarity and community. The right to free speech, for example, encourages truthful and open communication and ensures that people can freely speak to one another. This valuable right, therefore, has an unmistakable social character. Similarly, the right to nondiscrimination guarantees that the government will not exclude minority groups or subordinate their interests, but rather promote their integration into the whole community. These and other rights, therefore, are not antisocial but help cultivate communal harmony.[37]

Legal philosopher Ronald Dworkin described rights as "political trumps held by individuals." Rights have a certain "threshold weight against collective goals in general."[38] What Dworkin had in mind is that rights *generally* prevail when they compete with other concerns, such as maximizing profits or administrative expediency. Dworkin's language captures the idea that rights are powerful normative considerations in moral deliberations with at least a presumptive priority. A stronger thesis claims that while all natural rights are inviolable, there are some rights that are absolute. Absolute rights must *always* prevail against countervailing considerations.[39]

The notion of natural rights has a strong pedigree in the philosophical tradition. We find a doctrine of natural rights in both the liberal tradition of John Locke and the natural-law tradition of St. Thomas Aquinas. For Locke, the foundation of basic natural rights such as property is self-ownership: "by being master of himself and proprietor of his own person," a human person possesses natural rights.[40] According to Locke, "A law of nature . . . obliges everyone [that] no one ought to harm another in his life, health, liberty or possessions."[41] These rights to life, liberty, and property occupy a central place in Locke's political philosophy. Similarly, Thomas Aquinas intimates the concept of rights in his treatment of natural law. Persons have certain natural rights by virtue of the natural law, and those rights give normative recognition to our equality. Justice is achieved by respecting the rights of human persons, who are entitled to equal treatment.[42]

Each right, when properly specified, trumps all other competing factors, with the possible exception of a conflicting right that deserves priority. Contrary to a utilitarian viewpoint, natural rights cannot be set aside merely for the sake of the collective welfare. Most rights are not absolute, but the infringement of a right cannot be justified in consequentialist terms. An individual cannot be harmed by the deprivation of a right merely for the sake of the collective good. For example, when the right to a safe workplace is put aside because it supposedly burdens the corporation's economic welfare, there is every likelihood that some workers will be physically injured. Infringement is warranted only when rights conflict with each other, and this happens only in exceptional circumstances. Rights, therefore, have a moral force that is incompatible with utilitarianism.[43]

To understand this framework more fully, we must first consider the definition of a right. A right is an entitlement, a moral power to *do* or *have* something. More precisely, rights are *justified claims* that a person or group of persons can make upon other individuals or upon society. A claim right or a right in the strict sense differs from a liberty such as the liberty to smoke a cigarette under certain conditions. But a claim right is always a right not to be interfered with or treated in a certain way *or* a right to be given something or to be assisted in some manner. Rights provide a way of conceiving justice from the viewpoint of the "other" to whom something is owed and who would be injured in some way if he or she were denied that something.[44]

These claim rights, therefore, always imply *correlative duties* on the part of other individuals. Rights are the other side of many of those duties presented in the previous section. If a person possesses a right, that person is in a position to determine what others should or should not do. If someone has a right to property, others have a duty not to interfere with that right by stealing or destroying that property. Thus, rights are normative structures that usually require legal enforcement to make them effective. However, such enforcement is not essential to a right.[45]

A suitable natural-rights theory requires a secure foundation that consists of those goods that fulfill the human person. More fundamental than rights or duties are the basic goods of human nature, which allow us to rationally determine what rights people have. Morality is always ultimately concerned with what is good or bad for human beings. Every person seeks what is good and tries to avoid what is bad in order to live well and flourish. Certain goods are choice-worthy, not as a means to other ends but as ends in themselves. These intrinsic goods constitute the fundamental aspects of human flourishing and provide intelligible reasons for our choices and actions. Life, of course, is one such good, and this category includes health, safety, and bodily integrity. Knowledge is another good worth pursuing for its own sake, while ignorance is to be avoided. And since the person is also a social being who naturally seeks the companionship of others, living in friendship or community is an aspect of human flourishing. We can also add to this list other substantive goods, such as skilled performance at work (and play), along with marriage, aesthetic experience, and self-integration (the integration of one's feelings and practical intelligence). Finally, there are also instrumental goods, such as privacy and freedom, which make it possible to participate in some of the intrinsic goods that are so important for our fulfillment. This set of intrinsic and instrumental goods represents the ultimate ground of morality and expresses the moral force behind each natural right.[46]

Now that we understand the foundation for rights, we must articulate a set of rights that can guide all moral agents, including corporations. How can we determine which specific rights should be included in such a list? James Nickel suggests several criteria that legal and moral rights must satisfy. He argues that a right can be justified only if it protects something of great importance. The second condition is that there must be a "substantial and recurrent threat" to this claim for a right. Without the threat criterion, there would be too many potential rights. While racial discrimination can undermine someone's participation in one or more of the basic human goods, there would be no need for such a claim right in a society where there was no trace of discriminatory behavior. There must be a low threshold, so that even if a society experienced very little discrimination, it would still be worthwhile to recognize a moral and legal right against discrimination to handle the few cases that occurred. Thus, a "very important interest" must be secured by a specific right in order to protect it against some recurrent threat, even if that threat has a low intensity.[47]

The third and final condition stipulates that the obligations or burdens imposed by the right are affordable in relation to available resources, other obligations, and a fair distribution of burdens. Sometimes rights must be qualified or limited on the grounds of costs. When resources are scarce, the fact that a particular right is expensive to effectively implement may mean that such implementation is impossible. This condition pertains primarily to positive rights that call upon others to provide goods and services, such as education or health care.[48]

With the assistance of Nickel's suggestive framework, we can derive a reasonable set of rights that should be honored by all moral agents. To demonstrate that a specific right protects something of great importance, we can refer to those fundamental goods that promote human flourishing. As we have argued, general rights protect both intrinsic and instrumental goods that are basic to human well-being. Participation in these basic goods has certainly been threatened at many different times and in many different countries, and so they also deserve to be secured by rights. Also, the rights we propose satisfy the third condition, since, for the most part, they are negative rights rather than positive ones that often require a substantial amount of society's resources. Negative rights prevent someone or some community from acting in a certain way.[49]

Given the conditions articulated by Nickel, we present a list of 14 basic rights. All of these rights are under some threat, and all of them have the prospect of full ratification within a mature legal system. The list is fairly short because we try to avoid the assertion of rights that are not feasible to implement. All these rights are included in one form or another in the Universal Declaration of Human Rights, and many are found in other key documents such as the Bill of Rights in the U.S. Constitution. This list is not necessarily exhaustive, but the rights enumerated here express the most fundamental requirements of justice:

- Right to freedom or political liberty

- Right to be free from slavery or servitude

- Right to ownership of property

- Right to freedom from torture

- Right not to be subject to arbitrary arrest and to a fair trial (due process)

- Right not to be knowingly condemned on false charges

- Right to nondiscriminatory treatment

- Right to life, health, bodily integrity, and security of person

- Right to freedom of speech and association

- Right to political participation

- Right to minimal education

- Right to subsistence (a standard of living adequate for health and well-being)

- Right to privacy

- Right to freedom of thought, conscience, and religion[50]

These rights, of course, must all be precisely specified and limited by other rights and by certain aspects of the common good. Rights are inviolable, but they are not limitless: they may be *infringed* under certain conditions but not *violated*. Someone infringes on another's right when he interferes with the exercise of that person's right, and he violates that right only if he does so unjustly. Not every infringement constitutes a violation, but every violation is an infringement. The violation (or deprivation) of a right strikes at the heart of the particular good that right is supposed to safeguard. But there are sometimes conflicts. It may be necessary, for example, to trespass on someone's property without their consent to get access to water that will save one's life. According to Oderberg, rights can be infringed in these limited, well-defined circumstances where the more urgent right prevails because it is closer to the core of one's dignity and well-being. Life and health are more important than property, but one is still bound to respect the value of property and should only violate that right in the most unobtrusive manner that avoids a direct attack on the property owner's well-being.[51]

Only a select group of rights are absolute and subject to no exceptions. Given the great importance of the fundamental good of human life, a strong case can certainly be put forth for the absolute right of an innocent person not to have his or her life taken directly either as a means or as an end. Similarly, the right not to be tortured should be subject to no exception, since intentional damage to bodily integrity or health is intrinsically wrong. Even the right not to be knowingly condemned on false charges qualifies as absolute.[52]

As we noted earlier, duties are correlative to rights, and, according to Henry Shue, there are three categories of duties for every basic right. Of course, the most basic duty is not to wrongfully violate someone's rights, and Shue speaks about rights violations in terms of deprivation. In his estimation, all three of these duties must be performed if the right is to be fully honored. These generic duties include (1) duties to avoid depriving, (2) duties to protect from deprivation, and (3) duties to aid the deprived. For example, with respect to the right of physical security, there is a duty not to directly invade the good of personal security (by assault or rape), a duty to protect people against deprivation of security by other people, and a duty to provide security for those unable to provide their own. These three duties do not necessarily apply to all moral agents. For example, in most cases we cannot expect individuals or organizations to provide security for others. That task falls primarily on nation-states and their law-enforcement agencies.[53]

Corporations and their managers must assume at least the first two duties. Arguably, corporations are not required to assist those deprived of rights and correct rights abuses, since they are unsuited for this task, which may sometimes require them to educate the young and care for the sick. Thus, the corporation as moral agent should *avoid depriving* people of their rights and avoid cooperation in such deprivation by another party. In many cases, especially where corporate activities are directly involved, corporations must also help *protect* rights from being deprived. A corporation that outsources production to an overseas contractor with unsafe working conditions is not directly depriving these employees of their rights. But this corporation is obliged to protect this right to safety from being deprived by exercising its leverage over the employment practices of the contractor to demand that the work environment be safe.[54]

Unlike utilitarianism, a rights-based ethic anchors morality in the intrinsic worth of the human person. Every person's fundamental dignity and capacity for human flourishing is protected by these basic human rights. Rights properly justified express the norms of justice and what is owed to everyone alike. This framework inspires us to think about social life not just in terms of my rights but also in terms of solidarity and my duty to others. At the same time, those rights are firmly grounded in basic human goods, which are at the root of all moral norms.

Table 3.2 summarizes the four ethical frameworks discussed in relation to ethics and their application to the business world.

SYNTHESIS AND APPLICATION

While it is probably not possible to synthesize all these diverse theories into a coherent whole, we can recommend a holistic approach to moral reasoning that is labeled **DRJ (duties-rights-justice)**. It encourages managers to first identify their particular or universal moral obligations in a given situation. Within corporations, fiduciary duties along with duties such as transparency, fairness, and respect for property play a prominent role in the proper conduct of business. This simple framework also requires a precise consideration of what is owed to others in justice in terms of natural rights. Rights are correlative

TABLE 3.2 ■ Summary of Ethical Frameworks		
Theory	**Key Focus**	**Practical Question**
Virtue Ethics	Moral agency; character	Is my action in line with morally commendable traits and virtues?
Utilitarianism	Outcomes or results	What are the negative and positive effects of this action on stakeholder groups?
Morality as Duty	Natural and voluntary obligations along with obligations of solidarity	Is this action consistent with universal moral law; is it consistent with voluntary obligations incurred by consent or those arising from solidarity and co-responsibility?
Natural Rights	Protection of human goods and preservation of normative equality	Do these actions deprive anyone of his or her rights, or do they fail to protect rights from being deprived?

to natural duties. As we have discussed, both rights and duties constitute distinct markers, the unambiguous boundaries of permissible moral behavior.

In any situation where a moral duty arises, managers must comply with this obligation, even if noncompliance would yield better overall effects or consequences. Whatever the state of affairs a manager's actions may bring about, priority must be given to moral duty. A moral obligation directs itself to each manager's conscience as a necessary and universal demand inasmuch as it would be directed to any moral agent in the same situation. The only exception is whether a specific moral duty is superseded in a given context by a higher and more compelling duty. Similarly, in a conflict of rights, the more urgent right should always prevail.[55]

Thus, sometimes it is necessary to breach these clearly defined moral rules and thereby cause harm to others. But how do we discern when causing harm is reasonable and just? The notion of moral impartiality can be useful in resolving conflicts that involve a collision of rights or determining when exceptions to duties are valid. Justice demands rational impartiality to the type of actions or policies that are allowable in such circumstances. It is unjust and unfair for someone to choose a certain action or policy she would not allow others to choose. Consider a financially troubled company that decides to sell unsafe and potentially harmful electric heaters to remain in business. This action implies a general policy that permits the sale of unsafe merchandise that can harm people. But a rational person would not endorse such a policy, since it would allow others to do the same, and so that person would put herself and her family at an unacceptable level of risk.[56]

According to Bernard Gert, this blindfold of justice removes all knowledge of who will benefit and who will be harmed by one's choices. The central question for Gert is the following: would this violation of a moral rule be publicly allowed; that is, what would happen if everyone knew about this policy of selling unsafe products and chose to do it? Clearly, the consequences of allowing such a general policy would be unacceptable, since the risks of injury would be too high. This same veil of impartiality can be useful in reconciling rights conflicts. Karen, for example, has the right to exclude people from her personal property. But suppose that Mary must rush her extremely sick child to the local hospital and the quickest way is to drive through Karen's property? Mary infringes on Karen's property right in order to save her child's life. Any rational, impartial person (including Karen) would accept a policy that stipulates a need to temporarily breach the duty to respect a property right in order to save a person's life. Thus, others could also follow this rule that expresses a minor exception to a property right, and this exception could be publicly advocated. While some judgments about exceptions to moral rules will be agreed to by all rational, impartial people, in some cases there will be room for debate and disagreement.[57]

As we discussed in the previous chapter, corporate purpose is tied to the common good of all those who participate in the business. Since that common good includes fairness to these cooperating stakeholders, managers must create value and pursue their economic goals within legal and ethical boundaries that prescribe how that fairness can be achieved. We now appreciate that those ethical boundaries are determined by **duties**, including voluntary and natural obligations along with obligations of solidarity. They are also set by **rights**, which are the other side of natural duties and are owed to individuals by virtue of their rational personhood. Exceptions to moral rules that express duties or rights are sometimes possible, but not for egoistic or utilitarian reasons. In these cases, justice requires that these exceptions pass the impartiality test. We capture this approach with the acronym DRJ.

Figure 3.1 shows where this approach plays a role in the three obligations of corporations.

SCOPE OF CORPORATE SOCIAL RESPONSIBILITY

FIGURE 3.1   ■   Review of Corporate Obligations
• Pursue economic mission and create value
• Follow relevant laws and regulations
• Observe ethical principles according to the DRJ formula

Many ethicists and social activists have argued with some insistence that corporations have obligations that exceed respect for fundamental rights and rational moral principles such as "Do no harm." There is more to **corporate social responsibility (CSR)** than the creation of wealth, obeying the law, and observing ethical principles. The modern corporation must also be committed to a broad social agenda that includes philanthropic activities and contributions to the resolution of severe social problems. According to this view, corporations are not just bound to avoid depriving people of their rights while also protecting rights from being deprived; they must also assist those who are deprived of their rights, even if this means working for certain elusive but worthy objectives such as distributive justice.[58]

Although there is sometimes an overlap between these ethical and social obligations, it is useful to keep them distinct. As we have seen, ethical obligations primarily involve adherence to duties and respect for those basic human rights that protect fundamental goods. But social obligations are more philanthropic and proactive in nature and aim to address society's weaknesses and inequities. Corporate social responsibility in this thick sense adds corporate charity to the other three obligations. Corporations that embrace this thick version of CSR want to create wealth within the law and the bounds of ethical probity, but they also aim for social progress and the correction of social injustice.

There are many examples of altruistic companies that have adopted a generous social mission. Several major Indian firms like Tata are quite active in providing vital services, such as education and health care, for impoverished Indian communities.[59] Goldman Sachs has invested in a Utah preschool program that is designed to help "at risk" kindergartner students avoid special education classes.[60] The Dow Chemical Foundation contributes generously to Habitat for Humanity. And ExxonMobil has invested $125 million toward training teachers in science, technology, and engineering who will teach the skilled workers of the future. Sometimes these social investments are not purely altruistic. By committing funds to education, companies like ExxonMobil hope to indirectly benefit themselves in the long run through a better-educated workforce.

This type of pragmatic, win-win opportunity has been referred to as "shared value" by Porter and Kramer, who claim that companies can enhance their profits and address social problems at the same time. According to this theory, there are many ways in which corporations can create economic and social value simultaneously and thereby "reshape capitalism." They define shared value as "policies and operating practices that enhance competitiveness of a company while simultaneously advancing economic and social conditions in the communities in which it operates."[61] The authors point to Coca-Cola's commitment to better resource utilization, which will help the environment but also reduce costs. The soft-drink company is making progress toward the goal of reducing its water consumption by 20%. The prime advantage of the shared-value approach is the close integration of social and strategic goals. A greater commitment to shared value will redefine corporate purpose and encourage companies to expand their narrow view of value creation.

Of course, not everyone concurs that corporations should have such a broad social agenda, even if it seems to be in their enlightened self-interest. Critics of the shared-value approach are skeptical that business and social objectives can be so easily aligned except in atypical cases. How can ExxonMobil be so certain that its large investment in education will really pay future dividends toward its corporate performance? And if there is an abundance of these "shared value" opportunities, why haven't they been uncovered by other companies?[62]

The principal flaw of the shared-value model is a failure to acknowledge the inevitable tensions between social and economic goals. Some studies show the extreme difficulty of sustaining both of these objectives within the same organizational structure. In the face of these difficulties, there is a tendency to drift away from one of the two missions. In addition, while seeking win-win situations is constructive, there is little guidance in the Porter-Kramer model for how to proceed when social and economic outcomes diverge and cannot be aligned for all corporate stakeholders.[63]

Resistance to a social agenda for corporations has a long history in writings on corporate social responsibility. Milton Friedman and those who endorse the doctrine of shareholder primacy have steadfastly opposed the idea that a corporation is obliged to resolve social problems or contribute resources for such solutions. The priority of shareholder value is supported in the American legal system by cases such as *Dodge Brothers v. Ford Motor Company*, which directed companies like Ford to operate in the interests of shareholders and maximize profits. Corporations cannot pledge to "a general purpose and plan to benefit mankind at the expense of shareholders."[64] Friedman's view, confirmed by this ruling, is consistent with the property model of the corporation presented in the previous chapter.

According to Friedman, therefore, "There is one and only one social responsibility of business—to use its resources and engage in activities designed to increase its profits so long as it stays within the rules of the game, which is to say, engages in free and open competition, without deception or fraud."[65] The only responsibility for corporations is to increase long-term profits within the framework of the law and within certain ethical boundaries that preclude fraud and deception. Friedman also believed that the markets themselves would solve many of the "social" problems that resulted from market failures such as negative externalities. If people don't want sugary drinks or fatty foods because they are concerned about the health consequences, alert food and beverage firms will respond to these market demands accordingly. The result will be healthier foods and more wholesome drinks. When market failures or urgent social problems are not resolved by market forces, new laws or regulations should be enacted so that resources are directed to their optimal social use. Hence, corporations can count on markets and the laws that regulate those markets as a guide to any pursuit of social aims.

Friedman's skepticism about the corporation's social agenda was also based on his strong conviction that managers lacked the proper skills to prioritize and handle social objectives. Managers are not experts in social and political issues, and so the allocation of corporate resources to address complex societal problems such as obesity or low educational standards is likely to be in vain. Also, will managers be so distracted by achieving altruistic goals that they fail to create maximum value for shareholders and other key stakeholder groups?

However, when corporations push the idea of shareholder primacy too far, it quite often backfires. Consider the story of Valeant, a Canadian pharmaceutical company that reduced R&D investment and raised prices excessively in an effort to boost profits and share prices. Valeant faced a potent backlash and had to retreat from its ill-conceived strategy. When a company is single-mindedly devoted to profit maximization and nothing else, it is unlikely to prosper for very long. After the price hikes, the Valeant policy became a rallying cry against high pharmaceutical prices. As a result, revenues and profits declined and the stock price fell by 85%. While corporations must be wary of overextending themselves, they cannot abandon a commitment to some version of CSR in favor of fundamentalist tactics that will ultimately subvert their economic objectives.[66]

Whether or not prosperous corporations should have a social agenda and pursue "shared value" solutions to social problems is an open question that can spark lively debate. But what is not an open question is the need for corporations to be ethical. Porter and Kramer argue that capitalism has been discredited by a failure to address social problems that lie beyond the corporation's well-defined boundaries. However, haven't ethical scandals done far more to erode confidence in capitalism than the failure of corporations to be more altruistic? The shared-value model "presumes compliance with the law and ethical standards" and so pays little heed to ethics.[67] But in the face of so many recurring moral calamities, this is a big presumption. How much does capitalism benefit if a big retailer finds ways to cut costs and protect the environment by reconfiguring how it packages and delivers products but then engages in bribery and corruption in its overseas markets? There seems to be little doubt that ethical scandals such as the LIBOR fraud at Barclays bank, Volkswagen's Dieselgate, and Wells Fargo's sales scam foster distrust and suspicion as they lower expectations for fairness. Sometimes corporations that do well forget that it is more important to be right and to make reasonable moral choices that avoid harm and respect the rights of their constituencies.

CONCLUSION

Companies are organized to create wealth for their owners, but they must do so within the limits of the law and with a commitment to ethical standards. In this chapter, we defined ethics as an applied science because of its dual aim of knowledge and action. We reviewed several principles (virtue, utility, duty, rights) that have been at the center of an entire philosophical ethic. In the process, we considered some of the strengths and limitations of these avenues of moral reasoning. In our estimation, a focus on duties and rights, while not without its own limitations, offers the clearest and most direct approach for addressing ethical issues.

Duties fall in three categories, but the most important are natural duties that flow from our rational personhood. "Duty," explains Kant, "is the necessity to act out of reverence for the law."[68] That law is the categorical imperative, a universalization principle forbidding actions that put a manager's or firm's interest above that of everyone else.

Moral principles can also be expressed in terms of rights, which capture what is owed to others in justice. Rights offer moral protection to everyone and constitute the backbone of traditional legal systems. These rights are inviolable and in some cases absolute. Further, behind the notion of rights stands the more basic concept of human good. There are many potential rights, but a valid right must protect something of great importance, such as the intrinsic and instrumental goods necessary for human flourishing. The veil of rational impartiality can help conscientious managers determine when rights can be infringed and when exceptions to duties are warranted. While it is not always possible to be precise in these matters, most objective judgments about exceptions will be shared by rational impartial individuals.

We also considered the appropriate scope of a corporation's obligations. Should the corporation have a social agenda? Can it create economic value and achieve social progress at the same time? Wherever one stands on this issue, we can at least insist that corporate integrity is more fundamental than corporate charity. The reconnection of corporate success and social objectives advocated by Porter and Kramer is a positive tendency, especially as public expectations change on issues like pollution or safety. However, many companies, such as Apple, which prides itself on its social commitments, have been slow to resolve severe ethical problems, such as labor abuses and meager salaries in their supply chains.

Student Study Site

Visit **edge.sagepub.com/spinello.**

Key Terms

consequentialism 48	DRJ (duties-rights-justice) 57	normative ethics 44
corporate social responsibility	duties 58	rights 58
(CSR) 59	justice 59	utilitarianism 48

Review Questions

1. Explain how to use the three primary corporate obligations and the DRJ formula in ethical decision-making in corporations.

2. Explain the role the corporation plays in improving the future of the communities it functions in.

Discussion Questions

1. In an influential essay on legal education, Katharine Bartlett makes the following claim: "The dilemma is that we cannot be value-neutral in our teaching—indeed we should not be; but neither can we teach values—indeed in the most usual sense of the word 'teaching' we should not try." In your view, does her claim also apply to management education? Do you agree that we cannot "teach values" to managers or to aspiring managers? What are the key arguments that support your position?[69]

2. Niccolo Machiavelli (1469–1527) lived during the Italian renaissance and composed *Il Principe* (or *The Prince*) as a guidebook for princes or heads of state. In this extraordinary work, there emerges a far more pragmatic and cynical approach to human morality than we find in the frameworks presented in this chapter. Indeed, one of the greatest challenges for those aspiring to ethical conduct is this sobering admonition of Machiavelli: "A man who wishes to profess goodness at all times must fall to ruin among so many who are not good." For Machiavelli, the world is such an immoral and corrupt place that one cannot possibly maintain his moral values and be a success. Although Machiavelli is directing his comments at future political leaders, the following remark could easily apply to corporate managers, politicians, and other professionals: "And so, [the modern manager] must have a mind ready to turn herself accordingly as the winds and the fluctuation of things command her, and, as I said above, she must not separate herself from the good, if she is able, but she must know how to take up evil, should it become necessary." Is this good advice for today's executives and professional leaders? For example, is it always possible to be a virtuous manager in the "rough and tumble" world of modern capitalism?[70]

PERSONAL INTEGRITY IN THE WORKPLACE

Chapter 4.   The Person and the Corporation

PART II

THE PERSON AND THE CORPORATION

"Repose," says Holmes, "is not the destiny of man." Choice is your own. You answer for your choice. There are no rules to shoulder your responsibility.

—Karl Llewellyn[1]

The time is always right to do what is right.

—Dr. Martin Luther King Jr.[2]

We now turn to a set of short case studies that will put some of our theoretical knowledge about ethics to practical use. These cases provide learning opportunities that address themes of leadership, organizational behavior, and professionalism as well as ethical conduct. The acute challenges confronting the managers in these cases could easily have lasting implications for their personal character as well as their professional careers, especially if they are mishandled. However, when managers or young leaders are thrust into these dilemmas, they often walk away with greater clarity about their principles and commitments.

The cases range from a salesperson's quandary about her manager's tactics to situations that involve bribery, deception, whistle-blowing, religious liberty, and a potential conflict of interest. The moral problems in each case become a bit more intricate as we progress through the chapter. For the most part, these are real cases in which young or aspiring managers are caught up in demanding situations where processes are ill-defined and there are no straightforward solutions. We begin, however, on more familiar ground.

AN OVERVIEW OF THE CASES

In the first case, a college senior must make a difficult decision about his career before he leaves college—can he break a letter of agreement with an employer just to take a better job? When can implicit contracts or promises like this one be broken? And does this young man have a duty to his prospective employer?

The second case, called "Conscience and the Workplace," directly addresses the issue of religious liberty and the larger issue of employee rights. A young Buddhist finds her religious beliefs in conflict with some of her job requirements. Should she stand on principle or compromise her values? How far should employers go in accommodating the religious convictions and conscientious objections of their workers? This case is provocative in its own right but also anticipates the theme of religious liberty presented in the *Hobby Lobby* case in the next chapter. When perusing this case, students should bear in mind that while the First Amendment protects individuals only from government interference, Title VII of the Civil Rights Act of 1964 forbids discrimination on the basis of race, color, sex, national origin, or religion.

The next two cases involve salespersons who must face typical predicaments that sometimes arise in selling to the public. "Karen Preston's New Boss" describes a salesperson who uneasily confronts her new boss over unorthodox and questionable selling practices. "Confessions of an Appliance Salesman" introduces us to a novice salesman in a management training program who has reservations about steering customers to high-end products they don't really need. Are his selling techniques unethical, and if so, what does this say about his character? Both cases prompt us to think about the qualities that make someone a "good" salesperson.

In the case called "The 'Perfect' Job Offer," matters of right and wrong are complicated by the duty of family loyalty and the need to sort out competing moral obligations. A procurement officer at the Pentagon has to deal with the implications of seeking a favor for her son from one of her clients. Why is that client so eager to help her son find a job, and what are the probable long-term consequences of her efforts? Will her actions lead to the sort of conflict of interest that government workers should steadfastly avoid?

"The Product Manager" case is about a small bribe that can have broad ramifications for the managers involved. It seems that a small payment to a consultant is the only way the sales team can close a lucrative deal. This all-too-familiar scenario anticipates some of the themes in Chapter 13 about bribery in a foreign context where there is a conflicting set of values along with different expectations. Bribery, which has been called "the quintessential white-collar crime," harms others in subtle and often attenuated ways.[3]

The next case in this series is called "Telling the Truth about the Probable Sale of a Division." It highlights the problem of maintaining confidentiality concerning the possible spinoff of a conglomerate's medical systems business. There is a strong temptation to deceive or obfuscate in order to protect that confidentiality, and the moral question of deception is closely linked to other dynamics such as the high stakes involved for the firm. Is deception, which is defined as the intention to mislead, warranted in this case?

The case study on deception is followed by two cases that suggest the need for moral intervention or whistle-blowing. The first case, "Should an Engineer Inform the FAA about a Defective Fuselage Design?," explores the risks and perils of blowing the whistle on upper-level managers. It features a potentially serious safety matter that is being ignored or downplayed by the company's top managers. To what extent must a worker risk her job and livelihood to expose these negligent management practices? How strong is the duty to get involved when one is a witness to apparent indifference about safety?

The last case in this chapter, called "Who's Responsible?," describes the plight of a young attorney rather than a businessperson. It presents an opportunity to think about the issue of moral responsibility presented so thoroughly in Aristotle's philosophy. According to Aristotle, we are accountable or subjectively culpable for all our voluntary actions. An action is considered "voluntary" unless there is coercion or excusable ignorance, that is, ignorance, through no fault of one's own, "of the circumstances of action and the objects with which it is concerned."[4] Ignorance is inexcusable when it is deliberately willed or the result of negligence. Aristotle notes that "our action and inaction constitutes our being good and evil."[5] When does simple inaction, sitting on the sidelines, facilitate another's wrongdoing? In this case, does inaction represent a wrongful omission?

Although there are no obvious solutions to these troublesome cases, the ethical analysis presented in Chapter 3 offers objective criteria that can address some of the moral uncertainty and ambiguity. These tools can help frame the critical issues in these cases and provide fruitful avenues for thinking about a possible resolution. For example, one approach is to think about the moral duties implied in a particular situation. Another is to think about what a sensible and virtuous person would do under the circumstances. The Appendix provides a general guide for case analysis.

Finally, what adds further complexity to several of these cases is the need to take into account an individual's particular background along with his personal moral commitments. People must be true to themselves and to the convictions that have shaped their moral character. This mandate implies that in some situations we cannot overlook a person's "moral particularity" that is inherited from her family, community, and culture. As Alasdair MacIntyre points out, this inheritance, with all its debts, rightful expectations, and obligations, constitutes "the given of my life, my moral starting point."[6]

CASE STUDY 4.1

TROUBLE IN THE RECRUITING OFFICE[7]

©iStockphoto.com/andresr

As Jerry made his way across the campus to the recruiting office, he couldn't help but notice the long shadows thrown off the tall buildings on campus by the afternoon sun. He would miss the Gothic splendor of these grand buildings surrounded by the beautiful landscape. But his focus these days was on the future. Jerry had found himself in a quandary that could have significant implications for his career. He was now on his way to defend his decision.

Jerry Hogan was a finance major and had always looked forward to some kind of career in investment banking. Unlike many other members of the senior class, Jerry already had a job with a prominent but small investment bank located in the heart of Wall Street. Over the past summer he had interned with Trout & Donovan. They were impressed with his keen analytical skills and had offered him a letter of commitment, which he had gladly signed at the end of August. In that letter, Jerry certified that his résumé was accurate to the best of his knowledge and that he would begin his training program on July 1 after his graduation. He also consented to be available to lend support as a trainee to any projects where he might be needed.

During the early weeks of the fall semester, Jerry found out from his roommate that a more prestigious investment bank, Gold & Watson, absent from the recruiting scene for several years, was coming back to campus later in the fall for a recruiting trip. Jerry had always been impressed with this revered institution, an American banking empire known for its wealthy clients and financial aggression. He signed up for an interview "just to see what would happen." Weeks after this initial interview, he was invited to spend the day at Gold & Watson's ornate New York office on Broad Street. Of course, the bank had no idea he had already committed to one of its competitors. The Gold & Watson recruiters were especially impressed with Jerry's knowledge of French. They hinted that if he were hired, he might be assigned for a time to the Paris office. A few weeks passed, and Jerry put the interview behind him as he became immersed in his course work. He was convinced the bank would pass him by. But as the first winter snows blanketed the campus, Jerry received a thick letter from Gold & Watson. To his great surprise, they were making him an incredible offer—a $15,000 signing bonus and a starting salary 10% higher than the one offered by Trout & Donovan. Opportunities for advancement were better at this prestigious institution, which was also known for its generous bonuses. "What a great opportunity," thought Jerry, "a chance to work in Paris, a $15,000 bonus, and a 10% higher salary, not to mention the prestige of being a Gold & Watson banker! How can I possibly turn this down?"

But now Jerry found himself in a real predicament: he had proceeded under the assumption that he wouldn't make the cut at Gold & Watson, and yet he had now received this terrific offer. He had to decide quickly. On a blustery Sunday afternoon in December, he went to visit his best friend for advice. Together they thrashed out the pros and cons of each choice. Jerry wanted the new job, but he had the vague impression that reneging on his commitment letter would not be the right thing to do. Yet, he pondered to himself, didn't he deserve to come out of school with the best entry-level job possible? Besides, the $15,000 would let him pay off some of that massive college debt he had accumulated.

Jerry talked with his parents, but they were not able to give him much guidance. "It's your decision," his father said. "We can't make it for you." But Jerry's father also reminded his son about the importance of integrity and loyalty, a message that had been reinforced throughout his childhood. After more soul-searching, Jerry decided to accept the Gold & Watson job. He wrote a letter to Trout & Donovan indicating he would not be able to enter their training program this summer for "personal reasons." His friends generally supported Jerry's decision, but his family was more reticent.

However, word about Jerry's decision soon reached the college recruiting office, where there was considerable dismay over his choice and even worries about the potential for some fallout. The Trout & Donovan recruiting manager registered a mild complaint with her contact at the university. As a result, one of the placement officers called Jerry and told him he should have honored his original commitment. Jerry could understand her annoyance, but he was still convinced that he had made the right decision. He agreed to meet with one of the placement counselors to discuss that decision.

- Why is it important to keep one's promises? Does making a voluntary promise such as signing a letter of commitment create a moral duty to keep that promise?

- How would you evaluate this dilemma from the perspective of the DRJ framework? Was Jerry's decision a valid exception to the moral rule that requires a person to keep his or her promises and commitments?

- What should Jerry say to his placement counselor? How can he justify his decision?

CASE STUDY 4.2

CONSCIENCE AND THE WORKPLACE

Yeo Soo-Ae paced around her living room as she thought about an uncomfortable conversation she had just had with some of her closest friends. She wondered whether or not her friends were on to something. Then again, maybe they were blinded by a dose of religious zealotry.

Soo-Ae's family had come to America from Korea before she was born (her friends just called her Sue). They were devout Korean Buddhists who had taught her about the Buddhist tradition when she was a child. Her family sought to preserve their Korean heritage but loved the freedom

©iStockphoto.com/Tinpixels

and opportunity in the United States. Soo-Ae graduated with top honors from Taylor State University, a well-known college in Texas, where she had double-majored in public relations and biology. In a bioethics class, she researched Buddhist views on contemporary moral issues and learned about the Buddhist commitment to the sanctity of all human life, which flows from the Buddhist philosophy of nonviolence (*ahisma*).

After graduation, she began to work as a lab technician in a local laboratory. But she aspired to work in the biotech industry in her home state of California. The industry was expanding in California thanks in part to the state's commitment of $3 billion to fund embryonic stem cell research. The funds would be allocated by the California Institute for Regenerative Medicine located in San Francisco.

During a visit home for a well-deserved vacation, she decided to concentrate on finding a job in biotechnology. After a careful search, she applied to several firms, but only one, Biotech Medical Associates (BMA), offered her a position. The company was impressed with Soo-Ae's skills and experience, and it hired her to do public relations and marketing work for their new facility in Santa Clara, California. She would promote and explain the company's technological innovations to the media and to the general public. Her main responsibility was to manage the promotional pages on the company website. Sue was ecstatic about her new job: good salary and benefits, stock options, and a chance to live and work in the environs of Silicon Valley.

BMA was engaged in a wide variety of research, especially in the area of parasitic diseases, where it had developed several successful drugs. But in recent years, it had dedicated some of its resources to embryonic stem cell research. This technology, however, is quite controversial, since it involves the destruction of human embryos. To appreciate the ethical issues of the debate, it is necessary to review some basic elements of biology. Cells are the building blocks of each person's body. While most cells are specialized (for example, skin cells), stem cells are undifferentiated, that is, they have the capacity to become any kind of cell, such as a brain cell, a skin cell, or a bone cell. These undifferentiated stem cells are found in a blastocyst, which is a one- or two-week-old embryo. Embryonic stem cell research begins with obtaining unused frozen embryos; there is also the possibility of cloning embryos for biomedical research (this is sometimes referred to as "therapeutic cloning"). The stem cells are obtained by disaggregating the embryo. The hope is to use these stem cells as the basis for cures for certain degenerative diseases, such as multiple sclerosis or Parkinson's disease. It should be pointed out that adults also have a supply of stem cells, but adult stem cell research is considered ethically acceptable and is not the bone of contention in this debate. The principal moral difficulty with embryonic stem cell research is the need to destroy the human embryo. At the heart of the moral debate is whether the human embryo is a human being and whether the embryo should be treated with respect and not as raw material for scientific research.

BMA was quickly becoming a pioneer in this growing field of embryonic stem cell research. The company had already made great strides in developing retinal cells from embryonic stem cells, perhaps portending a cure for some forms of blindness. It had developed a new therapy for a retinal disease known internally as project "Restore Vision." This revolutionary treatment was going to be made public in a few weeks as clinical trials were about to get under way.

Soo-Ae had worked for BMA for only six months, and everyone was impressed with her skills and enthusiasm. She had worked on several projects, but her boss had a new assignment: develop a promotional and information campaign for "Restore Vision." Since he anticipated some criticism because of the use of embryonic stem cells, he also asked her to put together a justification for this technology that could be positioned on the website.

But Soo-Ae was keenly aware of Buddhism's opposition to this research. She herself had thought about this issue a great deal. Like many other Buddhists, she believed that embryos bear the karmic identity of a recently deceased individual and so are entitled to the same moral respect as adults.[8] As a result, she wavered on whether to work on this project. On the one hand, she would have a hand in justifying morally questionable research and in promoting a biotech product based on that research. On the other hand, she was not directly engaged in the embryo-destructive technologies; her job was far removed from the laboratory. Still, she decided to ask her boss if she could be removed from this project. She explained her conscientious objection to this type of work. Soo-Ae's manager was skeptical and quite puzzled by her objections. He told her that it wasn't possible to find a replacement. The deadlines were short and there was no one else to fill in for her. However, he mentioned there were no other similar projects on the horizon so she probably would not have to address these issues again in the immediate future.

Nonetheless, Soo-Ae felt uneasy. She could pursue her conscientious objection to this work with Human Resources or others at BMA, but she knew that an obstinate refusal could ultimately jeopardize her promising career. Soo-Ae sought the advice of some friends, who were supportive but noncommittal. She knew there were people of goodwill on both sides of the debate, and she would simply be presenting the company's side of the story. But one of her close friends, a devout Korean Buddhist, was quite blunt. He told Soo-Ae that if she took this assignment, she would be "cooperating in evil." He remarked that this was tantamount to "scandalous" behavior for a committed Buddhist. Soo-Ae was uneasy with this type of language, but she also felt there might be something wrong with technologies that destroyed human embryos. Given her religious convictions, wouldn't it be hypocritical for her to elaborate a moral defense of this technology for public consumption?

Soo-Ae stopped pacing about her apartment. She slid into her favorite chair and stared at the putty-colored walls. She knew this would not be an easy decision. Would she be doing anything wrong by working on this project?

- Explain as clearly as possible Soo-Ae's options. What are the costs and benefits of each option?

- What should Soo-Ae do? To what extent should her upbringing and religious convictions inform her decision?

- Should BMA respect Soo-Ae's strong moral sentiments about embryo-destructive research? To what degree can companies support workers' religious-liberty rights that involve moral issues like this one? Would dismissing her over this matter be a violation of her rights in any way?

- Think about BMA's corporate obligations in this case. Can the DRJ framework be applied? If so, how?

CASE STUDY 4.3

KAREN PRESTON'S NEW BOSS[9]

©iStockphoto.com/urbazon

On a steamy summer day, Karen Preston departed Chicago's O'Hare airport to return home to Atlanta, Georgia. The Delta flight seemed interminable. Karen slouched in her uncomfortable seat and stared at her computer as she thought about her first sales calls in this new territory to which she had just been assigned. Karen hoped that better days were ahead, but she wondered about her future with this progressive company in light of her experience with a demanding new boss. Would she really be able to work for him and accommodate his way of doing business?

Karen had recently graduated with high honors from the business school of a well-known Boston university. She was an enthusiastic marketing major and looked forward to a long career in sales and marketing. After considering a few job offers, Karen had headed south to work for Southeast Furniture, a major supplier of furniture to discount furniture stores and retailers such as Target. The company specialized in living and dining room furniture, a highly competitive market. But Southeast Furniture, headquartered for many years in Atlanta, was known for its good-quality merchandise, reasonable wholesale prices, and excellent service.

Karen had spent six long months in the training department learning the ins and outs of the furniture business. After working for another year in the company's small Providence sales office, she had been reassigned to Atlanta. Her new sales territory was the midwestern states of Illinois, Ohio, and Indiana. Southeast had few regional sales offices, so this territory was managed from the home office. With this new assignment came a new sales manager, Rich Peters, who was known throughout the company for his aggressive but highly effective sales tactics. Karen was familiar with company rumors about his penchant for pushing the envelope to make a sale. His salespeople usually won the big awards at the company's annual sales meeting, and they were consistently paid the highest commissions in the company.

Peters decided to accompany Karen on her first sales trip to visit a buyer for a chain of Chicago-area furniture stores. He had been with the company for over 30 years and was a personal friend of the owners. Karen was quite wary of working with him, but he had always been nice enough to her whenever they met or chatted in the past. After a few courtesy visits to several other Chicago-area customers, Karen and Rich called on corporate headquarters for Gordon's Furniture, located on top of its flagship store in downtown Chicago. The Gordon's buyer, Paul Staples, was quite interested in Southeast's new line of dining room and patio furniture. After reviewing the glossy sales material, Staples decided to place a $2.9 million order with an immediate shipping date. He pointed out that if the merchandise moved quickly, they would be prepared to buy even more furniture. "Not bad for your first day in this new territory," Karen thought to herself as the trio headed off to lunch.

After a leisurely lunch at Rich's favorite Chicago steak house, the Gordon's buyer said he would like the "usual arrangement." He thought that something was warranted, given the size of his order and his loyalty to Southeast Furniture. Karen kept silent, but she was puzzled. What was he talking about? A discount? A kickback of some sort? She knew the purchase didn't qualify for a discount, which was given only on exceptionally large orders of $5 million or more. Rich assured Paul that something could be worked out. Rich told him they would find a way to accommodate a small "bonus payback" to Gordon's of about $8,000. Paul was quite satisfied and ordered a brandy. Karen sipped her coffee and remained silent during this exchange. But Rich's assurance was enough to close the deal. The paperwork was signed when they returned to the Gordon's office building, and the shipping dates were set. Rich and Karen hurried to the airport for a late-afternoon flight back to Atlanta.

In the taxi to the airport, Karen questioned Rich about the special deal he had approved. "My understanding is that there are no discounts on orders under $5 million. And the Northeast sales manager followed this policy closely. So I'm a little confused. Did I miss something?" she said, somewhat sarcastically.

"That's the sales policy on the books," said Rich, "but in reality we usually can't close deals with Gordon's without giving them this sort of payback from time to time; this practice has been going on for five years in this territory with a couple of our biggest customers. Gordon's sometimes asks for a small 'informal' discount on big orders for new merchandise, and I make sure they get it. He won't bother you about another discount if the furniture sells and he reorders. Keep all this in mind when you do business with him in the future."

"Well, how does it work?" Karen inquired.

"There are a few different options. The Gordon's buyer might send you a claim for some kind of shortage at delivery time. Or he'll claim there was some 'unsatisfactory' merchandise equivalent to about eight thousand wholesale. Since it's so expensive to ship the stuff back to our manufacturing plant in Alabama, you have the option of just refunding the money. We'll work out the details later. Once you and I sign off on Gordon's claim, the company will issue them the appropriate credit payment. The big boss knows about this and looks the other way to make the sale, so don't worry about questions from upstairs."

But Karen was uneasy with this procedure. "I can't believe you give some customers these unauthorized discounts or special paybacks, whatever you call it. It seems so unfair to our other clients. And I'm also uneasy about making these bogus claims for defective or missing merchandise."

Rich was exasperated at Karen's apparent naivete: "If you want Gordon's business, you don't have much choice." He paused and then said in an angry tone, "Anyway, what's so wrong with gaming the system now and then if we get a big order like the one we bagged today! So we cut a corner or two. Big deal! The main thing is to do what it takes to close the sale. Take the money and run, I always say. And if we have to give a little back now and then, so be it."

With this outburst, the conversation came to an abrupt end in the taxi, and the two said only a few words on the flight back to Atlanta.

It was still rush hour as Karen settled into her car and began the long drive home from the crowded Atlanta airport. She thought about her eventful first day. She didn't like the idea of deceiving the front office with false claims of shortages or unsatisfactory merchandise. But Rich was probably right—how could she risk losing this big account that had become accustomed to these special deals now and then? She wondered if this clandestine discount "policy" went on elsewhere in the company, and what other irregularities occurred in Rich's sales territory.

- What should Karen do? Should she submit a false claim for unsatisfactory merchandise as her boss suggests? (Defend your answer by using ethical principles drawn from the DRJ framework or from other ethical theories presented in Chapter 3.)

- How serious a problem is this for Karen? Rich says this isn't a big deal, but is that a good assessment of the situation? Can Karen afford to compromise her integrity in this situation?

- How would you assess Rich's sales philosophy?

- Under what circumstances is it appropriate to disobey your superiors?

CASE STUDY 4.4

CONFESSIONS OF AN APPLIANCE SALESMAN[10]

©iStockphoto.com/Thomes_EyeDesign

My name is John Anderson, and I work for Consumer City, a West Coast chain of retail stores that specializes in consumer electronics and white-goods appliances. We sell a wide range of computers, televisions, and phones along with refrigerators, stoves, washers, and dryers. Consumer City carries the well-known brand names like Maytag and Whirlpool, but we also sell our own brand of white goods, which are made by a competent manufacturer in Shanghai, China.

I'm a recent business school graduate, and after many interviews I was one of a select group accepted into Consumer City's management training program. My goal is to work as a buyer or a manager in the company's corporate offices. After a few weeks of orientation and training, I was assigned to work as a salesperson in our large San Jose store, where I'll remain for two years as part of my training experience. I work in the appliance department selling all the white goods. I've spent a great deal of time learning the inner workings of products like stoves and dishwashers. During my training assignment, I am being paid like anyone else: a small base salary and 5% commission on anything I sell. An aggressive salesperson in one of our suburban stores like San Jose could easily make an annual salary of $80,000 to $100,000. However, this would require a lot of 12-hour days with few days off and limited vacation time. It's a tough and competitive environment, especially on days when sales are slow. But my colleagues have been very helpful, and the atmosphere is conducive to learning about sales and also about our different product lines. I enjoy the work and spend long hours on the selling floor.

During our orientation sessions, special attention was focused on the Consumer City brands of washers, dryers, refrigerators, freezers, and stoves. The company generated more profits on their own private-label goods as opposed to branded products like Maytag or General Electric. Our Chinese manufacturer doesn't sacrifice quality but has a low-cost structure, and this allows for a pretty high markup. There are two product lines: for example, the low-end washers that start at $429 and the premium-brand washers where prices start at $549. The company was especially keen to sell their own premium products because of the especially high margins. As a result, sales commissions on those particular products were 9% instead of the regular 5%. This is big incentive for a salesperson, and most of them pushed the Consumer City premium line quite vigorously. After a few weeks on the sales floor and some disappointing commission checks, I suddenly found myself doing the same thing. Some customers were determined to get a brand like Maytag or Whirlpool, but I tried to steer all my other customers to Consumer City's line of products. I wouldn't lie about the lower-end Consumer City products, but I would downplay their positive features and hint about possible stock shortages in order to persuade them to buy the higher-end products. On one occasion, I knew the cheaper washer would be suitable for an elderly couple (who did one load of clothes per week), but I cajoled them into buying the more expensive washer for an extra $130. It was a more durable machine with fancier features and options. I was quite proud of myself and I thought this was what good salesmanship was all about.

But now I have some qualms about my sales tactics. Should I encourage people to buy high-priced products they don't really need just to get a higher commission and perhaps a better evaluation? Maybe this is no big deal and not really a serious ethical problem. My colleagues on the sales floor seem to have no ethical reservations and push the higher-margin products relentlessly. But I wonder if I should make some changes in how I sell these products.

- Is Mr. Anderson right to be concerned about his conduct, or is this not such a serious problem?

- What should Mr. Anderson do—should he continue to sell products so aggressively for which he gets an extra commission? How might the DRJ framework or other ethical principles help him reach some resolution?

- Briefly outline the basic moral responsibilities of a salesperson as you understand them. Does Mr. Anderson live up to those responsibilities? Is he being fair and just to those customers who depend on him for advice and guidance?

CASE STUDY 4.5

THE "PERFECT" JOB OFFER

When Nancy Cooper was promoted to senior procurement officer at the Pentagon, it came as no great surprise to many of her colleagues. After securing her MBA at a prominent Virginia business school, Nancy took a job with the Pentagon, where she found herself on the fast track to success. The affable Ms. Cooper was the youngest person and the first woman to have been appointed to this high-level position. This was a tribute to her talent, tenacity, and tough negotiating style. She was now in a position to give final approval to defense contracts worth billions of dollars. Some of these were no-bid contracts up to $100 million where officers such as Cooper had significant discretion. During her long career, Ms. Cooper had developed a reputation for integrity, and she was widely respected throughout the defense industry and military community in Washington, DC.

But her integrity was about to be put to the test. Shortly after her promotion, Ms. Cooper's son, Keith, graduated from college with an engineering degree. His grades were decent and he graduated in the second quartile of his class. The job market in this field, however, was mediocre at the time. Jobs went to the top students while others struggled. He searched in vain for a position for over a year, but to no avail. His friends told him repeatedly that he should rely on his mother for some help, but Keith thought better of this approach. However, a year after graduation, Keith's prospects remained dim. Also, his fiancée was growing impatient. There were constant quibbles about money and his future career. Their wedding date was postponed and the whole event appeared to be in some jeopardy. So, out of sheer desperation, Keith finally decided to seek out his mother's assistance. During his senior year, he had interviewed at Dray Defense Systems. The Dray recruiters, however, were quite selective, and he didn't even make it to the second round. A year later he noticed an online job posting—Dray was once again looking for engineers in its prestigious defense research division. Keith showed the ad to his mother, and he asked her if she could talk to someone at Dray on his behalf. He believed this job ideally suited his skills and background.

Ms. Cooper, of course, had many contacts at Dray, which did a substantial volume of business with the Pentagon. The company had just been awarded a major contract for an X-85 Quick Strike fighter plane, thanks in part to Ms. Cooper's direct intervention. Dray was now battling with its competitors over contracts for rockets that would launch surveillance satellites into space. There was a $1 billion contract pending and another one likely next year. Ms. Cooper was working on this project, and she would have considerable influence over the awarding of these contracts.

After Keith approached his mother, she thought about calling Dray's chief financial officer, Michael Moffet. But she was reluctant to intervene. She told Keith to keep looking while she thought about his request. In a rare family argument, Keith expressed his disappointment and even accused his mother of lacking "family loyalty." Several weeks later, Ms. Cooper met Mr. Moffet for lunch to discuss the financial details of some service contract issues. It was a pleasant summer day, and as they lingered over coffee and dessert at an outside café, the conversation drifted to family matters. Ms. Cooper soon found herself mentioning something about her son's persistent job woes. Moffet seized on the anxiety in her voice, and he intimated that he would probably be able to "pull some strings" and get him "the perfect job offer." "After all," he said, "Dray is indebted to you, and we want the best relationship possible. Just give me a call and I will set the wheels in motion."

Ms. Cooper was flattered by his solicitude, and she was convinced that Dray would hire her son, who was qualified for the position. But should she use her power and influence to get him this job? If she called upon Dray for this big favor, could she continue to be an objective and responsible decision maker? Government ethics codes forbid employees to accept gratuities or to permit personal benefits to influence their official duties. On the other hand, wasn't this sort of thing commonplace? Ms. Cooper recalled that several of Keith's friends had gotten their jobs with some initial help from their parents or other relatives. Could she afford to ignore her son's need for assistance at this critical time in his life? His words about "family loyalty" still echoed in her mind. As Ms. Cooper thought about calling Mr. Moffet, she hesitated. Was she about to make a big mistake?

- Is there anything wrong with what Ms. Cooper is planning to do? Evaluate this dilemma from an ethical perspective using the DRJ framework or other relevant moral principles. Does this differ from the sort of favor most people seek all the time?

- Will this favor create a conflict of interest for her in the future? Or is it possible to put all this aside and deal with Dray objectively when it seeks new military contracts?

- What advice would you give to her? Should she tell Moffet to forget about the whole thing?

CASE STUDY 4.6

THE PRODUCT MANAGER

Rai Wu works as a product manager for Project Software Management or PSM, Inc. The Dallas-based company is a major producer and distributor of project management software systems primarily for use on IBM mainframes, midsize computers, and workstations. The company, with annual sales of about $50 million, is full of project management experts, many with advanced degrees from places like Stanford and MIT. While Rai certainly has some background in the essentials of project management from his MBA

©iStockphoto.com/baona

training, he thinks of himself as a "marketing guy," surrounded by techies and engineers. He's the one who has to convince the customer that this product is different from the competition and worth its premium price.

Project management software comprises an unglamorous but steady segment of the lucrative and dynamic software industry. These systems enable users to manage large, complex, high-value projects. Most packages, such as the one offered by PSM, integrate planning and scheduling capabilities along with a facility for cost management. PSM's products are widely used in the construction industry to manage large-scale construction projects; they are also used extensively by major utilities to assist in the management of outages.

For the past few years PSM has faced a saturated market in the United States, but growth prospects are much better abroad. Demand is especially strong in Europe and Southeast Asia. PSM is particularly anxious to sell its product in the European marketplace, where it does not have a very strong presence. The British-based firm Pattelle Technologies, Inc., has dominated that market for many years. But PSM believes that Pattelle is vulnerable because it has not kept up with state-of-the-art technological advances. In a major strategy statement, CEO Dan Nash identified Europe as a key target market and set high sales quotas for the first year of this revised strategy.

However, despite these quotas and expectations, sales in Europe have been slow to materialize. But now the company is on the verge of closing a substantial deal with an Italian construction company. As is customary in Europe, that company has hired an independent consultant to assist them in the selection process. This individual is a specialist in the intricacies of project management software, and his job is to help the company pick the right software package among PSM and its competitors, which are all vying to make this sale. Along with the construction company's IT staff, he studies the RFP (request for proposal), reviews a sample demonstration of each product, and conducts the interviews of the finalists. This consultant has a great deal of clout with the IT staff, and it seems likely that the construction company will purchase whatever product he recommends.

In the middle of this elaborate process, Pete has been sent to Italy to help close the deal. Product managers are often involved in the sale process for software and are usually called upon to explain their vision of the product and its future—how it will be enhanced in future revisions, and when those enhancements will occur. Upon his arrival, Rai immediately consults with the salesperson on the scene, Kathy Flaherty. Kathy tells him they are on the brink of closing the deal but the consultant would like to meet him to resolve "a few issues." They arrange to have dinner together. Kathy and Rai meet in the early evening and make their way through a maze of alleys to a smoky stone edifice called the Caffè Stella. On the way, Kathy informs Rai that she is a bit uncomfortable with this consultant, who seems to be "out for himself." After a fine dinner, the conversation finally turns to business. Still sipping his wine, the consultant informs Rai that PSM is definitely "in the lead" to win this big contract. Rai is elated and believes that PSM is winning because it has the best product and support services. But the consultant says that PSM would really be a "sure bet" if he could get something for himself. He proposes a "consulting contract" for $10,000. He tells Rai that he would do a superficial study of the Italian market for project management software "to make things look good," but in effect the $10,000 is his "fee" for ensuring the sale. When Rai balks at this, he is informed that "this is the way business gets done in Italy." It seems likely that if he and Kathy don't go along, the sale will probably be lost.

On the other hand, Rai knows that if he makes the sale, PSM will take in about $1.5 million in revenue, not counting the setup and service fees. There will also be substantial maintenance fees charged each year that will help the company's annual cash flow. Rai is confident that PSM's state-of-the-art and fine-tuned system is the best product for this particular client. But he has some serious questions about making this payment; should he really pay this person $10,000 for a few hours' work which would probably be of little or no value to PSM? Isn't this equivalent to a bribe of some sort? On the other hand, if he refuses to pay the fee, there is a strong likelihood that PSM will lose out to one of its chief competitors, such as Pattelle. In an early-morning phone call to his boss, the senior vice president of sales and marketing, he poses this dilemma and tries to solicit his advice. But his boss skirts the issue and simply tells him that he should do whatever is necessary to win this sale. There is little doubt in Rai's mind that the senior managers back in Dallas would have no problem with the consulting agreement if it's necessary to win over this customer. But the decision rests squarely in Rai's hands. Should he authorize the $10,000 consulting contract?

- Discuss the business strategy of PSM along with its competitive environment. How do these factors affect the decision Rai has to make?

- What are the *economic, legal, and ethical* implications of this decision?

- What would you do and how would you justify your course of action? What would a Kantian or a utilitarian say about this case?

- Is this consulting payment really a bribe? Is anyone really harmed by this payment? Does it make any difference if this is common practice in Italy as the consultant implies? Why or why not?

CASE STUDY 4.7

TELLING THE TRUTH ABOUT THE PROBABLE SALE OF A DIVISION

It was late afternoon when Tim Roake returned to his office after a long and tedious meeting with some of his top engineers. He immediately poured himself a cup of coffee and checked his voice mail. As he suspected, it included several urgent messages from a key prospective customer. Roake headed the Medical System Division (MSD) of OmniTech, a privately held technology conglomerate. The MSD sold MRI (magnetic resonance imaging) systems, ultrasound machinery, CT scanning devices, and other X-ray equipment to hospitals and medical centers. Roake was personally involved in a multimillion-dollar equipment

©iStockphoto.com/courtneyk

sale to the newly constructed Centerville Medical Center. Patricia Dalton, the center's executive administrator, had heard some disturbing rumors that the MSD might be spun off by OmniTech. As a result, she had been calling all day long to get some answers. But Roake avoided having a conversation with her. He had no choice, thanks in part to a string of meetings and appointments.

Unfortunately, there was some truth to these rumors. Despite Roake's efforts to strengthen OmniTech's commitment to the MSD business, OmniTech executives were contemplating the sale of this division to a bigger competitor such as General Electric or Siemens. They were discretely negotiating with these companies to see what they might be willing to pay for the MSD unit. A sale was by no means a sure thing, but it seemed more probable given recent developments. The MSD was hemorrhaging cash. It was also having a hard time innovating, and last week had come the announcement that one of its newest product innovations would be delayed indefinitely. Moreover, OmniTech was having trouble in some of its other divisions, and it needed to raise cash. Some corporate executives seemed determined to narrow the company's scope, but others believed in MSD's long-term prospects. Roake, of course, was somewhat biased, but he was also convinced that if MSD could quickly close a few big deals, he and his managers would be on firmer ground to argue against a divestment of his division.

As news of OmniTech's troubles leaked out, some of the managers at Centerville were becoming nervous about OmniTech's commitment to its medical systems business. Dalton was anxious to speak with Roake about the persistent rumors of a possible spinoff. She wanted assurances that the company would honor its service contracts, which were among the most generous in the industry. Otherwise, the sale might be off. She liked OmniTech's equipment, along with its pricing and financing package, but she wanted to be sure that this vendor would be around to honor its long-term commitments. The service contracts were subject to modification if the business was acquired by a new owner.

The medical equipment industry's customers were a close-knit and well-informed community, so Roake was not surprised that the possibility of the OmniTech divestment had managed to leak out. He certainly did not want to lose this important contract, which would go a long way toward helping the company's cash-flow problems. He believed in the viability of this division and its ultimate success within OmniTech.

Roake knew that he couldn't stall any longer. He would have to return Dalton's call tomorrow morning. But what should he say? Should he tell her the truth that a future sale to a corporation like GE was possible or even probable? This type of candor might scare her off and affect several other pending deals. Or should he allay her concerns and insist that the rumors were untrue? This posture might be the only way to save this deal. Roake realized that the stakes were high as he thought about how he would answer Dalton's pesky questions.

- What should Roake say to Dalton in his phone conversation? Should he stall, lie, deceive, or tell the truth? What's likely to happen if he is completely candid with her?

- In a famous article called "Is Business Bluffing Ethical?," the author, Albert Z. Carr, contends that in the workplace, executives must sometimes discard the Golden Rule and be guided by different ethical standards that call for deception or bluffing. Carr likens business to a poker game and writes that at times "every businessman, like every poker player, is offered a choice between certain loss or bluffing within the legal rules of the game; if he is not resigned to losing, if he wants to rise in his company and industry, then in such a crisis he will bluff—and bluff hard."[11] Is this one of those times?

- Deception has been defined as "the communication of a message with which the communicator intends to mislead, . . . that is, to cause a person to believe something that is untrue."[12] Is deception the morally proper strategy for Roake under these particular circumstances? How would the DRJ framework inform his decision-making?

CASE STUDY 4.8

SHOULD AN ENGINEER INFORM THE FAA ABOUT A DEFECTIVE FUSELAGE DESIGN?[13]

Janet MacArthur is a senior engineer, working for an airline manufacturer that has recently developed a new commercial airplane known as the DF-8. Janet has worked for this Los Angeles–based company for almost 15 years. She took this job after graduating from a top engineering program and has always felt at home here.

But the congenial atmosphere suddenly changed when she began to work on a demanding testing project for the DF-8. The aircraft is due to be delivered to several U.S. airlines within the next several months, given its recent approval by the Federal Aviation Administration (FAA). The FAA is the regulatory agency responsible for the oversight of general and commercial aviation within the United States. However, Janet is quite uncomfortable with this ambitious schedule.

Janet lacks confidence in the safety of the DF-8 unless some changes are made. She believes there is a defect in the design of this aircraft that could cause a fatal accident. She raised the issue several times as the development team worked its way toward the testing phase of this project. The problem is with the design of the system for the cargo doors, which are part of the fuselage. The cargo door is hard to close, and if the door is not closed correctly (for example, if ground service personnel force the door shut), it could become detached during flight. That catastrophic event could cause cabin decompression and a fatal crash. The DF-8 is unlike other planes, where the control cables are located above the passenger cabin. For various engineering reasons and cost factors, its control cables have been located below the cabin floor. As a result, decompression, which would most likely lead to collapse of the floor, would sever those vital cables and send the plane out of control. The initial testing on the fuselage prototype confirmed Jane's apprehension about this door's potential flaws. She discussed the matter several times with her superiors, who tended to agree with her overall assessment. However, they believed she might be overstating the risk. Nonetheless, they informed upper management of their concerns and urged them to delay the product's delivery schedule in order to study and correct the problem.

The company's executives, however, believed that the plane was safe. After reviewing their data, they concluded that any chance of a door failure and subsequent crash was "extremely remote," so remote that it did not warrant the kinds of costly changes sought by engineers like Janet. They did not believe that ground service personnel would improperly force the door shut. Janet, on the other hand, thought these managers were being imprudent and shortsighted. Over time, it would become increasingly probable that a careless ground crew member in a hurry might force the door shut and the end result would be catastrophic.

Executives balked at correcting the design flaw because it would push the plane behind schedule by at least six to nine months and appreciably increase cost. More importantly, the delay might cost the company the loss of a big order from a major airline. Its buyers were impressed with the DF-8 but required a timely delivery. Hence, no modifications were mandated. Despite Janet's disappointment over this inaction, her manager told her that nothing more could be done. "It's out of our hands," he explained. "We need to move on to the next project."

Six months later, Janet has learned that the jumbo jet has been certified by the FAA, since it has met all the agency's safety requirements. Janet is skeptical that the FAA was given all the relevant data, such as the test results on the prototype that indicated the presence of these flaws. A major U.S. airline has already taken delivery of the new plane, and it is scheduled to be in the air within a matter of months. But Janet remains deeply concerned. She again approaches her boss. He is sympathetic but tells her to let it go and that if she doesn't, her job could be in jeopardy. Janet is taken aback by this admonition. She is a single mother with two children to support, and she needs the substantial income provided by this job.

- Should Janet just "let it go" as her boss recommends, or should she come forward and register a complaint to the FAA? Can she really afford to be a whistle-blower?

- Has Janet fulfilled her moral obligations in this case by calling attention to the problem, or does she need to pursue the matter at a higher level such as the FAA? What is her moral duty in this situation?

- What are her options and what should she do next?

- Janet wonders whether she can afford to be a whistle-blower, but can she really afford not to be a whistle-blower under these circumstances? Comment on this question.

CASE STUDY 4.9

WHO'S RESPONSIBLE?[14]

I am a young attorney working in San Francisco for the law firm of Cornwall, Williams, and Wallace. Upon joining the firm, I was assigned to work with one of our new clients, a building contractor in the Bay Area. One of my primary responsibilities was to ensure that safety certificates and other compliance documents were obtained for new buildings. My liaison at the firm actually dealt with the city safety inspectors, but my job was to make sure everything was "in order" before occupancy could begin. During a briefing at the law firm about my work, the senior partner assigned to this account pointed out how

easily this contractor seemed to get these certificates compared to our other clients, who usually had to contend with delays and red tape. He speculated that there might be payoffs involved. Of particular concern was a new office building that was ready for occupancy in record time. This 10-story building, perched on one of the city's many hills, was built as a medical center where doctors and dentists could see their patients.

I was troubled, so I raised the issue with my contact at the firm. Once he felt comfortable that attorney–client privilege was in effect, he admitted that there was a "cozy relationship" between the contractor and several of the city's building inspectors. They were being paid off to "look the other way" and to expeditiously approve new buildings even if substandard material was sometimes used. I asked about the new medical building, and he affirmed that not all the construction material conformed to the building code standards. I pressed him for more specific information, but he refused to elaborate. As our meeting came to an end, he tried to offer me some reassurance: "Don't worry—we've put up commercial buildings all over this city and none of them have ever collapsed!"

After this meeting, I returned to my office at the law firm. I was not sure what to do about this revelation. I didn't want to be mixed up in some elaborate bribery scheme. Should I ask for a new assignment? Should I take steps to inform city authorities about the illicit activities of this company? I brought these matters up with the senior partner, but he seemed inured to such corporate wrongdoing and was much less concerned than I was. He reminded me that we had a duty to respect confidentiality and that we were bound by the ABA code of professional responsibility.[15] He was also somewhat upset that I had pursued this matter. "You should have stayed out of it," he exclaimed. "The less we know about these things, the better." I was then instructed to keep working for this client on several new projects until the partners could figure out how to proceed.

Four months later, much to my great dismay, there was a terrible fire at the new medical building. Three people trapped on one of the top floors were killed in the blaze, and several firefighters were seriously injured. It appears that the electrical wiring was inferior and not in compliance with the city's building code standards. There was a major scandal, and the contractor along with five city inspectors were quickly indicted on several criminal charges. Civil suits are sure to follow. But nothing happened to me or to anyone else at Cornwall. Rather, I am now assigned to the team defending the contractor in these criminal proceedings, so I must begin to collect evidence and prepare for the upcoming depositions.

Despite the apparent complacency of my colleagues, I can't seem to shake off the guilt I feel over this tragic incident. I could have probably done something about this contractor's corrupt payoffs, but I chose not to do so. Do I bear some of the responsibility for what's happened? I can't help but wonder what the victims' families would think about my lack of action. Maybe I'm just not cut out to be a lawyer.

- Is this lawyer in any way remotely complicit in the corrupt actions of his company and the city building inspectors?

- Should he have "stayed out of it," as the senior partner said, and not sought to confirm his suspicions of the corruption? Would his "ignorance" relieve him of responsibility for what transpired? What would Aristotle say about all this?

- Does the duty of confidentiality spelled out in the ABA code trump a lawyer's moral duty to expose the corruption?

CONCLUSION

As a way out of the dilemmas presented in these cases, it may occur to some managers and professionals to adopt a general strategy that separates their personal ethics from their professional conduct. Some business theorists have supported this viewpoint. As Albert Carr pointed out in his classic article, in their professional lives, managers "cease to be private citizens" and become "game players" who must be guided by a different set of ethical norms.[16] Game players adhere to a different set of rules geared for a competitive marketplace where people are not always fair and honorable. The avatar of virtue has scant chance in the brutal world of Wall Street. Recall the advice of Machiavelli: "A man who wants to act virtuously in every way necessarily comes to grief among so many who are not virtuous."[17] For instance, lying might be bad for my personal and family life but is sometimes necessary in the workplace. It is often suggested that a failure to make this separation puts at risk one's chances of professional success.

But this perspective stands in sharp contrast to Michael Maccoby's landmark article on corporate and personal integrity called "The Corporate Climber Has to Find His Heart." Maccoby argues that this gamesman mentality with its emotional detachment is quite damaging to individuals. He makes a persuasive case that integrity is achieved only by the person who prudently integrates his or her private and professional lives by following the same set of moral principles. To achieve success, executives often sacrifice emotions such as compassion along with their capacity to develop values that go beyond "winning the game." But good leadership and a fulfilling life depend not just on the head but also on the heart.[18]

In light of this discussion, it is also instructive to bear in mind an important observation taken from Aristotle's *Nicomachean Ethics*:

> The man, then, must be a perfect fool who is unaware that people's characters take their bias from the steady direction of their activities. If a man, well aware of what he is doing, behaves in such a way that he is bound to become unjust, we can only say that he is voluntarily unjust.[19]

Aristotle makes no distinction about whether those activities or actions that determine character are personal or professional. His point is that our free choices endure because through those choices the person creates his or her moral identity, either as someone just and reasonable or as someone unjust and unreasonable. A person's character is indelibly shaped by the choices he or she has made.[20]

Student Study Site

Visit **edge.sagepub.com/spinello.**

Review Questions

1. How might you summarize or characterize the type of moral dilemmas managers and leaders must deal with?

2. Which of the frameworks discussed in Chapter 3 are most useful for resolving these dilemmas?

Discussion Questions

1. What do you think about Albert Carr's opinion of managers as "game players"? Do you side with Carr or with Maccoby?

2. What are the dangers or pitfalls involved in applying ethical theories to cases like the ones in this chapter?

Appendix: How to Analyze a Case

For the most part, we will be using the case method throughout this book. The value of this method is that it gives students the opportunity of learning by doing. Almost every case calls for diagnosis of the problem along with a decisive action plan. Noted teacher and historian R. W. Southern once said that "men learn after all by being puzzled and excited, not by being told."[21] This sums up the philosophy of this book. The cases may not always "tell" you very much about what should be done, but they will help you to *think* in the presence of new and challenging business situations.

For those students who are new to the case method, a broad overview of how to analyze a business ethics case can be quite helpful. There are certainly many different ways to go about this process, but here is a concise guide outlining the major steps to follow.

1. After reading the case carefully, think about the principal and relevant facts of the case. How would you briefly summarize it to a friend or a colleague? What are your first impressions about the events described in the case—is there anything you find striking or surprising?

2. Think about the case from the viewpoint of *corporate purpose* and the company's *ethical, legal, and moral obligations* to stakeholders that allow it to fulfill that purpose (especially for cases in Chapters 6 through 14).

   a. What are the economic aspects of the case, and how might they affect leaders' decisions?

   b. What are the main ethical issues explicit or implicit in the case? Is the ethical problem one of deception, lack of transparency, unfair competition, disloyalty, cheating, extortion, promise breaking, bribery, or some other type of moral wrongfulness?

   c. Are there any legal issues in the case, and if so, how do they interplay with the moral issues? Are there any laws that are not being complied with?

3. How *serious* are these moral and legal problems? How could they affect the corporation's economic mission? For example, what financial or strategic impact are they apt to have? What about intangible effects on employee morale or on the company's reputation?

4. Develop a *diagnosis* for the origin of these problems. What are the organizational factors at the root of the ethical (or legal) crisis (for example, a flawed culture with weak norms, poor leadership, or lack of adequate controls)? And what are the individual factors (for example, lack of professionalism or moral indifference)?

5. After the diagnosis, it's time to turn to an *action plan*:

   a. What are the options for resolution of the ethical problem or dilemma in the case?

   b. What are the pros and cons of each option?

   c. Which option should be chosen?

      i. Based on the ethical frameworks in Chapter 3 and especially the DRJ formula, make the strongest case possible for your choice.

      ii. How would you carry out or implement this choice?

6. Finally, what are the main lessons or takeaways of this case, and how do those lessons fit with what you have studied so far in other cases?

CORPORATE VALUES AND RESPONSIBILITIES

PART III

5

THE RIGHTS OF THE
MODERN CORPORATION

I am compelled to say something about corporate "personhood." Human
beings are persons and it is an affront to the inviolable dignity of our
species that courts have created a legal fiction which forces people—
human beings—to share fundamental natural rights with soulless
creations of government.

—Justice James Nelson[1]

LEARNING OBJECTIVES

Upon completion of this chapter, you should be able to:

5.1 Discuss some of the constitutional liberties enjoyed by the modern
corporation.

5.2 Develop analytical skills and legal reasoning.

5.3 Relate the theme of corporate purpose presented in Chapter 2.

The remaining sections of this book dwell extensively on the theme of corporate
responsibility and misconduct. The cases in subsequent chapters bring into sharp
relief the corporation's moral obligation to respect the rights of others. But before
we turn to those case studies, it is instructive to review the corporation's own legal
rights. In Chapter 2 we suggested how those rights could be justified if the corporation

qualified for moral agency. Moral agency assumes the capacity to enter into relationships of duties and obligations, and it is difficult to comprehend how corporations could be morally liable to others without having the right to make their own moral demands. Agency and corporate accountability seem to require some sort of authentic moral reciprocity.[2]

In the eyes of the law, the corporation has many rights. The for-profit corporation enjoys the protection of the Fourteenth Amendment, which affords it due process and equal protection under the law. It is also entitled to Fourth Amendment protection against unreasonable search and seizure. In some cases, these rulings have been predicated on a theory of corporate personification that sees an analogy between the corporation and the human person. Many legal scholars and activists are quite concerned about this pro-corporate trend. They worry corporations will leverage their collective influence to overwhelm the interests of ordinary citizens. Also, if corporations invoke the rights of natural persons, will they end up burdening themselves with too many responsibilities?[3]

While the Supreme Court has sought to protect the corporation from government's coercive powers, there are limits to the corporation's constitutional liberties. Thanks to *Hale v. Henkel*, corporations do not have the right against self-incrimination (guaranteed by the Fifth Amendment). They do not have the right to vote or the right to keep and bear arms. Yet there are two key liberty rights they share with real persons that are the axis of discussion in this chapter: the right to free speech, which includes the right to spend money on political campaigns, and, under certain conditions, the right to the exercise of religion.

AN OVERVIEW OF THE CASES

The First Amendment to the United States Constitution states that "Congress shall make no law . . . abridging the freedom of speech." The Constitution protects forms of speech that other Democratic nations ban outright or severely limit. The First Amendment is designed to impose strict limits on governmental authority over speech and to prevent government from seizing a "guardianship of the public mind."[4] And speech does not lose its protection simply because the speaker is a wealthy corporation. Several pivotal rulings in which corporations received First Amendment protection laid a firm legal foundation for protection of free speech. One, *Citizens United v. FEC* (2010), is the first case study to be reviewed in this chapter. *Citizens United* invalidated provisions of the Bipartisan Campaign Reform Act and preserved the corporation's right to make financial contributions for political purposes. This highly contested decision along with its reasoning and assumptions is the focus of this challenging case.[5]

Four years after *Citizens United* was decided, the U.S. Supreme Court issued another landmark decision in *Burwell v. Hobby Lobby* (2014), the second case study in this chapter. Hobby Lobby, Inc., which operates over 600 arts and crafts stores, clashed with the federal government over certain provisions of President Obama's Affordable Care Act. Hobby Lobby's owners challenged the regulation requiring employers to cover in their health plans certain forms of emergency contraception that prevent a fertilized egg from implanting. Hobby Lobby executives believed this regulation contradicted the pro-life religious principles on which their company was founded. For the company's owners, religious expression is central to the company's mission. They invoked the First Amendment, "Congress shall make no law respecting an establishment of religion, or prohibiting the free exercise thereof," along with the Religious Freedom Restoration Act (RFRA) of 1993 as support for their claim that their religious liberty was being infringed upon. But do impersonal corporations have the right to free exercise of religion? In its 5–4 decision, the Supreme Court concluded that the word *person* in laws such as the RFRA included corporations and other organizations, and hence ruled in Hobby Lobby's favor. Justice Ginsberg and three other justices dissented, calling the ruling "a decision of startling breadth."[6] However, the majority believed that this right was valid based on the corporation's status as an association capable of defending the rights of its employees.[7]

This second case study examines the controversial aspects of the *Hobby Lobby* decision and what it might portend for the future of corporate constitutional rights. It also takes into account the implications for managers who must now determine how a corporation's religious expression can be reconciled with other corporate objectives and the needs of all employees, especially those who do not share its religious sentiments. In the words of one *Hobby Lobby* skeptic, does this ruling allow corporations to compel their female employees to "foot the bill for [their] religious beliefs"?[8]

Finally, the issue of corporate purpose, discussed in Chapter 2, surfaces quite directly in the *Hobby Lobby* case. Recall the proposition that corporate purpose is tied to the corporation's common good, understood as effective economic cooperation and fairness to those who cooperate to create economic value. Some businesses, however, are organized partly for altruistic reasons that become integrated into its common good. A corporation, for example, might espouse religious values and give away a large portion of its profits to religious charities. There is nothing wrong with broadening the corporation's purpose in this fashion, so long as core stakeholders, including investors, consent to this gratuitous arrangement.[9]

CASE STUDY 5.1

CITIZENS UNITED V. FEDERAL ELECTION COMMISSION

In January 2010, the U.S. Supreme Court handed down its eagerly awaited ruling in *Citizens United v. Federal Election Commission.* In this 5–4 decision, the court concluded that a federal election law could not ban general fund independent expenditures for political campaigns or electioneering communications. The justices opined that the law violated the First Amendment rights of corporations and other institutions. The decision immediately ignited a firestorm of protest and indignation. Within a short time, there were petitions circulated calling on Congress to initiate the process for a constitutional amendment to

overthrow the decision. But why the outrage? Isn't this ruling a logical extension of cases affirming a corporation's limited right to political participation? On the other hand, does this sweeping decision represent sound legal reasoning, consistent with a reasonable view of the corporation, or is it based on fatally flawed assumptions? These contested issues, which are carefully explored in this case, continue to be a topic of intense debate.[10]

Citizens United

Citizens United is a nonprofit advocacy corporation organized to support and defend various political causes. It was founded in 1988 by Floyd Brown, a well-known Washington political consultant. The group promotes corporate interests, socially conservative causes, and political candidates who advance their goals and values. Those values include "limited government, freedom of enterprise, strong families, and national sovereignty and security." Citizens United opposes progressivism and supports the cultivation of conventional virtues as part of America's inherited tradition. This organization champions political campaigns and conservative candidates, whom it supports through media promotion and advertising. Citizens United operates with an annual budget of about $12 million. Over the years Citizens United has been generously funded by several conservative foundations as well as businesspeople such as the Koch family. Some of its funding has also come directly from several for-profit corporations.[11]

Citizens United is perhaps best known for some of its provocative documentaries. Citizens United Productions, which is led by president David Bossie, has released over 20 feature-length documentaries. They include *ACLU: At War with America*, *America at Risk*, *Battle for America*, and *The Gift of Life*. It also produced *Hillary: The Movie*, a critical, feature-length documentary about the life and political career of Senator Hillary Clinton, who had entered the Democratic Party's 2008 primary to secure the presidential nomination. The ostensible aim of the 90-minute documentary, which was released in January 2008, was to damage her political campaign as the presidential primary season got under way.

Hillary was released both in theaters and on DVD. But Citizens United sought to increase viewership for the *Hillary* movie by also releasing it in a video-on-demand format, and by promoting the video format through short 30-second advertisements that would run on broadcast and cable television. The ads included a terse derogatory statement about Hillary Clinton, the movie's name, and its website address. If Senator Clinton won the primary election, Citizens United was poised to use its general funds to advertise and distribute the movie right before the general election in November 2008.

However, according to the terms of the Bipartisan Campaign Reform Act of 2002 (BCRA), also known as the McCain-Feingold law, corporations and unions are banned from making independent expenditures for political campaigns. They are also banned from "electioneering communication," that is, "any broadcast, cable, or satellite communication [that] refers to a clearly identified candidate for Federal office" that is made within 30 days of a primary or 60 days of a general election.[12] A company like Citizens United could not use its general funds to advertise and distribute a movie such as *Hillary* during the periods immediately before the election. The only alternative was to employ a political action committee (PAC) to make these expenditures. Thus, the law did not ban election ads by corporations, but those ads had to be financed through a PAC. However, given the rules governing PACs, Citizens United believed this option was too burdensome, and so it chose not to rely on a PAC.

Citizens United realized that advertising and distributing the *Hillary* video would bring it into direct conflict with the BCRA, and so it sought injunctive relief, claiming that the relevant section (441b) prohibiting "electioneering" was unconstitutional. In an initial hearing, a federal court in Washington, DC, ruled that Citizens United would be barred from advertising and distributing its film because it was within the 60-day period before the election. It refused to offer the injunctive relief sought by Citizens United. After a series of appeals the controversial case landed at the U.S. Supreme Court in March 2009.[13]

Citizens United at the Supreme Court

The *Citizens United* legal team was headed by talented attorney Ted Olson, who had represented President George W. Bush in the *Bush v. Gore* case of 2000. Olson was joined by another successful and experienced lawyer, Jim Bopp Jr., who also had a successful track record at the Supreme Court. Bopp, who worked out of a small law office in Indiana, was also known for his libertarian views on election expenditures by corporations or unions. He had previously represented ideological groups that sued to limit campaign finance law.[14]

During oral arguments, Olson claimed a First Amendment right to produce, distribute, and advertise the *Hillary* movie without any arbitrary restrictions. Nonprofit and for-profit corporations, Olson insisted, should be able to contribute their ideas or opinions to political campaigns and influence elections just as individuals do. He argued that the BCRA prevented this organization from exercising its political speech in accord with the First Amendment. The Bipartisan Reform Act, Olson said, was a "ban of speech by corporations." He went on to argue that there was no need for such a restrictive law since "there is no evidence that corporate and union independent expenditures" have a corrupting influence on the legislative process.[15] But the government's attorneys insisted that precedent was on their side and that the restrictions imposed by the BCRA were not unconstitutional. According to their claims, the government had the power under the Constitution to prohibit the dissemination or advertising of books, pamphlets, and movies under certain circumstances if they were made or sold by corporations.

On January 21, 2010, a divided Supreme Court handed down its famous ruling in Citizens United's favor. In a 5–4 decision, the justices claimed that the contested provision of McCain-Feingold barring corporations and unions from using general funds for political ads made independently of candidate campaigns was unconstitutional. There could no longer be a ban on the use of corporate general funds for expenditures associated with elections. Quite simply, as the court explained, corporations and unions have a First Amendment right to make expenditures for candidates in political elections, and since the BCRA burdened that right, it was unconstitutional.

According to Justice Kennedy, who wrote the majority opinion, "When government seeks to use its full power, including the criminal law, to command where a person may get his or her information or what distrusted source he or she may not hear, it uses censorship to control thought. . . . The First Amendment confirms the freedom to think for ourselves."[16] Even when it comes to corporate entities, including unions, government must not ban their speech or silence their voices. Kennedy went on to explain:

> Some may think that one group or another should not express its views in an election because it is too powerful, because it advocates unpopular ideas, or because it had a record of lawless action. But these are not justifications for withholding First Amendment rights from any group—labor or corporate. . . . First Amendment rights are part of the heritage of all persons and groups in this country.[17]

As its chief precedent, the court cited *First National Bank v. Bellotti*, where the Supreme Court had already ruled in 1978 that the political speech of a for-profit bank was protected by the First Amendment. The bank and several other corporations wanted to spend money on advertisements opposing a graduated income tax. The Massachusetts attorney general sued and the Massachusetts Supreme Judicial Court concluded that corporations possessed only those narrow speech rights that were necessary to protect their property and business concerns. But the U.S. Supreme Court overruled that decision, proclaiming that the First Amendment was written "to protect the free discussion of government affairs," no matter who the speaker is.[18] According to the court, "The inherent worth of speech in terms of its capacity for informing the public does not depend upon the identity of its source, whether a corporation, association, union, or individual."[19]

Subsequent to the *Bellotti* case, the Supreme Court nullified a New York state law that banned corporations from using their billing envelopes to express political views to their customers. But corporate speech was gradually undermined by several later decisions, including *Austin v. Michigan Chamber of Commerce* (1990). The court upheld bans on corporate contributions to candidates and committees and then a ban on "electioneering communications." The effect of those decisions was to silence corporate political speech and undermine the principles articulated in *Bellotti*.[20]

However, *Citizens United* strongly reaffirmed those principles: "The First Amendment protects speech and speaker, and the ideas that flow from each." And the identity of the speaker is immaterial: "Bellotti's central principle [is] that the First Amendment does not allow political speech restrictions based on a speaker's corporate identity."[21] In addition, argued Justice Kennedy, the First Amendment "has its fullest and greatest application to speech during a campaign for political office."[22]

These citations reflect how Kennedy's analysis was based on two well-established legal propositions. First, political speech is at the core of the First Amendment. While the scope of the First Amendment is sometimes debated, what is beyond dispute is the right to engage in political speech about whom to vote for or against. Second, a corporation could not be deprived of this right to endorse candidates through independent expenditures. Kennedy cited multiple cases in which the court endorsed full First Amendment protection for a corporate entity. Justice Stevens's dissent acknowledged this historical record and conceded that "we have long since held that corporations are covered by the First Amendment."[23]

To the surprise of some corporate rights advocates, the notion of corporate personhood is entirely missing from Justice Kennedy's opinion. The court granted broad free speech rights to corporations not necessarily because they were people. Instead, the *Citizens United* decision "obscured the corporate entity and emphasized the rights of others, like shareholders and listeners."[24] Rather than treating the corporation, independent of its members, as a legal person with rights of its own, it focused on the rights of the corporation's stakeholders. The Kennedy opinion is based on the assumption that corporations are associations of citizens, and that government cannot ban political speech "simply because the speaker is an association that has taken on corporate form."[25] The Kennedy opinion sharply rebuked the BCRA for oppressing "disfavored associations of citizens," that is, the for-profit corporation.[26]

Nonetheless, critics of the majority decision, including some of the minority justices, seized on the dissimilarity between the corporation and the person as the basis for denying First Amendment protection. Some of the justices, such as Elena Kagan, underscored substantial differences between corporate and human speakers. This sentiment was also captured to some extent in Justice Stevens's pungent dissenting opinion:

> Although they make enormous contributions to society, corporations are not actually members of it. They cannot vote or run for office. Because they may be managed and controlled by nonresidents, their interests may conflict in fundamental respects with the interests of eligible voters. The financial resources, legal structure, and instrumental orientation of corporations raises legitimate concerns about their role in the electoral process. Our lawmakers have a compelling constitutional basis, if not a democratic duty, to take measures designed to guard against the potentially deleterious effects of dissenting shareholders and national races.[27]

Thus, Stevens rejected the court's assumption that corporations are members of the political community who contribute to the discussion, debate, and dissemination of information and ideas the First Amendment seeks to protect. In his estimation, it is implausible to extend the right to political speech to the corporation: "The Framers [of the Constitution] . . . had little trouble distinguishing corporations from human beings, and when they constitutionalized the right to freedom of speech in the First Amendment, it was the free speech of individual Americans they had in mind."[28] When the First Amendment was drafted, the authors were concerned about protecting the free speech of American individuals, not groups or corporations. Moreover, Stevens insisted that the First Amendment allows for the regulation of speech based on the identity of the speaker. He noted that the government routinely imposes special restrictions on the speech rights of students, prisoners, and even members of the U.S. armed forces.[29] Because of their size and power and their ability to raise capital, why not impose limitations on corporations to spend money on elections?

Reactions to the Decision

After the Supreme Court decision was handed down, Citizen United's president, David Bossie, went out to greet the media. It was an arctic winter day in Washington, but there were many reporters gathered to record reactions about this controversial case. Bossie profusely thanked his legal team and told reporters that he was "grateful and humbled" by the Supreme Court's ruling. Corporations, he said, "could now participate fully and freely in the election process."[30]

The decision was highly unpopular in many circles. It was immediately condemned by President Obama and many other Democrats, who promised new legislation to counter the court's radical opinion. One congressman called it "the worst Supreme Court decision since the Dred Scott case."[31] A poll taken shortly after the decision was handed down indicated that 80% of the American public disagreed with the ruling. In the minds of many, the opinion radically altered the election calculus, because it offered greater opportunity for wealthy, for-profit corporations to speak their voices more effectively within the crowded national political debate. That corporate speech was likely to distort future elections. The fiction of corporate rights threatened democracy itself.[32]

Critics were also quick to point out that this ruling was a prime example of conservative judicial activism that represented a radical change in the law. The case quickly became a rallying cry against corporate personification and corporate liberty rights. Quite simply, Chief Justice Marshall got it right when he proclaimed in 1819 that a corporation is a "mere creature of law" that "possesses only those properties which the [state] charter confers upon it, either expressly or as incidental to its very existence."[33] While it was reasonable to treat a corporation like a person for matters of contracts or liability, this artificial entity could not be a bearer of rights. Corporate rights, which trump valid restrictions on excessive corporate influence, are a fabrication that will inhibit ordinary citizens from exercising their own rights.

Yet supporters of the *Citizens United* outcome could point to their own precedents, such as *Bellotti*, which laid the firm foundation for this decision. *Citizens United* did not represent a radical revision of the law but in fact was "the culmination of a two hundred year struggle for constitutional rights for corporations."[34] Those rights now included liberty rights as well as those property rights that corporations had been granted in the last century.

While the outrage over this case has subsided, there are still active efforts to overturn the *Citizens United* case by passing a Twenty-Eighth Amendment to the Constitution. Groups such as Common Cause, People for the American Way, US PIRG, and Free Speech for People have mobilized concerned citizens to get involved in this effort. It is called the People's Rights Amendment, and it is designed to strip artificial entities of any rights including the right to free speech. Section II of that Amendment disavows the idea that corporations are constitutional persons with rights:

> We the people who ordain and establish this Constitution intend the rights protected by the Constitution to be the rights of natural persons.

> The words *people*, *persons*, or *citizens* as used in this Constitution do not include corporations, limited liability companies, or other corporate entities established by the laws of any state, the United States, or any foreign state. Such corporate entities are subject to any regulation as the people, through their elected state and federal representatives, deem reasonable and as are otherwise consistent with the powers of Congress and the States under this Constitution.[35]

While such an Amendment would effectively overturn the *Citizens United* ruling, its successful passage is quite improbable.

- Consult the *Citizens United v. Federal Election Commission* Supreme Court case and outline the arguments on both sides of the debate. (The decision can be downloaded at the Supreme Court website: https://www.supremecourt.gov/opinions/09pdf/08-205.pdf.)

- In your view, should for-profit corporations be entitled to the same rights of free speech and political participation as individual citizens? Or should those rights be limited in some way?

- Does this ruling threaten free, fair elections in any way?

- How would you have decided this case if you were a member of the U.S. Supreme Court? What are the major reasons and assumptions underlying your decision?

CASE STUDY 5.2

THE *HOBBY LOBBY* CASE

In *Burwell v. Hobby Lobby*, five Supreme Court justices concurred that a closely held, for-profit corporation is entitled to the free exercise of religion without undue government interference. The justices exempted Hobby Lobby from providing several contraceptives mandated by the Affordable Care Act's contraceptive mandate because this requirement imposed a substantial burden on its religious beliefs. The four dissenting justices vigorously resisted this conclusion. In this case study we present both sides of the sharp debate on corporate liberties reignited by this case.

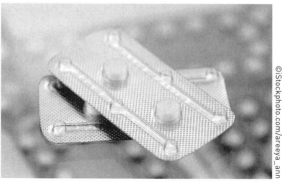
©iStockphoto.com/areeya_ann

The *Hobby Lobby* decision has brought little closure to the dispute about the scope of rights for the corporation and the whole question of corporate purpose. A key issue in this case is whether or not a for-profit corporation like Hobby Lobby can qualify as a "person" who can in some way "exercise religion."

Hobby Lobby Inc.

By any measure, Hobby Lobby is a unique and exceptional corporation. This privately held company was founded in 1970 by entrepreneurs David and Barbara Green along with their three children. The Green family began by making miniature picture frames in their garage. A few years later, on August 3, 1972, the Green family opened the first Hobby Lobby shop. It was a small store with only 300 square feet of retail space. Beneath its gray roof, the Greens began selling their picture frames, art supplies, and other items for hobbyists. The store was a big success, and Hobby Lobby has been growing at a rapid pace for the past four decades.

In 2016, Hobby Lobby Stores Inc., with corporate headquarters in Oklahoma City, Oklahoma, operated over 600 stores located across the United States, especially in the Midwest. It also has stores in China, Hong Kong, and the Philippines. The company currently employs 20,000 full and part-time workers. Each U.S. store has an average space of about 55,000 square feet. Hobby Lobby is an industry-leading retailer offering more than 70,000 arts, crafts, hobbies, and home decor products, along with an abundance of Christmas and seasonal products. Hobby Lobby is included in Forbes's annual list of America's largest companies. It ranks as the third-largest craft and fabric retailer (behind Michaels Stores and Jo-Ann Stores). Hobby Lobby is set up under Oklahoma law as a for-profit but nonpublic and closely held corporation. The company is in excellent financial health and still carries no long-term debt on its books. Its total revenues in 2016 exceeded $4 billion.[36]

What sets Hobby Lobby far apart from most of its corporate peers is its explicit Christian values. The Green family members are all devout practicing Christians, and they have designed a corporate structure and culture that embeds Christian values. The company's statement of purpose commits the owners to "honor the Lord in all they do by operating the company in a manner consistent with Biblical principles." Each family member signs a pledge to run the business in accordance with Christian ideals. To be true to that commitment, Hobby Lobby stores are closed on Sunday despite the fact that the company loses millions of dollars by doing so. Hobby Lobby also contributes substantial profits to Christian missionaries and different Christian ministries.[37]

In addition, Hobby Lobby takes out full-page ads during the Easter season in every city or town where it operates one of its stores. The company evangelizes through these ads, which provide some information on how to learn more about Jesus Christ. The ads are expensive and are not the most efficient way of reaching new customers, but the Greens see this evangelization initiative as part of their Christian duty.[38]

However, Hobby Lobby, the "dream store" for the hobbyist and amateur decorator, soon found itself thrust into a legal nightmare when its religious convictions collided with the country's new health care law. The landmark *Hobby Lobby* case has now become the center of legal and moral debates about corporate purpose and religious freedom. To explore how this happened, we must first turn to a cursory treatment of the Affordable Care Act and the Health and Human Services mandates that put the company into this moral and legal bind.

The Patient Protection and Affordable Care Act

When Barack Obama became president of the United States in 2008, he signaled that universal health care would be one of his chief priorities. In 2010, the U.S. Congress passed the Patient Protection and Affordable Care Act (ACA). This law mandates employers with 50 or more full-time employees to offer a group health plan or group health insurance that provides "minimum essential coverage."[39] Any employer who refused to comply with this group health plan requirement had to pay a fine for every affected individual worker. In addition, under the so-called individual mandate, every U.S. citizen had to purchase minimal essential health care coverage or be subject to a tax penalty.

Unless certain exceptions applied, the Affordable Care Act also mandated that the group health care plan provided by an employer include "preventative care and screenings" for women without any copayments.[40] It was left to the Department of Health and Human Services (HHS), which was responsible for implementation of the Affordable Care Act, to stipulate which types of preventative care should be covered. Accordingly, the department promulgated Women's Preventive Services Guidelines. Among those guidelines was a requirement that employers provide "coverage without cost sharing" for all Food and Drug Administration–approved "contraceptive methods, sterilization procedures, and patient education and counseling."[41] There were exemptions from this so-called contraceptive mandate for "religious employers," a category which included churches and their "integrated auxiliaries."[42] There was also an accommodation for other religious nonprofit organizations. An eligible organization such as a Christian school could exclude contraceptive and sterilization coverage from its health plan. However, the insurance issuer had to provide separate payments for those services without imposing any cost-sharing on the school or the employee who wanted that service.

The ACA's individual mandate was promptly challenged in the federal courts. Plaintiffs argued the ACA's attempt to regulate individuals who were not in the health care marketplace was unconstitutional, a violation of the commerce clause of the U.S. Constitution. The Eleventh Circuit federal court agreed with those arguments and ruled that Congress had exceeded its power under the Commerce Clause when it passed into law the individual mandate provision of the ACA. The Supreme Court, however, overturned that decision and upheld the constitutionality of the ACA's individual mandate. It reasoned that the ACA was constitutional because it was a tax.

The contraceptive mandate also became a source of some contention. For-profit corporations were not eligible for an exemption or an accommodation. But some of these corporations resisted the contraceptive mandate since it forced them to provide certain forms of contraception to which they objected. These employers worried that by subsidizing these medical treatments, they would share in the blame for the wrongful act of using contraceptive devices that behaved as abortifacients. Thus, they had grave conscientious objections to the contraceptive mandate. One of those employers was Hobby Lobby.[43]

Hobby Lobby and Religious Freedom

As a for-profit, closely held corporation, Hobby Lobby did not meet the criteria for an accommodation or an exemption from the HHS mandate. The company was not opposed to contraceptive coverage in general. But it objected to 4 of the 24 FDA-approved contraceptive methods because they prevented the fertilized egg or embryo from implanting on the uterus.[44] The Green family, following its Christian faith, believed that human life begins at conception. Since those 4 contraceptive methods functioned as abortifacients, they terminated a human life, and Hobby Lobby did not want to be complicit in this immoral act. Thus, while the Greens did not object to providing through their health care plan 20 of the 24 FDA-approved contraception methods, they vigorously objected to providing the four that could potentially destroy a fertilized egg or early-stage embryo. Moreover, Hobby Lobby's insurance had never covered contraceptive drugs or devices that could terminate a pregnancy.[45]

The majority Supreme Court opinion described Hobby Lobby's concern in this way: the owners of the business have religious objections to abortion; several FDA-approved contraceptive methods are abortifacients; if the owners comply with the HHS's contraceptive mandate, they will be facilitating abortions and complicit in the killing of an embryonic human being.[46] According to the court, "The owners believe that providing the coverage demanded by the HHS regulations is connected to the destruction of an embryo in a way that is sufficient to make it immoral for them to provide the coverage."[47]

Accordingly, the Greens and Hobby Lobby sued the Health and Human Services Department and challenged the contraceptive mandate, claiming the requirement to provide abortion-inducing drugs violated their right to properly exercise their religious freedom. The plaintiffs claimed the HHS mandate infringed upon their rights as guaranteed by the First Amendment, which states that "Congress shall make no law respecting an establishment of religion, or prohibiting the free exercise thereof." It is also guaranteed by a 1993 statute called the Religious Freedom Restoration Act (RFRA). In their view, the government requirement unfairly burdened their religious beliefs. The RFRA prohibits the "government from substantially burdening a person's exercise of religion even if the burden results from a rule of general applicability," unless the government demonstrates that the application of such a burden is "the least restrictive means" to advance a "compelling government interest."[48] The RFRA was amended in 2000 by the Religious Land Use and Institutionalized Persons Act in order to redefine the *exercise of religion* as any exercise of religion, "whether or not compelled by, or central to, a system of religious belief," that is to be "construed in favor of a broad protection of religious exercise, to the maximum extent permitted by the terms of this chapter and the Constitution." In 2006, the Supreme Court upheld the constitutionality of the RFRA in another landmark case, *Gonzales v. O Centro Espirita*.[49]

The Hobby Lobby lawsuit challenging the contraceptive mandate was filed in September 2012 in the U.S. District Court for the Western District of Oklahoma. Hobby Lobby could have been fined $1.3 million per day for failure to provide the four types of contraception to which it so strenuously objected on religious grounds. The company, therefore, sought injunctive relief. However, the district court denied Hobby Lobby's request for a preliminary injunction. The court held that Hobby Lobby did not possess the right to the free exercise of religion (as guaranteed by the First Amendment of the U.S. Constitution) and therefore that it was unlikely to prevail on constitutional grounds.

Several months later, another company, Conestoga Wood Specialties, also brought suit to challenge the HHS mandate on the basis of its religious liberty. Conestoga was a for-profit Pennsylvania woodworking business with 950 employees. It was operated by the Hahn family, two parents and three children, who were all active in the business. The Hahns were devout members of the Mennonite Church and owned all of Conestoga's stock. They also controlled the board of directors, and one of the sons was the company's president and CEO. Like the Greens, the Hahn family objected to providing their employees with the FDA-approved contraceptives that were considered to be abortifacients. As evidence of their deep-seated religious convictions, they cited the company's "Vision and Values Statement," which explains the corporate mission: "a reasonable profit in a manner that reflects Christian heritage." Years before the HHS mandate was issued, the company's board had also adopted a "Statement on the Sanctity of Human Life."[50]

Hobby Lobby appealed its case, and in March 2013, the U.S. Court of Appeals for the Tenth Circuit granted the plaintiffs a hearing. Two months later the Court of Appeals reversed the lower court's ruling and held that Hobby Lobby satisfied the conditions for a preliminary injunction. The court ordered the government to stop enforcement of the contraception rule on Hobby Lobby and sent the case back to the district court, which granted a preliminary injunction in July. In its ruling, the appeals court held that a closely held, for-profit corporation like Hobby Lobby qualified as a person under the RFRA and therefore had legal standing to bring forward this claim. Hobby Lobby "established a likelihood of success that their rights under this statute [were] substantially burdened by the contraceptive coverage requirement and have established an irreparable harm."[51] In September 2013, the Health and Human Services Department appealed the decision to the U.S. Supreme Court, and the two cases, *Conestoga Wood Specialties* and *Hobby Lobby*, were consolidated.

The Supreme Court Decision

In *Burwell v. Hobby Lobby, Inc.*, the U.S. Supreme Court ruled in favor of Hobby Lobby and Conestoga. It concluded that requiring family-owned corporations to pay for insurance coverage for some forms of objectionable contraception under the Affordable Care Act violated the RFRA, along with the owners' sincerely held religious beliefs. The majority opinion of the court concluded that "a federal government's restriction on the activities of a for-profit, closely held corporation must comply with the RFRA."[52] The *New York Times* wrote that the decision was characteristic of the Supreme Court under Chief Justice John Roberts: "an inclination toward nominally incremental rulings with vast potential for great change."[53]

Until this litigation and this ruling, no court had ever recognized a for-profit corporation's exemption from a law in the name of religious liberty. The 5–4 ruling appeared to open the door to many challenges from corporations over laws they claim violated their religious liberty. But Justice Samuel A. Alito, who wrote the opinion for the majority, emphasized the ruling's narrow scope. According to Alito, the court ruled only that a federal religious-freedom law applied to "closely held" for-profit corporations run on religious principles. It would not really apply to large publicly traded corporations, since the "idea that unrelated shareholders—including institutional investors with their own set of stakeholders—would agree to run a corporation under the same religious beliefs seems improbable."[54] Justice Alito concluded that "corporate giants" would be highly unlikely to assert RFRA claims.[55]

Despite its limited scope, the case represented a new landmark since it allowed at least some corporations the right to claim a religious accommodation in order to avoid compliance with federal regulations. What was the court's reasoning behind this decision? The justices had to resolve at least two major questions. The court had to determine whether RFRA protection included closely held, for-profit corporations, even though the law from which the exemption was sought was designed to aid their workers, some of whom did not share the owners' religious beliefs. The justices also had to determine that there was a "substantial burden" on the free exercise of religion in order to qualify for the RFRA exemption.[56]

The first question depends on how one interprets the RFRA statute and the legislative intent behind it. Does the for-profit corporation qualify as a "person" within the statute? Justice Alito affirmatively answers that question, and he relies on the proposition that within the law generally corporations qualify as persons. Moreover, reasons Alito, the government had already conceded that RFRA applies to nonprofit organizations, so why arbitrarily exclude for-profit companies? To suggest that a for-profit corporation cannot be included under the auspices of the RFRA "flies in the face of modern corporate law."[57] For Alito, it was simply unintelligible to include some kinds of companies within the purview of the statute but not others.[58]

The second question is whether requiring insurance coverage for employees for the four contraceptive devices at issue represented a "substantial burden" on the companies' exercise of religion. In making the determination that there was such a burden, Alito relied on two key factors. The first factor was the sincerity of the owners' beliefs. There was ample evidence to support the sincerity of both parties, Hobby Lobby and Conestoga. Their faith-based practices, such as closing stores on Sunday, along with their explicit mission statements, were quite convincing. Both companies sent a clear message of "religiosity" to their employees, shareholders, and other stakeholders.[59] Both companies sincerely believed the use of particular contraceptive devices that sometimes resulted in abortion was immoral, and in good conscience they did not want to provide that device through their insurance plans. On this point, Justice Ginsburg had argued that "the requirement is too attenuated to rank as substantial."[60] But the majority was convinced that the employers' connection to the use of the abortifacient was direct rather than remote and therefore constituted a substantial burden. The second factor was the onerous financial impact that would result from violation of the mandate. If these companies failed to include these contraceptives in their coverage, they would be fined $100 per day for each employee, and if they dropped insurance coverage, they would be fined $2,000 per employee per year.[61]

With these two threshold questions resolved, Alito easily resolves other issues such as the government's "compelling interest" and whether the denial of an exemption was the least restrictive means of achieving its objective. Alito assumed (without deciding) the presence of a compelling government interest, but he also found that the government did not use the least restrictive means to achieve its objectives. Instead of denying the exemption to all for-profit corporations, why not allow for the same accommodation available to religious nonprofits? Hence, he reached his conclusion that the contraceptive mandate violated RFRA as applied to corporations.[62] But Alito's opinion was always focused on the members of the corporation, rather than the corporate entity itself. His opinion did not draw on insights about corporate personification as a justification for this right to the exercise of religion. Nor did it imply that a corporation itself, apart from its members, can somehow exercise religion or practice its religious beliefs. Rather, the court concluded that we should grant free-exercise rights to the corporation as a means of protecting the free-exercise rights of the corporation's owners and employees.[63] According to Justice Alito, "A corporation is simply a form of organization used by human beings to achieve desired ends. When rights, whether constitutional or statutory, are extended to corporations, the purpose is to protect the rights of these people."[64] The Hobby Lobby corporation was entitled to assert its religious rights in order to protect the religious liberty of its owners. The case did not treat the corporation as an independent legal entity or "person," with rights separate from its members. Rather, the court emphasized a conception of the corporation as an association capable of asserting the rights of its members.[65]

The Dissent

Four dissenting justices took strong exception to Justice Alito's polished reasoning. Justice Ginsburg, who wrote a stinging dissenting opinion, said the court had mistakenly extended religious-freedom protections to "the commercial, profit-making world." In her view, the exercise of religion can only be done by natural persons and cannot be associated with the corporate format. Thus the application of the RFRA to for-profit corporations is a serious error, since it does not make sense to think of these corporations as exercising religion. "The court's expansive notion of corporate personhood," Justice Ginsburg wrote, "invites for-profit entities to seek religion-based exemptions from regulations they deem offensive to their faiths."[66]

Justice Ginsberg also found fault with Alito's conclusion that the contraceptive mandate substantially burdened a person's exercise of religion and therefore violated the RFRA. Congress, she explained, "meant the modifier 'substantially' to carry some weight."[67] She argued that the requirement does not include a directive that Hobby Lobby or Conestoga purchase or provide directly the contraceptive devices they find to be objectionable. These companies simply direct money into health insurance plans that finance a wide variety of benefits, and now, thanks to the ACA, must provide contraceptive coverage as well as other preventative services.

Justice Ginsberg's dissent also voiced a sentiment shared by many: what are the limits for allowing corporations to opt out of federal regulations with which they disagreed? She feared other religious objectors would eliminate from their insurance coverage treatments they determined to be in conflict with their religious beliefs. Ginsburg speculated about the possible repercussion of the ruling:

> Would the exemption the Court holds, RFRA demands for employers with religiously grounded objections to the use of certain contraceptives extend to employers with religiously grounded objections to blood transfusions (Jehovah's Witnesses); antidepressants (Scientologists); medications derived from pigs, including anesthesia, intravenous fluids, and pills coated with gelatin (certain Muslims, Jews, and Hindus); and vaccinations (Christian Scientists, among others)?[68]

The Ginsberg dissent is perhaps most noteworthy because it calls attention to the unmistakable contrast between religious communities and the for-profit corporation. Religious organizations exist for the purpose of fostering religious faith. But that is not true for the corporation whose workers are employed to sustain the operations of the corporation and who are not drawn from one religious faith or community. According to Ginsburg, "For-profit corporations are different from religious communities in that they use labor to make a profit, rather than to perpetuate the religious values [shared by a community of believers]."[69] Ginsburg wholly concurred with the government's case that RFRA was not meant to include for-profit corporations because their purpose is to make money and not to disseminate religious beliefs or values.

Thus the issue of corporate purpose explicitly arises in *Hobby Lobby* with Justice Ginsburg's attempt to draw a bright line between the for-profit business corporation and religious, nonprofit organizations. Following the lead of the attorneys who represented the government against Hobby Lobby, she portrays the business corporation as functioning within a secular sphere with one overriding goal: make a profit for shareholders. Dedication to that goal is incompatible with exercising religion within the meaning of RFRA. Ginsburg appeared to dismiss any possibility of a religious orientation for the corporation: "religious organizations exist to serve a community of believers; for-profit corporations do not fit that bill."[70]

But the court determined that a for-profit corporation could pursue religious objectives, sometimes at the expense of its own profits "so long as its owners agree."[71] The court's majority flatly rejected the government's argument that the for-profit corporation is secular by definition.[72] The commitment to making money or to maximize shareholder returns by no means precludes an exercise of religion. According to Justice Alito,

> While it is certainly true that a central objective of the for-profit corporation is to make money, modern corporate law does not require for-profit corporations to pursue profit at the expense of everything else, and many do not do so. For-profit corporations, with ownership approval, support a wide variety of charitable causes, and it is still not at all uncommon for such corporations to further humanitarian or other altruistic objectives.[73]

Even if state corporate law mandates shareholder wealth maximization as a "default rule of governance," that mandate can be altered by shareholder approval. There are clear implications in the court's language about corporate purpose, corporate social responsibility, and the corporation's commitment to social and religious values.[74]

Ramifications of *Hobby Lobby*

Public criticism of the *Hobby Lobby* decision was quite vociferous at times. There were ominous predictions that it would "unleash a parade of horribles."[75] Aside from this overheated rhetoric, however, more targeted and valid criticism centered on the "expansive" notion of corporate personhood that had presumably been adopted by the Supreme Court in this case. Is it really sensible to confer free-exercise rights on a corporate entity that has no conscience or beliefs?

Also, critics argued, while the decision is narrow, this sort of ruling has a history of becoming more broadly cited as a precedent in future cases. Will future courts, building on the logic of *Hobby Lobby*, begin to grant other requests for religious-based exemptions that will burden third parties? In their view, Justice Ginsburg's warning was quite apposite: to what extent can employers now refuse to abide by laws and regulations that conflict their sincerely held religious beliefs? For example, will the notion of corporate religious rights justify a refusal to cover other controversial therapies and medicines such as those derived from embryonic stem cell research?[76]

Some legal scholars have also noted that *Hobby Lobby* ignores the rights and interests of all corporate stakeholders except the owners. While the owners' religious convictions are internalized and acknowledged, the employees' religious beliefs and their interests in accessing certain forms of contraception are nullified in this decision. According to Ackerman and Cole, "The corporation owes nothing to anyone, except those who have an ownership interest." The owners' beliefs and rights seem to be the only ones that matter. Should the owners' religious rights take precedence over the rights of employees to free, unrestricted access to these contraceptive treatments that has been mandated by Congress as part of the ACA?[77]

At the same time, supporters of the *Hobby Lobby* decision echoed the reasoning of Justice Kennedy's concurring opinion. The religious beliefs of corporate owners (such as the Greens) are not confined to "what happens in their minds, homes, and houses of worship."[78] Rather, those beliefs also shape and influence their business dealings and their public lives and thus can even become embedded within corporate structures. To argue otherwise is to accept a narrow and arbitrary conception of religion's impact on the human person. Also, the for-profit corporation is not intrinsically secular. A commitment to profits and enhanced shareholder value need not rule out other objectives that require free-exercise rights guaranteed by the First Amendment. Therefore, the court was right to uphold the idea that U.S. citizens do not forsake their religious liberties when they form a family business. Companies like Hobby Lobby have every right to operate the company "in a manner consistent with Biblical principles," and the legal system must respect that decision.[79]

- Sketch out the arguments for and against Hobby Lobby Inc. In your view, what are the strongest arguments that support the company's position? Do you agree with Hobby Lobby's contention of "complicity" if it provided the abortifacient contraceptives to its employees as part of its insurance package?

- Do you agree with the reasoning behind the Supreme Court's decision? If not, do you agree with the elements of Justice Ginsburg's dissenting opinion which were presented in the case?

- Should for-profit (but closely held) corporations like Hobby Lobby have a right to the free exercise of religion as guaranteed under the First Amendment of the U.S. Constitution? Do you worry about the negative implications of recognizing such a right?

CONCLUSION

The two case studies in this chapter followed up on key themes in Chapter 2 concerning corporate purpose and corporate rights, especially the right to freedom of expression. That right for corporations has been affirmed in the *Citizens United* case, albeit in a ruling that remains highly controversial. According to that Supreme Court decision, the government cannot determine whose speech can be regulated, even if it is the "speech" of a company engaged in advertising for political purposes. The second case, *Burwell v. Hobby Lobby*, dwells on the corporation's right to religious liberty under some circumstances. That right has also been validated by the Supreme Court based not on the theory of corporate personhood but on the corporation's status as an association that can affirm the rights of its members. Finally, like some other corporations, Hobby Lobby has a broader purpose than most for-profit corporations because of its emphasis on altruistic activities. There are no problems with adopting such a broad corporate purpose, as long as its stakeholders, especially the stockholders, are in agreement.

Student Study Site

Visit **edge.sagepub.com/spinello.**

Review Questions

1. What are the constitutional liberties enjoyed by corporations today?

2. What skills are needed to apply analytical and legal reasoning in decisions of court rulings?

3. How does corporate purpose factor into the decisions made in these two cases?

Discussion Questions

1. Discuss the concepts of corporate personhood as it applies to these cases.

2. Looking to the future, discuss the impact these rulings may have on corporations versus individual citizens.

3. In general, do you agree with the concept of corporate liberties such as free speech? Do you accept the broad notion of the First Amendment implied in the *Citizens United* decision?

ETHICS IN THE INVESTMENT AND FINANCIAL SERVICES INDUSTRIES

Throughout the country there exists an idea that Wall Street is a very wicked place and that the New York Stock Exchange is a den of gamblers who would not hesitate to run the country if they thereby could make a dollar. . . . A demagogue can always win votes by denouncing the conspiracies, the trickery, the deceit, the corruption which are alleged to exist on Wall Street.

—Joseph French Johnson, 1917[1]

LEARNING OBJECTIVES

Upon completion of this chapter, you should be able to:

6.1   Practice case analyses and evaluation of corporate conduct.

6.2   Explain the economic, legal, and ethical implications of fraudulent behavior in financial markets.

6.3   Describe concepts such as fiduciary duty.

6.4   Assess corporate leaders' moral duties to investors, shareholders, and customers.

The investment and financial services industries have been plagued by multiple high-profile scandals. With large sums of money at stake, it is probably no surprise that the American financial sector is so vulnerable to dishonesty and market manipulation. Regrettably, several waves of derelict behavior have defined the recent financial era and shattered the trust of ordinary investors. The ill effects of the 2008 market crash have rippled through the global economy for over a decade.

In the 1980s and 1990s, the malfeasance was centered primarily within the savings and loan industry. Fraud and reckless real estate loans led to the abrupt failure of many savings and loans associations. In addition, there were several notable insider-trading cases on Wall Street that bilked unsuspecting investors out of huge sums of money. Ivan Boesky, the inspiration for the cult movie *Wall Street*, admitted to buying and selling securities of firms involved in pending takeover deals. There was also a scandal-ridden junk bond industry that led to the collapse of some bright Wall Street stars like Drexel Burnham Lambert. These events culminated in the Salomon Brothers bond trading incident in 1991 that ultimately led to that investment bank's untimely demise.

The second wave of scandals did not directly involve Wall Street investment firms, but it ensnared companies exploiting financial and accounting innovations such as Enron and WorldCom along with the accounting firm, Arthur Andersen. Enron, the failed energy company, relied on a tangled web of financial instruments to conceal its heavy debt. It also convinced its outside auditors to test the limits of acceptable accounting standards. Based on Andersen's role in enabling Enron's fraudulent practices, critics complained that accounting firms had gone from "watch dogs to lap dogs." Andersen began in 1914 by putting reputation for quality over profit, but it disintegrated in 2002 (its consulting branch survives as Accenture).

The third wave centered on the 2008 credit crunch and the subprime mortgage debacle. Lehman Brothers, Goldman Sachs, and J.P. Morgan were at the epicenter of this crisis. As the world looked on at Lehman's precarious financial condition, the beleaguered investment banking firm shifted assets off its balance sheet to reduce its leverage. All of this creative effort, however, could not avert bankruptcy.[2] The collapse of Lehman Brothers came perilously close to dismantling the world's financial system. At the same time, Goldman Sachs exploited fragilities in the system through opaque financial tools and intricate debt chains that magnified the losses associated with the collapse of the U.S. housing market. Other banks economized on safety measures and assumed too much debt. At fault was a Wall Street culture of greed along with careless government oversight.

In all of these cases, key financial institutions and their managers fell far short of their ethical and fiduciary obligations. Insider trading, dodgy accounting, imprudent investments, outright fraud, and interest rate manipulations have imposed steep financial costs on investors and consumers. Another result of this misbehavior is hostility toward the financial community, which has intensified in recent years. For some, the main culprit is complex financial innovations along with a feeble and reactive regulatory system that could not keep economic imbalances in check. For others, the persistent misconduct is chiefly due to Wall Street's incentive system—big potential bonuses and promotions create powerful incentives to cheat or take big risks with other people's money.

Whatever the causes, we must keep in mind that a well-functioning capitalist economy depends on strong and efficient capital markets. As William Cohan observes, Wall Street institutions provide "utterly irreplaceable" services.[3] Innovative companies like Apple,

Amazon, or Google could never have ramped up so fast without the indispensable help of Wall Street financiers. Similarly, an efficient consumer finance sector depends heavily on these institutions and their financial innovations. But how can unethical schemes be perpetrated so easily in efficient and heavily regulated capital markets?

This question is at the core of financial ethics, an important subfield of business ethics, and the topic of this chapter. Finance is not value-free. Capital markets presuppose moral rules and a sound regulatory framework that inspires trust among investors. If there is fraud, manipulation, or nontransparency, these markets cannot be fair or efficient. Market failures become profound moral failures when they are exploited by opportunistic moral agents. It is all too easy sometimes for bankers and traders, motivated by material gain, to manipulate information deficiencies and tilt the market in their favor. In this fashion, they expropriate value from unsuspecting parties. The economic problem with the expropriation (or theft) is not just the expropriation itself, but the negative expectations that cloud impending transactions and inhibit necessary capital formation.[4]

Thus, finance ethics focuses on preserving fairness, honesty, and cooperation in financial markets. The principal ethical problems in financial market transactions arise from unfair or fraudulent trading practices. Finance ethics also concentrates on the formal fiduciary duties of corporate executives, investment bankers, and other professionals in the banking industry. A **fiduciary** can be defined as a person trusted by others because that person has superior knowledge and expertise. Corporations hire investment bankers because they lack proficiency and need expert financial assistance with executing a merger or raising capital. These professionals have a duty to act in a principled way on behalf of their clients. They cannot breach these fiduciary duties for their own financial gain. **Corporate insiders** also have a fiduciary obligation to act in the best interests of the corporation and its shareholders. And investment bankers should certainly refrain from risky financial manipulation that puts investors and their own institutions in some peril.[5]

Ethical and honest conduct is an imperative for the entire financial services industry, including insurance firms, brokerage houses, and retail banks. These industries operate still through personal selling by insurance agents, personal bankers or loan officials, and stockbrokers. Fraud, which includes nondisclosure of material facts and breaches of trust, has been a perennial problem. Other abuses include churning, which is defined as excessive trading that generates commissions for a broker but does not benefit or enrich his or her client. The insurance industry has had to contend with twisting, a practice employed by some insurance agents to replace an older policy with a newer one. The retail banking industry, on the other hand, has been recently disrupted by the massive Wells Fargo scandal where bankers secretly opened banking or credit accounts without a customer's permission. Professionals in the financial services industry have a strong moral responsibility to the clients they serve, and some of the cases in this chapter underscore what happens when that responsibility is ignored.[6]

AN OVERVIEW OF THE CASES

The first cases in this chapter look at insider trading and provide background on its definition and the appropriate regulations. Insider trading refers to trades in securities based on material, nonpublic information to the detriment of shareholders or other investors.

Confidence in the stock market depends on the perception of fairness and the reality of a reasonably level playing field. It's not unfair that some investors have better information than others. But there is unfairness if some investors have access to certain information to which others are denied. There have been many insider-trading scandals, and some have even involved famous celebrities such as Martha Stewart. A briefing that explains the essentials of insider trading is followed by two short cases. The first case tells the story about Texas Gulf Sulphur, and it presents in classic terms the problems and motivations associated with insider trading. The next short case study, called "All in the Family," is about an investment banker who tips off his father about impending developments in the health care industry.[7]

The third case in this chapter chronicles the infamous LIBOR scandal and the brazen manipulation of this cornerstone interest rate used by banks to lend funds to each other. The London-based Barclays was one of the major banks behind this scandal, and, like Salomon Brothers, appeared to have cultural problems that contributed to the errant ways of its traders and senior managers. This case focuses on Barclays's traders and the bank's two-phased rigging of the LIBOR rate. Traders across Wall Street and London have one thing in mind: maximize profits by managing risk. Some agile opportunists found an easy way to achieve this goal by tinkering with an interest rate that had the capacity to spawn big profits with commensurate losses for many unsophisticated victims.[8]

In the next case we turn to Goldman Sachs and its alleged deceptive behavior involving the sale of packaged subprime loans through collateralized debt obligations (CDOs). Goldman invented the CDO, an obscure financial mechanism that became a main target of ethical controversies when the subprime market malfunctioned. Malfeasance, fraud, and complexity became a familiar formula for taking advantage of the U.S. real estate bubble before its collapse. Goldman itself prospered through nontransparency, which still remains the norm for some Wall Street transactions. While this case focuses primarily on Goldman Sachs, it also considers the complex chains of debt securities that contributed to the 2008 financial crisis and its aftermath.

The final case study in this chapter takes us to the West Coast, far away from Wall Street. The retail banking industry relies heavily on the strategy of cross-selling. Banks try to get their customers to purchase as many of their products as possible through various marketing techniques. But "The Wells Fargo Sales Scam" case details how this classic selling strategy was abused by this San Francisco–based bank. The bank's aggressive push to meet sales quotas along with its incentive compensation system induced some employees to sign up customers to sham checking accounts or bogus credit cards. Once again, we seem to be witnessing a broken culture with senior managers turning a blind eye to improprieties of some magnitude.

BRIEFING ON INSIDER TRADING

Despite the government's endless legal tussles with inside traders, someone always thinks that it's possible to evade the watchful eye of the Securities and Exchange Commission (SEC) and make quick profits by trading on inside information. In recent years there has been a steady progression of high-profile cases as federal prosecutors continue to aggressively pursue illegal insider trading and bring wrongdoers to justice. In the summer of 2014, for example, the SEC grew suspicious of Michael Lucarelli, a director at a financial relations firm in New York City. As head of market intelligence, Lucarelli knew about the firms' press releases prior to their publication. Lucarelli was suspected of using this confidential information to purchase securities before the news was publicly announced, in violation of insider-trading laws. Federal agents set a trap for Lucarelli and gathered enough evidence for a successful conviction. In 2015, Lucarelli pled guilty to securities fraud.[9]

While some scholars view insider trading benignly, most concur that trading on privileged information is immoral because it creates an unlevel playing field and punishes ordinary investors. Insider trading also undermines the efficient and proper functioning of financial markets. As a consequence, insider trading has been illegal in the United States for almost a century. However, there is considerable ambiguity about what exactly constitutes insider trading. Who are insiders, and when does trading on privileged information cross the line and become an illegal offense?[10]

The general law prohibiting insider trading is codified in the Securities and Exchange Act of 1934. Section 10(b) forbids any "manipulative or deceptive device or contrivance."[11] Also, according to Rule 10b-5 of that act, it is unlawful for any person (directly or indirectly) to "engage in any act, practice, or course of business which operates or would operate as a fraud or deceit upon any person . . . in connection with the purchase or sale of any security." While Rule 10b-5 is only a general antifraud provision, it has been relied upon extensively in insider-trading cases. The application of this rule, therefore, depends on demonstrating that an insider has engaged in some type of fraud or deceit during the purchase or sale of securities.[12]

When insider trading occurs, however, is not formally defined in a statute, so one must look elsewhere—to SEC rulings and federal case law—for proper guidance. In a landmark 1961 decision, *Cady Roberts & Co.*, the SEC set forth the basic rule that a corporate insider who possessed privileged information that would affect his or her judgment about a given securities transaction must either "disclose" such information or "abstain" from trading those securities. The court underscored the "inherent unfairness involved where a party takes advantage of such information knowing it is unavailable to those with whom he is dealing."[13]

Thus, the term **insider trading** generally refers to trading in securities that are based on *material, nonpublic* information in violation of a fiduciary or similar duty to a corporation and its shareholders or to the source of the information. Neither of the key terms, *material* or *nonpublic*, is defined in a statute. But **material information** is normally considered to be information that if made public would have a significant effect on the market value of a corporation's securities. **Nonpublic information** is information that has not yet been made available to the trading markets.[14]

Classical Theory of Insider Trading

According to the classical theory of insider trading, legal liability is contingent on a breach of fiduciary duty to shareholders by an "inside trader." Under this theory, a corporate insider violates Rule 10b-5 when he breaches a fiduciary duty owed to shareholders by using for his own benefit material, nonpublic information obtained in his role as an insider. Officers and executives of the company, along with directors and managers, have a fiduciary duty to the corporation and its shareholders. Hence they must avoid conflicts of interest, self-dealing, or taking personal advantage of "corporate opportunities." This means the use of privileged information for personal gain acquired in the role as a fiduciary is a breach of this duty. For example, consider top corporate officers who invest ample funds in their company stock based on secretive information about an impending merger. When the information about the merger becomes public, the price of the securities increases substantially and these insiders cash in. The individuals in this case would be clearly liable for insider trading because they breached a duty of loyalty owed to the company's shareholders, some of whom sell off their shares at a lower price unaware of the pending merger.[15]

The classic theory also extends to outsiders who become temporary insiders (or "quasi-insiders") and therefore subject to Rule 10b-5. An outsider might legitimately receive information from a corporate insider in the context of a confidential relationship with the company. **Temporary insiders** can include accountants, lawyers, and investment bankers who become privy to inside information in the performance of their professional services. If the company *expects* the outsider to keep this information confidential, he or she becomes a temporary insider with a fiduciary connection to the corporation's shareholders. Thus, an outside counsel working temporarily for company X could not buy stock based on confidential information he or she might learn about company X. This restriction assumes company X has clarified its expectation that the disclosed nonpublic information must remain confidential.[16]

In some cases, **tippees**, that is, those who receive information from a tipper (a corporate or temporary insider), also inherit a fiduciary duty to shareholders. There are two conditions that must hold for the tippee to assume this fiduciary duty to shareholders that precludes trading on material, nonpublic information. According to *Dirks v. SEC*, those conditions exist "when the insider has breached the fiduciary duty to the shareholders by disclosing the information to the tippee, and the tippee knows or should have known that there has been a breach."[17] Under those circumstances, the tippee becomes a "participant-after-the-fact" in the insider's misconduct. However, the inside tipper breaches a fiduciary duty only if "the insider personally will benefit, directly or indirectly, from his disclosure."[18] Unless something of value is received for passing along the information, there is no breach of duty to stockholders. Even secondary or "sub-tippees," that is, those who receive information from other tippees, can be held liable if they knew or should have known that the insider improperly disclosed the information.[19]

Misappropriation Theory of Insider Trading

The classical theory relies heavily on the fiduciary principle, but the courts have also adopted the "misappropriation" theory to demonstrate fraud in connection with the buying or selling of securities. According to this theory, wrongful insider trading occurs when there is a breach of fiduciary duty not to the shareholders of the insider's firm, but instead to the source of information that has been misappropriated. In *United States v. O'Hagan*, the defendant was a partner in the law firm that represented Grand Metropolitan, which was in the process of offering a bid to buy Pillsbury. O'Hagan did not work on the Grand Metropolitan deal, but he allegedly duped a fellow partner into revealing details of this hostile takeover. O'Hagan purchased both Pillsbury stock and call options (options to buy the stock) and made over $4 million on these transactions. Since he was neither an insider nor a temporary insider, O'Hagan had no fiduciary duty to Pillsbury shareholders, and so his purchase of stock would not have been insider trading under the classical theory. But under the misappropriation theory endorsed by the Supreme Court in this case, O'Hagan was liable because he breached a duty of loyalty to the source of the information, his law firm's client, Grand Metropolitan. According to that decision, a person is guilty of securities fraud if he or she "misappropriates confidential information for securities trading purposes, in breach of a fiduciary duty owed to the source of the information."[20]

The laws on insider trading have evolved over the years, and there are still ambiguities and generalities that leave much room for interpretation. However, the essentials remain the same. Insider trading involves material, nonpublic information, and the trader is the traditional corporate insider, a temporary insider, or a tippee who is aware (or should be aware) that the disclosure breaches a duty of trust and confidence.

- Explain in your own words the difference between the classical and misappropriation theories of insider trading.

- Law school professor Henry Manne has suggested that insider trading is not necessarily morally wrongful behavior.[21] Do you agree with his assessment? Also, are the insider-trading laws good for society?

CASE STUDY 6.1

TEXAS GULF SULPHUR

The New York mining company known as Texas Gulf Sulphur (TGS) was incorporated on December 23, 1909. Thanks in part to World War I, demand for sulfur, a yellow, nonmetallic element, had grown rapidly, as sulfuric acid became a critical component of military products. In 1916, TGS began exploring a mineral rich property known as "Big Hill," which eventually produced millions of tons of sulfur. By 1926, TGS had become the world's leading sulfur producer. After World War II, TGS tapped into four new sulfur mines in Texas to supplement its dwindling supplies. In 1959,

©iStockphoto.com/Pgiam

the company told shareholders it planned to broaden its operations into materials other than sulfur. TGS relied on operating efficiencies as a source of competitive advantage. It was always in search of new mines to maintain its sulfur reserves, just as oil companies continually explore for new reservoirs of oil. In 1959, TGS opened its first research lab in Stamford, Connecticut.[22]

As the new decade dawned, TGS remained the world's leading sulfur producer, but the sulfur market had turned soft. As the price of sulfur dropped from $28 a ton in 1956 to below $20 in 1963, so did TGS's earnings. In 1960, company president and CEO Claude Stephens announced that TGS would diversify into a potash field in Utah. Also, in 1959, TGS geophysicists, led by Richard Clayton, had begun conducting aerial geophysical surveys over the Canadian Shield, an area in Eastern Canada known for its mineral deposits such as gold. The company was in search of sulfides, that is, deposits of sulfur that occurred within other valuable minerals such as zinc or copper. On three separate occasions in 1959, an "anomaly" was detected on a piece of property that later turned out to be the Kidd Creek mine (or Kidd-55), an area of about 1 square mile located 15 miles north of Timmins, Ontario. Other anomalies were discovered in the same area during the winter of 1962.[23]

By June 1963, TGS was able to negotiate an option on this land that allowed it to drill on the northeast quarter section. The man in charge of the drilling project was geologist Kenneth Darke. After making the necessary preparations, he and his team began drilling in November. Darke was impressed by the first samples and called his boss, chief geologist Walter Holyk, at his home in Stamford. Vice President Richard Mollison and Executive Vice President Charles Fogarty were also immediately informed of the drilling results. All three men decided to travel to Kidd-55 to see for themselves. Holyk made an appraisal of the drill core: for an area of over 600 feet, there appeared to be an average copper content of 1.15% and an average zinc content of 8.64%. A Canadian stockbroker and specialist in the mining industry would later say that such mineral content "is just beyond your wildest imagination."[24]

Shortly after his visit to Canada, Charles Fogarty purchased 300 shares of TGS stock on November 12. He made additional purchases of 1,400 shares in three other November transactions. Richard Clayton, the TGS geophysicist, purchased 200 shares on November 15, and Richard Mollison purchased 100 shares that same day.[25]

By the end of the year, however, very few people at TGS, aside from the geologists and senior executives, knew about Kidd-55 and its high mineral content. Neither stockholders nor the company's directors were informed. There was only a vague reference to "metallic sulphide exploration activities" in Eastern Canada in the 1963 annual report. Stephens had insisted on strict confidentiality in order to facilitate acquisition of the land.[26]

One person who did know about the apparent strike was Kenneth Darke, the first geologist on the scene. In late December 1963, Darke traveled to Washington, DC, to enjoy some Christmas vacation. He visited two friends, Madge Caskey, a 64-year-old clerk in the National Bank of Washington, and her daughter, Nancy Atkinson, who worked for the Department of Commerce. Darke recommended TGS stock to Mrs. Caskey and her daughter, but he never discussed the Canadian drill hole. Rather, he spoke with these two women in general terms about the excellent prospects for TGS and told them the purchase of TGS stock would be a "tremendous investment." Darke claimed he had made similar recommendations to many other people, including his parents, but they never acted on his advice. The women told two other friends. Between December 30, 1963, and February 17, 1964, these four individuals purchased 2,100 shares of TGS stock along with calls (options to buy) on 1,500 additional shares.[27]

On February 20, 1964, Darke himself purchased 300 shares of TGS, his first ownership of the stock he had recommended so enthusiastically. During the next month he purchased 3,000 calls or options to buy TGS stock. Also, on February 20, with the approval of the board of directors, TGS issued stock options to 26 of its officers or executives whose salaries exceeded a specified amount. Stephens, Fogarty, Mollison, and chief geologist Holyk, who all knew about Kidd-55, were eligible for these options. At the time, neither the TGS Stock Option Committee nor its board of directors had been informed of the Kidd-55 results. All of these individuals accepted the options granted to them.[28]

With confidence in the initial drilling results, the company moved forward to acquire rights to drill on the land in question. TGS executives relied on one of its attorneys, Earl Huntington, to assist in the land acquisition effort. On March 16, Huntington drafted a letter to the Royal Trust Company offering to pay $57,000 for portions of the land that were still retained by trustees. On that same day, he purchased a call on 100 shares of TGS stock; a month earlier he had purchased 50 shares. Huntington claimed his purchases were based on "his evaluation of the total company business and prospects."[29]

By March 27, 1964, the necessary land acquisition of the drilling site was complete. TGS had either clear title or mineral rights to all segments of Kidd-55. The company drilled new holes to confirm its initial findings. The second operational hole was drilled in late March, the third was finished on April 7, and the fourth hole was immediately begun using the same rig. Another hole was drilled on April 10. All of this drilling revealed the contours of a vast ore deposit. The fourth drill hole established that the mineral vein was not just long but quite deep. Thus, these additional drill holes at Kidd-55 confirmed "there was real evidence that a body of commercially mineable ore might exist." There was little doubt at this point that the company had a workable mine of substantial proportions.[30]

By now, rumors were spreading throughout Canada and the close-knit mining industry. On the morning of Saturday, April 11, Claude Stephens read in the *New York Times* an article by a well-informed reporter speculating about the company's "rich strike" in Canada. Stevens called Fogarty, and both men concluded that TGS needed to promptly make a public statement. With the help of a public relations consultant, Fogarty drafted a press release designed to stifle the rumors about Kidd-55. The statement was issued at 3:00 p.m. Sunday, April 12, and appeared in most major newspapers the next day. Thanks to the TGS statement, some papers like the *New York Herald Tribune* retreated from their original stories of a major strike with headlines such as "Copper Rumor Deflated."[31]

Here are excerpts from the April 12 statement:

During the past few days, the exploration activities of Texas Gulf Sulphur in the area of Timmins, Ontario, have been widely reported in the press, coupled with rumors of a substantial copper discovery there. These reports exaggerate the scale of operations, and mention plans and statistics of size and grade of ore that are without factual basis and have evidently originated by speculation of people not connected with TGS.

Recent drilling on one property near Timmins has led to preliminary indications that more drilling would be required for proper evaluation of this prospect. The drilling done to date has not been conclusive, but the statements made by many outside quarters are unreliable and include information and figures not available to TGS.

The work done to date has not been sufficient to reach definite conclusions and any statement as to size and grade of ore would be premature and possibly misleading. When we have progressed to the point where reasonable and logical conclusions can be made, TGS will issue a definite statement to its stockholders and to the public in order to clarify the Timmins project.[32]

Drilling activities were finally completed by Monday, April 13. A last drill hole also confirmed substantial copper and zinc mineralization. A reporter from the *Northern Miner* was given a tour and briefed on the findings by Mollison, Holyk, and Darke. What they told the reporter made it clear these men knew they had a sizable workable mine. The reporter's article, which did not appear until Thursday, April 16, confirmed at least a 10-million-ton iron-ore strike. The story was checked and approved by Mollison.

At midweek, TGS was finally prepared to disclose its big discovery. A statement drafted by Mollison was given to the Ontario minister of mines for release to the Canadian media. TGS officials expected it to be read over the airways at 11 p.m. on Wednesday, April 15, but for unknown reasons, the press release was never read. Instead, on Thursday, April 16, at 9:40 a.m., an official, detailed statement announcing a strike of at least 25 million tons of iron ore was released to the Canadian and American financial media. It was read aloud from 10 a.m. to about 10:15 a.m. The news appeared over Merrill Lynch's private wire at 10:29 a.m. and then over the Dow Jones News Service ticker tape at 10:54 a.m.[33]

Between the release of the tentative first press statement on April 12 and the April 16 official announcement, several TGS officials purchased TGS stock. David Crawford, the TGS corporate secretary, ordered 300 shares at midnight on April 15 and another 300 the morning of April 16. Both orders were executed over the Midwest Exchange in Chicago. Crawford had apparently assumed the press release had gone on as scheduled for 11 p.m. the night of April 15. The geophysicist, Richard Clayton, ordered 200 shares of TGS stock on April 15, and the order was executed that day.[34]

At 200 Park Street, company headquarters, the TGS board of directors was meeting at 9 a.m. on the morning of the press release, and all the directors present were shown a copy of that release. When the board meeting ended at 10 a.m., reporters entered the boardroom for the formal reading of the press statement. At the end of the press conference, Francis Coates, a TGS director for many years, went into a small office next to the boardroom. He called his stockbroker in Houston around 10:20 a.m. and ordered 2,000 shares of TGS stock for family trusts. Coates was the trustee but not a beneficiary of those accounts. At about 10:40 a.m., Thomas Lamont, another TGS director, telephoned an associate at Morgan Guaranty Trust, Longstreet Hinton, and alerted him "to watch out for news of TGS on the [ticker] tape." According to Hinton, Lamont did not suggest that he purchase TGS stock. Without checking the Dow Jones tape, Hinton placed an order of 3,000 shares for Nassau Hospital, where he was the treasurer. Less than a half hour later, Hinton recommended TGS stock to the Morgan Guaranty officer in charge of pension funds, and he purchased 7,000 shares for the bank's pension fund and profit-sharing account (2,000 shares were purchased before the news appeared on the Dow Jones tape). At 12:35 p.m. on that same day, Lamont placed an order for 3,000 shares for himself and his family at a price of $34^{1}/_{2}$.[35]

On Wednesday, April 15, the share price of TGS was $29^{5}/_{8}$, and it opened Thursday morning at $30^{1}/_{8}$. By the time the Dow Jones ticker tape carried the big story, the stock was up to $32^{5}/_{8}$. By the end of the day the stock gained over six points, closing at $36^{3}/_{8}$. On

May 15, 1964, TGS stock was selling at 58¼. And by the end of 1966, when commercial production of Kidd-55 was well under way, TGS stock was selling at over $100 per share.[36]

The SEC undertook an investigation into these events and issued a complaint against Fogarty, Mollison, Darke, Huntington, Clayton, Crawford, Lamont, and Coates, who purchased either personally or through agents TGS stock (or calls) from November 12, 1963, to April 16, 1964, on the basis of material inside information. It also charged Darke, Coates, and Lamont with divulging such privileged information to others for the purpose of purchasing TGS stock or calls. Third, it alleged that Stephens, Fogarty, Mollison, and Holyk had accepted options to purchase TGS stock without disclosing relevant material information about Kidd-55. Finally, the SEC alleged that the first press release was deceptive.[37]

- Do you agree with the SEC's claims against *all* of the defendants in this case? Who among these individuals are guilty of insider trading and who are innocent?

- Should Darke's communication to his friends in Washington be considered "material" information? Also, did Coates and Lamont trade on nonpublic information, given that they placed their orders after the press release announcing the big strike?

- What are the major lessons of this case about insider trading?

CASE STUDY 6.2

ALL IN THE FAMILY: THE STEWART INSIDER TRADING CASE

On a warm August afternoon, 35-year-old Sean Stewart, a former managing director at Perella Weinberg, emerged from a crowded New York city courtroom. A jury had just found him guilty on nine counts of securities fraud. As he walked quickly to a waiting car, he was besieged with questions from the media, which had closely followed this unusual case. Several spectators, huddled in the shadows of nearby buildings, looked on with mild curiosity. Stewart allegedly had given tips to his father, who had then traded on the information to make a large sum of illegal profits. Yet Sean himself received no meaningful financial benefit from these transactions. The government's case, however, would hinge on whether it could prove that Sean received some "personal benefit" for disclosing this confidential information to his father.

AP Photo/Larry Neumeister

Mr. Stewart's problems began after he took a position as an investment banker at J.P. Morgan Chase. He became a vice president during his five years at Morgan, but in October 2011, he took a job at Perella Weinberg, where he worked on health care acquisitions and related transactions. While at both investment banks, he was privy to sensitive, inside information about the health care industry, including pending mergers and acquisitions. He allegedly tipped his father, Robert, about five different deals involving the prospective acquisition of health care companies. For example, in January 2011, while Stewart was still at J.P. Morgan, he became aware that Kendle Industries, a clinical research organization, was about to be acquired, and he informed his father, Mr. Robert Stewart, about this potential takeover. In February and March, Robert Stewart purchased thousands of shares of Kendle stock at prices ranging from $9.86 to $12.54 a share. After the close of the market on May 4, 2011, INC Research announced it would acquire Kendle for $15.25 a share (or $232 million). The next day Kendle's stock rose to $14.98 a share. On May 5, Robert Stewart sold off his entire position in Kendle stock for $14.99 a share, and he realized a profit of about $7,887.[38]

In March 2012, while Sean Stewart was employed at Perella Weinberg, he was assigned to work on Hologen's acquisition of Gen-Probe. He learned privileged details about this transaction, including the anticipated (per share) purchase price. Stewart tipped his father once again that Gen-Probe was likely to be acquired, and Robert began to purchase call options. On April 30, 2012, Hologen announced the acquisition of Gen-Probe for $82.75 per share. Robert Stewart promptly sold his Gen-Probe options and realized a total profit of approximately $181,000.[39]

Robert Stewart also shared the information with a friend and business associate, Richard Cunniffe. Mr. Cunniffe traded on this information and shared the proceeds with his friend Robert. According to court records, Stewart and Cunniffe made approximately $1.4 million. Mr. Sean Stewart, however, made no investments based on this non-public information, and he did not directly profit from those disclosures to his father.[40]

Both Mr. Cunniffe and Mr. Robert Stewart were charged with breaking insider-trading law. Sean Stewart was also charged. Robert Stewart and Cunniffe pled guilty and were sentenced to probation. But Sean Stewart chose to go to trial. In exchange for their plea deals, Robert Stewart and Cunniffe became cooperating witness in the case against Sean. In one incriminating statement, Robert recounted that his son had once said, "I handed you this on a silver platter and you didn't invest in this." This was an obvious rebuke for not taking full advantage of the inside information he had been given.[41]

At his trial, Stewart admitted he had discussed sensitive, privileged information with his father and with other family members on several occasions. But Stewart contradicted his father's testimony. He forcefully claimed he did not intend or expect that his father would use the information to make these securities trades. According to Sean Stewart, his father had "betrayed" him by using the information for his own material gain. "I never ever gave my father information expecting him to trade," he told the jury. "My dad made some terrible mistakes. He used me."[42] Prosecutors, however, hammered Mr. Stewart for lies he had originally told the J.P. Morgan compliance staff. Stewart conceded he had lied about giving his father information in order to protect his family and his career.

The most challenging part of the case for the SEC and the Justice Department was proving that Sean Stewart had received a "personal benefit" from his father in exchange for the confidential information. According to *Dirks*, the tipper must personally benefit from his or her disclosure. In a recent ruling (*United States v. Newman*), a federal appeals court upheld a narrow view of the personal benefit standard. The court ruling required the government to demonstrate the tipper dispensed the information as part of "an exchange that is objective, consequential, and represents at least a potential gain of a pecuniary or similarly valuable nature." That meant prosecutors had to prove that some tangible, pecuniary benefit was expected and/or received by the insider.[43]

But the government's case was thin. The prosecution showed that during the four years in which Sean disclosed confidential information to his father, Robert gave his son two pecuniary benefits. First, Robert Stewart spent some of his profits to hire a photographer (for $10,055) and to pay for the rehearsal dinner at his son's 2011 wedding. Second, Robert also gave his son $15,000. However, Sean Stewart's attorneys presented convincing evidence that these payments were not a quid pro quo, made in exchange for inside information. Robert Stewart had also paid $7,000 to a photographer for his other son's wedding, which took place shortly after Sean's wedding. Also, the $15,000 payment was a partial repayment of $35,000 that Sean had given to his father several weeks earlier, and thus did not represent some type of pecuniary advantage for Sean.[44]

The larger issue that emerged in this case was whether a close family relationship could satisfy the "personal benefit" standard in the absence of the tipper's pecuniary gains. Did Sean Stewart's conduct satisfy this standard because the relationship with his father inferred an exchange of personal benefit and at least the *potential gain* of a pecuniary or similarly valuable nature? Is the gratitude and warm feelings generated by the "gift" of confidential information to a family member enough of a benefit to meet this standard? Despite the recent *Newman* ruling, in her instructions to the jury the judge herself framed the personal benefit standard in broad terms: "the Government must prove beyond a reasonable doubt that Mr. Stewart anticipated receiving a personal benefit in return for providing material non-public information to his father. Personal benefit is broadly defined to include pecuniary gain, as well as the benefit one would obtain from making a gift of confidential information to a trading relative or friend."[45]

Even with the aid of the judge's instructions, the jury struggled with this issue. It was reported the jury's forewoman said they asked themselves, "What was he getting out of it?"[46] But on August 17, 2016, after six days of deliberation, the jury reached its verdict and convicted Sean Stewart. He was found guilty on nine counts of securities fraud and other charges.[47] On February 17, 2017, Stewart was sentenced to three years in prison and a $7,500 fine. The judge denied a request for leniency, remarking that he chose "personal appearance, convenience, and family benefits over the ethical duties his employer placed upon him."[48]

Media accounts of the trial pointed out that this whole affair had all the elements of Greek tragedy for the Stewart family. One newspaper poignantly cited an ancient Yiddish proverb: "When a father gives to his son, both laugh; when a son gives to his father, both cry."[49]

- Which theory (or theories) of insider trading applies here? (See the "Briefing on Insider Trading.") In what way did Sean Stewart breach his duty as an investment banker?

- Did the jury reach the correct verdict in this case?

- Should the gift of confidential information to a family member without a pecuniary quid pro quo be a sufficient personal benefit to satisfy the legal standard spelled out in the *Dirks* case?

- What do both of these insider trading cases suggest about the importance of fiduciary duties as part of the matrix of duties (cf. DRJ framework) leaders must consider when they make decisions?

CASE STUDY 6.3

MANIPULATING THE LIBOR

AP Photo/EMPPL PA Wire

During his testimony before the House of Commons Treasury Select Committee in 2012, Barclays CEO Robert Diamond acknowledged there had been a manipulation of **LIBOR** (London Inter-Bank Offered Rate) by some of the bank's traders and senior managers. Several other major banks, including UBS, Royal Bank of Scotland (RBS), Deutsche Bank, and Rabobank, were also conspicuously involved in this epic banking crisis. These five banks have been pilloried in the press and forced to pay huge fines for their misdeeds.

Some refer to LIBOR as the most important rate in finance. It is the key benchmark to set borrowing rates between banks. Thus, the rate banks charged other banks for loans was being surreptitiously rigged by the bankers themselves. An honor system that depended on trust, cooperation, and integrity completely collapsed. How could this happen, and why were bankers able to orchestrate these manipulations for so long? This case addresses these and other questions by examining how events unfolded at Barclays.

Barclays and the Banking Industry

Barclays is a British multinational banking and financial services company headquartered in London. It is regarded as a "universal bank" with a wide range of operations in retail, wholesale and investment banking, as well as wealth management, mortgage lending, and credit cards. It has operations in over 50 countries and territories. It now operates through two principal divisions: Barclays UK and Barclays International. Barclays UK offers banking services to retail customers in the United Kingdom, and Barclays International delivers products and services for larger corporate, wholesale, and international clients.[50]

Barclays traces its distinguished history back to 1690, when John Freame and Thomas Gould started trading as goldsmith bankers on Lombard Street, London. It took the name Barclays in 1736. The bank expanded rapidly in the first half of the 20th century by making acquisitions of many small English banks. In 1965, it opened its first offices in the United States, Barclays Bank of America located in the San Francisco area. Then, in 1986, the bank established an investment banking division now known as Barclays Capital.[51]

Since its founding, Barclays has been a leader in innovation: funding the world's first industrial steam railway, naming the United Kingdom's first female branch manager, and introducing the world's first ATM machine. In 1966, Barclays introduced to its customers the first credit card in the United Kingdom. About 20 years later, it launched its Connect Card, the first debit card in the United Kingdom. Thanks to its reputation for innovation and service, Barclays now has 48 million customers and clients worldwide.

The company asserts its strategy is to "build on its strengths as a transnational consumer, corporate, and investment bank anchored in our two home markets of the UK and the U.S." In its mission statement the company enunciates the following core values:

Respect: We respect and value those we work with, and the contribution that they make.

Integrity: We act fairly, ethically and openly in all we do.

Service: We put our clients and customers at the center of what we do.

Excellence: We use our energy, skills, and resources to deliver the best, sustainable results.

Stewardship: We are passionate about leaving things better than we found them.[52]

Barclays is currently the fifth-largest bank in Europe, with assets of £1.1 trillion ($1.4 trillion in U.S. dollars). In 2017, Barclays had total revenues of £21 billion and a net income of £1.3 billion. Its most profitable division continues to be investment banking. The capabilities of that division were greatly enhanced when Barclays absorbed the remains of the bankrupt Lehman Brothers for $1.35 billion. Retail banking has also accounted for a big percentage of its revenues and profits.[53]

In 2011, an American banker named Robert Diamond became its CEO. He attempted to help the bank navigate through the thicket of issues and controversies that ensued because of the LIBOR scandal. From 2005 through 2010, traders in this august British institution tried many times to manipulate the LIBOR. During that period the bank routinely submitted rates that were either set unrealistically low or were falsely inflated. Before we can assess the motivations behind the efforts to rig LIBOR, it is necessary to explain in more detail the significance of this interest rate.

What Is LIBOR?

The LIBOR was created in the 1980s at a time when banks were regularly making loans to each other. LIBOR is a global benchmark interest rate, which is used to set a large range of financial deals worth in the trillions of dollars. It is arguably the most important interest rate in finance and fundamental to the efficient operation of international financial markets. It helps to decide the price of transactions between banks and other financial institutions. LIBOR is also used as a measure of trust in the financial system and reflects the confidence banks have in each other's financial stability. Just as a high credit card rate might signal that a consumer is in financial distress, an especially high borrowing cost might indicate a bank's poor financial condition. As a benchmark rate, LIBOR is also an indicator of the overall health of financial markets. A spread between LIBOR and other benchmark rates could signal a change on the horizon in those markets.[54]

Why is LIBOR necessary? Banks do not make random loans to each other at arbitrarily set interest rates. A precise system has been put in place for these transactions. Every day leading banks around the world submit a figure to the British Bankers Association (BBA) based on the rate at which they estimate they could borrow funds from other banks. They suggest rates in 10 currencies covering 15 different borrowing periods, ranging from overnight to 12 months. The U.S. dollar LIBOR panel, for example, consists of 16 banks, and the rate calculation for each maturity excludes the highest four and lowest four submissions. The most important of all these rates is the three-month dollar LIBOR: the hypothetical rate at which a bank could borrow if it borrowed that money on the day the rate was being set. Banks on the LIBOR panel submit their three-month rates, and then an average of these rates is calculated after the highest and lowest 25% of submissions are eliminated. For example, let's assume that a LIBOR panel comprises eight banks, which submit rates of 2.0%, 2.5%, 2.75%, 3.0%, 3.25%, 3.5%, 3.75%, and 4% respectively as the borrowing cost for a three-month loan. The two top rates (3.75, 4%) and the lowest two rates (2.0, 2.1%) are discarded and the rate is set as an average, that is, 3.125%.[55]

LIBOR has become the reference rate for short-term floating rate financial contracts such as swaps and futures. These rates are typically expressed as "LIBOR + x," where "x" is the premium charged for a particular borrower on top of the LIBOR rate. According to the BBA, the LIBOR rates are used as the basis for many types of lending including commercial loans, personal loans, and residential mortgages. An estimated 45% of prime and 80% of subprime adjustable-rate mortgages had interest rates that were determined by LIBOR. In addition, about 50% of variable student loan rates are tied to the LIBOR. Thus, the LIBOR "touches everyone from large international conglomerates to small borrowers."[56]

Barclays and the LIBOR

There were apparently many traders and a number of banks involved in LIBOR manipulations, but Barclays was one of the most prominent banks at the forefront of this scandal. In theory, LIBOR is supposed to be an honest and reliable number. When the system was designed, it was assumed that banks would play by the rules and provide honest estimates of their borrowing rates. But in reality, the system had been corrupt for many years. The problem is that LIBOR is based on estimates rather than the actual rates at which banks borrow from each other. In addition, those bankers involved in using LIBOR and submitting LIBOR rates had big incentives to lie, since their banks could incur big profits or losses based on LIBOR. Thus the system was heavily prone to opportunistic behavior.[57]

In Barclays's case, there were two distinct phases of LIBOR fixing with different motivations. From 2005 to 2008, the rigging was orchestrated by traders who were motivated by profit. During the financial crisis from 2007 to 2010, Barclays senior managers authorized lowballing its LIBOR submissions in response to negative media comments about the bank's financial condition.[58]

Phase One

In the first phase of LIBOR fixing, traders encouraged rate submitters to submit higher or lower LIBOR rates that would benefit their own trading positions. Traders colluded with those in Barclays who submitted the LIBOR figures by encouraging them to submit rates that might alter the overall LIBOR rate. A small change in LIBOR, for example, could have a large effect on a derivatives contract and increase profits on their derivatives exposure. Very small moves in the value of LIBOR could translate into daily profits (or losses) worth millions of dollars. On occasion, Barclays colluded with other banks by influencing their LIBOR submissions. According to the House of Commons, "Where Barclays acted in concert with other banks, the risk of manipulation increased materially."[59]

How might the manipulation of LIBOR help a trader? As an example, consider derivatives tied to interest rates, known as interest rate swaps, which had become a common product offered by investment banks. Let's assume a company known as ACE Manufacturing borrowed $100 million from National Bank. The variable interest rate for the one-year loan was tied to the floating federal funds rate, and it stood at 3% when the loan was made.[60] If the federal funds rate increased during the year, its interest payments would also increase, perhaps quite substantially. As a result, ACE would hedge its position with an interest rate swap with an investment bank like Barclays. ACE would agree to borrow $100 million from Barclays at 3%, and Barclays would agree to borrow $100 million from ACE at a floating rate tied to LIBOR, such as LIBOR (currently 2.80%) + 0.2%. At the end of one year, whichever party, ACE or Barclays, owed more money would make a payment to the other party, while the $100 million itself would not change hands. If LIBOR remained unchanged, there would be no net payment made to either party. But if rates move up, including the federal funds rate and LIBOR, ACE would have a higher interest payment on its real loan from National Bank, but it would also collect a net payment from Barclays. However, manipulation of the LIBOR by Barclays, perhaps in collusion with other banks, could help reduce Barclays's payment. When the date for payment on the swap arrives, a Barclays banker successfully submits a false low bid so the LIBOR ends up at 2.85% instead of 2.88%. Instead of paying ACE $80,000 (3.08 [i.e., 2.88% + 0.2] × $100 million), Barclays pays ACE $50,000 (3.05 [i.e., 2.85% + 0.2] × $100 million. When swaps involve billions of dollars, a few LIBOR percentage points can make a big difference when it comes time to settle these swaps.[61]

The majority of requests for fixing the LIBOR came from Barclays's New York Interest Rate Swaps Desk, whose traders frequently requested certain rates for the U.S. dollar LIBOR. Between January 2005 and May 2009, at least 173 requests for U.S. dollar LIBOR submissions were made by traders to Barclays submitters. According to former CEO Robert Diamond, "They [the traders] were acting on behalf of themselves. It is unclear whether it benefited Barclays but I don't think they had any interest in benefiting Barclays, they were benefitting themselves."[62]

Many of these requests for rate fixes were done openly rather than in clandestine fashion. Collusion seemed to be fairly normal. According to one of the investigators, Lord Turner,

> One of the shocking things about this is that on some occasions the derivatives trader is not asking the submitter to change its submission on the basis of a hidden phone call or a note that he believes is hidden, but by shouting it across the trading floor.

Lord Turner wondered what this implied about the culture at Barclays. Wasn't there something "deeply wrong" with a culture that allowed this to happen? Only 14 of Barclays thousands of traders were involved, and defenders of the bank point out they were isolated in one area, so this was not something happening across the whole bank.[63]

But the question remains, how could this rate fixing go undetected by senior managers for such a long period? Why wasn't it picked up by compliance officers and flagged by other internal controls at the bank? How could this practice flourish for so long? Desk supervisors, who knew this behavior was wrong, did not report it to their supervisors or to compliance officials. At the same time, the management of the bank seemed to have turned a blind eye to the culture of the trading floor. Traders were not monitored carefully despite the high monetary incentives to make their trades as profitable as possible. In addition, LIBOR submission was regarded as a low-risk activity, and compliance functions were focused on riskier areas of the bank. As a result, LIBOR submissions were not a chief focus of compliance officers, and so there were no effective LIBOR-setting controls in place. Neglect of the LIBOR continued despite the fact the LIBOR's behavior had "departed from its historic patterns." Barclays later admitted it should have changed its compliance in recognition of this change, but remained "behind the curve."[64]

Also, despite Mr. Diamond's claims the bank sought to rectify the problem as soon it was recognized, it is important to note that Barclays's internal compliance department was notified three times about concerns over LIBOR fixing during the period in question. But these warnings were never passed on to senior management within the bank. Hence, there were serious failures of Barclays's compliance office that prevented the bank from acting sooner.[65]

Phase Two

The second phase of LIBOR fixing occurred during the financial crisis and can be traced back to 2007, with rising defaults on subprime loans and mortgages. The crisis peaked in the summer of 2008 as losses accumulated and liquidity strains on banks grew more severe. After the bankruptcy of Lehman Brothers, U.S. government bailouts prevented the collapse of other major banks. During this period, there was an understandable apprehension about the financial stability of all major banks, including Barclays, even though the British bank had largely escaped the subprime calamity. In this second phase of wrongdoing, Barclays engaged in "lowballing," lowering its LIBOR submissions in response to negative media comments about the bank.[66]

As the financial crisis intensified and implicated more major banks, LIBOR was perceived as an important indicator of a bank's financial health. In August 2007, Barclays borrowed £1.6 billion from the central Bank of England. A month later, a Bloomberg news article titled "Barclays Takes a Money Market Beating" questioned the bank's liquidity and highlighted Barclays's high LIBOR submission relative to other banks. The article wanted to know, "What is happening at Barclays . . . that is prompting its peers to charge it premium interest rates in the money market?" The report caused alarm both within and outside the bank.[67]

And so began this new phase of LIBOR manipulation. Barclays sought to manipulate LIBOR to prevent being singled out when compared to other banks on the panel of LIBOR submitters. As a result, in 2007 and 2008, senior managers in the bank's Treasury Group instructed submitters to lowball LIBOR rates. The aim was to convey to the media and the markets Barclays's strong financial condition and "to avoid further negative media comment." Rates had to be within 10 basis points of the rates submitted by other banks. According to one manager, Barclays should not "stick its head above the parapet" when it submitted LIBOR rates. It should not stand out too far from the submissions of other banks.[68]

Thus, the second phase of the LIBOR manipulation was not the result of actions by rogue derivatives traders colluding with the LIBOR submitters. Some of the bank's most senior managers sent instructions down the chain of command to reduce LIBOR submissions. By submitting these low rates, Barclays thought it was assuring a skeptical media that it could borrow funds at low rates. It was projecting an aura of stability and financial strength to the financial markets.

Barclays was joined by other banks on the LIBOR panel who were routinely submitting rates that were 30 to 40 basis points too low. However, the media were not fooled. "The LIBOR rates are a bit of fiction," wrote a *Financial Times* reporter.[69] In addition, in May 2008, an article in the *Wall Street Journal* questioned the credibility of LIBOR. It concluded that based on an extensive analysis, the LIBOR rates were artificially low. According to this report, 15 of the 16 banks on one of the LIBOR panels appeared to be understating their 6- and 12-month rates over a period of 7 months.[70]

The Role of Regulators

The Federal Reserve Bank of New York was informed in April 2008 that at least one major bank was reporting false interest rates. A concerned Barclays employee had a phone conversation with a New York federal official, Fabiola Ravazzolo, an analyst in the bank's Market Group. The employee stated the bank was not posting an honest LIBOR rate. The employee further indicated that other big banks made similarly bogus reports, claiming these institutions wanted to fit in with the rest of the crowd. Here is a portion of the conversation between Ravazzolo and the anonymous Barclays employee:

Barclays Employee: We were putting in where we really thought we would be able to borrow cash in the interbank market and it was above where everyone else was publishing rates. And the next thing we knew, there was, um, an article in the *Financial Times* charting our LIBOR contributions and comparing it with other banks and inferring that this meant we had a problem raising cash in the interbank market.

Ravazzolo: Yeah.

Barclays Employee: And um, our share price went down.

Ravazzolo:	Yes.
Barclays Employee:	So it's never supposed to be the prerogative of a money market dealer to affect the company share value.
Ravazzolo:	Okay.
Barclays Employee:	And so we just fit in with the rest of the crowd, if you like.
Ravazzolo:	Okay.
Barclays Employee:	So, we know that we're not posting, um, an honest LIBOR.
Ravazzolo:	Okay.
Barclays Employee:	And yet and yet we are doing it because, um, if we didn't do it, it draws, um, unwanted attention to ourselves.[71]

Despite the candor of this conversation, there is no evidence that Barclays employees like this individual provided such explicit signals to UK authorities.

After this phone conversation, the federal analyst notified senior management in the Market Group that a Barclays source had informed her the underreporting of LIBOR was prevalent in the markets. However, the New York Fed had neither jurisdiction nor regulatory authority over LIBOR. Hence it did not conduct a further investigation into these dishonest submissions. Rather, Timothy Geithner, president of the bank at the time, conferred with British and American regulators about the problems. He sent an email to the governor of the Bank of England with a memorandum attached called "Recommendations for Enhancing the Credibility of LIBOR." Thus, while reforms were recommended, no effort was made to stop the illegal activity, which persisted through 2009. British officials at the Bank of England claimed they could not act at that time because they did not have adequate proof then of wrongdoing by banks like Barclays. No one had reported any explicit wrongdoing. The Geithner memo was merely a recommendation for how LIBOR should operate in the future.[72]

Penalties and Reforms

Despite many red flags raised by the media, the full breadth of this scandal did not come to light until 2012. A number of government investigations in several countries revealed a widespread plot by some of the world's biggest and oldest banks. As many as 20 banks were named in investigations or lawsuits that alleged rigging of the LIBOR. The other major banks involved besides Barclays included UBS, Deutsche Bank, Rabobank, and the Royal Bank of Scotland (RBS). The magnitude of the scandal further corroded the little remaining public trust in banks and the managers who run those banks.[73]

Another big player in the broadening scandal was UBS. Its involvement became apparent in 2012 when the Swiss bank admitted that several of its traders, led by Tom Hayes, worked closely with traders from other banks to push the Yen LIBOR submissions up and down. Thanks in part to these manipulations, Hayes made profits of almost $260 million for UBS between 2006 and 2009. Hayes admitted working hard to keep the LIBOR "artificially high."[74]

Regulators in the United States, the United Kingdom, and the European Union have fined banks over $9 billion for rigging LIBOR. UBS was fined $1.5 billion for its role. Deutsche Bank was forced to pay a fine of $2.5 billion. Barclays agreed to pay U.S. and UK authorities $435 million in 2012; an additional $100 million was paid out to 44 U.S. states in 2016. Its CEO, Robert Diamond, and other leading executives have resigned for their mishandling of the LIBOR crisis.[75]

In addition, criminal charges have been brought against some traders and brokers for their roles in the rate fixing. Hayes, known as "Rain Man" by his colleagues, was convicted on eight counts of fraud due to his leading role in the scandal. He was sentenced to 14 years in prison. However, six brokers who allegedly helped Hayes were acquitted by a UK jury in 2016.[76] In 2015, two traders at Rabobank were convicted of "exploiting and abusing their role" in setting LIBOR rates.[77] These convictions lend support for the success of future class action lawsuits.

The LIBOR incident has had broad global ramifications, especially for banks that remain at the heart of capitalism by providing a necessary link between savers and borrowers.[78] Regrettably, it has confirmed the public's perception of greedy, amoral bankers who know no bounds to making money for themselves. According to one columnist, the LIBOR debacle is another sure sign of capitalism's moral decay.[79] The scandal has not only eroded trust in banks and in financial markets, but it has also drained banks of precious capital as they pay out fines and incur legal fees. Questions have also been raised about the credibility and efficiency of central banks that failed to address the scandal in a timely manner. It's surprising that regulators were not inspired to take action in 2008 when the New York Fed was tipped off about the rigging of this benchmark interest rate.

What's the future for the LIBOR in the wake of this scandal? Some argue the LIBOR has been discredited and should be abandoned for a new rate based on real transaction data. There have been many proposals for reform, such as increasing the number of banks on the LIBOR submission panels or giving government agencies authority over setting the rate. But LIBOR is still calculated in the same way and continues to be the primary benchmark for global lending rates.

- In your opinion, what is the root cause of the LIBOR scandal at Barclays? Who benefits and who potentially gets hurt when the LIBOR is rigged?

- How would you explain the interaction between the legal, ethical, and economic aspects of LIBOR manipulation by banks like Barclays?

- Is there any moral difference between derivatives traders manipulating the LIBOR to make profits and bank officials doing so to project an image of stability? How do you assess the actions of these individuals in light of the DRJ model?

- As noted at the end to the case, one observer sees this incident as indicative of capitalism's moral decline. How would you relate this case to some of the issues on capitalism discussed in Chapter 1?

CASE STUDY 6.4

FRAUD OR SHREWD BUSINESS? THE CASE OF GOLDMAN SACHS

AP Photo/Richard Drew

Goldman Sachs is an elite Wall Street firm, a powerhouse in the world of finance with a long, distinguished history. Thus, shock waves rippled through the Wall Street community when Goldman was charged with securities fraud by the Securities and Exchange Commission (SEC) in April 2010. Goldman promptly replied that the SEC's accusations were "completely unfounded in law and fact."[80] The focus of the SEC case was a complaint that Goldman deceived customers by selling them subprime mortgage securities secretly designed by a hedge fund firm that sold those securities short and made millions betting on the housing market's collapse. The Goldman scenario also illustrates the failure of financial regulators who were unable to identify and deal with a big "asset bubble" before it damaged a fragile financial system. The issues raised by this case go to the heart of the Goldman business model and suggest the need for greater transparency in the world of investment banking.[81]

Goldman Sachs: A Brief History

Goldman Sachs was founded in New York in 1869 by German-born Marcus Goldman. Goldman began by helping small businesses secure capital. He made short-term loans known as commercial paper to New York merchants. As the company's reputation grew, small and medium-sized businesses flocked to the bank to solve their financing needs. A number of years later in 1882, Mr. Goldman's son-in-law, Samuel Sachs, joined the firm. In 1885, Goldman took his son Henry and his son-in-law Ludwig Dreyfuss into the growing Wall Street firm, which adopted its current name, Goldman Sachs & Co. At this stage Goldman Sachs expanded into other areas of finance, such as handling overseas transactions of debt and currency. It also began to make inroads against the better-established investment banks by handling initial public offerings (IPOs) for progressive companies such as Sears Roebuck, which were selling equity shares for the first time.[82]

The investment bank survived the 1929 stock market crash, and during the ensuing economic depression, Sidney Weinberg took the helm. He was the first nonfamily member to head the firm. Goldman expanded yet again into arbitrage for securities and currencies. It continued to attract many choice IPO customers such as Ford Motor Co. and added commodities trading to its portfolio of businesses by purchasing J. Aron & Company. During the decade of the 1990s, the company enjoyed record-breaking profits year after year thanks to the broad scope of its banking activities. It made considerable money from Japanese equities and U.S. bankruptcy turnarounds.[83]

Goldman went public in 1999, and the capital it received made it one of the largest financial services firms on Wall Street. It utilized that capital to finance another $7 billion in merger and acquisition deals. As it entered the new millennium, Goldman ranked among one of Wall Street's leading firms in its core businesses, which included merger and acquisitions advisement and underwriting stock sales. In 2008, under pressure from the federal government, Goldman converted from an investment bank into a commercial bank so it could get access to inexpensive government funding to calm nervous investors. Although it still specializes in investment banking activities, in recent years Goldman has devoted more energy and resources to commercial lending and other banking products.[84]

Under the leadership of Lloyd Blankfein, who became CEO in 2006, Goldman sought to transform its knowledge of the market and its network of corporate clients into an awesome "money-making machine." It emphasized a corporate mantra called "Being in the flow," collecting and assimilating its vast market and corporate sources of information to inform its own trading and that of its clients. Goldman saw itself as the best-connected trader on Wall Street, continually absorbing information for use on behalf of itself and its clients. Its specialty was turning over capital quickly, extracting as much profit as possible from the same dollar. Goldman also stressed its resolute commitment to its clients, its willingness to help them achieve their aims, even if that meant profiting from a pessimistic view of the U.S. housing market.[85]

Goldman has been embroiled in a number of ethical controversies over the course of its long history. In 1929, for example, Goldman executives apparently sponsored a pyramid scheme investment cleverly disguised as a mutual fund. When the investment collapsed after the stock market crash, 42,000 investors lost almost $300 million. In 1970, Goldman was one of the banks at the center of the Penn Central catastrophe. A default on short-term paper marketed by Goldman produced damage claims exceeding the bank's net worth. In the late 1980s, Goldman, like many other investment banks at the time, found itself caught up in a web of insider-trading scandals. Goldman's head of risk arbitrage, Robert Freeman, was sent to jail for insider trading. During the same time frame, Goldman was implicated in an illegal scheme to prop up the insolvent businesses of the newspaper tycoon, Robert Maxwell. And in 2010, the Wall Street titan faced another ethical crisis, suffering a serious blow to its reputation. Wall Street observers claimed that Goldman's opaque financial mechanisms, which helped it to earn abundant profits, deceived some of its clients and exacerbated the effects of the subprime mortgage crisis.[86]

Subprime Mortgages, CDOs, and Credit Swaps

The subprime mortgage market was generating almost $500 billion in new mortgage loans each year by 2005. These were risky loans made to "subprime" borrowers with poor credit histories. The mortgage bankers making these loans sought ways to protect themselves from default and turned to the big Wall Street banks for help. Wall Street financiers devised several ingenious mechanisms to distribute or spread the risk by putting large numbers of these mortgages together into pools. A pool of mortgages packaged together from different geographical areas became a mortgage bond, commonly known as a residential mortgage-backed security (RMBS). An RMBS is simply a security backed by residential mortgages. Investors receive payments out of the interest and principal on the underlying mortgages. Like all bonds, RMBSs can be high- or low-investment grade, depending on the quality of the mortgages in the package. A subprime RMBS would be rated "Triple B" (BBB) by Moody's bond-rating agency, and represent the lowest investment grade. But many had high bond ratings based on the premise that geographical diversity diminished the overall risk of these pooled mortgages. By 2005, there was $625 billion in subprime or low-quality mortgage loans, and $507 billion of that amount found its way into mortgage bonds.[87]

The case against Goldman centers around two complex financial tools: the credit default swap and collateralized debt obligations. The credit default swap is not literally a "swap" of any kind but a type of insurance policy in which the seller agrees to compensate the buyer if a third party defaults on a loan or a bond. For example, someone might pay $120,000 to purchase a 10-year credit default swap on $100 million in AT&T bonds. The most an investor would lose is $1.2 million (10 years × $120,000). But that investor would gain $100 million if AT&T defaulted on its bonds and left its bondholders with nothing. Credit default swaps became a tool for hedging and were used with some frequency to hedge against subprime loans going bad.[88]

In addition, Goldman Sachs is credited with inventing synthetic subprime mortgage-backed collateralized debt obligations known as CDOs. The original CDO was similar to a credit default swap, since its aim was to redistribute the risk of holding government and corporate bonds. In a CDO, the debt securities were collateralized by debt obligations that included RMBSs. Many RMBSs, composed of pooled residential mortgages, were packaged together to create a "tower of bonds." The CDOs were carved up into "tranches" by degree of exposure to default. Most investors were attracted to the safer tranches because of their perceived low risk and high returns. These mortgage securities were packaged and held by a special purpose vehicle (SPV) that issued notes entitling their holders to payments derived from the underlying assets. Goldman was able to persuade rating agencies to give a CDO higher credit ratings since it represented a diversified portfolio of assets. In a synthetic CDO, the SPV does not actually own a portfolio of fixed income assets but rather enters into credit default swaps that reference the performance of that portfolio. Buyers of a synthetic CDO would receive premium payments, but short sellers could make a speculative bet on default of the bonds in that portfolio and be paid the value of those bonds if they defaulted. Short sellers would be paid nothing if the bonds proved to be good, but stood to make billions if they went bad.[89]

Goldman Sachs and Paulson

Goldman's troubles began when it allowed Paulson & Co., a hedge fund firm, to design a CDO built out of risky, subprime Triple B–rated mortgage bonds. Paulson, a rather obscure company founded in 1994, had created two funds known as Paulson Credit Opportunity Funds, which purchased credit default swaps to capitalize on its bearish views of the U.S. housing market. In 2006, Paulson identified 123 mortgage-backed securities it expected to decline in value. It approached Goldman about creating a synthetic CDO that would track or reference the value of those securities. Paulson would then purchase credit default swaps on the RMBS it had selected for this CDO, given its conviction that these bonds would experience "credit events." Thus, Paulson persuaded Goldman to let it participate in the selection of RMBSs for a synthetic CDO, which Paulson would then short by entering into credit default swaps to buy protection on specific layers (or tranches) of that CDO.[90]

The problem was that Paulson needed buyers of the CDO so it could be the short-seller. Goldman could structure the CDO, but it would find no buyers if it was known that Paulson was the short-seller and that it had played a significant role in the RMBS selection process. According to the SEC complaint, "By contrast, they knew that the identification of an experienced and independent third party collateral manager as having selected the portfolio would facilitate the placement of CDO liabilities in a market that was beginning to show signs of distress."[91]

As a result, in 2007, Goldman turned to ACA Management, an independent third party, to help design the portfolio and to serve as the "portfolio selection agent." ACA had previously constructed and managed numerous other CDOs for big fees. According to a Goldman internal email, "We expect the strong brand-name of ACA as well as our market-leading position in synthetic CDOs of structured products to result in a successful offering." ACA worked with Paulson to finalize the RMBS for this CDO, but it did not know that Paulson was planning on shorting that CDO through credit default swaps. Of the 123 RMBS originally proposed by Paulson, ACA included only 55. After long negotiations between ACA and Paulson, they agreed in late February 2007 on a reference portfolio of 90 RMBSs. An internal ACA email questioned Paulson's selection criteria: "Attached is the revised portfolio Paulson would like us to commit to—all names are at the Baa2 level. . . . Are we ok to say yes to this portfolio?" The response was "Looks good to me. Did [Paulson] give a reason why they kicked out all the Wells [Fargo] deals?" According to the SEC, Wells Fargo was regarded as one of the higher-quality subprime loan originators.[92]

The CDO structured by Paulson and ACA was known as ABACUS 2007-AC1. The marketing materials, which described ACA as the portfolio selection agent, omit any reference to Paulson. The 65-page marketing document described the deal as a $2 billion synthetic CDO based on a pool of residential mortgage bonds selected by ACA. The logos of Goldman Sachs and ACA were printed on almost every page.[93]

One of the major ABACUS investors was IKB, a German commercial bank with headquarters in Dusseldorf. Since 2002, IKB had been a purchaser of RMBS CDOs. In 2006, it informed Goldman it would not invest in the liabilities of CDOs that did not utilize an independent third-party collateral manager. In April 2007, Goldman sent IKB its marketing material for ABACUS, indicating that the RMBS portfolio was selected by ACA but with no reference to Paulson. IKB invested $150 million into ABACUS. By October 2007, 83% of the ABACUS mortgage portfolio was downgraded. As a result, the notes purchased by IKB were virtually worthless, and IKB lost nearly all of its $150 million investment. Another big loser was ACA Capital Holdings, the parent company of ACA, which operated a bond insurer that insured a $909 million piece of the CDO in return for a fee. According to the SEC, investors in ABACUS lost about $1 billion. Paulson's big gamble, however, paid off, and the company netted $1 billion in profit. Goldman collected its customary fees from all parties in these transactions.[94]

The SEC Complaint and Goldman's Settlement

The Securities and Exchange Commission filed a lawsuit in April 2010 and accused Goldman of securities fraud for the way it handled the ABACUS CDO. The SEC claimed that Goldman had made misleading statements and omissions in its marketing materials. Goldman had misrepresented its product and caused heavy losses for its investors. The main omission was the role of the Paulson hedge fund in choosing the RMBS portfolio for ABACUS. According to the SEC complaint, Goldman "recklessly or negligently misrepresented in the term-sheet, flip book, and offering memorandum for ABACUS 2007 that the reference portfolio was selected by ACA without disclosing the significant role in the portfolio selection process played by Paulson, a hedge fund with financial interest in the transaction directly adverse to IKB [and] ACA Capital."[95]

Goldman vigorously denied these damaging allegations, which stunned its senior managers. According to the *Financial Times*, "In a company that built its ethos and pay structure on hiring the best and being the best, the surprise news that Goldman stood accused of securities fraud was a bombshell."[96] Over the years, Goldman had adopted a loose trading ethic. The bank's executives believed they could execute virtually any trade regardless of the consequences for clients or the market, so long as that trade didn't break the law. Goldman defended its actions by saying it simply brokered a transaction between professional investors, who knew the risks, and it was not required to hold their hands. The ABACUS deal was a reflection of Goldman's use of market intelligence drawn from different sources to broker deals that other investment banks were incapable of doing. Goldman executives spoke of its ability to "embrace" conflicts of interest that arose from its pivotal position at the center of information and capital flows.[97]

Paulson & Co. was not named in the SEC complaint despite the fact that its request led to the whole controversy. The hedge fund company successfully deflected attention to Goldman. According to a statement released at the time, they "were not involved in the marketing of ABACUS products," and ACA "had sole authority" over the bond selection.[98] According to press reports, many banks on Wall Street had been reluctant to work with Paulson. A banker at Bear Stearns & Co. turned down their business as he questioned the propriety of selling deals based on risky mortgage assets that a bearish client had some role in assembling. Yet banks like Goldman Sachs and Deutsche Bank AG had no problem doing business with Paulson. Paulson earned $15 billion betting against the housing market in 2007.[99]

By July 2010, Goldman reached a settlement with the SEC. It agreed to pay a $500 million fine, which was one of the largest penalties ever paid out by a Wall Street firm; $300 million in fines was paid to the Treasury Department, with the rest serving as restitution to investors who lost money on the ABACUS deal. As part of the settlement Goldman did not admit wrongdoing, but it did concede that marketing materials for the investment "contained incomplete information." Goldman admitted it should have revealed Paulson's role. Goldman also agreed to change some of its business practices, specifically the way it developed marketing materials for complex mortgage securities. Goldman acknowledged it was conducting a comprehensive, firmwide review of its business standards.[100]

EXHIBIT 6.1 ■ Goldman Sachs Financials, 2014–2016 (in thousands)[101]			
	2014	**2015**	**2016**
Revenues	$34,528,000	$33,820,000	$30,608,000
Operating Income	12,357,000	8,778,000	10,304,000
Net Income	8,477,000	6,083,000	7,398,000

- In its press release announcing the Goldman settlement, an SEC spokesperson said that Goldman had violated "the fundamental principles of honest treatment and fair dealing."[102] Do you agree with that assessment? According to the DRJ framework, what was wrong with Goldman's actions?

- As an investment banker, would you do business with the Paulson hedge fund under the circumstances described in this case?

- How can Goldman improve its "ethical performance" as it moves forward? What changes need to take place at Goldman?

CASE STUDY 6.5

THE WELLS FARGO SALES SCAM

AP Photo/Cliff Owen

John Stumpf's appearance before the Senate Banking Committee was a nightmarish experience. Senator Warren from Massachusetts harshly upbraided the Wells Fargo chairperson as he sat docilely in front of disgusted committee members with a skeptical media looking on. Both Republicans and Democrats accused him of incompetence and moral laxity for not doing more in the wake of the banking scandal swirling around Wells Fargo. One senator told Mr. Stumpf that he should resign and that the bank fraud warranted a thorough investigation by both the Department of Justice and the Securities and Exchange Commission. The sharp, bipartisan criticism made headline news the next day.

The California-based bank had been accused of a massive fraud that bilked hundreds of its own customers out of millions of dollars. This was accomplished through "ghost" accounts for which customers were sometimes charged late fees and overdraft fees. Retail bank employees opened almost 2 million unauthorized accounts and credit cards in order to meet unrealistic sales quotas. Although the full scope of these offenses did not come to light until 2016, the bank began dismissing employees in 2011 for these irregularities. This case study explores the multiple dimensions of this banking scandal and its ramifications for Wells Fargo and the banking industry. That industry has been in some turmoil since the global financial crisis of 2008. The case begins with a history of this banking legend along with a brief summary of Wells Fargo corporate strategy.

Wells Fargo & Co.

In 1852, Henry Wells and William Fargo founded Wells, Fargo & Co. to serve the Western region of the United States during the Gold Rush years in California.

The new bank with branch offices in San Francisco and Sacramento offered both banking and "express" delivery services, including the delivery of gold and other valuables. The San Francisco–based company became especially famous for its stagecoach line, which transported these precious commodities from city to city. In 1905, Wells Fargo separated its banking and express delivery operations. By 1910, the express network, which now relied heavily on the U.S. rail system, linked 6,000 locations, including new offices in the Upper Midwest and Great Lakes regions. In 1918, however, the federal government took over this transportation system as part of a strategy associated with its participation in World War I. As a result, Wells Fargo was left with just one bank in San Francisco.[103]

But Wells rapidly expanded after the war and soon became the predominant commercial bank in the San Francisco region, supporting the West's growing businesses and especially the agriculture industry. It survived the depression era thanks to its conservative banking philosophy. World War II was an uneventful period for Wells, but it embarked on an ambitious expansion program in the 1950s with the purchase of banks in San Mateo and Antioch. By the 1960s, Wells Fargo had evolved into a premier regional bank with branch offices scattered throughout northern California. In the 1980s, Wells Fargo expanded into a statewide bank and became the seventh-largest bank in the country.[104]

The decade of the 1980s, however, began inauspiciously with a serious scandal that greatly embarrassed the Wells Fargo organization. In 1981, a $21.3 million embezzlement scheme by a bank employee was brought to light. At the time it was one of the largest embezzlements in the history of banking. Ben Lewis, a bank officer at the Beverly Drive branch, later pleaded guilty to the embezzlement charges. Lewis had routinely written phony debit and credit receipts to pad the accounts of his cronies, and received a $300,000 cut in return for his efforts.[105]

In the 1990s, Wells Fargo developed a national presence, opening new offices in many Western, Midwestern, and Eastern states. It pursued a series of acquisitions to expand its presence including a merger with Minneapolis-based bank Norwest Corporation. These mergers and acquisitions culminated in Wells's purchase of the financially challenged Wachovia Corporation in Wisconsin. The contested merger immediately created a coast-to-coast "megabank" with $1.4 trillion in assets and 48 million customers. It further extended Wells Fargo's operations into nine Eastern and Southern states. By acquiring Wachovia, Wells Fargo now gained the big retail banking network it had sought for a long time with a significant presence east of the Mississippi. Wachovia's retail banking management team was also considered among the strongest in the industry and complemented Wells's own expertise in this area. Wells Fargo maintained Charlotte as the central hub of Wachovia's operations, making it the headquarters for the combined company's East Coast operations.[106]

By 2013, Wells Fargo had overtaken J.P. Morgan Chase & Co. as the most valuable U.S. bank, with its market value driven up by its upward spiraling stock price. In 2017, Wells Fargo & Co. was the third-largest U.S. bank (by assets), right behind J.P. Morgan Chase & Co. and Bank of America Corp. It had $1.9 trillion in total assets and a loan portfolio of $904 billion. Wells had over 6,000 branches with about 40 million retail customers. It employed 269,000 people scattered throughout its global operations in 130 countries. Despite its extensive operations, retail banking continues to be its core business.

The CEO and Board of Directors

John Stumpf, who grew up on a dairy farm in Pierz, Minnesota, became chief executive officer of Wells Fargo in 2007. He assumed the chairman's title in 2010. Stumpf had begun his banking career immediately after college. He later joined the loan department of Northwestern National Bank, which merged with Wells Fargo in 1998. He quickly rose through the ranks at Wells Fargo and was appointed group executive vice president of the community banking division in 2002 and president in 2005. Thanks to his superior performance in these positions, he was appointed CEO. In 2015, Stumpf was among the country's highest-paid bankers, with total compensation of $19.3 million.[107]

While many banks retrenched during the financial crisis of 2008, Wells Fargo made some bold moves as it strived to develop a stronger national presence. Stumpf is credited with outmaneuvering arch rival Citigroup to acquire Wachovia. He also orchestrated an acquisition of key segments of GE Capital. Stumpf consistently praised the bank's spirit and teamwork, which he regarded as its "secret sauce."[108]

Mr. Stumpf was chairman of the Wells Fargo board of directors, which consisted of 15 independent board members. The board included top corporate executives, former federal government officials, and an academic. Like all corporate boards, the Wells Fargo directors were responsible for risk assessment in the company's various businesses, along with setting compensation for top bank officials, including the CEO. Stumpf made recommendations to the board's human resources committee, which was responsible for determining executive salaries and compensation packages. The human resources committee meets each year with the bank's chief risk officer "to review and assess any risks posed by our enterprise incentive compensation programs." The board is also responsible for monitoring a company's culture along with the tone set by its top managers. Two of the Wells Fargo directors, Elizabeth Duke and Cynthia Milligan, were former financial regulators with considerable experience in the area of retail banking.[109]

In recent years, prior to the scandal, some powerful stockholders attempted to compel Wells Fargo to hire an independent chairman while retaining Mr. Stumpf as CEO. They claimed the dual role of chairman and CEO gave Stumpf too much power and a better balance of power would be preferable. However, most U.S. banks, aside from Citigroup, do not split these two roles.[110]

Community Banking

Wells Fargo's banking operations were divided into three discrete segments: community banking, wholesale banking, and wealth and investment management. Wholesale or commercial banking provided loans and other services to major business customers. The elite wealth and investment management division offered a range of services including various premium investment products.

The community banking sector represented the retail division of Wells Fargo. It served more communities and customers than any other U.S. bank. The bank's diverse retail products included savings deposit accounts, debit cards, credit cards, checking accounts, certificates of deposit, IRAs, mortgages, and home equity loans or lines of credit. These products were available through the bank's 6,000 branches and 13,000 ATMs located across 39 states. The retail division has 40 million retail-banking customers (21 million households) along with 3 million small business relationships. For several years Wells Fargo has been the leading small business lender. Its loan portfolio is over $450 billion, and deposits total about $650 billion. In 2017, the community banking division generated revenues of over $48.7 billion, or 55% of Wells Fargo's total revenues. Net income for this division amounted to $12 billion.[111]

CEO Stumpf had risen through the ranks of the retail unit and became its leader in 2002. Since 2007, this division, which was at the center of the sales scam controversy, was led by Carrie Tolstedt, who had worked at the bank for 27 years. She oversaw the bank's branch network and was the architect of the division's sales goals and cross-selling tactics. Those sales goals shaped the bank's culture. Tolstedt, who was called "the watchmaker" by some of her peers, was known for her meticulous planning and attention to details. Under her leadership, the retail banking arm remained an important driver of the bank's revenue and profit growth. In 2015, her total compensation was $9.05 million. She also received $20 million in annual bonuses between 2010 and 2015 that were "justified by the company in certain instances because of the strong cross-sell ratios in her division."[112]

Culture and Sales Ethos

Wells Fargo has always sought to separate itself from Wall Street banks, particularly as Wall Street's reputation plummeted in the wake of the subprime mortgage debacle in 2008. It has leveraged its West Coast location in San Francisco to portray itself as the friendly bank of Main Street rather than Wall Street. It has long cultivated a "down-home culture" and "folksy image" in order to appeal to ordinary customers.[113] Insiders have also described that culture as "insular" and isolated from external influence or attention. This insularity was fostered by senior executives with decades of tenure at the bank who were not accustomed to being in the limelight or dealing with unwanted publicity.

Despite its outsider image, Wells Fargo, along with other major retail banks, could never completely escape the high-stakes "incentive-driven banking culture" that has long shaped the strategy of Wall Street investment banks like Goldman Sachs and Morgan Stanley. Wall Street banks, specializing in trading and underwriting stock sales, have been "bonus driven" for a long time. But many retail banks have also imitated the Wall Street model, which relies heavily on big financial rewards. The problem has always been that this culture, which motivates employees to push hard and take risks to generate sales, often lacks the proper internal mechanisms to moderate opportunistic behavior.[114]

Over the years, Wells Fargo cultivated a strong "sales consciousness," and that mentality pervaded its community banking unit. Wells was admired and emulated in the banking industry for its "sales prowess," its ability to attract new customers and maximize revenue from those customers by selling them multiple products. Branch managers were so obsessed with sales that they instructed their employees to hunt for potential customers at bus stops or retirement homes. Managers carefully monitored each employee's progress toward his or her sales goals and sent daily reports to higher-ranking managers. Sales quotas were set by product and were quite aggressive. For example, in Lincoln, Nebraska, branch account managers had a daily goal to open two new checking accounts and make eight other product sales. Those who questioned these unrealistic targets were told, "You're negative," or "You're not a team player." This sales-driven culture was deeply entrenched in the entire organization and especially in the retail division.[115]

Those managers and branch employees who consistently met their quotas were well rewarded with promotions and handsome bonuses. Bankers working in branches who reached their sales targets could earn bonuses of $500 to $2,000 a quarter. District managers could earn bonuses of $10,000 to $20,000 per year. Those who failed, on the other hand, were punished and sometimes fired for their lack of performance. Many capable workers left because of the excessive pressure. Incentive compensation practices like this one are common, but they can pose big risks for corporations if they inadvertently reward improper behavior. In this case they led to the questionable practices that put Wells Fargo in an intense international spotlight.[116]

Cross-Selling

The key to Wells Fargo's sales strategy was cross-selling. During the recent past, the banking industry evolved strong convictions about the unlocked potential of cross-selling its multiple products to each customer. Some of the new opportunities were made possible through deregulation of the financial industry. When Travelers Insurance and Citicorp merged in 1998, they formed the largest financial services company in the world and sought to take advantage of that deregulation.[117] The new company, known as Citigroup, aimed to establish a financial supermarket, which offered to customers a broad range of services and products under the same roof. Consumers could buy insurance, invest in securities, and have several bank accounts all at the same company. When the merger was consummated, Citigroup put into place an aggressive plan to market investment and insurance products to its many banking customers.

Cross-selling is popular with many other banks that often offer savings for customers when they exhibit brand loyalty and choose other products. Customers can get a better deal on a mortgage or get a waiver for certain account fees. However, cross-selling can also pressure consumers into buying products they don't really need or products that could have been acquired at a cheaper rate elsewhere. Some banks try to induce customers to purchase their services with bogus claims that the offer is time sensitive or exclusive for the bank's loyal customers. Cross-selling is so heavily favored by banks because it lowers the customer acquisition cost. These complementary products also create higher switching costs and thereby lock in consumers to the bank's related products. Banking services offer little opportunity for differentiation. They are essentially commodities. Thus, the success of cross-selling heavily depends upon the resources and skill of the bank's sales staff.[118]

Like most of the big multiservice banks, Wells Fargo has successfully relied on the cross-selling approach as one of its major strategic principles. Hence, its business model depended heavily on selling additional products and services to its existing customer base. When customers opened checking or savings accounts, account managers might also try to persuade them to apply for a Wells Fargo credit card. The objective was always to squeeze as much additional revenue as possible from the existing customer base. The bank's credit card business, for example, was built up primarily by targeting its own customers: 82% of Wells Fargo credit card holders have a checking account or some type of deposit relationship with the bank. Among the biggest American banks, Wells Fargo became known as "the king of consumer cross-selling."[119] The company pitched not only credit cards to its depositors but also home equity loans, mortgages, certificates of deposit, IRAs, and other products. As a result of this assertive sales strategy, the number of products per retail household at Wells rose from 5.5 in 2009 to 6.3 in 2015. The Wells Fargo cross-selling goal was eight products per customer. Stumpf himself was behind the bank's sales motto, "Eight is Great." Wells Fargo employees were constantly being reminded about the "great 8," or the need to sell eight financial products to every house-hold doing business with the bank. However, on average, bank customers had only 2.7 products at their primary bank. Observers have pointed out that this strategy was sure to hit "soft limits," since there are only so many credit cards, savings accounts, and mortgage loans that a customer really needs.[120]

The Sales Scam

Wells Fargo employees, sometimes desperate to meet their sales quotas, opened as many as 2 million savings, checking, and credit card accounts without a customer's knowledge or consent. An internal investigation by Wells uncovered 1.5 million deposit and checking accounts that were not authorized along with 565,000 unauthorized credit and debit cards.[121] Employees issued these debit and credit cards for customers without informing them, and assigned those cards personal ID numbers. In some cases, they temporarily transferred funds from a customer's regular account to a bogus one in order to make the account look real. These unauthorized transfers sometimes generated fees for insufficient funds when checks written on a customer's valid account could not clear. In certain instances, customers were told they were getting a credit card in the mail as a reward for being a loyal customer. For the most part, however, customers did not know that accounts or credit cards had been opened in their name until they were forced to pay late fees or they found strange banking statements in their mailbox. Some Wells Fargo bankers also created phony email accounts, such as noname@wellsfargo.com, along with fake PIN numbers in order to enroll unsuspecting customers in online banking services. It has been estimated that 14,000 of these fraudulent accounts generated over $400,000 in revenue through annual fees, interest charges, and other fees. Virtually all of this fraud was motivated by the drive to meet sales goals and quotas established by the retail division's executives.[122]

As the Wells Fargo story unfolded, hundreds of consumers came forward with countless examples of unauthorized accounts. In Culver City, California, a Wells Fargo employee opened five checking accounts for the owner of a facial care business. That owner was also charged $105 a month for three accidental-death insurance policies he had not authorized. He learned about the bank accounts only after the bank began send-ing letters saying he needed to put more money into his Wells Fargo accounts. On some occasions, Wells Fargo bankers took advantage of elderly and unsophisticated clients. Mr. Hing Chow was surprised to find that his 96-year-old father and 84-year-old mother had suddenly accumulated $690 in banking fees they could not explain. The reason was that a checking account with a minimum required balance of $25,000 across their Wells Fargo deposit accounts was opened without their knowledge.[123] And in Los Angeles a Mexican music star described how a Wells Fargo bank employee opened ghost check-ing accounts and credit lines in her name and moved $400,000 of her funds into these accounts. The employee covered his tracks by stopping by her house and stealing the Wells Fargo statements from her mailbox.[124]

Wells Fargo managers also pushed employees to sign up customers for expensive over-draft services they didn't need and didn't want. Overdraft services allow ATM debit card transactions to clear even if a checking account has insufficient funds. It usually generates a fee of about $35. In 2010, a Federal Reserve regulation required banks to get a customer's explicit permission to choose this strictly optional service. But in Tucker, Georgia, Wells Fargo branch managers told their employees to present debit card overdraft protection as a requirement for checking account customers, in clear violation of government regulation. In other areas, managers pressured bankers to sign up as many people for overdraft services as possible. Some bankers claimed they had to report at the end of the day how many customers they persuaded to opt in and felt "major pressure" to do so.[125]

Corporate Reaction

There have been conflicting reports about when senior Wells Fargo executives knew about these bogus accounts. As early as 2005, the year John Stumpf became president, some employees came forward to report they had witnessed the opening of ghost accounts and the forging of customer signatures. Several individuals wrote to human resources with their complaints, but nothing was done. Why didn't these complaints raise alarm bells within Wells Fargo at a higher level? And why were these sales tactics not picked up by internal auditors? The answer to that question has never been fully clarified. However, bank branches were given 24 hours' notice before internal monitors arrived, and this advanced warning gave employees adequate time to cover up their improper practices.[126]

Also, bank officials seemed largely indifferent to the complaints of employees who reported this bad behavior. One whistle-blower, Julie Tishkoff, was fired in 2009 after she reported her suspicions about fake accounts. Two of her supervisors were aware of her complaints but refused to act, and eventually Tishkoff was terminated. According to one branch manager, "Everyone knew there was fraud going on, and the people trying to flag it were the ones who got in trouble." As the bank's disgrace has grown, a number of former employees have indicated that senior executives should have heeded their warnings years earlier.[127]

In some branches, Wells Fargo managers alerted new employees about the need to come forward if they witnessed their colleagues opening phony accounts or issuing bogus credit cards. But often employees turned a blind eye to these infractions. According to one worker, "They warned us about this type of behavior and said, 'You must report it,' but the reality was the people had to meet their goals. They needed a paycheck."[128] As these events became more widely known within the community banking division in 2011, Wells Fargo dismissed several employees for opening fraudulent accounts. Two years later, in early 2013, 200 Southern California branch workers were released for questionable sales practices. Later in that same year, the *Los Angeles Times* detailed the scope of the fraudulent sales practices at Wells, and the company accelerated its efforts to deal with those employees who opened unauthorized accounts. By 2015, over 5,300 bank staff had been fired for improper behavior related to these sales practices over a five-year period. Finally, under continued political pressures, the bank's firings reached the higher echelons of management. In February 2017, Wells Fargo fired four senior managers in the bank's retailing business, including its chief risk officer and consumer credit executive.[129]

In November 2015, the *Wall Street Journal* reported that banking regulators were investigating Wells Fargo, including its sales tactics and product quotas. Wells, however, made no official disclosure about the investigation. By the summer of 2016, the story was front-page news, and in September, Wells Fargo was ordered to pay a $185 million fine for creating accounts without customer authorization. On September 9, 2016, in full-page ads in many newspapers, the bank proclaimed its "full responsibility" for the growing scandal. However, the ad did not include a formal apology to customers from CEO John Stumpf.[130]

As public pressure mounted on the bank's executives, Stumpf blamed some miscreant Wells employees and their managers for this debacle. He defended the firm and informed the media that the bank had taken the necessary steps to stop the behavior that included opening accounts for customers without permission. Stumpf also seemed to dismiss the idea that there was a systemic problem at the bank or that the behavior of these employees was the result of its cross-selling strategy or its incentive program. According to Stumpf, "There was no incentive to do bad things." Those employees who broke the rules did not properly respect the bank's culture by failing to put the customer first and honoring the bank's vision. But he indicated that the bank would eliminate some practices that may have contributed to the problem, such as branch-level product sales quotas. However, Stumpf continued to commend and defend the strategy of cross-selling.[131]

On September 20, 2016, Stumpf testified before the Senate Banking Committee, where he continued to blame rogue individual employees for the unauthorized accounts. He insisted the sales problems were not indicative of "deeper cultural flaws" within the company, nor did these actions constitute in any way some type of "massive fraud," as they had been portrayed by the media. In response to one senator's questions, Stumpf offered few specifics about when he actually learned about these abusive sales practices. However, the CEO acknowledged that the bank had not moved fast enough after it learned about the scope of the misbehavior in 2011. Nonetheless, the committee was quite dissatisfied with his responses.[132] At the end of her questioning, Senator Elizabeth Warren offered an especially harsh assessment of Stump's flawed leadership:

> Have you returned one nickel of the money that you earned while this scandal was going on? Have you fired any senior management, the people who actually oversaw this fraud? Your definition of accountability is to push this on your low-level employees. This is gutless leadership.[133]

Ten days later, Stumpf was grilled by members of the House Financial Services Committee. Once again he provided few specifics to defend the bank's actions or explain how these activities had gone on for so long without the knowledge of senior executives and auditors. Congressman Roger Williams seemed to sum up the committee's sentiment: "I'm amazed at what you do not know about your business."[134]

The Fallout and the Future

In a serious blow to Wells Fargo's reputation, the treasurer of California suspended many of its ties with the bank because of the "venal abuse of its customers." The bank could no longer underwrite certain California municipal bonds. The treasurer, John Chiang, also suspended purchase of Wells Fargo securities. The state's unusual move will likely cost Wells Fargo millions of dollars in lost fees, since California is one of the largest issuers of municipal debt in the United States.[135]

In late September 2016, the Wells Fargo board finally stepped into action as it withdrew $60 million in bonuses, $41 million for Stumpf and $19 million for Tolstedt. The board of directors also announced the immediate retirement of Carrie Tolstedt, the senior executive vice president of community banking where the phony accounts were created. There was no evidence that Tolstedt knew of these bogus accounts and questionable practices. However, Tolstedt was later singled out in a report prepared for the Wells Fargo board as the one who set the tone for the bank's retail operations. She is described as being "scared to death" over not making her sales quotas and of running her division in an "insular and defensive way."[136]

Not long after his appearance before Congress, chairman and chief executive officer John Stumpf stepped down from both roles. Feeling the pressure from within and outside the bank, Stumpf reluctantly concluded that he could not continue leading the bank through this ongoing sales-tactics scandal. The report prepared for the Wells board later criticized Stumpf for being too late and too slow to deal with this crisis. He failed to appreciate this was a systemic problem, and not one isolated to a few groups of corrupt employees and their managers. According to that report, "He refused to believe that the sales model was seriously impaired."[137]

Mr. Stumpf was replaced by chief operating officer Timothy Sloan. Sloan's primary task was to restore the battered reputation of Wells Fargo as he navigated the company through a host of federal and state investigations. Sloan also had to contend with the impact of the scandal on the retail business. Both consumer checking account openings and credit card applications were down over 20% in the latter part of 2016 when the scandal first broke. The company also had to work out a new incentive plan that would encourage sales without the risks of Wells Fargo's past approach. As a first step toward restoring credibility, the bank has embarked on a long process of refunding customers for improper charges. Sloan also indicated he wanted to focus on customer concerns and ensure that the bank had the right product and services. While the bank has ended its product sales quotas, it has no immediate plans to end its cross-selling strategy.[138]

Despite the change in leadership, a full year after the sales practices scandal, Wells Fargo was still losing ground to its rivals. Wells Fargo's shares badly underperformed those rivals during this period, and the firm's market value had fallen by $4.5 billion. On the other hand, Bank of America's market capitalization had risen by $82 billion and J.P. Morgan Chase & Co.'s had increased by $69 billion. The bank has had to contend with more investigations and lawsuits. In addition, in September 2017, Wells Fargo reported that it now believed 3.5 million ghost accounts had been opened by its employees, up from the 2.1 million reported in the fall of 2016. The new figures brought renewed attention to the scandal as investors wondered when the bank would begin to grow its revenues and improve its profit margins.[139]

EXHIBIT 6.2 ■ Wells Fargo Financials, 2013–2016 (in millions)				
	2013	2014	2015	2016
Total Assets	$1,523,502	$1,687,155	$1,787,632	$1, 930,115
Total Revenue	88,059	88,772	90,033	94,176
Net Profit	21,821	23,057	22,894	21,938

EXHIBIT 6.3 ■ Revenue Breakdown for 2016 (in billions)	
Community/retail banking	$49.3
Wholesale banking	$25.9
Wealth management	$15.8

- Explain the specific allegations against Wells Fargo. What is your assessment of these allegations? Which ones are the most troubling?

- How big a problem is this scam for Wells Fargo? Is it just a group of rogue employees or something more systemic and widespread?

- What organizational and cultural factors have contributed to its problems? How can the company's cultural problems be rectified?

- Has Wells Fargo lived up to its economic, legal, and ethical obligations? Which moral duties or rights have been violated by Wells Fargo employees (cf. DRJ model)?

- How well has Wells Fargo handled this crisis? What have they done right and what mistakes have they made?

CONCLUSION

Beyond those clearly defined fiduciary duties to shareholders and investors, there are moral duties as well. The insider-trading case series exposed the acute problems that arise when corporate insiders shirk their duties to shareholders in favor of their own vested interests. In the LIBOR and Goldman Sachs cases the focus shifts from fiduciary duties to extralegal considerations and common moral problems such as honesty, fraud, and conflicts of interest. Particularly disturbing in the Goldman case was the opaqueness of financial mechanisms that stymied regulators and confused investors. The final case on Wells Fargo anticipates the next two chapters by dealing with dysfunctional corporate cultures and their impact on maintaining corporate integrity.

Student Study Site

Key Terms

corporate insider   111

fiduciary   111

insider trading   113

LIBOR   122

material information   113

nonpublic information   113

temporary insider   114

tippee   114

Review Question

1. Explain as clearly as possible the concept of fiduciary duty. In addition to fiduciary duties, what moral obligations do managers have to their shareholders?

Discussion Questions

1. Are the general insider-trading laws in the United States beneficial for the economy? Should those laws be more precise and how could they be adjusted to better serve the public interest?

2. Based on these cases, what is your assessment of the ethical standards and behavior on Wall Street? Does the investment industry deserve its bad reputation (as depicted in movies such as *Wall Street*)?

7

PATIENTS, PATENTS, AND THE PHARMACEUTICAL INDUSTRY

Valeant's monopoly model operates at the expense of real people.

—Sen. Susan Collins (R-Maine)[1]

It would be theoretically possible for us to give away all our drugs. Everyone would get it for a while, and then we'd go bankrupt.

—David Barry[2]

LEARNING OBJECTIVES

Upon completion of this chapter, you should be able to:

7.1   State the rationale for patents and intellectual property protection.

7.2   Express the dynamics of the heavily regulated pharmaceutical industry.

7.3   Review and debate the economic, legal, and ethical duties of pharmaceutical firms to their stakeholders, especially doctors, patients, and society.

This entire chapter is dedicated to the pharmaceutical and biotech industries, which have created many revolutionary drugs thanks in part to the wonders of genetic engineering. However, the pharmaceutical industry has come under powerful scrutiny in recent years for high prices and excess profits, even as its biggest companies face declining returns on their research dollars. Mylan, for example, was pilloried in the press for excessive price increases of the EpiPen, which reverses allergic reactions. A pack of two EpiPens sold for $609 in 2016, up 548% since 2007. And Marathon Pharmaceuticals faced mounting criticism when it tried to launch its new treatment for muscular dystrophy at an annual cost of $89,000. Political leaders, doctors, and patients accused these and other firms of predatory pricing in order to fatten their bottom line. Responsible pricing and affordable access to lifesaving medicine remain critical issues thanks to the pricing policies of companies like Marathon.

Pharmaceutical companies seem virtually immune to economic cycles due to the high inelasticity of demand for their products—no matter what the price, people need certain drugs to alleviate pain or treat their illnesses. Moreover, many pharmaceutical products enjoy the benefits of patent protection. Patents provide a limited monopoly that constrains competition and leads to higher prices. Yet without a patent, Big Pharma companies would not invest billions of dollars in research. Some empirical data suggest that the industry needs patents to survive. But what can be done about those who are excluded from medical treatment because they cannot afford lifesaving medication? The issues in this industry are complex and will not likely be resolved by simplistic solutions such as the elimination of patents or exclusive reliance on market-based solutions.

We begin this chapter with a short briefing that provides essential background on patents and intellectual property protection. It includes the prime normative justifications for limited intellectual property rights based on the theories of utilitarianism and natural rights. This briefing is followed by an industry overview that examines the evolution of Big Pharma in the United States with a particular focus on the development of the regulatory infrastructure that governs this industry. Several moral and policy issues about pricing and patents are also considered. Special attention is devoted to the questionable strategy of "evergreening" that has been adopted by some firms facing the "patent cliff." We then turn our attention to several case studies.

AN OVERVIEW OF THE CASES

We begin with Valeant Pharmaceuticals, whose business model involved buying out other companies and sharply raising the price of their undervalued drugs. Also reviewed is Valeant's problematic relationship with Philidor, one of its main distributors. The Canadian drug company defended its hefty price increases by appealing to the argument that it had to maximize shareholder value, but is this defense tenable?

The next case in this chapter highlights the industry's tepid response to the AIDS crisis, especially as the HIV/AIDS virus took hold in Africa. It examines the political and economic factors at play in developing new therapies for AIDS along with the complications involved in dealing with impoverished Africans who could not afford this medicine at any price. Should drug companies have been more proactive in responding to this crisis? Who is responsible for ensuring impoverished AIDS patients get access to the medicine they need? Companies were committed to protecting their patents, but should patent rights be waived in times of severe medical crisis?

The final case shifts our attention to the biotechnology industry and the intricate issue of gene patents. The mapping of the human genome, which indicates the location of genes on various chromosomes, opened the door for the discovery of gene mutations tied to certain diseases. Do these scientific discoveries warrant intellectual property protection? Specifically, does the biotech company Myriad Genetics deserve a patent for its labor-intensive efforts to isolate the BRCA genes, mutations of which can increase the risk of breast or ovarian cancer? Although the issue of gene patents has been recently resolved by the U.S. Supreme Court, it is useful to consider the costs and benefits of awarding a patent for isolated genes. What are the likely implications of the court's decision for medical and scientific innovation?

A NOTE ON PATENTS AND INTELLECTUAL PROPERTY RIGHTS

This short background note is designed to provide an overview of intellectual property rights as a context for understanding the cases about Big Pharma and the biotech industry. We focus here on the nature of intellectual property and how it differs from physical property. Also reviewed are the legal forms that intellectual property protection takes, and the normative justifications that have been put forth to defend intellectual property rights. While copyright and trademark are important forms of legal protection, we do not include an extensive discussion of those formats in this chapter, which is confined to the subject of patents.

What Is Intellectual Property?

The most basic principle underlying the institution of private property is the assignment to individuals and organizations of control over individual assets. It creates a "one-to-one" correlation between owners and assets, and some scholars claim this decentralized control is the optimal means of treating all forms of property, including intangible property. The logic of individual ownership control makes property management workable and effective.[3]

The concept of property is a dynamic one, since property can include both physical and intellectual objects. Unlike physical property, **intellectual property** consists of intangible objects or assets. These intangible assets (such as software programs, music, or books) are public goods. Public goods are both *nonrivalrous* and *nonexclusive*. A good is nonrivalrous if someone's consumption of that good does not affect the consumption of others. A piece of cake, for example, is a private good; if I eat the cake, no one else can enjoy it. But a recipe for a cake is a public good—everyone can get access to the recipe and enjoy the cake. A good is nonexclusive if it is difficult or even impossible to exclude or "fence out" people who haven't paid.

National security and clean air are examples of **public goods**, which are the responsibility of government. But private companies may also provide public goods, which include certain information-based assets, such as a movie or the formula for a pharmaceutical product. Since public goods are nonexcludable, there is a likelihood they will be under-produced. There must be some type of protection or government intervention that will hinder the efforts of free riders who want to copy those goods and sell them at a cheap price. Important intellectual property markets will remain underdeveloped where the up-front investment cost is high, copying is simple and inexpensive, and free riders threaten to prevent the innovator from appropriating the value that has been created.[4]

The difference between intellectual objects and physical objects also means that ownership rights will be defined and configured in a different way. One cannot (or should not) "own" an abstract idea, concept, or principle. As a result, legal protection is given only to the original *expression* of an idea. If the idea is literary or artistic in nature, it must be expressed (or "fixed") in some tangible medium such as a book or a song in order to be eligible for a copyright. And if the idea is functional in nature, such as an invention, it must be expressed in terms of a new machine, an innovative process, or some new composition of matter. The dichotomy between idea and expression is central to the system of intellectual property rights.

Legal Protection

Intellectual property is legally protected in three ways: copyright, trademarks, and patents. Copyrights protect literary expression such as books, music, and even software code. Over the years, copyright protection has been given a broader scope and the term has been lengthened. A copyright now lasts for the life of the author plus an additional 70 years. Trademarks protect brand names and logos (such as the Disney brand or the Nike swoosh symbol) and have no time limit. Our focus is on patents because of their particular relevance for the pharmaceutical and biotech industries.

A **patent** is a form of legal protection given to individuals who create an invention or process. Patent protection is covered in Title 35 of the U.S. Code. The basis for patent protection can be found in Article 1, Section 8 of the U.S. Constitution, which recognized the need for exclusive intellectual property rights "to promote the progress of Science and the useful Arts." Patents offer a 20-year limited but exclusive monopoly over the patent holder's discovery. The first explicit U.S. patent law, the Patent Act of 1793, was passed when Thomas Jefferson was the administrator of the patent system. The present U.S. patent statute is based on the Patent Act of 1952, which was amended in 1995.

According to that statute, there are two classes of patents: **process patents** for a process or method of doing something, and **product patents**, which apply to inventions or functional devices such as machines, articles of manufacture, or "compositions of matter." Pharmaceutical products are eligible for both a process patent, since one can patent the method of producing a drug, and a product patent, since drugs are compositions of matter. In addition to the proper subject matter, the Patent Act requires three other conditions to be satisfied before a patent can be granted. First, an invention must have a certain *usefulness* or utility in order to be awarded a patent. "A patent is not a hunting license," remarked a famous judge as he refused a patent for a chemical process that had no useful result.[5] Second, the invention must be *novel* or new to qualify for a patent. One cannot simply modify an existing invention, unless the modification is significant enough to make a "qualified difference." Third, the invention or novel process must be *nonobvious*. An invention is considered nonobvious if someone "skilled in the art" would not know how to achieve the improvement over the "prior art" that is accomplished by this new invention.[6]

Current law allows for three forms of patents: design patents, utility patents, and plant patents. **Design patents** protect any new, original, and ornamental design for an article of manufacture, while **utility patents** protect any new, useful, and nonobvious process, machine, or article of manufacture. Whatever the form, patent protection always provides a corporate or individual inventor the right to exclude others from making, using, selling, or importing the claimed invention for a 20-year period.

From an economic perspective, patents are necessary to solve a market failure: the underproduction of public goods. By awarding a patent, the government confers upon the patent holder this exclusive property right to a certain asset, which means that it cannot be copied by rivals. This allows the company or individual awarded such a patent to reap higher rewards than would be possible in a competitive market. Without direct competition to drive prices down, the patent holder can charge the profit-maximizing price. The prospect of these big profits or high economic returns encourages firms to invest and take risks in order to innovate. Patents, therefore, provide an environment conducive to securing the capital needed to commercialize innovations and bring them to the marketplace.[7]

While patents may be necessary to ensure that certain public goods such as drugs are not underproduced, these limited monopolies have a social cost. The introduction of patents for pharmaceutical products solves one market failure but creates another. Patents allow companies to charge a price well above marginal cost, and this high price excludes some potential buyers from the market. For example, patients may need a certain patented drug but not be able to afford this drug's premium price, which is set to maximize profits. Patents therefore create an "exclusion" or "access" problem. This exclusion is morally troublesome in some cases, especially when lifesaving medicines are involved. The question of how to preserve patent protection while also addressing the access problem is at the heart of many moral conundrums that confront Big Pharma firms.[8]

Normative Justifications

What are the moral foundations of copyright and patent laws? Are intellectual property rights genuine moral rights or are they just legal ones that exist purely for the sake of expediency? There are two main avenues for addressing these questions.

Utilitarian Arguments

Intellectual property rights are commonly defended on moral or principled grounds from a purely consequentialist or utilitarian perspective. Utilitarian ethics evaluates actions or policies by their results. According to this theory, the right course of action is to promote the general good. This general good can also be described in terms of "utility," which simply refers to whatever produces pleasure or "happiness" and minimizes pain. Under this model, the moral propriety of intellectual property protection rests on cost/benefit calculations. Intellectual property rights such as copyrights and patents are justified because the benefits of increased creative or inventive activities outweigh the costs. In the absence of such rights, for example, an innovative company's new drug would be copied by competitors, and the company would find its economic returns too small to justify the costs of innovation. In such a situation, it would not develop new drugs, and social welfare would presumably suffer. According to *Mazer v. Stein*, the "philosophy behind the clause empowering Congress to grant patents and copyrights is the conviction that encouragement of individual efforts by personal gain is the best way to advance public welfare through the talents of authors and inventors in 'Science and useful Arts.'"[9]

The utilitarian or instrumental justification assumes it is society's duty to adopt policies and take actions that, ceteris paribus, yield the largest achievable net gain in expected utility.[10] To that end, a system of intellectual property rights is essential for a society that seeks to maximize innovation and creativity in order to enhance social welfare. Without the above-market rewards associated with these rights, there will be fewer creations or inventions that benefit society. Free riders will force the price of the intangible creation or physical invention down to its marginal cost of production. Over time, this free copying will erode the incentive to invest in expensive innovations such as new medicines.

This version of utilitarianism represents a classic ex ante justification of property rights. It is often referred to in economic terms as a "reward theory," because it claims that without those substantial monetary rewards, certain works would not be created or invented. The benefits of this system are weighed against the social costs, such as lost consumer surplus, monopoly rents, and limited access. Policy makers must strike the right balance to ensure that the number and quality of innovative products are maximized while minimizing the cost to society. Authors and inventors should receive only those rights that promote economic efficiency and enhance social welfare.[11]

Consider the case of patents. Kieff offers a convincing argument that a property right in the form of a patent is essential for facilitating investment in the invention *and* commercialization of new products, especially ones requiring a big up-front investment of research and development (R&D).[12] Popular alternatives such as cash rewards offered by the government to inventors do not address the commercialization activities that take place after an invention is developed but before it can be profitably exploited in the marketplace. On the other hand, an exclusive patent right provides an incentive to incur the costs necessary to commercialize this new innovation.

The primary problem with instrumental arguments is their ultimate indeterminacy—there is a lack of empirical data that can support the correct policy choices aimed at maximizing social welfare. There are some studies (such as those cited by Kieff) indicating that property rights play a limited role in promoting innovation, particularly in certain industries.[13] But for the most part the evidence is not adequate to help identify the optimal level of patent and copyright protection that will promote economic efficiency. According to Priest, "The inability of economists to resolve the question of whether activity stimulated by the patent system or other forms of protection of intellectual property enhances or diminishes social welfare implies . . . that economists can tell lawyers very little about how to enforce or interpret the law of intellectual property."[14]

Property as a Natural Right

A second normative justification is based on the work of John Locke, especially the arguments presented in the *Second Treatise on Government*. With Lockean theory there is a shift from the rhetoric of social utility and pragmatism to a discussion of intellectual property as a matter of justice and as a fundamental right.[15]

According to Locke, the foundation of a property right is within the person himself: "Man (by being master of himself, and proprietor of his own person, and the actions or labor of it) had still in himself the great Foundation of Property."[16] And since every person has "property in his own person," by extension he also has property in "the labor of his body and the work of his hands" (II, §27). According to Locke, it logically follows that if a person has a property right, understood as the right to exclude others, in her body, she must also have a property right in the labor she performs. The ownership of labor, which derives from the ownership of one's body, becomes the ground for legitimate appropriation, because it also follows that one owns what is produced by that labor. When a person takes something from the commons, "he has mixed his labor with it and joined to it something that is his own and thereby makes it his property. . . . For this labor being the unquestionable property of the laborer, no man but he can have a right to what that is once joined to" (II, §27). In summary, one owns one's body and the labor it produces, and mixing one's labor with common, preexisting resources gives rise to property rights.[17]

The "appropriative labor" described by Locke, which is the source of a valid property claim, must be *purposeful*, that is, it must transform what is held in common in some way to make it useful or valuable so it satisfies human needs. We must regard labor not as something that is literally mixed with things but as a purposeful activity whose aim is to satisfy basic human requirements, often by transforming nature. Labor personalizes objects and incorporates them within our sphere of influence so we can successfully pursue our plans and projects. According to Simmons, "We bring things within our purposive activities ('mixing our labor' with them) when we gather them, hunt them, enclose them, and use them in other productive ways."[18]

There are limits, however, to what people can validly acquire through their labor. According to Locke, a person should only appropriate property sufficient for his or her needs. This restriction is known as the Lockean proviso: "Labor being the unquestionable Property of the Laborer, no man but he can have a right to what that is once joined to, *at least where there is enough and as good left in common for others*" (II, §27). According to this moral principle, one can only appropriate an object from the commons through labor when there is enough and as good for others. This proviso includes the *sufficiency* limitation which implies that one should only appropriate what is sufficient for his or her needs. In addition, individuals should not be wasteful and take from the commons more than they can use "to any advantage of life before it spoils" (II, §31).

Although Locke had in mind physical property such as land, this theory is naturally applicable to intellectual property as well. Mental labor is no different from physical labor; both are extensions of the person and belong to the person. It's certainly logical that those who expend intellectual labor and transform resources in the intellectual commons into a unique creative product have a valid claim to ownership. In keeping with the Lockean proviso, however, a property right should be recognized only if an author or inventor's use or borrowing from the commons or public domain does not diminish the stock of ideas, algorithms, concepts, principles, and other resources found in that domain. Copyrights and patents, therefore, protect expression, not ideas, so that others can build upon those same ideas.

Summation

These two theoretical justifications of intellectual property rights are often invoked in legal rulings that reinforce patent or copyright protection. But patent and copyright doctrine tends to rely more heavily on the incentive justification based on the utilitarian reasoning that is found in the Constitution itself. According to Benkler, "The basic ideological commitment of American intellectual property is actually heavily utilitarian, not Lockean or Hegelian."[19] Nonetheless, the Lockean paradigm provides a cohesive argument for property rights based on a simple principle: one owns one's body, and thus one's labor, and therefore the product of that labor. While utilitarian arguments cannot be casually dismissed, Locke's approach gives the limited rights associated with patents and copyrights a strong philosophical and ethical foundation.[20]

BRIEFING ON BIG PHARMA AND INDUSTRY REGULATIONS

This industry background note dwells on the origins, history, and complex market structure of the pharmaceutical industry in the United States. It also reviews the genesis of the regulatory infrastructure governing this industry. The goal is to understand how firms like Merck and Pfizer became such global powerhouses along with the rationale for the state's "heavy hand." Industry regulations include patent protection, which resolves the public-goods problem, but they also include requirements for safety and efficacy testing.

This analysis concludes with a discussion of the industry's major current trends and ethical controversies. Big Pharma has been accused of "profiteering" at the hands of the sick, but it faces steep research and development cost increases. Big Pharma firms must also contend with the "patent cliff," as patents on its "blockbuster" drugs expire at a record pace, opening the way for generic competition. One of the issues considered is the dubious response of some firms that have adopted novel strategies to block or delay generic competition. We begin with a brief overview of the major global players in this industry.

Big Pharma: The Major Players

In the last century, medical research has led to the cure for many diseases while significantly reducing the pain and burdens imposed by others. At the forefront of that research in the private sector has been the pharmaceutical industry, which earns huge returns from these research breakthroughs. The sale and distribution of prescription or so-called ethical drugs is one of the most profitable and powerful industries within the global economy. This is a $1 trillion industry, and the United States is the largest market, with over $360 billion in revenues. The term *Big Pharma* refers to the major Western pharmaceutical companies, such as Pfizer and Merck in the United States, GlaxoSmithKline in the United Kingdom, Novartis and Roche Holding Co. in Switzerland, Bayer in Germany, and Sanofi-Aventis in France. These companies have dominated this fragmented industry for quite some time.

In 2017, the U.S. firm Pfizer was the world's largest pharmaceutical operation, with revenues of $52.5 billion. Pfizer was followed by Roche, Sanofi-Aventis, Merck, and Novartis.[21] The industry has been consistently profitable during its long history, which dates back to the end of the 19th century, when "proprietary" drugs (using the manufacturer's name) were first made available. The top drug companies have typically earned high profits, but in recent years (2014–2016), return on equity (ROE) has been 16.2%, well below that of some other manufacturing industries, such as aerospace and beverages.[22] In 2017, Pfizer's net income was $8.4 billion. While pharmaceutical products require massive amounts of capital and a willingness to take big risks, these firms compete within a favorable industry structure. There are high barriers to entry because of the exorbitant cost of R&D; it is also costly to commercialize and produce certain drugs. There are high switching costs for consumers because drugs are protected by patents. Patents are limited monopolies which preclude direct imitation and lead to high prices and substantial profit margins. All of these factors make the pharmaceutical industry quite attractive for its major incumbents.

Despite consistent profitability, growth has slowed over the last few years in both Europe and the United States. Pharmaceutical companies have usually depended on a few blockbuster drugs (those with over $1 billion in global annual sales), such as Lipitor, Cialis, or Viagra, to drive profits and revenues. Among Pfizer's top drugs is Lyrica, which generated over $4 billion in revenue in 2017. To control costs and prevent the potential for holdup by suppliers or distributors, Big Pharma firms have tended to be **vertically integrated**, performing all value-chain activities in house, from research and development to manufacturing and marketing. Most pharmaceutical companies still spend vast sums of money on R&D. In 2016, the two biggest U.S. companies, Pfizer and Merck, continued to make sizable investments in R&D. They spent $7.8 billion and $9.7 billion respectively, excluding special charges. Merck was the global industry leader in R&D expenditures, followed by Roche, which spent $8.7 billion.[23]

Origins of the U.S. Drug Industry

The pharmaceutical industry traces its origins back to the 19th century, when large wholesalers such as Merck and Smith, Kline & French began to offer proprietary drugs to pharmacists, druggists, and other retailers. They sold patented "ethical" drugs used for a specific purpose which later became prescription drugs. They also sold over-the-counter (OTC) drugs such as aspirin, which were available without a prescription. Most of their early concentration was on the blossoming OTC market. During this time, they invested far more in marketing and advertising than in research and development. In the early 20th century, drug companies marketed a broad range of OTC proprietary drugs and eventually expanded into related consumer markets such as soaps, shampoo, and toothpaste.[24]

Between the two wars, the pharmaceutical industry continued its low-level investment in R&D, since drug technology remained fairly stable. Things began to change in 1935, however, with the discovery of the antibiotic medicine called sulfa or sulfanilamide, a "miracle" drug that was effective against bacterial pneumonia and other infections. Sulfa drugs and their derivatives were revolutionary and played a pivotal role in the future of drug research.[25]

In the midst of World War II in the 1940s, the "therapeutic revolution" began. The war inspired the search for new antibiotics, and this led to the development of penicillin, whose antibacterial action was more potent than sulfa. The U.S. government spent $3 million subsidizing penicillin research. The first successful human use of the drug was in 1941, and, thanks to new production techniques, enough penicillin was being manufactured by 1943 to satisfy the military's urgent needs. After the war, the drug remained in great demand and was produced by 19 drug companies.[26]

The commercial success of sulfa and penicillin led to a surge of new research. The drug industry transformed itself from an ordinary manufacturing industry to one based on the continual progress of technical knowledge and scientific research. As a result, there were many important breakthroughs. There were new drugs for heart and lung disease, cancer, and diabetes. There was also a renewed focus on preventative medicine through the introduction of multiple vaccines and vitamins.[27] In the 1950s, the number of new drugs introduced each year rose to over 50 as companies devoted more capital to R&D. Thanks to this steady stream of new medications and scientific discoveries, not only did the traditional pharmaceutical industry change beyond recognition, but so too did the practice of medicine. In a profound shift, doctors were transformed into healers, and patients, who demanded sulfa drugs for almost every ailment, became consumers.[28]

The industry also depended more heavily on patents to protect its innovations and thereby ensure a return on its investment. The typical large U.S. drug company during the 1950s and 1960s was vertically integrated and grew by introducing new patented products and therapies. These products were sold by means of aggressive marketing campaigns. Profits were reinvested in R&D and expansion of production capabilities. This powerful combination of integrated operations and patent protection meant more new drugs, growing revenues, and higher profits.[29]

Regulating a Growth Industry

In the 19th century, the sale and distribution of drugs was not heavily regulated. Yet a significant piece of regulatory legislation was enacted by the U.S. Congress as far back as 1848. The Import Drug Act required that all imported drugs be labeled with the name of the manufacturer and the place of the drug's preparation. The drug must also be inspected and tested for its "quality, purity, and fitness for medical purposes." Drugs deemed improper or unsafe could not be imported into the United States.[30]

Regulators, however, did not set the same standard for domestic manufacturers. At this time, drugs were not prescribed by doctors, so there was no way to restrict access. Any concerns over the quality and safety of drugs were typically addressed within the industry, and the federal government played a minimal role. Drug manufacturers were more concerned with improving manufacturing processes than with the development of new medicines, so R&D spending was minimized.

As the industry grew, various safety issues soon came to the public's attention. At the same time, the calls for regulation grew louder. In the early 20th century, progressive reformers called for greater government regulation of both the food and drug industries. Given the few drugs on the market at the time along with their questionable effectiveness, demands for strict controls over the sale and distribution of drugs were easily dismissed. But there was also widespread concern over food spoilage and adulteration. One motivated government official, Harvey Wiley, chief of the Division of Chemistry in the Department of Agriculture, established the "Poison Squad" in 1902 to expose harmful side effects caused by dangerous food additives like boric acid. On the other hand, political pressure from the food and agriculture industries led to the defeat of "pure-food" legislation introduced in Congress multiple times between 1871 and 1905. However, the climate changed after a series of articles in *Collier's* by Samuel Hopkins Adams titled "The Great American Fraud" exposed the nascent drug industry's false testimonials and unfounded cures for cancer. These articles were followed by the timely publication of Upton Sinclair's novel *The Jungle*. This popular book was a vivid portrait of the lack of sanitation in the meat industry that created an outcry for legislative action.[31]

Not long after these publications appeared, Congress passed the Pure Food and Drug Act of 1906, more commonly referred to as the Wiley Act. This piece of legislation was dedicated primarily to food safety, but it also prohibited the adulteration and misbranding of drugs. A drug was considered "misbranded" if it was sold under a false name, sold in the package of another drug, or failed to identify the presence and amount of addictive, dangerous substances such as alcohol, morphine, or opium. The Sherley Amendment, passed a year later, mandated that labels should not contain "any statement regarding the curative or therapeutic effect . . . which is false and fraudulent."[32] The law, therefore, made misrepresentation and fraud illegal. The new law was administered by the Bureau of Chemistry. In 1931, the Food and Drug Administration became the successor of that bureau and began to oversee the pharmaceutical industry.[33]

The Wiley Act was followed by several key drug regulations in the 1930s, principally the Federal Food, Drug, and Cosmetic Act (FFDCA) of 1938. This landmark legislation was a response to the sulfanilamide scandal. An antibacterial syrup called Elixir Sulfanilamide manufactured by Massengill killed at least 75 people, many of them young children. Sulfa was being produced in greater quantities and in different forms. It had become apparent to manufacturers that children preferred syrup to tablets. Massengill's chemists found a way to suspend sulfa in water, raspberry flavoring, and diethylene glycol, a dangerous chemical sometimes used in the manufacturing of antifreeze. The company did not test the compound for safety and shipped 240 gallons throughout the United States. The deadly syrup was quickly recalled by the new FDA, but not after a number of tragic fatalities.[34]

The FFDCA established new labeling requirements, including directions for use and suitable warnings. More importantly, the new law also required drug manufacturers to prove to the FDA that any new drug was safe before it could be marketed and sold. This requirement meant the need for extensive tests on both animals and humans. The 1938 act marked the birth of the New Drug Application (NDA). This application included safety data that was submitted to the FDA, which had the final say in determining a drug's safety and marketability. If the FDA did not disapprove the NDA within a set time period after filing, the drug could be marketed. In addition, thanks to the FFDCA, certain drugs became available only by a physician's prescription and were put out of the consumer's direct reach. Now the government, not the market, would protect the consumer and determine which drugs could be sold or not sold.[35]

As research intensified during the 1950s, the drug industry more aggressively sought to protect their innovations from copiers and free riders. Since a drug is a composition of matter, it is eligible for patent protection so long as it is novel, nonobvious, and useful. Prior to the safety testing prescribed by the FDA, there was a higher standard of utility for medicinal products; courts were wary of placing a government stamp of approval on products that might not be safe. After the FDA was given its broad powers, functional utility (rather than safety) was all that mattered when patents were awarded. The industry benefited from several key rulings in the 1950s, such as the validation of "new use" patents. This meant that if a company discovered a new use for an existing chemical substance, the process of using the compound for this new purpose would be eligible for a patent. Also, while a natural substance was not eligible for a patent, chemical modifications of a known substance that resulted in a "new composition of matter" were now patent-eligible.[36]

The 1938 act was vague on what constituted a prescription drug versus an over-the-counter drug that could be purchased without a doctor's prescription. As a result, there was constant conflict between the industry and FDA over this matter. But thanks to the 1951 Durham-Humphrey Amendment to the FFDCA, the law identified fairly clear parameters for prescription medication; it also delineated under which conditions a prescription should be refilled. Doctors prescribe drugs for their patients, and their primary motivation behind the selection of a specific drug is efficacy rather than cost.[37]

The thalidomide scandal marked another turning point in the evolution of pharmaceutical industry regulations. In the late 1950s and early 1960s, a product called thalidomide was utilized as an antinausea drug by pregnant women in Europe and Japan. The drug was effective but caused serious birth defects. The FDA had refused to approve the drug for use in the United States, but American doctors got free samples, which they eagerly distributed to some of their patients. As a result, 40 American children were born with debilitating birth defects. The thalidomide scandal was a great embarrassment for the industry and led to a new wave of regulations.[38] The Kefauver-Harris amendments to the FFDCA in 1962 established a more rigorous procedure for the approval of new drugs by requiring for the first time additional tests for a drug's efficacy or effectiveness. In addition, the amended law obliged the FDA to grant explicit approval of new drug applications rather than allowing them to go into effect through the FDA's inaction. The FDA acknowledged the burden of additional testing, and it took steps to streamline the drug approval process, including a decision in 1975 to accept data from foreign studies.[39]

In 1983, the U.S. Congress passed the Orphan Drug Act to incentivize the pharmaceutical industry to invest in treatments for rare diseases. The Orphan Drug Act provided manufacturers with several key incentives, such as federal development grants and assistance from the FDA in planning their animal and clinical trials. There was also a tax credit of 50% of clinical testing costs and an exclusive right to market an unpatentable orphan drug for seven years from the date of marketing approval. This seven-year temporary monopoly functioned as a de facto patent because it protected orphan drug manufacturers from direct competition during that period. An amendment to the act, passed in 1984, defined a rare disease as a condition affecting fewer than 200,000 people in the United States.[40]

Finally, the modern generic drug industry was greatly assisted by the 1984 law known as the Drug Price Competition and Patent Term Restoration Act (or the Hatch-Waxman Act). The law was designed to keep regulatory barriers low for generic products so there would be a "fast path" for bringing generic versions of branded drugs to market. Manufacturers could submit to the FDA an abbreviated and simplified new drug application (ANDA) for a forthcoming generic *before* the patent on the branded drug expired. These drug applications needed only to provide evidence of "bioequivalency" and demonstrate that the generic had the same therapeutic characteristics as their branded counterpart. Generic manufacturers were also given latitude by the FDA to use their production lines for multiple drugs to contain costs.[41] At the same time, Hatch-Waxman authorized the extension of drug patents for up to five years to compensate for the time lost when drugs were going through the testing and approval process mandated by the FDA.[42]

With the advent of efficacy as well as safety testing, the drug development and approval process became much longer and complex as a drug made its way from the start of pre-clinical testing to final FDA approval. According to the Council of Advisors on Science and Technology, it now takes about 14 years to bring a new drug to market—this is an increase from 8 years in the 1960s.[43] Phase I and II testing using healthy volunteers is focused on the drug's safety. Phase III is a large study for efficacy and proper dosing in the intended patient population. Following the successful completion of Phase III testing, an application for approval is submitted to the FDA. A fourth phase of post-market monitoring is sometimes required due to the fact that even large clinical trials cannot accurately predict the occurrence of harmful side effects.

In more recent years, the number of new drug applications approved for markets has dropped dramatically. In 1996, 58 drugs were approved for sale in the United States, but from 2005 onward, the number of drug approvals has averaged just over 20 per year. Since the drugs that eventually reach the market take much longer to develop and test, they cost more. One of the underlying factors behind the decline of new drug approvals was another landmark event: Merck's 2004 controversial decision to withdraw the FDA-approved arthritis drug Vioxx over concerns that it was causing cardiovascular problems in patients. The result was a more pronounced "safety first" approach on the part of the FDA. This meant raising the bar for drug approvals.[44]

In summary, public-policy initiatives for the pharmaceutical industry have been based on two fundamental objectives: protect consumers and stimulate innovation, A secondary objective is promotion of the rapid introduction of generics in order to address the issue of affordability. Hence the requirements for stringent safety and efficacy testing along with a mandate to provide extensive data to the FDA, including proposed labeling information as well as records to verify production methods. According to Peter Temin, "The government, not the market, will weed out worthless products and misleading labels."[45] On the other hand, the government expanded the scope of patent protection and provided some additional incentives for new drug research. These two objectives, protecting consumers and incentivizing R&D, are in obvious tension with each other. The more safety and efficacy tests there are, the higher the costs of producing drugs and the less companies have to spend on R&D. Finally, through legislation like Hatch-Waxman, regulators have sought to balance adequate patent protection for original innovations with policies that support the prompt launch of generics once the patent protection has elapsed.[46]

There is an obvious trade-off between the expeditious approval of new drugs and the risk of negative side effects, which often take time to be properly identified. This accounts for the length of the clinical trials. Some industry critics, however, argue that over the years, the FDA has become increasingly risk averse, especially in the wake of the Vioxx controversy. There are repeated calls for allowing terminally ill patients access to medicines that may save their lives, even if those medicines are still in the testing phase. The FDA does allow access to experimental drugs on a limited basis through its compassionate use program, but the vast majority of people who need medicine do not gain access to experimental medication. One of the biggest obstacles is that drug manufacturers cannot charge above cost, so they have little incentive to participate. Darcy Olsen argues that terminally ill patients who have exhausted all conventional options should have a "right to try" an experimental treatment (under certain conditions). To qualify, a drug must have passed Phase I safety testing. Once it is ensured that a drug is safe and the patient's doctor concurs that this drug is necessary, the patient gets access to the experimental medicine without the FDA's approval. The issue of who should pay for the treatment (private insurers, Medicaid, etc.) is still a matter of heated debate.[47]

Internal Growth Followed by Industry Consolidation

Merck and Pfizer dominated the American drug industry well after World War II and the therapeutic revolution. But at the center of the industry stood the "old line pharmaceutical

TABLE 7.1   ■   Summary of Drug Regulation

Regulation	Year	Description	Comment
Import Drug Act	1848	Mandates examination of imported drugs for quality and purity	Remained in effect until 1922
Federal Food and Drug Act (Wiley Act)	1906	Labeling requirement—no adulteration or misbranding of drugs	*Collier's* exposé goads Congress to act
Federal Food, Drug, and Cosmetic Act (FFDCA)	1938	Safety testing required for all prescription drugs; birth of NDA	Sulfanilamide scandal: untested solvent led to many deaths and worries about safety
Durham-Humphrey Amendment to FFDCA	1951	Identified clear parameters for what constituted a prescription drug	1938 act vague on difference between prescription and nonprescription drugs
Kefauver-Harris Amendment to FFDCA	1962	Efficacy tests required for all prescription drugs; manufacturers must prove drugs are effective as well as safe	Thalidomide scandal induces Congress to strengthen drug regulations
Orphan Drug Act	1983	Tax incentives and 7 years' market exclusivity for nonpatentable orphan drugs with a patient population under 200,000	20 million Americans suffer from 5,000 rare diseases
Drug Price Competition and Patent Term Restoration Act (Hatch-Waxman)	1984	Abbreviates and simplifies application for generic drugs and facilitates manufacturing processes	Act also authorized patent extension for up to five years to compensate for loss of patent life during testing

companies" such as Eli Lilly; Squibb; Smith, Kline & French; Abbott; and Upjohn, which were all major industry players. These vertically integrated firms with their extensive research capabilities expanded abroad and diversified beyond proprietary drugs into the OTC market. Most of them moved quickly to exploit the new opportunities provided by biochemistry and enzymology.[48]

Eli Lilly, for example, became the primary producer of antibiotics in the United States. It pioneered new drugs such as Prozac (an antidepressant) and the highly effective antibiotic Ceclor. Both were blockbuster products that drove revenue growth in the 1980s and 1990s. Abbott Labs focused successfully on antibiotics, tranquilizers, and cardiovascular medicine. It diversified through acquisitions, but not always with great success. It also undertook a major transition into the growing field of medical diagnostic devices and supplies.[49]

The two principal U.S. firms, Merck and Pfizer, continued to consolidate the leadership positions they had developed after the war. Merck invested heavily in R&D and created the U.S. industry's largest research establishment. Its investments paid off, and during the 1980s, Merck produced more of the 50 best-selling drugs than any other U.S. company. It specialized in vaccines, drugs for high blood pressure and heart disease, and cholesterol drugs such as Zocor. During the mid-1980s, Merck's ROE peaked at 27% and the company boasted 13 drugs with over $100 million in annual revenue. Under the exceptional leadership of Roy Vagelos, it began to acquire technical capabilities in molecular biology and signed contractual agreements with new biotech firms such as Biogen and Genzyme. By 2000, Merck employed 62,000 people located in over 100 countries.[50]

Pfizer, a first mover in antibiotics during World War II, became the leading manufacturer of penicillin. It continued to exploit its capabilities by introducing a new "broad spectrum antibiotic" called Terramycin. These drugs were an improvement over penicillin, since they were effective against almost every sort of pathogenic bacteria (including eye infections, respiratory ailments, and even skin lesions). By 1952, Americans were spending over $100 million annually for these broad-spectrum antibiotics.[51] Pfizer also developed vaccines for polio as well as drugs for the treatment of diabetes. When demand for these drugs declined, Pfizer embarked on a bold diversification strategy into the OTC market. As a result, the company lagged behind rivals such as Merck in terms of research spending, but in the 1980s changed its strategy and concentrated on strengthening its prescription drug capabilities. Pfizer invested more heavily in basic research, and by 1992, R&D spending had reached $1.2 billion. This research led to the discovery of profitable breakthrough drugs such as Zoloft, Viagra, and Norvasc, which were successfully marketed in the 1990s.[52]

For decades, most of these American companies demonstrated exceptional financial performance: strong sales growth, high profitability, and impressive earnings per share. Merck, Pfizer, Eli Lilly, and Abbott Laboratories consistently had a return on sales of 15% to 20%, with Merck usually outperforming its rivals. Some of the pharmaceutical companies that did not perform as well as these four merged with other companies as the industry began to consolidate. Smith Kline, which pursued a flawed diversification strategy, merged with the British firm Beecham PLC to become SmithKline Beecham. It later merged with Glaxo Wellcome to become GlaxoSmithKline (GSK), one of the largest firms in the industry today. Squibb, which had delved heavily into cancer research, also struggled, and merged with Bristol-Myers in 1989 to form Bristol-Myers Squibb.[53]

In the last two decades, the industry has been further transformed as this consolidation trend has intensified. From 1995 to 2015, 60 pharmaceutical companies have been combined through a series of mergers and acquisitions into 10 global Big Pharma giants. Pfizer, for example, acquired Warner-Lambert in 2000 for $111.8 billion, which gave it control of the blockbuster cholesterol drug Lipitor. In 2009, Merck merged with Schering-Plough in a $41 billion deal. The Swiss firm and industry leader Novartis was created in 1996 from the merger of Ciba-Geigy and Sandoz Laboratories. And the French giant Sanofi-Aventis, which is the result of a series of mergers between Sanofi-Synthèlabo and Aventis, acquired the U.S. biotech firm Genzyme in 2013.[54]

Many factors, such as expiring patents and higher R&D expenses, have led to these strategic mergers. In Merck's case, the patent for its blockbuster bone drug Fosamax had expired, and the same thing was about to happen in a few years to its best-selling allergy and asthma drug called Singulair. The merger gave Merck access to several successful brand-name Schering products with much longer patents, such as the prescription allergy spray Nasonex. Merck also believed it could capitalize on Schering's extensive investments in promising biotechnology drugs.[55]

The Road Ahead: Challenges and Controversies

Despite the industry's historically high financial performance, difficult trials lie ahead. One of the pharmaceutical industry's biggest problems is the so-called **patent cliff**: the expiration of patents on well-known blockbuster drugs. Immensely profitable products like Lipitor, Plavix, and Zyprexa are no longer protected from competition. Pfizer was particularly hard hit when the patent expired on its highly effectual cholesterol-lowering drug Lipitor. Lipitor, with total sales of over $125 billion from 1996 until generic market entry in 2011, had been the best-selling drug in Big Pharma's history. The Lipitor annual revenue stream helped propel Pfizer into the industry leader. Similarly, in 2013, after years of profitable sales, Merck had to face fierce generic competition for its three top-selling drugs: Fosamax, which treats osteoporosis, Singulair, a therapy for asthma, and its popular blood pressure drug called Cozaar.

Generic products usually reduce a branded drug's sales by half during the first six months of competition. When a generic drug is introduced, it is initially sold at a 20% discount from the branded product for its first six months, and then the price drops off abruptly from that point. Most generics are eventually priced at an 80% to 85% discount from the branded medications. As a result, the brand-name drugs, still sold at a premium price, rapidly lose their market share.[56]

Pfizer's reaction to the patent cliff has been the source of some controversy. The company pursued aggressive strategies to extend its patent protection for Lipitor by filing patent applications that claimed the discovery of new uses for the drug. The U.S. Patent Office rejected these claims, but Pfizer was able to extend its patent for several months by appealing this negative decision.[57] Pfizer also engaged in a long battle with the first generic filer for Lipitor, the Indian pharmaceutical firm Ranbaxy. The complex litigation led to delayed entry for the generic version of Lipitor. In the 2008 settlement, Ranbaxy agreed to delay the release of its generic product until 2011, and in return, Pfizer gave Ranbaxy the exclusive right to market generic Lipitor in 11 international markets.[58]

Other companies have relied on techniques like "evergreening" to thwart generic competition. **Evergreening** is an attempt to "refresh" a patented product by making a modification to the drug's delivery mechanism, its dosage, or other characteristics. The goal is to make this new version of the drug eligible for a new patent. Several Big Pharma firms have used this tactic as part of a strategy known as "product hopping." As a patent is about to expire, a company makes a minor change to the patented drug and introduces the revised formulation as an entirely new drug. The new drug will be protected by a patent, so generic competitors will be blocked from this new market. The aim is to shift the market away from the old drug as it approaches the patent cliff. The pharmaceutical company takes advantage of its established market power to move pharmacists, doctors, and patients to this new version of the branded drug before the generic drug for the old version is released in the marketplace. Its sales reps, for example, will extol the benefits of the new drug and encourage doctors to write prescriptions for that drug instead of the old one.[59]

AstraZeneca, for example, orchestrated a very successful product hop as its famous drug Prilosec approached its impending patent cliff in 2001. The company's researchers made a slight molecular modification of this heartburn drug to create a brand-new drug called Nexium. The prescription drug Nexium received a new patent, and Prilosec became an over-the-counter drug. AstraZeneca then shifted the prescription market away from Prilosec to Nexium by persuading doctors to prescribe this new brand. Some doctors and health care experts, however, have argued that Nexium is no different from its predecessor, Prilosec. "Nexium is no more effective than Prilosec," said an insurance executive. "I'm surprised anyone has ever written a prescription for Nexium."[60]

Higher Costs and Premium Prices

Another critical issue for this industry is the exceptionally high cost of research and development. A new study by the Center for Drug Development at Tufts University estimates that the average cost for developing a new drug is $2.6 billion. This high development cost includes $1.2 billion for the cost of capital required for R&D. The remaining $1.4 billion is the average R&D cost for a random selection of drugs multiplied by the risk factors for failure at any stage in the development process. This takes into account the money spent by drug firms on many failed research projects (such as the $800 million Pfizer spent on a cholesterol drug that failed during the testing phase).[61] Critics, such as Doctors without Borders and other consumer groups, criticized the methodology for including the cost of failures. But the study's main author, Joseph DeMasi, argued that failures should be included as part of the cost, "since real money is spent." Fewer failures will lower the cost of drug development.[62]

In addition, in light of the high costs of research and development, major drug companies have sought to acquire new drugs instead of developing them. The industry is now reversing course, however, by narrowing its focus after many decades of acquisitions to diversify their drug portfolio. Companies want to focus on specific sectors where they believe they have the capacity and expertise to compete effectively. As a result, several companies like Novartis and GSK have grown much slimmer over the past few years.[63]

Higher R&D costs, of course, translate into higher prices. When a new drug called Dupixent, a treatment for atopic dermatitis (a common form of eczema), was released in 2017 at a price tag of $37,000 per annual dose, there was little protest. Industry analysts and health care executives recognized the high development and testing costs for this new medication, and hence they believed this price was "responsible." Sanofi did not make its cost data public, but documented the long research and commercialization process along with the complex testing phases. Researchers had to uncover the underlying causes of atopic disorders, and testing included three expensive, randomized, Phase 3 trials.[64] On the other hand, prices for older, patented drugs continue to spiral upward. Drug prices rose by an average of 14% a year between 2011 and 2015. Drug price increases have declined in the last few years. In 2017, the median price increase was 8.9%, still well above the U.S. inflation rate of about 2%.[65]

Anxiety over the industry's high prices has been aggravated by the scandalous behavior of several non-research-based pharmaceutical firms, such as Turing and Valeant. When Martin Shkreli became CEO of Turing, he immediately raised the price of Daraprim, a drug for treating certain infections, from $13.50 to $750 per tablet. Daraprim was an off-patent drug but had no competition. These two companies were soon joined by Mylan NV, which was thrust into a harsh media spotlight when it doubled the price of the EpiPen to over $600. Politicians accused these companies of price gouging, and its executives were summoned to testify about their pricing policies before congressional committees.

These recent scandals have put pressure on companies to limit price increases, especially in the United States. Doctors and patients have complained more vociferously about exorbitant prices, especially when there appears to be little justification based on cost. Cancer drugs are especially expensive, and a group of 100 oncologists, citing the burden on cancer patients, have called for new regulations to control prices. "What we're fighting is the greed," explained an oncologist at Mayo Clinic. "The greed and the additional maneuvering that is being exercised after you've already recouped what you've invested."[66]

When Pfizer introduced its new breast cancer drug, Ibrance, in 2015, the list price of $9,850 per month was met with a torrent of criticism. A doctor who heads the Women's Cancer Center at the Dana-Farber Cancer Institute in Boston called the price tag for this and other cancer drugs "pretty outrageous." Moreover, the high price structure seemed to bear little relation to the cost of research and development. The price was based on the need and benefits of this new drug, the price of potential competing drugs, and the attitudes of cancer doctors and health plan officials. A price too high, for example, might require physicians to document "medical necessity." An internal study showed a 25% drop in doctors' willingness to prescribe the new drug if it cost more than $10,000 per month. And so, Pfizer settled on $9,850 per month, a price that would maximize revenue without inhibiting health plans from providing coverage.[67]

The pricing strategy was clear: charge whatever the market will bear and maximize profits. The criteria of "reasonable return on investment" or "affordability" did not seem to factor into the company's pricing philosophy. Ibrance has become a blockbuster drug for Pfizer, with sales in 2017 of $3.5 billion.

Drug Patents

Patents also continue to be a source of contention and even disparagement. Some critics disagree that pharmaceutical products warrant patent protection despite the high R&D

costs involved in bringing new drugs to market. Michelle Boldrin and David Levine maintain that the case for pharmaceutical patents is much thinner than we have been led to believe. They point out that many drugs are discovered by government-sponsored research, especially the National Institutes of Health (NIH), and that Big Pharma is more focused on redundant research that yields "me-too" drugs rather than on real innovation. How can we be so sure, they inquire, that valuable medicine would no longer be invented if patents were abolished? They conclude that "far from encouraging great new health and life-saving products, the system instead produces too much innovation . . . of the wrong kind—me-too drugs to get around the other guy's patents and get a share of a lucrative monopoly."[68]

Ethicists Werhane and Gorman argue that intellectual property is different from material property and that, as a result, it is difficult to maintain that this form of property really belongs to an individual or to a company. The development of new ideas, inventions, and creations is the result of a "network of interrelationships, discoveries, research and development, and exchanges of ideas, some passed down over time." While some credit might be given to the person or group of persons who ultimately "discover" that idea and bring it to fruition, we must recognize that the property in question has many "ancestral roots." Therefore, a patent assigned exclusively to an individual or company may not be the proper vehicle for protecting these discoveries. The "communal qualities" of intellectual property suggest the need to reconfigure exclusive ownership rights as "shared rights" so that the discoverer does not have the absolute control associated with the current system.[69]

To be sure, there are serious abuses in the pharmaceutical industry such as evergreening, but there is another side to the patent story, which does not always get a fair hearing. As we have seen, it is expensive and financially risky to bring efficient and safe drugs to the market. Companies will not undertake these risks and bear these costs without the prospects of high profits as a reward. That reward is made possible by the exclusive protection of a patent, a limited monopoly that allows a company to charge a profit-maximizing price that enriches the bottom line. There is some convincing empirical evidence that the pharmaceutical industry needs patents to survive. Eliminating or weakening patents by enforcing new forms of "shared rights" could appreciably reduce the volume of research and development and hence the supply of new medicines.[70]

Also, a recent study of 35 profitable blockbuster drugs showed that while NIH-sponsored research played a role in development, private-sector research geared to applied science and commercialization was indispensable. Zycher and DiMasi, who authored the study, conclude that "without the scientific advances yielded by private-sector research, most drugs would not be developed." Hence, public policies (such as those affecting patents) that lead to a reduction in private pharmaceutical research and development will reduce the economic benefits of NIH research along with "the immense medical benefits derived from the continuous development of new and improved medicines."[71] Finally, there is even a reasonable case to be made for those so-called "me-too" drugs—the first product to market is usually not the best, and follow-up products often represent significant improvements. These drugs bring more choice for patients and typically help lower prices of expensive first-to-market drugs.

CASE STUDY 7.1

THE NEW ECONOMICS OF DRUG PRICING: VALEANT PHARMACEUTICALS INTERNATIONAL

AP Photo/The Canadian Press/Ryan Remiorz

On October 16, 2015, J. Michael Pearson glanced with dismay at the glaring headline in the *Wall Street Journal*: "Valeant Probe Reprises Focus on Drug Pricing." The article reported that congressional investigators were seeking information from the firm about its steep price increases. Valeant had been assailed in the press for many months because of its pricing policies. Exorbitant drug prices tend to attract a great deal of media attention, and Valeant had become a focal point of reporting about the high price of prescription medicine. Once again, this company was making front-page news for all the wrong reasons. The primary complaint was that Valeant was boosting drug prices to meet predetermined profit targets. Valeant insisted its price increases were justified and had little effect on patient access. Nonetheless, the endless negative publicity was tarnishing Valeant's image and helping to send its stock price into a tailspin. Valeant's executives had to figure out some solution. Was a change of strategy in order, or should the company simply seek to improve its message to the media and to other stakeholders?

Valeant Pharmaceuticals International

Valeant is a multinational pharmaceutical company headquartered in Laval, Quebec. The company was founded as ICN Pharmaceuticals in 1960 by a colorful entrepreneur named Milan Panic. Panic was known for the extravagant claims he made about the health benefits of his company's drugs, and for his brief stretch as the first prime minister of post-socialist Yugoslavia. Unfortunately, under Panic's leadership, ICN persistently underperformed its local and global rivals. In 2002, after years of lackluster performance, ICN's board of directors forced Panic to resign. At the same time, the company was renamed Valeant Pharmaceuticals International, Inc. However, Valeant continued its mediocre performance and lost money for another five years. During that period, a key clinical trial on an expensive hepatitis C treatment failed, and the company was forced to write off hundreds of millions in research expense.

In 2007, the company's chairman sought outside help from J. Michael Pearson, who ran the global pharmaceuticals arm of the McKinsey consulting group. Unlike other industry executives, Pearson had neither medical degrees nor any direct experience working for a pharmaceutical company. But in his 23-year career at McKinsey, he had developed a reputation for blunt business advice. When it came to pharmaceuticals, he believed in an unorthodox approach. Given recent research inefficiencies, Pearson had advised pharmaceutical companies to reduce their research budgets and instead focus on commercially successful market-proven drugs. At the same time, he advocated a policy of higher drug prices, underscoring the price inelasticity of most prescription drug products. People have no choice but to pay higher prices for products they need for the sake of their health and well-being.[72]

In 2008, the Valeant board persuaded Pearson to become Valeant's CEO and to put this bold business philosophy into practice. Pearson joined the company that year and became the architect of Valeant's new business model. He immediately closed down many of Valeant's costly lines of research. Most of its researchers and scientists, who had been with the company for many years, were abruptly dismissed in the process. At the same time, Pearson aggressively raised the prices of many drugs in Valeant's portfolio, sometimes by three or four times their original price. The net result was an extraordinary turnaround: the company began to generate more consistent profits and higher earnings per share, to the delight of its stockholders.[73]

Over the years, Valeant began to manufacture an array of prescription drugs along with generic pharmaceuticals and over-the-counter products. It specialized in dermatology, eye health, oral health, and neurology. Its basic strategy under Pearson's leadership was rapid growth through mergers and acquisitions rather than organic, internal expansion. Valeant has been described by some as a "platform company" that grows serially by acquiring other companies.[74]

In 2013, Valeant purchased Bausch & Lomb, the well-known manufacturers of contact lenses and related products. After a failed bid for Botox maker Allergan, Inc., it acquired Salix Pharmaceuticals in late 2015 for $10 billion. Salix primarily sells products for stomach disorders, and its top-selling drug is an antibiotic called Xifaxan, a treatment for diarrhea. After the acquisition, Valeant immediately set out to exploit synergies and to cut costs by $500 million. Much of this cost savings occurred through layoffs and sizable reductions in overhead.[75]

Valeant International currently states that its mission is "improving peoples' lives with our health care products." That mission is supported by "five pillars" or guiding principles: quality health care ("bringing value to our shareholders while delivering safe and effective products is at the heart of everything we do"); customer focus; innovation; efficiency; and people ("build and retain a strong team [of employees] by recognizing and rewarding excellence").[76]

The Valeant Business Model

When Pearson became CEO, Valeant departed from the traditional business model associated with the pharmaceutical industry. Big Pharma companies invest huge sums of money in R&D with the hope of developing a blockbuster drug that could reap big rewards. Valeant, however, invested only 2% to 3% of its revenue in research for new drugs. This was in stark contrast to Merck and Pfizer, which typically invested 15% to 20% of their revenue for R&D. But under Pearson, Valeant regarded R&D as too risky and inefficient. It pursued a "follower" strategy rather than trying to be a research leader that pioneers its own innovative products. According to Pearson's approach, it was better to focus efforts on promoting and selling proven products than to search for new blockbuster drugs in the laboratory. Pearson also sought to reduce Valeant's product scope by focusing on a few product lines such as dermatology, an area overlooked by big drug companies. In addition, the development of new skin treatments was more dependent on redesigning existing treatments than on discovering new ones, which made this R&D work far less risky.[77]

A major component of the new Valeant business model was the company's determination to pursue takeovers and acquisitions to build revenues and profits. It looked for drug companies that had developed promising drugs that were undervalued. Valeant relied on its well-honed turnaround skills to cut costs in those companies and thereby increase profit margins. It added immediate value by eliminating overhead, engineering significant layoffs, and sometimes rationalizing product lines. Also, once a company was purchased, Valeant always considered whether or not its drug products were underpriced. After that review, it typically raised the price of those products that further enhanced its profit margins.

This strategy was compatible with the Pearson philosophy that regarded higher prescription drug prices as the primary means to increase revenue dollars and enrich the bottom line. In 2015, Valeant raised prices on its brand-name drugs by 66%, according to a report published by Deutsche Bank. Drug research, which Pearson called "a hugely expensive game of trial and error," was further marginalized as the acquisition strategy bore positive results.[78] Some Wall Street investors, such as hedge fund manager William Ackman, praised Valeant's strategy of acquiring rivals rather than developing drugs internally. Others questioned whether or not a strategy of serial acquisitions over organic growth was sustainable. For several years the strategy appeared to pay off in terms of higher revenues and better profits. In 2014, the company's net income was $880 million on sales of $8.2 billion. On the other hand, the company was highly leveraged. After the takeover of Salix, it became saddled with much more long-term debt, which increased from $18 billion in 2014 to an estimated $30 billion in 2015.[79]

A Deal with Marathon Pharmaceuticals LLC

In February 2015, Valeant purchased from Marathon Pharmaceuticals the rights to two lifesaving heart drugs, Nitropress and Isuprel. Valeant was particularly interested in these two off-patent drugs because they did not face any generic competition, and the company believed both products were potentially undervalued. Isuprel's revenues were $103 million in 2014, and Nitropress recorded revenues of $58 million in that same year. Valeant also wanted these drugs because their acquisition would expand its portfolio of hospital-administered drugs.[80]

Nitropress is an emergency drug given to patients whose blood pressure has risen to a dangerously high level, while Isuprel treats abnormal heart rhythms. Valeant looked at the prices of both drugs and concluded the price structure did not reflect the benefits of these drugs for the patients who needed them. Nor did it take into account the costs saved by the hospital when these drugs were administered in lieu of more expensive treatments. Consequently, Valeant concluded the drugs were undervalued and decided to raise the price for both medications. Shortly after the purchase from Marathon, the list prices for the two drugs rose by 525% and 212%, respectively. The price of a 1-milliliter vial of Isuprel rose from $215.46 to $1,346.62. The price of a 2-milliliter vial of Nitropress increased from $257.80 to $805.61. A skeptical *Wall Street Journal* report noted that neither of the drugs was improved as a result of an expensive investment. Nor was there any increase in production cost. The cost of raw materials had not increased, and manufacturing operations did not shift to a more expensive plant or venue. The only change was the new ownership.[81]

Similarly, after its acquisition of Salix Pharmaceuticals, Valeant raised the price of one of its more popular brands, the diabetes pill known as Glumetza, by about 800%. A typical monthly supply of this product, which originally cost a patient $520, rose to $4,643 pursuant to the Valeant acquisition. At the time, there were no generic versions of Glumetza, which was due to come off patent by 2018. In most cases, patients still had access to the more expensive drugs (like Glumetza), since they were shielded from the burden of these price increases by health care insurance. For some patients, however, the insurance copay or out-of-pocket expense went up so high they could no longer afford the drug. Also, the increased costs were absorbed by insurers, hospitals, and taxpayers (who support Medicare), and those higher costs lead to higher copayments and premiums for everyone. Hospitals, for example, had to absorb the big price increases for Nitropress and Isuprel. Ascension Health, which operates 131 hospitals across the United States, estimated that these price increases would triple its spending on these two drugs to $8 million. The lack of viable alternatives in clinical situations requiring these medications left the hospital chain with little choice but to pay the excessive prices.[82]

These dramatic price increases enabled Valeant to grow its revenues by an impressive 27% in 2015. But the price increases for the two drugs purchased from Marathon almost immediately became the focus of a prolonged pricing controversy for Valeant. A steady stream of Canadian and U.S. newspaper reports caught the eye of Congress, which asked Valeant for information about revenues, costs, and expenses for the two drugs. The press repeatedly profiled vulnerable consumers who were frustrated by these pricing tactics and worried that insurers would terminate their coverage for these very costly drugs.[83]

The Philidor Connection

In addition to its high price increases, Valeant also faced criticism for its close and secretive relationship with Philidor Rx Services LLC. Philidor was a mail-order specialty pharmaceutical company that filled prescriptions for Valeant's drugs and dermatology creams. Valeant and other drug companies rely on specialty pharmacies such as Philidor to ensure that prescriptions are filled as often as possible with its brand-name drugs rather than lower-cost generics. In most cases, Philidor carried only the brand-name Valeant drug and did not make generic substitutes available. Doctors submit prescriptions for Valeant drugs to a specialty pharmacy such as Philidor, the Valeant drug is sent to the patient, and the pharmacy works with the insurance company to get reimbursement. Patients and doctors like these pharmacies for two reasons. They eliminate some of the inconvenience involved in filling a drug prescription, and sometimes a specialty pharmacy will subsidize the out-of-pocket cost. However, unlike traditional pharmacies, specialty pharmacies are far less likely to make any effort or commitment to switch a physician's intended prescription to a generic brand.[84]

Valeant never told its investors it had an option to purchase Philidor, which accounted for 5% of its sales. Valeant also had a sales plan, called the "Philidor Strategy," to use the pharmacy as a means of increasing sales for several drugs, including Solodyn, an antibiotic that treats acne. It was only in the wake of the pricing controversy that the tight relationship between Philidor and Valeant came to light. Pearson initially defended its lack of disclosure by observing that the use of such pharmacies was "one of our competitive advantages." However, Pearson later expressed Valeant's commitment to more transparency about its business ties.[85]

In addition to the lack of transparency, there were credible allegations that Philidor employees were directed to modify doctors' prescription orders to squeeze more reimbursements out of insurers. According to former employees and internal documents, prescriptions were altered so it would appear that physicians demanded that only Valeant's brand-name drug be dispensed rather than the less-expensive generic versions. In most cases, pharmacies such as Walgreens or CVS will sell a generic version of a drug if not told to do otherwise by a "dispense as written" indication on a prescription. The "dispense as written" order precludes the sale of generics, and this meant the guarantee of more sales for Valeant's higher-priced branded drugs. According to Bloomberg, former employees who worked at Philidor until 2015 confirmed that prescriptions were altered in this fashion, and the intent was to fill more prescriptions with Valeant products instead of generics.[86]

By November 2015, Valeant had terminated its relationship with Philidor Rx Services. Shortly thereafter, Philidor announced it would shut down operations. In announcing this change, Pearson was unusually contrite. "We understand that patients, doctors, and business partners have been disturbed by the reports of improper behavior at Philidor, just as we have been. We know the allegations have also led them to question Valeant and our integrity, and for that I take complete responsibility. Operating honestly and ethically is our first priority, and you have my absolute commitment that we will make it right." Cutting ties with Philidor, however, did little to allay investor concern, and the stock price of Valeant continued its precipitous decline.[87]

Valeant's Defense

Valeant faced mounting criticism, not only over its connections to Philidor but also because of its business model that depended on higher prices as the key driver of revenue growth. In its defense, Valeant Pharmaceuticals continued to insist that its drug-price increases were warranted because these drugs were undervalued and underpriced. According to Pearson, the company has a duty to shareholders to maximize the profit for each drug the company sells. When products are priced below market value, the company must seize the opportunity to appropriate as much value as possible. In many cases, argued Pearson, those older, neglected drugs acquired by Valeant sold at a discount compared to newer drugs for the same diseases. Valeant's price increases simply rectified this anomaly. According to Pearson, if "products are sort of mispriced and there's an opportunity, we will act appropriately in terms of doing what I assume our shareholders would like us to do."[88]

This has been a standard line of defense for other pharmaceutical firms that have also raised prices after acquiring a new drug in order to boost sales and profits. These practices have been common in the industry for years, although Valeant has taken them to a new extreme. Pharmaceutical companies frequently remind critics that they are not charities and are obliged to their shareholders to charge whatever price consumers and health care insurers are willing to pay. Moreover, claim industry executives like Pearson, prescription drugs deliver superior value: they improve the quality of life for patients and sometimes eliminate the need for costlier treatments such as invasive medical procedures.

Valeant spokespersons also repeatedly pointed out that the price hikes did not necessarily make these lifesaving drugs inaccessible to patients. Thanks to insurance coverage, patients were usually protected from the impact of higher prices. Yet, despite these claims, there were many patients who were burdened by Valeant's higher prices. For example, Bruce Mannes, a 68-year-old retired carpenter from Michigan, had been taking Cuprimine for over 50 years to treat Wilson disease, an inherited condition that can cause severe liver damage. In the summer of 2015, Valeant quadrupled the price of Cuprimine. Medicare now had to pay $35,000 per month for this medication, and the copay for Mr. Mannes jumped from $366 to $1,800. The higher copay put a great strain on this retiree's budget. Finally, Valeant defended some of its price increases as a way of dealing with the prospect of generic competition. Pearson informed industry analysts of the standard and acceptable industry practice to raise the price of a drug shortly before it is likely to face generic competition. Once generics enter the market, there is no longer an opportunity to extract substantial value from a product.[89]

Turing Pharmaceutical Joins the Fray

Valeant was not the only pharmaceutical company to come under fire for inordinate price increases. It shared the spotlight with Turing Pharmaceuticals, which was founded in 2015 by its CEO, Martin Shkreli. Shkreli purchased three drugs from his former company Retrophin to jump-start his new company named after the legendary computer scientist Alan Turing. Like Valeant, Turing was not a research-based company, but rather sought to "buy forgotten and orphaned assets from Big Pharma—any drug that's had weak supply or weak support." Those drugs could usually be acquired at a very low price. After the acquisition, Mr. Shkreli, who became known as "pharma bro," would usually raise the drug's price considerably.[90]

In August 2015, around the same time that Valeant's problems began, Turing announced that the price of its newly acquired anti-infection drug Daraprim would increase by 5,000%, from $13.50 to $750 per tablet. This meant the annual cost of the drug was now $634,000. There are no generic alternatives to Daraprim, which treats a dangerous infection known as toxoplasmosis. The drug was originally approved in 1953 and has been off patent for decades. When Turing acquired rights to this drug, it also maintained the restrictive distribution system used by the drug's former owner, Impax. There were no valid reasons for Daraprim's restricted distribution, such as safety concerns. Turing's motivation was most likely to make it more difficult for generic manufacturers to gain access to the drug in order to create the generic version.[91]

Shkreli became the target of widespread public ire, and he was soon the media's newest villain. Politicians of all stripes also quickly condemned the excessive price increase. In light of harsh media criticism, Shkreli promised to roll back the price of Daraprim, but then changed his mind. The actions of Turing and Valeant once again made drug pricing a hot political issue heading into the 2016 presidential election. Big Pharma executives were anxious to distance their companies from both of these rogue companies, claiming they were "outliers." Yet from May 2015 through May 2016, pharmaceutical prices rose by 9.8%, the second highest in the Producer Price Index.[92]

In the midst of the furor over high drug prices and industry profits, Shkreli was not reticent about defending Turing's pricing strategy, often citing his fiduciary duty to his shareholders to maximize profits. According to Mr. Shkreli,

> No one wants to say it, no one's proud of it. But this is a capitalist society, capitalist system, capitalist rules. And my investors expect me to maximize profits. Not minimize them or go half, or go 70 percent, but to go 100 percent of the profit curve that we're all taught in MBA class.[93]

When asked if he had any regrets, Shkreli said he should have raised prices even higher to maximize shareholder returns. His familiar arguments based on duties to shareholders loudly echoed the reasoning of J. Michael Pearson, but few people outside the pharmaceutical industry found those arguments to be very convincing.

Working toward Resolution

In late 2015, in response to its critics and falling stock price, Pearson announced a change in the Valeant business model. Valeant decided to increase R&D spending by 26%—for 2016, the company projected a $500 million investment in R&D. According to Pearson, through these tribulations, Valeant had come to appreciate the potential of R&D for providing more organic future growth. At the same time, the company committed itself to increasing revenues for existing products and paying down debt rather than further aggressive deal-making.[94]

In the wake of the unabated public fury over its pricing policies, Pearson apologized at a Senate hearing for the company's tactics. "Valeant was too aggressive and I, as its leader, was too aggressive," he told lawmakers.[95] Valeant also reduced the prices for both Nitropress and Isuprel but did not roll back prices on some of its other high-priced products, such as Glumetza. By the summer of 2016, Valeant stock had lost 90% of its value since its peak price in August 2015. From its highest share price of $262, Valeant's stock stood at about $25 per share. In April 2016, Valeant's board of directors decided to replace Pearson, the mastermind of the company's controversial strategy. It named Joseph Papa as the new CEO. Papa was a seasoned pharmaceutical executive with over 35 years of experience in the industry. Papa promised to initiate a "new chapter" at the struggling company.[96]

But Valeant's woes continued into the summer and fall of 2016 as Papa struggled to get his beleaguered company beyond this contentious affair. Federal prosecutors were claiming that Valeant had defrauded investors by not disclosing their close relationship with Philidor. This probe could lead to criminal charges for the executives of Philidor and Valeant.[97] In early 2017, Valeant sold off three skin-care brands to French cosmetics giant L'Oréal in order to sharpen its focus and pay down its massive debt. But many investors remain dubious about Valeant's prospects, and the stock price has not yet recovered to the lofty levels it had achieved before the pricing controversy.[98]

EXHIBIT 7.1 ■ Valeant Financials, 2014–2016 (in millions)			
	2014	**2015**	**2016**
Revenues	$8,206	$10,446	$9,174
Gross Profit	5,969	7,861	7,063
Operating Income	1,871	1,507	(566)
Net Income	880	(291)	(2,409)

- How would you assess the Valeant business model, and how does it differ from that of Big Pharma firms? What is a responsible pricing strategy for Valeant? For a firm like Merck or Pfizer?

- Discuss the economic, legal, and ethical issues involved in setting drug prices, drawing on the frameworks presented in Chapters 2 and 3. Do you assign any merit to Valeant's defense that it must charge these high prices in order to maximize profit for shareholders? What about the claim that sharp price increases are warranted when a drug is about to go off patent and face new competition from new generic products?

- What would you do if you were Papa and appointed CEO of this company? Defend your strategy to the board of directors.

CASE STUDY 7.2

BIG PHARMA CONFRONTS AIDS

The conflict over inflated drug prices was especially acute during the prolonged AIDS pandemic. The excessive price level of AIDS medication sparked many protests when these therapies were first introduced in the late 1980s. Prices were eventually reduced, and health insurers stepped in to provide coverage for many patients. But a more pressing and complicated issue arose as AIDS spread to developing countries like Africa. The world was slow to recognize the imposing barriers presented by poverty that severely limited access to AIDS medication. Several pharmaceutical companies had developed highly effective AIDS therapies, but they were inaccessible for many African patients because the price was out of reach. And patents protected these products from competition by generic manufacturers.

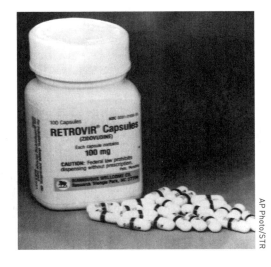

AP Photo/STR

The central theme of this case is the problem of patents and the developing world, where few can afford the cost of lifesaving medication. The critical conflict of "patient versus patent" is common in emerging economies. The case chronicles the rapid spread of HIV/AIDS in Africa and reviews the reasons behind the slow response of Big Pharma to that crisis. While many fault the response, the key question remains: how to balance the rights of patent holders and the rights of patients who need essential pharmaceutical products.

The AIDS Epidemic

Acquired immune deficiency syndrome, known as AIDS, was a major health calamity for the United States during the decade of the 1980s. For a long time, AIDS was a baffling illness that defied a cure or even an effective therapy. After considerable research, scientists were finally able to link AIDS to a deadly virus that was to be called the human immunodeficiency virus (HIV). Once the invading virus enters the bloodstream, it slowly destroys white blood cells, which play a major role in the body's immune system by fighting off germs and bacteria. With the immune system compromised, patients more easily die from diseases that a normal immune system can resist and fight off. This virus is not spread through casual contact but requires the direct interaction of bodily fluids.

The pharmaceutical industry began researching treatments for AIDS, but progress was slow due to the complexities of this disease. When HIV/AIDS first surfaced in the 1980s, there were few incentives for companies to invest resources for a treatment, since the disease population was relatively small. Working with a live deadly AIDS virus was also dangerous for researchers and technicians, and few were willing to take that risk. Many argued that given the infectious nature of the disease, pharmaceutical companies along with the NIH should have been much more proactive. According to some informed critics, government financing was woefully inadequate. They also blamed the U.S. Food and Drug Administration for not making available to desperate patients the first experimental drugs in the research pipeline.

Fortunately, one of those experimental medications emerged as the first effective therapy for HIV/AIDS. After a number of early drug failures such as Suramin, AIDS patients finally got some relief. A new therapy was developed by Burroughs Wellcome (BW), the American subsidiary of the British pharmaceutical company Wellcome PLC. This company, which was founded in 1880, had special expertise in antiviral research. In 1987, Burroughs Wellcome brought to market this antiviral medication, known as AZT or Retrovir. AZT (initially known as compound S) was actually discovered in 1964 as a treatment for cancer, for which it was ineffective. It was then resynthesized as an antiviral drug. The anti-AIDS drug was fast-tracked and rapidly approved by the FDA. Unlike other drugs, it was not too toxic if given in the proper dosage. It was first designated as an "orphan drug" under the terms of the Orphan Drug Act, with seven years of market exclusivity. It was later awarded a full 17-year patent.[99]

According to Nussbaum, Burroughs Wellcome executives worked behind the scenes to bypass bureaucratic red tape in order to secure quick FDA approval for its new medication. Smaller companies, however, lacked this opportunity. As a consequence, many drugs that could have been more efficacious than AZT were left undeveloped and never made it to market. These included drugs such as AL 721 and HPA-23, which showed great promise against the AIDS infection. But their sponsors were not "drug savvy" and could not navigate their way through the maze of complex regulations that governed the industry at this time.[100]

But like most drugs of this type, AZT was not cheap. The initial retail price was $9,500 to $10,000 per annual dose; the wholesale price was $8,200 or $1.88 per 100-milligram capsule. This high price put the drug simply out of reach for many AIDS patients. Some were uninsured, and for others their health plans did not cover the cost of prescription drugs. The exorbitant price ignited vehement protests by groups such as ACT UP, who contended that this price level was unwarranted and unfair. According to that group, Burroughs Wellcome had a monopoly on the treatment of HIV/AIDS and was exploiting that monopoly to maximize its profits. On the other hand, some anti-AIDS activists, such as Nussbaum, appreciated the company's efforts to develop a therapy when other companies (and the government) refused to get involved: "It is true that Wellcome is making enormous profits off AZT. Perhaps it is profiteering, perhaps not. But Wellcome at least delivers for the case, something the NIH cannot claim to do."[101]

Despite the objections, the company steadfastly insisted that $9,500 was an equitable retail price, given its heavy research and development expenditures. Burroughs also defended its pricing policy by claiming it would use AZT revenue to support research into new AIDS drugs. When asked to be more specific about its research expenditures, the company responded that it had spent over $80 million in R&D and related costs and that it required this high price to recoup its investment. But AZT was originally discovered by the government researchers. For this reason, it was not initially eligible for a full patent. Instead, under the Orphan Drug Act, it qualified as an orphan drug with seven years of sales exclusivity. There were certainly costs incurred by Burroughs for commercialization and clinical testing of the drug, but the $80 million figure seemed "suspicious" to some AIDS activists and politicians. However, Burroughs Wellcome was unwilling to provide any further data detailing costs for developing this drug and bringing it to market.[102]

Thanks to dosage reductions and other factors, the price of AZT steadily came down. By 1993, AZT was selling for about $2,000 for a year's supply. However, the company was deeply stigmatized by this whole affair. The controversy swirling around BW was part of a larger debate about high drug prices, a priority policy issue for the newly elected Clinton administration. A scathing congressional study accused the industry of making "excess profits" and pointed out that between 1980 and 1992 drug, prices rose 128%, whereas during that same period producer prices increased only 22% for other products.[103]

AIDS activists, insurers, and political leaders still balked at BW's lower price, because AZT remained inaccessible for many patients. But AIDS victims had little recourse until new and less expensive therapies came on the scene. AZT was followed by a drug called Videx (or DDI), produced at considerable expense by Bristol-Myers Squibb. Videx was discovered at the National Cancer Institute and licensed to Bristol-Myers, which commercialized the compound into a safe and reliable product. Aware of the furor over pricing for AZT, this image-conscious company was more sensitive to the issue of affordability and charged $1,745 for an annual dose. Bristol-Myers believed that a moderate pricing structure was warranted, especially given the role of the government in Videx's discovery. AZT finally had some real competition at an affordable price.[104]

Researchers later developed protease inhibitors that acted to prevent the infected cells from spreading the virus. Those drugs came to market in 1996. Eventually, drug companies developed an antiretroviral therapy consisting of a combination of at least three drugs (often called "highly active antiretroviral therapy," or HAART) that can suppress replication of the HIV virus. Three drugs are necessary in order to reduce the likelihood of the virus developing resistance to medication. HAART is not a cure but has the potential to reduce mortality rates among HIV-infected people and to improve their quality of life.[105] Thanks to these drugs along with proactive measures like preventive education, the AIDS epidemic finally began to recede in the United States during the late 1990s.

HIV/AIDS in Africa

However, just as the AIDS epidemic was waning in the United States and other Western countries, it began to grip several countries on the continent of Africa. According to the World Health Organization (WHO), by 2001, 25 million Africans were infected with the HIV virus that causes full-blown AIDS. Of that number, 5 million were ready for antiretroviral drugs. This meant they were sick enough to need these drugs, but not so sick they couldn't benefit from them.[106] South Africa was particularly hard-hit—an estimated 4.7 million people, or 30% of the population, were infected with the potentially deadly HIV virus.

HIV/AIDS also swept through the vulnerable populations of countries like Botswana and Zimbabwe. In Botswana, the United Nations estimated that 36% of the population was infected with HIV/AIDS; in 2001, 26,000 people, both adults and children, perished of the fatal disease.[107] Life expectancy had been on the rise, but now it plunged dramatically in this poor African nation. In Zimbabwe, there were 2.3 million people living with HIV/AIDS in 2001. Of this number, 240,000 were children. In that same year, there were 200,000 adult and children deaths from AIDS. The average life expectancy for a Zimbabwean was 33, the second lowest in the entire world. The disease was highly stigmatized in this country, and this made it difficult for the government and aid workers to address the problem.[108]

While the medicines on the market didn't cure HIV/AIDS, they kept the disease under control and prolonged the patient's life for many years. However, they were also quite expensive. Several major pharmaceutical companies marketed a potent drug cocktail of protease inhibitors combined with other medicines (HAART). Merck sold a drug called Crixivan, which prevents human immunodeficiency virus (HIV) cells from multiplying in the body. And Glaxo Wellcome PLC, the company that pioneered AIDS research, marketed Combivir. Combivir was another drug cocktail, a mixture of AZT and two other drugs that formed the basis of its AIDS therapy. When it was first brought to market in the United States, Combivir sold for over $10,000 per person for an annual dose. Thanks to private insurance and some government assistance, most HIV/AIDS patients in Western countries were able to afford these new medications.

But the same was not true in African nations like Botswana or Zimbabwe. Most Africans infected with HIV/AIDS were far too poor to afford this medicine, even if it was available at much lower prices. There was no health insurance and no other sources of aid. Governments in affected countries in sub-Saharan Africa lacked sufficient resources to buy these drugs at discounted price from Western companies in order to treat their afflicted citizens. In addition, they did not have the research capabilities, political will, or funds necessary to invest in manufacturing plants in order to make generic drugs. Further, most African countries lacked the necessary health care infrastructure to deliver and administer the drugs, monitor their use, and educate people about how to use them.

Some countries like Botswana increased their health expenditures and made a good-faith effort to deal with HIV/AIDS, but they needed outside assistance. Thus, the problem of AIDS in Africa did not lend itself to easy solutions even if drugs were more readily available. There were many "non-patent barriers" that impeded access to antiretrovirals.[109]

Nevertheless, as the impact of the disease intensified, nongovernmental organizations (NGOs) and other philanthropic groups tried to help. The French organization Doctors without Borders was willing to acquire at an affordable price enough antiviral medication to treat as many inflicted Africans as possible, but those efforts were in vain. In 1998, a new agency within the United Nations called UNAIDS asked the pharmaceutical companies for steep price reductions for their drug cocktails in order to make this medicine more accessible. But the industry politely refused their request. The $10,000 to $15,000 price would have to be cut by a factor of 10 before African economies or aid agencies could realistically afford them. Companies like Merck, Glaxo, and Bristol Myers would not agree to such steep discounting and argued that Africa needed to buttress its fragile medical infrastructure before it could make a commitment to provide drugs at low prices. In addition, these companies were worried that price reductions of this magnitude might make more transparent the industry's large profit margins on these products. Also, discounts are a politically sensitive matter. Drug companies worry about the slippery slope: if they discount AIDS drugs, will they have to deal with pressure to do the same for medicines for other diseases such as malaria?[110]

As a result, in 2001, at the height of the African AIDS crisis, only 10,000 people in Africa had access to the anti-AIDS cocktail drugs, even though 5 million Africans would have benefited from antiretroviral therapy. Millions of Africans, many of them babies, were suffering and dying for lack of drugs which were routinely available in the United States and the rest of the Western world. As the crisis intensified, the international media was beginning to pay close attention.[111]

Although African countries had few resources and low annual health budgets, they did not sit idly by and watch their citizens die helplessly of HIV/AIDS. South Africa had initially refused to face up to the spread of the disease within its borders, but eventually took action to establish some foundation for facilitating access to antiretrovirals. In 1998, the South African government passed the Medicine and Related Substances Control Act. The law authorized the use of compulsory licensing and "parallel importing" to provide low-cost medication for AIDS victims. Under the new law, South Africa could import pharmaceuticals from any source, including generic manufacturers, without the patent holder's permission. It would also allow for the manufacture of those patented medicines within South Africa without any licensing agreement.[112]

Given the industry's solicitude about the patent system, the response of Big Pharma was predictable. Thirty-nine Western drug companies along with a trade group, the South African Pharmaceutical Manufacturers Association (PMA), went to court to challenge the new law. The antagonistic lawsuit claimed that the new South African law infringed on intellectual property rights, broke international trade agreements, and "contravened the constitutional protection of property rights" by allowing the importation and manufacture of generic drugs at lower prices than those offered by the patent holders. In addition, the U.S. government added South Africa to its "watch list," which made it subject to trade sanctions. The lawsuit was immediately condemned by human rights groups, but Big Pharma was adamant. It was worried about the precedent of a government interfering with patent rights which might have far-reaching effects. According to a PMA spokesperson, "What's at stake here is more than just a narrow South Africa issue. It's about the ability of the entire pharmaceutical industry to protect its patents, which motivates it to innovate the development of new drugs."[113]

Generic companies like India's Cipla, the market leader for AIDS drugs in India, stood ready to help South Africa and other African countries. Cipla, headed by the outspoken Yusef Hamied, had reengineered patented AIDS drugs to make its own cocktail. The company filed a request with the South African government for a compulsory license to start selling its generic version of the drug. Cipla was prepared to sell its three-drug cocktail for $350 a year, its breakeven price. This price was a shocking 1/30 of the U.S. price. To the embarrassment of Big Pharma firms, Cipla candidly revealed that the active ingredients for making an annual dose of Combivir could be purchased on the international generic market for only $240. It was not clear how much this crusade would help AIDS patients because of the poor infrastructure that inhibited delivery of these drugs. Nonetheless, Cipla's proposal certainly caught the industry's attention.[114]

Big Pharma Responds

Under pressure from the media, AIDS activists, and the United Nations, the pharmaceutical industry dropped its lawsuit in 2001. The United States also removed South Africa from the Section 301 watch list. Big Pharma executives were at a crossroads as they pondered the plight of Africans stricken with AIDS, offers by generic manufacturers like Cipla, and the intensifying media spotlight on their refusal to act. Given their corporate mission, the broadening scope of the pandemic in hopelessly poor African countries, and the efficacy of their antiretroviral therapies, it was necessary to think more carefully about their moral obligations under these exigent conditions. What was their responsibility to society? Should they make lifesaving drugs available to all who needed them? Of course, there was still apprehension that weakening patents or waiving patent rights to allow generic competition in these situations would reduce profits needed to fund future research. What about the need to protect the integrity of the patent system, which is the precondition for new drug development? As the industry pondered these questions, they considered several options: waive their patent rights for AIDS drugs in Africa; license their products to generic manufacturers such as Cipla; lower their price structure for the AIDS cocktail; or maintain the status quo and their defensive posture.[115]

The companies selling AIDS drugs chose to go the route of price reductions. In May 2000, five Western drug companies, including Merck and Bristol Myers, had struck a deal to cut the price of AIDS drugs, but there were some strings attached to this offer. Merck, for example, declined to make its discounted prices widely known, asked the UN to help oversee the process, and engaged in country-by-country negotiations. Little progress was made. But a year later, with no conditions attached, Merck agreed to sell Crixivan for $600 a year per patient, and Stocrin for $500; both are critical components of its cocktail therapy. These figures, Merck claimed, represented "no profit" for the company. The total wholesale price of Crixivan and Stocrin was $11,700. Glaxo offered to sell an annual dose of the Combivir cocktail for $1,330, well below its $10,880 price tag in the United States. Merck president Raymond Gilmartin described his company's "evolving stance" on the issue of pricing for HIV/AIDS medication in Africa. At first there was an adamant refusal to discount prices, then the offer of some price reduction but with certain strings attached, and finally steeper price reductions with no conditions. According to Gilmartin, this was all part of "gaining experience" in how to handle such complex scenarios.[116]

Even these bold and dramatic price reductions, however, failed to bring the crisis to closure or to mute the criticisms of activists and African country officials. It took time to make these drugs available and to develop better medical facilities for the delivery and monitoring of the medication. For several years after the price drop, Africa still accounted for 70% of the world's HIV/AIDS victims. The new price structure led to increased access, but wider and broader access to antiretrovirals was still necessary. AIDS activists continued to demand even lower prices, and by 2006 the average cost of a three-drug cocktail had been reduced to about $1 per day. But the actual cost of treatment, including health care personnel, infrastructure requirements, and laboratory monitoring, was higher than the cost of the drug itself and a tremendous burden for destitute African economies.[117] This was remedied to some extent by an infusion of foreign assistance, such as President Bush's initiative in 2004, which made available several billion dollars to provide care for AIDS patients. By 2015, the price of antiretrovirals in Africa had dropped to $100 for an annual supply. The steady price decline has enabled many more Africans to benefit from this therapy.[118]

Over time, a concerted world effort has also begun to address the African AIDS crisis more comprehensively by focusing on education and prevention. Charitable foundations and NGOs have played a pivotal role in finally getting affordable medicines to the poorest Africans who cannot afford to pay anything for this treatment. They have also helped to build the supporting health care infrastructure. As a result, many countries like South Africa have made great strides against the HIV/AIDS epidemic. However, Africa still has an abnormally high infection rate, and about 1 million people still die from AIDS across the continent. Also due to an inadequate supply of medicine and a dearth of health care providers, only half of HIV patients in Africa receive treatment.[119]

EXHIBIT 7.2 ■ HIV/AIDS in Africa Timeline

1981: First AIDS cases reported by Centers for Disease Control (CDC) in the United States

1983: CDC reports 3,000 cases of AIDS and over 1,000 fatalities

1985: HIV virus isolated and identified by researchers working in France

1987: AZT developed by drug company Burroughs Wellcome receives approval from the Food and Drug Administration as the first therapy for AIDS; AZT's initial retail price is $9,500 ($8,200 wholesale)

1988: AIDS cases rise to a cumulative total of 80,000 with 20,000 fatalities

1989: National Institutes of Health (NIH) endorses "parallel track" testing to hasten development of new AIDS drugs

1996: First protease inhibitors made available, followed by HAART

1998: As AIDS spreads through Africa, South African government passes Medicines and Related Substances Control Act; pharmaceutical companies respond with a lawsuit

2000: Big Pharma multinationals make concession on prices of their AIDS cocktails (but with strings attached)

2001: 25 million Africans infected with HIV; lawsuit against South African government is dropped; companies like Merck agree to lower costs to break even without any conditions

2006: The price of the antiretroviral drug cocktail drops to $1 per day

- Did Burroughs Wellcome charge a fair price for the first AIDS therapy, AZT? If not, what would have been a fair price? How would you compare this company to Valeant or Turing?

- How would you assess Big Pharma's handling of the African AIDS crisis—why were these companies so reluctant to adjust prices or license their products to generic manufacturers like Cipla? Do you agree with their rationale?

- Did Big Pharma firms selling antiretrovirals make the right decision in 2001 to lower the price of their drugs to breakeven levels? Evaluate this decision from an ethical perspective using frameworks described in Chapters 2 and 3, such as DRJ.

CASE STUDY 7.3

MYRIAD GENETICS: PATENTING THE GENOME

©iStockphoto.com/Altayb

The discovery of DNA represents a biological revolution that continues to ramify through the health care industry. Thanks to the pioneering work done on mapping the human genome, medical researchers and doctors have gained greater insight into the genetic factors underlying diseases such as cancer. Because of DNA sequencing, doctors are now able to determine which genetic mutation might contribute to a patient's ailment. This research has also created opportunities for genetic testing and screening along with more tailored medical treatments.

But the field is still in its infancy, and commercializing these discoveries on the edge of scientific research is an expensive and risky business. At the forefront of this work are bio-tech companies such as Myriad Genetics, which owned the exclusive rights for tests that check for genetic susceptibility to breast cancer. The company believed it earned those rights by discovering the location and sequence of genes whose mutations can increase the risk of cancer. The central issue in this case is whether unaltered but isolated human genes such as the ones discovered by Myriad should be eligible for patent protection.[120]

Myriad Genetics

Myriad Genetics is a molecular diagnostic company, founded in 1991 in Salt Lake City, Utah. Its first breakthrough came two years later in 1993 with the discovery of the *p16* gene associated with hereditary melanoma. Myriad has grown steadily over the years and now employs about 1,650 people. It has tested and screened over 3 million people for cancer and other diseases. In 2017, it had net income of $22 million on worldwide revenues of $771 million.

Myriad was founded 10 years before the human genome was sequenced, making it one of the first genomics and genetic testing companies in medical history. It operates through three divisions: research, molecular diagnostics, and companion diagnostics. The research division focuses on the discovery of genes related to cancer and other common diseases. Molecular diagnostics, the core business of Myriad, provides testing designed to assess an individual's risk for certain diseases, usually based on their genetic history. Products include tests for hereditary cancer, urological cancer, lung cancer, autoimmune disorders, and other diseases. Once risks are assessed, preventive action can be taken if warranted. These tests also assess the likelihood that a person will respond to different drug therapies and guide doctors in providing the right dosage of that medication. The companion diagnostics division provides testing products and services to pharmaceutical and biotech companies.[121]

In addition to the *p16* gene, Myriad scientists, in collaboration with other researchers, have discovered many important genes whose mutations can cause deadly diseases. These include the *BRCA1* and *BRCA2* genes associated with hereditary breast and ovarian cancer, the *PTEN* tumor-suppressor gene involved in the development of many other cancers, and the *ELAC2* prostate cancer gene.

In 1996, Myriad introduced the first genetically based diagnostic test for hereditary breast and ovarian cancer. This test, known as BRCA Analysis, quickly became the standard for predicting a person's risk of developing breast cancer because of a genetic mutation. Myriad charges $3,340 for this test, which accounts for a major proportion of its annual revenues. In 2001, it launched Melaris, a genetic test for hereditary melanoma. These successful products have been followed by a series of other innovative molecular diagnostic tests for breast, colon, lung, pancreatic, prostate, ovarian, and uterine cancers. According to the company, its highly regarded hereditary cancer tests have already benefited more than 1.5 million patients.[122]

Cancer has been at the forefront of genetic research and medicine since the mapping of the human genome was completed and published in 2003. Scientists are now convinced that cancer is a genetic disease: it originates in a genetic mutation that is aggravated by environmental factors. Smoking, for example, doesn't poison cells directly but promotes mutations in those cells' DNA. Genomics has led to limited success in cancer treatment with therapies such as PLX4032, which inhibits the activity of mutated proteins in patients with melanoma and causes those cells to die. Many similar therapies are on the horizon and the whole biotech industry stands to gain, but who appropriates the value from these discoveries depends to some extent on how the thorny issue of patents gets resolved.[123]

Like most medical research and biotech companies, Myriad Genetics has depended on patents to protect its innovations. Myriad secured a number of process patents for the methods underlying its diagnostic testing. It also secured product (or structure) patents for the isolated *BRCA1* and *BRCA2* genes, which it had discovered and isolated from the chromosomes in which they reside. Those gene patents soon became a source of contention in the industry and they were promptly challenged in court. Myriad was convinced that the labor and investment that led to the discovery of those genes entitled them to a patent as a pecuniary "reward" for that effort. But many researchers and competitors disagreed and claimed that a patent would give the company exclusive control over products of nature.

Genes and DNA: An Overview

To appreciate the issues in the dispute about gene patents and genetic testing, some background on cell biology and genetics is essential. Cells are the basic units of all living organisms. Within the cells of a body are chromosomes or "threadlike units" that contain our genes. Half of a person's chromosomes are received from his or her biological father and the other half from his or her biological mother. A human's chromosomes contain approximately 23,000 genes, packed into 23 pairs of chromosomes. The complete set of genes is known as the human genome.

Each gene is encoded as DNA, which takes the familiar form of the "double helix." Genes, therefore, are stretches of DNA that contain information for creating strings of amino acids that produce certain proteins. There is about six feet of DNA within the nucleus of every cell. In effect, each gene is analogous to a sentence with a four-letter alphabet, A, T, C, and G (representing the nucleotide bases that form the genes: adenine, thymine, cytosine, guanine), which combine in pairs to communicate with the cell and instruct its development in certain ways. It's this genetic information that, for example, instructs cells to make black hair instead of red hair or brown eyes instead of blue ones.[124]

The Human Genome Project mapped and sequenced these genes. Mapping the human genome was the key to unlocking our understanding of the genetic factors underlying human diseases. This effort has enabled genetic testing and screening and opened the way for gene therapies that could repair defective genes. Through a blood test or tissue sample, an individual's genetic status can be compared to the human genome map, allowing doctors to determine if that individual has a defective gene that might predispose him or her to a chronic illness. These tests help both diagnosis and treatment, allowing doctors to choose the proper drugs or some other therapy. For example, the disease known as phenylketonuria is triggered by a mutation to a gene that breaks down the molecule called phenylalanine, which can cause brain damage if it builds up in the bloodstream. The optimal remedy is to repair this defective gene once it is detected so that the person's metabolism is restored to a normal state.[125]

For a long period, genes were considered to be patentable material. Approximately 4,000 isolated human genes have been granted patents in the United States. The Patent Office reasoned that while the Patent Act would not cover the gene as it occurs in nature, an isolated gene should be seen as a modified substance. In the laboratory, scientists can isolate and purify DNA so it can be extracted from a chromosome. In defending its patents, Myriad claimed that an isolated DNA molecule is patent-eligible because it is "a non-naturally occurring composition of matter" with a "distinctive name, character, and use."[126] This conclusion seemed consistent with the U.S. Congress's apparent intention that the patent statute cover "anything under the sun that is made by man."[127] The Supreme Court's decision in *Chakrabarty v. Diamond* set out the framework for deciding the patent eligibility of isolated DNA molecules, since in that case the court ruled that a living microorganism qualifies as a patentable composition of matter.[128] Three types of gene patents are possible: structure patents, covering the isolated and purified gene; function patents, covering a new use for the DNA in question (such as a diagnostic test or gene therapy); and process patents, which cover a new method of isolating, purifying, or synthesizing this DNA material.[129]

The Myriad Genetics Patents

Gene patents did not go unchallenged, and Myriad Genetics suddenly found itself at the epicenter of the gene patent controversy. The company's most famous patents were based on its discovery of the precise location and sequence of the *BRCA1* and *BRCA2* genes. Mutations in these genes can greatly amplify a woman's risk for both breast and ovarian cancer. Before Myriad's discovery, it was known that heredity played a role in the risk for breast and ovarian cancer, but the genes associated with those cancers had not been identified. Knowledge of the location of these two genes enabled Myriad to determine the typical nucleotide sequence, and that information allowed the company to create medical tests for the purpose of detecting genetic mutations in a patient's *BRCA1* and *BRCA2* genes in order to evaluate whether that patient has an increased risk of cancer. It was awarded patents in 1997 covering these two DNA sequences. The patents were granted on these two genes in their isolated and purified form.

These structure or product patents have a "preemptive effect," since they exclude any-one from working with these isolated BRCA genes without Myriad's permission. Patents gave Myriad the exclusive right to isolate an individual's *BRCA1* and *BRCA2* genes by breaking the covalent bonds that connect the DNA to the rest of a person's genome. This isolation is necessary to conduct genetic tests for BRCA mutations. Therefore, only Myriad could commercialize the discovery of these two genes through the development of diagnostic screening tests, gene therapies, or other products. In addition to the pat-enting of this isolated DNA, the patent holder also claimed a product called cDNA, which is the "mirror image" of the DNA sequence. cDNA does not normally exist in the human body, and is naturally created only through the operation of certain retrovi-ruses. Transforming normal DNA into cDNA, however, provides a more efficient tool for researchers and health care professionals who wish to study, diagnose, and treat the disease associated with a gene.[130]

Along with its patents for the BRCA genes, Myriad was also given patents for its meth-ods of comparing and analyzing a patient's BRCA sequence with the normal sequence in order to identify the presence of a mutation that might predispose the patient to cancer. Finally, Myriad received a patent for the method of determining whether a particular cancer therapy is efficacious by growing cells containing the relevant gene and determin-ing whether those cells grow more slowly when subjected to that therapy.

After the patents were awarded, Myriad Genetics filed patent infringement lawsuits against other companies that performed BRCA testing. Those companies ceased their infringing activities, and Myriad had a monopoly on BRCA genetic testing. A number of years later, a group of patients, advocacy groups, doctors, and medical researchers filed a lawsuit seeking a declaration from the U.S. Patent Office that the Myriad patents were invalid. In that lawsuit the plaintiffs maintained that the BRCA genes are "natural human genes" or products of nature. As such, they are unpatentable subject matter. The Patent Act clearly defines patentable subject matter:

> Whoever invents or discovers any new and useful process, machine, manufacture, or composition of matter, or any new and useful improvement thereof, may obtain a patent therefore, subject to the conditions and requirements of this title.[131]

But the courts have held that this provision of the patent law includes important exceptions, which are not explicitly stated: "laws of nature, natural phenomena, and abstract ideas" are not patentable.[132]

The plaintiffs also argued that the monopoly rights over these genes enabled by the patent interfered with the capability of patients to obtain better cancer screening tests. In 2010, in the case of *Association of Molecular Pathology v. United States PTO*, a federal district court agreed with the plaintiffs and rejected all the Myriad patents, reasoning that since the purification of natural DNA does not alter its inherent characteristics, isolated DNA remains a product of nature. The court concluded that "because the claimed isolated DNA [was] not markedly different from native DNA as it exists in nature, it constituted unpatentable subject matter."[133] The court also invalidated Myriad's method claims.

On appeal, however, a federal appeals court ruled in favor of the Myriad Genetics patents, reversing the decision of the lower district court. Following the framework laid out in the Supreme Court's decisions in the *Chakrabarty* and *Funk Brothers* cases, it ruled that both isolated DNA and cDNA were patent-eligible according to U.S. patent law. It reasoned that due to human intervention, the isolated DNA did exist in a distinctive chemical form and therefore was different from DNA in the human body (or native DNA). Isolated DNA has been cleaved or severed from chemical bonds so that it consists of just a fraction of the naturally occurring DNA molecule. Since isolated and purified DNA has this "markedly different" chemical structure, it is eligible for a patent. Moreover, after decades of genetic patents and a pattern of firm judicial precedent, including the *Chakrabarty* case, the court concluded that it could not now call isolated DNA as non-patentable and thereby disrupt the "settled expectations" of the scientific community. The court also rejected the plaintiff's argument that isolated DNA and native DNA are not different because they have the same genetic function of transferring information. According to the court, it's not the use of this isolated DNA that determines patent eligibility but its distinctive nature. As a result, the court declined to extend the "laws of nature" exception to include isolated DNA sequences. At the same time, the appeals court ruled that the method for comparing and analyzing DNA sequences was not patent-eligible. But it concluded that the second method for screening potential cancer therapeutics by way of changes in cell growth rates was patentable subject matter.[134]

The Case against Gene Patents

Critics of this favorable ruling from the federal appeals court resisted the conclusion that isolated DNAs are patent-eligible compositions of matter. The simple isolation of the BRCA genes by extracting them from their natural location and incidentally changing their molecular structure in the process seemed an insufficient basis for a patent. It is quite dubious, they argued, that the cleaving or breaking of chemical bonds transforms the isolated genes into a new substance as the court supposed. Thus, this innovation appeared to still fall on the side of products of nature as something discovered but not invented. As an amicus curiae brief for the plaintiff stated, awarding a patent for the discovery of the BRCA gene was like awarding a patent for the discovery of a chemical element such as lithium. On the other hand, there was far less concern with cDNA, which cannot be isolated from nature but must be created in the laboratory.

Researchers or biotech companies like Myriad, critics concluded, should therefore not be able to obtain patent rights to isolated and purified DNA sequences. Patent scope is broad, but there are three general exceptions to the law's patent eligibility principles: "laws of nature, physical phenomena, and abstract ideas."[135] Although different in molecular structure, those DNA sequences have not been sufficiently modified, so they are still fundamentally the same entities as they were in their natural state. Isolated DNA is not "markedly different" from the natural product. Also, why isn't the issue of utility relevant in this case as it is in other patent cases? Isolated DNA offers no new utility, since it serves the same function it did in nature.

According to opponents of gene patents, the biggest social problem associated with these patents is that other researchers are preempted from using the isolated genes for their own scientific work. As one dissenting judge in the *Molecular Pathology* appeals case stated, "Broad claims to genetic material present a significant obstacle to the next generation of innovation in genetic medicine—multiplex tests and whole genome sequencing."[136] The purpose of patent protection is to stimulate innovation but sometimes too much protection can impede rather than promote innovation. As Harrison observes, progress in biotechnology research will become "unduly burdened by the existence of too many intellectual property rights in basic research tools."[137] There is considerable risk that excessive ownership of information inputs, such as genes or even genetic data, will impose high costs and formidable burdens on the flow of critical scientific information. Biomedical research depends upon the open availability of genetic data resources.

Thus, substances like genes or genetic data, which are upstream in the research cycle, must be made easily accessible for downstream research and testing. According to Horn, "This kind of information is considered basic research and provides the data that is necessary for making end products such as drugs, diagnostic tests, and other treatments based on genes and their products."[138] The gene is a basic tool of research, and according to some critics, seeking an exclusive right to a gene by means of a patent is like "trying to gain ownership of the alphabet."[139] It is a mistake, therefore, to award proprietary rights too far upstream in the research and development value chain for biotech products. Gene patents limit the research that can be done on isolated genes such as *BRCA1* and *BRCA2*, and they make it difficult for new competitors to succeed in this nascent industry.

Given these valid preemption concerns and the close proximity of these modified genes to native DNA, opponents of the appeals court ruling argued that the justification for BRCA patents appeared to be based on tenuous legal and moral ground. Also, like all intellectual property rights, gene patents create monopolies that lead to market failures including the lack of access for patients who cannot afford to pay premium prices for genetic testing.

The Case for Gene Patents

But there is also a strong case to be made for gene patents that has been put forth by legal scholars along with the investors and principals of biotech ventures such as Myriad Genetics. In response to the claim that companies should not be given ownership over the human genome, supporters argue that this notion does not reflect the reality of the gene patent. The patent owner merely has exclusive rights to the isolated gene that is extracted from its natural state. The patent does not imply control over the genetic information encoded in that gene.[140]

In addition, isolated DNA does not exist in nature. As Myriad and other gene patent holders have consistently argued, isolated DNA exists in a chemical form distinct from that of DNA in the human body or native DNA. Isolated DNA has been cleaved—that is, its covalent bonds have been severed—so it consists of a fraction of the naturally occurring DNA molecule. According to the appeals court that ruled in Myriad's favor, "Human intervention in cleaving or synthesizing a portion of a native chromosomal DNA imparts on that isolated DNA a distinctive chemical identity from that possessed by native DNA."[141]

Proponents of gene patent protection further contend that without the promise of a patent and the exclusivity which it provides, there will be minimal investment in the discovery of isolated genes or DNA sequences like *BRCA1* and *BRCA2*. The isolated gene is not an obvious "product of nature" just waiting to be discovered. In the case of the BRCA genes, it took 17 years of research and sophisticated genetic mapping techniques to isolate these molecules that make the breast cancer test possible. Awarding of patents for the discovery of the precise location and sequence of these genes gives companies the time and space to work without the worry that other companies can quickly copy their new discoveries. This opportunity is especially important for smaller companies that may not have the financial resources to compete with larger, more established companies.[142]

Patents stimulate research and lead to incremental innovations in the field of biotechnology. Moreover, as the cofounder of Myriad Genetics has observed, real innovation requires money—scientific acclaim is not adequate. Patents and the promise of a big payoff will attract investors, who must take substantial risks and wait a long time before there is any payback for their investment. Only some type of patent protection can ensure that innovators will capture the value of their innovations without the interference of free riders. According to Kevin Kimberlin, "Two decades passed before Myriad recouped its enormous investment—an investment that would not have happened without patent protection."[143] The elimination of patents would drive away much-needed capital and lead to fewer major discoveries.

Also, on the basis of intellectual property rights theory, there is a plausible case that a property right is well deserved, given that there is substantial labor involved on common property (the human genome). The laborious and time-consuming efforts in mapping the physical location of the BRCA genes (with the help of DNA samples), the determination of the exact nucleotide sequences, and the cleaving and purifying efforts to isolate the DNA seem to warrant a property right of some sort. The question is whether this work is merely a discovery rather than a transformative and creative invention that justifies a property claim.

The Supreme Court Decides

The 2011 ruling in favor of Myriad Genetics and other gene patent holders was appealed to the U.S. Supreme Court. In June 2013, in a surprising unanimous ruling, that Court reversed the federal appeals court's decision. It concluded that Myriad's claim for a DNA patent on the *BRCA1* and *BRCA2* genes was invalid because it fell within the law of nature exception. Myriad's contribution was discovering the precise location and genetic sequence of these two genes, but this did not render those genes patentable. In the court's view, separating those genes from the surrounding genetic material was not equivalent to an act of invention. According to the justices, "groundbreaking, innovative, or even brilliant discovery does not by itself satisfy the § 101 inquiry."[144] Moreover, reasoned Justice Thomas, who wrote the majority opinion, ownership rights over "building blocks" of nature "would be at odds with the very point of patents which exist to promote creation."[145] The justices were also unpersuaded by the claim that the Patent Office's established practice of awarding gene patents is entitled to some recognition.

On the other hand, cDNA did not face the same obstacles to patentability as the naturally occurring isolated DNA segments; cDNA is distinct from DNA from which it was derived. While the nucleotide sequence of cDNA is "dictated by nature," the lab technician creates something new when cDNA is produced. Therefore, it is not a product of nature and so is patent-eligible.[146] Also, the court did not take up the method patents of Myriad, which were not challenged in this case.

Thus, the Supreme Court in this unanimous decision has resolved the matter of gene patents. Whether this decision is fully equitable and prudent is a matter of debate. Beyond the patents for *BRCA1* and *BRCA2*, the court's decision invalidated patents for thousands of other genes, including several that can help predict birth defects and certain heart conditions. The medical community was generally in accord with the Supreme Court's decision, while some biotech firms disagreed. Myriad Genetics stressed the patent claims the court did not invalidate, particularly for synthetic DNA. After the decision was announced, several medical companies announced their plans to compete with Myriad by introducing their own genetic-testing products for detecting mutations in genes linked to breast and ovarian cancer.[147]

- Do you agree with the Supreme Court's decision in this case? What are the likely consequences for the biotech industry? What about patents for cDNA and Myriad's method claims?

- Will entrepreneurs invest in the technologies developed by companies like Myriad Genetics without the promise of protection from free riders?

- If you were defending Myriad Genetics' DNA patent claims before the Supreme Court, how would you argue this case?

- How do you assess the Lockean argument for gene patents? (See the "Note on Patents and Intellectual Property Rights" at the beginning of this chapter for more background on Locke's theory.)

CONCLUSION

After a cursory review of the pharmaceutical industry structure, this chapter traced the evolution of industry regulations in the United States and reviewed some of the current controversies that confront industry executives. A pivotal issue is the high-profile matter of patents and exorbitant prices for lifesaving pharmaceutical products such as cancer drugs. The industry has been quite determined to protect its patents, which are the key to the promotion of future research. The Valeant case also exposed the problems associated with non-research-based firms that buy drugs and raise prices to reflect their true value. These price increases are more awkward to justify because they do not reflect a company's research investment. The chapter concluded with the case on gene patents which provides an opportunity to think about the scope of patent protection and apply some of the intellectual property theories underlying that protection.

Student Study Site

Visit **edge.sagepub.com/spinello.**

Key Terms

design patent 151	patent cliff 162	utility patent 151
evergreening 163	process patent 150	vertically integrated 155
intellectual property 149	product patent 150	
patent 150	public goods 149	

Review Questions

1. What is the basic rationale for patent laws, and how do they help stimulate research and innovation?

2. What is the primary purpose behind the extensive regulations that govern the pharmaceutical industry?

Discussion Questions

1. The pharmaceutical industry is quite dynamic and complex. It will continue to challenge regulators, who must somehow balance the need to protect consumers without destroying incentives for research and development. How would you define the role of government? Is the FDA too paternalistic and too cautious? Should it do more to control steep price increases? What are the risks of price regulations?

2. Do patients have a *right* to access experimental drugs that have not completed the testing cycle?

3. How would you assess from a moral point of view the techniques used by some firms to deal with the "patent cliff"?

4. How would you adjust the patent system in the United States? If you had a chance to design a patent system from the ground up, what would it look like?

8

PROTECTING THE CONSUMER

Product Safety and Marketing

The responsibilities of bigness demand leadership. Leadership by its very nature is highly visible. In February of 1974 then Chairman [of General Motors] Richard C. Gerstenberg told an audience of investors, educators, and the press "We must do well before we can do good." The gist of his message was that the corporation had to make money—profit—before it could exercise its public responsibilities. This may sound naïve to many but the opposite is true. That by doing good, exercising a role of leadership and public responsibility, General Motors, or any American business, will do well and promote its long-term health and viability.

—John Z. DeLorean[1]

(Continued)

8.2 Describe the moral dimensions of marketing decisions.

8.3 Apply the DRJ model to examine the ethical basis of duties of disclosure and product safety.

8.4 Manage and respond to product safety controversies.

The last chapter reviewed the duties of pharmaceutical companies to provide products that are safe, effective, and affordable. The theme of duties to customers continues in this chapter. The case studies in this section look at several critical consumer issues, including responsible marketing and product safety. The primary purpose of these cases is to help aspiring managers understand the moral aspects of marketing and to recognize, analyze, and respond to product safety issues.

What is the scope of the corporation's obligations to its customers? Two general but contradictory philosophies have prevailed: *caveat emptor* and *caveat vendor*. Under caveat emptor ("let the buyer beware") corporations have narrow responsibilities, and the burden is on the consumer to be circumspect about the products they choose to buy. Savvy companies will certainly attempt to win the customer's business by meeting his or her expectations by providing reliable and reasonably safe products, but consumers are generally at the mercy of market forces. If consumers demonstrate a willingness to pay for safer products, companies will make their products with added safety features. However, if they show no preference for safety, they will not get these features unless government regulators intervene. In recent decades, however, there has been a demonstrable shift to the philosophy of *caveat vendor* ("let the seller beware"). The reason for this shift is the asymmetry between the seller and the buyer. Sellers know far more about their products, including their risks and possible defects, than the buyer. Hence the seller has a duty to exercise "due care" to protect consumer welfare. Products should perform as promised. They should be reliable, function "as advertised," live up to the claims of their service life, and be safe. A product is safe if its risks are known to the consumer and they are judged to be acceptable or reasonable by that consumer based on the benefits he or she expects to receive from using that product.[2]

Companies also have an obligation to avoid or restrict the sale of "predatory" products that are highly dangerous. This product category includes addictive substances such as cigarettes. Some predatory products are banned altogether while others are confined to a subset of customers. The sale and marketing of these predatory products raises many ethical concerns. Should customers even be allowed to assume the risk of consuming these products? Do companies have ethical responsibilities to their customers to refrain from marketing these products or even remove them from the market?[3]

Most companies seek to win new customers or induce customers to switch from competitors through commercial advertising. The purpose of advertising is to provide consumers with product information and persuade them to purchase that product. Advertising works by creating a desire for the seller's product or by fostering a belief that this product is the best means to satisfy some desire the consumer already has. Advertising has been condemned for being manipulative because it plays on people's perennial desires for "social acceptability" or "personal beauty." The debate about manipulation is one that cannot be opened here, but advertisers have ethical duties to avoid deception because it impairs consumer autonomy. In Kantian terms, deception that interferes with autonomy implies using the person as a means to achieve the goal of higher sales. However, it is not always easy to draw the line between deceptive ads and those with harmless puffery or hyperbole.[4]

AN OVERVIEW OF THE CASES

This set of cases on duties to the customer begins with a history of the controversial tobacco industry in the United States, which reviews the industry's growth, especially during the first half of the 20th century. This case also chronicles the epic struggle between the tobacco industry and government regulators once the causal link between cancer and cigarette smoking was established. Also reviewed in this briefing is the moral propriety of the targeted marketing campaigns deployed by companies like Philip Morris and R. J. Reynolds, which were desperate to attract new customers. Campaigns like "Joe Camel" seemed to cross the line by appealing to young children and impressionable teenagers. Also explored are hostile public policies, which imposed major restrictions on the industry, along with a brief discussion on the industry's current structure and challenges.

This industry overview is followed by a case study about the latest chapter in the "smoke wars" between the industry and regulators. In some countries, such as the United Kingdom and Australia, government regulators have mandated that cigarette manufacturers abandon their fancy packages for plain ones without logos such as the Marlboro red-and-white chevron. Those plain packages come with graphic warnings about the dangers of smoking. Will this trend continue and spread to the United States? And should tobacco companies switch to plain packaging for the sake of placating policy makers who want to suppress any vestiges of marketing tobacco products in order to further limit smoking consumption?

The chapter continues with a briefing on the history of the automotive industry in America. It includes a summary of the chief safety disputes in the industry such as the Ford Pinto debacle and the problems with the ill-fated Chevy Corvair. For many decades, automobile manufacturers did not take product safety seriously enough, and industry executives became masters at shifting blame. In their view, bad or negligent drivers, not vehicles, caused accidents. Is there any evidence that attitudes about safety have sufficiently evolved or that the industry has a higher level of "safety consciousness"? The briefing concludes with a look ahead at some of the potential controversies surrounding the driverless cars of the future.

The next case details General Motors' faulty ignition switch, which led to the recall of almost 5 million Chevy Cobalt cars in 2014. The company even faced criminal charges for covering up the defect. Consumers began complaining about the ignition switch in 2005, but GM never took adequate steps to investigate or resolve this safety problem. Failures to communicate within the organization and a sense of moral indifference seemed to contribute to GM's poor handling of this catastrophe which has exposed it to hundreds of potential lawsuits.

The second case on automotive safety examines Takata's defective airbag. The Japanese company has been in the crosshairs since 2014 for these dangerous devices which can disperse shrapnel throughout the vehicle when they are activated. The company initially resisted the efforts of regulators to replace all the malfunctioning airbags, and some of its managers falsified test results. What happened at Takata, the leading manufacturer of safety airbags, and why did this matter go unresolved for such a long stretch of time?

The final case in the chapter reviews the safety problems associated with the Samsung smartphone known as the Note 7. The popular phone, the leading competitor of Apple's iPhone, sometimes spontaneously erupted into flames thanks to a faulty battery. Samsung responded slowly to these problems but eventually orchestrated a comprehensive recall. The company has struggled to rebuild trust with consumers and overcome the adverse economic impact of this untimely product safety controversy.

BRIEFING: SPOTLIGHT ON THE TOBACCO INDUSTRY

Since the 1964 surgeon general's report indicating a strong link between cancer and cigarette smoking, the tobacco industry has faced a stressful and hostile business environment. Out

of concern for the health and welfare of its citizens, policy makers throughout the world have enacted many punitive measures to curtail smoking. These include high excise taxes, age requirements, and substantial restrictions on advertising and promotion. The end result has been a massive decline in cigarette consumption. Nonetheless, more than 15% of American adults smoke cigarettes on a regular basis, and there are still 1 billion smokers throughout the world. Despite all this turmoil and bad publicity, the industry continues to find new ways to lure customers, sometimes deploying questionable methods. Although their established brands are cash cows that require little investment, the major firms have not abandoned their marketing strategies or product innovation efforts.

Before it exposes the current challenges for the cigarette manufacturers, this industry overview will explore the dynamics of the tobacco industry and its quest for continued viability. How responsibly has this industry coped with the social and ethical challenges that have complicated its business plans and strategic decisions? Was it ethical, for example, to aggressively pursue foreign markets where there were fewer advertising restrictions? Is target marketing to susceptible segments of the population morally permissible? What should companies like R. J. Reynolds and Philip Morris have done differently? The following analysis investigates these and other questions, but we begin with a broad historical overview.

Industry Origins and Growth

The modern cigarette was invented by James "Buck" Duke. His North Carolina company, W. Duke Sons & Company, made chewing tobacco and other products, and first began producing cigarettes in 1879. Human cigarette rollers were soon replaced by the Bonsack machine, which could produce 100,000 cigarettes a day. W. Duke Sons & Company became American Tobacco, which immediately appreciated the benefits of heavily promoting its products. By 1890, it was already spending close to $1 million on advertising. Other competitors joined with American Tobacco to form a Tobacco Trust. The trust was dissolved in 1911 because it violated the Sherman Antitrust Act. After the "trust bust," there were 16 small firms competing for customers. Those companies eventually evolved into the Big Six, which have dominated the cigarette market for almost a century.[5]

In 1913, one of the Big Six, R. J. Reynolds, introduced the first national branded cigarette known as Camel. This non-filter-tip brand quickly captured a 35% market share. Its broad mass appeal was attributed to its mild taste and especially to the clever "Coming of the Camel" advertising campaign. Soon after the successful debut of Camel, L&M brought Chesterfield to the market and the American Tobacco Company introduced Lucky Strike. Both were heavily advertised and soon became national brands that rivaled Camel's market power. American Tobacco spent more than $100 million advertising Lucky Strike during the brand's first 10 years.[6] The "Reach for a Lucky" campaign introduced around 1925 was a huge success. By the mid-1920s, R. J. Reynolds, American Tobacco, and L&M had accumulated an imposing 80% share of the expanding cigarette market. Lorillard's Old Gold made its mark but never achieved the popularity of the other three brands. However, years later, Lorillard would have a big success with its menthol brand, Newport.[7]

These four major tobacco companies were soon followed by Brown Williamson, which launched two new brands, Viceroy and Kool, the first menthol cigarette. Finally, in 1932, Philip Morris joined these five companies by introducing its elite Marlboro brand, which was originally pitched to women because of its "ivory tips." Philip Morris remained the smallest of the six companies until it transformed Marlboro into a virile man's cigarette in the 1960s. Through World War II, three brands, Chesterfield, Camel, and Lucky Strike, continued to rule the U.S. market. The industry reached its peak during the 1950s, when Americans consumed more than 350 billion cigarettes per year.

By 1975, the Big Six accounted for 99.8% of the market. This was a powerful oligopoly that controlled virtually every aspect of the value chain. There was little price competition among these popular brands, and companies competed on the basis of marketing and limited product innovation. The cigarette is really no more than a commodity, so sales were driven by aggressive advertising and other creative promotions.[8]

Companies like American Tobacco and Philip Morris had followed Reynolds's early example and invested millions of dollars to build their brands. There seemed little doubt that in the postwar consumer culture, demand could be generated and directed by the marvels of advertising. As a result, cigarette brands like Camel and Lucky Strike became iconic fixtures in American culture and became extremely valuable. According to *Fortune* magazine, "There can be little doubt that if Reynolds, Liggett & Myers, or American had to give up either their secret formulas or their brand names, they would keep the brand names."[9] In the 1980s, despite the rise of health concerns, advertising and marketing expenditures averaged about $2 billion per year.

Thanks in large part to the success of its flagship Marlboro brand, Philip Morris's market share surged from 11.3% in 1950 to 37.9% in 1987, when it overtook R. J. Reynolds as the undisputed market leader in the industry. The power of advertising and promotion was not lost on Philip Morris. In the 1950s, Marlboro was repositioned as a man's filter cigarette. In 1962, new ads depicted cowboys on the open range beckoning smokers to come to Marlboro country "where the flavor is." This innovative "Marlboro Man" ad campaign rapidly propelled Marlboro to be the number-one brand in the United States.

Other popular brands in the 1970s and 1980s included Winston (RJR), Salem (RJR), Kool (Brown and Williamson), and Camel (RJR). But these products now had to contend with the potent appeal of Marlboro Man, who would not shrink from facing up to anxiety about the risks of smoking. According to Brandt, "Rarely, if ever, had marketing so brilliantly combined American values, traditions, and symbols with a promotional message. The campaign offered images rich in denial and escapism, in reassurance and immortality. The Marlboro Man would find an enduring place at the American campfire."[10]

The decline in demand that began in the 1970s thanks to health concerns had little adverse effect on the industry's ability to generate large profits. Well-established brands such as Marlboro were entrenched cash cows with a dedicated customer base and low production costs. This steady stream of profits provided Philip Morris with the capital necessary to diversify and to make strategic acquisitions such as Miller Brewing Co. and Seven-Up. Philip Morris successfully used its marketing acumen to revive dormant brands such as Miller, although it had less success with Seven-Up. R. J. Reynolds diversified into the food business with its takeover of the cookie maker Nabisco in 1985. A subsequent leverage buyout created RJR Nabisco Corp. However, in 1999, the cigarette business was spun off, so Reynolds was once again just a tobacco company. As the new century dawned, the industry was on the brink of a wave of consolidation that would reshape the tobacco business.[11]

Health and Safety Issues

As far back as the 1930s, many doctors and scientists had strong suspicions that cigarette smoking was hazardous to a smoker's health. But there was only anecdotal and insufficient evidence to support these suspicions. It took some time and commitment to accumulate more objective and convincing scientific proof. In addition, the tobacco industry vociferously insisted that smoking was safe. They often ran ads like "More Doctors Smoke Camel" to reassure present and future customers. However, by the mid-1950s, researchers had gathered empirical proof of the strong connection between cigarettes and cancer. After a study commissioned by the American Cancer Society in 1954, one of the study's authors declared that "all the evidence to date certainly points strongly to the conclusion that cigarette smoking does increase the probability of developing lung cancer."[12] The growing consensus about the dangers of cigarette smoking would soon pose an existential threat to the whole thriving tobacco industry.

The public was barely cognizant of these dangers, but that situation changed dramatically during the Kennedy administration (1960–1963). In response to mounting political pressures, the surgeon general, Luther Terry, formed a committee in 1962 to study the issue of smoking's effect on human health. The surgeon general's report was released to the public in January 1964. In ominous terms, it concluded that cigarette smoking "is a health hazard of sufficient importance in the United States to warrant immediate action." The report went on to declare that "cigarette smoking is causally related to lung cancer in men; the magnitude of the effects of cigarette smoking far outweighs other factors. The data for women, although less extensive points in the same direction."[13] The blunt report took an unsuspecting public by surprise. This was an alarming and unwelcome revelation to a nation of contented and addicted cigarette smokers. The report was also an economic shock for the tobacco industry and the Big Six. There was an immediate but temporary decline in cigarette sales as well as a decline in the stock price for the major tobacco firms. The resilient industry fought back with its own studies and claims that disputed the surgeon general's findings. As a result, cigarette sales soon began to rebound.

The surgeon general's report, however, was followed by a series of governmental regulatory actions along with research projects to corroborate the report's findings. The Federal Trade Commission (FTC), for example, initiated tar and nicotine studies. By June 1974, 13 major federal laws pertaining to smoking and health were put into place by the federal government.[14] The first of these happened in 1965: the Trade Regulation Rules on Cigarette Labelling and Advertising required a health warning on all cigarette packages, forbade ads directed at youths under 25, and prohibited advertising at schools and colleges. Suddenly the tobacco industry found itself in an adversarial relationship with policy makers. According to Miles, "What had once been fairly benign environment and an unquestionably lucrative domain had now become turbulent, interconnected, and complex."[15]

In 1967, the U.S. government mandated that broadcasters run one public-service antismoking ad for every three cigarette commercials. This mandate was followed by additional antismoking legislation, which included the banning of cigarette ads from all broadcast media, including radio and television. The ban was part of the Public Health Cigarette Smoking Act, passed by Congress in 1970. It was challenged by the tobacco industry but ultimately upheld by the Supreme Court. Two years later, health warnings were made mandatory in all print cigarette ads. At the same time, many states began to raise the cigarette excise tax, and some passed laws banning smoking in public buildings. The Federal Trade Commission began to monitor the industry by checking warning labels and studying the effects of advertising content on consumers. Antismoking forces continued to coalesce to create restrictive regulations for the industry.[16]

The tobacco industry assumed a defensive and combative posture during this trying period. It continued to insist that smoking was safe, refuting or obfuscating the evidence whenever possible. Industry executives categorically denied that smoking endangered one's health and pointed to the government's lack of conclusive evidence. Edward Horrigan, the chairman of Reynolds, appeared on many television programs claiming that "there is another side to these emotional issues." According to Horrigan, science had still failed to establish a "causal link" between smoking and cancer. Rather, the adverse health effects remain an open case.[17] As Richard Kluger observed, the industry always tended "to dispute, distort, minimize, or ignore the unfolding evidence against it."[18]

Despite the protests of the industry, most rational consumers became convinced that the surgeon general's report was quite accurate: cigarette smoking is hazardous to one's health and a leading cause of lung cancer. Complicating the health issues was the fact that cigarette smoking is so addictive. Nicotine enters the bloodstream, affecting the smoker's mood and psychological state. When a smoker attempts to stop, he or she has to deal with painful withdrawal symptoms. Many smokers are so addicted they cannot quit smoking despite their best efforts and fears for their future health.[19] At the same time, industry supporters argue that smoking reduces stress, which often leads to other health problems like overeating. So perhaps, they surmise, the benefits of smoking outweigh or at least offset its costs.

Restrictions on tobacco smoking continued unabated. In the United States smoking was banned from all domestic flights in 1990. At the same time the public's support for the tobacco industry was continuing to steadily erode. Universities like Harvard and CUNY divested their tobacco company investments. Harvard's president, Derek Bok, observed that the university did not want to be associated with companies "engaged in significant sales of products that create a substantial and unjustified risk of harm to other human beings."[20] Many other institutions such as California Public Employees Retirement System, the state pension fund, followed suit and accelerated the tobacco divestment drive.

The Tobacco Industry's Strategic Response: A Search for New Markets

How did the tobacco industry respond to this turbulent environment where it was constantly under siege? The Big Six employed a number of defensive strategies to protect their domains. The first was brand proliferation. In 1962, two years before the surgeon general's report, the number of domestic brands on the market was 47. By 1975, there were 100 different brands being sold on the domestic market. Many of these new brands were targeted to small segments of the tobacco market. Marginal brands were quickly eliminated to make shelf space for new brands.[21]

A related strategy was targeted marketing to help sell these new brands. Some of these campaigns, however, were quite controversial. In 1990, R. J. Reynolds introduced a new menthol cigarette called Uptown, which was expected to appeal "most strongly" to blacks. Marketing cigarettes to minorities was nothing new, since billboards with black and Hispanic models could be found throughout many minority communities. But civil rights groups viewed the Uptown brand as an escalation in target marketing that exploited blacks, especially the poor. According to an NAACP leader, "With the poor health of many black folks today, we do not need anything else to cause even more health problems. R. J. Reynolds' targeting of blacks is unethical." For its part, RJR said they were not trying to attract new smokers: "taking away business from our competitors is the only thing that Uptown is about." Nonetheless, the heavy criticism forced Reynolds to cancel the test marketing it had scheduled in Philadelphia and withdraw the brand.[22]

On the other hand, the industry demonstrated more success in targeting women smokers. Philip Morris introduced Virginia Slims in the late 1960s, and it remained the predominant brand with women, with a 3.1% market share in 1989. With this in mind, Reynolds sought to market a new brand for women smokers called Dakota. Dakota was aimed at 18- to 20-year-old blue-collar "virile females," white women with only a high school education or less. A marketing campaign was designed to target these young women in an effort to cut into Marlboro's domineering market share without diluting the appeal of Reynolds's Camel brand to males. After test marketing in several cities, however, Dakota failed to yield the desired results, and the brand was withdrawn.[23]

In general, while cigarette smoking had continued to decline in the 1980s and 1990s, the industry found it worthwhile to cultivate certain consumer groups, including blue-collar workers, women, and blacks, because these groups were the slowest to quit smoking. Its goal was to use their marketing skills on groups such as the less educated, women, and blacks that were quitting smoking less quickly than the general population.

But women's groups and other industry critics were sharply critical of targeted marketing. According to a spokesperson for the Women vs. Smoking Network, "When you target for marketing, you target for death."[24]

In one of the most disputed marketing campaigns, R. J. Reynolds introduced Joe Camel. This was a cartoon figure of a camel with an oversized nose, a "smooth character," often depicted wearing sunglasses and a T-shirt or a baseball cap turned backward. Joe Camel always appeared in a "heroic pose," surrounded by palm trees or in a barroom encircled by adoring cartoon women. The campaign ignited consumer interest, and soon Reynolds was spending $75 million to promote the Joe Camel character.[25]

It certainly appeared that Reynolds was targeting young people, even underage smokers. The company denied these claims, however, and insisted the Joe Camel campaign was simply conveying that Camel was a fun and exciting brand. But even if youth were not directly targeted, the ads appealed to young people, and Reynolds could not discount the spillover effect on children. Research demonstrated that 51.1% of all preschoolers knew Joe Camel far more than any other cigarette brand. Three surveys concluded that the Joe Camel mascot "was highly effective in reaching children."[26] Despite this evidence and the cries of antismoking activists, Reynolds vowed to maintain Joe, and there were good economic reasons for their obstinacy. Thanks to this ad campaign, the market share for the Camel brand was showing steady growth trends. But in 1997, the FTC issued a "cease and desist" order against Reynolds that forbade the use of the Joe Camel figure in ads in magazines or on billboards. Rather than challenge the FTC, Reynolds decided to end the Joe Camel campaign.[27]

A second strategy of Big Tobacco to compensate for falling domestic demand was the exploitation of opportunities abroad, especially in Asia, where health issues were not taken too seriously by some local governments. Between 1975 and 1995, cigarette consumption in the United States declined by 20%, and companies sought to fill the gap in sales through exports. To some extent, this effort did not represent a major new strategic direction, since the industry had always been committed to the idea of "global brands." As it moved more forcefully into foreign markets like India, the cigarette companies used novel advertising approaches to promote interest in cigarette smoking. In the 1990s, Japan became a lucrative market for foreign tobacco companies. Japanese consumers were attracted to U.S. brands by ads depicting groups of people enjoying a cigarette while engaged in activities like riding a motorcycle or singing songs. For the Japanese smoker, the American cigarette became a symbol of "high style." Antismoking activists blamed these ads for the sharp rise in the number of female smokers in Japan during this decade. Eventually an antismoking movement put an end to these ads and successfully lobbied for other steps to curb cigarette consumption. But for a long while, Japanese and foreign tobacco companies enjoyed a free hand in Japan.[28]

During the 1990s, the U.S. tobacco industry also found a hospitable environment in Eastern Europe. After the breakup of the Soviet Union in 1989, these Eastern bloc countries like Poland and Czechoslovakia represented fertile new markets with high potential demand. Through heavy advertising of their brands, the U.S. companies sought to use their popular "Western image" to get young people to start smoking. When confronted about these ambitious ad campaigns, Philip Morris executives said that they were only taking advantage of "latent demand" that would exist "whether or not Philip Morris plastered the countryside with posters and billboards."[29] Most countries, including those in Eastern Europe, have since signed on to the World Health Organization's 2003 treaty, which lays out universal standards limiting the promotion and advertising of tobacco-related products.

However, in India, where marketing regulations are slightly more permissive, companies can still advertise at the point of sale. Cigarettes can be advertised on small billboards outside shops where tobacco products are sold. Product displays and advertisements inside those shops or kiosks are also permissible. Some shop owners receive payments from tobacco firms in the form of monthly fees or free cigarettes to put up these "hoardings" or displays that promote a specific brand.[30]

For the most part, the tobacco companies' foray into foreign countries was a big success and sustained its revenues and profits throughout its travails in the West. Philip Morris, for example, still depends heavily on its Asian operations. During 2013, Asia accounted for 34.2% of Philip Morris's revenue. The company shipped about 301 billion cigarettes to Asia during that year, out of a total of the 880 billion cigarettes sold by Philip Morris globally during the period.

Antismoking activists in Asia and the United States claim that Philip Morris is targeting low-income families within Asia. According to one prominent critic, "The bulk of the smokers in Asia are people with low income so the revenue earnings are from selling an addictive and hazardous product to poor people." Moreover, Asian governments can afford to spend only small sums of money to stop the spread and prevalence of smoking. People in these countries are also more vulnerable because they lack information about the health risks and dangers of smoking.[31]

Current Industry Structure and Strategy

In 1998, the industry reached a deal with 46 states and the federal government to settle lawsuits from states seeking compensation costs associated with the treatment of smoking-related illnesses. Both sides estimated the payment would be about $206 billion over 25 years. Industry payments to the "master settlement" have already amounted to about $120 billion. While the settlement was a financial blow to the industry, it also brought closure to the industry lawsuits over product liability.[32]

The industry has also consolidated over the last two decades as scale has become increasingly critical for a mature industry under pressure. British American Tobacco (BAT) acquired its former parent, American Tobacco Company, which brought brands such as Lucky Strike and Pall Mall into its portfolio of products. Philip Morris renamed itself Altria in 2003, as the parent company of Philip Morris USA. Altria spun off its international division, Philip Morris International, in 2008. In 2014, Reynolds purchased Lorillard Inc. to acquire its highly popular Newport brand. Consolidation has rationalized the U.S. market from the Big Six to two predominant players: Altria with a 46.6% market share and Reynolds America with a 33.6% share. Thanks to their scale and market power, these two companies have been able to reduce costs, increase prices, and remain quite profitable. Operating profits of U.S. tobacco manufacturers grew 77% from 2006 to $18.6 billion in 2016.[33]

In 2017, British American Tobacco announced its purchase of Reynolds for $49.4 billion. International companies have renewed interest in the U.S. market, where they see some opportunities for growth. Aggregate cigarette sales in the U.S. have grown from

$71 billion in 2001 to $94 billion in 2015. The deal will give Reynolds better access to faster-growing emerging markets in South America, the Middle East, and Africa, where BAT has a strong presence. It will also give Newport, Reynold's leading brand, a chance to increase its share in the European market.[34]

Tobacco companies continue to emphasize new marketing campaigns to preserve their customer base and lure new smokers to their brands. Altria, for example, has designed Marlboro Black, a bolder tasting offshoot of the original Marlboro brand, which is aimed at millennials. The lower-priced cigarette represents a "bold, modern take" on the traditional Marlboro brand. According to one description of Marlboro Black, "Think tattoos, black jeans, and motorcycles instead of Stetsons, blue jeans, and horses." The brand is marketed to young adults through an elegant direct mail campaign that takes the form of a VIP party invitation. Marketing representatives also hand out coupons for $1 packs at dance clubs and neighborhood bars. The product appeals to young adults for another important reason: it is less expensive than traditional brands. Introduced in 2016, Marlboro Black has already captured a 1% share of the U.S. cigarette market, or about $320 million in revenues. This fashionable product has given the Marlboro brand new credibility with younger smokers.[35]

Epilogue

By now, everyone is keenly aware that smoking is unhealthy and likely a contributory cause of diseases such as cancer and emphysema. Tobacco remains responsible for one in nine adult deaths. Despite the health risks and the battery of regulations passed by countries to fight smoking, Big Tobacco has not faded away. Companies continue to contend for market share, to invest in new marketing campaigns, and to innovate by developing reduced risk products such as e-cigarettes.[36]

The beleaguered tobacco industry has always defended itself based on the premise that consumers are free to choose their products. Smokers willingly assume the risks associated with these products. Free choice is an important principle and cannot be overlooked in the debate about smoking. That argument, however, overlooks the addictive nature of smoking and the limits of free choice. Also, what about the social costs of smoking? Is it right for society to have to bear the burden of medical costs of smokers who contract lung cancer, emphysema, and other calamitous diseases? Are those costs high enough to ban consumption altogether? Such a move seems inconsistent with recent trends to legalize other potentially harmful substances such as marijuana. Arguably, governments should continue on the same path, following a consistent policy of "legalize and discourage."[37]

- If you were writing a history of American business, what would you say about the tobacco industry from a moral and social perspective? Is the industry's success a notable accomplishment for free-market capitalism? (Consult Chapter 1 for relevant background on capitalism.)

- Was it right for the industry to engage in "regulatory arbitrage," that is, to take advantage of weak regulations in emerging economies where it sought to compensate for lost business in the West? Should tobacco companies feel free to advertise in countries where there are no restrictions on ads?

- How do you assess the targeted marketing campaigns of companies such as R. J. Reynolds? What about Altria's new Marlboro Black brand targeted to urban millennials? Which ethical principles support your position?

- What are the tobacco industry's duties to consumers? Given the product's predatory nature, is there a duty to refrain from any kind of marketing?

CASE STUDY 8.1

PLAIN PACKAGING AND THE ONGOING TRIALS OF BIG TOBACCO

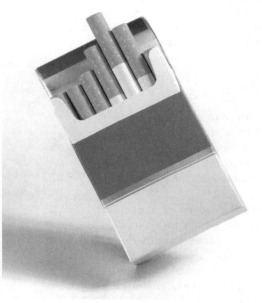

©iStockphoto.com/Grafissimo

Big Tobacco continues to be the object of restrictive regulations including higher excise taxes, bans on advertising, more pronounced health warnings, and public smoking restrictions. These measures, which have been adopted by both mature and developing economies, are consistent with the World Health Organization's concerted effort to inhibit the prevalence of smoking throughout the world. But do any of these regulations go too far and perhaps even deprive these companies of their "free-speech" or trademark rights?

Governments in the developed world have adopted many diverse tactics to curtail cigarette consumption and dissuade new smokers. They have been successful in stifling ads and marketing promotions, and now they want to do something about packaging. In the tobacco trade, product, package, and promotion are closely linked together. Distinctive packaging has always been one key success factor in the marketing of tobacco products. Packages are carefully designed with reliance on "color experts" and top graphic design artists. American Tobacco spent millions to redesign its Lucky Strike package so it would better appeal to consumers. Marlboro's legendary red-and-white logo displayed on a "crush-proof," cardboard flip-top box has been one of the main factors in the extraordinary success of this famous brand. Few other products have been able to boast of such an enduring achievement of package design and promotion.[38]

Given the importance of packaging, therefore, it is no surprise that it would become the next target of regulators determined to restrict the remaining traces of promotional efforts by tobacco firms. With smoking consumption in decline and advertising severely restricted, tobacco companies are forced to entice smokers to their products with quality and brand image communicated partly through smart packages. In some countries, like the United Kingdom, the tobacco firms have become quite innovative in designing packages, using vibrant colors like pink to appeal to young women smokers.[39]

In 2012, a plain-packaging law was passed in Australia. It came under immediate attack by the tobacco industry but survived a lawsuit by British American Tobacco. The Australian law passed amid opposition from some retailers and merchants who saw little benefit from this new restriction. Would a plain package really deter cigarette smokers? According to one report, "The Plain Packaging legislation is not supported by any research or evidence and would have the unintended consequences of job losses and a potential increase in illicit trade with no public health benefit."[40] However, supporters of the Australian law argued that the cigarette package clearly promotes the brand image, and hence this law should be an integral part of a comprehensive ban on advertising and marketing.

In May 2017, the same type of plain-packaging regulations went into effect in the United Kingdom. The law was passed in 2014 but delayed by several court challenges. The tough UK law bans branding or promotional messages on all cigarette packs. Thus, the legendary red-and-white chevron will be banished from all Marlboro packages. Cigarettes must be sold in drab greenish-brown packs without any logos or colors. There are large health warnings covering 65% of the package. On the side of each package, there is a message such as "Smoking kills—stop now" or "Smoking Causes Emphysema." There is also a graphic photo of a diseased lung or a cancerous tongue that further conveys the great health risks of smoking. All cigarette packs must contain at least 20 cigarettes so they can be big enough for all the requisite health warnings.[41]

Many other countries including France, Ireland, Hungary, and Norway have passed similar plain packaging laws, so it is likely this trend will spread at least throughout the European Union. The French law also went into effect in 2017. French authorities hope that neutral packages will change tobacco's image and deter new smokers from taking up the habit. However, the First Amendment and strong free-speech laws in the United States will most likely preclude government regulators from mandating plain packaging, though this result is far from certain.[42]

The tobacco industry led by British American Tobacco vigorously challenged the UK law, the latest step in a very restrictive regulatory regime throughout the United Kingdom. A ban on newspaper and billboard ads went into effect in the early 2000s, followed by a law that bans tobacco products from being displayed in stores. The industry first took its case to the European Court of Justice (ECJ), but that court ruled that the packaging restriction was lawful. The UK Supreme Court refused the industry's request to appeal their case any further.

In its defense, the industry has claimed these new plain-packaging laws have infringed upon their trademark and intellectual property rights. By forbidding the use of the trademark on a package, the companies are being deprived of their property without the appropriate compensation. It should be pointed out that while trademark law prevents a trademark from being misappropriated, it does not give someone a positive right to use that trademark. Companies also argued the legislation is unnecessary since, in the words of one spokesperson, "no one starts or continues to smoke because of the color of the pack." However, these arguments failed to persuade the legal authorities in the United Kingdom and countries in the European Union.[43]

- Do you agree with this recent trend toward plain packaging? Do the industry arguments regarding their trademark rights seem plausible? Will plain packaging make any difference in reducing smoking consumption?

- Should U.S. policy makers move in this direction? Is this a free-speech issue as the tobacco industry contends?

- Do tobacco companies have a duty to refrain from any kind of marketing?

BRIEFING ON SAFETY AND THE U.S. AUTOMOTIVE INDUSTRY

Ralph Nader's popular book *Unsafe at Any Speed* was a landmark work in the annals of books and articles dealing with the issue of automobile safety. Written in 1964, Nader concluded that the industry was myopic about safety issues and the situation

was not likely to change very much in the immediate future. Indeed, popular cars in the 1960s and 1970s, such as the Chevy Corvair and the Ford Pinto, were notorious for their unsafe designs. For a long time, safety was not a prime concern of automobile manufacturers who attributed accidents to careless drivers rather than to unsafe cars. They refused to believe the improper design and inferior quality of some vehicles was a contributing factor to many fatal accidents. At the same time, the U.S. government procrastinated putting into place a set of suitable safety regulations.

This briefing chronicles the long road to safer cars taken by the major players in the automotive industry along with U.S. policy makers. It also provides some background about the evolution of this industry so current safety issues can be viewed in their proper historical context.

The U.S. Automotive Industry

In the industry's earliest years, Ford Motor Co., founded by Henry Ford, was the undisputed market leader thanks to its famous Model T, nicknamed the "Tin Lizzy." Ford was followed by General Motors, which was founded by William C. Durant in 1908 as a holding company. Initially, General Motors operated only the Buick Motor Company, but it soon acquired several other young car companies including Oldsmobile, Cadillac, and Oakland (which became known as Pontiac). Another round of acquisitions from 1918 to 1920 added Chevrolet and General Motors Trucks to its expanding product range.

Ford wanted the car to become ubiquitous in the United States as a replacement for the horse and buggy. The company committed itself to large-scale high-volume production of the Model T. Accordingly, Ford innovated modern mass-production techniques at his new Highland Park plant in Michigan, which opened in 1910. The assembly line was introduced at that plant in 1914. Mass production led to lower costs and lower prices. By the time the Model T coupe was withdrawn from production in 1927, its price had been reduced to

$290, making it affordable for many middle-class Americans. The Model T was challenged by GM's Chevrolet as prospective drivers demanded different styling and new features.

After World War I, there was a striking transformation in the industry. A 1920 recession left an overly ambitious GM with excess inventory and resulted in a cash-flow crisis. Durant, who resigned in 1920, provided little central guidance and no sensible growth plan. Alfred P. Sloan became president of General Motors in 1923 in order to rescue the firm from its severe financial crisis. Sloan developed a new organizational structure that simultaneously emphasized decentralized operations and coordinated controls. Leaders of divisions like Chevrolet and Buick had freedom to operate, but certain controls were put in place to ensure those operations conformed to GM's overall growth and performance plans. Thanks to Sloan's brilliant management, GM took over first place in the industry and Ford fell into second place. GM held that leading market position for many decades.[44]

The third member of the "Big Three" automotive manufacturers in the United States was created during the 1920s. Walter Chrysler, formerly of General Motors, formed the Chrysler Corporation in 1925. The fledgling company's growth was accelerated by the acquisition of the Dodge Brothers company in 1928. Chrysler soon broke into the sizable low-priced car market with its famous Plymouth brand. Chrysler has had an especially turbulent history as the third largest of Detroit's auto companies. It was highly respected in the years after World War II for its well-engineered cars, but it has spent the last several decades "bouncing between highs and lows."[45]

Despite the rise of the automotive industry in Europe thanks to companies like Volkswagen, the Big Three dominated domestic and world markets until after World War II. They were joined by American Motors, which was founded in 1954, but always remained a minor industry player. In the postwar period, demand for automobiles peaked and the industry prospered. Detroit made big stylish "muscle" cars with high-performance V8 engines that were the envy of drivers throughout the world. The Ford Thunderbird, the Cadillac El Dorado, and the Chrysler Imperial became immensely popular and profitable brands.

But as foreign manufacturers made inroads into global markets, quality issues began to plague the industry. By the mid-1960s, American-made cars were being delivered to retail buyers with an average of 24 defects per unit. Federal regulations also upended the industry's cherished autonomy. Controls of emission of pollutants and energy consumption followed the oil shocks of 1973 and 1979. Demand for small, more fuel-efficient cars increased, and Japanese manufacturers like Toyota and Honda did a far better job of meeting that demand than GM and Ford. The industry was a victim of its own success and insularity. As David Halberstam points out,

> The weaknesses of the system, the inherent dangers of being a part of a domestic monopoly in an industry open to other countries, had not yet revealed themselves. So, while other areas of the American economy remained competitive, no one challenged the auto industry until the full-scale assault of the Japanese in the seventies. When it finally came, the extent of American vulnerability surprised even those who had been critical.[46]

After peaking at a record 12.87 million units in 1978, sales of American-made cars fell to 6.95 million in 1982 as imports increased their share of the U.S. market from 17.7% to 27.9%.[47]

Japanese manufacturers were particularly adept in penetrating the huge American market. The Big Three struggled to downsize their models in order to meet fuel efficiency standards with poor quality cars such as the Chevy Vega and Chevy Malibu. There were also public embarrassments such as the massive Ford Pinto recall. Chrysler, the weakest of the Big Three and battered by competitive pressures from abroad, found itself in financial chaos in the late 1970s. By 1979, Chrysler teetered on the brink of bankruptcy. But a $1.5 billion loan guarantee from the U.S. government helped save the company along with tens of thousands of jobs. Chrysler paid off the loans early in the 1980s, when it enjoyed success thanks to its minivans and a family of fuel-efficient autos called K-cars.

In 1980, Japan became the world's leading auto producer, a position it continues to hold. Honda and Toyota remain leading global brands with a high reputation for quality and reliability. In response to these events, the American automobile industry in the 1980s and 1990s underwent a massive restructuring effort, which included the introduction of new technologies to create a new generation of smaller and more fuel-efficient vehicles.[48] The era of the attractive, gas-guzzling muscle car was over. There was also the beginning of a consolidation trend during this decade. In 1987, Chrysler bought the number-four automaker, American Motors, but the subsequent consolidation prompted another financial calamity that led to a restructuring of the company. In 1998, Chrysler was acquired by Daimler-Benz of Germany and spent the next eight years as part of DaimlerChrysler. It was spun off in 2007 and once again became a stand-alone U.S. company.

The other major manufacturers also purchased or invested in foreign automakers. GM, for example, purchased a controlling interest in Swedish carmaker Saab and in Daewoo Motors. Ford invested in foreign manufacturers of Volvo, Aston Martin, and Jaguar. But under CEO Alan Mulally, Ford divested its interests in these elite brands to focus more intently on strengthening its own brand and enhancing manufacturing efficiency.

After difficult years battling resilient foreign competitors, fortunes improved somewhat in the late 1990s thanks to the popularity of sports utility vehicles (SUVs) such as the Ford Explorer and Chrysler's Jeep Cherokee. These vehicles have much higher profit margins, which helped Ford and GM to fatten their bottom lines. But in 2005, oil prices began to rise again, and demand for SUVs and light trucks suffered. Declining sales put a strain on industry profitability that culminated in near bankruptcy for Chrysler and GM. At the beginning of the 2008 recession, the Big Three were all in fragile financial condition, though Ford had the foresight to raise $23 billion in cash in 2006 by mortgaging some of its assets. According to conservative estimates, in 2008 the U.S. government directed $65 billion of taxpayer money to GM and Chrysler to avert financial disaster.[49] This "bailout," which has been repaid, averted tragic bankruptcies at a time when the U.S. economy was quite vulnerable. The Big Three have enjoyed more prosperous times in recent years. In early 2012, as the U.S. economy showed stronger signs of recovery, demand for U.S.-made cars, including trucks and SUVs, rallied. As a result, General Motors posted a record net profit of $7.6 billion. Chrysler announced a profit of $183 million, its first net profit since its near bankruptcy in 2008.[50]

Industry Indifference: "Safety Doesn't Sell"

The first known automobile fatality occurred in 1898, just one year after the automobile was invented in 1897. Since 1900, 3.5 million Americans have been killed in automobile accidents and over 300 million people have been injured. As automobile sales increased during the early part of the 20th century, so did fatalities. By 1946, automobile sales exploded in the United States thanks to pent-up demand after World War II. At the same time, highway deaths rose to 32,000 people per year. The number of fatalities continued to rise, and some safety advocates and policy makers took notice. The main problem was the so-called second collision after the initial impact of an accident. This was the collision of the occupants with the interior of the car, or with the road if they were thrown from the vehicle. For example, in a serious accident, a driver could be impaled by the steering column. To limit the physical damage from the second collision, safety experts recommended seat belts, collapsible steering wheels, "double-grip" door latches to prevent ejection, and other restraints.[51]

But for a long time, the general public regarded automobile accidents and fatalities as part of the "acceptable risk" of driving a car. Hence much of the early advocacy for safety improvements fell on deaf ears in Detroit, home to the corporate offices of the Big Three. During the high-growth era after the war, there was no recognition that safe design was a responsibility of the automobile industry. Safety simply meant safe and careful behavior by drivers. In the mind of Detroit, it had nothing to do with improved safety design (such as "deep-center" steering wheels to prevent impalement) or higher quality. Without the market pressure of demand from consumers for safer cars, safety was not a high priority for the Big Three. According to Joel Eastman, "Automobile manufacturers, echoing the reasoning of the highway professionals, took the position that it was not normal for a motor vehicle to be involved in an accident, and therefore they were under no obligation to design for that circumstance."[52] The industry mantra was clear: "cars are safe, drivers cause accidents." As one General Motors executive exclaimed, "If the drivers do everything they should, there wouldn't be accidents, would there?"[53] Some states such as Massachusetts were considering meaningful safety regulations, but they met with fierce resistance from the industry.[54]

Instead of safety, the industry was far more concerned with design, style, and performance. They wanted to build and sell cars that consumers wanted. At the time, there was big demand for fashionable muscle cars with powerful V8 engines and 300 horsepower. The Chevy Camaro, the Ford Thunderbird, and the Pontiac GTO were all top-selling brands. None of these cars were constructed with safety in mind—they usually had mediocre handling and inadequate brakes. They were designed to accelerate quickly and to appeal to younger drivers who often pushed them beyond reasonable safety limits.[55] During the 1950s and 1960s, the Detroit oligopoly chose to emphasize annual styling and horsepower enhancements rather than new safety technologies such as seat belts (available in 1959), rollover protection, and disc brakes (introduced by Mercedes-Benz in 1958).[56]

The Safety Crusade Begins

Attitudes about car safety finally began to change in the mid-1960s. Fatalities were on the rise, peaking in 1966 at 51,000 lives lost in car crashes. It was slowly dawning on the public and the media that this was a big problem that needed to be addressed. A catalyst for change occurred in 1965 when consumer advocate and lobbyist Ralph

Nader published his book *Unsafe at Any Speed*. Here was Nader's bleak assessment of the situation:

> For over half a century the automobile has brought death, injury, and the most inestimable sorrow and deprivation to millions of people. With Medea-like intensity, this mass trauma began rising sharply years ago, reflecting new and unexpected ravages by the motor vehicle. . . . A transportation specialist, Wilfred Owen, wrote in 1946, "There is little question that the public will not tolerate for long an annual traffic toll of forty to fifty thousand fatalities." Time has shown Owen to be wrong. Unlike aviation, marine, or rail transportation, the highway transport system can inflict tremendous casualties and property damage without in the least affecting the viability of the system. Plane crashes, for example, jeopardize the attraction of flying for potential passengers and therefore strike at the heart of the air transport economy. They motivate preventative efforts. The situation is different on the roads.[57]

The book documented in detail the many egregious flaws of the Chevrolet Corvair models from 1960 to 1963. Before its redesign, this car was infamous for its poor handling and lack of stability. *Time* magazine listed the Corvair as one of the 50 worst cars of all time. The Corvair was distinctive because it was a rear-engine car. There are certain benefits to putting the vehicle's heaviest component behind the rear axle. However, this design produces cars with a tendency to spin out. Chevrolet executives refused to spend the extra money to make the swing-axle rear suspension more manageable. The car had many other problems. It leaked oil profusely and its heating system tended to pump noxious fumes into the cabin. The end result was an unsafe vehicle that was heavily accident-prone.[58]

The remainder of Nader's book focused on other notably neglected safety issues, ranging from poor brake performance to the fate of drivers who were being impaled by noncollapsible steering wheels. In general, Nader hit hard on the theme of poor accident protection. There was a big gap, he argued, "between existing design and attainable safety."[59] Nader's book and his subsequent safety campaign got a great boost from General Motors itself. The company was caught having private investigators follow him around. GM offered various excuses but all lacked plausibility, and General Motors formally apologized. Thanks to this publicity, by the spring of 1966, *Unsafe at Any Speed* was a runaway best-seller for nonfiction books.[60]

At the same time that Nader's book appeared, Senator Abe Ribicoff held hearings on "Traffic Safety" during the spring and summer of 1965. Among the many issues discussed was GM's lack of attention to the Chevy Corvair's documented safety problems. The hearings raised the profile of automotive safety and showcased a defensive and combative industry, reluctant to confront the challenge of making safer cars.

Thanks in part to the growing higher safety consciousness of the American public, Congress passed landmark safety legislation in 1966: the National Traffic and Motor Vehicle Safety Act, which created the National Highway Traffic Safety Administration (NHTSA). The Highway Safety Act of 1966 was also passed at the same time, and it led to many changes in vehicle design. Thanks to new federal guidelines empowered by this law, vehicles were built with new safety features, including front head restraints, energy-absorbing steering wheels, shatter-resistant windshields, and safety belts. For example, despite the objections of the automobile industry, in 1968 all passenger cars were required to come equipped with seat and shoulder belts for front seats. This regulation was widely regarded as a monumental step forward for passenger safety. According to NHTSA research, new safety standards, especially the seat belt and the airbag, saved more than 600,000 lives between 1966 and 2012.[61]

Subsequent to these laws, there has been a series of government mandates to enhance passenger safety. In 1974, the national speed limit was set at 55 miles per hour. The national maximum speed limit law was repealed in 1995, and the speed limit has since been modestly increased in most states. In 1984, states began to enact laws obligating drivers to wear their seat belts (or face fines). And in 1998, all new passenger cars were required to be equipped with frontal airbags. Airbag technology had been invented decades earlier, and it was commercialized in the 1960s when Mercedes-Benz developed airbags for its vehicles. But this proven safety technology did not find its way into most vehicles until the 1990s, perhaps another sign of safety indifference on the part of the Detroit oligopoly.[62]

Since the imposition of the airbag requirement, there have been several other key NHTSA mandates. The agency has upgraded roof-crush standards for vehicles. In 2012, the NHTSA required electronic stability control (ESC) in all vehicles. ESC improves a car's stability by detecting and reducing loss of traction. These regulations along with a steady stream of other technological improvements have led to a sharp drop in automotive fatalities. In 1950, there were 70 deaths per billion vehicle-miles traveled, but in 2015, there were only about 10 deaths per billion.[63]

Nonetheless, the industry has still not demonstrated a capability to recognize and deal promptly with defective cars. There have been numerous safety scandals involving automobile manufacturers like Ford, General Motors, Chrysler, and Toyota along with suppliers such as Firestone and Takata. The Pinto catastrophe still casts a dark shadow over the image of Ford and the entire automobile industry. The subcompact Pinto was a poorly made, unsafe car, subject to explosions and fire in the case of a rear-end collision. As the NHTSA investigative report into the Pinto's rear-end collisions concluded, "The fuel tank and filler pipe assembly installed in the 1971–1976 Ford Pinto is subject to damage which results in fuel spillage and fire potential in rear impact collisions by other vehicles at moderate closing speeds."[64] The report also indicated that between January 1975 and June 1977, there were 33 fatal Pinto accidents involving fire that resulted in 41 fatalities. After the NHTSA report was issued, Ford announced it was recalling 1.5 million Pintos, but the damage to Ford's reputation represented a huge setback for a company struggling to compete with the Japanese.

In addition to the Pinto controversy, Ford had to contend with safety problems with its popular Explorer SUV about 15 years later. The Ford Explorer was prone to rollover crashes, which were blamed in part on its Firestone tires. Ford acknowledged that it had been slow to detect and respond to the deadly Firestone-Ford combination. Given its reactive response to the radial tire recall in 1978, it is reasonable to assert that Firestone already had a poor safety record. From 2002 to 2010, reports of unintended acceleration in several Toyota models became another tragic example of industry safety problems. At least 56 people were killed because of defects linked to unintended acceleration. The Chrysler Jeep fires, which led to the recall of

1.7 million vehicles in 2013, and Chevy Cobalt's ignition switch debacle brought to light in 2014 are further evidence of the industry's continuing safety problems and its poor responsiveness. General Motors itself found a pattern of incompetence and neglect in its handling of the defective ignition switch. Thus, while progress has been made, new safety defects, inaccurate reporting, and delayed recalls continue to beset the automotive industry.[65]

"Driverless Cars" and the Future of Automotive Safety

Despite enhancements such as airbags, seat belts, ESC, and many other effective safety devices, there are still far too many automotive fatalities. According to the NHTSA, there were 35,000 traffic fatalities in 2015, about 90% of them attributable to human error, including drunk driving. The leading cause of accidents continues to be driving too fast, with "driving under the influence" in second place. Auto accidents also cause over 2 million serious injuries per year.[66]

Many cars now come equipped with high-tech safety gear such as autonomous braking and systems that prevent drivers from drifting out of their lanes. Enabling these safety features are cameras, sensors, and microprocessors. These safety technologies along with autopilot systems are a precursor to the driverless car, which should help reduce fatal automobile accidents. Tesla Motors has introduced a system that provides not only automatic braking and cruise control but also steers the car more actively (and accurately) than other semiautonomous systems. While some say that intelligent cruise control and self-driving vehicles will prevent accidents, others argue these technologies lull drivers into a false sense of security. According to Tesla, "Autopilot is by far the most advanced such system on the road, but it does not turn a Tesla into an autonomous vehicle and does not allow the driver to abdicate responsibility."[67]

The driverless car, still in its experimental stage, may be the next step in the steady evolution of automobile safety. The industry is certainly convinced that autonomous driving systems are on the horizon. Ford Motor Company announced it would introduce fully driverless cars without steering wheels by 2021. Other automobile manufacturers such as Nissan and Volkswagen have also committed to putting self-driving cars on the road as soon as possible. Eventually this technological race will engulf the entire global automobile industry. Even software giant Google is involved in a project to leverage its software and technology skills to make a driverless car. Carmakers need the cooperation of regulators, who tend to be quite cautious. The first mover in this new market, whether it be a company in Detroit, Silicon Valley, or Singapore, will gain a huge advantage in deploying driverless car technology throughout the world.[68]

These safer vehicles may come along just in time. Within the last few years, car-crash fatalities have been on the rise as people have spent more time on the road and attempted to multitask with their smartphones or other devices. High-tech safety packages and eventually the driverless car can perhaps compensate for the human error and negligence that still cause the vast majority of automobile accidents.[69]

CASE STUDY 8.2

THE CHEVY COBALT IGNITION SWITCH CRISIS

Kelly Ruddy was only 21 years old when she lost her life in a deadly crash on Interstate 81 in Lackawanna County, Pennsylvania, in January 2010. It was a dark and dreary winter night, and Kelly was driving north on the highway near the Bear Creek exit. For no apparent reason and without warning, she suddenly lost control of her 2005 Chevy Cobalt. The car flipped over, and Kelly was thrown from the vehicle. She was struck immediately by passing cars, which had no opportunity to stop. The accident was carefully investigated by Pennsylvania State Police. It was later determined that due to a faulty ignition switch, Mary's car

AP Photo/J. Scott Applewhite

had lost all power, become uncontrollable, and then flipped over, leading to her tragic death.

Her parents, Mary and Leo Ruddy, fought General Motors for four years and often met denial and corporate resistance. Finally, in October 2014, they received a large financial settlement for their daughter's death along with an apology from the company. "It took us a whole four years. It was extremely difficult dealing with GM. They just set up road blocks and didn't want to deal with us and give us any acknowledgment," said Leo Ruddy. The distraught father went on to say, "It's ten years too late, they should have did something back in 2004 when they knew about it, our daughter would still be here and still would God knows how many other people."[70]

This case explores the design flaws in the Chevy Cobalt that led to numerous tragic accidents. It also explores the corporate attitudes and bureaucratic morass that prevented General Motors from expeditiously getting at the root cause of the problem.

The Chevy Cobalt and General Motors

The early 2000s were once again difficult times for General Motors and the automotive industry in the United States. From 2001 to 2007, GM's global market share declined from 15% to 13.3%, and the trends for the future were not too promising. In 2005, General Motors lost over $10 billion, and during that year the company initiated widespread cost-containment measures. The company eliminated 30,000 manufacturing jobs to reduce excess assembly capacity by 1 million units. Despite these measures, in 2007, GM was still losing $729 per vehicle. Against this backdrop, GM sought to develop a more successful line of compact cars to shore up the declining sales of its trucks and SUVs. Rising gasoline prices increased consumer demand for smaller and more efficient vehicles, and GM sought to respond with new models.[71]

This new line of cars included the Saturn Ion, introduced in 2003, and the Chevy Cobalt, launched in 2005. The Chevy Cobalt replaced the very successful Chevy Cavalier, but it had a higher price point than its predecessor. The Cobalt was a compact car that was designed to compete with the Ford Focus, the Toyota Corolla, and the Honda Civic. The Cobalt SS was a sports coupe, which was described in ads as the Corvette's "little brother." GM hoped the Cobalt's smart design and contemporary styling would attract younger drivers looking for cars with a more European look and feel. Its marketing efforts were heavily directed at drivers in the 18-to-34 age segment. Buyers could test drive the Cobalt in showrooms and also during Chevy tours across the country. These targeted marketing efforts paid off. The Cobalt was a big hit with younger drivers. More than 212,600 Cobalts were sold in 2005. Within a short period of time, the car delivered the highest number of buyers under age 34 for all GM vehicles. By the end of 2008, 40% of sales of the Cobalt Coupe were made to drivers under 30.[72]

In developing vehicles for its small car line, GM relied on platform technology or common vehicle architectures that could be deployed on a global basis. This platform approach was adopted to help reduce development costs. Delta was GM's compact platform for front-wheel-drive automobiles and SUVs. Vehicles using the same platform shared key design and architectural components. The Delta platform included the Saturn Ion, Chevy Cobalt, the Chevrolet HHR, and the Pontiac G5. The platform debuted in 2003 with the Saturn Ion. All platform vehicles used the same four-speed automatic transmission and the same engines. They also used the same ignition switch.[73]

The Cobalt and other Delta platform cars were described as "cost conscious vehicles," produced and sold with only the slimmest of margins. Every effort was also made to keep production costs low and all suppliers were pressured to lower their costs. GM sought to reduce material costs by $1 billion by 2008 by setting cost-cutting targets for individual parts. Also, in an effort to increase revenues, the Cobalt was sold in large volumes to fleet buyers and to rental companies at steep discounts.[74]

Choosing an Ignition Switch for the Cobalt

All Delta platform vehicles used the same ignition switch, which was located on the steering column of each vehicle. When the driver turns on the ignition switch, the engine turns over, and a signal is sent to activate the vehicle's systems, such as the antilock brakes and the airbag. When the switch is in the off position, all power is shut off, including the power for the airbags. In accessory mode, limited functions remain on (such as the radio). Key supporting components of the ignition switch include the shaft, the housing, the key cylinder, and the detent plunger, which holds the switch in the proper position (such as the run position). An essential design issue is the amount of force or rotational torque needed to turn the ignition switch from the off to the accessory or run position and keep the switch in that desired position.[75]

In 1997, GM engineers designed a new "low current" ignition switch system known as the Discrete Logic Ignition Switch (DLIS). The innovative new system was designed to be less expensive and less prone to failure. It was developed as a "common" switch that could be used on multiple vehicle platforms. One of its main suppliers, Eaton Corporation (later acquired by Delphi), was chosen to develop and produce the DLIS ignition switch.[76]

From its inception, however, this ignition switch had extensive problems. The prototype switch built by the supplier performed so poorly that the entire electrical concept needed to be reconfigured. But the redesigned switch also failed to meet GM's mechanical specifications for ignition switches. Specifically, the rotational torque, or the amount of effort required to rotate the ignition switch, was too low, allowing it to inadvertently move from the run position to off or accessory. The reason behind the low torque was that the detent plunger, which holds the switch in position, was too short. A longer spring along with a tighter and longer detent would have increased the rotational torque and prevented inadvertent shut-offs of the ignition switch when the car was in motion. But the lead engineer, Ray DeGiorgio, initially approved production of the switch with the low torque and shorter spring, since he believed this deviation would not affect the car's performance. Subsequent torque tests conducted in the fall of 2001 demonstrated very poor results: torque values required to rotate from the run to accessory position were well below the norm. The report states "Not OK" next to the test results. DeGiorgio received and reviewed these test results, but it is not clear whether they were seen by anyone else at GM.[77]

Despite the negative test results with torque values below specification, DeGiorgio signed off on the ignition switch for production. No other approvals were necessary. He instructed Delphi to take no action to enhance the rotational torque because he was concerned that changing the detent would compromise the switch's electrical performance. DeGiorgio's email to Delphi, signaling his frustration, was signed, "Ray (tired of the switch from hell) DeGiorgio."[78]

While DeGiorgio knew he was approving a substandard ignition switch, there is no evidence that other GM managers knew the switch did not meet GM's specifications. With DeGiorgio's knowledge and approval, the switch went into production even though it had these torque values well below standards. The fact that an inferior ignition switch had been authorized by DeGiorgio was not known to the engineers who would be investigating the Cobalt's accidents for the next decade. This lack of knowledge was due to a failure within the organization to track authorizations and accompanying test results for the vehicle's different technologies.

The switch was first installed in the Saturn Ion in late 2002. It was then approved for use in the Chevrolet Cobalt, Pontiac G5, Chevrolet HHR, Pontiac Solstice, and Saturn Sky. Ion production had begun in the fall of 2002, and by October 2003, performance reports indicated ignition switch problems. There were 65 reported moving stalls thanks to the ignition switch being accidentally rotated to the accessory or off position. But nothing was done to address the problem. The Cobalt went into production in the summer of 2004 with the defective switch. It was common practice for a group of new cars to be tested by GM employees, who were responsible for identifying problems before full-scale production began. During those tests, there were three cases of moving stalls as a result of the ignition switch being inadvertently turned to the off position. But the head of this testing group did not report these stalls, since he did not consider them to be significant.[79]

When some of the first Cobalt cars coming off the assembly line were tested, there were also reports of inadvertent ignition switch shut-offs that resulted in moving stalls. But the engineers categorized the problem with the ignition switch as a "convenience" issue rather than a safety issue. Instead of implementing a solution, the engineers debated short-term fixes and their possible costs. In November 2004, as the Cobalt was about to arrive in showrooms, the moving stall problem was classified as a nonsafety issue despite the fact that this "stall" also deactivated the power steering, the power brakes, and the airbag system.[80]

Around the time of the Cobalt product launch, there were two other reports of moving stalls triggered by a driver bumping the key chain with his knee. One was a journalist from Santa Barbara who informed Doug Parks, the Cobalt chief engineer, of the incident. Parks directed someone to look into the problem, but both incidents were once again regarded as "isolated events with no safety implications." Nonetheless, in late November 2004, GM personnel opened a PRTS (problem resolution and tracking system) report to address the complaints. Engineers reviewed the problem and possible solutions, but the PRTS was closed in March 2005 with no action taken.[81]

By May 2005, General Motors had received many disturbing reports about moving stalls from Cobalt drivers. Some of those drivers demanded that GM repurchase their Cobalts because the ignition switch shut off during normal driving conditions. While GM engineers continued to disavow that this was a safety issue, Cobalt drivers had a much different perspective. According to one disgruntled customer,

> This is a safety/recall issue if there ever was one. . . . The problem is the ignition
> switch is poorly installed. Even with the slightest touch, the car will shut off
> while in motion. I don't have to list to you the safety problems that may happen,
> besides an accident or death, a car turning off while doing a high speed must
> cause engine and other problems in the long haul. I am forwarding this letter
> to the NHTSA as I firmly believe that this ignition switch needs to be recalled,
> reexamined and corrected.[82]

As a result of these complaints, GM opened a second PRTS on May 17, 2005, as two committees took charge of the issue: VAPIR (Vehicle and Process Integration Review) and CPIT (Current Production Improvement Team). Both committees discussed various solutions such as changing the key head design. They also considered longer term solutions such as replacing the ignition switch in future model year vehicles. DeGiorgio was consulted by both committees, and he argued for changing the ignition switch.[83]

VAPIR signed off on the short-term fix, a new key head design that would put less weight on the key chain. GM issued a technical service bulletin to dealers explaining that the company now had an insert to change the key from a slot to a hole along with a smaller 13-millimeter key ring. However, in September 2005, the same committee rejected the new Cobalt ignition switch, called the GMT 191, that had been recommended by DeGiorgio. The long-term fix was scrapped because it was "too expensive" and would not result in "offsetting changes in savings on warranty costs." In an email to engineers working on the problem, it was explained that "the con of the change is that the piece cost of the ignition switch went up around $0.90 and would require $400,000 in retooling . . . [while] the warranty offset for the new switch is in the $0.10 to $0.15 range."[84]

It was clear from the committee's deliberations that they still saw the problem as a convenience issue that could be solved by a simple measure, such as changing the key head and warning drivers to remove unessential items from their key chain. By this point, there were reports coming into GM about fatal Cobalt accidents due to airbags not deploying, but GM committees and managers did not grasp the connection to the flawed ignition switch, which they declined to treat as a safety issue.

To complicate matters further, the same GM engineer, Ray DeGiorgio, who approved the faulty ignition switch reversed course several years later without telling anyone. In 2006, he authorized a change in the ignition switch that would increase the torque required to turn the key. The original detent plunger was replaced by a new one that had a longer and tighter spring. The new ignition switch was installed in the Cobalt and other vehicles beginning with the 2008 model year. However, the part number was not changed, and this made the change difficult to track. This failure to assign the new switch a different part number became a source of great confusion for engineers and others investigating the problem. When asked in 2009 and on subsequent occasions if the ignition switch had changed, DeGiorgio said it had not. DeGiorgio even testified under oath that he did not remember making a change from the 2005 to 2008 models.[85]

By June 2006, GM engineers had been investigating the problem of moving stalls in the Cobalt for two years. At the same time, there were fatalities being reported due to airbag nondeployment. Those reports began to reach the GM legal department. But none of the investigators, committees, or lawyers perceived the connection between airbag nondeployment and the ease with which the ignition switch could be rotated to the accessory or off position. These two matters were regarded as separate and unrelated problems. Aside from changing the key head, no other solutions had been implemented to fix the low-torque ignition switch. DeGiorgio had approved a redesign of the ignition switch to take effect with the 2008 models, but this change did not address the problems with 2005, 2006, and 2007 Cobalts.[86]

Cobalt's Fatal Accidents

On July 29, 2005, Amber Marie Rose died in a head-on collision in her 2005 Chevrolet Cobalt. This was the first death to be attributed to the defective switches. A contractor hired by NHTSA found that the Cobalt's ignition had moved out of the run position and into the accessory position, which cut off power to the steering, brakes, and airbags. In October 2006, three teenage girls returning from a trip to a Wisconsin Walmart store were involved in a serious accident when their 2005 Cobalt lost power and the car smashed into a tree. The airbags did not deploy, and as a result, two of the girls died, while the third suffered severe brain damage.

Many other accidents were reported to GM, including Kelly Ruddy's in January 2010. Just two months later, in March 2010, 29-year-old Brooke Melton was killed when her car stalled and lost control. It slammed into an oncoming Ford Focus. Other fatal crashes included the Cobalt that wrapped around a tree in Baldwin, Louisiana, in November 2005 and the Cobalt that struck a light pole in Lanexa, Virginia, in February 2006. Every time GM received notice of a crash, it opened a file, but there was no follow-up action. In 2007, the Wisconsin State Police sent to GM a detailed report on a different accident, detailing how a Cobalt crash had led to a fatality thanks to a moving stall and the subsequent nondeployment of the airbag. The report indicated that the ignition switch was in the "Acc" position and that the loss of power was the most likely reason for the airbag's failure to deploy. Outsiders had figured out the connection between the ignition switch failure and airbag nondeployment, but this fact continued to elude GM engineers.[87]

According to a *New York Times* investigation, federal safety regulators and General Motors received more than 260 complaints from 2005 to 2014 about GM vehicles that suddenly turned off while being driven. Reports about Cobalt accidents and airbag nondeployment also continued to arrive at the company. However, while the NHTSA "expressed interest" in Cobalt airbag nondeployments in 2007, it refused to investigate these accidents more thoroughly. The NHTSA made no formal request to GM and did not ask the company to report back about the issue. Every time GM received notice of an accident, the company opened a new file. But GM engineers could not figure out the source of the problem until 2013. Many of the complaints detailed frightening and harrowing scenes in which moving cars abruptly stalled out at high speeds. This happened on highways, in the middle of city traffic, and even while crossing railroad tracks. Some consumer complaints warned of "catastrophic consequences" if remedial action wasn't taken.[88]

When in-house lawyers began to see a troubling pattern in these accidents, they urged GM executives to initiate a more comprehensive investigation. This time the investigation was handled by GM's Product Investigation Unit. It was assigned to a team led by Brian Stouffer. But despite the growing number of Cobalt crashes, "the investigation moved with no sense of urgency." Stouffer was given all the results of the previous investigations, including outside reports like the one from the Wisconsin State Police. Stouffer and his team were especially puzzled that later models had no problems with airbag nondeployment. They did not know of the ignition switch change authorized by DeGiorgio beginning with the 2008 models. The Stouffer investigation proceeded slowly and produced no results—it became "stuck" by early 2013. However, there were several lawsuits in litigation against GM, and in one of the court proceedings in 2013, a plaintiff's expert revealed there was a difference between the ignition switches used in the later Cobalt models (beginning in 2008) and those found in the 2005 to 2007 models. Only then were GM executives fully aware that the early-model Cobalts had a different ignition switch than the later models and that the first defective switch most likely had severe torque problems that might be responsible for airbag nondeployment.[89]

With this evidence in hand, GM investigators had finally gotten to the root cause of the problem. But Stouffer wanted reconfirmation, so he hired his outside expert to review the conclusions of the plaintiff's expert. Around this time, GM lawyers and outside counsel, which formed the Settlement Review Committee, reviewed the matter again. According to their report, "Airbag non-deployments in Cobalts . . . may be at least partially linked to the ignition switch issue. We know of approximately 20 non-deployments of frontal airbags in Cobalts where the crash forces are sufficient to have properly deployed the frontal airbag. [But] the ignition was in the 'Acc' position. In the Cobalt the airbag will not deploy with the key in 'Acc.'"[90] Stouffer received his own report from the outside expert in November 2013, which confirmed that the defective ignition switch had been changed. At this point, he too came to the same conclusion as the Settlement Review Committee, a conclusion that had been reached six years earlier by Wisconsin state troopers.[91]

The Recall and Settlement

One month later in December 2013, a recall was proposed and reviewed by the Executive Field Action Decision Committee (EFADC). The committee was hesitant to approve a recall because GM's chief engineer still questioned the extent and severity of the problem. Also, the EFADC members were not presented with fatality data and hence felt no strong pressure to take immediate action. Thus, even when GM became aware of the root cause behind this pattern of airbag failures, there was still a lack of urgency, a reluctance to "elevate" the issue, and a lack of leadership to drive the investigation to a conclusion.[92]

Finally, in February 2014, GM issued its first recall of 780,000 cars with faulty ignition switches; vehicles included both the Chevy Cobalt and Saturn Ion models. The cost was estimated to be $32.3 million. Later that month, the recall was expanded to an additional

842,000 vehicles at a cost of $34.3 million. In March, GM officials learned that older ignition switches had been used to fix 2008–2011 Cobalts and Ions, and so the recall was expanded again by another 970,808 vehicles at an additional cost of $39.7 million.[93]

GM hired the law firm of Jenner & Block to investigate the entire Cobalt saga. GM also hired an attorney, Kenneth Feinberg, to ascertain precise numbers of accidents, deaths, and injuries due to the faulty ignition switch. GM originally claimed there were only 13 deaths attributable to this defect, but Feinberg found this number was much too low. Of all the claims for physical injury or death received up to 2015, Feinberg determined that 399 were valid. There were 124 deaths and 17 victims with very serious injuries (such as quadriplegia or permanent brain damage). Many other victims suffered modest injuries.[94]

In April 2014, Mary Barra, who became GM's CEO in January 2014, testified before a congressional hearing. She admitted many mistakes had been made but reassured the congressional panel, "We will not shirk from our responsibilities now and in the future." She authorized a victims' compensation fund of $625 million. In 2015, the U.S. Attorney for the Southern District of New York announced that a deal had been struck with General Motors. The carmaker would admit to concealing defects that led to the death of 15 people and it would pay a $900 million fine. No GM employees were charged with criminal wrongdoing.[95]

EXHIBIT 8.1   ■   Timeline of Events

1997–2001: Specifications determined for ignition switch for Delta platform (including Cobalt)

2002: DeGiorgio approves ignition switch for production in Cobalt and Ion models

August 2004: Cobalt goes into production

Fall 2004: Early reports of Cobalt moving stalls

November 2004: PRTS opened but moving stalls classified as nonsafety issue

March 2005: PRTS closed with no solution

May 2005: Cobalt VAPIR Committee considers short-term and long-term solutions to moving stall issue

September 2005: VAPIR rejects proposal to change ignition switch

2006: Litigation involving fatalities begins

May 2006: DeGiorgio approves ignition switch design change without change in part number

2007: Outsiders discover solution (Wisconsin trooper's report) but GM remains unaware

2009: GM declares bankruptcy as investigations continue

2011: Production Investigation Unit headed by Stouffer begins new investigation

April 2013: Plaintiff's expert demonstrates that ignition switch was redesigned in 2006

November 2013: GM's outside expert reconfirms redesign of switch and Stouffer arrives at his conclusions

December 2013: EFADC meeting to consider recall

February 2014: Recall of Cobalt (and Ion) model years 2005, 2006, 2007 gets under way

EXHIBIT 8.2 ■ GM Selected Financial Data, 2009–2013 (in millions)					
	2009	**2010**	**2011**	**2012**	**2013**
Revenues	$57,474	$135,592	$150,276	$152,256	$155,427
Operating Income	(4,928)	5,084	5,656	(30,363)	5,131
Net Income	(4,428)	4,668	7,585	4,859	3,770

- What was the competitive environment for GM when the Cobalt was introduced, and how might this have affected the company's decision making about safety issues?

- What are the implications of this case for how safety crises should be managed?

- How do you assess the actions of engineer Ray DeGiorgio?

- Did GM shirk its ethical obligations in this case? Were rights violated by GM's refusal to take action earlier?

CASE STUDY 8.3

TAKATA'S AIRBAG: UNSAFE IN ANY CAR?

©iStockphoto.com/jpgfactory

One of the most propitious developments in the history of automotive safety was the introduction of the airbag that inflates on impact to protect drivers and passengers in the event of a dangerous collision. In the United States, the front-seat airbag became mandatory equipment in 1998. All vehicles now include front-seat driver and passenger airbags, and most cars are also equipped with seat-mounted and door-mounted side airbags. Airbags save lives and reduce the number of traumatic injuries that can result from accidents. But what happens when the airbag itself is defective? Auto manufacturers and motorists were forced to deal with this unfortunate situation when they learned that the airbags made by the Japanese company Takata could explode and disperse shrapnel throughout a vehicle's cabin.

After providing some background on the dynamics of the airbag industry, this case examines the root causes of the Takata-made airbag's defects. It also presents Takata's reactive response to this crisis, which frustrated automakers and regulators. The tragedy of the Takata airbag and the subsequent recriminations and lawsuits have had a profound impact on this once proud pioneer in automotive technology.

Takata AG

Takata AG was founded in 1933 in Shiga Prefecture, Japan, by an entrepreneur named Takezo Takada. The company began by manufacturing the lifelines that were used for parachutes. It also produced a number of other textile products. In the early 1950s, the company started to do research on seat belts based on its knowledge of parachute technology. Mr. Takada and other principals eventually incorporated as Takata. In the 1960s, Takata started to sell seat belts to automobile manufacturers. Takata soon developed a reputation as an innovator. The small company built the world's first crash-test plant for testing seat belts under real-world conditions. Takata was also a pioneer in the development of child restraint systems. In the early 1980s, the company changed its name to the Takata Corporation. Takata began making airbags in 1988. It soon expanded into Korea, Europe, and later to Ireland, where it manufactured and sold its seat belts. In the late 1980s, Takata established a U.S. subsidiary in North Carolina called TK Holdings Inc.

In 2000, the Takata Corporation acquired a German competitor, Petri AG, forming the European subsidiary Takata-Petri, which was renamed Takata AG in early 2012. Takata went public in November 2006, listing its shares on the Tokyo stock exchange. The Takada family and trust retained 80% ownership stake in their company. The founder's son, Juichiro Takada, became CEO and chairman that year, but several years later, in 2011, leadership was handed over to his son, Shigehisa Takada. In addition to its core products, airbags and seat belts, Takata AG makes steering wheels, child seats, and various plastic parts for cars and other machinery. By 2016, this major Japanese supplier to the global automotive industry employed over 48,000 workers in its worldwide operations, with revenues of $6.6 billion.[96]

Over its long history, Takata built a global reputation for reliability and quality. It was a company noted for its innovative product development and careful product testing. Takata's whole philosophy and mission has been tied to the goal of consumer safety:

> Takata has been engineering the precision of our products to the millisecond for over 70 years. We have been driven by our dedication to save human life while embracing a pioneering spirit in developing innovative products. Takata has spread this same thought process to all of our locations worldwide. "Somewhere on earth, Takata products have saved the preciousness of human life today." We continue to challenge ourselves and our affiliates all over the world to develop new technologies so that people will be able to experience the joy of life. Our dream is that someday there will be zero victims due to traffic accidents. And we hope the day will come when the word "TAKATA" becomes synonymous with "safety."[97]

Airbag Technology and the Airbag Industry

Airbag technology is an integral aspect of automotive safety. The purpose of the airbag is to impede the driver or passenger's forward motion during a collision within a fraction of a second. The airbag system consists of a bag made of thin, nylon fabric, the sensor that tells the bag to inflate, and the inflator, a steel canister encasing the propellants that release gases which cause the bag to inflate and cushion the driver's forward motion. Inflation must happen quickly but not too quickly or the bag will blow up and burst, sending shards of metal at the vehicle's occupants. An essential element for a safe airbag is the use of stable propellants.[98]

The global airbag industry has been highly concentrated in the hands of a few major producers for the last several decades. Steady global demand for autos and trucks along with tighter safety regulations have in turn fueled an escalation in demand for component products like airbags. Growth has been highest in North America, with Asia and Europe following close behind. One challenge for the industry has been a change in consumer expectations. Consumers have become more demanding and want superior safety equipment in their vehicles. But some structural aspects of the industry favor the rivals. Barriers to entry are high due to the need for substantial capital investment in plant and machinery coupled with technical expertise. In addition, the airbag is not optional equipment so there are no available substitute technologies for automakers.

The whole airbag industry is dependent on the original equipment manufacturers, or OEMs (automobile manufacturers), which are required by law to install airbags. This dependency makes the industry vulnerable to fluctuations in demand for new automobiles and trucks. If automobile industry sales decline, so too will sales for the airbag industry. Also, automakers have forced down their cost structure by techniques such as "just-in-time" production, which frowns on inventory and requires parts to be delivered as they are needed. These demands can create challenging delivery schedules and the need for quick production ramp-ups by suppliers.[99]

There is fairly intense rivalry among airbag industry incumbents, which include the US-Swedish firm Autoliv, TRW, Takata, and Delphi, the principal supplier of General Motors. The number of viable competitors lowers the bargaining power of airbag module manufacturers, since OEMs can easily transition to another airbag manufacturer. These low switching costs give OEMs considerable leverage over their airbag suppliers. Airbags are a necessary but expensive component of every vehicle. The addition of the airbag as standard equipment drove up the price of cars, especially in developed markets like the United States and Europe. Since the high cost of airbags can adversely affect the margins of OEMs, they pressure suppliers for cost containment whenever possible.[100]

By 2014, the year when Takata's recalls were beginning to mushroom, the company held an impressive 20% share of the market for automotive airbags. It followed behind market leader Autoliv (40% share) and TRW. Airbags accounted for about 40% of Takata's sales to outside customers. The Takata safety airbag could be found in many vehicles made by prestigious manufacturers like Honda, Toyota, Fiat Chrysler, and Volkswagen. Honda was Takata's biggest customer, accounting for over half of the company's net sales in fiscal 2015. Honda also held a small equity stake in Takata.[101]

The Takata Recalls

Takata's good fortune and commercial success soon unraveled when complaints about its defective airbags began to proliferate in 2007. At first, there were isolated cases of airbag inflator explosions that led to fatalities. When the inflator explodes during a collision that triggers the airbag to inflate, it can spread deadly shrapnel throughout the vehicle. As complaints mounted, Takata was pressured by regulators such as the NHTSA to cooperate with manufacturers and recall cars that had defective airbags. By May 2013, the recall of defective Takata airbags had expanded to 3.5 million. But how could Takata identify which of its airbags were defective or prone to explosion?

The Japanese firm initially believed the problem was confined to manufacturing deficiencies at two of its plants in North America. The first problem was at the Moses Lake plant in the United States, and the second at the Monclova Plant in Coahuila, Mexico. The latter plant was operated by Takata's North American/Mexican subsidiary. The initial batch of recalls involved airbags made at both of those manufacturing facilities. Takata believed the mishandling of the propellants used to trigger the airbag's inflation was the source of the problem.[102]

But by 2014, Takata began to see the problem was more pervasive, and the recall was extended to 19 million vehicles with Takata airbags. The recall, worked out in conjunction with automakers, was now one of the largest in the automotive industry's long history. The company concluded that high humidity levels might be causing the propellant to deteriorate and lead to a malfunction of the airbag. As a result, vehicles in a number of states with high humidity levels (such as Florida, Georgia, Texas, Louisiana, and South Carolina) were added to the recall list. The theory was that moisture was invading the inflator and destabilizing the propellant.

However, industry analysts and regulators were less confident about this new explanation for the defective airbags and argued the recall still did not go far enough. After airbag explosions involving vehicles operating outside the high-humidity states surfaced, the NHTSA demanded the company recall all vehicles with potentially defective airbags in the United States, not just those in "high humidity" states.[103] Takata, however, initially resisted the NHTSA's request. It insisted the safety agency had no legal authority to coerce an auto supplier to conduct a recall.

Regulators, however, had begun to grasp the ultimate source of the problem, which stems from the airbag's inflator. The culprit was the ammonium nitrate encased in those metal inflators as the propellant. According to the NHTSA, airbags with inflators that use an ammonium nitrate-based propellant without a chemical drying agent are susceptible to the risk of rupture. If that rupture occurs in a crash, metal shrapnel can be sprayed throughout the vehicle cabin. Scientists and regulators believe this volatile chemical compound is predisposed to destabilization. Ammonium nitrate is sensitive to temperature changes and moisture that can cause it to deteriorate over time. Thus, environmental humidity, high temperatures, and age are the key factors that break down the propellant and make it susceptible to explode and rupture the inflator during a crash. To date, there have been 13 deaths and more than 100 injuries due to this problem in the United States. Despite evidence to the contrary, Takata had remained skeptical for a long time that ammonium nitrate was the root cause of the problem.[104]

By 2016, the total recall expanded to 100 million vehicles worldwide, with airbag inflators needing to be replaced before 2019. Any airbag that employed ammonium nitrate as a propellant without a drying agent was subject to the recall. In the United States, 42 million vehicles with 70 million Takata airbags were scheduled for recall. Adding to Takata's woes was the defection of most OEMs to new suppliers. In 2015, Honda, which was Takata's largest customer, announced it would no longer manufacture automobiles with the Takata airbag. A year later, Fiat Chrysler Automobiles announced it would end market production of vehicles with ammonium-nitrate Takata airbag inflators.

Manipulating the Test Data

Takata's struggle with ammonium nitrate can be traced back to the 1990s, when airbag manufacturers eagerly sought alternatives to the airbag propellant sodium azide, which could cause toxic fumes. Takata first replaced sodium azide with tetrazole, but concerns over high cost and unpredictable supply led Takata to choose ammonium nitrate for its propellant, which generated the gases that inflate the airbag. However, as far back as 1995, one of Takata's patent applications indicated that this volatile compound was so vulnerable to temperature changes that it could be unreliable. Nonetheless, Takata was confident it could stabilize this propellant. In 2000, it went ahead with phased stabilized ammonium nitrate (PSAN) as its airbag propellant. Executives and engineers at Takata were convinced that PSAN was safer to manufacture and more efficient, thus allowing for smaller and lighter inflators that were more easily integrated into compact and subcompact vehicles.[105]

Prior to the choice of this propellant, Takata's airbag business had experienced some formidable setbacks. A previous generation of airbags sold to Nissan had deployed too forcefully and were linked to at least 40 serious eye injuries in the 1990s. In 1997, an explosion at its inflator plant in Moses Lake, Washington, destroyed equipment and severely limited production. The company had to purchase inflators from competitors to make up for the shortage. These events set the stage for Takata's choice of the cheaper new compound, ammonium nitrate. Former engineers at Takata, like Mark Lillie, claim that considerations of cost induced the company to use this compound, despite its dangers. Takata's replacement for sodium azide, tetrazole, is produced in limited quantities and can be expensive. According to Lillie, tetrazole was squeezing margins at Takata at a time when the industry was more competitive and being pressured to lower costs. Ammonium nitrate is about one-tenth the price of tetrazole.[106]

On the other hand, engineers at Autoliv who were asked to study Takata's cheaper airbags believed the risks posed by aluminum nitrate were too high. According to an Autoliv chemist, when the airbag is detonated, sometimes "the gas is generated so fast, it blows the inflator to bits." Autoliv scientists considered the evidence against ammonium nitrate to be irrefutable. Autoliv's concerns were also backed by ample research about the volatility of ammonium nitrate.[107]

Airbag manufacturers were all seeking the "perfect propellant" that could inflate an airbag in microseconds and yet remain stable in an automobile for many years, sometimes in hot and humid climates. Despite evidence and advice to the contrary, Takata believed that ammonium nitrate was still the best choice. And it had the added advantage of being "unbelievably cheap." But other large airbag manufacturers besides Autoliv stayed away from ammonium nitrate, following the advice of scientists like Paul Worsey, an expert in explosives engineering at the Missouri University of Science and Technology. He claimed ammonium nitrate should never be used in airbags because it is so unstable; it is far more suitable for large demolitions in mining and construction.[108]

Takata immediately encountered problems with PSAN, even before the first airbag shipments began. As Takata was preparing to manufacture bags with the new propellant, it conducted process validation tests. Those tests showed the product did not meet the process validation specifications prescribed by carmakers like Honda. Some of these failures involved rupture of the inflator. But the final version of those test results omitted this information on these failures or substituted altered test results. Internal Takata documents reviewed by Honda revealed serious discrepancies. Several documents clearly indicated that a June 2000 report sent to Honda misreported several instances of "pressure airbag failure" (airbag ruptures) as "normal airbag deployments." One of the reasons given by Honda for the termination of its relationship with Takata was the fact that the airbag company had "misrepresented and manipulated data."[109]

In 2001, Takata began to ship airbags using this propellant to automobile manufacturers including Toyota and Honda. Just two years later, Takata learned that an inflator had ruptured in a vehicle in Switzerland. In May 2004, there was another rupture that seriously injured a passenger in Alabama. The company was notified about the accident and inflator rupture by Honda. Alarmed by the Alabama incident, Takata secretly conducted tests on 50 airbags that it had retrieved from scrapyards. The steel canisters holding the propellants in two airbags cracked during the test. This failure could easily lead to the inflator's rupture and spraying of debris inside the vehicle. However, according to two former employees who conducted these tests, Takata did not alert federal safety authorities about the dangers of these rupture-prone airbags. Instead, Takata executives ordered the testers to delete the testing data from their computers and dispose of the airbag inflators. The testing, which took place at Takata's American headquarters in Auburn Hills, Michigan, was "hush-hush," according to a former employee. "Then one day, it was, 'Pack it all up, and shut the whole thing down.'" Takata had told the NHTSA that the first time it conducted tests in response to complaints about the airbags was in 2008.[110]

In the summer of 2007, Honda reported to Takata three accidents involving driver-side airbag inflator ruptures. In late 2007, Takata began testing 86 airbag inflators and determined the airbags involved in these accidents had all been made in 2000–2001 and came from its Moses Lake, Washington, facility. It recommended to Honda a limited recall of vehicles with airbags coming from the same production lots. As more ruptures in Honda vehicles were reported in 2009, Takata widened the scope of its recall. Additional inflator ruptures were linked to isolated manufacturing issues at its plant in Mexico, where manufacture of the propellant had been mishandled. Once again, the scope of the recall was broadened. The NHTSA launched its own investigation into Takata in late 2009 but closed it six months later because the company had identified the source of the problem. Critics claim that if the NHTSA had investigated Takata more thoroughly, the burgeoning recall crisis might have been avoided.

As additional complaints were received by Honda and Takata, Honda expanded recalls to 2.5 million. In 2013, Takata filed a "defect report" with the NHTSA explaining that some passenger-side airbags could rupture due to "manufacturing errors" at its Monclova, Mexico, plant. As more and more bags erupted in high-humidity states, more regional recalls were launched in those states. By 2016, both Takata and the NHTSA recognized that the problem was even more widespread, and the recall was expanded to include all airbags with inflators using ammonium nitrate that did not contain a drying agent. At this point, there was incontrovertible evidence that the cause of the problem was ammonium nitrate's volatility. Also, inflators using this substance become more unsafe over time especially when exposed to high humidity and high temperature fluctuations.[111]

For many years, Takata had assured regulators at the NHTSA that the airbag explosions were linked to isolated manufacturing issues. But thanks to multiple tests, the company knew better, or should have known better. In 2010, for example, Takata sought the help of outside experts at the pyrotechnic lab at Pennsylvania State University. The goal was to determine whether ammonium nitrate was at the heart of the defective inflator problem. A 2012 study released by scientists at the lab cast severe doubt on the use of ammonium nitrate because it was so unstable. However, Takata dismissed those results and waited two years before it shared that vital research with regulators such as the NHTSA. The study reflected the same concerns raised by some of Takata's own engineers in the late 1990s.[112]

As the safety crisis unfolded, other instances of test data manipulation came to light in a set of emails released as part of a personal injury lawsuit. In 2005, a U.S. engineer had accused his Japanese counterparts of "dressing up the data" by removing or glossing over unfavorable testing results about airbag failures. He complained that testers were changing graphics to divert attention from problematic test results. Four airbag exerts asked by the *New York Times* to review the emails said they strongly suggested the company was trying to misrepresent or alter testing data presented to customers. The emails underscored concerns about tests on airbags conducted at a high temperature. A Takata spokesperson admitted problems in Takata's past reporting, including the validation test reports given to Honda in 2000. According to that spokesperson, "There have been instances in the past when Takata provided inflator validation testing reports to automotive customers that contained selective, incomplete, or inaccurate data."[113] The pattern of manipulating testing data that began in 2000 strongly imply that this practice had become a systemic problem at Takata.[114]

Postscript

After much delay and defensiveness, Takata finally accommodated regulators by recalling all cars with ammonium nitrate propellants and agreeing to phase out the use of this substance. But the crisis was far from over. In 2018, 19 auto manufacturers were still in the process of recalling an unprecedented 42 million U.S. vehicles with Takata airbags that risk rupturing. Auto manufacturers faced numerous logistical problems in replacing defective inflators and tracking down cars with faulty airbags that have been sold by the original owner.

In January 2016, Takata's CEO and grandson of the company's founder, Shigehisa Takada, resigned. Many automakers and regulators expressed their frustration at the way Mr. Takada had handled the prolonged airbag problem. They highlighted the company's poor governance and lack of transparency.[115] After resisting the idea of a fund to compensate victims of the exploding airbags, Takata reversed course in February 2017 and set up a $125 million fund for that purpose. Several months later, in June 2017, Takata, facing billions of dollars in costs and liabilities, filed for bankruptcy. Finally, Takata pled guilty to criminal charges and agreed to pay $1 billion in penalties for providing misleading testing reports to automakers like Honda. Of that amount, $850 million would be paid to automakers that had had to absorb huge recall costs.[116]

- How important is this product for Takata's long-term success? What percentage of Takata's sales does this product represent? How is this product distributed to the end consumer? What is the competitive environment for this product? What difference might these factors make in Takata's handling of the safety crisis?

- How has Takata handled this product safety crisis? What could they have done differently?

- What are Takata's economic, legal, and ethical duties in this situation? How would you assess Takata's ethical performance throughout this controversy?

CASE STUDY 8.4

THE SAMSUNG RECALL: A GALAXY OF TROUBLES

When passengers on board Southwest Airline's flight 994 noticed smoke billowing from a smartphone, there was panic and chaos throughout the cabin. Fortunately, the plane bound from Louisville to Baltimore had not yet taken off. The Southwest crew quickly evacuated the plane's anxious 75 passengers, and the faulty device was disposed of. That device was a Samsung Galaxy Note 7. This was the latest in a series of incidents for Samsung that led to a recall of the troubled phone and then a halting of the Note 7's production and sales. The product recall joins a list of similar historic events, such as Johnson & Johnson's recall of Tylenol in 1982, Toyota's recall of 8 million vehicles in 2008, and the massive Takata airbag recall initiated in 2016.

AP Photo/Ahn Young-joon

In the wake of this crisis for one of Korea's most renowned companies, there were many questions to be answered. Were these phones properly designed and tested? Was Samsung too passive in its response to this crisis? Why did some regulators fault the company for botching the initial recall? And could Samsung rebound from this disaster and rebuild trust with its customers? This final case of the chapter examines this product safety controversy and illustrates the challenges of making a strategic decision about a product recall with little time and a lack of sufficient information.

Samsung Electronics

The Samsung Electronics Company is a South Korean electronics giant headquartered in the city of Suwon, South Korea. It is the flagship division of the Samsung Group, a diversified, global conglomerate. The Samsung Group, founded in 1938, includes Samsung Heavy Industries and Samsung C&T, which is one of the world's largest construction companies. Its other businesses include financial services and shipbuilding. The conglomerate employs around 370,000 people in its various operations and production facilities scattered throughout the world. Under the leadership of chairman and CEO Lee Kun-Hee, Samsung has narrowed its broad focus by divesting some of its defense and chemical businesses.

Despite its diversity, the core business of Samsung is electronics, which accounts for about 70% of the group's revenues. Samsung ranks as the second-largest information technology company, just behind Apple. The electronics business is divided into four segments: mobile communications, consumer electronics (including TVs), semiconductors, and display panels. Products from the latter two divisions include DRAMs (memory chips), flash memory, and LCD panels. In recent years the company has made major capital expenditures on technologies such as 3-D NAND flash memory and organic light-emitting diode (OLED) displays to drive the profits of these divisions.[117]

The mobile communications division, which accounts for 46% of Samsung Electronics's revenue, produced the Samsung line of smartphones. Like Nokia and other competitors, the company initially lagged behind Apple, the pioneer in smartphones, but soon surpassed its American rival. By 2016, the company was selling over 300 million smartphones a year. Samsung Electronics earned $18 billion in 2016 on revenues of $167 billion. About 50% of its sales come from the Asia/Pacific region.

The Galaxy Smartphone Series

In 2007, Steve Jobs unveiled to the world the first version of Apple's smartphone technology. The iPhone was a "revolutionary" product that reinvented the phone and changed the course of mobile telephony. The iPhone ran on a modified version of the Mac operating system (iOS), and its touch-screen interface allowed users to navigate the system without a physical keyboard. Compressed into a small device was a powerful networked computer. Apple worked with wireless carriers such as AT&T and Verizon, which provided phone service. A key driver of the iPhone's phenomenal success was the plethora of applications or apps that ran on the phone, available for download at Apple's App Store.[118]

Samsung had competed for some time in the mobile device industry, jockeying for competitive positioning against companies like Blackberry and Nokia. Soon after Apple's iPhone debut, Samsung introduced its own line of smartphones. Most of the company's smartphone profits come from its two premium phones, the Galaxy S and the Galaxy Note, even though they accounted for only a small proportion of overall shipments. For a time, the Galaxy S2 was its flagship product. The Galaxy Note Series was launched by Samsung in 2011. It was a "point of pride" for the Korean company, which had been seen as a follower and imitator rather than a technology leader. The phone had a bigger screen than the Apple iPhone, and this feature appealed to many consumers. It also had a handsome design. The shift to bigger handsets led to the nickname "phablet," an amalgam of a smartphone and a tablet. By the time Samsung released the Note 3, the product was a big hit, and it sold 10 million units in its first two months on the market. Riding a wave of success, the company decided to skip revision number six and jump right to number seven. This decision conveyed its desire for direct, head-to-head competition with Apple's iPhone 7, which was released in the fall of 2016.[119]

Like the vast majority of Samsung's smartphones, the Galaxy series ran on the open-source Android operating system made by Google. Android was free and open for customization, so manufacturers could modify this platform to suit their needs. Other companies like HTC, Huawei, and LG also ran on the Android OS, but Samsung quickly dominated the expanding Android market. Many app developers quickly realized Android's potential and provided products for this platform. Unlike other smartphone manufacturers (such as HTC), the mobile division was vertically integrated. The company designed its own phones and did not outsource manufacturing the way Apple did. Samsung was also integrated "upstream"—it made many of its own components such as chips, batteries, and LCD screens. Its Super Amoled display screen was considered to be one of the brightest and best in the entire industry.[120]

But while Samsung has been the undisputed leader in Android devices, it has faced stiff competition from upstart companies like China's Xiaomi and Huawei, who were challenging Samsung in the key China market. Both companies undercut Samsung on price to gain competitive advantage. Samsung also had to contend with newer products like Google's Pixel. But in the premium market segment, its toughest competitor continued to be Apple Inc., which now relied on the iPhone as its core technology. Apple sells other products, such as its Macintosh computers, and services such as iCloud, but the lion's share of its revenues and profits derive from the iPhone. In mid-2016, just before the Note 7's release, Samsung had a 22% share of the smartphone market. Apple was in second place with a 14% share.[121]

Exploding Batteries

On August 19, 2016, the company launched its new Galaxy Note 7 to much excitement and fanfare among its loyal customers. It came to market just weeks ahead of Apple's new iPhone 7, which incorporated only incremental improvements. The Note 7 was by far Samsung's most advanced smartphone technology. It was loaded with new features, such as an iris scanner, water resistance, and about 16% more battery life than its predecessors. The phone was an immediate success, and Samsung hoped that increasing sales would cement its position as the undisputed industry leader.[122]

Almost immediately, however, Samsung began receiving reports that its new smartphone had spontaneously caught fire and exploded on several occasions. The reports of overheated batteries and phones catching fire began to spread in September and capture headlines. Within a few short weeks after the product debut, the company received 92 complaints about batteries overheating in the United States, with 26 reports of burns and 55 reports of property damage. Samsung engineers promptly began a series of tests. They admitted the batteries on the Galaxy 7 could ignite, yet they were not able to get a phone to explode. Nonetheless, the company soon realized the Note 7 batteries of one of its suppliers, its affiliate, Samsung SDI Co., had these overheating problems while the batteries of another supplier did not. Scans of faulty devices showed the Samsung SDI battery protruded slightly.[123]

By early September 2016, the company was in crisis mode as investors reduced the company's market value by $20 billion. Samsung executives now had to determine what course of action to take. Some were skeptical that the incidents amounted to anything serious and recommended a "wait and see" approach. But others thought the company needed to take decisive action without delay. D. J. Koh, who headed the mobile communications unit, believed he had adequate evidence to conclude that the problem lay with Samsung SDI's batteries. Koh wanted to do the "the right thing" and remove an unsafe product from the market. Others pressed him to wait for more information, but Koh's supporters argued that waiting would leave customers in the dark and perhaps allow the crisis to get even worse. Koh made the final decision to shift all battery production to its other supplier, Amperex Technology Ltd., and to recall the 2.5 million Note 7 phones that had been sold. The recall would cost Samsung $5 billion, including lost sales.[124]

When the recall was announced, frustrated Galaxy users were told to stop using and power down their phones. They were urged to trade in their Note 7's for new phones with different batteries (made by Amperex) at their wireless carrier or at the retail store where they purchased the phone. Consumers were also given the option of a full refund.

But how could Samsung efficiently manage the logistics of a recall of 2.5 million smartphones that had been distributed in 10 countries? Could the company supply enough replacement phones with different batteries? These were major challenges for Samsung. Unlike Apple, Samsung does not have a network of retail stores in the United States and relies on carriers to sell its phones. Despite these challenges, the recall proceeded smoothly. About 90% of customers turned in their phones and eventually got a replacement.[125]

However, there were some "hiccups" in the recall. First, Samsung did not inform the Consumer Product Safety Commission (CPSC) in the United States, which coordinates all U.S. product recalls. Rather, Samsung acted unilaterally without working in conjunction with this safety agency. However, it's illegal for a company to recognize that it has a hazardous product and not inform the CPSC. The commission usually announces recalls in cooperation with manufacturers, but that did not happen in this case. The CPSC sets a framework for those recalls that all companies must follow, but Samsung's voluntary recall bypassed CPSC requirements. Second, some U.S. customers ran into trouble returning their phones to U.S. wireless carriers due to conflicting information and communications problems. Customers were told by Samsung that they could get a loaner from their carriers, but when they went to stores like T-Mobile, they were unable to get a loaner. Samsung had sent replacement Galaxy Note 7 phones to carriers, but the carriers had to wait for CPSC approval before distributing those phones.[126]

As the company rushed to deliver these replacement smartphones, they hoped their product-safety nightmare would abruptly end with minimal damage to this flagship brand. But then there were more complaints. Batteries in these replacement phones were also overheating, causing phones to catch fire. There were at least four incidents of phones smoking up and causing fire, including the one on Southwest Airlines. These batteries were not made by SDI but by its other battery manufacturer, Amperex. Samsung engineers thought they had properly diagnosed the problem, which was isolated to the batteries made by Samsung SDI, but they were wrong. It was now apparent that the first sweeping recall was based on incomplete evidence. On October 10, 2016, Samsung pulled the plug on the ill-fated phones. The drastic move is unusual in the technology industry, where companies try to improve a product rather than pull it from the marketplace. The discontinuation of the Galaxy 7 culminated in a two-month period of chaos during which the company was under intense scrutiny from investors, consumers, and regulators. It was highly unusual that two separate sets of defective batteries made by two different suppliers had ended up in Samsung phones, especially when that phone was supposed to be its "marquee" product to rival Apple's iPhone.[127]

Despite its prompt action, Samsung was criticized for a lack of urgency or nonchalance in how it handled the second recall. The company seemed to downplay the gravity of the situation and the risks posed by the overheating batteries. For customers to determine the status of the troubled smartphone, they had to click on a link on the company website titled "Updated Consumer Guidance for the Galaxy Note 7." Buried on that page was a notice that Samsung had stopped production of the Galaxy Note 7 along with information telling customers to contact the outlet where they bought the phone for a refund or an exchange. The company did not communicate this information through its Twitter account or on its Facebook page. For crisis management experts, this was an "overly passive" way to deal with a prominent safety problem. The notice should have been far more visible and accompanied by some expression of care and concern on Samsung's part. As one consultant pointed out, "This is a phone that can literally catch fire and burn your house down with you in it," and this threat needed to be better highlighted in Samsung communications.[128]

As Samsung's smartphone safety crisis came to a head in October 2016, the South Korean conglomerate's heir apparent, Lee Jae-Yong, stayed in the background. Mr. Lee made the final decision to close down production of the Galaxy Note 7, but the leader of the mobile division, D. J. Koh, was most prominent throughout the controversy. As Samsung shares tumbled further, executives at Samsung wondered whether Mr. Lee should continue to remain behind the scenes or assert himself more publicly to allay investor concerns.[129]

Testing Batteries and Diagnosing the Problem

Samsung engineers continued to research the problem as the company's battery testing procedures came under scrutiny. To sell smartphones in the United States, producers are required to test phone batteries at one of the 28 laboratories that have been approved and certified by the U.S. wireless industry trade group known as the CTIA. Samsung is the only smartphone manufacturer that uses in-house battery testing facilities for CTIA certification. Other companies, including Apple, use third-party CTIA-certified labs to test their batteries. These test labs have autonomy from smartphone manufacturers—they are in a separate building and under separate control. The use of independent CTIA-certified testing labs has greatly reduced the battery safety failure rate in cell phones and smartphones. Samsung said its internal testing revealed no problems with these batteries. But some industry insiders say that allowing manufacturers to test their own batteries creates the potential for conflicts of interest.[130]

Also, Samsung's situation may have been compounded by the company's rush to market to compete with the iPhone 7. The Samsung phone was a sophisticated device with many new features that complicated technical issues and made thorough testing more challenging, especially when suppliers and quality assurance testers faced tight deadlines.

Samsung has acknowledged that it did not have adequate quality controls to identify battery problems before phones were sold to consumers. To prevent a recurrence of the battery problems, Samsung said it would put into place "multi-layer" safety measures during the design phase of its smartphone projects. Samsung will do more testing for durability and leakage, and it will open the battery cell to inspect tab welding and insulation tape conditions; in the past, suppliers did the latter test, but now both the supplier and Samsung will run this test. Also, both Samsung and suppliers will use X-ray tests to look for any internal abnormalities. Samsung has taken responsibility for its lack of quality controls, but it puts the primary blame on its suppliers for the defective batteries. However, does Samsung also share more of the blame than it recognizes because of the specifications and deadlines it set for the Note 7 batteries in its haste to get this product to market before the launch of Apple's iPhone 7?[131]

Months after the Galaxy Note 7's discontinuation, Samsung finally believed they had uncovered the likely causes of the battery problem. According to the company, the batteries provided by one of its suppliers, Amperex Technology Ltd., had "manufacturing flaws" that were most likely linked to the rapid ramp-up in production. There were apparently welding issues caused by a manufacturing defect, which didn't appear until after the battery was pulled from the market. The other supplier, Samsung SDI Co., a subsidiary of Samsung, used battery cases that were not big enough. In one case the problem was the flawed manufacturing process, but in the other it was a design issue—there was inadequate space inside the battery casing to allow the battery's electrodes to expand. According to one expert, "The design of the cell pouch did not provide enough room."[132] With this disclosure, Samsung hoped to put the Galaxy Note 7 controversy behind it.

Restoring the Samsung Brand

The valuable Samsung brand has been damaged by these battery problems. The company has apologized, but will that be enough to placate frustrated consumers? Concerns about public safety continue to weigh on the brand as it tries to restore consumer trust after fumbling the initial recall. The company must also contend with a global slowdown in smartphone sales, which will not help its recovery.[133] Thanks to the discontinuation of the Note 7, Samsung lost its number-one position to Apple in the last quarter of 2016, the first quarter in two years in which Samsung was not the leader in smartphone shipments.[134]

In April 2017, Samsung introduced the Galaxy S8, its first product launch since the Note 7 was pulled from the market. Samsung hoped the phone's innovative features, such as its new virtual assistant, Bixby, would counter competitors like Apple and some of its lower-cost rivals making strides in China. According to Koh, "If the product is really good, it will help bring back the loyalty and trust in the Galaxy brand."[135] Early sales for the Galaxy 8 were quite promising. Five million smartphones were sold within the first three weeks of the product launch. Most of these sales were in Samsung's domestic market.[136]

EXHIBIT 8.3 ■ Samsung Electronics: Selected Financial Data (in millions)			
	2014	2015	2016
Revenues	$187,606	$170,655	$167,327
Operating Income	22,676	22,464	24,232
Net Profit	21,000	15,899	18,580

- What grade would you give the Samsung recall? What things did they do right and what did they do wrong? How could the company have better managed this product safety controversy?

- What are the most pressing ethical issues in this case? In your view, has Samsung acted in a morally responsible way in how it handled these defective batteries?

- What can Samsung do to restore trust with its smartphone customers?

EXHIBIT 8.4 ■ Market Share by Shipments (fourth quarter, 2016)[137]	
Apple	18.3%
Samsung	18.1%
Huawei	10.6%
Oppo	7.3%
Vivo	5.8%
Others	40.0%

CONCLUSION

The general theme of this chapter has been the corporation's duties to its customers. The philosophy of *caveat vendor* generally prevails over the simplistic notion of *caveat emptor*. Adherence to the former principle helps to overcome the information asymmetries between companies and their customers. Those duties to customers include the requirement that products be safe and possess reasonable quality and durability. The chapter also addressed the question of responsibility in marketing, especially when the promotion of predatory products is involved. The cigarette industry represents the paradigm case of the challenges involved in selling and marketing such products. Safety is obviously a major concern in the automotive industry, but the cases in this chapter demonstrated how much the industry has struggled with providing safe products for its customers. However, as we saw in the Samsung case, the lack of due diligence in matters of safety can also be found in other industries.

Student Study Site

Visit **edge.sagepub.com/spinello.**

Review Questions

1. How would you summarize the corporation's obligations to its customers?

2. What are some guidelines for responding to product safety controversies?

3. Can the market find the necessary equilibrium in these matters, or does government need to exercise more control?

Discussion Questions

1. How could an organization like General Motors prepare itself to deal with product safety issues more efficiently?

2. How would you define a "safe" product?

3. Have your opinions about marketing or the cigarette industry changed after reading the cases in this chapter?

GLOBAL CAPITALISM, CULTURE, AND JUSTICE

PART IV

9

BUSINESS AND THE ENVIRONMENT

Environmentalists are . . . in search of the motives that will defend a shared but threatened legacy from predation from its current trustees.

—Roger Scruton[1]

LEARNING OBJECTIVES

Upon completion of this chapter, you should be able to:

9.1 Discuss the corporation's responsibility to society and the importance of environmental issues.

9.2 Demonstrate how social and political concerns about the environment can impact corporate strategies.

9.3 Use additional analytical tools to help evaluate proper response to environmental crises.

In early 2016, General Electric finally finished its expensive cleanup of the Hudson River. General Electric had dumped hundreds of thousands of tons of polychlorinated biphenyls (also known as PCBs) into the river for several decades. It stopped the practice in the late 1970s when it was forced to do so by the U.S. Environmental Protection Agency (EPA). GE, like many other companies, used the water and land as a source for toxic waste without paying much attention to the possible dangers and long-term consequences. Despite its massive cleanup efforts, the largest river-dredging project in the nation's history, the river is still not clean enough. Environmental groups complain that GE should continue its efforts until human beings can safely eat fish caught in the Hudson. They point out that only 65% of the contaminants have been removed from the river. The PCBs (and other chemicals) have done so much damage that fish may not be safe to eat from the Hudson River for several generations to come.

But the GE dredging project is over. Now the company must turn its attention to cleaning up its factory sites at Fort Edward and Hudson Falls. That could take another decade and many more millions of dollars. The total tab for GE for its damage to the river and its ecosystem will most likely exceed several billion dollars.[2]

Since the days of GE's poor environmental performance, considerable progress has been made. Most companies are far more attentive to environmental issues, although there is still room for more enlightened policies. There are also stricter laws in place to prevent pollution of land and waterways. These laws seek to resolve the market failure of public goods (such as clean air and water) and free riders who pollute and damage those goods, imposing social costs on others.

Despite a network of laws that protect the environment, there are still severe problems that plague the fragile global ecosystem. These include stratospheric ozone depletion, global warming, pollutants in the air and water (including pesticide residue), and toxic waste disposal. Wetlands and coastal erosion are also a principal long-term concern. While some of these problems seem to be local in scale, they can have a broad impact. Air pollution in a small city affects not just the citizens of that city, but also neighboring communities and at some level the whole ecological system.

Arguably, the most prominent environmental issue of this era is climate change. Most scientists are in accord that the planet is growing warmer and that this warming trend is caused by excessive reliance on greenhouse gases emitted from fossil fuels such as oil and coal. There is less consensus on what should be done in response to the risks associated with climate change, which include rising sea levels, pressure on water and food supplies, changing weather patterns, and human health risks. The probable consequences of climate change, along with the social costs and regulatory changes that those consequences may drive, are major issues for the private sector. Many companies are already striving to improve energy efficiency and to develop sustainable energy solutions that are less dependent on fossil fuels.[3]

Environmental issues and problems are complex and multidimensional. They can be conceptualized and described in many different ways. There are ethical, aesthetic, and economic dimensions of environmental studies. Our focus is not on aesthetics, but on ethics and to a lesser extent on economics. From a purely economic viewpoint, pollution and waste represent the market's failure to deal with environmental externalities. An **externality** is "an effect of one economic agent on another that is not taken into account by normal market behavior."[4] Externalities can be positive or negative. Negative externalities are costs imposed on others that directly impair their social welfare. These costs can occur, for example, when manufacturing plants spew pollutants into the air that adversely affect the health of nearby residents and reduce the market value of their property. When private and social costs are misaligned, the goods of those manufacturers will be overproduced, which leads to a misallocation of society's resources. To protect the environment, markets must ensure that firms internalize all of their production costs by providing incentives to minimize pollution and waste. However, markets have not always been successful in dealing with economic agents who escape some of the costs of their transactions. In these cases, where markets are not self-correcting, government intervention is warranted.[5]

Many environmental problems such as oil spills and excessive air pollution go beyond market inefficiencies and imply deliberate moral failings, especially when firms refuse to improve their environmental performance. Environmental degradation that exceeds an acceptable level of pollution associated with industrial activity is ethically problematic if it is intentionally caused by human actions or if it is the foreseeable and preventable side effect of such action. Some environmental harms, such as those due to careless waste disposal or negligent oil spills, directly threaten human health or affect the quality of life for those people who are at risk. Other forms of environmental damage may affect non-human nature, such as the habitat for a rare animal species. The extinction of a certain species will probably have no real impact on human health or the quality of life, but its loss is still of some concern. These goods that do not bear on human welfare are referred to as "**pure environmental goods.**"[6]

The social demands for environmental improvement when human health and welfare is at stake are easily defensible. The tendency to regard the environment as a "free good" must always be tempered by how different forms of pollution affect human well-being and human rights to health and safety. How seriously one takes damage to pure environmental goods depends upon one's viewpoint. Those who opt for an anthropocentric perspective will give such damage limited attention, but those who endorse a biocentric perspective will have a very different attitude. We cannot enter into this debate here, but let it suffice to say that most forms of environmental damage will affect human beings in the long run.[7]

Unfortunately, most U.S businesses were indifferent to the environment prior to legislation such as the Clean Air Act of 1970, which regulated emissions coming from vehicles or industrial sources. Manufacturers routinely externalized the costs of waste and disposal onto innocent third parties and future generations. But they now rely heavily on regulatory systems to manage environmental impacts within their businesses. This reliance is appropriate, but managers should also ask what other complementary mechanisms might be used for the proactive management of environmental risks.[8]

Environmental ethics is about aspiring to a high level of environmental performance by competently managing those risks and choosing strategies consistent with environmental sustainability. Sound environmental performance and ethical responsibility implies making every realistic effort to avoid (or at least minimize) negative externalities associated with operations such as mining and drilling for natural gas and oil. Even under optimal circumstances, those externalities may occur, but if that happens, companies must swiftly correct the problem and provide compensation for the environmental harms the community has endured. Ideally, environmental concerns, which includes sensitivity to global warming and the issue of intergenerational justice, should be well integrated into every corporation's strategy and operating policies. Environmental problems are fundamentally problems of morality that go beyond economic or legal reasoning.

AN OVERVIEW OF THE CASES

The four cases in this chapter review instances of poor environmental performance due to negligence, indifference, and an unwillingness to invest in environmental protection beyond what the law required. The first case provides some historical perspective. It documents Hooker Chemical's disposal of chemical waste, which poisoned the land in the region of Love Canal near Niagara Falls. Hooker was looking for inexpensive solutions and chose to bury chemical by-products rather than incinerate them. At the time, there was no comprehensive legal framework that prescribed the handling of dangerous toxic waste. This legal vacuum adds complexity to this case, but should moral common sense have led the firm to seek more viable alternatives for its waste disposal?

The Love Canal case is followed by a case study on Deepwater Horizon that chronicles British Petroleum's massively expensive oil spill in the Gulf of Mexico. BP has been subject to endless recriminations and lawsuits since that oil spill occurred in 2010. This catastrophic event, along with BP's mishandling of the crisis it triggered, has badly tainted the company's reputation. The massive fire and oil spill that killed 11 oil rig workers was a tragic accident. But BP's cost-cutting along with careless and imprudent decision-making set in motion a chain of events that led to Deepwater's explosion and its aftermath.

The next case in this chapter is not about an environmental accident but describes a deliberate attempt to cheat on emissions standards. Those standards have been set by government regulators to curtail the emission of greenhouse gases and mitigate the effects of global warming. However, Volkswagen engineers installed "cheating software" on its diesel engines to rig the results of emissions tests in several countries, including the United States. As the scandal unfolded, it became apparent that 11 million vehicles worldwide had the cheating device. This case provides an opportunity to examine the cultural and organizational factors contributing to the scandal along with the fallout for Volkswagen and its executives.

The final case also deals with the oil industry, which has often been in the crosshairs of environmentalists and regulators. Texaco, now owned by Chevron, drilled numerous oil wells in the Amazon region of Ecuador when oil was discovered there. Thanks to irresponsible environmental policies, there were numerous oil spills along with leakage from buried toxic waste that contaminated this pristine rain forest environment. This case study looks at Texaco's alleged negligence and the liability of its partner Petroecuador. It also reviews the subsequent lawsuits and considers whether any reparations are owed to the people of Ecuador. The drama of these events is still being played out in the international court system.

Three of these four cases involve companies abusing the environment of the foreign countries in which they were operating, evading liabilities, and deflecting responsibility. Despite our more proactive environmental policies, this failure to think about environmental consequences of actions in someone else's homeland is a common pattern. As Roger Scruton points out, "It is this carelessness towards 'other places' that underlies environmental catastrophes like BP's oil-rig spill in the Gulf of Mexico, or the 'slash and burn' cropping by multinational agribusinesses in the Amazon rainforest."[9]

CASE STUDY 9.1

POISONED LAND: THE TRAGIC HISTORY OF LOVE CANAL

In the postwar era, as corporations expanded to accommodate the great economic boom, they were often quite careless about the disposal of toxic waste. The result was a number of serious tragedies that adversely affected the lives of many innocent people. In Massachusetts, a famous lawsuit (which was the basis for the movie *A Civil Action*) alleged that two companies in Woburn had improperly disposed of chemicals, contaminating two municipal wells, and was responsible for the deaths of several children in the area. One company, W. R. Grace & Company of New York, owned and operated the Cryovac Division manufacturing plant, which produces equipment for the food-packing industry and used chemical solvents to clean tools and dilute paint. The Cryovac plant is just 2,400 feet northeast of the Woburn wells. The other company, known as the John J. Riley Tannery, was owned by Beatrice Foods. The tannery allegedly contaminated 15 acres of nearby property by dumping chemicals that flowed about 700 feet northeast into the same wells.[10]

AP Photo

But the most famous of these incidents was undoubtedly the saga of Love Canal. This community is located in upstate New York, close to Niagara Falls. This case explores the actions of Hooker Chemical Company, which dumped 2 tons of toxic chemicals into a canal that later leached into residents' water supplies and basements. It focuses on the legal, environmental, and ethical aspects of the situation in which Hooker was immersed due to the disposal process. During remediation of this vast toxic dump, residents were relocated. But the area has since been resettled and is now called Black Creek Village. Hooker's actions happened decades ago, but this classic pollution case, a controversy lasting over half a century, deserves not to be forgotten.[11]

Developing Love Canal

The story of Love Canal has a strange history as a development project with inauspicious origins. Love Canal was supposed to be a model industrial city, located a few miles from the scenic tourist attraction, Niagara Falls. It was the brainchild of William T. Love, a 19th-century entrepreneur with big dreams for the environs of Niagara Falls. The charismatic Mr. Love envisioned a city with 2 million people arising from the fields and pastures of Lewiston. A big part of that utopian dream was the harnessing of the power source of the falls. Love persuaded investors of the viability of his plans as he sought to entice factories to relocate with the promise of free power. Prominent New York politicians became some of his most enthusiastic supporters. He planned to build a canal to help deliver the hydroelectric power from Niagara Falls to the model city's factories and residents. In May 1894, workers began to construct this canal or artificial waterway in the town of Lasalle near the falls. The canal would run to Lewiston 7 miles from Niagara Falls to the Lewiston area.[12]

But the great canal project was never finished. Love's efforts failed, thanks to a severe economic recession and fears about the ill effects of industrial development in this region. He ran out of money to continue building the canal and to purchase the farms that would constitute his new model city. After several years there was precious little to show for Love's efforts. Only the partially dug out canal remained as a bleak "monument" to the defunct dreams of William Love. According to one historian, "Being a non-technical person he hoped for more than was possible. He dreamed too big for the time and came off looking like a charlatan."[13]

Nonetheless, despite the failure of Love's ill-fated project, the area of Lasalle (annexed by Niagara Falls in 1920) and its surroundings was eventually developed as a major industrial center, thanks in part to cheap electricity. The Niagara region's economy expanded, and this led to a thriving residential community in the vicinity of the canal. Niagara Falls quickly became home to a booming chemical industry that produced huge amounts of industrial-grade chemicals with the help of hydroelectric power. By World War II, Niagara Falls' chemical sector was the global leader in the production of chlorine, pesticides, plastics, and explosives.[14]

Hooker Chemical Corporation

Hooker Electrochemical Company was founded by Elon Huntington Hooker, described as one of the "captains of industry" before and during the Great Depression. He built Hooker's first plant in the Niagara Falls area in 1905. It was situated on the upper part of the Niagara River and used the power of the falls to generate its electricity. Hooker Chemical's operations expanded rapidly. Hooker manufactured a variety of chemical products, including chlorine and caustic soda. The company sold its products to the chemical industry for use in many consumer products. In 1915, as a response to shortages caused by the war, Hooker built the first monochlorobenzol plant in the United States and produced 1.5 million pounds of this chemical per month.

After World War I, Hooker diversified into many other organic and inorganic chemical compounds. It built another chemical plant in Tacoma, Washington, to service the West Coast, and it opened corporate headquarters on Wall Street. In 1938, Elon Hooker died in an automobile accident, but his absence had little effect on Hooker Chemical's future financial performance. By the mid-1950s, Hooker was a global leader in the manufacture of many common chemicals that now included explosives and defoliants. From 1940 to 1953, its sales grew from $7.1 million to $38.7 million. In 1968, Hooker was acquired by Occidental Chemical Corporation. Its sales peaked at $450 million in 1970.

For decades Hooker employed over 3,000 workers at its sprawling Niagara Falls plant. However, there were always questions about safety at the plant. In its early years, the plant ran two 12-hour shifts with no holidays and no vacations. Pay was 15 cents an hour in 1907. Workers faced many potential hazards from the dangerous chemicals they worked with. There was a lack of suitable equipment for the workers, who often had to "improvise" their own protective gear. Workplace safety eventually improved, but it came about slowly through a painful process of trial and error.[15]

Hooker's increased production of chemicals also meant a surge in its industrial waste. A big challenge for the company was how to deal with its heavy waste disposal needs. Hooker had few good options, but it became interested in the nearby Love Canal site as a landfill for the wastes coming from its Niagara Falls plant. In April 1942, Hooker received a license from the Niagara Power Development Corporation to initiate waste disposal operations. Within a short time, it acquired title to the property. The canal area was undeveloped and unpopulated at the time of Hooker's actions, and there was no zoning restriction on the canal's use. The site offered several advantages. Its proximity to the plant reduced transportation costs and avoided the hazardous problem of moving toxic chemicals over long distances by truck.[16]

Love Canal is a rectangular 16-acre site located on the outskirts of the city of Niagara Falls. In 1928, the area immediately west and east of the canal had been subdivided into building lots as the population of Niagara Falls spread toward and past Love Canal. The unfinished canal area was flat and had poor natural drainage along with a high water table. Hooker did little analysis of the soil and drainage conditions. Hooker deposited caustic waste materials from its Niagara Falls plant into the canal for 12 years. This waste disposal operation ended in 1954. At the time, there were no residents at the northern end of the canal, where the dumping first took place. Hooker widened the canal for waste disposal. Chemicals were buried in pits 30 to 50 feet in diameter and 20 to 30 feet deep. The company had determined there were no legal restrictions on dumping "so long as the property is either owned or leased by the party doing the dumping." However, the law called for the property's protection "to prevent the possibility of persons or animals coming in contact with the dumped materials." Therefore, the original development plan called for a fence to enclose the areas in which chemicals were to be dumped.[17]

By 1946, Hooker had finished its dumping in the northern section and began dumping at the southern end of the canal and then to the central section. Hooker did not install a fence around the southern and central section of Love Canal, where 75% of the dumping took place. There was also no fencing around the residential property lines bordering the west and east sides of the canal. Nor did Hooker post warning signs in any of these locations.[18]

Hooker's routine was to accumulate between 500 to 2,000 drums of chemical waste at the plant before transporting those drums to Love Canal. The 55-gallon metal or fiberboard drums weighed about 300 to 500 pounds when full. The majority of drums storing these chemicals were either used or reconditioned. Some witnesses described them as "rusty and leaking," while others said they were in "pretty good" condition. The drums were dumped to within ½ to 4 feet of the ground surface. The original plan was a 4-foot cover, but this guideline was not always followed. In many places the cover was only 6 inches deep.[19]

Hooker records indicate the company dumped 25,000 tons of different chemicals into the canal site from the time it began to use the site in the early 1940s until 1954. Those records do not accurately report the types and quantities of waste materials buried at Love Canal. But it is known that the chemical found in the largest quantity was benzene hexachloride (BHC, or "spent cake"). BHC, sometimes called lindane, is commonly used in the production of insecticides. This BHC waste was being dumped at a rate of 300 tons per month, primarily at the southern end of the canal. BHC is a highly toxic substance, and Hooker's files show that company officials were well aware of its toxicity. A quarter of an ounce of BHC for adult humans amounted to a fatal dose. There could also be severe effects such as liver damage if this substance was absorbed through the skin. Some of the other toxic chemicals buried in Love Canal included thionyl chloride, used in dyes, dioxin (or TCP), and dodecyl mercaptan (or DDM). Hooker knew that DDM residues were lighter than groundwater and could easily rise to the surface if it seeped out of drums in which it was stored. DDM is similar to hydrogen sulfide and is one of the most toxic gases in existence. Exposure can cause "convulsion, paralysis, and finally death." In 1944, Hooker realized that DDM residue was seeping out of drums and rising to the surface but took steps toward better disposal. There were no further reports of leakage migrating to the surface.[20]

Love Canal Site Purchased by Niagara Falls School Board

In 1952, shortly before Hooker closed down the chemical waste landfill, the Niagara Falls Board of Education approached the company and indicated their interest in purchasing part of the site to build a school. Hooker initially resisted the sale of land for this purpose. One Hooker executive said the sale was inappropriate "because of the toxic nature of some of the materials that were being dumped there, and [it] wouldn't be right for utilization for other than commercial or industrial development."[21] They told the school board to look for an alternate site.

But Hooker eventually changed its mind. It reached the conclusion that it would be prudent to turn over the property to the school board under one condition: assurance that Hooker would not be held liable for future claims or damages resulting from the storage of its chemicals. The reasons for this shift in thinking are unknown, though some intimate the school board might have suggested it would attempt to seize the property through eminent domain. Hooker's change of heart about the sale caused some consternation and opposition within the company. Nonetheless, Hooker proceeded with the transfer of property. In April 1953, the school board acquired the land encompassing the dump and some of the adjacent area for $1.

The city of Niagara Falls immediately began to develop its newly acquired property. It launched a construction project to build an elementary school in an area that encompassed the central part of the chemical dump and surrounding lots. But it did not take long before construction crews ran into problems. The foundation sank into one of the big chemical pits and the school had to be moved 30 yards north. Despite such challenges, the school opened in 1955. The city sold some of the remaining land to developers, who built rows of houses adjacent to the school with their backyards jutting into the waste site. More land was sold to private developers in 1957, and more houses were built close to the dump. These subdivisions had great appeal—this was a new neighborhood away from congested cities and near playgrounds and schools. By the early 1960s, 150 homes had been built. Churches and stores were also built along with the Summit Park Mall.[22]

In building up this area, construction crews removed thousands of cubic yards of topsoil, and this process severely damaged the integrity of the clay covering. Removal of this protective topsoil made the toxic chemicals buried at Love Canal more exposed.

Even in the mid-1960s, some residents sensed something was not quite right with their property. On windy days the area was permeated by the odor of chemicals and fumes. Over time, water from rain and snow seeped through the thin clay covering and entered the chemical-filled basin. The basin overflowed, and residents had to contend with noxious chemical gases seeping into their basement and surfacing to the ground throughout the area. Cold, snowy winters (especially 1977) aggravated the problem, pushing more chemical leachate into sewers, backyards, and basements around Love Canal. Residents complained, and officials were quickly convinced that unhealthy and hazardous conditions existed in some of the homes adjoining the chemical dump site. Tests revealed that DDM and BHC had migrated from the dump and now posed a massive environmental hazard.[23]

The leakage problem intensified, and by 1978 the New York State Health Commission took action. New tests were done and teams were dispatched to Love Canal to initiate a house-to-house health survey. For years, residents complained of health issues including headaches, nausea, and chemical burns. Health studies indicated there was an unusually high incidence of cancer, miscarriages, birth defects, nephrosis, epilepsy, and respiratory ailments. There was little doubt this was a major public health hazard, but officials were slow to come up with solutions. The chemicals were now migrating beyond Love Canal into the surrounding land, water, and air.[24]

The health commissioner finally recommended that the school be temporarily closed. The governor of New York announced that the state would purchase the 235 houses nearest to the chemical dump and assist in the relocation of the displaced families. President Carter declared Love Canal a disaster area, which qualified families and the community for federal assistance. In the early 1980s, the Environmental Protection Agency sealed the dump more securely with a 3-foot-thick clay cap and built a chain-link fence around the central area. A containment system was also built that could process 160 gallons of leaking waste per minute. The containment system was refined in Phase II of the EPA's operation, and the 227 homes built nearest to the dump were razed. By the late 1980s, the containment project came to a close.[25]

In a remarkable turn of events, Love Canal was resettled in the 1990s, much to the chagrin of former homeowners. Houses were priced at 10% to 20% below the market rate. By 1995, 170 houses had been sold. The new community renamed itself Black Creek Village. But it would not be long before these new residents had their own health problems, such as birth defects and reproductive disorders. New lawsuits were filed, and by 2014 there were over 1,000 claims pending against Occidental from past and present residents of this neighborhood.[26]

Hooker's Moral and Legal Liability

Hooker Chemical is probably far removed from the minds of the residents of Black Creek Village struggling with a new set of environmental issues. But this company is the source of the health disorders and lawsuits that still persist. Occidental/Hooker has been battling lawsuits from Love Canal residents for decades. It has also been forced to deal with legal action initiated by the federal government under the auspices of the Superfund Act, the federal program that cleans up polluted sites. In February 1988, a federal court found Occidental "partially responsible" for its inadequate storage of chemicals at Love Canal. As a result, Occidental was responsible for the costs of cleaning up Love Canal, and it reimbursed the federal government $250 million. The company had argued unsuccessfully that the city of Niagara Falls bore sole responsibility for these events, since it had developed the land and disrupted its hydrology, which led to the leakage. But in 1994, that same court decided not to hold Occidental liable for punitive damages. The company was "negligent" but did not act with "reckless or wanton disregard for human rights."[27] In June 1994, Occidental agreed to pay New York State $98 million for damages and expenditures for its ongoing cleanup work at the site.[28]

Hooker's voluntary response to Love Canal prior to these legal actions has been described by some as apathetic and insufficient. In 1978, Hooker announced its support of remediating the dump and offered to provide $200,000 for the cleanup. It also provided technical assistance and some personnel. But for the most part, Hooker adopted a defensive posture and insisted that it was not liable for what had happened. According to Vice President Bruce Davis, the company "is not liable for any claims of damage or harm that may result from this unfortunate situation."[29] Hooker consistently denied liability because it had no connection with the school or homes that were built once it transferred ownership. The city of Niagara Falls through its contractors and housing developers had breached the dump and their actions were the direct cause of all the contamination. Hooker also claimed it had always followed "best practices" when dealing with hazardous chemical waste. Hooker claims its method of toxic waste disposal was standard industry practice in the 1940s and 1950s. The company diligently obtained the necessary permits and permissions to use Love Canal as a disposal site, and it proceeded openly to fill the canal with its waste products. When Hooker sold the property to the city of Niagara Falls, it warned the school board and city officials about building on or near a waste disposal site. Hooker believes its sincere attempts to dissuade school and city officials from public and private development of the Love Canal area were not appreciated.[30]

Critics of Hooker remain unconvinced by these arguments and claim it should have made greater efforts to use incineration as an alternative to landfilling. In the 1994 trial, the State of New York argued that Hooker chose landfilling rather than incineration because it was easier and cheaper. It cost about twice as much to burn the chemical residues as it did to bury them. Hooker had made several attempts to use incineration in the 1940s, but the operation was suspended because it caused too much air pollution. Hooker began working on a properly designed incinerator in 1957, which was built in 1961. This incinerator, however, permitted the incineration of only liquid, not solid waste. In addition, some chemicals such as DDM are difficult to destroy by incineration, and effective air pollution controls did not exist at the time. Efficient air pollution control for solid waste and chemicals like DDM was not developed until the 1970s. Hence, incineration did not appear to be a viable alternative for every form of chemical waste during the decades of the 1940s and 1950s.

Postscript

The entire Love Canal affair represents a sordid chapter in America's environmental history. According to Newman, Love Canal symbolizes the "toxic legacy of industrial expansion in the Chemical Century."[31] Some degree of pollution and environmental damage seemed to be an inevitable by-product of a healthy industrialized economy.

However, in this case, the risk of imminent harm due to buried toxic waste should have been apparent to all the parties involved, including Hooker and Niagara Falls city officials.

Occidental/Hooker has been persistently maligned for its poor environmental performance. Yet Hooker violated no laws and had few other viable alternatives for the disposal of its hazardous chemical waste. Do we ask too much of companies to invest in more environmental protection than is required by law? Should Hooker have foreseen the development of this area and adjusted its plans accordingly? The Love Canal case continues to evoke many such lingering questions about externalities and the assumption of risk.

- Who is to blame for the Love Canal fiasco? How could this dreadful affair have been prevented? How could it have been better managed by public health officials?

- To what extent do you accept Hooker Chemical's defense for its actions? As the company points out, they followed the law at the time and got permission to dump the chemicals in the canal. Is there any moral turpitude in the actions of Hooker?

- Do you agree with the court's decision not to assign punitive damages to the Hooker chemical settlement?

CASE STUDY 9.2

DEEPWATER HORIZON: BP ON THE EDGE

The popular movie *Deepwater Horizon*, which played to big audiences in 2016, reopened some old wounds for BP. BP's catastrophic oil spill in the Gulf of Mexico was the lowest point in the company's long history. The 2010 explosion on the oil-drilling rig named Deepwater Horizon killed 11 of its workers, injured 17 others, and sent over 3 million barrels of light crude oil into the Gulf of Mexico. It was the worst environmental catastrophe since the Exxon Valdez oil spill in Alaska in 1989. For a company struggling to move on, the dramatic re-creation of these events was most
unwelcome. BP executives were portrayed in Hollywood's rendition of this disaster as uncaring bureaucrats worried only about budgets and schedules instead of safety and the fragile ecology of the gulf.[32]

But what are the basic facts behind this immense oil spill, and what factors led to the deadly explosion? Was BP criminally negligent, as the U.S. government alleged? This case explores these fundamental questions and provides a detailed account of the events on that tragic day in April 2010. It also examines the underlying causes of the explosion along with the cultural and organizational factors that shaped the decision-making of BP managers. The case concludes with an overview of the oil spill's impact on the wildlife, ecology, and residents of the gulf area and a brief summary of the legal proceedings against BP, culminating in its historic settlement with the U.S. federal government.

BP: A Short History

British Petroleum, or BP, was incorporated in 1909 as the Anglo-Persian Oil Company (AP). The company had discovered oil in Persia (now known as Iran) prior to World War I. After drilling several major oil fields, AP signed a lucrative contract with the British Admiralty for a supply of fuel oil to be used by the Royal British Navy. After the war, the British government invested 2 million pounds in the Anglo-Persian Company in exchange for a substantial ownership stake. This influx of much-needed capital enabled investment in refineries and further oil exploration. Soon AP was selling oil to both British and European customers.

As this corporation expanded after World War II, it emerged as one of the world's largest oil companies. It was soon a formidable rival to Royal Dutch Shell and Standard Oil of New Jersey. However, this distinctively British oil company, which had been renamed Anglo-Iranian Oil in 1935 (the year Persia became Iran), became subject to nationalistic hostilities. In 1951, the Iranian oil industry was nationalized, but after the overthrow of Iranian leader Mussadegh, the company was allowed to return. It changed its name once again in 1954 to British Petroleum Company as it sought to diversify away from its heavy dependence on Iranian oil. British Petroleum, with a keener appreciation of political risk, increased its output from neighboring countries like Iraq and Kuwait. It also embarked on a campaign of oil exploration in many other places, including the Arabian Gulf, Canada, and Australia. Major oil discoveries in Alaska and the North Sea provided BP with an abundance of oil as the oil giant now consolidated its position as market leader. BP's strategy focused the company's operations primarily on upstream activities in the value chain, such as oil exploration, production, and refining.[33]

The oil price shocks of the 1970s caused turbulence for the entire oil industry, including British Petroleum. It lost access to crude oil supplies produced in countries that belonged to OPEC (Organization of the Petroleum Exporting Countries). Also, its oil assets were nationalized and expropriated in Libya in 1971 and in Nigeria in 1979. The oil industry's structural changes led to more diversification and acquisitions. British Petroleum acquired Britoil, among other companies, in the early 1980s, which doubled its capacity for oil exploration in the North Sea.[34]

Under CEO Robert Horton, known as "The Hatchet," British Petroleum undertook Project 1990, a fundamental transformation of its corporate structure. Horton's goal was to reshape the organization by eliminating layers of bureaucracy and reducing costs. There were substantial job cuts and an uneven distribution of remaining workloads that led to low morale and Horton's eventual departure. Horton was succeeded by Sir David Simon, who cut another 9,000 jobs between 1993 to 1995. Analysts praised British Petroleum's dramatic strides toward becoming a leaner organization with greater strategic flexibility. When E. J. Browne took over the helm in 1996, he promised to build on these reforms and grow the company by adding $1.5 billion to its bottom line.[35]

Under Browne's leadership, British Petroleum pursued an ambitious acquisition strategy and became more vertically integrated. It merged with its rival AMOCO in 1998 and acquired ARCO in 2000. These strategic maneuvers gave the British firm a stronger presence in downstream value chain activities like the retail sale of petroleum products. As BP Amoco, the company become the largest oil producer in the United States. In the late 1990s, Browne introduced a rebranding campaign centered on the slogan "Beyond Petroleum," which implied the company was now committed to seeking out alternative sources of energy. In 2001, the British company shortened its name to BP. BP is now the United Kingdom's largest corporation, with 53,700 employees and sales in 2016 of £44.7 (US $69.8) billion.[36]

During the last two decades, BP has also promoted and financed its so-called "deep-water" strategy. As part of that strategy initiated by Browne, it acquired 500 oil leases in the Gulf of Mexico, which had previously been considered a wasteland for oil reserves. Other oil companies had avoided the gulf because of the enormous risks involved in exploring and drilling for oil in such a difficult physical environment. Oil wells in this area took many months to build and cost about $200 million, but an oil field here could produce high volumes of oil. BP's deep-water strategy paid off, and soon it was pumping 450,000 barrels a day at several gulf off-shore drilling sites. Its first big oil find was Thunder Horse, which nicely fit BP's new high-risk, high-return strategy.[37]

Another integral part of the BP strategy during this time was relentless cost-cutting throughout the entire organization. As a consequence, BP's per barrel production costs were the lowest in the entire industry. Instead of vertical integration, BP switched to a more "disaggregated" model, with the company now outsourcing technical support for its oil-drilling projects to subcontractors. Commercial interests seemed to always supersede engineering ones. According to Tom Bergin, "BP was no longer a technical company, but a commercial one. Its primary role was to decide which projects to back, and where possible to have others do the work."[38] The company had always prided itself on the high dividends it paid out, but those dividend payments come with an opportunity cost: less money to spend on maintenance facilities and engineering management.[39]

In 2007, Tony Hayward succeeded E. J. Brown as BP's CEO. Hayward inherited a prosperous enterprise that had largely succeeded at cost-cutting along with consistent revenue growth. However, BP had experienced a series of unfortunate accidents, which raised suspicions with regulators and NGOs about its level of commitment to safety issues. A catastrophic explosion at a BP refinery in Texas City in 2005 had been the direct result of BP's failure to promptly fix many safety violations. Budget cuts and poor maintenance were cited as the underlying causes of this accident, which killed 15 workers and injured 180. Browne did not discount safety issues, but his achievements "masked failures in assuring process safety" in places such as the BP Texas refinery.[40] This accident was followed by the Prudhoe Bay oil spill in March 2006, when almost 250,000 barrels of oil spilled into Alaska's pristine north slope. The pipeline failure that caused the damaging spill was later attributed to the careless use of inferior corrosion inhibitors that safeguard the pipeline from water corrosion.[41]

Finally, in 2009, under Hayward's leadership, the Occupational Safety and Health Administration (OSHA) imposed a $51 million fine on BP for its failure to correct the safety problems at the Texas City refinery. According to the OSHA complaint, "When BP signed the OSHA settlement from the March 2005 explosion, it agreed to take comprehensive action to protect employees. Instead of living up to that commitment, BP has allowed hundreds of potential hazards to continue unabated."[42]

Shortly after becoming CEO, Hayward restructured BP once again. In May 2007, he laid off 7,500 workers, sold assets, and sharply reduced the company's "unacceptably high overhead costs." Hayward wanted to decentralize and streamline the business into two basic units, exploration and production on one side, and refining and marketing on the other. According to BP's 2009 fiscal plan, budgets were cut in the Gulf of Mexico's operations by over 20%, and managers were instructed to stay within their tight budgets or face unpleasant consequences. In March 2010, Hayward announced that BP's principal strategic priority was cost-cutting and higher productivity. His goal was to save an additional $3 billion by reducing costs and enhancing operational efficiency, especially in the refining unit of the business.[43]

Consultants and former BP executives warned BP that its management changes and relentless cost-cutting were putting profits and productivity too far ahead of safety. Too often, cost-cutting leads to pushing limits on dangerous projects and taking big risks to save time. One former employee called attention to BP's poor risk management practices, which might have prevented the gulf accident. Workers, for example, had no "stop work authority" to challenge unsafe or dangerous conditions. On Deepwater, that authority might have been invoked by BP or Transocean workers to challenge and address the negative pressure test results. Similarly, the U.S. National Commission investigating the accident highlighted BP's lack of a proper "safety culture."[44]

Macondo

In March 2008, the Minerals Management Service (MMS), the U.S. federal agency that regulates offshore drilling, sold to BP the rights to drill for oil in a spot in the gulf called Mississippi Canyon. The price tag was $34 million. The site was 5,000 feet deep and 48 miles offshore. BP geologists estimated there were 60 million barrels of oil about 18,000 feet below sea level. The site was renamed Macondo. BP also submitted its drilling proposal to the federal government to secure permission to drill a well in this area. Their request was approved by federal regulators at the MMS, despite the fact that its contingency plans for an oil spill or "blowout" were not clearly delineated. The MMS has been criticized for taking a minimalist or "light-handed" approach that was focused more on facilitating than regulating offshore drilling. MMS also had budgetary constraints that prevented it from closely monitoring the oil industry.[45]

Drilling an oil well at the Macondo site proved to be a daunting geological challenge. BP geologists had underestimated the fragility of the strata or rock formations through which the BP crew would drill. This was one of several lapses of planning that plagued this project from its inception. Companies like BP first drill an exploratory well to verify the presence of hydrocarbons (gas and oil) and take initial measurements of the strata. After the presence of hydrocarbons is verified or disproved, most companies usually abandon such exploratory wells.

The next stage is an appraisal, which assesses the volume and nature of the "pay zone." This assessment can be done by taking measurements from the exploratory well or by abandoning that well and drilling a separate appraisal well. The final stage is production, which involves extracting the hydrocarbons or crude oil. Production requires the installation of a production casing, which is simply a pipe inside the well that connects to the pay zone and allows for a controlled flow of oil into a production system such as a pipeline or a facility for oil tanker ships. Oil companies can add production capabilities to the exploratory or appraisal well or drill a whole new well. Thus, companies can drill one, two, or three wells depending on budget and scheduling issues, but the decision is also contingent on geological issues, such as the fragility of the formation. According to experts, in the difficult underwater terrain of the Gulf of Mexico, the conservative and more common approach was to drill three wells or at least two wells. But BP chose to use the first exploratory well for appraisal and for production, declaring that Macondo was a "keeper," a viable long-term production well. It was described as "an exploratory well with a production tail," which meant it was an exploratory well in which a production casing would be installed. The inclusion of the production tail *within* the exploratory well combined with the fragile nature of the formation added to Macondo's risks.[46]

Following its customary procedures, BP leased an oil-drilling rig called Deepwater Horizon from an outside contractor, Transocean, at a cost of $1 million per day (including the cost of salaries and material). While BP engineers designed the well and laid out the specifications for drilling the well, the actual drilling was done by Transocean and Halliburton workers. Halliburton was an oil services firm that assisted in drilling deep-water wells like Macondo. The work began in January 2010, and the first task was to install the blowout preventer (BOP), the massive flow-control device used to deter the uncontrolled release of hydrocarbons. With the BOP installed, the process of drilling the exploratory well began.[47]

Since this well was a "keeper," it had to be prepared for later production and excavation of oil. To that end, workers installed the production casing after the exploratory work was finished. BP used a "long-string" production casing that ran the full length of the well from the ocean floor into the pay zone. Foamed cement was used to hold the production casing in place at the bottom of the well. The long-string design was riskier than alternatives but also less expensive. Competitors such as Royal Dutch Shell and Chevron used long-string production casing far less frequently than BP. These casings were especially uncommon in wells like Macondo, a deep-water well with unfamiliar geology, requiring a "finesse cement job." The choice of a long-string production casing may not have directly contributed to the blowout, but it increased the difficulty of getting a reliable primary cement job.[48]

BP had also purchased the rights to a site in the gulf known as Kaskida, and it had to drill an appraisal well before the regulatory deadline of May 16, 2016. If an appraisal well was not drilled by that time, BP would lose its lease. This regulation has been implemented by MMS to prevent oil companies from stockpiling territories. The Kaskida site was estimated to be 60 times larger than Macondo, so the stakes were quite high. There are only a fixed number of oil rigs available, and BP planned to use the Macondo rig to drill at Kaskida. As a consequence, the rig was scheduled to leave Macondo on April 26 so it could be transported to Kaskida in time to make the deadline. Thus, there was intense pressure to finish the Macondo project on schedule.[49]

The Deepwater Horizon Explosion

On the fateful night of April 20, 2010, Deepwater Horizon exploded and became engulfed in flames. Before the rig sank, it floated on top of the Gulf of Mexico's 5,000-foot-deep waters. A surge of natural gas forced its way through the concrete core that had recently been installed with the help of Halliburton in order to seal the well for future use. The cement core or seal was apparently too weak to withstand the pressure caused by the pay zone's high temperature (243 degrees Fahrenheit) and the fragile formation. The seal was composed of a concrete mixture that used nitrogen gas to accelerate curing, but it was ineffective. The blowout preventer failed as the invisible gas rose above it and expanded. It soon flooded the Horizon's deck. The rig had suffered a catastrophic blowout and a total loss of well control. The hydrocarbon gases were ignited by a flame and caused the fatal explosion.[50]

The accident resulted in the death of 11 workers on the Deepwater Horizon. The remaining 115 workers on board the rig survived, but 17 were severely injured. Thanks to the Coast Guard and vessels in the area, they were promptly plucked from the fiery sea. Two days after this massive explosion, Deepwater Horizon sank into the ocean. When it sank, the pipe connected to the well broke, and oil began spewing into the gulf at a relentless pace. When the explosion occurred, the crew tried to activate the emergency disconnect system that would prompt the sealing of the well, but this "deadman system" did not work.[51]

Over 3 million barrels of oil flowed from the damaged Macondo well over an 87-day period. It was by far the largest spill of oil in the history of marine oil-drilling operations. The well was finally capped on July 15, 2010. By that time, the damage done to the gulf's fragile ecosystem was virtually incalculable. BP immediately set up a $20 billion trust fund to pay expenses of the cleanup. The total cost to BP is expected to be about $62 billion.

As oil kept pouring into the gulf, the company made a valiant effort at damage control, but it was vilified by the media for weeks. Despite its best attempts, it could not seem to plug the hole and stop the oil spill. It first tried to install a containment dome, but that did not work. Desperate measures like "top kill" and "junk shot" were also futile. The hole was finally plugged using a technique known as a capping stack.[52] BP wasn't helped by the miscues of its CEO, Tony Hayward, who stepped forward as the public face of BP's response. Hayward said the oil spilling into the Gulf was "tiny" when compared to the size of the ocean.[53] At the height of the crisis, he was photographed participating in a yacht race with his son. Hayward tried to deflect blame from BP and minimize its role in the spill. Later he remarked that "this is not BP. It is an industry accident."[54] Hayward made other awkward statements during the crisis and eventually resigned in late July, several days after the well was capped.

The BP blowout and its aftermath had profound social, economic, and environmental consequences. But how could this explosion have happened? Hadn't BP taken adequate safety precautions during the process of closing the well? Oil well cement jobs and "abandonments" are routine in the gulf, and the Horizon crew had certainly performed these tasks many times. The abandonment process involved sealing off the hydrocarbon zones with bottom plugs composed of cement. But what went so drastically wrong this time?[55]

The Causes of the Deepwater Blowout

Engineering experts concurred that BP made several critical mistakes that contributed to the terrible explosion and subsequent oil spill. First, the well was probably not properly drilled. BP engineers had originally planned on a depth of 18,260 feet for the well, but then a decision was made to go 100 feet deeper. According to one drilling expert, that decision was reckless and "totally unsafe." As a result, the well was left in an "extremely fragile condition."[56] The crew was now drilling and operating in a formation where the mud weight was so great that primary well control was no longer possible. Nonetheless, at this depth the crew had uncovered an abundance of oil, and Macondo was officially classified as a major discovery, a pay zone with 50 million gallons of oil. Also, BP relied on the riskier long-string production casing despite the fact that it was disfavored by competitors.

Second, there are questions about the way BP handled the cementing of the oil well once the drilling was complete. For BP, there was some urgency in closing the well and moving the rig, since it cost $1 million a day to remain on-site and the Macondo project was already $60 million over budget. Also, as noted earlier, they had to drill an appraisal well at Kaskida before May 16, 2016, or BP would lose its lease. Cementing an oil well to isolate the hydrocarbon zone at the bottom of the well is a difficult task, especially in these deep-water regions. In this process, engineers pump mud inside the well to push down a slug of cement so that it "turns the corner" at the bottom of the well and flows up into the annular space to create a long and consistent seal around the production casing.[57] BP engineers, who were assisted by workers from the oil services firm Halliburton, were worried that the cementing procedure might place too much pressure on the unstable geological formation. BP decided to pump cement into the well at a lower rate (4 barrels per minute) to decrease that pressure, even though higher flow rates increase the efficiency of a cement job. BP also limited the volume of cement that would be pumped down the well, even though more cement is standard industry practice and reduces the risk of contamination. Finally, the company chose to use nitrogen foam cement, a substance with which it had little experience. It had the advantage of curing more quickly, but the destabilizing effects on foamed cement by oil-based mud are severe, and most engineers do not use it. Finally, while BP had good standards for cementing, it had devoted few resources to enforcing those standards, either among its own employees or subcontractors, such as the Halliburton workers on this project who decided that foamed cement was acceptable. BP's lack of oversight contributed to the problems with capping the well in a safe manner.[58]

The primary cement job was finished on April 19. The pumps were turned off and BP personnel performed tests to see if the float valves were closed and holding firm so that there was no flow on the drill pipe. They concluded the valves were holding and the cement job was a success. At 7:30 a.m. on April 20, BP engineers, convinced the cement job was effective, sent home a team of technicians from Schlumberger who were waiting to perform additional tests on the primary cement job. The decision saved time (about 10 hours) and also approximately $128,000.[59]

The next step was temporary abandonment, which secured the well, before untethering the Deepwater Horizon rig. This procedure involved installing a lockdown sleeve at the top of the well and a 300-foot-long cement "surface" plug 3,300 feet below the ocean floor as a backup for the cement plug at the bottom of the well to isolate the hydrocarbon zones. The BP Macondo team made numerous changes to the temporary abandonment procedures in the two weeks leading up to April 20, but none of those changes were subject to any formal risk assessment. One problematic decision was to replace 3,300 feet of mud below the ocean floor line with seawater. However, replacing heavy drilling mud with lighter seawater places excessive stress on the cement job at the bottom of the well. In its defense, BP has stated it prefers to set surface cement plugs in water rather than mud, but there is no evidence that other operators have set a surface plug so deep in seawater without additional barriers. On April 20, crews hurriedly began work on displacing all the mud, and this displacement process probably stressed the new cement job that sealed the well. The mud had also acted to equalize pressure at the bottom and relieve some of the strain on the newly constructed cement barrier.[60]

As a result of these factors, the cement barrier failed to contain the dangerous hydrocarbons, which seeped through and eventually led to the well blowout. It did not help that BP was so pressed for time. Engineers who voiced their concerns about the cement job or mud displacement were ignored. In one email message, a manager complained about an engineer who had identified some problems with the abandonment process: "Paranoia . . . from engineering leadership."[61]

Third, BP disregarded the test results for the oil well seals. After giving the cement time to cure, the crew conducted a test for well integrity known as a "negative test." The test revealed that at 8 p.m., two hours before the explosion, there was pressure on the drill pipe connecting the well to the rig. This was an indication that fluids were moving through the cement casing. The test should have caused alarm and triggered a "high-alert" status, but BP engineers on the rig ignored the results and continued to affirm the cement job a success. The negative pressure test is a binary pass/fail test, and by all accounts, BP had failed. At a minimum, further tests should have been conducted immediately, but that didn't happen.[62]

Thus, drilling a well that was too deep within a fragile formation, a poor job of cementing the well and implementing temporary abandonment procedures, and an inexplicable indifference to negative test results—all three of these factors contributed to the tragic explosion on the night of April 20. The production casing, the cement at the bottom of the well hole that also seals that casing, and the well formation form a tight system that can isolate hydrocarbons from the well. But BP did not create a properly functioning and effective system. Also, if the company had taken a "conservative" approach to drilling wells in the gulf, it might have built a new production well instead of using the well drilled for exploration.[63]

As a result of this combination of factors, the barriers or plugs isolating the hydrocarbon area failed. Massive amounts of gas rose above the blowout preventer and caused the explosion on the rig. For unknown reasons, the BOP failed, and when the gases reached the rig, they were ignited by an unknown spark that caused the explosion. The most important safety requirement of well construction and maintenance is well control, holding hydrocarbons temporarily in check, but Deepwater Horizon could not sustain well control.[64]

Environmental and Economic Effects of the Oil Spill

As the Deepwater Horizon rig sank slowly into the gulf waters, it began flowing light Louisiana crude oil into this biodiverse environment. The spilling of oil lasted

87 straight days and amounted to over 3.2 million barrels (134 million gallons). The environmental damage was quite extensive. The oil contaminated a wide area of wildlife habitats, pristine beaches, and wetlands. Over 1,100 miles of coastline and 1,200 square miles of the deep ocean floor were spoiled by oil and tar balls. About 22 tons of that oil washed up on the shores of the gulf coast. According to one resident, we witnessed "an entire culture being washed away by crude oil and chemicals."[65]

The wildlife impacted by the spill included fish, shellfish, birds, sea turtles, marine mammals (whales and dolphins), and plankton. According to the National Resources Defense Counsel (NRDC), over 1,000 sea turtles, 170 marine mammals, and close to 1 million coastal and offshore sea birds were found dead after the oil spill. Coastal bird mortality was especially high. A record high number of dolphin illnesses and deaths have been reported in the gulf region since the spill. Scientists estimate that 12% of bluefin tuna larvae were contaminated by oil, which will lead to heart defects and deaths of many bluefin tuna. The National Wildlife Foundation also determined that 12% of brown pelicans, 32% of the northern gulf laughing gulls, and 13% of royal terns had died thanks to the toxic effects of the oil spill. The pelican population was especially hard-hit because it was their nesting season.[66]

Long-term ecological damage, especially to marine and estuarine habitats, was widespread, and years after the spill it was still being assessed by researchers. A 10-square-mile area of seagrass that provides food and shelter for many organisms was contaminated by oil. Marsh and mangrove habitats were oiled and experienced a loss of vital vegetation. Lower supplies of snails, a key food source for birds, have also been documented. Diverse seaweed habitats and deep-sea coral communities were severely damaged.[67]

The adverse effects on the ecology and the wildlife will most likely persist for many more years. Oil was buried beneath the sand and periodically gets churned up when the waves are especially rough. Oil is still on the bottom of the ocean throughout the gulf, and tar balls continue to surface. Dolphin and sea mammal deaths in the contaminated areas still occur, although not at the high rates recorded directly after the spill. In Barataria Bay, mangrove islands full of mangrove trees have been destroyed because oil coated the roots of the tree and they slowly died. Experts fear that without the mangroves to hold the islands together, other islands will soon vanish as well.[68]

Food safety also became a big problem in areas of the Gulf Coast. After the spill, fish and shellfish became contaminated and no longer safe to consume. Estimated losses for the gulf area fishing industry are $247 million as a result of fisheries closures. At the height of the oil spill, 37% of federal waters in the gulf were closed to fisheries. Some of those closures lasted for years due to the persistence of the oil and tar balls. Shrimp landings in Mississippi and Louisiana state waters dropped precipitously. The thriving oyster and shellfish industries were irreparably damaged. The lack of fish and shellfish severely impacted the local food and restaurant industries, which have struggled for many years to recover.[69]

The local economy, of course, was also devastated by the oil spill. Tourists disappeared from the oil-tainted beaches of Louisiana, Alabama, Mississippi, and the Florida panhandle. In 2010, tourists canceled their reservations in many gulf area hotels, and most hotels had difficulty booking future events. The loss of tourism dollars and the "brand damage" attributable to the oil spill were estimated to cost the gulf area economy about $23 billion.[70]

The Aftermath: BP on Trial

Early on in this unfortunate saga, the Obama administration appointed a bipartisan presidential commission to investigate the causes of the Deepwater explosion and make recommendations for the future. The commission's comprehensive report, issued in January 2011, was harshly critical of BP. The report concluded that the loss of the Macondo well could have been prevented. There were a series of "identifiable mistakes" made by BP that revealed "systematic failures in risk management."[71] It also sharply critiqued BP's safety culture. The failure of that culture was reflected in the actions of BP workers who "did not adequately identify or address the risks of an accident—not in well design, cementing, or temporary abandonment procedures." BP made a series of decisions that saved the company time and money, but without a full appreciation of the accompanying risks.[72]

There were many legal proceedings directed at BP, but the most significant was the federal government's criminal case. Corporations themselves are usually not charged with homicide, but the Justice Department believed homicide charges were warranted in the case of three corporations: BP, Transocean (owner of the rig), and Halliburton. There are precedents for such charges against a corporation, such as the indictment of Ford Motor Co. by the state of Indiana for the death of three teenage girls killed in a rear-end accident of a Ford Pinto that Ford knew was unsafe. BP pled guilty to "seaman's manslaughter" and paid a $4 billion fine. In accepting the settlement, the presiding judge rebuked BP for its negligence. According to Judge Vance, the tragic accident would not have occurred if "BP employees had properly supervised the negative pressure testing of the well, had not ignored multiple indications that the drill pipe was not secure, [and] had not failed to respond to obvious signs of pressure on the drill pipe."[73]

The federal government also filed a civil suit against BP, and the trial, which was divided into three phases, began in February 2013. The government's case revolved around BP's gross negligence and willful misconduct. BP's defense was that there was no negligence or "willful" misconduct but simply a series of independent acts and omissions that led to the overcoming of its safety systems. According to BP, there was no proof of a "culpable mental state" that would suggest egregious and willful misconduct on its part.[74] The judge disagreed with BP and ruled that its actions manifested both "gross negligence" and "willful misconduct." In the second phase, the judge ruled against the plaintiffs, finding they were not eligible for punitive damages, since BP had made sincere efforts to clean up the oil spill. As the trial moved into its third phase, BP reached a deal with the federal and state governments that amounted to a payment of $20.8 billion. The largest portion would reimburse the state and federal governments for their past and ongoing efforts to deal with natural resource damages. This was the largest environmental settlement in the history of the United States. The deal was finalized and approved in April 2016, six years after the explosion.[75]

BP has calculated its total costs from the oil spill at $61.6 billion. Its disclosure of that figure in July 2016 came a month after BP agreed to pay investors $175 million to settle allegations that it had failed to fully disclose its business risks. The company said it had also resolved most of the litigation related to the oil spill. However, the disaster has drained the company of vital resources for the past six years and forced it to embark on new downsizing projects. BP's woes have also been aggravated by the steep drop in oil prices that began in 2014. At $61.6 billion, the BP oil spill is the most expensive environmental disaster in history. It dwarfs the $4.3 billion paid out by ExxonMobil for the Valdez oil spill when an Exxon tanker spilled oil into Prince William Sound in Alaska.[76]

- Do you agree with Hayward's statement that "this is not BP" but an industry-wide problem? Is this such a risky industry that accidents like Deepwater Horizon are almost inevitable?

- What went wrong on the Deepwater Horizon rig, and what was the root cause of the problem? In what ways did BP fail to live up to its corporate duties—create value, obey the law, and observe ethical standards?

- In your estimation, should the U.S. government allow offshore deep-water oil drilling in places like the Gulf of Mexico, or are the environmental risks too high? If not, how would you deal with the economic impact of a drilling moratorium?

- Is BP guilty of manslaughter? Should corporations like BP and Ford be charged with committing crimes, or should the government stick to filing civil suits?

CASE STUDY 9.3

VOLKSWAGEN'S DIESELGATE

Wolfsburg is a major industrial city in the north of Germany that has been known for a long time as the birthplace of the "people's car," produced by Volkswagen. The prosperous town is full of amenities, including a water park and a soccer stadium. Volkswagen's offices and factories dot the urban landscape. The company provides 72,000 jobs at this central Wolfsburg facility. Next to that complex is Autostadt, a prime tourist attraction where VW showcases its vehicles. The city's economic vitality is closely linked to the fortunes of Volkswagen. Tensions ran high, therefore, when a big emissions scandal erupted in the United States. The reaction of city officials was described as one of "stunned silence." Conversations around the city, in its cafés and restaurants, were full of anxiety about the repercussions of this scandal. What would happen to the company? Would the jobs and pensions of autoworkers still be secure? Many citizens found themselves in a pensive mood about this eruption of corporate corruption that had attracted global attention.[77]

Julian Stratenschulte/picture-alliance/dpa/AP Images

This case provides a detailed account of the Volkswagen diesel emissions scandal, including necessary background about this old German company, its management, and its organizational culture. Dozens of managers and engineers were involved in this fraud: a manipulation of diesel engine emissions tests to meet environmental standards. The incident has been quite costly to VW, and it has even led to the criminal indictment of several executives.

Company History

Germany's Volkswagen is the second-largest carmaker in the world, after Toyota. Its 590,000 employees produce nearly 41,000 vehicles daily. It currently owns 12 subsidiaries, including Volkswagen Passenger Cars and Audi, along with legendary luxury brands such as Bentley, Lamborghini, Porsche, and Ducati. Ferdinand Porsche, designer of the Beetle, and the Porsche family led this company for many years and greatly influenced Volkswagen's history.

Volkswagenwerk was founded in 1937 by Ferdinand Porsche during the height of Nazi Germany's rise to power. It was set up with the help of the Nazi trade union organization, and its first factory was built in 1938 in Wolfsburg. As its name suggests, the company's purpose was to build an affordable "people's car," which became known as the Volkswagen Beetle. Hitler had ambitious plans for Volkswagen, and its preoccupation with bigness has been evident throughout the company's history. After World War II, production of this subcompact vehicle increased dramatically, and sales reached 1 million units in 1955. In 1964, Volkswagen purchased Auto Union's premium Audi brand, which became its first luxury offering. The company's growth prospects were constrained by a small domestic market, and so it quickly turned to export markets to remain competitive and take advantage of scale economies.[78]

When sales of the subcompact Beetle began to decline, VW made the transition to a new generation of cars with front-wheel drive and water-cooled engines. These cars included the Passat, Jetta, Scirocco, Golf, and Polo. In 1975, VW Group was created as a holding company for the growing carmaker. These models sold extremely well, especially in Europe, and sales of the compact Golf eventually exceeded sales of the Beetle. But Volkswagen struggled in the United States against competitors like Honda and Toyota. By 1992, sales reached 3.2 million units, but during the worldwide recession global sales declined and high labor costs eroded its profit margins. In 1993, Ferdinand Piëch, grandson of Ferdinand Porsche, became CEO. Piëch began an efficiency campaign with a new "platform strategy" where as many vehicles as possible shared the same parts. The efficiency efforts paid off, and by 1997 profits once again exceeded 1 billion deutsche marks ($650 million). In 1998, VW made a series of major acquisitions of famous names, buying up Britain's luxury carmaker Bentley, France's Bugattian, and Italy's sports carmaker Lamborghini. It also purchased 49% of Porsche. In 2012, VW bought the remaining half of Porsche's car-making operations along with Italian motorcycle manufacturer Ducati.[79]

When Piëch stepped down as CEO in 2002, Volkswagen's sales had doubled to €87 billion, and the number of cars produced annually grew to 5 million. Piëch's successor, Bernd Pischetsrieder, resigned in 2007, and Volkswagen turned to Martin Winterkorn, head of its Audi unit, to become the new CEO. Winterkorn had a grand plan for the company, and in early 2008 he announced his new goal: VW would sell 10 million cars a year by 2018 and be the leader in the world's top three markets, the United States, Europe, and China. VW was selling about 6 million vehicles in 2008, and to meet that target, its sales would have to exceed sales of companies like General Motors and Toyota. But Volkswagen was "bent on world domination."[80]

VW reached Winterkorn's target four years ahead of schedule in 2014. The auto manufacturer became the biggest foreign carmaker in China. In Europe, one out of every four cars sold was a VW brand. With global sales of 10 million vehicles, VW surpassed General Motors and Toyota in the first half of 2015 as the world's largest auto manufacturer. By 2015, Volkswagen had become one of the biggest firms in the world. It had factories located in 31 countries, although a majority were in Germany. And its products were sold in 153 countries across the globe.[81]

The Diesel Engine and the Emissions Scandal

During 2008, Winterkorn informed U.S. executives of his ambitious objective for the U.S. market: a tripling of its current sales. The target was to sell 800,000 vehicles a year as part of the company's 10-year plan. To help reach that target, Volkswagen would heavily market small cars powered by diesel engines. In 2008, diesel-engine vehicles were just 5% of the U.S. car market, and Winterkorn saw a great opportunity for growth. As a result, the diesel became the centerpiece of the U.S. sales strategy. The diesel engine was quite popular in Europe, so why not make it more popular in the United States?[82]

The diesel engine, which was invented by Rudolph Diesel, is more efficient than the gasoline engine, which powers most of the cars in the world today. Both diesel and gasoline engines convert fuel into energy through a series of small explosions or combustions. The difference is how these explosions occur. In gasoline engines, fuel is mixed with air, compressed by pistons, and ignited by sparks from a spark plug. In the diesel engine, air is compressed first and then fuel is injected. Since air heats up when it's compressed, the fuel ignites. Diesel engines are more fuel-efficient because the compressed fuel and air burns more completely than the fuel in a gasoline engine.[83]

Diesel-powered vehicles emit much less carbon dioxide than gasoline cars but more noxious nitrogen oxides along with fine soot particles. Nitrogen oxides (NO_x) are serious pollutants that are harmful to human health and to the environment. Breathing air with a high concentration of NO_x gases can irritate the airways in a person's respiratory system. They can cause or aggravate health problems such as cancer and bronchitis and increase susceptibility to respiratory infections. People with asthma as well as young children are at greater risk of suffering from the ill effects of NO_x. These gases also have harmful environmental effects, since they react with sunlight to produce smog and are a main contributor to acid rain.[84]

Carmakers have relied on three basic technologies to reduce these dangerous nitrogen oxide emissions. A technology known as BlueTec treats the nitrogen oxide gases with a solution of urea that breaks down those gases while they are in the exhaust into harmless nitrogen and oxygen. The drawback is the need for a tank to hold the urea solution, which takes up valuable space, especially in smaller cars. A second technology was the lean NO_x trap that contains the gases in a chamber and transforms them into oxygen and diatomic nitrogen molecules. Fuel supplied by the engine was used to act as a cleaning agent and periodically flush out the trapped gases. Thus, a nitrogen oxide trap requires more fuel to allow the trap to work, but the car's computer could save fuel by allowing more nitrogen oxide gases to pass through the exhaust system. A third pollution control technology for diesel engines was exhaust gas recirculation or EGR, which recycles some of the gases and pumps them back into the cylinders. The gases lowered the temperature in those cylinders and led to lower production of NO_x. The problem with EGR is that it caused the engine to create more fine soot particles, which imposed a heavy burden on the filter that trapped those soot particles.[85]

Volkswagen began developing more diesel models when demand grew sharply during the 1970s thanks to the gasoline shortages. Diesels have remained common in Europe, where they account for more than half of all vehicles sold, but they never caught on in the United States. In this new market drive, Volkswagen would target environmentally conscious U.S. drivers with a powerful, German-engineered car that met emissions standards by burning high-performance "clean diesel" fuel. Drivers could enjoy high fuel economy, great performance, and environmental efficiency. The clean diesel theme begun a decade ago was seen as one of the key forces behind the growth of the U.S. market.[86]

The decision to develop the new EA-189 diesel motor was driven in part by Volkswagen's ambitions in America. Existing diesel technology had no chance of passing the U.S.'s stricter emission standards. The EA-189 diesel engine was designed and engineered over several years at great expense. VW decided not to use a more expensive diesel-emissions technology it had engineered in an alliance with Daimler-Benz and turned to the EA-189 technology instead. Company hopes were riding high on the EA-189, which included both 1.6- and 2.0-liter versions. Unfortunately, production fell behind schedule over an internal debate about the fuel injection system. Many VW people wanted to retain the existing technology known as *Pumpe Düse* (unit injector), while others favored the newer "common rail" system, which eventually won out. But the project was now two years behind schedule, and engineers were in a hurry to make up for lost time and get this product to market for the 2009 model year. The engines were to be used in Golf, Passat, Beetle, and Jetta models that were scheduled to be delivered to dealers in the United States in late 2008.[87]

However, there was one flaw in this grand plan: this new diesel engine could not meet the higher emission test standards in the United States. The VW engine developers came to this conclusion in the middle of 2006, trying to meet deadlines that would get the EA-189 into production in time for the 2009 model year cars. The exhaust gas recirculation (EGR) system in the new engine would put too heavy a burden on the particle filter and cause it to wear out prematurely. Also, the nitrogen oxide trap was not capable of keeping emissions under control without help from the EGR system. VW had several options. They could follow the path of their rival BMW and equip their new diesel engines with all three emissions technologies: exhaust gas recirculation, nitrogen oxide trap, and the urea-based system. But these technologies would have added hundreds of dollars to the cost of these compact and subcompact cars and taken up valuable space.[88]

Instead of incorporating all of these emission technologies, VW's engineers decided to solve the engine's emissions problem by installing software that had been developed to cheat on emissions tests. It was known as "acoustic function" software. This defeat device could recognize when a car was undergoing an emissions test, and it would set in place temporary pollution controls so the car would pass the test. The engine control software could activate the equipment to reduce emissions whenever a test was in process. However, during normal day-to-day operations, an automobile with an EA-189 engine could emit up to 40 times the legally permissible amount of nitrogen oxide, one of the most harmful pollutants. The nitrogen oxide trap captures NO_x gases but must be flushed frequently by increasing the ratio of fuel to air, which lowers fuel economy. The use of a defeat device meant that the NO_x trap could capture less of these noxious gases and flush less frequently when the car was not being tested. Cars from the 2009 model year began to arrive in the United States with these new diesel motors and emission systems equipped with the defeat device. Over the years the device was installed on 11 million vehicles worldwide, including 2 million in Germany.[89]

Several engineers, including James Liang, later came forward to admit that in November 2006, he and his colleagues were aware that the new EA-189 diesel engine could not meet customer expectations for fuel economy as well as U.S. emissions standards. As a result, they designed software that turned on the emissions controls when the car was undergoing an emissions test. These devices allowed the company to obtain approvals necessary to sell these cars in the United States. Mr. Liang came to the United States from Germany to help launch the "clean diesel" vehicles. When questions first arose in 2014 about Volkswagen emissions, Liang and other engineers involved in this "conspiracy" pursued a strategy of stonewalling and disclosing as little as possible.[90]

A total of 600,000 VW diesel cars sold in the United States were equipped with the emissions cheating software, including the popular Passat made at the new $1 billion factory in Chattanooga, Tennessee. Engines from VW's Audi luxury brand were also implicated in the emissions scandal. The Audi V6, 3.0-liter engine used in Audi sedans and SUVs included a defeat device as part of the software that controls the engine. Without the device, the Audi sedans could not have complied with U.S. environmental regulations.[91]

Exposing "Clean Diesel"

VW's emissions cheating was first discovered in 2013 by independent researchers at West Virginia University. The university was home to the Center for Alternative Fuels Engines and Emissions (CAFEE), which specializes in emission testing. The center's researchers had portable testing equipment that allowed them to test for emissions under driving conditions. They had received a $70,000 contract from the International Council on Clean Transportation (ICCT) to determine why diesel cars in the United States polluted much less than diesel cars in Europe. As part of their analysis, they tested whether diesel engines produced more emissions during normal driving than they did in standardized laboratory road tests. The research team chose to conduct the test in California, where these NO_x emissions are of some concern. Their tests found that cars like Jetta and Passat passed standardized lab tests but emitted unusually high levels of NO_x gases during normal driving conditions. The tests showed emissions of noxious NO_x gases at up to 35 times the legal levels. Their further investigations confirmed major discrepancies between nitrogen oxide emissions in lab tests and on the road. The researchers recalibrated their equipment several times throughout these various tests but eventually reached the only reasonable conclusion: "It had to be a defeat device."[92]

The CAFEE team released its findings in March 2014. It did not mention anything about illegal software and concealed the identity of the cars that were tested. CAFEE also dutifully reported the test results to the EPA and to the California Air Resources Board (CARB) and sent a copy to VW. The EPA conducted its own internal investigation and contacted VW about the discrepancies. But for months VW engineers and executives frustrated regulators seeking to get to the bottom of the irregular test results. According to court documents, VW "intentionally made . . . false and fraudulent statements" in order to convey that this was nothing more than an "innocent mechanical problem."[93]

In the spring of 2015, VW issued a voluntary recall and said the discrepancies were due to technical issues that could be fixed by means of a software update. But more sophisticated follow-up tests by CARB showed only a small improvement on cars receiving the update, and it continued its investigation. In August 2015, as regulators closed in on VW's scheme, engineers destroyed incriminating documents. On September 3, 2015, the German automaker finally admitted to the EPA that the NO_x emissions were concealed by software that reduced emissions to legal standards during testing but allowed the pollutants to spew forth while cars were being driven. The EPA publicly disclosed the emissions fraud later that month and gave VW a formal notice that it had violated EPA regulations.[94]

VW worked with U.S regulators on another recall to fix the 600,000 vehicles with the illegal defeat device. But the relationship with the EPA was tense. The company fought with U.S. regulators over details and publicly criticized the EPA's testing methodology. Volkswagen has a history of defying the EPA and questioning its motives. It has suggested in the past that the EPA was trying to stifle foreign competition. When the EPA told the company that the cheating software was in the Audi as well, the company contested the claim until it was confirmed by Audi engineers. Volkswagen admitted their initial response to the scandal was retarded by management changes and the whole scope of this crisis.[95] VW's lackluster response was supported by attitudes in Germany, where people believed the U.S. was overstating its case in order to damage a foreign automaker.[96]

Volkswagen also believed it had been fairly proactive in addressing the scandal. After the scandal was revealed, the company was candid and apologetic. In a widely reported speech to VW dealers gathered in New York City, Michael Horn, head of Volkswagen of America, admitted that VW had been dishonest with the EPA and the California Air Resources Board. "We've totally screwed up," he said.[97] Its CEO, Martin Winterkorn, resigned in late September, and the company pledged to prosecute those involved in this scandalous scheme. In his statement, Winterkorn said he would take full responsibility for these "irregularities." "I am stunned," said the CEO, "that misconduct on such scale was possible in the Volkswagen Group."[98] Soon after Winterkorn's resignation, VW suspended eight managers, six at Volkswagen and two from the Audi division. Winterkorn was succeeded by Matthias Müller. Müller apologized for the scandal and committed VW toward developing a fix for all the affected vehicles. In November 2015, U.S. consumers were also offered a "goodwill package" that included a $500 prepaid Visa card, a $500 credit for dealer services, and a three-year roadside assistance package. However, while VW was able to come up with a quick fix for vehicles in Germany equipped with the cheating device, the solution for U.S. cars was more complicated. Months after the scandal erupted, customers and car dealers in the United States remained in the dark about how and when their vehicles would be repaired.[99]

In the summer of 2016, Volkswagen finally gave their U.S. dealers a detailed timeline of its "buyback and repair" program. Owners of the tainted VW diesel cars could sell back their vehicles or have them repaired beginning in October 2016. For those seeking the latter option, a software fix would be available right away, with a hardware modification to follow.[100]

The Volkswagen Culture

Mr. Winterkorn, who was shocked by the scandal, initially said the misconduct was just the result of moral lapses by only a few VW employees. But VW's own internal investigation unveiled a scheme involving dozens of engineers and managers. Some actively participated, while others looked the other way. In May 2014, a senior Volkswagen executive warned CEO Winterkorn that regulators were getting suspicious about emissions tests, but there is no evidence of any prior communication to Winterkorn or other top-level executives. The failure of people within the company to sound the alarm about the installation of these defeat devices is an embarrassing aspect of the scandal for VW. Why did no one come forward earlier or pass the information up the VW chain of command?[101]

Former employees blame VW's traditional culture of centralized decision-making, which was reinforced by Winterkorn's autocratic style. This environment, with strong top-down management, discouraged open discussion of problems and deficiencies and pushed engineers to the limit. Middle managers were often silenced under CEO Winterkorn and his predecessor, Ferdinand Piëch. Piëch had a "dictatorial style." He intimidated managers and engineers, who in turn behaved the same way to the workers they supervised. Failure to achieve goals or complete technical assignments was not an option. According to Ewing, there was a saying around Volkswagen that exemplifies this culture: "*Geht nichts, gibt's nicht*," which loosely translated means "Impossible doesn't exist." This attitude, which often fostered unrealistic expectations, was not lost on the engineering team charged with getting cars with the new diesel engine to the U.S. market by the end of 2008. There was no way for the EA-189 to meet U.S. exhaust standards within the required time frame and budget.[102]

Pischetsrieder had tried to modify the rigid, top-down management style of Piëch, but it was revived by Winterkorn. Like Piëch, he ruled by force and intimidation. Management based on centralized authority, however, has many liabilities, such as delays and decision-making bottlenecks. In addition, this management style perpetuated by Winterkorn created a climate in which people were most likely afraid to come forward and speak up about the illegal software.[103] In an interview with Reuters, five former VW executives described the management style under Winterkorn as one that often fostered a climate of fear and retribution. Unlike other German car companies, such as BMW, there was a "special pressure" at Volkswagen. As a consequence, problems remained hidden because workers never felt comfortable challenging or arguing with their supervisors.[104]

VW's leaders also acknowledged a "culture of tolerance" for breaking rules in order to achieve results. This cultural climate probably allowed the deception to continue for almost a decade without detection. There was a mindset in some areas of the company that accepted breaches of company standards and ethical norms. In addition, an internal investigation found there was a lack of internal processes and monitoring to detect instances of fraud. For example, there were insufficient testing procedures in the engine department that enabled engineers to push engines out the door without "a second set of eyes to corroborate their findings." The company seemed to realize that cultural and organizational changes, such as removing the Wolfsburg bottleneck, would be essential to avoid a recurrence of this paralyzing crisis.[105]

Throughout the aftermath of the scandal, there were many signs of an urgent need for cultural reform. Even months after the scandal erupted, Volkswagen leadership did not seem to grasp the level of public indignation nor appreciate the full implications and gravity of the company's misdeeds. In January 2016, while attending the Detroit Auto Show, a National Public Radio reporter asked Matthias Müller about ethical problems at Volkswagen. His response: "It was a technical problem. An ethical problem? I cannot understand why you say that. . . . We had some targets for our technical engineers, and they solved this problem and reached targets with some software solutions, which haven't been compatible with American law."[106]

Fines and Criminal Prosecutions

As part of a historic settlement with the U.S. federal government, Volkswagen agreed to spend the necessary $14.7 billion to settle civil complaints and numerous consumer lawsuits. Some of these funds were dedicated to buying back or fixing the nearly half a million 2.0-liter diesel vehicles with tainted software. It also agreed to pay an additional $1.3 billion to owners of the 80,000 3.0-liter diesel vehicles (mostly Audi and Porsche brands) affected by the defeat devices. However, the actual amounts spent will depend on how many car owners take advantage of the offer. VW will also pay $5 billion into a trust to support environmental programs and promote zero-emissions vehicles.[107]

In March 2017, in a separate settlement with the U.S. Department of Justice, Volkswagen pleaded guilty to criminal charges for rigging its VW diesel vehicles in order to cheat on emissions tests. The specific criminal charges were conspiring to defraud the United States, violation of the Clean Air Act, and obstruction of justice. The $4.3 billion plea agreement includes a $2.8 billion criminal fine along with an additional $1.5 billion civil penalty. In most situations, prosecutors dismiss criminal charges so long as companies cooperate in investigations, but prosecutors saw this case differently since it was an attempt to execute a bold, systematic fraud over a number of years.[108] VW must also pay $600 million to state attorneys general to satisfy claims made by states against the company. And in September 2017, the company revealed it would need to spend an additional $3 billion to fix engines in the United States because the job was far more "technically complex" than they had estimated. Thus, the total bill for the German carmaker stands at close to $30 billion. This massive payout represents the largest settlement in U.S. history with an automaker. Also, in the wake of the scandal, Volkswagen's U.S. sales dropped 7.6% in 2016 from 2015, down from their peak of 430,000 in 2012.[109]

On January 12, 2017, a federal grand jury separately indicted six Volkswagen executives for the role they played in the emissions scandal. They were charged with conspiring to defraud the U.S. government and violation of the Clean Air Act by lying to regulators about the ability of VW's "clean diesel" technology to meet U.S. emission standards. One of the executives, Oliver Schmidt, head of VW's environment and engineering office, was arrested at Miami International Airport while preparing to fly home to Germany. The other five executives all reside in Germany and are unlikely to face any jail time unless they return to the United States.[110]

Finally, in May 2018, former CEO Martin Winterkorn was indicted in Detroit, accused of conspiring to mislead U.S. regulators about VW's defeat devices. According to U.S. attorney general Jeff Sessions, the scandal went "all the way to the top." Winterkorn is not accused of being involved in the design of the device or of authorizing its use in 11 million vehicles. Instead he is accused of playing a role in the cover-up that began in May 2014 when VW was first confronted about the devices. According to the indictment, Mr. Winterkorn "pursued a strategy of concealing the defeat device in responding to U.S. regulators, while appearing to cooperate." VW acknowledged that Mr. Winterkorn received a memo about the "Dieselgate" affair in May 2014, but the account of the testing irregularities was written "selectively, briefly, and in an undramatic manner." Since Germany does not have an extradition agreement with the United States, it is unlikely that Winterkorn will ever be put on trial.[111]

- Do you agree with Müller's claim that this is a technical issue rather than an ethical issue? What did Müller have in mind in making this statement?

- What are the economic, legal, and ethical dimensions of this epic scandal? In what ways has VW fallen short of its tripartite corporate duties (see Chapter 2)?

- What is your reaction to the penalties imposed on VW? Do you agree that the company was guilty of a crime and should pay criminal as well as civil penalties? Should Winterkorn have been indicted?

- In your opinion, what is the root cause of VW's ethical problems? Can you draw any normative generalizations from this case?

CASE STUDY 9.4

CHEVRON IN THE AMAZON: ANATOMY OF ENVIRONMENTAL DEGRADATION AND ITS AFTERMATH

Despite the strong push for alternative sources of energy, oil remains one of the most sought after fuels in the world because of its cheapness, reliability, and portability. Oil is still the most important transportation fuel and accounts for 93% of transportation in the United States. Oil is also one of the most versatile raw materials for making synthetic products. Oil's dominance leads to continuous investment in exploration and excavation by the supermajors such as Chevron and ExxonMobil.[112]

AP Photo/Dolores Ochoa

But oil companies have been the target of environmentalists' ire for the way they have sometimes operated in foreign countries, especially emerging economies. Royal Dutch Shell, for example, has been justly censured for the environmental debacle in the Niger Delta, where it has drilled for oil since the 1970s. Oil spills, contamination of land and waterways, and flaring have been persistent problems. Similarly, Texaco (now part of Chevron) has been criticized for the environmental problems associated with oil drilling in the Amazon region of Ecuador. This case study explores Texaco's environmental performance in Ecuador along with the legal ramifications of its questionable actions.

Texaco in Ecuador

The Texas Company, which changed its name to Texaco in 1959, was founded in Texas in 1902. It didn't take long before Texaco became a well-known brand in the United States. In 1932, the company introduced its Texaco Fire Chief gasoline, a higher-octane gasoline delivering better vehicle performance. It also added new brands, such as Havoline oil. Texaco's legendary marketing campaign, "Trust your car to the man who wears the star," helped drive sales growth in the 1970s and 1980s. In 2001, Texaco and Chevron merged to become ChevronTexaco.[113]

Texaco has always had a keen interest in oil exploration in Latin America. After making big oil finds in Colombia, Texaco set its sights further south on Ecuador. In March 1964, the oil giant signed an exploration concession agreement with the Ecuadorian government, which gave the company the right to search for oil on a wide area encompassing 3.5 million acres of land. Its silent but equal partner in the deal was the subsidiary of another American oil company, Gulf Equatoriana.

Several years later, on March 20, 1967, Texaco discovered oil in the "jungle country" of northeastern Ecuador. Texaco struck oil with its first well, called Lago Agrio ("sour lake") No. 1, and then struck oil again with its second well. It capped these two wells and continued to drill other exploratory wells. Texaco's oil strikes confirmed the existence of oil-rich fields in Lago Agrio but also in the area to the south and southeast. Texaco drilled all of the wells that became the source of extensive oil pollution and the later lawsuits.[114]

Regrettably, life was never again quite the same for many people in the Oriente region of this Latin American country where that oil was uncovered. The Oriente is an area in east Ecuador that includes the eastern slopes of the Andes Mountains along with lowland areas of the Amazon rain forest. The rain forest area is biologically diverse, and local Indian populations have flourished in these lands where they raise their crops. The Indians hunt the land and fish its rivers and lakes for their livelihood. The oil exploration zone was home to eight indigenous groups, including the Cofan, the Siona, the Huaorani, and the Secoya.

Over the decades, many major oil companies made substantial investments to search for oil in Ecuador. Their search was often in vain, but Texaco's efforts had paid off. The company celebrated its great find and looked forward to a long working relationship with the Ecuadorian government. With the exploration phase complete and the necessary infrastructure in place, the oil wells were uncapped, and full-scale commercial production began in June 1972. For almost two decades, Texaco and Gulf operated in Ecuador through an oil concession agreement. The partnership between Texaco and Gulf became a three-way joint venture when the state oil company Petroecuador took a 25% stake. Although Texaco's ownership stake was now only 37.5%, it was given full authority and control over the day-to-day oil operations. Three hundred twenty-five production sites were constructed along with 18 crude oil processing facilities. The Texaco consortium also built the necessary infrastructure, including interconnected roads and pipelines. These oil-rich wells in and around Lago Agrio produced 1.7 billion barrels of oil over a 20-year period. The crude oil flowed through a 312-mile trans-Ecuadorean pipeline that had been constructed to run from Lago Agrio across the Andes to the ocean terminal in Esmerald on the Pacific coast. From there it was shipped to refineries in California, where it eventually made its way into the gas tanks of American drivers. In 1976, after Ecuador raised its royalty rate on the oil, Gulf chose to sell out its stake in this venture to Petroecuador, which gave the government company a controlling interest of 62.5%.[115]

The Ecuadorian government profited handsomely from the Texaco-managed drilling operations. Deals for oilfields and royalty payments can be opaque, but this one was fairly transparent. Ecuador charged an 11.5% royalty rate on all the oil shipped by Texaco. It steadily increased the tax rate from 44.5% to 87.3%. And it required Texaco to invest $55 million to upgrade local infrastructure. The government itself made $23.5 billion from royalties, taxes, and the sale of this oil, though little of this fortune made its way back to the Ecuadorean people. Texaco itself made $1.6 billion. Citing the high taxes and royalties, other oil companies followed Gulf's example and sold back their concessions to the government by the mid-1970s. This gave the consortium virtual monopoly control over Ecuador's oil exploration and drilling.[116]

While Texaco crafted careful strategic plans to guide its operations, there was less consideration given to ecological and human rights issues. Some indigenous Indian populations, such as the Huaorani, had to be displaced to accommodate the drilling and pipeline sites. With the government's help, they were taken to a reservation, where they received food and protection from rival tribes. The Oriente region is also home to many rare species of animals, such as cicadas, squirrel monkeys, scarlet macaws, boas, leafcutting ants, and freshwater pink dolphins. Many of these species have small populations, making them vulnerable to environmental disruptions. The ecosystem of the rain forest is fragile and easily imbalanced by environmental externalities such as soot-laced acid rain.[117]

Environmental Degradation

Texaco's Lago Agrio oil wells were productive, but at a high social cost. A Spanish priest who lived in the area at the time described the local scene as "oil world hell." The air was thick with black smoke from gases and oil waste being burned off at separation stations, and the tropical rains were full of soot. Some residents with no other options collected and drank the contaminated water.[118]

Three major environmental issues were identified. The first problem was the number and magnitude of oil spills in the region. Over the 18 years (1972–1990) that Texaco operated the 312-mile trans-Ecuadorean pipeline, there were 27 major pipeline ruptures resulting in the spillage of 17 million gallons of oil, most of which was not cleaned up. Some of the oil spills have flowed down into neighboring regions of Peru. It's not known how much oil has spilled from the secondary pipelines. By comparison, the 800-mile Alaskan pipeline spilled about 1.6 million gallons of oil over a 25-year period. For many, this record is evidence that Texaco's environmental performance was well below industry norms.[119]

Second, the disposal of toxic waste was not handled properly. During the process of creating and testing a well for commercial production, toxic "formation water" rises to the surface and must be disposed of along with the drilling mud. Over 4 million gallons of this toxic waste was dumped into unlined, open pits, and some of that toxic waste (drilling mud, formation water, and oil) eventually found its way into rivers, streams, and shallow wells. Also, the pits were not fenced off, so sometimes wandering livestock would slip into the oily ooze. Texaco could have fenced off the pits and lined them with concrete or metal to prevent leaching but chose not to do so. The company created between 800 to 1,000 of these large pits, which are each about the size of a big swimming pool. They were 7 feet deep, which put them in the proximity of subsurface waters. Texaco inserted pipes or "siphons" on the side of the pits in order to drain them and prevent them from over-flowing during the tropical rains. The aim was to siphon off the water from underneath the oil waste, but there is considerable evidence that this technique did not work. As a result, dozens of adjacent streams below the pits were contaminated to some degree.[120]

The third environmental problem was flaring. When oil is extracted, it must be sep-arated from formation water and natural gas. With no viable options available to collect the gas with the help of pipelines, it must be burned off. This leads to the problem of flaring, natural gas burning incessantly, etched into the dark Amazon sky. Soot from the burning gas sometimes coats the nearby trees and plants. Once the natural gas was burned off, what remained was oil and more formation water, which was stored in large tanks. The oil floated to the top and was skimmed off and shipped away, leaving only the contaminated water. This "produced water" was piped into another set of open pits, where the residual petroleum, which rises to the top, was supposed to be skimmed off and the water treated with cleansing compounds. The petroleum-exposed water was then released into rivers, streams, and lagoons.[121]

U.S. regulations require any gas flares to be vertical and sufficiently oxygenated so that they produce little or no smoke. In Lago Agrio, however, Texaco sometimes directed the flames to burn horizontally so they would burn off the petroleum in the produced water pits. The oil would ignite and produce billows of black smoke that poured soot particles into the Amazon's forests, waterways, and villages. Petroecuador put an end to that prac-tice when it inherited control of the oil operations.[122]

Experts and environmentalists believe that Texaco's antiquated equipment and gener-ally low environmental standards were partly to blame for this ongoing ecological disas-ter. For example, strict environmental standards call for the reinjection of toxic waste deep into the ground rather than the use of unlined pits. Texaco acknowledged that it used these pits and that it could have lined them with concrete or metal. But they argued that reliance on unlined pits for hazardous waste was standard industry proce-dure. Unlined pits were common at the time in a few states like Texas, but they were used only to hold drilling muds temporarily before they were reinjected into the ground. Also, by 1970, most states, including Texas, had outlawed the use of unlined pits even for temporary storage. Ecuador has produced evidence that a considerable amount of toxic waste has leached from these poorly protected pits. In the 1980s, Texaco considered lining its pits to bring the company into conformity with its oil-drilling operations in countries like the United States. The estimated cost was about $4.1 million. Company executives concluded this was disproportionately expensive, and they decided to leave the pits unlined.[123]

Nonetheless, the company has always vaguely insisted that it abided by "international standards" and that most of the oil spills on the primary pipeline were the result of natural disasters rather than corporate negligence. Even if this were true, what is the rationale for not thoroughly and promptly cleaning up those oil spills? Texaco has also argued the pits were self-lining because the soil was composed of impermeable clay. Soil samples, however, indicate the oil waste has leached into nearby soil. Geological reports reveal an excessively high level of toxins in the soil and water in the vicinity of the Texaco production sites and these unlined pits. Texaco has disputed this geological data, however.[124]

In 1990, Texaco sold off its operations to Petroecuador, and it left the country in 1992. As the company was planning its departure, Texaco was confronted with demands from the Ecuadorian oil company and the government for environmental remediation. Consequently, Texaco signed an agreement to clean up some of the waste-oil pits and surface oil spills. It embarked on an extensive cleanup operation from 1995 to 1998 at a cost of $40 million. By mutual agreement, Texaco's obligation was confined to just one-third of the oil well and separation sites it operated. Petroecuador assumed responsibility for the other sites. Ecuador had leverage with Texaco at the time but accepted these restrictions. Texaco made no commitment to treat any of the contaminated waterways, but it did clean up the remaining surface oil spills. Texaco workers skimmed the oil sitting on top of those waste pits the company was responsible for cleaning, and they recycled that oil through pipelines. The petroleum-exposed liquid beneath the oil was treated with chemicals and channeled into nearby rivers and streams. The contaminated soil was then removed from the pits and treated with cleansing chemicals. The pits were then refilled with that soil and covered with fresh dirt and new plantings.[125]

Texaco has claimed this agreement relieves it of any further responsibilities. According to Texaco, the government of Ecuador had "released, absolved, and discharged" Texaco forever from any claims or litigation arising from its oil operations in the Ecuador rain forest. That release of legal claims, however, did not prevent civil suits by private citizens or class action suits.[126] Chevron has defended itself by claiming it has lived up to its obligations to remediate the oil waste sites that were part of its agreement with the Ecuadorian government. According to Chevron, "Texaco left Ecuador in 1992 and at that time it fully remediated its share of environmental impacts arising from oil production. The $40 million remediation operation was certified by the Ecuadorian government responsible for oversight and Texaco received a complete release from Ecuador's national, provincial, and municipal governments."[127]

In the 1990s, after ownership exchanged hands, environmentalists visited the Lago Agrio area to assess the ecological damage. In his preface to the book *Amazon Crude*, environmentalist and attorney Robert F. Kennedy described vast environmental destruction that was "reminiscent of war." He witnessed "antiquated equipment, rusting pipelines, and uncounted toxic waste sites." Here is a portion of Kennedy's graphic account of the environmental damage:

> Everywhere we saw spots like tar pits where discharges from production pits blackened the earth. The pits spewed poison through their effluent pipes into the stream's tributary to the Rio Aguarico. Areas of red dust, now blackened, surrounded an oil derrick and the hulking storage tanks of PetroEcuador. . . .
> Past the petroleum camp, a large river, recently burned, still ran black, its banks

charred and devoid of vegetation. Oil wastes streamed from the broken berm of a nearby production pit. On the horizon, dense plumes of inky smoke rose from burning production pits and gas flares, linked by dirt roads stained with oil, sprayed to subdue the dust.[128]

Lawsuits and Reparations

In 2001, Texaco merged with Chevron to create ChevronTexaco, and this new corporate entity has been dealing with the fallout from its Ecuador investment for many years. A class action lawsuit on behalf of indigenous Ecuadoreans was filed against Petroecuador and Texaco. The lawsuit contended that these companies caused serious environmental harm as a direct result of their oil and drilling operations. In addition, the plaintiffs claimed that some Ecuadorians had been poisoned by Texaco's toxic waste and suffered adverse health effects.[129] These plaintiffs, who are mainly from the indigenous tribes in the hardest-hit area of Lago Agrio, sought $1 billion in damages from Chevron. Judge Rakoff, a federal U.S. judge, dismissed the case. But the plaintiffs sued again, and the venue was changed to Ecuador. Thanks to the plaintiffs' enterprising lawyers, this time the trial gained much more media attention. The lead attorney, Stephen Donziger, was especially zealous, although he was later accused of dishonest tactics. Donziger hoped the extensive publicity would help his cause. The *Wall Street Journal* even called it "the globalization trial of the century."[130]

During the drawn-out proceedings, Rafael Correa was elected Ecuador's populist president. He spoke out frequently against Texaco, helping to keep the case in the spotlight. He accused Texaco of "savage exploitation" that had "killed and poisoned people." He also claimed that Texaco's cleanup was a "charade" and a sham.[131] As the case in Ecuador proceeded, a global expert appointed by the court to study the damage concluded that Chevron should pay $16 billion in damages. So what began as a $1 billion lawsuit in New York turned into a $16 billion lawsuit in Ecuador. Despite waves of negative press, including a *60 Minutes* exposé that excoriated the company, Chevron adamantly refused to settle. The company continued to insist that its 1998 agreement with the country of Ecuador absolved it from any legal liability.

In 2011, the Ecuadorean court found for the plaintiffs and awarded them a staggering $19 billion in damages. At the time, this was one of the largest environmental verdicts ever handed down. The damages were calculated at about $9.5 billion but doubled due to Chevron's failure to apologize. On appeal, an Ecuadorean high court upheld the ruling but reduced the settlement amount to $9.5 billion. The outcome looked like a triumph for the voiceless victims of the oil pollution, especially the indigenous tribes of the Oriente region. The money has yet to be paid, however, and will probably never be paid.[132]

Later that same year, Chevron filed a racketeering lawsuit in the United States against Donziger and the Lago Agrio plaintiffs. A six-week trial was held in 2013, and one year later in 2014, federal judge Lewis Kaplan ruled for Chevron. Based on evidence presented by Chevron's legal team, the judge concluded that Donziger and his team fabricated certain evidence and even coerced Ecuadorean judges into letting them ghostwrite portions of the expert's independent report and even some of the final ruling. Mr. Donziger has steadfastly denied any wrongdoing. Judge Kaplan issued an order banning Donziger and his clients from collecting any money from Chevron.[133]

The case was appealed, and in August 2016 a federal appeals court upheld the decision. This ruling prevented the Ecuadorean plaintiffs from collecting any of the multibillion-dollar award handed down in Ecuador. A three-judge panel reaffirmed that the judgment against Chevron was tainted by fraud and corruption. However, this ruling is unlikely to bring a closure to this legal saga, which is now one of the longest in corporate history. The judges indicated that while the $9.5 billion judgment cannot be enforced in the United States, plaintiffs can still pursue legal action to enforce the judgment in other jurisdictions.[134]

- What are the specific environmental allegations against Texaco? Which are the most serious? Did Texaco behave in a morally responsible manner? Use the DRJ and corporate duties frameworks to develop your response.

- According to the Ecuadorian constitution, its citizens are guaranteed a "right to live in an environment free of contamination."[135] Do you agree there is such a right, and has that right been violated in this case?

- Should environmental reparations be paid to Ecuador and its people, especially the indigenous tribes of the Oriente? If so, what would be just settlement? $500,000 million, $1 billion, $10 billion?

- Should oil companies like Texaco and Petroecuador be drilling for oil in environmentally vulnerable areas like the Amazon rain forest?

CONCLUSION

Environmental problems such as climate change persist and have the potential to affect our aggregate well-being. Social and political demands have induced many corporations to integrate environmental concerns into their corporate strategies. Those strategies must find a way to deal with environmental externalities more responsibly. But the four cases in this chapter reviewed egregious instances of poor environmental performance. The first case on Love Canal challenged us to ponder how to deal with environmental responsibilities when there are no laws to guide the way. Will companies be truly proactive, or will they refuse to expend more resources for environmental protection than what is required by law? While the Deepwater Horizon case was about negligence and unwarranted cost-cutting, the VW case described a deliberate attempt to bypass environmental regulations. Finally, as the Chevron case illustrates, a typical corporate failure in this area is the unwillingness to take into account the environmental consequences of corporate activities in other countries, especially those with substandard regulations.

Student Study Site

Visit **edge.sagepub.com/spinello**.

Key Terms

environmental ethics   235   externality   234   pure environmental goods   235

Review Question

1. Explain the notion of negative externality along with the public goods problem. What is the importance of environmental matters from society's viewpoint? How can environmental concerns be properly factored into corporate strategies?

Discussion Questions

1. Are there better ways of handling environmental issues than the ones chosen by the companies in this chapter's case studies?

2. Do we need stricter environmental laws, or can market forces solve the problem of negative externalities?

INFORMATIONAL PRIVACY AND CYBERSECURITY

If people had access to the means to encrypt their private communications, there could be a place to hide and a universal means to privacy.

—Steven Levy[1]

LEARNING OBJECTIVES

Upon completion of this chapter, you should be able to:

10.1 Explain the responsibilities to customers and to society, with a focus on the unique challenges posed by digital information networks.

10.2 Explore the scope of a corporation's responsibility for helping to maintain public safety.

10.3 Discuss the rationale underlying the right to privacy.

The cases in this chapter dwell on the interconnected issues of privacy and cybersecurity. Networked information technologies facilitate the gathering of consumer information but also magnify the risk of data breaches that affect employees and customers. At the same time, many Internet companies such as Facebook and Google have developed business models that are based on the collection and use of personal information provided by their customers. These companies must calibrate the proper level of privacy protection for their users as they seek to transform this personal information into a reliable stream of profits.

We begin with a briefing that provides a descriptive and normative account of privacy. It also defends privacy's status as something we value instrumentally rather than intrinsically. Nonetheless, there should be a presumption against depriving people of their privacy, because privacy is necessary to secure certain goods necessary for human flourishing. Therefore, it is valid to argue that privacy is not a mere interest or a good that we might strive to achieve, but a fundamental moral right. The right to privacy, however, is not absolute, and sometimes security requirements are so demanding that they override this right.

The second topic in this chapter is cybersecurity, which is also reviewed in the briefing. The United States has moved large portions of business and commerce online, including management of much of its critical infrastructure. This reliance on networked information systems leaves the United States and its institutions highly exposed and vulnerable to cyberattack. Yet despite this reality, there are too many public and private sector organizations that have not taken the necessary steps to ensure adequate security and data protection. In a world that has al-Qaeda, nation-state economic espionage, black hat hackers, and myriad forms of terrorism, how do we get communications and information security right?[2]

AN OVERVIEW OF THE CASES

The briefing is followed by two cases. The first is about security issues at the pioneering Internet company, Yahoo. This Internet portal experienced two massive data breaches, which were not discovered until several years after they first occurred. This case study examines Yahoo's response to those data breaches and presents some evidence that this company did not live up to its responsibilities as a custodian of customer data. There are many vulnerabilities that beset data storage systems used by companies like Yahoo, but did its executives adopt adequate security countermeasures to ensure the personal information of their users was as secure as possible?

The second case, "Going Dark," is particularly intricate and complex, and it underscores the difficulty of balancing privacy and security. This case study tells the story of the potentially epic struggle between Apple and the Federal Bureau of Investigation (FBI) over encrypted devices such as smartphones. After a terrorist attack in San Bernardino, California, the FBI sought access to one of the terrorist's phones with Apple's help. But the company declined to offer any assistance to the law enforcement agency. Apple's software locks the contents of all its iPhones with strong encryption code to ensure virtually absolute privacy for its users. But is this "absolute privacy" warranted? Criminals and terrorists also use iPhones, and Apple's policy seems to tie the hands of police and the FBI by making their investigations more difficult. At the center of the Apple case, which became a cause célèbre for privacy activists, lies the tension between individual privacy rights and national security.

BRIEFING ON PRIVACY RIGHTS AND SECURITY

Thanks to the emergence of networked information technology systems, the protection of personal privacy rights has become a major technological and ethical concern. Many communications and transactions occur online through mobile phone systems, email, websites, and social networks. Digital information that is often exchanged in those transactions is easy to collect, store, recombine, and transmit. In this era of "informational capitalism," market players transform digital information into fine-grained knowledge of their customers or potential customers in order to gain advantage and create economic value.[3] These market actors also use their leverage to shape legal and policy discourse about property rights and appropriate levels of data protection.[4]

In this dynamic digital environment, the continuous online access provided by platforms like Facebook or Google presumes a right to collect each user's personal information, including buying and search habits. That information, which is gathered and analyzed, becomes monetized through sales to online advertisers or data brokers. Those brokers aggregate vast amounts of personal data (such as age, sex, address, browsing habits) into dossiers and sell it to companies for slick targeted market campaigns.[5]

The online world is also a world of extensive monitoring. Web browsers, for example, download not only our favorite videos from YouTube but also trackers that trace our movements across different websites. Almost every commercial website relies on cookies or small data files to track every movement we make on that site. If you visit amazon.com looking for a wristwatch, you'll soon be getting ads for watches when you visit other sites. The motivation for this online surveillance is not some sinister Orwellian plot. Rather, the objective is to achieve competitive advantage through personalization that is often accompanied by special discounts and other privileges.[6]

Where's the harm with these practices that deliver more targeted ads and personalized marketing pitches to our computer screens and smartphones? One problem is that bits of information collected with the help of our web browser can be turned against us or taken out of context. Hunting for a new job online, googling the morning-after pill, searching for a book on ISIS terrorism (only for research), an angry Facebook post—any of this information could be damaging if it falls into the wrong hands.[7] Also, consumers have no idea how data is being recombined and synthesized to create revealing data profiles. It might be that a discrete piece of information, such as a Google search for subprime loans, is innocuous on its own. But when combined with other data, the pattern of information flows might steer a data broker toward profiling that consumer as someone in financial distress who is not a good credit risk.

Given the pervasiveness of digital networks, can we still have a reasonable expectation of privacy? And how important is it to preserve one's privacy in the age of informational capitalism? In this briefing, we examine why privacy has been such a significant value in the philosophical tradition. Our main goal is to provide a reasonable definition and theory of informational privacy. But we also demonstrate that privacy is an instrumental value that deserves to be secured by a claim right. We end with a brief discussion of how privacy and security issues are closely intertwined.

What Is Privacy?

The philosopher Judith Thompson once wrote that "the most striking thing about the right to privacy is that nobody seems to have any very clear idea what it is."[8] With this observation in mind, it is necessary to provide a description or working definition of privacy. The matter is complicated because there are many forms of privacy. **Communications privacy**, for example, involves the extension of constitutional protections to oral, written, and electronic communications. Privacy in electronic communications was affirmed by the Supreme Court in *Charles Katz v. United States*, a ruling that stipulates the right to privacy of telephone calls.[9]

Our primary concern is **informational privacy** or **data privacy**, that is, the protection of someone's personal data. Once we provide a sound definition of informational privacy, we can proceed to a normative account of privacy: why is privacy valuable, and should privacy be considered a fundamental human right? Over the years, many different descriptions of privacy have been put forth, and so we begin with a brief survey of various theories of privacy.

One of the first and most widely cited privacy theories was articulated in 1890 by U.S. Supreme Court justices Warren and Brandeis, who famously claimed privacy is "the right to be let alone."[10] The Warren-Brandeis theory puts an emphasis on physical privacy, or privacy as nonintrusion into a person's private physical space. A more recent approach has interpreted privacy in terms of secrecy. According to this simple model, privacy is violated when information that was previously concealed or kept confidential is publicly disclosed. According to Posner, our "privacy interest, concealment of information, is invaded, whenever private information is obtained against the wishes of the person to whom the information pertains."[11] One has privacy, therefore, if one is able to conceal facts about oneself, even discreditable facts.[12] Another theory postulates that privacy is control over one's personal information. According to Charles Fried, "Privacy is not simply an absence of information in the minds of others, rather it is the control we have over information about ourselves." Privacy depends on a person's ability to control the flows of his or her personal information by setting the terms for its disclosure and use.[13]

While these and other theories are suggestive, they have certain deficiencies. For example, the broad definition of privacy as the "right to be let alone" must be further qualified. A material witness to a crime cannot conceal evidence from the police by claiming that he or she has a right to be let alone. Likewise, the theory of privacy as control is too broad and needs more specification. Loss of control does not necessarily mean a loss of privacy. I may not "control" how my health care provider discloses or uses my personal medical history and information, but that does not necessarily mean that my privacy has been compromised.

Contemporary scholarship offers more nuanced theories that are worth serious consideration. Helen Nissenbaum proposes a conception of privacy in terms of "**contextual integrity**." She contends that our sense of privacy is disturbed when there are inappropriate flows of personal information. Inappropriate information flows are those that violate "context-specific" informational norms, such as the norms that would apply when a patient confides in her doctor about her medical history. Whether an information flow is appropriate is determined by these informational norms, which are defined by several factors: the type of information in question, about whom it is, by whom and to whom it is transmitted, and the conditions under which the transmission occurs. Thus, we must consider *actors* (subject, sender, recipient), the *information type* (such as a patient's medical diagnosis or a student's learning outcomes), and the *transmission principle*. That principle might include a range of options, such as that the information is provided "in confidence" or that it can be given to a third party only as "required by law." Informational norms are based on these three independent parameters—actors, information types, and transmission principles—and reflect our privacy expectations. For example, if John applies for a mortgage, he provides bank employees (actors) with his financial information, such as his salary and job history (information type), and he presumes his information will be shared with others but only to verify the information so the mortgage application can be processed (transmission principle). He does not expect this information will be transmitted or sold to a third party, and that action would be inconsistent with the informational norms in this context and hence represent a violation of contextual integrity.[14]

Privacy understood as contextual integrity exists when actions and practices involving information sharing are in conformity with context-specific informational norms. But when those actions or practices defy or exceed expectations because they disrupt expected information flows, they violate contextual integrity. Nissenbaum's approach of seeing privacy through the lens of contextual integrity represents an improvement over one-dimensional theories that emphasize a single aspect of privacy, such as control. Control plays a role as a transmission principle in most situations, but always with respect to specific actors and particular information types, and is always specified in accordance with a particular social context.[15]

In a similar vein, Jim Moor and Herman Tavani present another comprehensive theory that describes informational privacy in terms of "restricted access/limited control." This theory captures the critical importance of establishing a zone or sphere of privacy that restricts others from access to our personal affairs and data flows. It concedes that our information must sometimes be shared with others, so the proper use of information must fall somewhere between total privacy (or secrecy) and complete disclosure. The "restricted access" paradigm suggests the ability to shield personal data from some parties while sharing it with others. Thus, according to this perspective, an individual has privacy "in a situation with regard to others if and only if in that situation the individual is normatively protected from intrusion, interference, and information access by others." The notion of "situation" encompasses many states of affairs normally regarded as private, including the "storage and access of information."[16] The theory distinguishes between a "naturally private situation" (camping in a secluded forest) and a "normatively private situation." Our natural privacy may be lost, but when this happens, there is no violation of a privacy right. But in a normatively private "situation," which can include information such as a student's grades and performance measures, privacy rights can be violated because there are clearly defined norms that protect this situation. Thus, a student enjoys privacy only if there is a condition of *restricted access* such that this student's information is accessible only to her parents, her teachers, and certain school officials in accordance with the laws and ethical norms that protect those records.[17]

The capacity to exercise "limited control" is also essential for protecting privacy. Individuals need as much control as realistically possible over their personal data and data flows in order to help ensure the reality of restricted access. The control that enables information privacy relies heavily on ideas such as informed consent to mediate networked transactions and data exchanges.

In summary, privacy can be defined in many different ways, though some definitions are too simplistic. We might settle on the Moor/Tavani approach, which does not neglect the issue of contextual integrity set forth by Nissenbaum. Informational privacy can best be defined as a *condition of restricted accessibility* where access to one's personal information is limited based on the situation or context along with the prevailing moral and legal norms.

The Right to Privacy

Philosophers regard privacy as a value or a good, but is it a fundamental and intrinsic good, or an instrumental one? According to Innes, "Privacy is intrinsically valuable because it acknowledges our respect for persons as autonomous beings."[18] Many other philosophers accept this position that privacy is something we value intrinsically. However, it is more plausible to claim that privacy is an instrumental good. Life, health, and bodily integrity (including physical and psychological security) along with friendship and marriage are intrinsic goods; they are ends in themselves and sought for their own sake because they are fundamental aspects of our human flourishing. We form close bonds with others not just for instrumental purposes but because of the fulfillment provided by joining together in a wide arrangement of close associations and communities.[19] Knowledge is another intrinsic good we value and seek out for its own sake, because it too directly contributes to our well-being. When one acts in order to know something, that action is immediately intelligible. As Martha Nussbaum observed, Aristotle's proposition that all humans desire to know is verified by "the most refined anthropological analysis."[20]

Privacy, however, cannot be considered as a basic good, since it is not intrinsically valuable and it does not directly contribute to human flourishing. Privacy is always an instrumental means to some further end, such as security or friendship. Consider some of the reasons why a person desires privacy. First, we require privacy to ensure that certain personal relationships will adequately conserve a proper level of intimacy. The intrinsic goods in jeopardy by the erosion of privacy are intimate friendships and marriage. But privacy allows us to participate in these goods without self-consciousness and without the inhibition that comes from worrying about the prying eyes of others. According to DeCew, "The desire to protect a sanctuary for ourselves, a refuge within which we can shape and carry out our lives and relationships with others—intimacies as well as other activities—without the threat of scrutiny, embarrassment, judgement and the deleterious consequences they might bring, is a major underlying reason for providing information control" or privacy protection.[21]

People also desire privacy to preserve their security and safety, which is an integral aspect of the fundamental good of life, physical integrity, and health. In the information age, informational privacy is essential for our security. As we pointed out, without privacy (understood as the condition of restricted access), we might be subject to various harms such as the misuse of our credit card data when our credit card company gets hacked. Our Google search records might be used against us by a legal adversary, or they might find their way into a report to our supervisor, who fires us for looking for a new job. Invalid access to our social media or Facebook account can lead to online stalking or cyberbullying.

Privacy's status as an instrumental good does not devalue its importance. Since privacy supports intrinsic objective goods such as friendship and security, it is a critically important instrumental good. And since privacy is *necessary* to secure the benefits of these intrinsic goods, a strong case can be made for a right to privacy in order to ensure justice or fairness. According to H. L. A. Hart, "The core of the notion of rights is neither individual choice nor individual benefit but basic or fundamental individual needs."[22] Rights are based on need and necessity. As we discussed in Chapter 3, rights protect something of great value and neutralize substantive and recurrent threats. Individuals require the strong and stable protection provided by privacy rights in order to be free from harm and from interference with the pursuit of intrinsic goods that can occur in real space or cyberspace when a person cannot safeguard his or her personal data. A claim right and its correlative duties, which require identified parties to respond in certain ways to rights holders, are the best form of protection against the specified threats.[23]

Thus, our basic argument is that in the various situations where normative protection of information is necessary and reasonably expected, a person has a right to the condition of restricted access to his or her information. Individuals and organizations have a correlative duty to uphold and protect this right in these circumstances by respecting this person's desire to restrict access to his or her personal information and by giving that person the means to exercise limited control over that information. Like most rights, this right to privacy is not absolute. Privacy rights must be limited by the comparable rights of others along with morally justified exceptions for the sake of the common good.

Privacy and Security

Security is another important value that is closely related to privacy. We can identity three levels of security. First, security gives individuals control over their lives and physical well-being, their projects for work and play, and their personal property. At the personal level, "privacy and security come bundled together."[24] As we have argued, privacy is one way of protecting ourselves from physical, emotional, and economic harm. If someone gains access to a person's confidential financial data or credit card information, that person is at risk for theft or credit card fraud. Also, too much exposure in cyberspace could make us insecure and put our welfare at some risk. Consider the website StalkScan.com, developed by a hacker, that lets non-friends search Facebook accounts for public posts, pictures, tags, and likes. All of this can be material for online stalkers who seek to cause great psychological or physical harm to certain people.[25]

A second level of security pertains to groups, civic associations, and corporations. They too need security or protection from intrusion and unwarranted interference. Companies could not survive without being able to secure their assets, including their physical and intellectual properties. Businesses are the constant prey of cyberthieves. The Society for Worldwide Interbank Financial Transactions (SWIFT), which moves bank payment orders around the world, is the lifeblood of the global banking system, where trillions of dollars flow between banks every day. In 2017, despite tight security precautions, cyber-criminals used malware to steal bank codes and place fake transfer orders and appropriate $90 million from the central banks of Bangladesh and Ecuador. This incident shows that without better security, the whole banking system could be in some jeopardy.[26]

Of course, security at the corporate level deeply affects security at the personal level. Many companies are the custodians and stewards of valuable consumer data. Without adequate security measures that restrict access to thieves and other unauthorized users, that information could be compromised and peoples' lives disrupted. Companies must protect their information assets and be on guard against corporate security breaches and cyberthreats. Cyberspace is especially difficult to secure because of the capabilities of malicious actors who operate from all over the world and the complications involved in protecting complex cyber networks.[27]

When building a security infrastructure in an information intensive environment, corporations should have three goals in mind: confidentiality, integrity, and availability, sometimes called the CIA triad. The goal of confidentiality implies that information technology systems must keep valuable data private. Sensitive personal data collected by corporations along with transactional data must be carefully protected. **Confidentiality** is achieved by tools such as access controls and encryption software. **Encryption** entails the conversion of data into a secret code that prevents unauthorized access. **Integrity** means protecting information systems from being improperly altered or compromised. This goal is achieved with the help of firewalls, antivirus software, and other tools that thwart the efforts of hackers to infect a system with malware, such as worms and viruses that can sabotage a computer system. **Availability** means that employees and customers are able to use an information technology system without disruption. Websites, for example, must be safeguarded from denial-of-service attacks that employ computers and software to crash the site and disrupt service. Specialized firewalls equipped with router-based filtering can usually prevent these and similar attacks and sustain system availability.[28]

Finally, national security must also be considered. Every nation and its institutions need protection from foreign invasion or attacks carried out as part of a terrorist campaign. We value national security primarily because it is necessary to ensure the safety and well-being of a nation's citizens, who turn to their government for protection. According to Ken Himma, "Security is the ultimate value that the state is morally obligated to protect."[29] Thus, national or collective security is closely related to our personal security. If we live in a society that has deficiencies in collective security, there will most likely be a lack of personal security. A competent armed services, local police, intelligence agencies, and a well-functioning legal system are necessary to provide that collective security.[30]

While security and privacy are interdependent to some extent, there are obvious tensions and trade-offs that complicate cybersecurity and privacy issues. For example, although privacy-protecting architectures like encryption can be a useful means of countering cybersecurity threats and protecting our civil liberties, they can also be used by criminals and terrorists to plan unlawful acts and impede law enforcement investigations, thereby making innocent people less secure. How do we reconcile these conflicting demands, and how do we determine when national security interests must trump privacy rights or other civil liberties? As networked information technologies continue to evolve, we can only assume these problems will become even more complex over time.[31]

CASE STUDY 10.1

DATA BREACHES AT YAHOO

©iStockphoto.com/4x6

In September 2016, Yahoo announced to the public it had experienced a serious data security breach two years earlier in which 500 million records were compromised. Several months later, in December 2016, Yahoo informed its users of another newly discovered data breach. This one had happened in 2013 and affected more than 1 billion Yahoo users. The second breach involved more sensitive data, so Yahoo forced the affected users to reset their passwords. Yahoo's share price dropped 6% after the announcement of the second hacking incident.

While data breaches are quite common thanks to the ubiquity of malefactors, the magnitude of these breaches caught the attention of the financial community and even some members of Congress. People began wondering why it took a sophisticated Internet company so long to uncover these breaches, and whether they could be attributed to a weak security culture. Was Yahoo an innocent victim or a culpable party by virtue of its negligent failure to protect the sensitive data of its customers?

The Rise and Fall of Yahoo

Yahoo was founded in 1994 by a pair of precocious Silicon Valley entrepreneurs, David Filo and Jerry Yang. The Yahoo service originally functioned as a portal, that is, a gateway and comprehensive guide to the Web. This Internet "guide" evolved into a full-fledged commercial website, offering a plethora of services for its user base. It quickly became a thriving business for Filo and Yang, who called themselves the "Chief Yahoos." As the company grew, the two young founders realized they needed the help of a professional manager at the helm. Accordingly, in 1995 Yahoo took on an experienced executive, Tim Koogle, as its chief executive officer. Mr. Koogle oversaw Yahoo's growth into a Silicon Valley giant and dominant presence in cyberspace. Yahoo launched its initial public offering in 1996, and by 1999, Yahoo shares surged above $400. But after the dot.com bust in 2000 along with poor financial results, the stock value plummeted, and Koogle was forced to resign.

From the outset, Yahoo saw itself as a media company, a major platform for content and not just a search engine or gateway to the Internet. During 1996 and 1997, Yahoo added critical communication facilities, including services such as email and instant messaging. Yahoo's offering also included many "properties," such as e-commerce properties for shopping and making travel arrangements. Like eBay, Yahoo hosted user-based auction sites, and it also provided search technology. Millions of users soon flocked to Yahoo for its email services, instant messaging, scheduling, and personal web pages. It developed significant online content such as Yahoo News, Yahoo Sports, and Yahoo Finance, which also became quite popular with users.

In 2005, Terry Semel was appointed to the CEO position at Yahoo. The former Warner Brothers executive was responsible for a key investment by securing a stake in the Chinese company Alibaba. Since then, Alibaba has grown into an e-commerce giant and a principal player in China's Internet industry. Semel also engineered key acquisitions such as the photo-sharing site Flickr and the search market service Overture. However, Semel also committed some serious missteps. In retrospect, one mistake was particularly egregious—he missed out on the chance to acquire Google because he thought the company was overpriced.[32]

Like Google and other Internet companies, Yahoo was directed in its business dealings by a core set of values following its inception in 1995. In 2006, the company reasserted those guiding values with its strong libertarian overtones. "Information is power," proclaimed the company, and citizens across the globe can benefit from Yahoo's services in order to access the information they need. Among its key principles, Yahoo included the following;

- We believe the Internet is built on openness, from information access to creative expression. We are committed to providing individuals with easy access to information and opportunities to openly communicate and exchange views and opinions.

- We are committed to maintaining our customers' trust. Hundreds of millions of consumers around the world have put their trust in Yahoo for more than a decade. We take our users' privacy very seriously and never forget users come to us by choice.[33]

Those values were challenged, however, by Yahoo's unfortunate experience in China. When Yahoo entered the Chinese market in 1999, it promised China's Internet users access to the widest range of its services. However, to placate Chinese officials, Yahoo signed the "Public Pledge on Self-Discipline for the Chinese Internet Industry," thereby committing itself to "refuse access to those Websites that disseminate harmful information to protect Internet users of China from adverse influences of the information."[34] Yahoo had effectively agreed to function as a censor on behalf of the Chinese government.[35]

Yahoo also handed over information to Chinese authorities about a Chinese reporter by the name of Shi Tao, who had used Yahoo's email service to send a message to a nongovernmental organization called Democracy Forum explaining that the Chinese government would not allow any memorials or marches on the 15th anniversary of the Tiananmen Square massacre. With the help of that information, Chinese law enforcement located Shi Tao, who was promptly arrested and sent to prison for 10 years. It seemed that Yahoo's commitment to privacy and free expression did not apply to its own Chinese customers. When Yahoo's actions came to light, there were loud international protests along with an embarrassing congressional investigation.

In the wake of this disquieting scandal, the cofounder of Yahoo, Jerry Yang, took over as CEO at the request of the company's board of directors. Yang tried to restore Yahoo's reputation by making overtures to Tao's family. He settled a lawsuit filed against Yahoo by Tao's mother under the auspices of the Alien Torts Claims Act (ATCA). Along with Semel, he was responsible for bringing to closure the company's substantial 40% investment stake in Alibaba, which allowed Yahoo to lower its profile in China. But Yang was widely criticized in 2008 for rebuffing a lucrative buyout offer from Microsoft for $44.6 billion.

By the time Carol Bartz took over as head of Yahoo in 2009, things had begun to unravel. The former CEO of Autodesk was brought on board to reverse Yahoo's dismal fortunes in the display ad market, now dominated by Google. During Bartz's short tenure, profits increased but revenue dropped from $7.2 billion in 2008 to $5 billion in 2011 (the year she left). Yahoo had to contend with the rising threat of Facebook, but Bartz failed to catch up to either Facebook or Google. Yahoo continued to lag behind in the big growth markets: mobile telephony, social media, and cloud computing. Bartz focused primarily on efficiency, cutting staff to reduce costs and closing underperforming businesses. She spent little money on acquisitions. The company struggled in overseas markets, and directories in France, Germany, Italy, and Spain were closed. Bartz was fired two and a half years later, replaced on an interim basis by chief financial officer Timothy Morse, who made plans for a strategic review and a possible buyout. She was ultimately replaced by Scott Thompson, but he lasted only four months after an error in his résumé was exposed.[36]

In 2012, Marissa Mayer became the new CEO. The former Google executive initially embarked on a bold acquisition spree, including the $1 billion deal to purchase Tumblr. But she soon ended Yahoo's acquisition strategy and tried to focus on building up the core assets of the company. Yahoo's stock price surged under Mayer, as investors appeared confident in a turnaround. That turnaround, however, never really materialized. Mayer initiated major cost-cutting measures to get the company's expenses under control, but its financial performance remained mediocre.[37]

After three more years of turmoil, there was a growing crisis of morale within the company and the board was being pressured by investors to sell the core business. The company's advertising business had continued to deteriorate despite some uptick in Web traffic. The Yahoo board had overseen seven chief executives in the past decade. Yet despite investor demands for a comprehensive breakup plan, Mayer and her allies on the board resisted the pressure to sell out.[38]

However, in 2016, after a series of further setbacks and failed turnaround plans executed by Mayer, the company decided to sell its core business to Verizon Communications for the price of $4.8 billion. Verizon hoped that by combining Verizon, AOL, and Yahoo, a new powerful competitive rival in mobile media would emerge that would attract publishers and advertisers. Financial analysts who followed the company argued that despite its status as a digital pioneer, the diverse nature of Yahoo's "properties" and businesses had led the company to lose focus. As a result, its best hope for a more promising future was a buyout or merger. In their view, Yahoo had done a poor job over the years of defining what it is and what value it provides.[39]

Security at Google and Yahoo

Yahoo, like most Internet companies, is no stranger to data breaches and hacker attacks. By 2010, both Google and Yahoo had built up substantial business interests in China. Yahoo had entered the Chinese market in 1999 seeking first-mover advantages. Google followed in 2006. Both companies seemed to underestimate the ethical and political risks of competing in China. In 2010, the systems of Yahoo and Google were penetrated by Chinese military hackers. The technique used was spear phishing, which targeted company employees with infected email. There were several media reports about the incident. The *Guardian* reported that Yahoo had been targeted by a Chinese attack similar to the one that affected Google Inc. The *Washington Post* also claimed that at least 34 companies—including Yahoo, Symantec, Adobe, Northrop Grumman and Dow Chemical—had been attacked. These reports cited both congressional and industry sources.[40]

Unlike Google, however, Yahoo did not confirm the hacking incident or make any public announcements. A company spokesperson said, "Yahoo does not generally disclose that type of information, but we take security very seriously and we take appropriate action in the event of any kind of breach." Some companies do not always notify customers and law enforcement authorities of a breach if it doesn't cause serious harm, since they prefer to handle these acts of vandalism quietly. They worry that going public could inadvertently expose flaws in code that malicious attackers might exploit.[41]

Google and Yahoo took very different approaches to cybersecurity issues after this data breach. Google invested hundreds of millions of dollars in its security infrastructure and vowed it would never again permit hacking into the accounts of Google customers. Cofounder Sergey Brin made it clear to everyone at the search engine company that security was to be a top priority. Yahoo, on the other hand, did not immediately alter its security strategy or invest in its security infrastructure. Despite the pleas of its security analysts, Yahoo did not make security a top priority. When Marissa Mayer assumed the helm of Yahoo in 2012, she emphasized creating a "cleaner look" for core services such as Yahoo Mail along with the development of new products. She invested in improvements for Yahoo's search engine and in the creation of new mobile apps. The goal was always growth by attracting new customers. However, there was little funding provided for security improvements. Yahoo employees contend that under her leadership, the company continued to adopt a reactive and passive approach to security issues.[42]

On the other hand, after the 2010 data breach, Google took a number of proactive steps to enhance its security. The company hired freelance bug hunters and paid them "bounties" if they uncovered security holes in their computer systems. Yahoo, however, did not do the same until almost three years later after it had lost many frustrated security engineers to competitors and had experienced another data breach in 2012. In the 2012 incident, 450,000 Yahoo accounts were hacked. In early 2013, Yahoo also endured a series of humiliating spam attacks.[43]

According to the *New York Times*, disclosures in 2013 by Edward Snowden, who had worked for the National Security Agency (NSA), revealed that Yahoo was a favorite target of spies and state-sponsored hackers because of its weak security. Yet despite this disconcerting revelation, it took Yahoo a full year to take further action by hiring a new chief information security officer, Alex Stamos. The Internet community took this hiring in 2014 as a positive sign that Yahoo was finally prioritizing user security and privacy. Mr. Stamos immediately urged Yahoo to implement new security measures, including end-to-end encryption, that would encrypt user messages so they could not be read or intercepted. This technique employs a strong encryption code to which even Yahoo would not hold the key. But the company strongly resisted this proposal because it would impair their efforts to mine message data for the possibility of introducing new services. Stamos tried other tactics to enhance security. For example, he hired a team of "Yahoo Paranoids" who tried to break into Yahoo systems so that holes could be detected and fixed. He also planned to shore up Yahoo's defenses against intruders with more secure code and the use of encryption to protect traffic flows between Yahoo's data centers. However, Marissa Mayer, Yahoo's embattled CEO, denied Stamos and his team the necessary financial resources to provide upgraded security infrastructure, including proactive security measures such as advanced intrusion-detection software used by other companies. The Paranoids were slowly hired away by competitors, and a frustrated Stamos left Yahoo for Facebook in 2015.[44]

The 2014 Data Breach

In the fall of 2016, Yahoo revealed yet another breach, this one of historic proportions. The Internet company informed the world that in 2014, hackers had once again penetrated its systems and stolen the personal data of more than 500 million users. The pilfered data included email addresses, dates of birth, telephone numbers, and encrypted passwords. The company claimed that to the best of its knowledge, credit card data or bank account information had not been affected by the breach. Yahoo insisted this was the handiwork of state-sponsored Russian hackers, but this theory was disputed by some skeptical security experts. The intrusion in 2014 came at a time when there were similar attacks on other Internet companies and retailers such as LinkedIn, TJX, Target, and Home Depot.[45]

When the breach occurred, Yahoo assumed it involved only 26 users. Yahoo reported the intrusion to the FBI and the affected users, but took no further action. They did no further probing into this incident. But Yahoo became suspicious in the summer of 2016 when hackers offered for sale on an online forum the usernames and passwords of 280 million Yahoo customers. At that point, the company investigated the 2014 breach more thoroughly and discovered that 500 million records had been stolen.[46]

Security experts claim that two years is an exceptionally long time to identify the full scope of a hacking incident. According to the Ponemon Institute, which tracks data breaches, the average time it takes organizations to identify such an attack is 191 days, and the average time it takes to contain a breach is 58 days after discovery. Yahoo, on the other hand, clearly failed to identify the scope and magnitude of its 2014 breach. Why didn't it have the hardware and software tools necessary to uncover this sort of breach rather than wait for a list of customer data to show up on the black market?[47]

Several security professionals interviewed by the media concurred that a sophisticated technology firm like Yahoo should have developed capabilities to discover major data breaches with far more expediency. Without knowing more about the details of the hack, it's hard to identify the vulnerability that led to the breach and why it went virtually undetected for two years. But cybersecurity experts identified a number of factors that were likely at play, such as sloppy security practices, lack of investment in security systems (such as high-level intrusion detection programs), instability from high turnover on Yahoo's security team, and the companywide tensions associated with its search for a buyer. Particularly disturbing was the rapid turnover for those holding the executive position of chief information and security officer. Alex Stamos, one of the industry's leading security specialists, remained at Yahoo for only 16 months before going to Facebook. His replacement, Ramses Martinez, lasted only two months before leaving for Apple. All these distractions most likely made the company's security a secondary priority.[48]

After the breach was exposed, some security professionals also questioned the quality of Yahoo's response and its communications with users. Yahoo did not force users to reset their passwords after it disclosed the 2014 breach in September 2016. Passwords were stolen, but they were encrypted, so Yahoo assumed there would be little damage to its user base. However, security protocols at most companies prescribe resetting passwords as standard policy after a data breach, even if the passwords are encrypted. But Mayer and Yahoo executives worried that forcing users to reset passwords would induce some of them to abandon Yahoo services such as email at a time when revenues were declining and the user base was dwindling. Moreover, Yahoo executives were able to assure their investors that the breach wasn't material, since users were not required to reset their passwords.[49]

A New Yahoo Breach Startles Users

Yahoo's security woes did not end with its alarming revelation of the 2014 data breach and its aftermath. Yahoo was still reeling from its September disclosure when several months later, in December 2016, the company reported another data theft that had happened in 2013. This one involved over 1 billion records, twice as large as the

2014 hack. Unidentified hackers once again had penetrated into the insecure Yahoo network and stolen the names of Yahoo users along with email addresses, telephone numbers, dates of birth, and passwords. Yahoo said the incident was distinct from the 2014 incident and that those malicious attackers no longer had access to its corporate network. The two attacks are the largest-known security breaches of one company's computer network. Yahoo declined to comment on why it had not made this discovery earlier. It learned about the 2013 breach in November 2016 when a federal law enforcement agency provided the company with evidence that its data files were in the hands of a third party.[50]

The newly disclosed 2013 attack involved considerable sensitive user information, including names, telephone numbers, dates of birth, and encrypted passwords along with encrypted and unencrypted security questions, such as the maiden names of users' mothers, that could be used to reset a password. Yahoo announced it would compel many of the affected users to change their passwords, because some of the stolen data wasn't encrypted while other data was protected by an outdated encryption code. The company also invalidated the unencrypted security questions so users would be obliged to choose new questions. Yahoo had declined to take the more urgent step of requiring users to reset their passwords in September in response to the 2014 breach. This hack was particularly disturbing for users precisely because security questions and answers were pilfered by these hackers. The information frequently used for security questions, such as the maiden name of the user's mother, doesn't change and might be used to gain access to accounts for other online services.[51]

The Yahoo breaches revealed in 2016 could bring about expensive class action lawsuits in addition to other costs. The revelations also came at a delicate time, right in the middle of Yahoo's negotiations with Verizon. Verizon would have to assume future liabilities associated with both hacks, and that uncertainty now clouded the whole deal. Moreover, the full impact of the two breaches was not fully known. For example, how would these events affect Yahoo's dwindling user base? Would user confidence in Yahoo be severely compromised and lead to further major defections? Forcing users to reset their passwords was likely to cause a number of users to flee to rivals like Google. Password resetting also meant this hack must be classified as a material breach, with investors being informed accordingly.[52]

The 2013 breach also raised new questions about the fundamental causes underlying the insecurity of Yahoo's IT systems. The theft of personal information along with unencrypted security questions and answers posed troubling new risks for Yahoo users. Shouldn't Yahoo have taken stronger security measures to protect this user data from malefactors? Information security firms recommend that this sort of sensitive "metadata" associated with a user's account should always be encrypted with up-to-date software in order to ensure adequate protection against the intrusions of hackers.[53]

Verizon and Yahoo

In March 2017, the U.S. Justice Department indicted several Russian security officers who had paid for and directed the 2013 Yahoo data breach. Hackers had been hired to steal data useful to the Russian government by penetrating the accounts of users such as diplomats, journalists, and financiers. Also indicted was

Alexsy Belan, who had masterminded the plot. Belan and his team of hackers had broken into the user database of the Yahoo system, which was a treasure trove of vital customer information. Yahoo had hidden its users' passwords with a technique called "hashing" that supposedly made them difficult to decrypt. But Belan was able to fool the system with the help of small files called cookies and gain access without those passwords.[54]

Earlier in the year an internal review, conducted by an independent board committee, had chastised Yahoo executives, including CEO Marissa Mayer, for failing to "properly comprehend or investigate" the 2014 security breach that hit 500 million accounts. According to the report, there were "failures in communication, management, inquiry, and internal reporting" that contributed to a failure to comprehend the scope and gravity of the 2014 security incident. In late 2014, senior Yahoo executives and lawyers were aware that a state-sponsored hacker had accessed user accounts, but they believed the security breach was confined to 26 users. The report said that Yahoo's lawyers and its security team had sufficient information to justify a deeper probe. Their failure to dig deeper meant that Yahoo remained in the dark about the magnitude of the breach. It was unknown, however, how clearly this situation was communicated to Yahoo's upper management. The report concluded there was no "intentional suppression of relevant information." As a result of the report, Yahoo's top lawyer, Ronald Bell, resigned, and the board refused to give CEO Marissa Mayer her 2016 bonus.[55]

In the wake of these two massive data breaches, Verizon renegotiated its deal with Yahoo. Instead of $4.83 billion to buy Yahoo's Internet business, Verizon agreed to pay $4.48 billion, a $350 million reduction. The two companies agreed to split any future costs from the data breaches. Verizon also relinquished its right to sue over any allegations that Yahoo had covered up the hacking incidents.[56]

This sale marks the end of an era for Yahoo. After a bright beginning at the dawn of the Internet age, Yahoo had a troubled history. Its CEOs made major mistakes and were unable to gauge the future trajectory of Internet technologies. Arguably, the rapid turnover in the executive suite adversely affected Yahoo's commitment to a more robust security infrastructure. The company's quest for growth along with its financial constraints during the Mayer years seems to have distracted it from paying more attention to cybersecurity. But that distraction has proven to be quite costly.

EXHIBIT 10.1 ■ Timeline of Yahoo History and Data Breaches

- **January 1994:** Jerry Yang and David Filo create "Jerry's Guide to the World Wide Web," later renamed Yahoo.

- **March 1995:** Yahoo is incorporated and initiates its commercial website, which includes advertisements and news feeds from Reuters. Tim Koogle is also named CEO of Yahoo.

- **1999:** Yahoo acquires Geocities for $4.58 billion in stock.

- **February 2000:** Yahoo is the victim of a distributed denial-of-service attack that temporarily shuts down the website.

(Continued)

(Continued)

- **April 2001:** Terry Semel becomes the new CEO of Yahoo.

- **February 2002:** Yahoo acquires HotJobs.

- **December 2002:** Yahoo acquires the search engine company Inktomi.

- **July 2003:** Yahoo acquires Overture Services to help it deliver targeted ads.

- **March 2004:** Yahoo launches its own search engine technology and competes directly with Google.

- **August 2005:** Yahoo acquires 40% of the Chinese company Alibaba for $1 billion, and Alibaba takes over the day-to-day operations of Yahoo in China. Yahoo is heavily criticized for revealing the identity of Chinese reporter Shi Tao for using Yahoo email to complain about China's restrictions on events commemorating the 15th anniversary of the Tiananmen Square incident.

- **June 2007:** Yahoo exits the auction business, and Yahoo cofounder Jerry Yang replaces Terry Semel as CEO.

- **January 13, 2009:** Carol Bartz is hired as the new CEO.

- **January 2012:** Scott Thompson is appointed as CEO of Yahoo following the board's dismissal of Bartz.

- **Spring 2012:** Yahoo lays off 2,000 employees, and restructuring is announced.

- **July 2012:** Yahoo Voices is hacked, compromising approximately half a million email addresses and passwords.

- **July 16, 2012:** Marissa Mayer is appointed CEO and soon makes a $1 billion acquisition of Tumblr.

- **June 28, 2013:** Yahoo announces the closure of 12 services, including Alta Vista.

- **January 3, 2014:** Another major hack is detected in Yahoo's ad network by Fox-IT.

- **July 25, 2016:** Verizon agrees to purchase Yahoo's operating business for $4.8 billion, but the deal is clouded by possible liabilities stemming from the 2014 hacking incident.

- **September 2106:** Yahoo reveals that hackers penetrated its network in 2014 and stole the personal data of 500 million users.

- **December 2016:** Yahoo announces a newly discovered data breach that happened in 2013 and affected over 1 billion users; Yahoo requires some users to change their passwords and security questions.

- **March 2017:** Yahoo is sold to Verizon for $4.48 billion.

EXHIBIT 10.2 ■ Yahoo Financial Data, 2014–2016 (in millions)

	2014	2015	2016
Revenues	$4,618	$4,968	$5,169
Operating Income	45	(4,759)	(766)
Net Income	7,521	(4,359)	(214)

EXHIBIT 10.3 ■ Major Selected Data Breaches by Size[57]		
Company	**Breach Size**	**Year**
Yahoo	1 billion	2016
Yahoo	500 million	2016
Sony	100 million	2011
TJX	90 million	2015
Anthem	80 million	2015
Home Depot	46 million	2014

- In your view, what are the fundamental causes of Yahoo's insecure systems?

- How would you assess Yahoo's handling of the 2010 security breach, allegedly at the hands of the Chinese? How do you compare Yahoo's response with Google's?

- Drawing from the frameworks in Chapters 2 and 3 (such as DRJ), how would you frame ethical issues in this particular case? In what ways (if any) has Yahoo been lax in its approach to securing the data of its users? Was Yahoo morally negligent, or was it just a victim of circumstances?

- How could Yahoo have handled this situation more responsibly? What should it have done differently?

CASE STUDY 10.2

GOING DARK: APPLE VERSUS THE FBI

On December 2, 2015, a young married couple, Syed Rizwan Farook and Tashfeen Malik, who were both allegedly followers of the ISIS terrorist group, opened fire at a Christmas party in San Bernardino, California. The San Bernardino County Department of Public Health was hosting that party along with a training event in a banquet room. With homemade bombs and assault rifles, they killed 14 innocent people and severely injured 22 others. Most of these individuals worked for the county. Farook also worked for the health department as a county health inspector. The motive behind the shooting has remained somewhat obscure, though authorities suspect there was some sort of workplace grievance. Both Farook and his wife were killed in a gun battle with police.

AP Photo/Ng Han Guan

Mr. Farook, a young man of Pakistani descent, was born in the United States. He and Malik began plotting this terror attack before they were engaged to be married and before Malik moved to the United States from Pakistan in 2014. This wanton act came only a month after a terrorist attack in Paris that shocked the world. In that attack, 120 people were killed in a series of bomb explosions throughout the city of Paris. The atrocity in Paris heightened security concerns throughout the United States and around the entire world.[58]

After the San Bernardino episode, the FBI rapidly moved into action. Its investigators were able to recover one of the murderer's iPhones among his or her belongings. The bureau's agents sought access to the iPhone's hard drive for leads and clues among the messages, contacts, and other data. They were anxious to learn whether the couple worked with any collaborators and whether there were plans for future terrorist attacks. The FBI suspected the couple might have had more targets in mind. The phone was locked, however, and it was not possible to break through the robust encryption that protected its data. Despite appeals from the FBI, Apple, which was worried about setting the wrong precedent, refused to give the FBI investigators any technical assistance that might help them access the encrypted data. "This isn't about trying to set a precedent or send any kind of message," said FBI director James Comey, "it is about the victims and justice."[59] With that remark and the FBI's refusal to stand down, the stage was set for a titanic struggle between Apple and the FBI. But why did Apple allow this confrontation with the FBI to escalate? Before addressing that question, it is important to review the basic aspects of Apple Inc.'s history and overall strategy.

From Apple Computer to Apple Inc.

Apple was founded in 1976 by the creative genius Steve Jobs and his friend Steve Wozniak. Jobs sought to bring an easy-to-use personal computer to market, and he introduced the Apple II in 1978. That computer was replaced by the Macintosh in 1984. The Mac competed with the IBM PC, and despite its elegance and ease of use, it did not fare so well. Its failure was due to poor performance and the lack of application software. As a result, Jobs was forced out of the company in 1985. But Apple continued to struggle under different CEOs who tried different and often contradictory strategies. Eventually Steve Jobs returned to the company in August 1997. Jobs introduced the colorful iMac, and in 1998 the company earned $309 million in profits after losing $1 billion in 1997. The iMac represented new vigor for Apple and its beleaguered employees. Yet the premium-priced Mac remained a niche business, a distant second to computers that ran Microsoft Windows.

Steve Jobs wasn't satisfied with a new computer system, and he set out to expand the Apple product line by introducing the iPod in 2001. With the iPod and its companion technology iTunes, Apple was on its way to becoming an electronics giant, not just a computer company. The popular iPod was followed by the iPhone, introduced in 2007. The iPhone ran on a modified version of the Mac operating system (iOS), and its touch-screen interface allowed users to navigate the system without a physical keyboard. Compressed into a small device was a powerful networked computer, destined to alter consumer habits in areas like music and books.[60] Apple worked with wireless carriers such as AT&T and Verizon that provided phone service. A key driver of the iPhone's phenomenal success was the plethora of applications, or apps, that ran on the phone, available for download at Apple's App Store. Since the iPhone's launch, customers have been willing to pay a premium for better features found in products like the iPhone 7 Plus, which was released in the fall of 2016. Apple's high prices have allowed the company to aggregate over 50% of the industry profits.[61]

The next product was the iPad, introduced to the market in 2011. While Jobs's iPhone shook up the mobile-phone world, the iPad "ushered in a whole new category of mobile gadgets that consumers didn't even know they wanted."[62] The company changed its name from Apple Computer to Apple Inc. to reflect its diverse product line. The company's product portfolio also extended to the Apple Watch, which was introduced in 2015 by CEO Tim Cook. The watch was the first major strategic innovation after the death of the legendary Steve Jobs. Apple's iCloud service, which allows integrated data storage on the Internet, and Apple Pay round out the product line. Apple Pay is the company's mobile-payment service, which allows users to easily add credit or debit card numbers on their iPhone. The company's core business in 2017 remained its lucrative iPhone.

Cook has not only introduced new products but put more emphasis on Apple's values and its corporate responsibility. Cook articulated his commitment to all of Apple's stakeholders, including customers and employees and not just its shareholders. The Apple CEO was not reticent about stressing the company's commitment to moral values: "We believe that a company that has values and acts on them can really change the world. There is an opportunity to do work that is infused with moral purpose."[63]

One of the company's biggest challenges in recent years has been smartphone competition from the likes of companies such as Samsung Electronics, the world's largest handset maker. In 2016, Apple's share of the smartphone market fell to 14.6%, several points behind Samsung. Apple is also being tested by less expensive Chinese brands such as Huawei and Oppo, which have penetrated the expanding Chinese market. All of these companies rely on Google's Android operating system, while Apple has its own proprietary system, the iOS, based on the operating system for its Mac computers.[64]

One way in which Apple continues to improve with each new version of its iOS for the iPhone is enhanced security and privacy protection. Encoded into the iOS 8 and subsequent versions is encryption software that prevents anyone other than the iPhone user from accessing the data stored on that phone. All the important data on a user's smartphone—photos, messages, contacts, reminders, call history—is now encrypted by default. Nobody but that user can access the iPhone's contents unless his or her passcode is compromised. The decryption key is tied to the phone's password, and it is only stored locally on the phone. There is no master key to decrypt or unscramble the data locked on a user's phone.[65]

Apple's decision has been followed by other high-tech companies. Google's latest version of Android, called Lollipop, also enables this device encryption by default. Similarly, WhatsApp, an instant messaging service owned by Facebook, has implemented end-to-end encryption, which means these messages cannot be decrypted by any third parties, including law enforcement agencies. In all these cases, the encryption takes place using keys that are only in the possession of respective device owners. These policies of Google and Apple threaten to ignite a new "Crypto War," since users' communications and stored data cannot be intercepted or read by law enforcement agencies.[66]

What Is Encryption?

Encryption is a means of securing or protecting data exchanges between two parties. Stored data can also be encrypted to prevent unwanted access. Through the use of this common security technique, information can be protected against interception and tampering so that eavesdroppers cannot know what is being said. Data encryption has its roots in the ancient science of cryptography, that is, the use of ciphers or algorithms that allow someone to speak and to be understood through secret code. When a message is encrypted, it is translated from its original form or plain text into an encoded, unintelligible form called *cipher text*. Decryption, which is usually accomplished with a secret key, is the process of translating cipher text back into plain text. Only someone with the correct key can decrypt the information and translate it from cipher text back to plain text.

Private key encryption, where the same key is used to encrypt and decrypt messages, was widely used when computer technologies were first developed. But this technique has been surpassed by public key encryption, which is far superior. With public key encryption, introduced in 1976, the key used to encrypt a message is linked to but distinct from the key used to decrypt that message. Someone could create and widely distribute a public key that functions only to create messages. But only the owner of that public key would have the private key to decrypt those messages transmitted to her. Unlike private key encryption, the public key method enables two or more parties to communicate privately and securely even if they have never previously met.[67]

The innovation of public key cryptography has been the foundation for a host of technologies on the Web used to protect commercial and interpersonal transactions. All major Internet companies now employ highly dependable public key encryption systems. Techniques like RSA can ensure that electronic mail messages can be kept private. Both Secure Sockets Layer (SSL) and Transport Layer Security (TLS) have become industry standards. SSL is used to encrypt data between Web browsers and servers. Thanks to SSL, data such as credit card numbers can be exchanged with a server through a secure conduit that prevents potential intruders from pilfering that data. Encryption has also become stronger, and most methods are virtually unbreakable. Keys are composed of bits of data that can have a 1 or 0 value. Originally, keys were 56 bits long, but they could be hacked. Strong encryption uses a 128-bit key such that there are 2^{128} possible values, and this algorithm cannot be decoded even with the help of supercomputers.

Reliable encryption is now an integral part of modern commerce and communications. Encryption protects medical records and credit card numbers, secures mobile phone calls from eavesdroppers, and safeguards the financial networks that link the world's major banks. However, while encryption brings privacy, it also gives cover to villains, thieves, and terrorists.[68]

Going Dark: Apple Takes on the FBI

The origins of the Apple/FBI controversy can be traced back to Apple's critical strategic decision to incorporate hyperstrong encryption into its smartphone. For several years, Apple had employed "end-to-end" encryption to protect customer communications through its iMessage and FaceTime services. In this form of encryption, information is encrypted at the end points of a communication channel and only the sender and recipient have the keys needed to decrypt the message. Apple or any other intermediary would have no access to the keys and therefore no means to decrypt the communications. Apple enhanced security even further by implementing full-disk or "device" encryption beginning with the iOS 8. This means that everything on the iPhone—iMessages, email, calendars, contacts, FaceTime calls, etc.—is locked up tight. A decryption key is linked to the user's passcode, and that key is stored on the phone and nowhere else. The encryption is seamlessly integrated into the system so that the encryption and decryption happen automatically and by default. And Apple no longer retains any kind of master key to unlock the content on these phones. Only the phone's user, therefore, can access the data by means of his or her passcode. The same holds true for all subsequent operating systems, including the iOS 9.[69]

When Apple first released this new operating system, it was quite candid about the security implications of its new encryption architecture. Company officials issued the following statement: "For all devices running iOS 8 and later versions, Apple will not perform iOS data extractions in response to government search warrants because the files to be extracted [including photos, messages (including attachments), and email] are protected by an encryption key that is tied to the user's passcode, which Apple does not possess."[70]

Some data that resides on the phone is also stored outside the phone. Incoming and outgoing phone numbers and lengths of conversation are saved by wireless carriers. SMS texts are also stored by wireless carriers. Email (such as Gmail messages) and social network data are stored on servers that are accessible from anywhere. Other data, such as messages, notes, contacts, photos, and videos, reside only on the iPhone. However, if data from those apps is backed up to iCloud, it becomes accessible on Apple's servers. The iCloud service, which allows for storage of data in a centralized location controlled by Apple, is enabled by default on Apple computers and other devices such as iPhones. Apple encrypts iCloud backups, but it holds the key to those backups, and it complies with valid legal requests to produce data stored on the Cloud.[71]

Since the San Bernardino assailant's iPhone ran iOS 9, the encrypted phone data could not be accessed by the FBI as part of its investigation into these horrific shootings. The last iCloud backup had occurred on October 19. This meant that subsequent photos, notes, contacts, messages, and videos resided only on the device. Since the shooting had happened on December 2, 44 days of information was only on the phone.[72] And, by its own deliberate design, Apple did not have the key to decrypt the encrypted disk. Thus, Apple could not comply with the FBI's request to provide this evidence even though the bureau had a valid warrant to search the content of the terrorist's phone.

Accordingly, the FBI beseeched Apple with the help of a court order to create new software that would simply overcome the phone's built-in hypersecurity. The FBI did not ask Apple to relinquish its security keys or construct a master key. Rather, its request was quite specific: an alternative operating system software for this one phone that would allow them to break into this locked device. Among other things, this software would disable a feature that erases data stored on the phone after 10 unsuccessful password attempts.

There are no specific laws, however, that directly bear on the privacy rights at stake in Apple's dispute with the FBI over the encrypted iPhone. The Communications Assistance for Law Enforcement Act (CALEA), which pertains to telecommunications, requires telecommunications carriers to retain the capability to comply with a court order for the capture of call-identifying information. But the Apple case involved data on a cell phone at rest rather than data in motion. And there are no statutes that apply to data extracted from encrypted cell phones. Consequently, the FBI and Justice Department lawyers turned to a broad source of legal authority and obtained a search warrant under the auspices of the obscure All Writs Act, which stipulates that "all courts established by Act of Congress may issue all writs necessary or appropriate in aid of their respective jurisdictions and agreeable to the usages and principles of law."[73] Thanks to the All Writs Act, courts have the discretionary power to issue warrants and orders in order to "achieve the rational ends of the law." In accordance with this statute, in February 2016, magistrate judge Sheri Pym of the federal district court for Central California ordered Apple to cooperate with the FBI and provide technical assistance so that it could unlock the terrorist's iPhone.[74]

Apple refused to comply with the judge's order. Its outside counsel prepared briefs explaining the grounds for the company's opposition and outlining the big picture to the courts and to the public. There was certainly ample legal precedent for providing data about terrorists to law enforcement agencies like the FBI. But Apple accused the government of taking an unprecedented step that threatened the secure personal privacy of its customers. Apple was concerned that the software tool requested by the FBI, which bluntly overrode the iOS 9, could be stolen or somehow fall into the wrong hands. If that happened, it would threaten encryption on all iPhones. How could Apple be confident that this software would be either properly secured from malefactors or permanently disabled? Also, could compliance lead to a "slippery slope" in a vague legal terrain where there were no explicit laws or regulations? In Apple's view, the FBI's case was less narrow and targeted than it appeared to be on the surface.[75]

Apple fought the FBI because of its convictions about the privacy rights of its users. Giving in to this request could set a precedent for future requests by law enforcement agencies that might eventually lead to demands for a "back door" into all iPhones or the restoration of a master key that had been available until late 2014. Backdoor technology would permit law enforcement authorities to bypass encryption codes and access relevant data by means of encryption keys held in escrow by a government agency such as the FBI. But how could Apple or other companies be assured that those keys held in escrow would be secure from hackers? For Apple, this was a matter of principle: to protect user privacy in the fullest way possible, the company had not incorporated a "back door" into its newest iPhones. Apple CEO Tim Cook has repeatedly insisted that strong encryption without backdoor access is the only suitable way to protect the privacy of Apple's customers: "I don't know a way to protect people without encryption. . . . You can't have a backdoor that's only for the good guys."[76]

Apple was vigorously supported in its standoff with the government by many other companies in Silicon Valley, including Google and Facebook. Facebook executives maintained that weakening digital security by embedding back doors into smartphones was not the way to fight terrorism. "I don't think building back doors is the way to go," said Mr. Zuckerberg, "so we're pretty sympathetic to Tim and Apple."[77]

The FBI, on the other hand, took its case to the public, where it hoped to receive a sympathetic hearing. A Pew research report said that 51% of Americans agreed that Apple should unlock the iPhone to assist the FBI, while 38% said Apple should not help.[78] Prior to the San Bernardino case, the bureau had already been outspoken about the perils of strong device encryption, and it was joined by other Washington agencies such as the Central Intelligence Agency and the National Security Agency, which had also been stymied by strong encryption architectures. Their message was simple: use of this encryption without a back door or a master key would hinder efforts to investigate or stop terrorist attacks. The FBI pointed out that ISIS operatives in Syria were recruiting Americans to kill people through the use of mobile messaging apps, but thanks to end-to-end encryption, the bureau was powerless to monitor or intercept these communications.[79] According to FBI director James Comey,

> Unfortunately, the law hasn't kept pace with technology, and this disconnect has created a significant public safety problem. We call it "Going Dark," and what it means is this: Those charged with protecting our people aren't always able to access the evidence we need to prosecute crime and prevent terrorism even with lawful authority. We have the legal authority to intercept and access communications and information pursuant to court order, but we often lack the technical ability to do so.[80]

The FBI continued to publicly pressure Apple, but the company remained steadfast in its refusal to cooperate in providing the encryption-breaking software. Its lawyers looked for a basis to appeal the judge's decision. Tim Cook continued to insist that the FBI's request for new software that allowed access to the encrypted data was unprecedented. According to Cook, "We can find no precedent for an American company being forced to expose its customers to greater risk of attack."[81] Both sides geared up for a protracted battle in the courts. However, with the assistance of an "outside party," the FBI uncovered a different method to unlock the iPhone, so it no longer needed Apple's help. The court showdown was avoided, but this only delays the inevitable battle over whether the government can compel companies like Apple to break the security of its mobile devices.[82]

Ethical Questions: Security versus Privacy

Despite the surprise resolution, this watershed case raises many provocative ethical issues about how to set the proper balance between privacy and security. Law enforcement officials certainly have a valid interest in preventing criminals and terrorists from "going dark," planning out crimes or terror plots on their encrypted devices that are inaccessible to law enforcement agencies. Those agencies regard strong encryption in the wrong hands as a tool that thwarts their ability to pursue criminals guilty of kidnapping, child pornography, gang violence, and terrorism. Full-disk encryption, they argue, limits their capacity to investigate crimes and undermines efficiency in the fight against terrorism. According to one official, to investigate terrorism cases without smartphone data "is to proceed with one hand tied behind our backs."[83]

One solution for high-tech companies like Apple is to cooperate with authorities on an ad hoc basis to provide exceptional access if possible in case of an emergency. Another is to restore the master key with backdoor access into these locked smartphones so that data can be retrieved by law enforcement (with a warrant). But such backdoor access might have security flaws, and it would certainly become a favorite target of those malicious actors that lurk throughout cyberspace. The backdoor/master key solution might undermine encryption and make users vulnerable. In 2010, China accessed email of Gmail users by breaching Google's back door, which had been created as a "lawful access system" to respond to U.S. search warrants. Also, as Cohn points out, if the FBI is given an escrow key for backdoor access, won't other governments make similar demands? Can countries like China, Iran, or Turkey be trusted in these delicate matters? Couldn't Chinese law enforcement authorities demand escrow keys and use them to expose the communications and data of dissidents?[84]

These questions put Apple in a difficult position, since it cannot neglect the needs of its international customers. In general, Apple must take into account two perspectives: civil liberties and national security. Some analysts argue that every corporation has a duty to the public and some responsibility to help maintain public safety. They frame the issue in terms of "corporate patriotism," and reason that in this situation there is a moral obligation on Apple's part to help the U.S. government learn vital facts about vicious crimes or terrorist attacks such as the one in San Bernardino. But do such responsibilities supersede Apple's duty to protect the privacy rights of its customers? Apple's CEO Tim Cook operates this company based on certain values, but is absolute privacy encoded in its products the *right* value for Apple to champion? Is it hyperbole to suggest that complying with the court order to help the FBI would threaten everyone's civil liberties? At the same time, if we compel Apple and other high-tech companies to compromise the security of their products by means of a mechanism like a back door, we might all be less secure. All of these issues and questions must be thoughtfully considered before rushing to judgment about who's right and who's wrong when criminals and terrorists "go dark."[85]

Postscript

Not long after the San Bernardino shooting, there was a wave of terrorist attacks in Europe. On December 19, 2016, a truck driven by a Tunisian national deliberately crashed into a Christmas market in Berlin, killing 12 people and injuring many others. After Anis Amri was tracked down and killed in a shoot-out in Milan, German police arrested a collaborator: a 40-year-old Tunisian man whose contact information appeared on Amri's cell phone. There was strong evidence that he too was involved in the brazen attack, and police would not have found him without access to the data on Amri's smartphone. Also, in France, smartphone data was key to uncovering information about the terrorists involved in the Charlie Hebdo attack in January 2015. These cases underscored the importance of preserving the ability to collect evidence from a smartphone in terrorist investigations. But there are no signs that Apple has softened its stance on full-disk encryption and the absolute privacy rights of its smartphone user base.[86]

EXHIBIT 10.4 ■ Apple Financial Data, 2013–2016 (in millions)				
	2013	2014	2015	2016
Revenues	$170,910	$182,795	$233,715	$215,639
Net Income	37,037	39,510	53,394	45,687
Total Cash and Marketable Securities	121,251	146,761	205,239	227,000

EXHIBIT 10.5 ■ Smartphone Market Share, 2014–2016 (leading vendors)

Manufacturer	2014	2015	2016
Samsung	24.5%	24.0%	21.2%
Apple	14.8%	15.0%	14.6%
Huawei	5.7%	6.0%	9.5%
Lenovo	7.4%	7.0%	7.7%
LG	4.6%	4.0%	——

EXHIBIT 10.6 ■ Apple iPhone Sales, 2014–2016[87]

	2014	2015	2016
Net Sales (millions)	$101,991	$155,041	$137,700
Total Sales	56%	66%	63%
Unit Sales	$169,216	$231,218	$211,884

- What are the key sources of Apple's phenomenal success, and what is Apple's strategy?

- Explain the economic, legal, and moral issues that are at stake in this complicated case. How does Apple's moral conviction on privacy hurt or help its overall smartphone strategy?

- What is motivating Apple to take such a strong and unyielding stand against the FBI? Is some sort of compromise possible between the two sides?

- Do you side with Tim Cook and Apple or with the FBI and Director James Comey? Defend your argument as persuasively as possible. Is Apple's principled stand consistent with its values?

CONCLUSION

In the digital era, there are no more important concerns than privacy and data protection. Data-driven technologies impact both the right to privacy and other rights, such as self-determination, that depend on privacy. The first case on Yahoo described how this Internet firm failed to give adequate priority to cybersecurity even after its vulnerabilities were apparent. Its negligence put many of its trusting customers at risk. The second case on Apple centered on how firms can strike the right balance between protecting customer data and complying with national security demands. Should information on smartphones be inaccessible as intentionally designed by Apple and other companies through the use of encryption software code? In this case, there is a powerful conflict between technology and law that ultimately challenges the law's normative force.

Student Study Site

Visit **edge.sagepub.com/spinello.**

Key Terms

availability   276

communications privacy   271

confidentiality   276

contextual integrity   272

data privacy   272

encryption   276

informational privacy   272

integrity   276

Review Question

1. What is the moral justification for strong privacy rights? To what extent should corporations like Apple assume responsibility for public safety?

Discussion Questions

1. How would you define privacy in your own words? Assess the importance of your own personal privacy.

2. How can companies do a better job securing their data? Why haven't companies like Yahoo taken security issues more seriously?

FAIR COMPETITION IN THE ERA OF INFORMATIONAL CAPITALISM

And therefore if any two men desire the same thing, which nevertheless they cannot both enjoy, they become enemies; and in the way to their end, which is principally their own conservation, and sometimes their delectation only, endeavor to destroy or subdue one another.

—Thomas Hobbes[1]

LEARNING OBJECTIVES

Upon completion of this chapter, you should be able to:

11.1   Discuss ethical concepts such as fair and positive competition.

11.2   Describe the ethical, legal, and economic dimensions of competition strategies to win market share against rivals.

11.3   Explain the basic rationale underlying U.S. and European antitrust laws.

Competition is the essence of capitalism. Thomas Hobbes's stark analysis applies to corporations as well as individuals, since they too vie with each other in the marketplace and sometimes their very survival is at stake. When companies feel threatened, they sometimes resort to predatory tactics to preserve their market position and subdue the competition.

A corporation has an adversarial relationship with its rivals, especially in industries with a zero-sum game where the rival's gain is its loss. We must also interpret the notion of rivalry more broadly, since competition occurs not just between rival firms within an industry but also between those firms and their buyers and suppliers who seek to appropriate more of the value added generated by industry incumbents. Competition can also come from firms outside the industry that provide substitute products or technologies.[2]

The opposing interests of businesses do not imply the acceptance of an "anything goes" mentality in the competitive arena, nor does it mean the absence of ethical and legal obligations. There are different ways to compete, and some of those ways will have a negative impact on stakeholders.[3] Fair and open competition, on the other hand, can enhance consumer welfare. Open markets, where there are minimal entry barriers and low switching costs, encourage new rivals. And more rivalry leads to competitive prices, innovation, and higher-quality products. Anticompetitive markets, on the other hand, can create harm for consumers, especially when firms blatantly bypass the law and ignore the ethics of fair play. But what are the boundaries of fair competition, and how do we prevent these free markets from descending into the "law of the jungle"?

This issue of fair and open competition has taken on a new urgency in the digital economy, where "monopoly is becoming the rule, not the exception."[4] Software products and information platforms (products like an operating system that run other applications or that support an ecosystem of related products) can yield monopolylike power when an industry standard is implicated. There is considerable alarm these days about the size and clout of the Internet's biggest firms, including Amazon, Facebook, and Google. Ideas for certain products or services, such as Internet search, can be quickly scaled up, and these companies have taken advantage of that opportunity. Capturing a significant share of the global market has been crucial for their success. Once these firms gained a foothold, they raised capital, entered bigger markets, and tried to grow as quickly as possible.[5]

Just as the old monopolies of Standard Oil and AT&T were once crucial to the U.S. economic infrastructure, today's technology titans are the gatekeepers to the vast Internet economy. Google, Facebook, and Amazon have aggregated just as much monopoly power as their industrial predecessors. Google accounts for almost 90% of all searches in the United States, and 75% of all electronic book sales are made on Amazon. The big question for policy makers is whether the sheer size of companies like Facebook and Google leaves consumers worse off. These companies certainly don't charge high prices like the monopolies of the past, and in some cases their services are free. But if market dominance means reduced competition, it might also mean less innovation, and that anticompetitive effect will hurt consumers in the long run.[6]

Most of these Internet success stories, such as eBay and Google, have relied heavily on the power of network effects: the greater the number of users who adopt a particular platform, the greater the value of that platform to each user. For eBay, more buyers meant a better market for sellers, and more sellers attracted new buyers. Microsoft's dominance in the 1990s was also due to network effects. In the case of operating system software, the greater the number of people running the same system (such as Windows), the greater the ease of communicating with others and sharing files. In addition, as the installed base of users expands, so does the number of complementary applications that are written for that system. An abundance of applications in turn attracts more users in a virtuous cycle. A winner-take-all dynamic often characterizes information platform competition because of these communication and complementary network effects. And winner-take-all signifies monopoly power.[7]

Once companies like Microsoft or Google achieve that power, the moral standard of fair and constructive competition sometimes gets obscured. Google, for example, has a huge "data advantage" because it knows what people search for and what they want to buy. This knowledge plays a role in how it auctions off leads to would-be sellers. Problems arise when Google uses that data advantage to gain advantage in related industries. A platform that confers monopoly power in one market can sometimes be leveraged to gain a big foothold in another market. Facebook's massive user base, for example, has allowed it to become the largest photo-sharing website, thanks to its acquisition of Instagram in 2012.[8]

Sometimes monopolies like Microsoft promote an elastic interpretation of fairness as they seek to preserve their monopoly power, especially when there are disruptive new technologies on the horizon. In the fast-paced digital world, monopoly power is not easily sustained, and the struggle to preserve market dominance can trigger anticompetitive behavior. While some types of competitive behavior are clearly wrong, others are more ambiguous. When Microsoft's operating system was threatened by web browser technology, it bundled its own browser, Internet Explorer, with Windows in an attempt to defeat the market leader, Netscape. Was this an unjust strategy or a natural and morally valid response? Unfortunately, there are not always bright-line rules for how to compete with integrity in a dynamic marketplace.

One general guideline for corporations that aspire to fairness has been described as **positive competition**, that is, competition without negativity that is based securely on the merits of one's products or services. Positive competition implies the principle of "constructive effort," which requires a competitor to refrain from sabotaging a rival's business operations to secure a competitive advantage. This includes disparaging a rival's reputation or undermining key relationships with that rivals' suppliers, customers, or other stakeholders. A second requirement of positive competition is "respect for the rules," which forbids companies from gaining competitive advantage by violating the rules of the game that are usually expressed through the legal system. Finally, positive competition implies the "level-playing-field" principle, which prevents corporations from using or leveraging certain advantages such as size in their competitive efforts. This principle, which is especially relevant for the cases in this chapter, is grounded in the idea of equal opportunity. While competitors are rarely equal, there should be formal equality so that they all play by the same rules in a way that permits genuine competition that tests the resources of all participants. Even if you're a monopolist, providing a better product is fair, but what's not fair is leveraging your monopoly power to sell that product and wipe out the competition.[9]

Regrettably, the ethical norm of fair competition and just treatment of one's rivals, which is embodied in the spirit of antitrust law, has been overlooked by corporations, in part because vigorous competitive rivalry tends to bring out combative intensity. Some companies that climb their way to success will zealously leverage their imposing scale in the face of new competition. In many situations, therefore, competition tends to be "ruthlessly practiced" and "exploitive of others."[10] Under the pressure of competition, managers too easily ignore ethical standards that call for restraint and moderation. At best, companies tend to follow the letter of the law and look for loopholes in their quest for market supremacy. As a result, there is inadequate emphasis on internally imposed ethical standards to constrain competitive activities. The matter is not helped by the fact that this theme receives scant attention in the field of business ethics. As Cooke points out, "Many writers talk about ethics without mentioning competition," which is especially "disturbing in business ethics works."[11]

AN OVERVIEW OF THE CASES

In the cases for this chapter on high-tech giants Microsoft and Google, we consider the alleged anticompetitive behavior of these two platform leaders. The primary goal is to understand the basic parameters of ethical competition. Both cases raise many provocative questions. To what extent can companies use a dominant platform to gain advantage against competitors who endanger their market leadership? And to what extent can any monopolist leverage his or her advantage in one business into an ascendant position in other businesses? The ultimate question is, when does the competition of a monopolist cross the bounds of ethical probity and undermine the competitive process in a way that damages consumer welfare?

The first case reviews Microsoft's questionable practices in the so-called browser wars. Netscape initially dominated the browser market with its innovative browser called Navigator, but it was quickly vanquished by Microsoft's Internet Explorer browser. The U.S. Justice Department and many others argued that Microsoft's tactics were illegal and unethical. While Microsoft's opponents acknowledged that the boundaries of fair competition are sometimes rather blurry, they argued that Microsoft transgressed those boundaries through its obstructive behavior. Since the browser was regarded as a new platform for which applications could be written, it was a partial substitute for the Windows operating system. According to the Justice Department, which hoped this case would establish the ground rules for competition in the digital economy, Microsoft sought to neutralize Navigator's threat to its Windows monopoly by ostracizing it from the marketplace.[12]

The high-stakes browser war triggered by Microsoft is a paradigm case for reflecting upon the legal and ethical boundaries of fair play, especially when there are platform technologies and network effects at work. By studying this case, we discern how platform leaders like Microsoft can behave responsibly with due respect for the level-playing-field principle. The larger issue is whether or not technology has changed the need for strict antitrust enforcement. The economy is no longer as static as it was during the late 19th century, when the Sherman Antitrust Act was enacted. Digital monopolies tend to be undermined and displaced by the next new technology. Is the rapid pace of technological change the best answer for monopoly market power? Or is strict antitrust enforcement still necessary to ensure the economy is not swallowed up by big monopolies?

The second case considers Google's struggles with the European Union, which has accused the Internet search company of unfair competition because of the way it gives preference to its own services and products when it returns search results. The European Union contends that Google altered its algorithms to favor its own comparison-shopping service to the detriment of competitors like Yelp. Google has responded that its algorithms are designed to give Google Search customers the results they want. Is there anything morally repugnant or unfair about Google's conduct, or is this strategy simply part of the corporation's natural evolution into new markets? Also at issue in the Google case is the critical matter of transparency. Google's opaque algorithms are a trade secret, so it is difficult to know the extent to which any bias is built into their code.[13]

Both cases are complex and include some technical detail. But they provide an avenue to discuss matters of some urgency in the volatile information economy, where consumers should demand both fair competition and greater transparency. A study of the dubious behavior of Microsoft and Google can help to clarify the moral obligations of digital monopolies along with the responsibilities of policy makers who are charged with safeguarding consumer welfare.

CASE STUDY 11.1

MICROSOFT ACCUSED: THE BROWSER WARS AND THE ANTITRUST CASE

The Microsoft case has been called *the* antitrust case of the new millennium. It was certainly the first significant test for the application of antitrust law in an economy ruled by purveyors of information and networking technologies. Microsoft's legal troubles began when it integrated the Internet Explorer browser into its Windows operating system in a way that thwarted its main competitor, Netscape. One writer for *Forbes* magazine wrote that "everybody plays rough in Silicon Valley," but did Microsoft play too rough?[14]

To appreciate the gravity of the claims against Microsoft, it is instructive to review the special characteristics of software markets, especially the role of network effects on the demand side. With this in mind, the case begins with an overview of Microsoft and its strategic goal to achieve a winner-take-all advantage in the market for PC operating systems.

Jerzy Dabrowski/picture-alliance/dpa/AP Images

The Microsoft Corporation

Microsoft was founded in 1978 by two gifted college dropouts, Bill Gates and Paul Allen. In 1975, six years before the introduction of the IBM personal computer (PC) to the market, Gates and Allen had formulated a vision for the future of computing: "a personal computer on every desk and in every home."[15] As the PC emerged, the computer industry switched from a vertical structure to a horizontal one. Companies like IBM and AT&T had always been vertically integrated and controlled all activities in the value chain. For the PC, however, a strategic decision was made by IBM to outsource the development and production of the PC's main internal components: the microprocessor, the central processing unit of the computer that manages memory, and the operating system, the software that runs other software applications. The two pioneers, IBM and Apple, did not make their own microprocessors but chose products made by Intel and Motorola, respectively. Apple wrote its own operating system software, but IBM looked to an outside company to supply this critical component.

Microsoft got its big break when IBM selected Microsoft's MS-DOS (the precursor of Windows) to be the operating system for its IBM PC. MS-DOS would work in conjunction with Intel's microprocessor to power the PC by running applications and controlling all peripheral connections. Unlike Apple, IBM allowed other vendors to clone their system. Those clones also ran on the MS-DOS operating system and the Intel microprocessor. Compaq, Hewlett-Packard, and Dell became industry leading suppliers of personal computers along with IBM. Thanks to IBM's cloning strategy, the installed base of systems running MS-DOS grew rapidly, and this growth attracted many independent application software vendors. Within a short period of time, 90% of the world's computers ran on Microsoft's operating system. The PC world had evolved from a "playground" to a "multi-billion dollar arena" with a host of companies fighting fiercely for market share.[16]

Windows was sold through OEMs (original equipment manufacturers) such as Compaq, IBM, Hewlett-Packard, and Dell. The OEMs were shipped a copy of the latest version of MS-DOS on a master disk, which they would copy and install on PCs that were to be shipped out to retail stores and dealers. Thus, while operating systems were quite costly to design and develop, Microsoft's variable production costs were virtually zero.

In 1995, Microsoft introduced its graphical user interface (GUI), called Windows, to better compete with Apple. The Wintel (<u>Win</u>dows and In<u>tel</u>) standard, Microsoft's Windows operating system and Intel's Pentium Processor chip, was rapidly becoming the clear favorite for new PC buyers, who were anxious to take advantage of the Internet and the newly invented Web. The introduction of Windows, which resembled the Mac's GUI, clearly propelled Microsoft's growth. And the greater the number of users who purchased personal computers with Windows, the greater the number of software applications and other tools made available for this operating system. Microsoft also entered the application software market. It developed a word-processing product, Microsoft Word, along with the Excel spreadsheet. Once Microsoft bundled Word, Excel, and PowerPoint into the suite known as Microsoft Office, it began to seize control of this segment of the software market as well.

During 1998, the year in which the antitrust trial commenced, Microsoft reported $4.5 billion in net profits on revenues of $14.5 billion. By 2000, Microsoft had a 95% share of all operating systems for the PC, while Apple's share had dropped to around 3%. Also, new competition was unlikely. An operating system like Windows required three to four years to develop at a cost of about $1 billion. This high development expense constituted a major barrier to entry that kept potential new rivals away from this market.

There was another barrier to entry that became a salient issue in the antitrust case. An operating system like Windows generates network effects, which occur when the benefits of using a product for each individual increase with the number of users. Interconnectivity and compatibility are critical purchasing criteria, since no one wants to be running an operating system that is not widely used. Also, consumers prefer operating systems like Windows for which a large number of applications have already been written, and most software developers prefer to write software for systems with a large customer base. This situation ensures the applications will be written for the dominant Windows platforms rather than for new rivals. This is known as the **applications barrier to entry**.[17] These barriers to entry allowed Microsoft to preserve its industry leadership for an extended period of time.

As Microsoft rose to power in the 1990s, it struck fear in its rivals and provoked anxiety in government offices. Mitch Kapor, president of Lotus 1-2-3, a rival of Microsoft, claimed, "Policy makers don't understand the real character of Microsoft yet—the sheer will-to-power that Microsoft has."[18] Bill Gates had cultivated an extremely aggressive culture where managers and executives liked to describe themselves as "hard-core." Microsoft used its clout in the market to pressure smaller competitors, retailers, and journalists. The company was shaped by Gates's personality, which has been described as a blend of "ruthless competitiveness and planned paranoia." Gates believed there were critical moments in history where "discontinuities" emerged that could lead to failure. The Microsoft leader had witnessed the downfall of companies like IBM, and he wanted to avoid such a fate for his company.[19]

The Browser Wars

As Microsoft rapidly evolved into a software behemoth, officials at the U.S. Department of Justice (DOJ) became especially concerned about the company's assertive behavior during the infamous "browser wars." A web browser is a piece of application software allowing computer users to navigate the Web and its hyperlinks and to download various web pages. Google's Chrome and Microsoft's Internet Explorer are two of the most popular browsers in use today.

When the World Wide Web emerged in the early 1990s, so did new companies offering browsers. One of the first competitors to enter this new market was Netscape Corporation. Founded in 1994 by Jim Clark and Mark Andreesen, Netscape immediately exploited the growing popularity of the Web. The browser market was in its infancy and the technology was immature, but one product called Mosaic stood out. It had been developed at the University of Illinois and became popular because of its easy-to-use interface. Clark and Andreesen set out to build a much better and faster browser, a "Mosaic killer," known as Navigator.[20]

Netscape's Navigator browser quickly became an indispensable tool for savvy computer users, and by mid-1996, Netscape dominated the web browser marketplace. Netscape's executives sensed this was a winner-take-all market, so Navigator's initial price was only $49. The low price was designed to acquire market share early. The strategy worked. By the summer of 1995, the installed base of Navigator users was approaching 10 million. By 1996, Netscape had distributed almost 40 million browsers and had captured 85% of the web browser software market.[21]

Microsoft was so preoccupied with perpetuating its Windows monopoly that it paid little attention to the Internet or to the Web. But that all changed when Bill Gates went on one of his famous retreats or "Think Weeks" in the secluded mountain area of Washington state. While drinking Orange Crush and eating grilled cheese sandwiches (his typical diet on these retreats), Gates came to the conclusion that Microsoft needed to take the Internet more seriously. Accordingly, he developed a strategy, articulated in a May 1995 memo called "The Internet Tidal Wave," that would "embrace and extend" the Internet across Microsoft's product line. Microsoft products would be redesigned to take advantage of a networked world.[22]

As part of that strategy, Gates decided to introduce its own web browser. In his Tidal Wave memo, Gates called attention to Netscape's browser, which held the potential to "commoditize the underlying operating system." Gates worried the browser and other forms of "middleware" could threaten Windows because they were platforms for applications.[23] Some software applications, like video and audio players, readers, and email, could be plugged into a browser that ran on any operating system such as Windows or Mac. Microsoft purchased the rights to use the Mosaic browser technology from its owner, Spyglass, and transformed it into Internet Explorer (IE). The new product hit the marketplace in February 1996. Microsoft had "extended" its operating system to include this browser in its latest version of Windows. Microsoft was giving away Internet Explorer to Windows users in order to gain market share, and this was a strategy no other company, including Netscape, could afford to pursue at the time.[24] Microsoft also struck deals with Internet service providers like America Online (AOL) to make IE its default browser in exchange for putting the AOL icon on the Windows desktop page.

Thanks to these and other tactical moves by Microsoft, Netscape's market share began to plunge. When Internet Explorer 5.0 was introduced in 1999, the slow and bug-ridden Navigator browser was all but dead.[25] Netscape's executives cried foul, arguing that Microsoft had unfairly leveraged its monopoly power to beat them in the marketplace. The DOJ agreed, and the stage was set for an epic legal battle

The Antitrust Trial Begins

The DOJ was convinced that some of Microsoft's competitive tactics against Netscape had gone too far and represented unfair competition. Joel Klein, who led the DOJ's antitrust team, saw sufficient evidence of monopoly abuse. In his assessment, Microsoft had stepped over the bright line established by the Sherman Antitrust Act of 1890. The Sherman Act, the cornerstone of antitrust litigation in the United States, had been designed to prohibit and penalize anticompetitive behavior and the abuse of monopoly power (see Exhibit 11.1). The act outlawed restraints of trade and banned companies from monopolizing markets. According to subsequent case law, the offense of monopolization has two elements: (1) possession of monopoly power in the relevant market and (2) the "willful acquisition or maintenance of that power as distinguished from growth or development as a consequence of superior product, business acumen or historic accident."[26]

EXHIBIT 11.1   ■   The Sherman Antitrust Act (1890)

Section 1: Every contract, combination in the form of trust or otherwise, or conspiracy, in restraint of trade or commerce among the several States, or with foreign nations, is declared to be illegal.

Section 2: Every person who shall monopolize, or attempt to monopolize, or combine or conspire with any other person or persons, to monopolize any part of the trade of commerce among the several States, or with foreign nations, shall be deemed guilty of a felony.

On May 18, 1998, an ominous day for Microsoft, the DOJ filed a lawsuit, charging the company with antitrust violations. There were many pretrial moves and countermoves as both sides sought to avoid an expensive showdown in the courtroom. Settlement negotiations began but soon collapsed. Neither side would compromise, and so Microsoft and the government headed to court. The historic trial commenced on October 19, 1998, in the federal district court of Washington, DC. It took place on the second floor in Courtroom No. 2 with seats for just 100 spectators. The presiding judge was Thomas Penfield Jackson. The government's legal team was headed by Joel Klein and David Boies, who laid out a detailed case against Microsoft. Their goal was to present a lineup of witnesses and an array of documents that portrayed Microsoft as a paranoid, predatory monopoly and to paint Netscape as a hero and a victim. Microsoft, on the other hand, was ready to defend its right to add features to Windows, such as browser technology, and to defeat the government's attempt to meddle in the design of its operating system.[27]

The Government's Case against Microsoft

The case against Microsoft centered on its deliberate efforts to dethrone Netscape Navigator as the preeminent web browser. The DOJ argued that Microsoft's behavior constituted three distinct violations of the Sherman Act: (1) Microsoft maintained its monopoly power through anticompetitive behavior; (2) Microsoft was guilty of exclusive dealing arrangements; and (3) Microsoft engaged in unlawful tying or bundling of its Internet Explorer browser to the Windows operating system.[28]

To prove the first allegation, the Justice Department had to demonstrate that Microsoft had abused its monopoly power, since it is not illegal per se to be a monopoly. Windows accounted for a 95% share of the PC operating system (OS) market, so its monopoly status was not an issue for the court. Microsoft's market power derived from huge barriers to entry that prevented new competitors from entering the marketplace. One barrier is the cost of developing a new OS, estimated at about $500 million for Windows 98 (and $1 billion for the latest version). Microsoft was also protected by the "application barrier to entry." Since new rivals would have only a small installed base of users, they would not be able to attract independent software vendors to write applications for their system, and this factor deters their market entry.

But the emergence of browser software threatened to disrupt the OS market. If such "middleware" software were to succeed, it would begin to erode these barriers. Middleware refers to software such as browsers that expose their own APIs (application programming interfaces), which are blocks of code embedded in a software system allowing applications to "plug in" and function. These applications, such as email, PDF readers, and audio players, could run on any computer with a browser, regardless of the underlying operating system.[29]

Thus, the browser posed a threat to Microsoft because it was a *partial substitute* for the OS. If applications were primarily written for the browser instead of the OS, the underlying operating system might quickly become irrelevant and commoditized. According to one legal analysis, "If a consumer could have access to the applications he desired—regardless of the operating system he uses—simply by installing a particular browser on his computer, then he would no longer feel compelled to select Windows in order to have access to those applications. . . . Therefore, Microsoft's efforts to gain market share in one market (browsers) served to meet the threat of Microsoft's monopoly in another market (operating systems) by keeping rival browsers from gaining critical mass of users necessary to attract developer attention away from Windows as the platform for software development."[30]

Microsoft allegedly sought to prevent Navigator from consolidating its market position and attracting software developers away from Windows by aggressively promoting and distributing its own browser. After its introduction of Internet Explorer 3.0, Microsoft began an assertive distribution and marketing campaign. Key to that campaign was preinstalling IE with Windows at no charge and strategically positioning the Internet Explorer icon on the desktop. The desktop is the first screen the user sees when he or she turns on the computer. Moreover, Microsoft's licensing restrictions effectively prevented OEMs from distributing browsers other than IE in the same way.

In proof of its claim, DOJ lawyers pointed to Microsoft's policy toward its original equipment manufacturers regarding the distribution of browsers. Computer makers such as Compaq, Dell, and Gateway were forbidden from promoting Netscape's browser by prominently displaying its icon on the desktop screen, which they had been doing. They could only promote Internet Explorer in this way. During the trial, Microsoft admitted that it prevented deletion of the IE icon on the desktop in favor of a competitor's browser icon, arguing that the IE browser was an essential feature of the operating system and should not be tampered with. License restrictions prohibited the removal or modification of desktop icons, folders, and "Start" menu entries without Microsoft's permission. The government argued that this provision of Microsoft's license agreement was anticompetitive because it prevented OEMs from modifying Windows "in ways that might . . . generate usage for Navigator." In other words, "it thwarts the distribution of a rival browser by preventing OEMs from removing visible means of user access to IE."[31]

On the other hand, Microsoft never prohibited OEMs from preinstalling other browsers (including Navigator) on their PCs and placing icons for those browsers within the "Start" menu (rather than on the desktop). OEMs, however, were reluctant to install a second browser such as Netscape, since the presence of both a Navigator and IE icon might confuse consumers and lead to numerous phone calls that would overwhelm their customer support facilities. Rather than risk this confusion and chaos, they opted not to preinstall Navigator in addition to the mandated installation of IE. As a result, the government's case asserted that Microsoft had succeeded in virtually ostracizing Netscape from the OEM distribution channel, since it was infeasible for the OEMs to install a second browser.[32]

Exclusionary Deals and Tying

The second allegation against Microsoft focused on its many exclusionary deals, especially agreements with various Internet access providers (IAPs). The IAP category includes both Internet service providers (ISPs), which make available Internet access, and online service providers (OSPs), which provide proprietary content in addition to Internet access. America Online (AOL) is considered an OSP. Because of the monopoly position of Windows, IAPs have a strong interest in being favorably located on the Windows desktop. Microsoft was especially keen on exploiting its relationship with AOL and engineered an agreement to incorporate Internet Explorer into AOL software so it would become AOL's default browser. In exchange for this arrangement, Microsoft agreed to place an AOL icon in a prominent place within a folder on the desktop that allowed users to sign up for online services.[33] AOL was forbidden to promote or support any non-Microsoft web browser or provide software using any non-Microsoft browser except at the customer's request. If AOL subscribers wanted to use Netscape instead of Internet Explorer, they would have to locate the Netscape website and download the software. At the trial, David Colburn of AOL admitted that Microsoft's browser hadn't been chosen because it was superior. The decisive factor was "Microsoft's ability to give the AOL's icon prime placement on the Windows desktop."[34] Microsoft had made similar deals with other OSPs.

Thus, by ensuring the majority of Internet subscribers were offered IE as the default browser or only browser, these deals had the effect of preserving Microsoft's monopoly. They kept usage of Navigator below the level of critical mass necessary to attract applications that would pose a threat to Microsoft. Microsoft sought to "divert enough browser usage from Navigator to neutralize it as a platform."[35]

Perhaps the most involved and contentious aspect of the government's case against Microsoft centered on the third allegation. The DOJ maintained that Microsoft was culpable of unlawful technological tying, that is, bundling its IE browser with the Windows operating system. Initially, Microsoft relied upon contracts with its original equipment manufacturers to ensure that its browser functionality was included with Windows. For Windows 98 and beyond, however, the company modified the design of its Windows code to incorporate browser functionality. By commingling the browser code with the code for Windows 98, Microsoft made it more difficult to disable the browser.

The essence of a tying claim is that a company has improperly linked or bundled together two separate products. This arrangement violates the Sherman Act if "the seller has appreciable economic power in the tying product market, and if the arrangement affects a substantial volume of commerce in the tied market."[36] In the Microsoft case, the Windows operating system is the tying product and the IE browser is the tied product.

In previous cases, the Supreme Court has focused on damage to consumer welfare as the touchstone for inappropriate tying. The court has also proposed a "consumer demand" test for determining tying in difficult contexts where there is a question of the functional relation between two products. In those situations, it is necessary to examine the empirical evidence of demand for the tied product separate from the tying product.[37]

On the surface, the bundling of the two products in this case (the OS and IE) seemed to benefit consumers and not harm them, since IE was given away for free. It was alleged, however, that consumers were being harmed through loss of their ability to freely and easily choose their own browser. Also, this bundling was problematic because the browser was potentially a partial substitute for the operating system. The web browser was an alternative platform for applications, and this could mean the imminent commoditization of the Windows platform. By tying the browser to the operating system, which ran on 95% of all computers, Microsoft foreclosed competition from other browsers that could challenge the hegemony of Windows.

The DOJ argued that Microsoft tied IE to Windows not for any valid technical purpose, but as another strategic maneuver to preserve its monopoly. In their view, Microsoft had artificially bolted together these two separate products in violation of the Sherman Act. Late in the trial, Microsoft released a video purporting to illustrate 19 benefits resulting from the integration of the browser and Windows. But in a dramatic cross-examination by David Boies, Jim Allchin, senior vice president of Microsoft, was forced to admit that those same benefits could still be achieved by running Windows with a stand-alone version of the browser.[38]

The government's case, which centered primarily around these three alleged violations of the Sherman Act, was compelling, and it was corroborated with ample supporting evidence. There were many damaging emails and memos indicating the motivation behind Microsoft's decisions. In one such memo, Jim Allchin had written, "Memphis [the in-house name for Windows 98] must be a simple upgrade, but most importantly it must be a killer on OEM shipments so that Netscape never gets a chance on these systems." Another memo talked about "eradicating" the "Netscape pollution."[39] There was also an AOL email describing an offer from Bill Gates: "Gates delivered a characteristically blunt query: 'How much do we have to pay you to screw Netscape? This is your lucky day.'"[40] But Microsoft had strong rebuttals for all three allegations, which were capably put forth by its team of attorneys.

Microsoft's Defense

In response to the first allegation, Microsoft's lawyers argued that Microsoft had a right to impose restrictions on OEMs and prevent unauthorized alteration of its copyrighted operating system. They stressed that OEMs could preinstall a second browser in addition to IE, albeit in a less conspicuous position within the "Start" menu. The company rejected the narrative that two browsers would lead to "consumer confusion," despite the testimony that fear of such confusion impeded many OEMs from preinstalling multiple browsers. Two executives from OEMs that installed multiple browsers denied any awareness of consumer confusion. However, in a presentation to OEMs, Microsoft itself had noted that having only one icon for different functions would be "less confusing for end users."[41] Finally, Microsoft argued that despite the restrictions of the OEM license agreement, Netscape was not blocked from distributing its product. Navigator could easily be downloaded from a number of different locations.

Thus, in Microsoft's view, it did not prevent a competitor from reaching the marketplace but defeated that competitor through improved products, more efficient distribution, and lower prices, thereby increasing consumer welfare.[42] Microsoft's design of Windows and IE did not foreclose competition from rival web browsers. Microsoft attempted to maximize IE's share of the browser market at Netscape's expense, but this was compatible with a pro-competitive intent.

The second allegation regarding the agreements with Internet access providers was defended primarily on the grounds that exclusive contracts and cross-marketing agreements were commonplace in a competitive market economy and especially in the information technology (IT) industry. According to one supportive brief, "They represent vigorous competition on the merits, serving the legitimate purposes of facilitating entry into new markets and preventing IAPs from misappropriating the free advertising provided by placement on the Windows desktop."[43] These agreements did not deny Netscape access to the marketplace—Netscape was able to distribute Navigator in the PC marketplace despite Microsoft's IAP arrangements.

In response to the third allegation, Microsoft pointed out that tying these two products together was benign and did not harm consumer welfare. On the other hand, freezing Windows and forbidding the integration of new functionality like a web browser posed a great danger to the future of innovation in the software industry. As Microsoft's attorneys argued, "Had Microsoft not added Internet technologies to its products, it would be an anachronism today, [because] the Internet has become both a major inducement for consumers to buy PCs for the first time and a major occupier of time and attention of PC users."[44] Preventing firms from integrating into their products previously provided stand-alone products would chill innovation to the detriment of consumers. Word processors now included spell checkers and PCs now included modems, even though both features had been sold separately as add-on products. Software products were dynamic and must be allowed to evolve; if not, consumers would suffer from outdated technologies. On the contrary, consumers enjoyed tangible benefits from Microsoft's integration of IE and Windows. They got a browser for free, and there was no need to install additional software. Bundling in this case clearly saved distribution and consumer transaction costs, which meant it was welfare-enhancing.[45]

In Microsoft's view, product ties were illegal only if they coerced buyers to "forgo their free choice between competing products."[46] But Microsoft's actions did not preclude consumers from freely choosing a competing web browser such as Navigator. Also, should a tying question be raised every time Microsoft or any other software company wanted to bundle substantial new features into an existing system? From Microsoft's perspective, bundling had "redeeming virtue" and its prohibition would be a loss to society.[47]

The Outcome[48]

Microsoft lost the first round of this case. Judge Jackson ruled that the company violated the Sherman Antitrust Act by engaging in anti-competitive behavior to preserve its monopoly and by unlawfully tying its Internet Explorer browser to Windows. He also ruled there was insufficient evidence to conclude that Microsoft's exclusionary arrangements violated Section One of the Sherman Act. Jackson's remedy was extreme: a breakup of Microsoft into two companies, an operating system company and an applications company.

The case was promptly appealed, and on June 28, 2001, the U.S. Court of Appeals for the District of Columbia overruled the divestiture order approved by Judge Jackson. The court also ruled that the tying issue needed to be reconsidered and so it was remanded back to the lower court. Nonetheless, Microsoft was not completely exonerated. The judges affirmed that Microsoft employed anti-competitive means in order to maintain its monopoly in the operating system market. The case was returned to the district court, where a new judge urged both sides to work out a settlement. That settlement was reached in November 2001.

- Outline the government's case against Microsoft. What are the most serious charges? How would you have decided this case if you were in Judge Jackson's shoes?

- Discuss the economic, legal, and ethical dimensions of this case. In your opinion, did Microsoft compete fairly in the browser wars? For example, even if the exclusionary dealing did not violate the Sherman Act, was it ethically responsible?

- Was Microsoft an "ethical" company in the late 1990s?

- How persuaded are you by Microsoft's defense against the allegations presented in the antitrust trial?

CASE STUDY 11.2

CHALLENGING THE GOOGLE MONOPOLY

©iStockphoto.com/loops7

When Chinese citizens visit the San Francisco area of Northern California, they go to the usual tourist attractions, such as the Golden Gate Bridge, Pier 39, and the secluded Alcatraz prison. But another popular destination is Silicon Valley and the bland-looking corporate headquarters of Facebook and Google. Tourists are particularly fascinated by the sprawling Googleplex, the international headquarters of the giant search engine company. Chinese are keenly aware of how influential these high-tech firms have become throughout the world, and they are excited about touring the grounds of these pioneers. While Google and Facebook are regarded with considerable suspicion by the Chinese government, the country's aspiring entrepreneurs look to these companies for inspiration and guidance.[49]

But Google has also attracted unwanted attention from regulators who claim the company has abused its monopoly power. For many years, Google has been locked in a battle with the European Union, which has filed formal antitrust charges against the search engine company. At issue is whether Google uses its dominance in search to favor its own shopping services and whether such a policy is ethically suitable for a monopoly. Google has evolved into a diversified enterprise offering an array of services and products. But can the company validly use its search engine technology to promote its own content while demoting the content of its competitors?[50]

Google's History

Google was founded in 1998 by two Stanford graduate students, Sergey Brin and Larry Page. The company has remained faithful to its original mission: "to organize the world's information."[51] The World Wide Web was a relatively new technology, and users desperately needed a reliable search engine to navigate the Web and locate useful information. Page and Brin set out to create software that facilitated the searching of the Internet's expanding pools of information by relying on "crawlers" and bots to index the Web. Their sophisticated PageRank algorithm was the key to reliable search results. Thanks to PageRank, Google overcame the frivolous spam and irrelevant outcomes that had previously sabotaged search engine technologies. PageRank, named after Larry Page, delivered more dependable search results than its rivals by giving priority to web pages that were "linked to" or referred to by other web pages. The PageRank algorithm tracks the "votes" by all other web pages that signal the importance of the web page that is the object of those links. The more websites link to another page, the more votes they get, and the more votes of support they receive, the more relevant they become in returning search results. When search results are returned, they are sorted by relevance. The result was a search engine functionality far superior to established competitors like Alta Vista.[52]

In addition to its reliability, Google's simple technology and user-friendly home page encouraged users to adopt its search engine. Google has kept the home page reserved for Internet searches. So far, no amount of money can purchase ad space on the coveted Google home page. In 2000, to monetize its search service, Google became an online ad broker as it began to sell sponsored advertisements that were associated with search key words. A Boston-based electrician, for example, could purchase an ad displaying his company's information whenever a local user searched for the term "electrician" or "electrical work." Ads or sponsored links and official search results were kept separate. Google also generated revenues by licensing its advanced search engine technology. Both Yahoo and America Online have used the Google search engine on their websites.[53]

In 2001, Page and Brin hired an experienced Silicon Valley executive, Eric Schmidt, as CEO to manage the company's rapid growth. From its earliest days, Google has been guided by a set of core values, including "Technology innovation is our lifeblood," "Earn customer and user loyalty and respect every day," and "Do the right thing—don't be evil." Google sought to build the world's best technologies and products, but it also aspired to honesty and integrity. "Doing the right thing" meant preserving impartiality and objectivity in the way search results were delivered to users.[54]

Thanks to its technology and proficient management, Google enjoyed an impressive record of financial success. By 2004, it was already being employed for over 50% of all website searches and had fostered a strong brand identity. Its total revenues that year surpassed $3 billion. Google had also amassed over 150,000 advertisers, nearly 50% more than would-be competitors like Yahoo. Its launch of Gmail the same year, a free email service that offered users a gigabyte of storage, attracted many new customers. At the same time, Google benefited immensely from the steady shift of advertisers from traditional media to the Web. The popularity and critical importance of search engine technology enticed powerful new competitors like Yahoo and Microsoft, which were set to enter this explosive market.[55]

However, despite these early challenges, Google has solidified its position in the last decade, and it remains the most popular search engine on the Web. Google has about a 78% share of the global search engine market, with rival companies Yahoo and Microsoft falling way behind (see Exhibit 11.2). After constructing their own search engines to compete with Google, neither company has been able to achieve any momentum in this competitive industry. Microsoft launched Bing in 2009, which is a Google-equivalent search engine, but so far it has not managed to turn search into a profitable business, despite spending billions of dollars in the process.[56]

EXHIBIT 11.2 ■ Global Desktop Search Engine Market Share, 2017[57]	
Search Engine	**Share**
Google	77.90%
Bing	7.80%
Baidu	7.71%
Yahoo	5.05%
ASK	0.15%
AOL	0.05%
Other	1.24%

Google has expanded its reach in cyberspace in many different directions. In 2007 it purchased YouTube for $1.7 billion, and in 2008 it purchased DoubleClick, the online advertising network, for $3.1 billion. Google has also introduced a multitude of innovative products like Google Maps, Google Docs, and a leading web browser called Google Chrome. It has also developed its Chrome operating system to be ideally suited for powering small laptop computers. It has opened Google Shopping as a rival to Amazon and acquired Zagat, the famous restaurant reviewer. The company has also expanded into social networking with services such as Google+.

In addition, Google entered the mobile-phone market with its open-source Android operating system, which is the platform for many smartphones made by companies like LG, Huawei, Lenovo, and Samsung. Samsung is the market leader in the smartphone industry, and Android vies with the Mac iOS for predominance in this high-growth market. In 2012, Google purchased Motorola's cell phone business, but sold it off two years later. Google makes no money on Android, since it gives away the operating systems to handset manufacturers like Samsung who can also modify the code. But Google profits from ads that appear in apps like Google Search and Google Maps. In 2010, mobile advertising was already generating $1 billion a year in revenue. Google also receives a cut of sales from apps that are sold through the Google Play store and has written its own library of online apps for Android.[58]

By 2018, Google had over 80,000 employees. There are 3.5 billion search queries on the Web each day, the vast majority of which take place through Google. Google's phenomenal growth and competitive viability are reflected in its superior financial performance. In 2017, Alphabet, Inc., the parent company of Google and a collection of other small businesses, earned $12.6 billion in net income on revenues of $110.8 billion. For the past few years, revenues have been growing at an astonishing average rate of 23% per year. Alphabet's market capitalization in June 2018 was $776.4 billion.[59]

Advertising and Ad Auctions

Google is by far the preeminent player in online advertising. In 2016, it captured 31% of digital ad revenues, about $79 billion. Facebook, the second-largest seller of online ads, is far behind. Google has built a massive advertising business by selling ad space on more than 2 million third-party websites and on its own properties, including YouTube. These ads target people based on demographics and interests associated with their profile.[60]

Advertising revenue also comes from the ads that appear on top of (or beside) Google's search results. The user signals her interests with her queries, and Google delivers relevant ads that are tailored to those interests. Those ads are determined by millions of complex auctions that take place every minute. Every time a user conducts a Google search that calls for display of an ad, Google generates an automated auction in a fraction of a second that considers where the ad ranks and how much advertisers pay. Marketers choose the bid prices and terms for their ads, and submit their ad text to Google along with how much they are willing to pay if a user clicks on that ad. Google then determines ad placements based on its secret algorithm that weighs the bids along with the ad's relevance and its quality. Advertisers pay only if a user clicks on their ad.[61]

Google introduced text-based advertising in 1999, and over the years the company has allocated much more space to ads and created new forms of advertising. The ad growth has pushed the "organic" or unpaid search results farther down the user's screen, despite the fact that consumers trust organic results and click on those results more often than ads.[62] The ad placements have a bigger effect on smartphones, which have a smaller display area. There has also been a proliferation of product listing ads (PLAs), which incorporate pictures, descriptions, and prices at the top of search results. These ads are more effective, since consumers are more likely to click on image-based ads rather than text ads. Retailers rely heavily on leads from Google searches to drive their online sales. Some say the "billboard space" that accompanies Google searches is the Web's most valuable real estate for advertising. Google maintains that for consumer inquiries, users find the relevant ads and offers "extremely useful."[63]

Industry observers, however, worry that Google's steady "ad creep" will begin to diminish the value of its organic search results. But more problematic for some Google watchers has been the company's adoption of paid inclusion. In its early years, Google was irrevocably committed to the separation of paid material from its organic search results. Such separation was a guarantee of objectivity and impartiality. In its founders' letter, issued at the time of Google's initial public offering in 2004, Larry Page and Sergei Brin insisted that this objectivity was central to their "don't be evil" pledge:

Don't Be Evil

Don't be evil. We believe strongly that in the long term, we will be better served—as shareholders and in all other ways—by a company that does good things for the world even if we forgo some short term gains. This is an important aspect of our culture and is broadly shared within the company.

Google users trust our systems to help them with important decisions: medical, financial and many others. Our search results are the best we know how to produce. They are unbiased and objective, and we do not accept payment for them or for inclusion or more frequent updating. We also display advertising, which we work hard to make relevant, and we label it clearly. This is similar to a well-run newspaper, where the advertisements are clear and the articles are not influenced by the advertisers' payments. We believe it is important for everyone to have access to the best information and research, not only to the information people pay for you to see.[64]

However, in 2012, Brin and Page reversed their position on paid inclusion and its distinction between paid and unpaid content. This happened when Google introduced two new vertical search services: Google Hotel Finder and Google Flight Search. With paid inclusion, payment to Google played a role in being added to the organic search results. Google has said they could not rely on just "crawled data" to retrieve accurate results for users, and so it also depended upon paid relationships. Google's paid inclusion results appeared when a user searched for hotels or flights, and came with a disclosure through a small "sponsored" label at the top of the box. In addition to Google Flight Search and

Google Hotel Finder, Google Shopping also has a paid inclusion program. Critics of Google argue that in these categories it becomes harder to know whether the appearance of a hotel or hotel finder service in the organic search results reflects its quality or simply its willingness to pay for a visible position in those results.[65]

Google, the FTC, and the European Union

Google's market power is so great that it's always at risk of antitrust suits at home and in foreign countries. With a predominant share of the European search market, this U.S. company is an obvious target for European Union officials, especially the office of the directorate-general of competition. As this digital monopoly expanded into new markets, there were concerns that Google had abandoned its early commitment to search neutrality by favoring its own comparison-shopping service in its search results. Google was certainly in a unique position to give itself an unfair advantage over competing shopping sites and ad competitors.[66]

Google's practices were investigated in the United States by the Federal Trade Commission (FTC), and staff members determined that Google used anti-competitive tactics, abused its monopoly power in ways that helped its own business, and injured both rivals and consumers. In a 160-page critique that was supposed to remain private, FTC staff concluded that Google's conduct resulted in "real harm to consumers and to innovation in the online search and advertising markets."[67]

The FTC report concluded that Google had harmed vertical competitors by favoring its own comparison-shopping and travel sites over those of its rivals. These findings corroborated intentional search bias as alleged by rival comparison-shopping sites such as Yelp. The company also restricted advertisers' ability to run ad campaigns on rival search engines. In its investigation, FTC staff said Google's conduct had "helped it to maintain, preserve, and enhance Google's monopoly position in the market for search and search advertising in violation of the law." However, in 2013, the FTC ended the investigation and Google agreed to change some of its practices. Google still promotes its specialized search services at the expense of rivals, but it revised its policies to give advertisers more control over their ad campaign data.[68]

Things have been quite different in Europe, however, where Google handles 90% of all Internet searches. Google's undisputed monopoly status makes the search engine highly attractive for advertisers, but Google's competitors insist that it tilts the playing field to Google's services like comparison shopping. In 2010, several of those competitors filed complaints against the search engine giant with the European Commission. They included the British price comparison website known as Foundem and a German online shopping site called CIAO. Both businesses offered specialized or vertical search functionality for product searches and price comparisons. They claimed Google disadvantaged their business by either blocking them completely from its organic search results or by prioritizing Google's services when users searched for particular products.

According to former EU antitrust commissioner Joaquín Almunia, Google violated Europe's antitrust law in the following ways:

> First, in its general search results on the web, Google displays links to its own vertical search services. Vertical search services are specialized search engines which focus on specific topics, such as restaurants, news, or products. Alongside

its general search service, Google also operates several vertical search services of this kind in competition with other players.

> In its general search results, Google displays links to its own vertical search services differently than it does for links to competitors. We are concerned that this may result in preferential treatment compared to those of competing services, which may be hurt as a consequence.[69]

Google did not deny that it systematically promotes its own comparison-shopping service. Thus, if you search on Google for "iPod," above the organic search results and the text ads is a box titled "Shop for iPod on Google." These picture ads, which sometimes offer special deals, link to retailers' sites, and those retailers pay Google each time a user clicks on that ad. Other comparison-shopping sites operate in the same way, charging retailers by the click. But these competing shopping sites, which also offer iPods and perhaps even include better deals, are demoted in the Google search results, sometimes coming after the first page, which causes them to lose traffic.[70]

Foundem claimed that thanks to Google, it could never transform its critical acclaim and reputation in Europe into a large user base. Google blocked Foundem from its front pages in its organic search results when users searched for price comparisons. According to Google, however, Foundem was a low-quality site, composed primarily of links to other sites rather than original content. It insisted that the algorithm worked properly by protecting users from "link farms." But Foundem contended that Google downgraded their popular service to give priority to its own offerings. Was Foundem's exclusion a side effect of Google's efforts to give users the best results with no spam or link farms? Or was this an attempt to demote an up-and-coming competitor in vertical search? As Frank Pasquale points out, we can't possibly make this determination, because the Google algorithm is a "black box" and no one outside of Google is privy to how it operates.[71]

Based on the complaints of Foundem and other comparison-shopping sites, the EU engaged Google in a series of discussions to reach a reasonable resolution. Negotiations broke down, however, when all of Google's settlement offers were rejected. For example, in 2014, Google offered to change the search results pages that display Google shopping ads so that they would also include results from other shopping comparison rivals. Those results would be displayed in a shaded box to the right of Google shopping ads. The complainants rejected this offer, however, and claimed that this placement was not prominent enough. They also objected to the fact that Google would make them bid for this space by means of its elaborate auction system.[72]

In 2015, under the leadership of Margrethe Vestager, the EU's commissioner for competition, the EU issued a "statement of objections," an indictment of Google that formally accused the company of abusing its dominance in the search engine market. Ms. Vestager wanted to set "broad principles of fairness that Google would have to adhere to."[73] In 2016, the EU added a new antitrust charge against Google. It claimed that Google also obstructed website operators from placing ads on their websites if those ads competed with Google's own advertising business.[74]

But the core of the EU's complaint against Google is that it consistently uses its search results to steer customers away from rival services and toward its own. There is considerable empirical evidence to support the claim that Google favors its own specialized results for local and travel search (which includes flights and hotels) along with its shopping service, Google Shopping. Google seems to provide as much information as possible to keep users within its own "virtual universe." In the past, a user's search for a hotel might return a dozen or so text links to online travel agencies and hotel operators. But more recently, the search displayed a Google shopping services page with reviews, photos, and an offer to book a room. Google has promoted its own reviews even if other sites like Yelp have more information. Also, from inside the Google Maps app on a smartphone, a user can hail a car from Uber Technologies, a company in which Google has invested hundreds of millions through its venture capital unit. Google does not provide a similar link to competing apps like Lyft and Sidecar. But these competitors argue that users should have more than one choice when using Google Maps.[75]

A recent independent study, conducted by the *Wall Street Journal* and the search ad data firm SEMrush, also confirmed that Google promotes its own products through its search results as well as its comparison-shopping services. According to their study, ads for products sold by Google and its "sister companies" appeared in the most prominent spot in 91% of 25,000 searches related to those items. For example, an analysis examining 1,000 online searches of terms like "laptop" or "phone" demonstrated that Google used its search engine prowess to boost its own products and give it an edge over the competition. A Google search for "phone" gave the highest positions to three ads for Google's Pixel phones. All 1,000 searches for "laptop" started with a Chromebook ad. Similarly, a search for "watches" began with an Android smartwatch 98% of the time. And a search for "smoke detector" led with two ads for Internet-connected smoke detectors made by Nest, a company owned by Google.[76]

Google claims that its ads appeared on top of the results of the tests conducted by SEMrush only because of the ad's quality and the prices it was willing to pay. But because Google's secret algorithms are so black-boxed and opaque, we can never know whether this claim is true. As one marketing specialist said, "You have to take Google's word for it." Also, Google's ads can affect the price and placement of customer ads; ad spots are limited, so Google's ads can induce others to increase their bids for the remaining slots. Despite Google's claims, the *Wall Street Journal* analysis demonstrates at least a potentially serious conflict of interest, where the leading seller of online space competes with its customers for that space through algorithms known only to Google.[77]

Google has also said that when it promotes its own content, including its comparison-shopping services, the user base benefits. Google claims, for example, that users like the Google shopping ads on top of search results because they prefer links that send them directly to a retailer's site to buy a product rather than to another comparison-shopping site. For this reason, links to those sites appear much lower in Google's search results. In addition, according to Google, its services that deliver customers to different retail stores help these European merchants to compete against Internet giants like Amazon and eBay.[78]

The EU Fines Google

Google could not placate the EU's concerns about how it displayed its shopping search results. As a consequence, in June 2017, Google was fined €2.42 billion ($2.71 billion) by the EU's European Commission on Competition for abusing its dominance in the search engine market. The company has vowed to appeal this ruling. According to the commission's complaint, Google has systematically given prominent placement to its own comparison-shopping service, with results showing up in rich format at the top of search results or on the side. Rival comparison-shopping sites and consumers are the injured parties. The commissioners found that these rival services were demoted by two Google algorithms. According to the commission, "Google has abused its market dominance in general internet search by giving a separate google product . . . an illegal advantage in the separate comparison shopping market." The commission found that Google's practices meant a huge drop in traffic for rivals once Google Shopping was introduced. There was an 85% drop in the UK along with a 92% drop in Germany.[79]

In her announcement of the record fine, Margrethe Vestager stressed the basic principle of antitrust law in both Europe and the United States: dominant companies have a special responsibility not to hinder competition. According to Vestager, "They are not allowed to abuse their power in one market to give themselves an advantage in another."[80] The EU also ordered Google to alter its shopping search results so that the company treats competitors' offerings and its own shopping service on an equal footing. Google can decide on how precisely to change its service, but if its remedy falls short, it will face additional penalties.[81]

Google's original formula was quite simple: organic search results preserve neutrality and impartiality, while paid content and ads generate the revenue. So Google gets to have it both ways. But that formula has definitely evolved as Google has adopted paid inclusion and moved into new business opportunities and services such as Google Shopping.[82]

EXHIBIT 11.3 ■ Google versus European Union: A Timeline

2010: The European Commission first investigates allegations that Google abuses its quasi-monopoly power in search.

2014: Google and the EU commissioner cannot agree on a reasonable settlement.

2015: In April, the EU files formal charges against Google; the main accusation is that Google skews search results to favor its own comparison-shopping service.

2015: In August, Google rejects the EU's demands to change the way it displays comparison-shopping services.

2016: In June, the EU indicates it will go forward in the case against Google as it brings new antitrust charges (claiming that the company unduly restricts its advertisers and also abuses its dominance with its mobile operating system, Android).[83]

2017: In June, Google is fined €2.42 billion by the European Commission for abusing its dominance in search.

- Do you agree with the EU's decision that Google has unfairly stacked the deck and hindered competition? Does Google compete fairly? Take a stand on this issue and defend your arguments as cogently as possible, using ethical frameworks and concepts presented in Chapters 2 and 3.

- Are you convinced by Google's arguments for why it favors its own comparison-shopping business, Google Shopping? Should Google have found a way to put its comparison-shopping service and those of its rivals on equal footing without the EU's intervention?

- Are there any similarities between this case and the Microsoft antitrust case?

CONCLUSION

Companies have an obligation to compete fairly based on the principles of positive competition. The cases in this chapter, both Google and Microsoft, illustrate the difficulty of assessing the boundaries of fair competition, especially for companies that wield monopoly power and seek to enter new markets. Antitrust laws such as the Sherman Act are general, vague, and ill-suited to the information age, where, thanks to network effects, monopolies are the norm in many industries. In addition, case precedent is sometimes too nebulous to be applied in new contexts. In the Microsoft case, many others have concluded that Microsoft went too far in the infamous browser wars. The Google case, on the other hand, is subtler and more nuanced. Despite the ambiguities in setting fair competition boundaries, an integrated approach to corporate social responsibility will not overlook the question of fairness.

Student Study Site

Visit **edge.sagepub.com/spinello.**

Key Terms

applications barrier to entry   300

positive competition   297

Review Question

1. Explain the concept of positive competition. Do you agree with this standard? What is the basic rationale underlying U.S. antitrust laws such as the Sherman Act?

Discussion Questions

1. Why don't many companies take more seriously the norms that prescribe fair competition?

2. What are your general thoughts about the behavior of Microsoft and Google? Was Microsoft an ethical company during the 1990s?

12

EMPLOYEE RIGHTS AND SEXUAL HARASSMENT

The answer is to ensure dignity and respect in the workplace for women and men. . . . Finding the right balance may not be easy but it is the only way forward if we are to accept the human—and sometimes sexual or romantic—reality of our working lives.

—Cathy Young[1]

For workers, the American corporation used to act as a shock absorber. Now it's a roller coaster.

—Rick Wartzman[2]

LEARNING OBJECTIVES

Upon completion of this chapter, you should be able to:

12.1 Explain the responsibilities of corporate leaders and managers to employees.

12.2 Discuss concepts such as employment-at-will and employee rights.

12.3 Articulate the dangers of sexual harassment and the various forms it can take within the workplace.

Previous chapters have dealt with corporate leaders' duties to stakeholder groups such as investors, shareholders, and customers. In this chapter we review the obligation the corporation has to its own employees. As we discussed in Chapter 2, employees cooperate with other stakeholders toward the common good of the corporation. In return for their cooperative efforts, they deserve just compensation and appropriate working conditions where they are safeguarded from physical and psychological harm. They should not be treated merely as the means for producing the company's goods or services. With these principles in mind, this chapter reviews the issues of job security along with specific employee rights in the workplace such as privacy. The major question is how managers can deliver on their ethical responsibilities when dealing with their employees.

Special attention will be given to the matter of sexual harassment. The #MeToo movement that emerged in the United States in 2017, which encouraged women to share their sexual harassment stories online, led to many shocking disclosures of sexual misconduct. The wave of harassment allegations has begun to transform the culture of the American work environment by fostering better working conditions with more scrutiny of personal relationships among employees. While corporate boardrooms have not typically addressed the issue of sexual harassment, more directors are getting involved in formulating and enforcing harassment policies. However, it is not always easy to differentiate sexual harassment from behavior that is not intended as abusive or demeaning in any way. Some employees wonder what kinds of communications and interactions are suitable at work. Prudent policies and cultural change will help, but they cannot automatically resolve every problem.[3]

AN OVERVIEW OF THE CASES

The cases in this chapter examine three topics that address this broad theme of the corporation's duties to employees. The first case study looks at a scenario that illustrates some of the common dimensions of sexual harassment in a workplace or similar environment. It focuses on a young woman employed as an intern at a Washington think tank who believes she is a victim of sexual harassment, however subtle it may be. The case also delineates the different responses of those in authority who learn about her situation. The purpose is to understand the myriad forms of harassing behavior and to demonstrate its negative impact on the victim and on the organization's culture.

The second case, "Voluntary Redundancies at PSA Group," describes the history and financial troubles of this famous French automaker. PSA manufactures Peugeot among other well-known European brands. As part of its restructuring program, PSA wants to buy out the contracts of 1,300 older workers, despite some union opposition. The case highlights new laws in France that make it easier to remove workers especially during economic downturns. Do these laws strike the right balance between employer freedom and worker protection, and are the modest PSA layoffs morally responsible?

The final case shifts our attention to the issue of employee rights and workplace privacy. Privacy is one of several essential employee rights that prevent employers from collecting or using nonrelevant employee information. The case, which includes extended excerpts from a recent legal ruling, centers on the use of electronic monitoring devices to identify unproductive or dishonest workers. But did the New York State Department of

Labor go too far when it put a GPS tracking device on an employee's personal car without notification? New technologies have made the workplace a virtual panopticon, where a worker's every move can be tacked and analyzed. But where should the line be drawn in the use of these technologies to monitor employee behavior?

BRIEFING ON DUTIES TO EMPLOYEES

Before turning to the three case studies in this chapter, we offer a concise briefing with some theoretical background about the complicated issues they cover.

Employment-at-Will and Job Security

As discussed in Chapter 6, the corporation has certain fiduciary duties to its shareholders. Hence, they are protected by law from the negligence or conflicted interests of corporate managers. But there are no fiduciary duties to the corporation's employees. The doctrine that prevails in the United States is known as **employment-at-will** (or EAW). Employees without contracts work "at will," which means they can quit or resign whenever they like, but they can also be discharged or fired without notice. From a legal perspective, EAW has been interpreted as a rule allowing that employers "may dismiss their employees at will . . . for good cause, for no cause, *or even for causes morally wrong*, without being thereby guilty of a legal wrong."[4] EAW has been defended on the basis of two principles: managerial freedom and property rights. Managers and corporations have the right to freely decide who will work for their business and should not be coerced into activities that limit their choices or their freedom to initiate and terminate contracts. Second, since employers have property rights in the assets of the corporation, they are entitled to control the employment status of their laborers whose performance directly impacts the productive capacity of those assets. When a recession or economic downturn reduces the work to be done, workers must sometimes be released to avoid inefficiencies that are unfair to employers and investors.[5]

Nonetheless, in the past, despite the flexibility provided by EAW doctrine, there was much greater job security in the private sector, especially at big companies like General Electric, Xerox, General Motors, Sears Roebuck, Coca-Cola, and Kodak. There was an implicit or informal social contract between employers and employees often forged with the help of unions. This "contract" was based on deep ties of loyalty between the corporation and its faithful workers. If workers did their jobs, they would be rewarded with job security, higher wages, expanding health care coverage, and generous pensions. Many companies like Sears Roebuck were willing to share the rewards of their economic success with all their employees. According to a top executive at Coca-Cola, "At Coke, a job had always meant a job for life."[6]

But this attitude of a "job for life" changed dramatically in the 1970s and 1980s. The U.S. economy stagnated during this period, and many companies struggled to keep up with their more efficient Japanese competitors. As a result, there were massive layoffs among some of America's best-known corporations, like the paternalistic Kodak, which was known as the "Great Yellow Father" of Rochester. Embattled Kodak was in a competitive struggle with Japan's Fuji and needed to reduce its costs. In 1983, it offered an early retirement package to 5,000 workers. This was followed up in 1986 by the discharge of 13,000 people, a move that shocked Kodak employees along with the people of Rochester. There were also big layoffs at General Electric, General Motors, AT&T, U.S. Steel, and the chemical giant DuPont. One out of every five jobs at DuPont in the early 1980s was erased by the end of the decade.[7]

Thus, the old social contract between American corporations and their employees unraveled during this period. There are many reasons underlying the fraying of this ideal and the demise of the corporation's loyalty to its workers. Aside from the poor economy, the most prominent include globalization, the diminished influence of unions, the introduction of automation and robotics, and, arguably, a revival of corporate culture that gives priority to shareholders over employees. Executives still valued their employees but abandoned the philosophy that the corporation was an instrument of employment rather than investment.[8]

According to some observers of the current labor scene, shareholders now come first, while employees find themselves near the end of the line. Not only has job security all but disappeared, but profit sharing and pensions have become a rare commodity for rank-and-file employees while executives appropriate a bigger share of corporate wealth.[9]

Many companies still find it essential to periodically restructure and diminish the size of their employee base in order to remain nimble and resilient. They outsource jobs and replace regular employees with contract workers to get more control over costs. Executives believe the transfer of noncore jobs out of the company allows for greater efficiency and concentration on what the company does best. For example, the flexibility of outsourced labor helps companies like Southwest Airlines to protect its employees from the revenue fluctuations in the airline industry. Without the support of a principle like EAW and the freedom to discharge workers, companies would be constrained from taking the best measures to increase efficiency and productivity.[10]

Nonetheless, the adverse effects of layoffs cannot be taken lightly or ignored by corporations. Layoffs take a deep emotional toll on those who are released as well as their families. Layoffs are often accompanied by bouts of depression along with a loss of confidence and self-esteem. In the short run, a layoff often precipitates a financial crisis, and even in the long run there are negative financial effects. Some research indicates that on average, laid-off workers face a persistent reduction in income levels. Also, large-scale layoffs that happen within a specific city or community have a multiplier or ripple effect on spending that damages the local economy.[11]

While employers have a right to control assets and hire and fire employees, they cannot abuse their authority. This happens when layoffs are chosen instead of other viable alternatives, the layoffs are poorly managed, or there is a lack of fairness in the process, such as the use of arbitrary criteria. The corporation's prerogative to hire and fire workers employed "at will" must be balanced by other considerations, including employee rights. Thanks to the power asymmetry in the workplace, employers and managers can take advantage of their position and release workers without just cause. Workers should not be arbitrarily fired, discharged, or demoted, and layoffs must follow some fair and objective guidelines to ensure procedural justice. Workers also have the right to organize to protect their interests. The law has reaffirmed that employers have a right to discharge their workers when necessary, but employees also have a right to "self-organization . . . to form, join, or assist labor unions."[12]

Finally, given the negative effects of layoffs and loss of a job, companies must consider the moral issue of how a layoff is conducted and when it is morally permissible.

Companies should strive to do no harm, but sometimes a harmful layoff is necessary in order to avoid the much greater harm of bankruptcy. However, this good end does not warrant using unjust means, so layoffs must be handled as fairly and equitably as possible. Arguably, layoffs should only be done in situations of economic crisis or when they are necessary to save the company from bankruptcy. A substantial layoff might be the only way to prevent all of a corporation's workers from losing their jobs and stockholders from losing their investment. Proactive or anticipatory layoffs, on the other hand, which are done to prepare for future challenges or enhance efficiency beyond industry norms, are morally questionable. Second, if a layoff is necessary, the proper criteria must be used to determine who is to be laid off and who is to remain. Seniority (last in, first out) has been the most common way of making layoffs, but some companies choose performance as the major criterion, since it allows the organization to retain its better workers. Any criterion chosen will have costs and benefits, but corporations should not let ideological factors or favoritism creep into these decisions.

Employee Rights

The concept and language of rights can be useful to express the requirements of justice in the workplace, especially involving the employer–employee relationship. Natural rights correspond to moral duties that apply to everyone. These fundamental or natural rights are owed to all rational persons by virtue of their personhood. As we discussed in Chapter 3, they include the rights to life, health, and safety, the right to freedom or political liberty, the right to nondiscriminatory treatment, and the right to freedom of conscience. A person's natural rights are not suspended or nullified merely because he or she enters a factory or an office. These rights are not limitless, of course, and their exercise in the workplace may be subject to certain morally justified constraints.

Rights protect human dignity along with those basic human goods that contribute to human flourishing. These goods include life, safety, and health along with knowledge and friendship. No one, including employers, should arbitrarily interfere with another person's pursuit of these aspects of human well-being and their prospective benefits. Employee rights, therefore, direct employers and managers to act or refrain from acting in certain ways out of respect for the welfare and dignity of their employees. A recognition of these rights also provides employees with a foundation for defending themselves when basic goods are denied or they are put in harm's way. Human health and safety, for example, are goods to be preserved, but some environments and working conditions place those goods in jeopardy. An employee's right to health and safety, which cannot be overruled by utilitarian considerations, is designed to protect these goods and safeguard a worker's welfare.[13]

Employee rights are also implied by the definition of corporate purpose presented in Chapter 2. Corporate purpose is best expressed in terms of the corporation's common good: efficient economic cooperation in the value-creation process, and fairness to all participants, including employees, who voluntarily agree to contribute to that process. A truncated common good that overlooks fairness to cooperators implies that employees and other core stakeholders are merely an instrumental means for achieving the corporation's end result. If employees are to be treated fairly in exchange for the work they perform, they are entitled to a just wage, a reward commensurate with their contribution, along with other benefits. We can express the requirements of fair treatment consistent with the corporation's common good in terms of rights, these presumptive moral entitle-ments to receive certain benefits and be protected from physical and psychological harms in the workplace.[14]

It might seem that the EAW principle and the recognition of employee rights are incompatible. Can those rights coexist with the need for efficiency and productivity? However, a *proper interpretation* of EAW allows managers to control their businesses and discharge workers when necessary, but in a way that conforms with the fair and just treatment of those workers. For example, the employers' authority to dispose of corporate assets and discharge workers when necessary must be balanced by a recognition of each employee's right to due process. **Due process** does not mean that employees may not be dismissed, but rather that the employer must not act arbitrarily and must meet reasonable standards during the layoff (or firing) process. Due process implies the right to appeal, to arbitration, or to some other fair procedures to evaluate hiring, firing, promotion, and demotion decisions. As Werhane points out, due process in the workplace extends the accepted view that every accused person is entitled to a fair, impartial hearing and objec-tive evaluation of one's guilt or innocence.[15]

In addition to due process, workers have many other rights, such as the right to a safe environment where workplace hazards are minimized. It is not always clear how much employers should do to reduce the risks of workplace accidents or injuries. But under OSHA (Occupational Health and Safety Act) standards, employers must keep the workplace free of recognized hazards likely to cause injury to workers, regulate exposure to dangerous substances, and mandate safety precautions. More difficult questions center on the prerogative of workers to accept the risks associated with haz-ardous jobs. Specifically, how much risk should employers and society be willing to tolerate for their workers?[16]

Included on this list of basic employee rights is the right to equal treatment in mat-ters of hiring, firing, and promotion. Corporate policies should prevent individuals from discriminating intentionally against other individuals. Affirmative action policies aimed at achieving a proportional representation of minorities within a business may also be appropriate, but that issue is beyond the scope of our discussion.[17] Employees also need the right to freedom of conscience, so that they are not punished or penalized for refusing to carry out directives that are based on unjust laws or that violate common moral norms. Within reason, employees should not be forced to cooperate with an activity that violates their personal moral conscience. And employees have a right to privacy, a right to keep their employers from intruding into their family life and personal affairs.

We cannot dwell extensively on these and other important employee rights. But let us consider in more depth the right to workplace privacy, which has become particularly vulnerable thanks to a plethora of surveillance and monitoring technologies. The use and misuse of these technologies has led to many contentious legal disputes and workplace conflicts. Privacy has been defined as the condition of restricted access or as contextual integrity. A person possesses privacy when he or she can limit information to the appro-priate context. Information needs to be shared, but that sharing must be governed by the contextual norms within a given situation (see Chapter 10). The employee's right to privacy is violated whenever personal information is collected, used, or shared with oth-ers for any purpose that is irrelevant to the employer–employee relationship or context.[18] Employers should collect and have access to only job-relevant information about their workers, and they should protect this information from being shared beyond the work-place context without the employee's permission.

Most employers concede that their employees have privacy rights and they have no interest in prying into their personal lives. However, employers usually acknowledge a narrow right to privacy, whereas civil libertarians argue for more robust rights. As a result, there are frequent disagreements about the scope of privacy rights that escalate into litigious conflicts. Let us briefly consider two of these disputed areas that will shed light on the concept of employee privacy rights.

First, should employers be entitled to test their employees for illicit drug use? Many U.S. workers are routinely tested for drugs by companies like Quest Diagnostics. Those tests have revealed that more American workers are using drugs, both recreational marijuana and more dangerous drugs like cocaine. This testing seems quite intrusive, but most state laws allow workplace drug testing for both current employees and job applicants. For some jobs that affect public safety, such as school bus drivers and airline pilots, drug testing is mandated by federal rules. Employers can fire or choose not to hire someone who tests positive for marijuana or other illicit drugs, even in states like Colorado where marijuana is legal. However, although drug testing may be perfectly legal, is it morally justified?[19]

The general justification for drug testing is that drug use impairs a worker's performance. However, while information about an employee's level of performance is certainly job-relevant, it is hard to make the case that information about the underlying causes of that performance are relevant. A person who cannot perform his or her job needs to be disciplined or discharged, but the employer has no right to know the cause of the unsatisfactory performance unless the employee chooses to make it known. A stronger argument is that drug testing is justified because it provides knowledge that can prevent harm to others. Drug use by a cab driver or a train operator can put many other people in grave danger. However, not every job has the potential to cause harm if it is done by someone who is using drugs. It is necessary to identify those jobs where there is a "clear and present danger" to others if they are performed under the influence of drugs. In summary, job performance provides a dubious moral foundation for drug testing, but drug testing to prevent harm is warranted, so long as that testing is confined to jobs where the potential for harm is evident and obvious.[20]

The second issue involves employee monitoring or surveillance of workplace behavior, such as the monitoring of employee email. As soon as email became the preferred mode of communication in the workplace, firms began to routinely inspect their employees' email accounts. Employers contend that they have the right to read incoming and outgoing email to make sure their employees are not using company assets for illegal purposes or even for transmitting corporate secrets. Courts have given corporations wide latitude in this regard. In *Smyth v. Pillsbury*, a federal court established an important precedent: corporations have a right to monitor their employees' email even if they do not inform them about their intentions. The court stated that company email does not warrant privacy protection because email by its very nature is a public form of communication and employees should have no expectation of privacy when using email to communicate in the workplace.[21]

Some corporations monitor their employees through global positioning systems (GPS), which can be used to track the location of company vehicles. The deployment of GPS tracking has also become a bone of contention and source of legal disputes. However, reliance on these devices is now the norm in the transportation and delivery services industries. They are also used sometimes to investigate alleged misconduct. There is a growing trend to track electronic devices like smartphones, but these efforts have met with greater resistance. Federal privacy laws offer relatively little protection for employees or guidance for employers, who must develop responsible monitoring policies based on ethical grounds. When does GPS monitoring become too intrusive by collecting information that is not job-relevant? Employers can surely monitor company-owned vehicles, but can these vehicles be tracked if they are being used by workers during off hours? And what about monitoring an employee's personal vehicle that the employee uses to perform job-related activities?

Despite the statutory vacuum, several legal cases have suggested just how far companies can go in using these GPS devices to track their employees. In *Elgin v. Coca Cola*, for example, the employer attached a GPS tracking device to a company-owned vehicle to track the movements of an employee it suspected of taking cash. The employee drove the car not only for work but during weekends and other off hours. The employee sued for a privacy rights violation, but the court said that the intrusion upon the plaintiff's privacy was not "offensive to a reasonable person." The GPS provided information about only the whereabouts of the company vehicle, and vehicle location did not rise to a harmful invasion of privacy, since there was no reasonable expectation of privacy.[22]

In *Cunningham v. New York State Department of Labor*, the court ruled that personal vehicles are not off-limits for GPS devices. This case involved a state agency that wanted to track the movements of an employee who was allegedly submitting false time reports. The court recognized that employers have a valid interest in tracking employees on duty, even if they are driving their own car, in order to make sure they carry out their job-related responsibilities. However, in this case the court also ruled that employers do not have a valid interest in tracking employees when they are "off duty."[23]

Both of these privacy disputes bring to light the duties of employees to their employer. Employees are obliged to work with diligence and to respect the authority of their employer. They must respect corporate property and refrain from any form of misappropriation of corporate funds, however trivial it may seem. When these obligations are not fulfilled, employers have a right to take corrective and punitive actions. But in the process they should not transgress the employee's rights like due process and privacy, despite the fact that it is sometimes difficult to set the proper parameters for job-relevant information.

Rights are a consequence of justice, and every employer must strive for a just working environment. Above all, employers should not abuse their authority and treat workers as commodities rather than as associates in a common effort. Overemphasis on increasing profits by maximizing production and minimizing costs can lead to low wages, long hours, and indecent working conditions. But when the authority of employers is shaped by a proper understanding of corporate purpose and exercised for the common good, there will be appropriate working conditions, just compensation, and suitable benefits.[24]

Sexual Harassment

Among the requirements of workplace justice is the right to appropriate working conditions where employees are safeguarded from physical harm but also from the psychological harm that comes from unwelcome sexual advances or requests for sexual favors. Work environments that tolerate sexual abuse, sexual assault, and sexual harassment or put employees at risk of these harms fall far short of protecting this right.

The issue of sexual harassment exploded onto the political and corporate scene in 2017 thanks to some high-profile cases that featured members of the media and the rise of the spontaneous #MeToo movement. Companies like Wynn Resorts, Sterling Jewelers, Uber, and the fast-growing start-up Social Finance (SoFi) were suddenly thrust into the intense media spotlight. Some women at Uber, for example, described a male-dominated work-place with a toxic culture, rife with harassment and sexism. The company investigated 215 complaints and found 115 to be credible.[25] After that investigation, 20 executives were fired. Female workers at the online lender Social Finance claimed they had been repeatedly propositioned by their supervisors. According to lawsuits, the CEO of Social Finance encouraged and empowered managers to engage in offensive sexual conduct in the workplace. One woman described the company as a "frat house."[26]

While these cases of sexual harassment are quite obvious, it is sometimes difficult to discern whether there is real harassment or just a misunderstanding. Sexual harassment includes a range of activities from sexual assault and physical groping to sexual innuendo or sexist dialogue. Even giving someone personal gifts could be construed as a form of harass-ment. Thus, in some specific cases it can be difficult to categorize behavior as harassment, since judgments about unwanted sexual advances or dialogue are in the eye of the beholder. Does all sexual innuendo, for example, rise to the level of harassment? In 2017, the literary editor of the *New Republic* stepped down after being accused of sexual harassment. He had allegedly engaged in "low-level lechery" toward some women at the magazine. Accusations ranged from sexual innuendo and compliments on a woman's appearance to hugs and kisses (mostly on the cheek but sometimes on the lips). While some women were offended and claimed the behavior created a "hostile work environment," others saw this misconduct as a "little gross" and ridiculous, but not malicious in any way.[27]

Despite the difficulty of capturing the reality of sexual harassment in a nice formula, it is still important to present a working definition or guideline. In general, **sexual harass-ment** is unwanted physical behavior and dialogue of a sexual nature, either overt or covert, that is exacerbated when the behavior is an abuse of workplace relationships. The harassing behavior interferes with a person's work performance and creates an offensive work environment. The person responsible for this behavior has an attitude that seeks sexual ends for their own sake with no regard for the person who is the object of the harassment. This attitude typically produces an unwelcome and unpleasant response in the person, who feels harassed and abused.[28]

To determine if someone is morally culpable for sexual harassment, it is necessary to sort out the mental states of the harasser and the person who is harassed. Only by looking at intentionality, attitudes, and perceptions can we differentiate between valid sexual overtures or interactions and sexual harassment.[29] What are the specific intentions and attitude of the harasser, and what is the perception of the person who is harassed? We cannot just consider the physical characteristics of the act (such as an abrupt hug and kiss on the cheek), but we must also take into account what this person *intends* as an end and chooses as a means. The *New Republic* editor might only have had the friendly intent to display affection and gratitude rather than condescendingly seeking some sexual favor from a subordinate, even if he made a faux pas in the process. Finally, it is important to underscore that while most sexual harassment involves imbalances of power where someone takes advantage of their superior position by harassing a vulnerable subordinate, sometimes harassment occurs between parties who have equal status in the workplace.

The waves of sexual misconduct allegations have struck a sympathetic chord in corpo-rate boardrooms because harassment of a sexual nature can have such a malignant effect on a person's welfare and psychological well-being. How can we more precisely identify the moral evil in this misconduct? The fundamental moral problem is that people who are harassed feel used instead of respected, in violation of Kant's second version of the categorical imperative. Similarly, personalist philosophers like Karol Wojtyła emphasize that the rational person must always be affirmed for his or her own sake. In *Love and Responsibility*, he argues that we can either treat other persons with loving-kindness and respect or use them in such a way that they are objectified and treated only as subpersonal beings. According to Wojtyła, "When someone treats a person exclusively as a means to an end, then the person is violated in what belongs to his very essence and at the same time constitutes his natural right."[30] Harassment leaves women (or men) feeling used and abused, valued less for their contribution to the corporation and more as a sexual object. At Goldman Sachs, a vice president boasted at a company party that he could unhook a woman's bra over her shirt, and he attempted to demonstrate his technique on a woman colleague. This inexcusable behavior, which led to the vice president's termination, is an example of using a person exclusively as a means. It represents a form of depersonalization that can escape our attention but fails to show others the respect due to them as persons. This woman, who lives out of her own autonomous center, should not be a mere instrumental means for the sexual amusement of others at an office party.[31]

Sexual harassment can assume many forms and affect people in different ways, and this complexity makes it a unique managerial problem. Managers and coworkers must be attuned to the reality of sexual harassment's different manifestations and also appreciate the perceptions of the person who claims to be harassed as well as the intention of the alleged harasser. They must also realize how deeply sexually abusive and offensive conduct in all of its various permutations can affect the quality and integrity of the work environment. Sexual harassment and abuse is a moral challenge for every organization, a challenge that has previously been handled quite poorly in many organizations.

CASE STUDY 12.1

SEXUAL HARASSMENT OR IMPRUDENCE?[32]

It was twilight as Dr. Adams pulled into the driveway of his suburban home in Fairfax, Virginia. It had been an unusually warm day in early September, and he enjoyed the cool evening breeze as he walked toward the house. But Dr. Adams was troubled. He had been summoned to the director's office for a meeting tomorrow. At first, he had naïvely assumed she was going to commend him for his acclaimed work in Argentina and perhaps give him the salary increase he had sought last year. However, he had learned from the director's secretary that he would have to respond to an accusation of sexual harassment by one of the female interns. The accusation was totally unfounded, he believed, but what would he tell

his wife if this compliant led to some sort of disciplinary action? He remembered a real sexual harassment case a few years back and the descent of a good colleague into the dark abyss of disgrace.

Dr. Adams was a senior fellow and board member at the Institute for Latin American Strategy and Policy Studies, a highly regarded think tank located in the heart of Washington, DC, on Pennsylvania Avenue. The institute sought to guide public policy makers and leaders in government and business through its publications, conferences, and policy briefings. Its economic studies and surveys along with its policy briefings were frequently cited by members of Congress and used by corporations to help plan their business strategies in different Latin American countries.

Dr. Adams, who was 39 years old, had left a university teaching position to join the institute, where he had been employed for the last five years. He was also an adjunct professor at one of the local universities in the Washington area. His area of expertise was Latin American foreign policy and economic history with a special focus on the countries of Venezuela and Argentina. He was a prolific author, a sought-after speaker, and someone quite distinguished in his field. The senior fellows authored the institute's policy briefings and edited its other publications. They were supported by research associates and a small administrative staff. The institute employed over 200 workers. To subsidize its research, the institute received grants from foundations and the federal government. It also generated revenues through the sale of its research material and briefings.

Several years ago, the institute had received external funding to support a summer internship program. Every year five college students were chosen to participate in this highly selective program that lasted from early June through mid-August. Many students from across the country applied for the five coveted spots. The applicants were carefully screened, and 15 were invited to Washington for interviews and a battery of tests. The five individuals chosen for the internships were then assigned to work with senior fellows and their research associates. They would assist in the organization of conferences or in doing research for policy briefings. Students realized this would be a valuable experience to add to their résumé. Also, it was possible a permanent employment offer might be extended to a student who really excelled at the institute. Finally, if the university concurred, students could receive three academic credits for the experience.

In June 2018, one of the selected interns, Emily Walker, an international studies major, was assigned to work with Dr. Adams and his research associates. He petitioned for one of the five interns to assist in the preparation of a comprehensive policy briefing on the economic prospects of Argentina and the political risks of doing business there. Adams interviewed all the interns and chose Emily for this temporary position. He was impressed with her knowledge of the issues and believed she could make an immediate contribution to this project. His hope was that she could even write several sections of the draft report. Since Emily's school was willing to grant her three credits for her work at the institute, Dr. Adams was considered Emily's mentor, and he would be responsible for writing the performance review that would determine her grade.

Dr. Adams had limited interactions with Emily before the work began on the policy briefing. He was extremely cordial to her from the moment she arrived in his department. He also made a point of conversing with her whenever they met. In late June, Dr. Adams and his research team traveled to Argentina to get a firsthand look at the situation and do some interviews of business leaders and government officials. Much to her delight, Emily was asked to accompany the team on this trip. On the plane ride from Washington to Buenos Aires, Dr. Adams sat next to Emily. Bored with reading, they began to converse about a wide range of topics. As Dr. Adams felt more at ease with Emily, his conversation began to veer off into personal areas, which made Emily feel quite uncomfortable. Dr. Adams even confided in her about his recurring marital problems. He talked for a few minutes about the tensions in his marriage that had resurfaced during an extended visit of his in-laws, who lived in Omaha.

After arriving in the capital city of Buenos Aires, the team witnessed some of the turmoil unleashed by the last election. Argentina's ailing currency and stock market would be major topics of their study. Emily was an observer and not an active participant, as the team conducted interviews and did research at the city's major newspapers and libraries. After a hectic seven days, they were on their way back to Washington. Dr. Adams once again tried to sit next to Emily, but this time it didn't work out. He had virtually no interactions with her during the week in Argentina, and on the plane ride home she was able to sit with Rose, one of the more amiable research associates.

They flew into Washington's Dulles Airport on Friday evening, and on Monday, Dr. Adams had a staff meeting to discuss the next steps of the project. There were some intellectual fireworks as the team debated the magnitude of political risks for U.S. corporations doing business in Argentina. When the debates subsided, it was time to divide the work. Different team members were assigned sections to write. Dr. Adams planned to prepare the conclusions and policy recommendations. Usually interns did not write these reports, but Dr. Adams surprised his staff and assigned Emily a section on the recent political history of Argentina. He was confident that she could handle the assignment, and he looked forward to receiving her material. Everyone was given a two-week deadline to hand in their initial drafts for his review.

Dr. Adams frequently stopped by Emily's small cubicle to see how she was doing. During these impromptu visits, he would sometimes comment on her appearance, complimenting her on a nice dress or smart-looking shoes. After a week, he invited her to lunch at one of his favorite restaurants a few blocks from the institute's offices. He wanted a progress report on her work. Once again, his conversation was full of compliments about her appearance. After lunch, Dr. Adams ordered a cognac and spoke with her about his personal life. Emily was always polite, but she was uncomfortable with the personal tone of this conversation and hoped her diffidence would discourage it. She was also increasingly dismayed with all the unwanted attention. She talked with Rose and learned that none of the other team members had a luncheon date with Dr. Adams for a similar progress report. She thought about ways to avoid Dr. Adams and even considered wearing baggy, unflattering clothes so he wouldn't comment so much on how nice she looked.

Two days before the report was due, Dr. Adams swung by her cubicle again. She hadn't seen him in a few days, since he was preoccupied with his own writing and the institute's business. This time he told her there was "a lot riding" on this assignment. "If it's really good," he said, "I'm going to recommend you for a full-time position as a research associate when you graduate." Emily was surprised and delighted, but she did not display much enthusiasm. Tactful silence seemed like the best approach. Nonetheless, she had grown to like the institute, and this kind of research work and writing was her "dream job."

Although the unwanted attention from Dr. Adams made Emily distressed, she didn't know what to do. Dr. Adams was a senior fellow and sat on the institute's board. He had power, and a complaint might end her chances for a permanent job and perhaps lead to a bad performance review and a poor grade. So she kept silent. A week passed by and Emily finished her report. She sent it along to Dr. Adams on Thursday evening. He called her the next day and said he needed to speak with her about what she had written as soon as possible. Emily told him she'd be happy to drop by his office anytime during the day. But Dr. Adams said he was tied up all day with meetings and conference calls.

"What about getting together after work," suggested Adams.

"OK," Emily said, "I'll stop by your office around 5:30 before I leave for the day."

"No," responded Adams, "why don't you meet me a few blocks from here at Penny's Bar at 6 p.m. I have to visit someone nearby later in the evening, so that would be a perfect spot to meet."

Emily was reluctant, but she agreed to meet him at Penny's, a favorite "watering hole" for the Washington elite.

"Great," replied Adams. "See you this evening, and don't be late."

Emily arrived at Penny's Bar shortly after 6 p.m. Dr. Adams had already had a drink or two and felt quite "relaxed." He talked for a few minutes about her work assignment and suggested some minor revisions. Emily thought Dr. Adams had wanted to see her because there were significant issues with what she had written, but overall he was full of praise for her writing. Soon the conversation shifted yet again to his personal life and marital problems. He discussed the most recent argument with his wife and commented that Emily, unlike his wife, was a woman who could understand him. The conversation filled Emily with anxiety. She was polite, but after an hour, she excused herself and said she had to be heading home.

"Oh no," said Dr. Adams. "Why don't we go to dinner across the street?"

"I'm not feeling so well," answered Emily. "I need to go home."

By this time, Emily had enough, and she spoke to her friend Rose on Monday morning. She was worried things might escalate and that Dr. Adams might put demands on her. Rose encouraged her to speak with the associate director, Dr. Pierson, who handled some of the human resource issues for the professional staff of the institute. Rose was sympathetic with Emily's plight, but she also mentioned that Dr. Adams was a "needy individual, even a little immature," and that he often spoke "too freely" with women colleagues, especially the new ones. It was not unusual for him to make flattering comments about their dress or appearance.

Two days later, Emily met with Dr. Pierson and described her situation. He listened attentively and then asked a few probing questions: Had Dr. Adams ever propositioned her? Had he ever hugged her or touched her inappropriately? Had he ever retaliated against her for resisting a sexual advance? Had he ever embarrassed her in front of others by making inappropriate sexual comments? Had there been any unwanted sexual looks or gestures? The answer to all these questions, of course, was no. As a result, Dr. Pierson refused to get involved. "In my estimation," he said, "this is a personal relationship issue, not a management issue that affects the institute or violates our policies. I must admit his behavior seems rather odd and imprudent, but I don't think it rises to the level of harassment. The best way to handle this is just to have a candid conversation with Dr. Adams and tell him how you feel. I'm sure he'll understand. Also, you're an intern! You'll be gone from here in few weeks, and you can put all this behind you."

Emily was not satisfied with this response, but she took the matter no further. In her remaining weeks at the institute, she avoided Dr. Adams as much as possible. He was busy finalizing the briefing on Argentina and took a week off in early August. Dr. Adams had also learned about her meeting with the associate director, even though it was supposed to have remained confidential. All of a sudden his whole demeanor changed toward her—he was cool and aloof. He gave her an excellent recommendation, but nothing more was said about a permanent job at the institute.

Before the interns left to return to their university studies, it was customary to be given an exit interview by the director of the institute, Dr. Elaine Sherman. Dr. Sherman was interested in their perception of the institute and its personnel. Emily was still perturbed over all that had happened during the summer, and so she recounted the unpleasant experience with Dr. Adams that had clouded her work at the institute. Dr. Sherman expressed far more concern than the associate director and offered Emily her apologies. She said she would look into the matter further and certainly speak to Dr. Adams about his "imprudent" behavior.

- In your opinion, does the behavior of Dr. Adams represent sexual harassment of Emily? What do you think was his mental state or intentions throughout these interactions with her?

- If you were in Dr. Pierson's position as associate director, how would you have responded to Emily's complaint? What would you say to Dr. Adams?

- If Dr. Sherman concludes that Dr. Adams is culpable for harassing behavior, what should the consequences be?

CASE STUDY 12.2

VOLUNTARY REDUNDANCIES AT PSA GROUP

European companies have been largely immune to the large-scale corporate downsizings that have taken place in the United States. On the contrary, the socialist French government under François Mitterand cut work hours and increased paid holidays. In 2000, France capped the work week at 35 hours. This shortened work week along with a decade of generous wage deals became a burden for some companies in globally competitive industries. At the same time, government policies and union power made it difficult to discharge workers or close unproductive plants. By 2007, average salary and benefits in France were higher than in America, Germany, and Britain. But things have begun to change under the leadership of

French president Emmanuel Macron, who has retreated from the socialist policies of his predecessors.[33]

This case is about a French auto manufacturer attempting to take advantage of new French laws that make it easier to discharge workers. The company has reversed its financial fortunes, and yet it still wants to buy out older workers with long-term contracts. Some acts of corporate downsizing are morally valid, but does the situation at Peugeot warrant these buyouts of "protected" workers?

Company History

Peugeot is a 200-year-old French company that manufactured its first cars in the late 19th century. It survived two world wars, and for some it has become an "emblem of France." In 1976, the merger of Citroën, SA, and Peugeot, SA, led to the creation of the Peugeot Citroën Group. After the purchase of Chrysler Europe in 1978, this auto manufacturer became Europe's number-one group. The takeover left Peugeot encumbered with debt; however, it was rescued by the Peugeot 205, a first-generation "hot hatch." Peugeot sold millions of the 205, and those revenues helped save the company.[34]

Under the leadership of Jacques Calvet and Jean-Jacques Martin Foltz, PSA underwent a series of restructurings to sharpen its competitive edge. Like its American counterparts, Ford and General Motors, it adopted common-platform technology to reduce production costs. PSA also put more emphasis on international growth, expanding its presence into China, Brazil, and Eastern Europe. It built plants in both Slovakia and the Czech Republic. In 2008, it built its first plant in Russia, and in 2017, PSA opened a plant in Shenzhen, China.

In addition to realizing some of its global ambitions, PSA ramped up its research-and-development activities and developed proprietary technologies. In 2000, it began development of the particulate filter, which culminated in the introduction of its three-cylinder EB Pure Tech Engine in 2012. This innovative engine reduced CO_2 emissions by 18%. But the company struggled with meager 1% profit margins for over a decade. Industry analysts said it was still too Eurocentric and lacked overall scale in an industry where scale economies are decisive and "bigger is better." Peugeot began a restructuring campaign in July 2012, but, hamstrung by French law and public opinion, it could only close one plant even though its capacity utilization was at 61% (versus 135% for Ford). In 2014, on the brink of bankruptcy, PSA received a €3 billion bailout from the French government and the Chinese automaker Dongfeng Motors.[35]

In 2014, Carlos Tavares was chosen as chairman to help PSA escape from the throes of bankruptcy. Two years later, in 2016, he presented his "Push to Pass" (named after an engine-boost button that aids overtaking another vehicle) strategic plan. In that same year, PSA Peugeot Citroën became simply PSA Group. The Tavares strategy sought to make PSA a global car manufacturer on the cutting edge of efficiency as well as a provider of mobility services favored by customers. Aside from global expansion, Tavares put a great deal of emphasis on cost-cutting and streamlining manufacturing to boost profits.[36]

Despite its financial woes and low profits, in August 2017, PSA Group consummated a deal with General Motors for the purchase of Opel and Vauxhall for €2.2 billion (or $2.6 billion). General Motors sold its money-losing European operation to PSA, which had a better record of profiting in the small-car business in Europe. Opel had 38,000 workers, with most of its plants located in Germany. In 2016, the year prior to the take-over, Opel suffered a net loss of $257 million. The PSA Group will build the next Opel Corsa on the same platform as the Peugeot 208 and Citroën C3 models, aiming to achieve scale economies by building 5 million cars a year.[37]

Restructuring and Layoffs

Group PSA was now faced with the challenge of restructuring Opel and integrating its operations into the PSA organizational structure. The restructuring plan called PACE centered on the development of several new car models by 2020. Four of these new models were fuel-efficient, electric-powered vehicles. But in the short term, austerity measures would be necessary. These measures included placing workers on "reduced hours" at three factories in Germany, a partial retirement program, and a reduction in the number of temporary workers. There would be no drastic measures, however, such as plant closings. The 19,000 employees at Opel's German factories were protected from plant closures by German law.[38]

The restructuring plan also included job cuts at Opel. PSA intends to eliminate 3,700 jobs primarily through voluntary departures, but that plan has not yet received union approval. Shortly after the takeover, PSA attempted to negotiate with unions over a proposed pay increase for German factory workers. Workers were asked to forgo a $4.34 pay increase in 2018 in exchange for PSA's investment in production of a new SUV at the German plant in Eisenach. The union, however, accused PSA of "blackmail" for demanding this wage freeze for all 19,000 German workers as a condition for investment in the Eisenach plant.[39]

Group PSA took over the struggling Opel operation just as its own revenue stream and financial condition were beginning to improve. In 2017, its total revenues were $73.5 billion, with net income of $2.2 billion. The 1% profit margins were a thing of the past. Its operating margin of 7.3% in 2017 set a new historic high for PSA and was well above the profit targets set forth in Tavares's strategic plan. The results were a considerable improvement over the company's performance in 2014, when it had been on the edge of bankruptcy.[40]

Nonetheless, as part of a broader restructuring plan, Group PSA announced in January 2018 that it planned to eliminate 2,200 French jobs in addition to the cuts at Opel. The plan called for 1,300 buyouts along with the elimination of 900 jobs through early retire-ment. The job cuts were facilitated by new labor reform laws instituted by French pres-ident Emmanuel Macron. Those laws expedited negotiations with workers and unions and eased the requirement for proving financial difficulty. Some unions opposed the job cuts and claimed they were unnecessary, merely an effort to cut costs at the expense of "protected" workers.[41]

French Labor Reform

Emmanuel Macron's labor and economic reforms have been designed to stimulate economic growth and reduce France's unemployment rate, which has stagnated at about 9% to 10% for a decade (2007–2017). The persistently high unemployment can be attributed to the fact that businesses in France have been reluctant to hire new full-time permanent workers because it is so difficult to discharge them even in an economic downturn. As a result, they have chosen alternative strategies and often turned to hiring short-term, temporary workers. France's high unemployment rate, well above the rate of eurozone countries like Germany, is a main source of the country's economic malaise.

Macron's reforms have also been conceived to emulate the Scandinavian economic model found in countries like Denmark, which introduced the idea of "**flexicurity.**" The objective is to create a more flexible economy without destabilizing the job security provided by the Denmark welfare state. Employers can fire or lay off workers when necessary and without notice, but the state will provide generous unemployment compensation along with more education and retraining programs for those who find themselves unemployed.[42]

Flexicurity seems to have worked in Denmark, which prides itself on a number of globally competitive firms such as Oticon, which makes hearing aids, the legendary toy company Lego, the drug company Novo Nordisk, and Carlsberg, the Danish brewery. These and other Danish companies do not hesitate to maintain off-shore jobs or release workers during a downturn, confident that displaced workers will be eligible for wage insurance and retraining. At the same time, thanks to competent management, Denmark's major companies, which typically thrive in well-defined global niches, consistently generated high-quality jobs through their innovative activities.[43]

Macron's model of "flexible security" closely parallels the Denmark template, which tries to balance employer rights with worker protections. The French labor reforms will make it easier to hire and fire people in France, but there will also be retraining programs for those who lose their jobs. The new rules allow French companies to negotiate job reductions or layoffs due to restructuring directly with labor or union representatives within the business. In the past, employers were bound by industry-wide collective bargaining agreements. Companies also face less risk of legal action over dismissals with legal damages limited. For example, an employee with 30 years' seniority would be entitled to no more than 20 months' salary if he or she was wrongly discharged. French firms can also hire new workers immediately after a layoff.[44]

The biggest change is that global companies or multinationals will be able to downsize even if the overall business is highly profitable. Under French law all layoff and worker discharge plans need the approval of the Chamber of Commerce before going into effect. Before the Macron reforms, if an employer wanted to lay off French employees, a Chamber of Commerce judge would consider the company's global financial health to determine whether layoffs were justified. Thanks to the reform, the judge's determination of the company's financial health is confined to France's geographic borders, thereby preventing the judge from taking into account global circumstances and global-level profits.[45]

These measures give firms like Group PSA more flexibility to lay off or buy out workers, a procedure known in France as "voluntary redundancies." PSA immediately took advantage of this opportunity. In early 2018, it announced the buyout of the 1,300 workers, much to the surprise of the French auto industry. The company said it would fill most of those vacancies with younger and less costly employees on full-time contracts. PSA obtained the agreement of unions representing over 50% of their workers, as required by law. But one of the unions representing PSA factory workers saw these job buyouts as an opportunity for corporations like PSA to hire a new generation of cheap labor at the expense of older, experienced, and protected workers with long-term contracts. According to Phillippe Martinez, the leader of the powerful General Confederation of Labor (GCL), "This is a means for companies to get rid of high-cost employees with seniority and therefore considered too highly paid, while at the same time recruiting precarious and disposable workers."[46] GCL leaders argued that PSA was trying to turn permanent contracts into insecure jobs. They also claim there were numerous cases where "volunteers are forced."[47] Many PSA workers agreed with this sentiment and opposed the Macron reforms. One PSA factory worker told the French newspaper *Le Monde*, "The Macron executive orders are a way of pushing people toward unemployment."[48]

There is little doubt that PSA's restructuring will help improve its bottom line even further, since new workers hired will not be paid nearly as much as those headed out the door. The bigger question for France is whether these reforms will make the country more economically competitive or simply unravel its social welfare model.[49]

EXHIBIT 12.1 ■ PSA Group Financials, 2015–2017 (in thousands)[50]			
	2015	**2016**	**2017**
Revenues	$60,653,253	$59,765,500	$73,541,170
EBITA**	4,100,052	4,966,590	5,903,819
Net Income	997,280	1,913,630	2,175,447
Total Assets	53,692,082	47,487,485	62,988,891
Total Debt	8,564,931	6,946,489	9,255,705

**Earnings Before Interest, Taxes, and Amortization (a measure often used in industries with heavy assets and a big depreciation expense).

- In your opinion, are the modest PSA job cuts or voluntary buyouts morally justified (based on the company's financial condition and other factors)? What if the job cuts were not voluntary but took the form of traditional nonvoluntary layoffs?

- Unions have opposed PSA's efforts to make changes at Opel, which is a money-losing operation. Should the unions accept PSA's restructuring plan?

- Do you agree with the French labor law reforms? What are the benefits and costs of this new policy? Do you think "flexicurity" or "flexible security" is a sound idea? If so, could this principle work in bigger countries like the United States?

CASE STUDY 12.3

GPS MONITORING AND EMPLOYEE PRIVACY RIGHTS: EXCERPTS FROM *CUNNINGHAM V. NEW YORK STATE DEPARTMENT OF LABOR*[51]

In this case, a GPS monitoring device was placed on the personal vehicle of Michael Cunningham, a 30-year employee for New York State's Department of Labor who was thought to be submitting false time reports. The GPS device tracked the whereabouts of Cunningham and his family for a month, and this tracking of the family vehicle included evenings, weekends, and even a week-long vacation. While a person's home and personal possessions are protected by the Fourth Amendment from search and seizure without a warrant, there is a workplace exception as articulated in the Supreme Court

©IStockphoto.com/Tzido

case of *O'Connor v. Ortega*. Therefore, employers do not need a warrant to search an employee's desk, locker, or other workplace belongings.[52] The primary question in this dispute is whether a personal vehicle used during the work day also qualifies for the workplace exception that allows for warrantless search or monitoring.

Below are extended excerpts from the judgment in this case by the New York State Court of Appeals in favor of the plaintiff, who claimed his constitutional right to privacy had been violated. The appeals court ruled that the Department of Labor had acted illegally when it put the GPS device on this employee's car and tracked his movements outside business hours. The opinion sheds light on how the courts are drawing the line in the use of these devices and their reasoning behind this determination.

Summary and Appeals Court Decision

Mr. Michael Cunningham, the "petitioner" in this case, began to work for the New York State Department of Labor (DOL) in 1980. Nine years later, in 1989, he was appointed the director of staff and organizational development for this state agency. Cunningham was suspected of submitting false time reports, and as a consequence, the state launched an investigation into his alleged unauthorized absences. The state believed that Cunningham was falsifying records to conceal his absences from work. The investigation uncovered enough evidence to warrant a disciplinary proceeding that resulted in a two-month suspension. In addition, a second investigation was launched because Cunningham eluded an investigator who was trying to follow his car. The DOL, suspecting the wrongdoing was more extensive than it could verify, referred the case to the Office of the State Inspector General, which initiated a new investigation into Cunningham's activities.

The first phase of the inspector general's investigation was the attachment of a GPS device to Cunningham's personal vehicle without his knowledge. This was done on June 3, 2008, while the car was in the parking lot next to the DOL offices. According to DOL policy, no notification to Cunningham or his family was necessary. This initial device and two later replacement GPS devices recorded all the car's movements for a month, including evenings, weekends, and even several days when Cunningham was on vacation with his family in Massachusetts. The GPS device was removed one month later on July 3, 2008. At the same time, the inspector general sought to collect information from other sources of investigation: discreet surveillance of an apartment building Cunningham was suspected of visiting during working hours, issuing subpoenas for E-ZPass records, and conducting interviews with Cunningham and his secretary.

After the department received the inspector general's lengthy report, it brought 11 new charges against Cunningham. Four of those 11 charges were derived from the evidence obtained from the GPS device that had been attached to his car. The extensive GPS information showed that the petitioner's times of arrival at and departure from his office were inconsistent with the number of hours he claimed to have worked, based on the time records he had submitted. One of those four charges against Cunningham was based on his approval of time records that showed that his secretary was working during hours when the GPS information clearly indicated that he was visiting her home. Four other charges were supported by GPS evidence (along with other evidence collected by the inspector general's office). Those charges involved the time period when Cunningham claimed he and his secretary returned home from a business trip to Syracuse. Both GPS information and E-ZPass records demonstrated they had returned in the middle of the workday, not at the end of the workday, as documents submitted or approved by Cunningham had indicated. The GPS information was irrelevant to the remaining three charges brought against Cunningham.

After reviewing the results of this second investigation into Cunningham's actions, the commissioner of labor terminated Cunningham's employment on August 24, 2010. But Cunningham immediately filed a lawsuit to challenge the commissioner's decision. Among other things, the lawsuit asked the court to declare that the DOL's deployment of the GPS tracking technology without a warrant violated Cunningham's constitutional rights against unreasonable search and seizure. The case was transferred from the New York Supreme Court to the Appellate Division, which confirmed the commissioner's decision and dismissed Cunningham's petition. Cunningham then appealed his case to the New York State Court of Appeals, which decided to reverse the Appellate Division's judgment.

Here is the appeals court's reasoning behind that decision:

> The attachment by law enforcement officers of a GPS device to the automobile of a criminal suspect, and the use of that device to track the suspect's movements, was a search subject to constitutional limitations. What happened in this case was a search also, within the meaning of Article I, § 12 of the New York Constitution and the Fourth Amendment; the State does not contend otherwise. But the State argues, and we agree, that this search is within the "workplace" exception to the warrant requirement recognized in *O'Connor v. Ortega*.

O'Connor involved the warrantless search by a public employer of the office of an employee suspected of misconduct. The Supreme Court upheld the search. The plurality opinion explained: "In our view, requiring an employer to obtain a warrant whenever the employer wished to enter an employee's office, desk, or file cabinets for a work-related purpose would seriously disrupt the routine conduct of business and would be unduly burdensome. Imposing unwieldy warrant procedures in such cases upon supervisors, who would otherwise have no reason to be familiar with such procedures, is simply unreasonable."

Petitioner here does not challenge the existence of a workplace exception to the warrant requirement, but argues that it is inapplicable because the object of the search in this case was petitioner's personal car. Petitioner asks us to confine the exception to "the workplace itself, or workplace-issued property that can be seen as an extension of the workplace." We reject the suggestion, at least insofar as it would require a public employer to get a warrant for search designed to find out the location of the automobile an employee is using when that employee is, or claims to be, working for the employer.

The *O'Connor* plurality observed that such items as a personal photograph on an employee's desk, or a personal letter posted on an employee bulletin board, are part of the workplace (480 U.S., 716). The location of a personal car used by the employee during working hours does not seem to us more private. Petitioner was required to report his arrival and departure times to his employer; this surely diminished any expectation he might have had that the location of his car during the hours he claimed to be at work was no one's concern but his. We are unpersuaded by the suggestion in the concurring opinion that, on our reasoning, a GPS device could, without a warrant, be attached to an employee's shoe or purse. People have a greater expectation of privacy in the location of their bodies, and the clothing and accessories that accompany their bodies, than in the location of their cars.

The reason that led the *O'Connor* Court to dispense with the warrant requirement was the serious disruption that such a requirement would entail, and the burden it would impose on supervisors. We thus conclude that when an employee chooses to use his car during the business day, GPS tracking of the car may be considered a workplace search. The Inspector General did not violate the State or Federal Constitution by failing to seek a warrant before attaching a GPS device to petitioner's car. While the search did not require a warrant, it did not comply with either the State or Federal Constitution unless it was a reasonable search. We conclude that the State has failed to demonstrate that this search was reasonable.

Thus, the court claimed that the GPS device placed on Cunningham's personal car clearly fell under the workplace exception and therefore did not require a warrant. As the court explained, requiring a warrant for workplace searches would be too burdensome and disruptive. And tracking an employee's car used for work during the business day should be considered a workplace search. But the search also has to be reasonable, and the court goes on to explain why in this case it did not meet that standard.

The *O'Connor* plurality summarized the approach of courts to the question of reasonableness in this way: "Determining the reasonableness of any search involves a twofold inquiry: first, one must consider whether the action was justified at its inception; second, one must determine whether the search as actually conducted was reasonably related in scope to the circumstances which justified the interference in the first place. The search will be permissible in its scope when the measures adopted are reasonably related to the objectives of the search and not excessively intrusive in light of the nature of the misconduct."

Under *O'Connor*, a workplace search based on a reasonable suspicion of employee misconduct is "justified at its inception." The search in this case clearly meets that test. Petitioner's employer had ample grounds to suspect him of submitting false time records.

The appeals court concluded that the search met the first criterion of reasonableness because it was based on a just foundation. There was adequate evidence over a long period to suspect that Cunningham was submitting false time reports. But what about the scope of the search that is the basis for the second criterion? The appeals court had problems with the search's scope, because it considered the GPS tracking to be too intrusive under these particular circumstances. The judges' comments on the scope issue constitute the most decisive part of their opinion:

> We cannot find, however, that this search was reasonable in its scope. It was, in the words of *O'Connor*, "excessively intrusive." It examined much activity with which the State had no legitimate concern, i.e., it tracked petitioner on all evenings, on all weekends and on vacation. Perhaps it would be impossible, or unreasonably difficult, so to limit a GPS search of an employee's car as to eliminate all surveillance of private activity especially when the employee chooses to go home in the middle of the day, and to conceal this from his employer. But surely it would have been possible to stop short of seven-day, twenty-four hour surveillance for a full month. The State managed to remove a GPS device from petitioner's car three times when it suited the State's convenience to do so, twice to replace it with a new device, and a third time after the surveillance ended. Why could it not also have removed the device when, for example, petitioner was about to start his annual vacation?
>
> It is true that none of the evidence used against petitioner in this case resulted from surveillance outside of business hours. Ordinarily, when a search has exceeded its permissible scope, the suppression of items found during the permissible portion of the search is not required. But we hold that rule to be inapplicable to GPS searches like the present one, in light of the extraordinary capacity of a GPS device to permit constant, relentless tracking of anything. Where an employer conducts a GPS search without making a reasonable effort to avoid tracking an employee outside of business hours, the search as a whole must be considered unreasonable.

In presenting its case, the State of New York had acknowledged that GPS tracking was intrusive, but it claimed that Cunningham's prolonged pattern of misconduct and the difficulty of "constant in-person surveillance" justified the use of this technology. The court sided with Cunningham's lawyers, however, who argued that in this case the use of GPS technology involved an "unprecedented degree of government intrusion."[53]

Although it had problems with the intrusive GPS tracking, the appeals court did not suggest that Cunningham should be spared from discipline by DOL, since only 4 of the 11 charges depended on GPS evidence. Below are the judges' concluding remarks:

> The consequence of suppression in this case is not to preclude the State from disciplining petitioner. As the majority and the dissenting Justices in the Appellate Division agreed, only four of the 11 counts on which petitioner was found guilty depended on GPS evidence, and only those four charges need be dismissed. As to the others, the GPS evidence was either substantially duplicated by E-ZPass records or was wholly irrelevant. Whether the seven surviving charges warrant the same or a lesser penalty is a matter to be decided, in the first instance, by the Commissioner of Labor on remand.
>
> Accordingly, the judgment of the Appellate Division should be reversed, with costs, charges one, two, three and six against petitioner dismissed, and matter remitted to the Appellate Division with directions to remand to the Commissioner of Labor for redetermination of the penalty.

- Do you agree or disagree with the ruling in this case? Was this individual's right to workplace privacy violated? Should a worker's personal vehicle used during the workday be exempt from the workplace exception established in *O'Connor v. Ortega*? Do you agree with the State's contention that given the prolonged misconduct, the use of GPS technology was warranted?

- More generally, are privacy rights violated when workplace searches are conducted without a warrant (as allowed by *O'Connor v. Ortega*)?

- What should be the moral and legal limits of GPS monitoring? If you were a human resource executive, how would you craft a GPS monitoring policy for your company?

CONCLUSION

While previous chapters have examined the corporation's obligations to external constituencies, this one focuses on obligations to internal constituencies such as the corporation's employees. The axis of discussion is the rights of those employees, especially the right to a safe environment, free from all forms of abuse, and the right to privacy. While employees do not have a right to their jobs, they do have the right to due process when there is a layoff or when they are dismissed for cause. The right to a decent and safe work environment, free of harassment and sexual pressures, is given special emphasis. The case on sexual harassment, however, illustrated some of the obstacles involved in discerning whether sexually oriented behavior rises to the level of harassment. Finally, the case on employee privacy rights underscored the acute legal and moral problem with tracking employees (for valid reasons) through potentially intrusive technologies such as GPS.

Student Study Site

Visit **edge.sagepub.com/spinello.**

Key Terms

due process   322

employment-at-will   319

flexicurity   333

sexual harassment   325

Review Question

1. Explain the corporation's duties to its employees. What is meant by employment-at-will, and how is this idea tempered by employee rights? What is wrong with sexual harassment?

Discussion Questions

1. In your opinion, what are the most important employee rights? Do employees have the right to express themselves publicly on issues of concern to them? Which rights are least tolerated by employers?

2. What do employees "owe" their employer?

GLOBALIZATION AND CORPORATE RESPONSIBILITY

PART V

13

GLOBAL POLITICS AND DISINVESTMENT STRATEGIES

Modernity is inherently globalizing.

—Anthony Giddens[1]

The global corporation has become a major actor in world politics.

—Richard Barnett and Ronald Müller[2]

LEARNING OBJECTIVES

Upon completion of this chapter, you should be able to:

13.1 Illustrate the economic and ethical challenges multinational companies face when they do business abroad.

13.2 Explain the history, dynamics, and moral challenges of globalization.

13.3 Apply the course framework to the moral dilemmas that arise in an international context.

In the final three chapters of this book, we turn our attention to globalization issues, which add another layer of complexity to ethical decision-making. Multinational firms are the primary drivers of the flow of goods and capital across borders as measured by foreign direct investment (FDI). Multinationals are companies that engage in FDI through acquiring an existing firm in a foreign country or by making a greenfield investment involving construction of a new operation. These companies invest in countries with moral and cultural differences along with diverse interpretations of political sovereignty. They often do business in emerging and frontier economies that are suspicious of foreign investment and wary of a large foreign presence.

The general theme of this chapter is the interactions between multinationals and their host governments. In some countries, there is excessive political and ethical risk that stems from unstable governments or institutional voids such as weak judicial systems that are supposed to enforce the law and set rules for businesses. Companies must learn to navigate these risks and to manage them as prudently as possible. A multinational might suddenly find itself suddenly confronted with a threat to its economic viability when there is a surge of nationalist sentiment or there are changes in a country's political leadership. United Fruit, for instance, enjoyed a fairly stable relationship with the Guatemalan government for decades until a socialist president was elected to office and threatened to seize all its property. What is the proper political behavior of multinationals in such a situation, and to what extent can they become politically engaged to protect their interests? Are political maneuvers aimed at regime change ever justified, or should companies always be politically neutral?

In some countries, the political situation can deteriorate so badly that the only option seems to be economic disengagement. Many multinationals thrust in this situation, however, have avoided this strategy. In the 1930s, some American firms doing business in Germany refused to leave even though they found themselves providing indirect assistance to the Nazi war effort. Companies have offered different rationales for remaining in countries with unjust laws or repressive regimes, such as Burma in the 1990s. Despite pressures from stakeholders, the French energy firm, Total, remained in Burma, and justified this policy by claiming that its presence there helped the Burmese people by providing jobs and enhancing the local infrastructure. But is this justification ethically warranted? Under what circumstances should companies refrain from doing business in countries where there are human rights abuses and rampant corruption?

The chapter commences with a briefing that provides a working definition of globalization. It also considers the history of global capitalism along with the disruptions that can lead to deglobalization. This discussion will provide some historical context for the cases in this chapter as well as those in the next two chapters. The briefing also examines in some depth the three prime challenges for multinationals in developing economies, including the political and ethical risks of expanding into countries where there are different social norms, and where free-market principles are less firmly entrenched.

AN OVERVIEW OF THE CASES

The globalization briefing is followed by two comprehensive case studies. The first case examines the issue of political activism and the extent to which a corporation can engage in political activities to safeguard its vested interests in a particular country. International Telephone and Telegraph (ITT), a major U.S. conglomerate, found itself in an awkward situation when the Marxist leader Salvador Allende was on the brink of being elected to the presidency of Chile. ITT had sizable investments in Chile, including a majority-ownership stake in its national telecom company. Its properties were threatened, and ITT responded with a heavy-handed political strategy. Was it proper for ITT to work against Allende's election by financing the campaign of the opposition right-wing candidate?

The second case treats the intricate issue of disinvestment or economic disengagement. In the case called "Rubber at any Price: Firestone and the African Strongman," the Ohio-based tire company must decide about retaining its rubber plantation in the midst of a brutal civil war. The only way it can remain is to make payments to the despotic leader, Charles Taylor, who will use this money to help finance his bloody revolution. At the same time, many Liberians working on the plantation depend on Firestone for their livelihood, education, and medical care. Should this paternalistic corporation remain in Liberia and make the payments to Taylor, or abandon its plantation along with the Liberians who work there?

Both cases confirm that, despite their economic power, multinationals are often ill equipped to understand or shape the social and political environment in which they operate. The cases also highlight the exceptional risks and moral ambiguities of doing business in emerging economies where there is periodic political instability along with nationalist or socialist sentiments that lead rulers to turn against foreign multinational corporations (MNCs) as a way of asserting their own power.[3]

BRIEFING ON THE HISTORY AND CHALLENGES OF GLOBALIZATION

Before we plunge into the globalization cases, it is instructive to develop some historical perspective. There is a common assumption that globalization is a purely contemporary phenomenon that has only recently sprung forth with the help of modern technologies. However, **globalization**, broadly defined as the "process of increasing integration in world civilization," is not a new paradigm.[4] It first gained momentum in the 19th century when Europe and other parts of the world, including the Americas, became increasingly interdependent. Globalization should be distinguished from *globalism*, which is an ideology or mindset. Globalism represents the conviction that globalization is something natural and positive and that global governance should take precedence over national sovereignty whenever possible.[5]

Globalization can be more precisely defined in economic, political, social, or cultural terms. Since our focus is on the economic aspects of globalization, a more instructive definition is the following: "the integration of economic activities across borders, through markets."[6] Goods, capital, and people move freely across borders, driving an expansion of national economies. Economic forms of globalization can lead to cultural globalization, the development of global forms of identity and activity. This occurs, for example, when diverse people from various cultures rely on smartphones and apps made by Apple or play the same video games.[7]

Globalization is often interpreted as an inevitable by-product of Western capitalism and modernization. New and innovative technologies are often a primary driver of globalization. Also, in order to sustain revenue and profit growth, companies eagerly expand abroad when their domestic markets are saturated. Thus, globalization seems to be a permanent feature of capitalist markets. This sentiment is echoed in the writings of Marx and Engels, who foresaw the continuing expansion of global capitalism as one of its abiding perversions. In *The Communist Manifesto*, they write, "The need of a constantly expanding market for its products chases the bourgeoisie over the entire surface of the globe. . . . In place of the old local and national seclusion and self-sufficiency, we have intercourse in every direction, universal inter-dependence of nations." [8] However, there is certainly room for disagreement with Marx's polemical analysis. While the process of global capitalism's expansion seems inexorable, history tells a different story. Global expansion is contingent on many historical and political forces and is not a fixed attribute of capitalist markets. [9]

Globalization: A Brief History

The precariousness of globalization is reflected in its long but nonlinear history, which can be divided into four distinct periods. The first era of economic globalization extends from the mid-19th century until 1914, the outbreak of World War I. The second extends from World War I through 1950. During this time the globalization movement suffered a series of shocks that set back the progress made during the 19th and early 20th centuries. The third period, beginning around 1950 and extending to 1980, represents the rebuilding of the global economy through liberal trade policies and increases in foreign direct investment (FDI). In the fourth period, about 1980 to the present, there has been a potent revival of globalization with a concomitant acceleration in worldwide economic growth. [10]

Globalization has strong Eurocentric origins. During much of the 19th century, there was relative peace and political stability in Europe. As a result, economies expanded in European countries such as the United Kingdom and Germany, and there was a significant increase in international trade. That expansion of trade was enabled by the adoption of liberal economic policies in most European countries, which overcame mercantilism and its brand of noninclusive capitalism. These countries shunned high tariffs or restrictive quotas that protected favored local producers. The integration of this first global economy was driven primarily by technological developments in transportation (such as the railroad and steamship) and communications rather than by policy changes. [11] Thanks to the telegraph, electronic communication between Europe and the United States became possible for the first time when a trans-Atlantic cable connection was completed in 1866. Imperialism, which kept colonies captive to the economic demands of the empire, also defined this era of globalization.

During this period, Europe was the export leader in manufacturing goods while it was also the net importer of primary products. [12] The world was prospering on global trade. The report of a bad harvest in Australia might mean lower prices on the London stock exchange the next day. European imperialism augmented these global linkages—advertisements in London newspapers recommended holidays in India or the Sudan. [13] Foreign direct investment also increased substantially during the prewar years. There was a high level of multinational manufacturing but also foreign investment in agricultural and raw materials. Buoyed by success in their domestic markets, companies like Bayer and Siemens in Germany and Lever Brothers in the United Kingdom built manufacturing plants around the world. Lever Brothers' plants could be found in 33 countries, including the United States, Canada, Australia, and South Africa.

By 1913, with the world on the brink of war, foreign direct investment reached $14.5 billion. World trade grew from about $8 billion in 1896 to $18 billion in 1913. Multinational companies had extensive operations in countries ranging from Russia to Australia. Globalization had clearly begun to impact many aspects of human life in the 19th century, although its impact was imbalanced. Despite rising political tensions, there was optimism that the world was too economically interdependent to afford a strong reassertion of the nation-state and sustained armed conflict.[14]

Nonetheless, the first era of globalization came to an abrupt end with a series of violent political shocks beginning with World War I, which created economic turmoil and disintegration. The war was accompanied by the Russian Revolution that led to the systematic expropriation of foreign property in Russia.[15] The new Russian government nationalized the banking system and confiscated all private enterprises. Many U.S. companies, including Singer, Kodak, and Otis Elevator, lost their substantial Russian assets.[16]

The war traumatized most of Europe and led to the demise of Great Britain as a commercial and financial power. The burdensome reparations demanded from Germany at the Treaty of Versailles not only sowed the seeds for future conflict but destabilized the world financial system. And just as the world economy was recovering in the postwar period, economic growth in the United States began to stall, and an inflated stock market crashed in October 1929. As international financial markets collapsed along with it, much of the world found its way on the pathway to autarky or economic self-sufficiency. In America, the tariffs authorized by the Smoot-Hawley Act (1930) put major restraints on foreign trade. In retaliation, tariffs were substantially increased throughout Europe.[17]

The world also had to contend with a fascist economic order: Hitler in Germany, Franco in Spain, and Mussolini in Italy. Relations between business interests and these states were tense, and economies suffered due to government controls and the diversion of resources to the military. The Japanese government also assumed many of fascism's worst features. The rise of fascism led to the final shock of World War II, which began in Europe in September 1939 when Hitler's troops crossed over the Polish border, and in the United States after Japan's bombing of Pearl Harbor on December 7, 1941. The heavy resources demanded by the war effort put the global economy under severe strain and stifled economic growth. The war impacted international trade policies immediately as trade between warring military blocs ceased completely.[18]

As relative calm descended on the world after the defeat of Germany and Japan, rebuilding efforts got under way, and globalization began a steady renewal process. This postwar period beginning in 1950 marks the third period of globalization. Liberalization displaced protectionist policies in most countries, and foreign trade expanded. The United States led the way in foreign direct investment. Major corporations like IBM, General Electric, Pepsi, and Ford began making sizable capital investments abroad in new plants and distribution networks. Like the United States, Japan was especially committed to foreign investment during this period. Most of its biggest companies expanded globally through inexpensive capital made available through Japan's insulated financial markets. Japan's targeting of certain strategic industries led to the rise of companies like Hitachi and Fujitsu, which challenged IBM on the world stage. Japan, the United States, and Europe were now the undisputed leaders in foreign direct investment. By 1973, the United States had already invested $200 billion around the world, almost three-quarters of it in the advanced industrialized countries.[19]

However, there were still many restrictions on the flow of goods, capital, and people across borders. Investment in developing countries such as those in Latin America and Asia remained modest, thanks to the risky political climate and poor economic conditions. In addition, the Soviet Union and China excluded multinational companies and remained essentially isolated from the global economy. In some cases, decolonization in countries like India led to hostile reactions against corporations of the former colonial power and against FDI in general.[20]

The fourth period of globalization and economic expansion began in the early 1980s. One of the prime drivers of this phenomenon was the new telecommunications and computing technologies that facilitated information flows. Networked digital technologies, which have reshaped the global economy, are inherently connective, and they can greatly reduce the transaction costs of producing and selling products in the global marketplace. They can also help large and small enterprises to cultivate markets for globalized forms of mass culture.

Also significant was the collapse of communism in Russia and Eastern Europe. The implosion of these autarkies drove these nations outward. They opened their economies, privatized some industries, and began the massive task of deregulation. In addition, China began implementing free-market policies in the 1980s and joined the World Trade Organization (WTO) in 2001. China's low wages and tax structure became a major catalyst behind the sudden rise of offshoring, as companies moved factories to China and other low-wage countries in order to dramatically decrease their cost structures.

There was also a further decline in protectionism during these decades, as trade once again became an engine of growth. To some extent, falling tariffs reflected the growth in regional trade groups such as the European Union, NAFTA (U.S., Canada, Mexico), and Latin America's Mercosur. NAFTA led to an expansion of U.S. investment in Mexico during the 1990s. Moreover, most developing countries no longer opposed or restricted the entry of multinationals. Instead, there was an eagerness to attract foreign direct investment, which was welcomed as a partial solution to high unemployment, poverty, and other social ills.

What distinguishes this second wave of global expansion from the first wave that ended in 1914 is the absence of formal imperialism and the emergence of non-Western forms of globalization and capitalism. Top-down or state-guided capitalism as currently practiced by China is proposed as a better path to prosperity and global power. This second wave also has a broader scope, with Asian economies playing a bigger role in the shape of global markets. Unlike the first wave, there is a high level of foreign direct investment originating from Asian economies. India's conglomerate, Tata Group, has invested heavily in Western companies such as Tetley Tea. Chinese companies have also invested heavily in the West. In 2010, the Swedish Volvo brand was purchased by Chinese carmaker Zhejiang Geely. In 2016, the giant Chinese white-goods manufacturer Haier purchased the appliance business of General Electric to solidify its market presence in the United States.[21]

Global foreign direct investment flows reached their peak in 2007, hitting a record $2 trillion. More than half of that amount went to developing countries like China. In 2016, global FDI flows were $1.6 trillion, which represented a 7% drop from 2015. Some see this decline as a sure sign of globalization's prolonged retrenchment.[22]

What does the future hold for economic globalization? Will a new surge of nationalism curtail economic integration and expansion? England's exit from the European Union (Brexit) and the election of nationalists like President Donald Trump have been construed as tectonic forces that will cause globalizing forces to recede. Populist politicians have consistently highlighted globalization's weaknesses and flaws. In addition to the drop in FDI, there are other tangible signs that globalization may be taking a U-turn. Since the 2008 financial crisis, global trade has fallen from 32% of GDP (gross domestic product) in 2008 to about 28% in 2016.[23] Many companies are localizing production and importing fewer components for assembly. According to the World Bank, global supply chains stopped growing around 2011 after expanding 4% a year for almost two decades.[24]

As we have seen, the history of globalization is nonlinear, with upward surges and sharp reversals. In some parts of the world, like the Middle East, the legacy of history trumps the expansionist logic of capitalism. A resurgence of similar political or ethnic conflicts in Thailand or other Southeast Asian countries could also curtail investment by global firms. Globalization is historically contingent, and there is no proven way to prevent its contraction. It's possible that globalization's expansion over the last four decades is a historical anomaly. If more countries adopt inward-looking polices, we might witness a "return of history," with globalization forces in another dramatic retreat. The future of economic globalization remains as uncertain and unpredictable as ever.[25]

Challenges for Multinationals

Crossing borders raises unique strategic, organizational, and ethical challenges for multinational firms. They encounter alien practices, policies, and cultures, along with a different set of moral norms and laws. One author tersely expresses this experience as "the liability of foreignness."[26]

Cultural Distance

The extent of this liability correlates to the distance between the home economy of a multinational and the host economy. There are four dimensions of this "distance": political, geographic, economic, and cultural. **Economic distance** implies a different economic system or reliance on economic policies alien to those in an MNC's home country. The rules for competing under state-guided capitalism will usually be far different from the rules of competition in a traditional capitalist economy. **Political distance** implies an unfamiliar policy environment along with different regulatory processes. **Cultural distance** includes dissimilarities in linguistic heritage, religious or philosophical beliefs, ethical standards, and social norms. Each type of distance can affect a multinational in different but dramatic ways.[27]

If MNCs invest in countries within reasonable geographic proximity to their home country and with similar political systems, distance issues are minimized. But consider the case of the fast-food chain McDonalds. Opportunities for growth in the United States and in most developed economies have been constrained for some time by an oversaturation of restaurants. So it has turned to countries like Russia, which it now designates a "high-growth market." McDonald's has even opened a restaurant in the Siberian town of Tomsk. In Siberia, every dimension of "distance" is great—the restaurant chain must operate in a country with a difficult and hazardous climate, along with an immature infrastructure and underdeveloped supply. The political scene differs vastly from that of the United States, and the cultural divide includes dissimilarities in social norms and linguistic heritage.[28]

Cultural Relativism

While the cases in this section touch on political and policy issues, our principal focus is the moral and social tensions that inevitably arise from foreign direct investment. How can the multinational corporation accommodate cultural distance by handling normative differences with both moral sensitivity and strategic effectiveness? In effect, corporations must typically make a difficult choice: *either adapt to new cultural and moral norms or challenge those prevailing norms, even if it threatens a host country's sovereignty.*

In some cases, this represents a stark choice and even a "no-win" situation for a multinational. For example, should a multinational endorse the inferior workplace safety standards in certain emerging economies? If they adapt to these lower safety norms, which are culturally acceptable in these countries, they might be accused of having a double standard. On the other hand, if they challenge those norms by introducing higher "Western" standards, they can be accused of cultural imperialism.

To some extent, how companies resolve this dilemma depends on their views about **cultural relativism**, which claims that morality is relative to a given culture. Moral rightness is measured in terms of local custom and social tradition. Intercultural comparisons of moral values are considered pointless. A moral claim such as "adultery is wrong" means only that "adultery is disapproved in culture X." This standard assumes some semblance of objective validity only through the settled habits and attitudes of that culture. Moral norms, therefore, are regarded strictly as a matter of cultural and social consensus. If this proposition is true, the philosophy of cultural relativism provides a warrant for a corporate policy of adaptation to local ethical standards. If there are no universal standards, multinationals have little choice but to play by local rules when doing business abroad.[29]

The rise of relativism has been motivated to some degree by cultural and anthropological studies that seemed to confirm moral cultural diversity. Margaret Mead, for example, presumably demonstrated that Western moral standards were nothing special and actually worse than the more libertine standards of the Samoans. However, other anthropologists have demonstrated that Mead's research was ill informed and inaccurate. There are also conceptual problems with cultural ethical relativism. Relativism in its extreme form degenerates into moral nihilism, since there are no objectively valid moral laws governing interpersonal behavior. Anything approved by a particular culture, including genocide or racism, must be tolerated by other cultures. Most reasonable people cannot accept these consequences and prefer the teaching of Aristotle, who argues for a "universal law" or "law of nature," binding on all persons, "even on those who have no association or covenant with each other."[30] Given our common humanity, there must be *some* transcultural standards or rights that protect human life and health and forbid abuses such as slavery.[31]

Also, social relativists have not been clear and consistent on the standard or "unit of measurement" they are adopting in order to determine a society's consensus about a specific moral practice. Is morality relative to a culture, a society, a whole country, or an ethnic group within that country? This arbitrariness in the determination of a standard is a major flaw in the theory of cultural ethical relativism. The implication of repudiating the claims of cultural relativism is that the international marketplace is not a "moral-free zone," where companies can adapt to local cultural norms with impunity.[32]

If there is a small set of transcultural moral principles, which Donaldson and Dunfee call "hyper-norms," they provide "a thin universal morality" but also leave room for the "moral free space" that allows respect for intercultural diversity.[33] Those standards can be concretely described in terms of universal rights, as we discussed in Chapter 3. Rights give normative recognition to our fundamental equality as human beings. Without the cover of normative ethical relativism, which is an implausible theory, MNCs face a more difficult ordeal when doing business in different cultures. They must find a way to be sensitive to cultural differences without accommodating injustice by violating these basic rights.[34]

Political and Ethical Risk

Companies that do business abroad are usually prepared for the economic risks associated with foreign direct investment, trade, and outsourcing. That risk can be exceptionally high, particularly in capital intensive industries. Consider the supermajor oil companies that invest billions in exploration projects in foreign locales. Sometimes their efforts to find oil or natural gas are futile and they end up losing their sizable up-front investment.

But companies are often ill prepared to navigate the political and ethical risks associated with FDI and trade. **Political risk** simply refers to the possibility that political decisions or events in a particular country will cause foreign investors there to lose money or fail to capture their expected returns. Political risk in developing countries usually arises from feeble legal and judicial systems, provisional institutions, volatile urban areas, and fragile political regimes. In countries like China and Russia, there is a different breed of political risk. Under state capitalism, government favoritism toward domestic firms can threaten a multinational seeking to gain market share. Also, within these economies business is sometimes used as an instrument of state power. Deals with Russia's state-controlled natural gas giant, Gazprom, can be easily complicated by political considerations. The effects of taking on such risks can be an unjust resolution of legal matters, expropriation of foreign holdings, or just a loss of business thanks to biased government policies that promote domestic companies. The most severe of these risks is expropriation. No business will invest in a country where there is a likelihood that the sovereign authority will seize its properties. Whenever government policy decisions or political events can affect the profitability of foreign investments, political risk exists.[35]

Consider the abnormally high political risk of investing in the Middle East. This region still has an abundant supply of oil and gas and remains a highly attractive venue for industries such as oil, petrochemicals, and aluminum smelting. Governments are eager to attract new firms in an effort to diversify their economies. The opportunities are great, but the political risk is excessive. The dual threats of terrorism and ethnic strife still hover over much of the region. As the world has witnessed, countries such as Libya, Iraq, and Syria, which were once promising investment destinations, can easily turn into violent conflict zones.[36]

Multinationals are even less prepared to prudently manage ethical risk that is most often found in countries with weak political institutions or countries with a history of corruption. **Ethical risk** can be defined as the risk that a company will violate its core values and participate in the deprivation of human rights or fail to protect those rights. When MNCs operate in dangerous environments or in countries where laws are poorly enforced, the risks of violating their values increase exponentially. After a series of scandals, Chiquita Banana developed a set of core ethical principles as a guide for its managers in foreign environments. But in Colombia, where law enforcement once ceded authority to paramilitary groups, the company was asked to make extortion payments to one of those groups in order to protect its employees and its property. It reluctantly agreed, even though it knew the money would be used to buy guns that might kill innocent civilians. But in these exigent circumstances, Chiquita saw little choice but to transgress its code of conduct along with common moral values.

Ethical risk also arises for companies operating in places where domestic law fails to uphold and protect certain fundamental human rights. China does not have the same regard for democratic free expression as most Western countries. Thus, dissident political speech, which is protected in Western liberal democracies, is forbidden throughout China. Internet companies like Yahoo and Google, which pride themselves for being platforms for free expression, complied with China's censorship demands in order to have a presence in China. These companies sacrificed one of their core values, support for free and open communication, because they were motivated by the economic potential of this new and expanding market.

At a minimum, complex economies like China require careful planning that proactively anticipates and manages the possibilities of ethical risk, including the risk of human rights incidents and their potential fallout. The most important recommendation for multinationals is to take politics and ethics more seriously when doing business abroad and to understand that political economy is a far more intricate subject than pure economics.[37]

Disinvestment

One of the most vexing questions for any multinational is disinvestment or economic disengagement. Sometimes MNCs must abandon a foreign operation on moral grounds, either because the regime is repressive or because its laws are transparently unjust. During World War II, many companies like IBM and ITT chose to stay in Germany until the war began despite the fact that they were forced to comply with the racist laws of Nazi Germany and discriminate against their own Jewish workers. Their reputations were tarnished with disgrace for many years for failing to disassociate themselves from Nazi ideology and the palpable evils of the Third Reich. But there are other cases where the decision to withdraw is not so simple or obvious.

In some situations, economic sanctions will be imposed to prevent multinationals from doing business in countries where human rights are being violated on a significant scale. Many countries, including the United States, imposed sanctions on Iran because of alleged human rights abuses and the country's close ties to terrorist organizations. Those sanctions were lifted in 2016 in exchange for restrictions on Tehran's nuclear weapons program. But companies like Boeing were criticized for doing business with Iran and for not maintaining a corporate policy of disengagement. In 2017, Boeing negotiated a deal with the Iranian government for the sale of 60 of its most popular jets to an Iranian airline. But critics of the deal pointed out that despite the lifting of official sanctions, Boeing should refrain from selling aircraft to Iran. Iran remains a staunch ally of the Syrian government, which has allegedly used chemical weapons against its own citizens. There are also concerns about ongoing human rights abuses and the role of Iran's powerful Revolutionary Guard Corps, a hard-line paramilitary force with members who have wide and sometimes opaque economic interest. Without the shield of sanctions, multinationals must decide whether to invest in or trade with Iran, or if they should continue to avoid commercial relations with this country until there are more salutary political changes.[38]

As a guideline for those multinationals that must make these hard choices, Thomas Donaldson has proposed a "condition of business principle" that centers on the violation of human rights. The violation of rights causes great harm, and third parties such as MNCs should not be complicit in bringing about this harm. Every country, including democracies like the United States, sometimes violates fundamental human rights. The arrest of all Japanese U.S. citizens during World War II is just one example. We cannot expect MNCs to confine their business activities to perfect democracies.

Hence, it is more realistic to argue that a country must be a *systematic violator of basic human rights* before it is subject to trade sanctions or other forms of economic disengagement. The basic human rights we have in mind were discussed in Chapter 3 and include free expression, the right to life and health, the right to own property, and the right to be free from slavery and torture. Recall that these fundamental rights, which are rooted in our common humanity, were defended as necessary conditions of human flourishing. Although there is some room for a culturally informed interpretation of how to specify and properly limit some of these rights (like free speech), there comes a point where such limits become unreasonable if they virtually nullify the right in question. There is a big difference between limiting the right of free expression by forbidding pornography for minors (United States) and forbidding any form of political dissent (China).

With these observations in mind, we offer this modified version of Donaldson's condition of business principle:

> Ceteris paribus, business transactions by an MNC with a foreign country are morally unacceptable when that country is a systematic violator of fundamental rights, unless those transactions actually discourage the violation of rights or harm or, at a minimum, fail to benefit that country in consequence of its rights-violating activities, or unless the withdrawal of that MNC's business will cause a moral catastrophe or severe injury to innocent people (such as deprivation of vital goods or services).[39]

The exemptions from the condition-of-business principle must be carefully and conscientiously applied. The termination of business in any country will injure some people, but such injury usually doesn't rise to the level of a moral catastrophe. But if a pharmaceutical company's abrupt departure from a rights-violating country meant that innocent people would no longer have access to life saving drugs, a case could be made for its continued presence. The general moral principle is simple: it is unjust to transact business within corrupt regimes that systematically violate the human rights of their innocent citizens. These transactions presuppose a mutual economic advantage between the multinational and the host country. Therefore, a multinational's presence in a rights-violating country means that it unjustifiably helps that country to benefit from its unjust policies and actions.

Summation

Regrettably, the history of global capitalism has a dark side. There are many examples of multinationals that have behaved irresponsibly in order to remain in a country and take advantage of profitable markets. Others, such as firms in the tobacco and oil industries, have been content with regulatory arbitrage, that is, following the weaker regulations of a host country rather than the more stringent standards established by their home countries. Still other MNCs have simply been inept at managing social and political interactions in foreign countries. In the cases that follow this briefing, we will have an opportunity to see firsthand the acute challenges of trying to be a responsible multinational in the midst of economic tensions and radically diverse cultures. Success or failure will depend on many factors. But, above all, multinationals should be more aware *in advance* of the potential for abuse or misconduct and the sympathetic chords any allegations of abuse will strike in their home countries.[40]

CASE STUDY 13.1

ITT IN CHILE: CORPORATE EXECUTIVES AND MARXIST PRESIDENTS

Thanks to the emergence of nationalism and socialism after World War II, multinationals struggled to preserve their financial empires. In some countries, MNCs were unable to protect their assets from expropriation by sovereigns eager to assert their independence from the West. Those companies unwilling to relinquish their assets sometimes resorted to tactics that were ethically questionable and largely ineffective.[41]

This case describes the experience of the U.S. conglomerate ITT in Chile. When a Marxist president, Salvador Allende, came to power, ITT sought to thwart his regime's progress and bring about his downfall. ITT's actions have become a symbol of corporate aggrandizement. But was its strategy an abuse of corporate power or merely the realpolitik of doing business in risky foreign environments? Above all, this case highlights the close relationship between foreign investment and a country's political environment.

The Rise of ITT

The 1960s in the United States was the age of the conglomerate. Successful companies diversified into different industries to spread their economic risk. One such conglomerate was International Telephone and Telegraph, or ITT. The original International Telephone and Telegraph was created in 1920 by two brothers in the Virgin Islands named Sosthenes and Hernand Behn, who began their careers as sugar brokers in Puerto Rico. They recognized the potential of the telephone and purchased the bankrupt Puerto Rico Telephone Company that eventually became ITT. Their goal was to build the first worldwide system of interconnected telephone lines.

At first, the company operated inconspicuously in Puerto Rico and Cuba. But it expanded rapidly through key telecom acquisitions, such as Compania Telefonica de Espana (now Telefonica) in 1923 and the purchase of numerous telephone patents. In the United States, it purchased several companies from Western Electric. ITT was backed by J.P. Morgan in these acquisitions, and several Morgan partners served on its board. The end result was the creation of a major international provider of telephone-switching equipment and telecommunications services.[42]

ITT's growth slowed during World War II but accelerated again in the postwar period. Harold S. Geneen, a former accountant, became CEO in 1960. He was known for his "tight, buttoned-up control system," and his intimidation of subordinates. Under Geneen's leadership, ITT was transformed from an electronics company into a "global service bazaar."[43] Geneen, the principal architect of ITT's conglomeration strategy, led ITT through 250 acquisitions that incorporated 2,000 separate business units. The diverse portfolio of businesses included Sheraton hotels, Avis Rent a Car, Hartford Insurance, and the maker of Wonder Bread. When he retired as ITT CEO and chairman of the board in 1979, revenues had grown from $800 million to $22 billion. ITT's earnings had grown from $30 million to $560 million. ITT was a global economic powerhouse that employed over 400,000 workers. It was the fifth-largest employer in the United States.[44]

The conglomeration model, however, quickly fell out of favor on Wall Street as investors began to prefer more focused companies. These highly diversified companies were hard to manage due to their size and complexity. It became difficult for big conglomerates like ITT to cope with the demands of specialized markets and rapid change. Soon their performance began to falter, and massive conglomerates had to make rapid market adjustments. The stock market imposed a "conglomerate discount" on companies like ITT. Investors still wanted diversity but preferred well-defined strategies of related diversification and narrow scope.[45]

Subsequent to its prosperous conglomerate years, ITT began a painful restructuring process. It divested itself of many businesses and acquired others in an effort to achieve the right mix. In 1995, ITT split into three separate and independent companies: ITT Corporation, which was focused on the hotel and gaming businesses; ITT Hartford, which became a stand-alone insurance operation; and ITT Industries, a group of manufacturing companies. Only ITT Industries retained the name, and in 2011 it split into three again: ITT Corporation, a maker of sophisticated pumps and brake pads; Xylem, a water technology company; and ITT Exelis, a defense company.[46]

Early Ethical Controversies

From its founding, ITT had a strong presence in international markets. By the early 1970s, it was making half its profits from operations located outside the United States.[47] Throughout its long history, ITT was no stranger to controversy in its international business dealings, especially in prewar Nazi Germany. In 1930, ITT acquired the giant electronics firm Standard Elekrizitäts A.G. which included two manufacturing plants. On the board of Standard Elekrizitäts was Baron Kurt von

Schröder, a Nazi banker and prominent leader of the Nazi movement. ITT also purchased C. Lorenz AG of Berlin, which became its major German subsidiary.

Like IBM, which operated in Germany throughout the decade of the 1930s, ITT apparently saw no ethical conflict in doing business within the Nazi regime. It made no efforts to distance itself from the Nazi war machine. ITT and its leaders had cordial relations with both Hitler and Goering before the war. In August 1933, Sosthenes Behn, who was then the CEO of ITT, met with Hitler shortly after his election. In addition, Colonel Behn flew from New York to Madrid to Berne during the war to help offer some advice for the improvement of Hitler's communication systems. There have also been allegations that certain ITT subsidiaries made cash payments to the notorious SS (Schutzstaffel) leader Heinrich Himmler. These payments allowed ITT to protect its various assets and investments in Germany.[48]

Regrettably, ITT companies continued to supply communications equipment to Germany despite the clearly racist policies and atrocities of the Nazi government. Even after World War II began, ITT fulfilled its contracts to the German military for switchboards, telephones, alarm gongs, air raid warning devices, radar equipment, and 30,000 fuses per month for artillery shells used to kill British and American troops. ITT's communication services provided direct support for the Nazi war machine all throughout the war.[49] In addition, its German subsidiary, C. Lorenz AG, with the approval of Colonel Behn, purchased a 25% stake in Focke-Wulf AG, a Bremen company that made sophisticated fighter planes for the German Luftwaffe. The investment was made in 1939 at the outbreak of World War II. The Focke-Wulfs dropped bombs on much of London during the early phases of the war and were later used on British and American troops.[50] At the same time, ITT equipment was being used by the Americans. Anthony Sampson points out the paradox: "While ITT Focke-Wulf planes were bombing Allied ships, and ITT lines were passing information to German submarines, ITT direction finders were saving other ships from torpedoes."[51] Sampson goes on to conclude that "the only power [Behn] consistently served was the supranational power of ITT."[52]

ITT and Allende's Chile

During the 1960s, ITT had expanded its operations into Latin American countries, including Chile. One of ITT's many foreign-owned properties was Chitelco, the national Chilean Telephone Company. ITT had a 70% interest in this company while the remaining 30% was held by the Chilean Development Corporation. The estimated book value of Chitelco was about $153 million. ITT also owned two major hotels in Chile along with an international cable company. The total value of ITT's Chilean investments was estimated to be $160 million. With such a substantial presence in a country with a volatile political history, the political risk was exceptionally high, and ITT executives were always vigilant during the country's elections.

Harold Geneen paid particular attention to Chile's 1970 presidential election and the candidacy of Salvador Allende, an avowed Marxist. The president at that time, Eduardo Frei Montalva, a Christian Democrat, was completing his six-year term and was ineligible for reelection. At first, Allende's chances of success were dismissed by political experts. This was Allende's third attempt to win the Chilean presidency. In 1958 and

1964, he ran on a Marxist/communist platform and was soundly defeated. The other two candidates in 1970 were Rodimiro Tomic Romero from the Christian Democrat Party and Jorge Alessandri Rodriguez, who was the candidate of the right-wing National Party. Allende campaigned on a program of extensive land reform and the nationalization of basic industries. Alessandri, on the other hand, gave his unequivocal support to the free-market system.[53]

As Allende's campaign gained momentum in the late spring of 1970, ITT became increasingly apprehensive about his victory and its future prospects in Chile. Other U.S. companies operating in Chile, including PepsiCo, Chase Manhattan, Kennecott Copper, Anaconda, and Ford, also voiced their concerns about the economic consequences of a possible Allende presidency.

Unlike most of its corporate counterparts in Chile, however, ITT took decisive action. It wanted to help ensure Allende's defeat, and so it approached the U.S. Central Intelligence Agency (CIA), which was also opposed to Allende. John McCone, an ITT director, held conversations with CIA director Richard Helms. McCone asked Helms if the United States intended to intervene in the election since Allende's policies were in opposition to the American national interest. But Helms told McCone that a decision had been made by Secretary of State Dr. Henry Kissinger that nothing of consequence would be done. Geneen was greatly disappointed by this news. On July 16, 1970, Geneen met with William Broe, chief of the CIA's Clandestine Services. At that meeting, Geneen offered to accumulate a "substantial" election fund for Jorge Alessandri that would be controlled and channeled through the CIA. The CIA, however, rejected ITT's magnanimous offer. In this hour-long meeting, Broe informed Geneen that the CIA was not supporting any candidate in the Chilean election.[54]

But ITT was undeterred. It asked the CIA's advice about a reliable individual who could funnel money to the Alessandri campaign. At another series of meetings, the CIA gave ITT representatives some advice about how to securely transmit funds to Alessandri and the National Party. With the help of reliable intermediaries recommended by the CIA, $350,000 was passed by ITT officials to the Alessandri campaign in the weeks prior to the September election. The CIA knew about these donations, but it did not directly assist ITT.[55]

ITT also funded a right-wing, anti-Allende newspaper known as *El Mercurio* by means of increased advertising. In August 1970, Ned Gerrity, ITT's vice president for corporate relations, instructed Chitelco to increase its ads in *El Mercurio* and other conservative publications by 50%. Later he explained that the ad campaign was designed to boost revenues for these papers "to keep editorial voices alive." ITT officials also encouraged the United States Information Agency (USIA) to circulate *El Mercurio*'s anti-Allende editorials throughout Latin America.[56]

On September 4, 1970, Salvador Allende narrowly won the election by a margin of 39,000 votes. He had 36.3% of the popular vote compared with 35.3% for Alessandri. However, since no candidate had an absolute majority, the Chilean constitution mandated that its congress had to choose between the first- and second-place finishers. The congressional election was scheduled for October 24, 1970. On September 9, Alessandri announced that if he were elected by the congress, he would resign, and this would open the way for President Frei Montalva to run again. The consensus was that Frei Montalva would easily defeat Allende. This plan became known as the Alessandri formula.[57]

In addition, on September 9, the ITT board of directors met in New York, and Geneen again expressed his dismay over the political situation in Chile. He told McCone after the meeting that he was prepared to spend up to $1 million in support of a U.S. government plan to galvanize a coalition of those opposed to Allende in the Chilean congress in order to stop Allende's election. The offer was made to both Kissinger and Helms through McCone, who told them that Geneen would be willing to come to Washington to discuss his interests in Allende's defeat. But Geneen's offer was turned down.[58]

A week later Bernard Goodrich, an ITT public relations man, visited the offices of the USIA in Washington. He told the agency that ITT was supporting *El Mercurio* with increased advertising, and he once again encouraged them to circulate *El Mercurio* editorials opposing Allende throughout Latin America. Goodrich asked if ITT could do anything more, but USIA officials told him that ITT should not do anything that could be interpreted as intervention.[59]

However, as the Allende election became more likely, Dr. Kissinger advised President Nixon to mobilize U.S. efforts to oppose Allende covertly but as strongly as possible. The president agreed, and Kissinger instructed the CIA to implement Track I and Track II. Track I entailed taking political action, such as providing monetary support for opposition candidates, while Track II called upon the CIA to arrange for the possibility of arranging military intervention in Chile. CIA officials secretly contacted Chilean military officers to determine if there was the possibility of a coup. For a number of reasons, however, the Track II initiative was not carried forward.[60]

As part of the Track I initiative, the CIA's William Broe proposed a plan to ITT executives in late September to foment "economic chaos" in Chile as a means of putting pressure on the Christian Democrats in Chile's congress to vote against Allende. The idea was to work with other multinationals and U.S. banks with a stake in the country to freeze American business contacts with Chile by denying technical assistance, bank loans, and so forth. However, the plan was rejected by Geneen as unworkable and unrealistic, and he decided not to implement it.[61]

On October 18, 1970, Alessandri withdrew from the run-off election in the Chilean congress. On October 24, Salvador Allende was elected president, receiving 153 of the 195 votes cast. He was sworn in as president of Chile on November 4. Upon his election, Allende promptly extended diplomatic recognition to communist countries including North Korea, North Vietnam, and Cuba. From the inception of his presidency, Allende was perceived as an existential threat to the U.S. multinationals operating in Chile. His rise to power was regarded by the Nixon administration as a portentous development and cause for alarm.

Cold War politics infused American perspectives at the time. With Allende's election, there was now another communist threat in this hemisphere, a new populist leader to stand alongside Cuba's Fidel Castro. In 1961, President Kennedy had authorized the Bay of Pigs invasion of Cuba to overthrow the communist government of Fidel Castro. But this attempted coup was a fiasco, and Castro remained in power. In 1971, Nixon and Kissinger worried that Chilean Marxism would spread to other countries. There was undoubtedly concern that funding from Moscow might be forthcoming. Kissinger's advice to Nixon was to mobilize "quietly and covertly . . . to oppose Allende as strongly as we can and do all we can to keep him from consolidating power."[62]

However, Allende was not another Castro. He had won the presidency in a peaceful, democratic election. He opposed the Cuban economic model as too extreme, and also opposed armed struggle to achieve political power. This belief set him apart from revolutionaries like Che Guevera. His chief concern was to cure Chile of economic injustice, which, in his view, had been partly inflicted by multinational corporations that had been doing business there for decades. He advocated a doctrine of "geo-political sovereignty" and Chilean self-determination. He accused multinationals of making "excess profits" while paying Chile's workers meager wages. Allende simply wanted Chile to determine its own economic destiny and become a "U.S. free" economic zone.[63]

Expropriation

After Allende's election, ITT changed its strategy toward Chile. In January 1971, ITT executives persuaded other American companies like Anaconda and Bank of America to form an ad hoc committee on Chile for the purpose of "pressuring Kissinger and the White House." One purpose of this pressure was to get the U.S. government to block loans to Chile from the World Bank and other institutions. These maneuvers would foster economic problems in Chile, and the prospect of economic collapse might make Allende more willing to negotiate with ITT and perhaps desist from taking expropriatory action.[64]

Nonetheless, with Allende in power, ITT knew that its property was in grave danger of government seizure. Allende had campaigned on a platform calling for the expropriation of the assets of American corporations. On May 26, 1971, ITT was informed that Chitelco would be nationalized and that a commission headed by the Ministry of the Interior was being organized to negotiate the terms of this confiscation. ITT's response was that the Allende government had to pay the full book value of the company, $153 million. But the Chileans agreed to pay only $24 million for ITT's interest in Chitelco. On September 29, 1971, the new president, true to his word, took full possession of Chitelco, confiscating the books of the company. The government took immediate control and fired all the workers at the telecom company because it claimed that Chitelco was deliberately allowing service to deteriorate. ITT vehemently denied those allegations.

Shortly after this confiscation of ITT's property, the Allende government also nationalized the copper mines of Kennecott and Anaconda. These companies along with ITT protested vigorously, but to no avail. Kennecott, however, filed lawsuits in France, Sweden, Germany, and Italy to block all payments to Chile for any nationalized copper sold in those countries.[65] The Chilean president loudly rebuked ITT during a speech at the UN General Assembly in late 1971. He denounced ITT as an agent of "economic imperialism" that had attempted to bring about "civil war" in Chile.[66]

ITT did not sit idly by while its properties in Chile were being seized by the new government. After its property was confiscated, ITT continued to put pressure on the Nixon administration to do something about Allende. In October 1971, a year after Broe proposed his plan to instigate economic chaos in Chile, William Merriam, head of ITT's Washington office, proposed to Peter Peterson, special assistant to the president, a similar plan to "accelerate economic chaos" in Chile with the goal of destabilizing the Allende regime. The detailed plan included a number of specific measures such as loan restrictions, bringing about a scarcity of U.S. dollars in Chile, delaying purchases from Chile for six months, and using American copper instead of buying from Chile. The hope was to prevent Allende from getting through the next six months, but the 18-point plan was never directly acted upon by Peterson.[67]

Aftermath

On September 11, 1973, a coup organized by Chile's military forces overthrew the Allende regime. The coup was led by Augusto Pinochet. As Pinochet's troops invaded the presidential palace, Allende committed suicide rather than facing capture and imprisonment. General Pinochet succeeded Allende and ruled the country as a military dictator for 17 years. The CIA has admitted knowledge of the plot but insists it had no direct involvement. According to a CIA report on these events, the agency "was aware of coup-plotting by the military, had ongoing intelligence collection relationships with some plotters, and—because the CIA did not discourage the takeover and had sought to instigate a coup in 1970—probably appeared to condone it." [68]

ITT certainly played no direct role in the violent coup that eventually overthrew Allende. But it soon had to face up to serious allegations that it had interfered in Chile's internal political affairs. Before Allende's victory, ITT had attempted to manipulate the election by offering a substantial fund to the CIA to support the conservative candidate. When that offer was turned down, it had still found a way to funnel $350,000 to the Alessandri campaign just before the popular election. It had also been willing to spend $1 million to support a U.S. government plan to build a coalition in the Chilean congress to stop Allende's election. ITT had supported the country's anti-Allende newspaper with increased advertising and urged the USIA to circulate its editorials throughout Latin America. It had also seriously considered CIA plans to sow the seeds of economic chaos in Chile, but rejected those plans not on ethical grounds but because they were too impractical. After the Allende election, ITT had been the moving force behind an ad hoc committee dedicated to persuading Kissinger and the White House to put economic pressure on Chile. And it had proposed to President Nixon's office plans for a concerted campaign to weaken the Allende government through the acceleration of economic turmoil in Chile.[69]

During the hearings of the U.S. Senate Subcommittee on Multinational Corporations, ITT was chastised for its belligerent attitude toward the Allende regime. But the company seemed generally unrepentant. "What's wrong with taking care of number one?" asked ITT executive Ned Gerrity. But should taking care of number one imply that multinationals ought to have some role to play in setting the operative U.S. foreign policy in countries like Chile?[70]

- Describe the history and culture of ITT and how they might have influenced its behavior in the context of its challenges in Chile.

- How do you assess ITT's behavior in this case? Were any of its political activities in Chile morally valid? Is it legitimate to support political candidates in foreign countries through political contributions?

- What kind of political action would have been morally permissible in Chile under these circumstances?

- How could ITT have managed the political situation in Chile more responsibly? What might you have done if you were in Harold Geneen's shoes?

CASE STUDY 13.2

RUBBER AT ANY PRICE: FIRESTONE AND THE AFRICAN STRONGMAN

Firestone Tire and Rubber, one of the world's oldest and largest tire companies, sourced a sizable portion of its natural rubber from a massive plantation in the African country of Liberia. When the autocratic dictator Charles Taylor thrust the country into civil war in the early 1990s, Firestone was faced with a painful choice. It could either abandon its plantation or do business with Taylor, who was a true menace on the African continent. The company chose the latter option and made "tax" payments to the Taylor regime of several million dollars. This case is about Firestone's fateful decision to

cooperate with Taylor and his rebel forces. It also surveys the criticism that unfolded when these events came to light in 2014 thanks to the work of reporters from the Public Broadcasting System (PBS) and Pro Publica.

There have certainly been other countries with repressive leaders who have denied their citizens fundamental rights and flaunted the use of violence in the name of progress. Multinationals cannot always confine their business activities and foreign investment to cooperative and peaceful democracies. But how bad does it have to get before a company is morally obliged to leave a country where there are egregious human rights abuses? When is disinvestment the only morally reasonable option?

Firestone Tire and Rubber

The Firestone Tire and Rubber Company was founded in 1900 by Harvey S. Firestone. It remained a family-owned and -managed business for much of its long history. In its early years, Firestone forged a close commercial relationship with Ford Motor Company. It began supplying Ford with rubber tires for its Model T in 1908 and remained a chief supplier of original equipment (OE) tires for many more decades. In addition to OE tires, Firestone sold replacement tires directly to consumers in its own chain of 1,500 stores and in other retail stores such as Sears Roebuck. It produced its tires in several domestic plants located throughout the United States and in 12 plants located in nine foreign countries. Firestone established its corporate headquarters in Akron, Ohio, which became known as "Rubber City."

In this highly concentrated industry, where scale economies were a key success factor, Firestone's rivals included Michelin, Bridgestone, BF Goodrich, and Goodyear. These companies vied for market share in an intensely competitive world market. By the 1970s, Firestone was the second-largest tire manufacturer. During the decade before, the tire industry had been disrupted by a new technology: the radial tire. Although French tire maker Michelin had introduced radial tires to the U.S. market in the late 1960s, Firestone and other American companies resisted the trend. BF Goodrich, however, quickly responded and introduced its own radial brand in 1967. Radials were in demand because they were safer and lasted longer than regular bias-ply tires. Firestone soon realized the radial tire was the future of the tire industry and began to retool its factories. Automakers like Ford and GM insisted that tire manufacturers, including Firestone, supply radial tires for their new cars and trucks. In 1972, Firestone made commitments to supply both manufacturers with 433,000 radial tires per month.[71]

Although it was late to the radial market, Firestone soon leapt ahead of its rivals when it became the first company to produce steel-belted radial tires. The Firestone 500, the company's flagship brand, became the leading selling radial on the market. However, rather than build a dedicated radial factory to produce the 500 series, Firestone decided to convert its factories and modify its existing equipment. In this way, it could ramp up production more quickly to forestall the progress of Michelin and Goodyear and achieve automakers' requirements. Regrettably, this "quick fix" led to serious quality and safety problems. The tire's steel cords failed to properly adhere to the rest of the tire.[72]

From 1972 through 1978, Firestone was entangled in a critical product safety controversy over its Firestone 500 tire. Safety defects such as the adhesion problem led to numerous accidents and eventually a major recall of 14.5 million tires that cost the company $160 million. Despite substantial evidence of safety problems, Firestone remained in denial and on the defensive. Firestone CEO Richard Riley said that his company agreed to the recall not because the tires were defective but only because of the unfair negative publicity. Firestone recovered from this debacle in the 1980s but lagged behind industry rivals with only a 13% market share.[73]

In 1988, Firestone merged with its Japanese competitor, Bridgestone, which purchased a 75% equity stake in the U.S. company. The challenge of integrating these two organizations, with their diverse structures and cultures, was formidable. The effort was overseen by Yoichi Kaizaki, who took control over the process upon his arrival in Akron in 1991. He divided the company into 21 operating divisions, cut costs, and rationalized production. In March 1993, he was chosen as CEO of Bridgestone Firestone (BFS) and returned to Japan.[74]

BFS still relied heavily on sales of original equipment tires to manufacturers like Ford. It supplied its ATX radial tires for the popular Ford Explorer, introduced in 1990 to take advantage of the expanding SUV market. In 1992, drivers began to complain about tire failure and tread separation, which could cause the Explorer to roll over. The complaints mounted, but neither Ford nor BFS took decisive action. By 2000, BFS had received 1,500 claims for property damage and injuries. There were also several fatalities attributed to rollovers caused by the defective tires. As retailers like Sears pulled the radials from their shelves, Ford and BFS announced a recall. BFS found itself in the midst of its second prominent tire controversy in 20 years, complete with congressional hearings, lawsuits, and endless recriminations from Ford.

BFS survived the ill effects of this second recall and safety dispute, and in 2013 it proudly celebrated the 25th anniversary of its historic merger. Thanks to that merger, BFS has become the world's largest tire company, with a 22.4% market share, followed by Michelin with a 20.3% share. It had impressive revenues in 2017 of $32 billion.[75]

Firestone in Liberia

Liberia is a rather unique African country. It is the oldest of Africa's republics with a Western orientation that is not present in other African cultures. But Liberia's image has been tainted by a long-running civil war along with its role in the rebellious history of its neighbor, Sierra Leone. Liberia is composed of 16 ethnic and cultural groups. In addition, with the help of a charity known as the American Colonization Society, it was settled in the early 19th century by freed American slaves. This colony declared its independence in 1847, when it chose the name Liberia, or "Land of Freedom." The freed American slaves who migrated to Liberia hoped it would become a haven for other escaped or freed slaves who fled from the United States. However, full citizenship of this sovereign country was confined to this elite group of "Americo-Liberians," while members of the country's indigenous native tribes were denied equal rights. Liberia's repatriated leadership built a political and economic system that mirrored the plantation economy of the American South. It distinguished between the so-called "masters" or "*kwi*" and the "second-class" members of the different tribes. This inegalitarian system laid the groundwork for much of the political and social upheaval in Liberia during the last century.[76]

Liberia has an agrarian economy, but due to incessant internal strife and its long civil war, there is a legacy of high unemployment, poor health care, and low literacy. A succession of revolutions devastated the infrastructure, and the government has been slow to rebuild. Most of its inhabitants are extremely poor. Nonetheless, the country is blessed with ample natural resources, especially its abundant rubber trees. Its primary exports are rubber, timber, iron, diamonds, and cocoa. The void created by Liberia's diminished capacity to provide vital services for its citizens has often been filled by multinationals with concessions to extract those resources. Like many African countries, Liberia inspires both opportunities and wariness for multinationals.

In the 1920s, entrepreneur Harvey Firestone set out to find new sources of natural rubber, the main raw material for tires. Rubber trees grow only in very warm climates near the equator. Firestone's explorers soon uncovered a huge swath of rubber trees in Liberia. At the same time, this impoverished country was anxious to attract foreign investment to boost its economy. Hence it welcomed the opportunity to do business with Harvey Firestone and his expanding enterprise.

In a remarkable deal, the Liberian government signed a concession agreement with Firestone for a 99-year lease for a million acres of land full of rubber trees. The price was only 6 cents an acre. This tract of land constituted close to 10% of Liberia's arable land mass. Initially, Firestone developed two separate plantations: the 220-square-mile Harbel plantation in Margibi County with 8 million rubber trees, and the 31-square-mile Cavalla plantation in Maryland County. It later sold off the Cavalla plantation. At the peak of their production, these plantations employed almost 20,000 workers, half of whom were "tappers" who extracted the rubber (or latex) from the trees. However, as the demand for natural rubber declined during the 1980s, Firestone contracted its operations and laid off a large number of workers.[77]

The Harbel plantation, which employed about 8,000 workers, had its own latex-processing plant as well as its own infrastructure, including a water supply and electricity. There were 40 U.S. expats directing operations on the plantation. They resided in executive housing immersed in a beautiful section of the plantation known as Harbel Hills. Firestone managers could relax at their own country club situated on a nine-hole golf course. The African workers lived in huts scattered about the property. Firestone provided many community services, including schools, churches, clinics, electric power stations, and even two radio stations.[78]

The production of natural rubber involves three basic stages: planting, production (or tapping), and processing. The process revolves around the life cycle of the rubber tree. The rubber tree is fragile, especially after it is first planted. These trees reach maturity in seven to eight years but are ready to be tapped for their latex after three years. The rubber is collected from trees in a cup attached to the tree below a deep cut made in the tree's bark. The tappers gather the cups full of lumps of rubber and return them to the field stations. The rubber is then sent to an initial processing facility on the plantation, where it undergoes heat treatment. It is then packed into slabs ready for export.[79]

Nearly half of all rubber output is used for automotive and truck tires. Thanks to the expanded use of synthetic rubber, natural rubber accounts for only 44% of world rubber consumption. With Firestone's help, rubber quickly became the foundation of Liberia's economy. The rubber plantations were the primary source of employment, and rubber was the chief export. The rubber industry employed 30% of the population. Firestone's Harbel was by far the country's most productive and efficient plantation. It was also Liberia's largest employer and its biggest source of exports. However, the rubber industry in Liberia was confined to extracting latex from the trees and forming it into slabs for shipping. There was no secondary rubber processing, which entails shredding, hanging, and drying this raw material so that it could be formed into finished rubber blocks. Given the plenitude of this natural resource, Liberian leaders often spoke about industry expansion, perhaps even inviting companies to invest in rubber-processing plants. But that possibility never materialized. Part of the problem was undoubtedly the unstable political environment along with the country's poor transport system and weak infrastructure.[80]

Charles Taylor and Liberia's Civil War

Firestone was deeply enmeshed in the volatile political scene of Liberia. The company always strived to promote positive relationships with Liberia's despotic and mercurial leaders, such as William Tubman, who was president of Liberia from 1944 to 1971. Tubman ruled the country as a virtual dictator, but he welcomed FDI and cultivated policies to increase exports. He had a positive and cordial relationship with Firestone. Tubman was succeeded by William Tolbert, whose relationship with Firestone was more antagonistic. In the mid-1970s, he renegotiated the Liberian government's contract with Firestone, which raised taxes and mandated more Liberians in senior management.[81]

The Tolbert presidency was later thrust into turmoil during a dispute over an increase in the price of rice. Riots broke out in 1979, and the "settler rule" imposed by the Americo-Liberians was in jeopardy. Tolbert suppressed the riots with brute force, but a full-scale revolution was soon under way. After a violent coup in which Tolbert was executed, Samuel Doe came to power in 1980. Doe was far more friendly to Firestone than some of his predecessors, but things took a terrible turn for Firestone when Charles Taylor began his ruthless pursuit of the Liberian presidency.[82]

Charles Taylor was born in 1948. As a young man, he spent some time in the United States, taking business courses at Bentley University in Waltham, Massachusetts. Upon his return to Liberia, Taylor joined up with the revolutionary forces of Samuel Doe. Taylor took part in the uprising of April 12, 1980, under the leadership of Samuel Doe. The successful coup was supported by a large segment of the population who hoped that Doe was serious about economic reforms. A new military rule was established by Doe's party, the People's Redemption Council. Doe appointed the young and well-educated Taylor as the director general of the General Services Agency (GSA), an organization that was responsible for making procurements for the government. In 1983, he was removed from the post because he had allegedly stolen about $1,000,000 from the GSA for his own personal use. When Taylor fell out of favor with Doe, he became a marked man and sought refuge in the United States, where he had once studied. When President Doe requested his immediate return from the United States, Taylor was captured and arrested. But while awaiting extradition, he made a daring escape from the Plymouth County House of Corrections in Massachusetts. He eventually made his way to Libya, where, with the help of Muammar Gaddafi, he was trained in military and revolutionary tactics.[83]

Taylor then moved to the Ivory Coast in West Africa and in 1989 formed the National Patriotic Front of Liberia (NPFL), a group of revolutionaries. From the Ivory Coast, the NPFL began preparing for war, with the aim of ousting President Samuel Doe. When Doe took control of the government, he was heralded as a reformer, but little changed under his leadership. Instead he became quite unpopular thanks to his brutal tactics and erratic behavior. There was rampant corruption and theft along with the torture and murder of dissidents. Under Doe, there was the same autocracy and repression that had poisoned the political climate of Liberia for many decades. Also, his ethnic group, the Krahns, progressively aggravated ethnic tensions in Liberia while Doe was in power. The failed economic reforms and the ethnic tensions were enough to give Taylor a base of popular support, especially with Gio and Mano ethnic groups.[84]

Taylor was convinced that the presidency of Liberia was his destiny. He built up his army as he recruited soldiers of all ages, including young children, who became known as the infamous Small Boys Unit. Members of this unit were as young as eight years old, and they were often given drugs to stiffen their nerve for battle. Soon his troops invaded Liberia, and the First Liberian Civil War began. As Taylor's undisciplined "Freedom Fighters" marched to Monrovia, Liberia's capital, they terrified everyone in their path. Within the next year, under Taylor's leadership, the NPFL took over a sizable segment of this war-torn country.[85]

Many towns and villages were devastated by the fighting. Liberians faced the grim knowledge that they would be mired in this bloody conflict for many long years. Charles Taylor's and the NPFL troops are estimated to have been responsible for thousands of deliberate killings of civilians. They targeted innocent civilians of the Krahn and Mandingo ethnic groups, both of which the NPFL considered supporters of President Doe's government. Doe's tribe, the Krahn, were slaughtered in especially high numbers, and almost two-thirds of the tribe took flight from their country. Troops loyal to Doe also killed many Gio and Mano people who were sympathetic to Taylor. Accordingly, Human Rights Watch warned about a possible genocide. In 1990, 20,000 Liberians were killed, most of them civilians.[86]

In June 1990, on their way to Monrovia, Taylor's army met with few pockets of resistance. Soon they invaded the Firestone plantation. The young soldiers terrorized workers, commandeered trucks and other vehicles, and killed anyone suspected of being an ally of Doe. They were quickly repelled, however, by the Liberian army. Government troops used their own brutal tactics to suppress the NPFL, and their oppressive behavior inspired many young men on the plantation and in the region to join forces with Taylor's insurgency. During the fighting, Firestone's plantation manager, Donald Ensminger, and his fellow expats took refuge in his house, an elegant Georgian-style mansion known as House 53. But they were not safe from these warring factions, and Ensminger informed Firestone headquarters that they had to abandon the plantation. On June 14, 1990, with the help of U.S. military personnel from the Liberian embassy, Firestone's American expats were safely evacuated and returned to the United States. They were quite relieved to be back in Rubber City, far removed from the ongoing hostilities on the Liberian plantation in Harbel. According to a Firestone spokesperson, there was "little that could be done" for the 8,500 Liberian workers left behind.[87]

Firestone's Bargain with Taylor

In late 1990, a new Interim Government was established under a West African Regional Peace Initiative. Its president was Amos Sawyer. The Interim Government replaced Doe, and its military forces controlled the small enclave around Monrovia. By this time, Taylor and his band of mutineers had overtaken much of the country, but they had still failed to capture Monrovia. Every attempt to seize the capital had failed. At the same time, government troops could not snuff out the NPFL insurrection. Taylor set up his own government, choosing the village of Gbargna as his capital. He appointed a cabinet of ministers and continued to fortify his army. Taylor also controlled the country's prize commercial possession: the sprawling Firestone plantation and its valuable rubber trees. His soldiers occupied the plantation territory, but without proper leadership and know-how, there was very little rubber production.[88]

Meanwhile, Firestone had to decide what to do about one of its most precious and irreplaceable resources. Firestone wanted to get its stored rubber out of Harbel and resume production on the plantation. The company was concerned not only about the fate of its Liberian assets but also about the welfare of its former workers. Thousands of Liberian workers and their families depended on the plantation for their livelihood. They were cut off from receiving vital services from Firestone (such as food supplies and medical care) that they had relied on for many years. Also, Harbel was a profitable operation in what had become a challenging economic environment for Firestone. In its last full year of operations (1989), the plantation had reported $104 million in revenue and about $16 million in profits. Firestone's new partner, Bridgestone, seemed keenly interested in keeping the plantation in the company's hands. The giant company was struggling after this merger, and every source of profit and positive cash flow was welcome.[89]

To preserve the plantation's value as a productive asset, time was of the essence. It would be suicidal to leave the plantation in the hands of Taylor and his rebel troops for an extensive period. Trees were not being planted, the fruitful rubber trees were not being properly cared for, and the plant and equipment were rapidly falling into disrepair. A well-qualified and properly managed workforce was necessary in order to plant, maintain, and harvest the trees. The weeding and pruning of fields and the young trees were being neglected, yet all of this was integral for efficient production. The longer the plantation was neglected, the longer it would take to restore the plantation and reach adequate production levels.[90]

Despite the turbulence of Liberia over many decades, Firestone had done little contingency planning in the event it lost this source of rubber. It soon located alternative sources of rubber in Asian countries like Vietnam, but the quality was inferior to the rubber produced in Liberia.[91] The Harbel plantation supplied about 40% of the U.S. market for latex and 10% of the world market. The value of the plantation, including the land, the trees, the processing plants, buildings, and equipment, was estimated at about $200 million. If Firestone cut ties with Liberia, it would lose this source of high-quality rubber, and it would not be able to salvage its valuable assets.[92]

With these factors in mind, Firestone executives in Akron deliberated about how to proceed, hoping the conflict would be soon resolved. But when that did not happen, the company decided to initiate the process to resume operations in Liberia. Since the NPFL controlled the plantation, Firestone had to deal with Taylor rather than Amos Sawyer and the Interim Government. One notable obstacle for Firestone was the policy of the U.S. government. The State Department had instructed U.S. companies to refrain from establishing commercial relations with Taylor and the NPFL. But Firestone decided to ignore the State Department's advice. In a memo outlining its plans for Liberia, there is the notation "State Department consent not expected."[93]

Firestone officials met with Taylor on July 3, 1991, and both sides agreed on a process to resume operations in Harbel with NPFL support and protection. But in exchange for its safe return to Liberia, the company was required to treat Taylor's government as the official government of Liberia. This meant that all fees and taxes would be paid to Taylor and the NPFL. The company also had to consent to hire all the workers left stranded by its abrupt departure. Firestone reluctantly agreed to all of these terms. They also committed to a major capital investment to repair and refurbish the plantation. In return, Taylor's security forces would protect the plantation and its workers and the seized housing would be returned. The Firestone board agreed to the plan, and in January 1992, Firestone managers were on their way back to Liberia. Full-scale operations were resumed by May.[94]

According to a memorandum of understanding signed in January 1992, Firestone agreed to pay Charles Taylor and the NPFL an annual sum of $2 million in exchange for NPFL protection. In early 1992, Firestone began making its payments to Taylor. Company records show that by the end of 1992, Firestone had paid out $2.3 million in taxes, rents, and other fees to the NPFL. An additional $35.3 million was spent to rebuild the plantation. Battered buildings were fixed and new equipment was purchased.[95]

The nature of these payments to the NPFL and the way this money was spent has become a source of significant debate. First, Taylor himself has verified that the funds were used to finance his revolution. According to Taylor's testimony at his war crimes trial at the Hague, Firestone's payments "became at that particular time our most significant principal source of foreign exchange." Second, while Taylor controlled much of Liberia, his forces had not yet captured Monrovia, so the NPFL wasn't the official government of Liberia. How could these payments be considered legal or classified as a "tax"? The United States and other Western countries had not given any diplomatic recognition to the rogue Taylor regime. They officially recognized Sawyer and the Liberian

Interim Government. But, in the eyes of Firestone, Taylor and the NPFL were the de facto government, and what they paid were government taxes and not some sort of bribe or extortion payoff. U.S. officials in Monrovia, however, including Ambassador William Twaddell, claimed that they were unaware of these "tax" payments.[96]

The new plantation manager, Ronald Weihe, kept his promise to Taylor and rehired thousands of Liberians. More than 6,500 Liberians were soon back at work, planting saplings, pruning, and tapping the mature rubber trees. Other Liberians were rehired to help run the plantation's operations. By September 1992, the production level had reached 4 million pounds of latex. At Taylor's insistence, the workers were paid half in Liberian currency and half in U.S. dollars. Without access to Monrovia, Weihe was forced to create a new transportation system that enabled Firestone to use the port in nearby Buchanan to export its liquid latex. The port was controlled by Taylor, who pocketed the fees paid by Firestone for the privilege of using this facility to ship its products. Taylor, still in hot pursuit of Monrovia, also used the plantation as a "staging ground" for some of his military escapades. About 1,000 men belonging to Taylor's rebel force lived on the plantation.[97]

During this same year, Taylor initiated Operation Octopus, aimed at seizing Monrovia. Once again the Firestone plantation functioned as the "launching pad" for the attack. But after weeks of savage fighting, the NPFL was unable to establish a foothold in the devastated capital city. The government's troops went on the offensive against Taylor, who was planning the attacks in his war room, one of the plantation's guesthouses. A counterattack by the government's small air force targeted the plantation. Some planes dropped bombs while others strafed innocent workers below. Forty-two people were killed and over 200 others were injured in the prolonged assault. After the bombing spree, Weihe and his managers once again concluded that they could not safely remain on the plantation. On November 20, they departed for the Ivory Coast and then returned to the United States. Bridgestone Firestone's CEO, Yoichi Kaizaki, pointed out that Firestone hoped to return and restore operations at Harbel, but for now it was just too dangerous to stay in this war-ravaged country. Nonetheless, Firestone estimated that it had made about $1.1 million in profits during this period when its plantation operations were resumed.[98]

In the ensuing years, Taylor made one last effort to retake Monrovia, but his efforts failed. The civil war dragged on, and there was still no peace in Liberia. After a series of transition governments, Taylor and the Liberian ruler Sami Abacha reached an agreement to hold elections. Taylor was elected as Liberia's president in 1996. The results were a surprise to many, but the Taylor forces were well organized. People also feared that if they didn't vote for Taylor, the country would be thrust back into another prolonged civil war.

During his time as president, Taylor was as ruthless and avaricious as ever. He had little regard for basic human rights or a free press. He siphoned off money from the government for his own personal use. Over the years, the government of Charles Taylor became increasingly intolerant of dissent. Liberia became known for its harassment of civil society and human rights groups. Taylor was also intolerant of Liberia's independent media. Journalists who criticized the government were usually promptly arrested. In addition, members of the rival Mandingo and Krahn tribes were singled out for indiscriminate persecution based on their ethnicity.[99]

Evidence shows that Taylor was also directly involved in Sierra Leone's bloody and protracted civil war. Tax payments went right into Taylor's personal accounts, and he used some of that money to finance the rebellion in Sierra Leone. The Liberian leader supplied weapons to the country's Revolutionary United Front (RUF) in exchange for blood diamonds. The RUF committed many atrocities against civilians and were notorious for hacking off limbs to terrorize the population into submission. Taylor also helped plan the capture of diamond mines and the invasion of Freetown.[100]

Despite his lofty promises, there were no serious economic reforms under Taylor. As a result, in 1999, a rebellion against his government began in northern Liberia by the Liberians United for Reconciliation and Democracy (LURD). By early 2003, the rebels had gained control of northern Liberia. They were joined by new factions and quickly proceeded to seize Monrovia. Taylor's troops, greatly outnumbered, were easily subdued by the rebels, and Taylor soon surrendered. He was forced into exile in Nigeria and was succeeded several years later by a new president, Ellen Johnson-Sirleaf. There were still political tensions in Liberia, but the incessant turmoil and brutalities of its protracted civil war had finally come to an end.

When Taylor was elected president, Firestone concluded that the political situation was stable enough to resume operations as Kaizaki had promised. The Liberian government, unable to operate the plantation without Firestone's help, eagerly sought the company's return. In 1996, Firestone began rehiring workers to make repairs, and by March 1997, Firestone had exported 370,000 gallons of its latex to France. The company has remained in Liberia since 1996, and it is once again the country's largest employer, with 6,100 workers at its Harbel plantation. Firestone has invested $147 million in the country, including infrastructure, a new high school on the plantation, and the renovation of worker homes. The plantation boasts one of the best hospitals in Africa.[101]

In March 2006, Taylor was arrested for crimes against humanity and sent to Sierra Leone. He was tried at the Hague, where he was convicted by an international tribunal of arming and abetting a rebel movement that committed mass atrocities during its civil war in the 1990s. However, the tribunal judges ruled that the prosecution failed to prove that Taylor had directly commanded the rebels responsible for the atrocities. Nonetheless, he was the first head of state to be convicted by an international court of perpetrating "war crimes" since the Nuremberg trials of World War II. Prosecutors claimed that Taylor's role in the devastation of Sierra Leone was motivated not by ideology but by greed, his insatiable quest for money and power. Taylor was sentenced to 50 years in prison. In 2013, Taylor was sent to the United Kingdom to serve the remainder of his sentence, and he is currently locked up in a British jail cell.[102]

In the eyes of its supporters, Firestone's commitment to Liberia and its natural rubber industry over the years is commendable. It has helped the Liberian economy through its know-how and its employment of so many workers. It has given Liberia a chance to be a world player in the export of rubber. With only small rubber plantations, the Liberian rubber industry had been far less productive prior to Firestone's arrival. The company also improved the quality of life in Liberia through its investment in infrastructure, schools, and community development. According to *Fortune*, Firestone "has been an unquestionable force for good and a rare source of economic livelihoods."[103] However, Firestone has also been strongly critiqued for its payments to the Taylor regime, especially before his election. How could it support such a ruthless leader even after he became Liberia's democratically elected president?

Firestone Responds

In 2014, when the story broke about Firestone's payments to Taylor in 1992, the company answered several questions for PBS reporters who were planning a documentary for its *Frontline* series focused on these tragic events. According to their statements, the company had to acknowledge the Taylor government and work with it or abandon its plantation along with all of the Liberians who depended upon it. Accordingly, Firestone made the difficult decision to preserve its operations in Liberia. A Firestone spokesperson summed up the company's rationale to stay thus: "Because the company did not abandon its operation, employees had work. . . . The Firestone operation was critically important to the economy of Liberia and to the lives of the tens of thousands who depend on it for wages, healthcare, housing, and education."[104]

Firestone was especially defensive about its 1992 payment to Taylor and the NPFL even though it was not the legitimate governing authority in Liberia. The company insisted that the NPFL was acting as the government in every way and that, as a private corporation in a foreign environment, it had negotiated the best terms possible. It also asserted that there had been no "well-established" record of Taylor's human rights abuses, which only emerged years later. Firestone admitted that Taylor used the plantation as a staging ground for his various incursions into Monrovia, including the vicious "Operation Octopus." But the company firmly denied having a "collaborative relationship" with Charles Taylor, as some of its critics claimed. Its activities were exclusively for the purpose of protecting its employees and its property. Firestone "had no role in the rise of Charles Taylor, [and] no role in his ability to hold power in Liberia." Firestone believes it did the right thing, but regrets the war criminal that Taylor eventually became. In the company's mind, the disputable decision to remain in Liberia was quite costly, but it preserved an "important economic asset" for this needy country and for its destitute citizens.[105]

EXHIBIT 13.1 ■ Timeline of Events

1847: Liberia becomes a sovereign country with a constitution modeled on the U.S. Constitution; only Americo-Liberians are eligible for full citizenship.

1926: Firestone begins doing business in Liberia, and rubber becomes the cornerstone of the economy.

1980: Samuel Doe leads a successful military coup; President Tolbert is executed.

1985: Doe wins the presidential election.

1989: Civil war begins under Charles Taylor, who forms a rebel group, the National Patriotic Front of Liberia (NPFL).

1990: Taylor invades Firestone's Harbel plantation, and Firestone expats are evacuated; the Interim Government is installed to replace Doe.

January 1992: Firestone expats return to Harbel and initiate "tax" payments to Taylor.

November 1992: Firestone managers once again abandon the plantation after a bombing spree.

1996: Taylor is elected president; Firestone returns to Liberia a second time.

1999: Insurgents mount a new civil war against the Taylor regime.

2003: Taylor's forces are defeated, and Taylor is sent into exile to Nigeria.

2005: Ellen Johnson-Sirleaf becomes president.

2006: Taylor is arrested and sent to Sierra Leone.

2012: Ex-president Taylor is convicted of war crimes and sentenced to 50 years in prison.

EXHIBIT 13.2 ■ Profile of Liberia[106]

Capital:	Monrovia
Population:	4.2 million people
Population growth:	4.3%
Infant mortality:	79 per 1,000 births
Location:	Southwest corner of the African continent
Area:	99,067 square kilometers
Languages:	English, Mande, Kwa
Religions:	Christianity and Islam
Currency:	Liberian dollar
Exports:	Rubber, cocoa, iron ore, coffee
Economic growth:	4.6% GDP (2010–2015)

EXHIBIT 13.3 ■ Bridgestone Firestone Financials, 1989–1993 (in millions)

Bridgestone Corp	1989	1990	1991	1992	1993
Sales	$11,750	$13,138	$14,134	$13,981	$14,328
Net Income	67.0	33.2	59.8	227.0	254.3
Net Profit Margin	0.6%	0.3%	0.5%	1.7%	1.8%
Return on Equity	N/A	N/A	1.9%	6.5%	6.1%

- Imagine that you are a board member of Firestone Tire and Rubber Company and have to vote on the plan to return to Liberia in 1992.

- Outline the pros and cons of this plan.

- How would you vote? Explain your reasoning.

  ○ Firestone claims that these payments to Taylor were legitimate (even though he wasn't the official president) because they could still be classified as taxes paid to a foreign government. Do you accept that argument?

  ○ Did Firestone act responsibly by making this decision to return to Liberia and pay taxes to Taylor and the NFLP? Which ethical theories support your conclusion?

  ○ Should Firestone have returned again in 1996, given Taylor's record of human rights abuses? Or is "economic disengagement" the right policy at this point?

  ○ Firestone asserted that there was no "well-established" record of Taylor's human rights abuses until much later. Do you accept its position on Taylor's human rights record?

CONCLUSION

What is the moral reasoning appropriate to companies when they do business abroad? Should a multinational apply the moral norms of its home country culture, should it rely on universal transcultural moral norms, or should it adjust morality to the new cultural standards of its host country? The introduction to globalization focused on this question of cultural relativism, among other key issues. The cases in this chapter centered on how major multinationals have dealt with political and social issues in foreign terrains. The ITT case study described this conglomerate's questionable efforts to nudge Chile's politics in a certain direction. There has been a pendular swing, however, as most companies recoil at ITT's overt political activities. Instead, they advocate political neutrality. But how far should that philosophy be taken—does it mean standing by as a government tramples on the rights of its citizens? The second case on Firestone was about how to handle international outlaws. Disinvestment may be the only reasonable option in countries where there are repressive or illegitimate regimes. The condition-of-business principle was proposed as a general guideline for making these decisions.

Student Study Site

Visit **edge.sagepub.com/spinello.**

Key Terms

cultural distance   349

cultural relativism   350

economic distance   349

ethical risk   351

globalization   345

political distance   349

political risk   351

Review Question

1. Explain the challenges multinationals confront when they engage in foreign direct investment. What are the lessons to be learned from the history of globalization?

Discussion Questions

1. What might be some of the problems with a strategy of political neutrality?

2. How can companies prepare more diligently to handle the political and ethical risks of foreign investment?

BRIBERY AND CORRUPTION IN FOREIGN MARKETS

Every day, funds destined for schools, health care, and infrastructure in the world's most fragile economies are siphoned off and stashed away in the world's financial centers and tax havens. Corruption, like a disease, is eating away at people's faith in government. It undermines the stability and security of nations. . . . It also undermines the preconditions for growth and equality.

—Ngozi Okonjo-Iweala[1]

LEARNING OBJECTIVES

Upon completion of this chapter, you should be able to:

14.1 Discuss the root causes and effects of bribery and corruption.

14.2 Explain the economic, legal, and ethical implications for multinationals that choose to engage in bribery in developing economies.

14.3 Use the tools provided to assess foreign business practices.

Guinea is one of several African countries rich in natural resources like iron ore. Foreign mining companies are eager to do business there. Sometimes a little too eager. Take the case of Rio Tinto, the British-Australian mining giant, and the Israeli company BSG Resources. Both companies allegedly tried to outmaneuver each other by making payments to corrupt Guinean officials to win the rights to mine a lucrative iron ore vein in the remote Simandou mountain range. These hills have some of the world's largest high-quality iron ore deposits. Rio Tinto originally had the rights to Simandou thanks to a deal made with the government in the 1990s. But Guinea stripped the company of its rights in 2008 because it was moving too slowly to extract the iron ore. Two top Rio Tinto executives allegedly paid $10.5 million to several Guinea officials as part of an effort to retain the Simandou concession. However, the rights were given to BSG, and the Guinea government claims that BSG won those rights by paying bribes to the wife of its ex-president. The ongoing scandal has embarrassed both companies and key executives who probably viewed these payments as a commercial necessity.[2]

As multinational corporations (MNCs) continue their global expansion, they must come to terms with the reality of rampant corruption in many developing countries. Corruption is a particularly severe problem in countries with autocratic leaders and weak institutions. Some MNCs resort to bribery in those environments because they are convinced they have no other recourse if they want to retain their business or obtain new business. Economic necessity is the motivation and justification. Bribery is certainly not confined to emerging economies or countries dominated by corrupt leadership. It is a pervasive social problem with a long and sordid history.

This chapter begins with a briefing on bribery that provides a working definition as well as some theoretical background. It then reviews the legal landscape by first discussing the Foreign Corrupt Practices Act of 1977 that all U.S. firms are obliged to follow when they engage in business in foreign countries. We also look at the relevant laws of other countries such as the United Kingdom, which passed a strict anti-bribery law in 2010.

AN OVERVIEW OF THE CASES

This briefing is followed by three case studies. The first explores bribes paid by GlaxoSmithKline employees to doctors and hospital employees in China. The purpose was to influence these doctors to prescribe their medications. The problem for GSK is that local Chinese drug companies practice informal bribery payments as a common marketing strategy. This case reveals the motivations of bribery recipients along with the high cost of relying on bribes to increase sales abroad. It also illustrates the particular risks pharmaceutical companies face when they attempt to do business in countries with a dysfunctional health care system.

The second case looks at Monsanto's bribery scandal in Indonesia, where cash payments and other amenities were used to help sell their genetically modified cotton seed and influence government policy. One $50,000 bribe was paid to the minister of the environment as an inducement to cancel an environmental impact study. In other cases, modest "gifts" were made to other Monsanto officials, but did those gifts rise to the level of bribery?

Beyond the legal issues, both of these bribery cases demonstrate the apparent ineffectiveness of corporate ethical codes of conduct unless they are reinforced by the right incentive structures and internal controls.

The final case examines how the extraction of natural resources can breed corruption and social disorder. Several African nations have been especially vulnerable to the predations of corrupt leaders working in tandem with multinational corporations to exploit a country's mineral resources. The case focuses on the forlorn country of Equatorial Guinea, which is enriched with natural resources like oil but full of people living in dire poverty. It probes what companies like ExxonMobil should be doing to prevent rapacious leaders from amassing great wealth from oil revenue while ordinary people in the country suffer.

BRIEFING ON BRIBERY AND THE U.S. FOREIGN CORRUPT PRACTICES ACT

Eli Black was the CEO of United Brands (later known as Chiquita Bananas), the largest banana enterprise in the entire world. By all accounts, Mr. Black was a taciturn man, rather grim and serious. On a wintry Sunday afternoon in February 1975, Mr. Black's chauffeur drove him from his Park Avenue apartment to United Brands headquarters in the Pan American Building just a short distance away. He worked alone in his office on the 44th floor for a short while and then plunged to his death on Park Avenue after breaking the tall window behind his desk with his briefcase. It was a striking scene: a well-dressed executive stretched out on the ground, stories below the shattered glass window of one of Manhattan's most iconic buildings.

What would possess such a powerful and privileged corporate leader to commit suicide? How could things in the banana industry be so bleak? The answer is simple enough. United Brands had been caught up in a notorious bribery scandal. The banana industry was difficult terrain, with high fixed costs, low profit margins, and volatile banana prices. United Brands had been losing money, and Black was struggling to turn things around. In 1974, a catastrophic hurricane in Honduras wiped out the crops at United's banana plantation, and the company lost $70 million. Also, United Brands would soon have to absorb a sizable new expense in Central American countries where it grew most of its bananas. Honduran officials were set to impose a dollar-per-box tax on all exported fruit, including bananas. Black knew this tax would have a catastrophic effect on the bottom line and on United's fragile financial condition. Consequently, he reluctantly agreed to authorize $1.25 million in secret payments to persuade Honduran officials to reduce the tax to $0.25 per box. The bribery payment worked, but Black could not live with this dirty secret. He was painfully aware that news of this graft would surely leak out and be a source of humiliation for him and his family. It would also tarnish the reputation of United Brands. Burdened by guilt, Mr. Black, a former rabbi, apparently believed suicide was the only way out. The United Brands scandal, along with many others which were brewing in the 1970s, led Congress to take action and pass a law prohibiting bribery payments to foreign officials.[3]

International Corruption and Bribery: A Perennial Problem

It is no surprise to the world's oil companies that natural resources can often breed corruption and malfeasance. Too often leaders of countries with abundant resources seek to profit from the country's good fortune at the expense of their citizens. Nigeria's oil rents, for example, led to persistent corruption within the ranks of its political leaders. In Nigeria, suspicious deals and payoffs have cost the oil industry over $30 billion in the last decade.[4] The World Bank defines **corruption** as the "abuse of public office for private gain."[5] This is a sound definition as far as it goes, though corruption can also occur exclusively in the private sector. Public sector or government corruption can take many forms, including patronage and nepotism, the theft of state assets, or the diversion of state revenues. Some corruption is isolated to a few officials, but the worst type is systemic and pervasive. Government corruption is often cleverly concealed and difficult to detect. Powerful officials have the resources to cover up their corrupt activities behind the facade of their position and identity.[6]

One of the primary tools of dishonest political leaders and the corporations that appease them is **bribery**. But before we can intelligibly discuss the topic of bribery, we need a working definition. According to Stuart Green, X is bribed by Y if X accepts or consents to accept something of value from Y in exchange for X's acting or agreeing to act to further some interest of Y's by violating some duty of loyalty owed by X as a consequence of X's office, official position, or involvement in some practice. Thus, the briber (Y) offers or gives something of value in exchange for some service provided by the bribee (X). That "something of value" can be money, but it could also be an offer of future employment, tickets for athletic events, a paid vacation, or even sexual favors. Bribes are sometimes confused with gifts or rewards, but a gift is given without any condition of reciprocation.[7]

In some legal statutes, the bribee can only be a public official, but from a moral viewpoint, it is also wrong to bribe employees or managers of private firms. Payments made to a retail buyer or to other private-sector agents in exchange for "something of value" are just as immoral as payments made to government officials.[8] In a foreign setting, bribes can be used by multinationals to win government contracts, to reduce taxes or fees, and to influence the distribution of government benefits. Companies are often under great pressure to make such payments, especially when they are perceived to be the customary local practice. In many countries, bribes and payoffs appear to be a valid mode of doing business. There may be local laws against bribery, but those laws are often unenforced and ignored, especially in emerging economies. Should multinationals adapt to a foreign culture when doing business in these countries? Or are bribes intrinsically wrong and simply off-limits everywhere?

The answer to those questions may be open to some debate, but what is not debatable is the fact that bribery has been rampant in the world economy for centuries. Bribes are so customary that some companies have actually booked bribes or "gifts" as a tax-deductible expense. The problem for multinationals is that in certain markets without bribery payments, there is a "first mover disadvantage." The first company fighting for a rewarding contract immediately puts itself in a weakened position unless it bribes its way to winning the contract. Accordingly, the *Economist* refers to bribery as the "worm that never dies," the worm that "gnaws at the fruits of economic endeavor."[9]

Bribery is a murky business conducted in the shadows rather than out in the open, so it is always difficult to get the full picture of its scope and penetration into various industries. Recent studies, however, confirm that the most "bribery-riddled" sectors of the global economy are oil, gas, mining, construction, and transportation. On the other hand, the financial services and retailing industries have been devoid of widespread bribery payments. Most bribes are paid to managers of state-owned companies and to customs officials. Bribes are not typically the work of rogue employees. In 53% of cases, bribes were made or authorized by high-level corporate managers, and in 12% of cases, the authorization for a bribe came directly from the corporation's CEO.[10]

Most economists concur that a pattern of bribery actually hurts a country's economic growth. Corrupt economies get high marks on the corruption index and consequently struggle to attract new foreign investment. Often, bribery is encouraged by countries that pay their civil servants quite poorly. They look the other way as those workers collect bribes to supplement their meager salaries. In addition, businesses do not necessarily gain in the long run from fostering bribery practices. Companies that are caught are forced to pay out big fines and conduct expensive internal probes. Siemens, for example, was entangled in a series of bribery scandals that cost the company $2.4 billion.[11]

Finally, the impact of bribery is far-reaching, since bribery negatively affects the economy by diminishing competition and distorting free-market dynamics. Thanks to corruption, a contract is not awarded to the efficient low-cost producer in an industry but to the inefficient producer who pays the highest bribe. Nonetheless, market forces have been somewhat effective in fighting bribery, since bribery falls short of acceptable global business standards and taints a company's reputation. Thus, firms are punished in the market when word of a bribery scheme leaks out. But market forces have not been a sufficient deterrent. As a result, policy makers have turned to the law with some new statutes and better enforcement of old ones. For a long time, countries were unwilling to legislate the offshore activities of their multinational companies. But now there is new comprehensive bribery legislation in countries like Brazil and Britain that restricts the behavior of MNCs. The United States has been a pioneer in this effort with its Foreign Corrupt Practices Act, passed in 1977.

Bribing Foreign Officials

The U.S. federal bribery statute, which makes it a crime to "corruptly" give or receive something of value in return for influencing an "official act," does not apply beyond U.S. borders.[12] Companies seemed to believe this legal void gave them permission to bribe within a foreign culture whenever necessary. The U.S. government became increasingly apprehensive about the damage being done by American multinational firms engaged in bribery to win foreign contracts. In addition to United Brands, companies like Northrup, Gulf Oil Corporation, and Lockheed were involved in major corruption scandals that implicated top executives and sullied the reputation of American business.

Gulf, for example, had a thriving business presence in South Korea. When Gulf was informed that it had to contribute $10 million to the country's incumbent president, its executives settled on a payment of $3 million. Gulf president Bob Dorsey approved the payment, which was recorded as a transfer to Bahamas Ex. At the time, the payment was no crime under American law and perhaps not even a crime in Korea. When queried about the payment, Dorsey said that "the opportunity to continue a profitable business, without unwarranted and inhibiting government interference, warranted it."[13]

In one of the most publicized cases, Lockheed executives admitted making payments in Europe and Japan. The defense contractor paid $12.5 million to Japanese government officials to win a lucrative contract from Nippon Air for its TriStar plane. When word of these bribes leaked out, Lockheed rationalized these payments as an "acceptable" way of doing business in Japan, where bribery was supposedly a common practice. In the company's eyes, the total amount paid out was less than 3% of what Lockheed expected to receive on the sale of its 21 TriStar planes, so the payments were definitely "worthwhile."[14]

Lockheed actually resisted the notion that these payments constituted bribes. Rather, in their words, "gifts" were given to these foreign officials for their cooperation in securing certain business contracts. In a bold statement, Lockheed's president, Carl Kotchian, later wrote, "I should also like to stress that my decision to make such payments stemmed from my judgement that the TriStar payments to ANA [All Nippon Airlines] would provide Lockheed workers with jobs and thus redound to the benefit of their dependents, the local communities, and the stockholders of the corporation."[15]

Kotchian's rationale for these payments is a model of utilitarian reasoning. It justifies the payments based on the positive consequences of jobs that help workers and their families along with profits that benefit shareholders. A refusal to pay would mean an inability to compete against foreign competitors and the loss of a lucrative contract. Some academics have apparently concurred with this line of reasoning. James Q. Wilson, for example, did not believe bribery of this sort should be stigmatized. In an article called "Corruption Is Not Always Scandalous," he suggested that we must differentiate between "those forms of corruption that impede the attainment of social objectives and those that may facilitate it." He argued that there is such a thing as "honest graft" that brings profit to the briber and bribee and no harm to the public.[16]

On the other hand, from a nonutilitarian viewpoint, it is difficult to dismiss the harms caused by bribery, which cannot always be neatly quantified. How might we explain the moral wrongfulness of bribery on the part of those who accept or offer a bribe? First, the use of bribery to win contracts or close a business deal represents unfair competition, since the briber is seeking a market advantage not based on price or on the merits of the company's product or service. Those who accept the bribe participate in this harm of unfairness. Also, from a Kantian perspective, the practice of bribery cannot be universalized because the briber's maxim promotes an action that would be inconsistent with his purpose if everyone tried to act on it. If everyone bribed, the bribes would cancel each other out and defeat the whole purpose of a bribe.[17] Second, bribery often interferes with the duty of public officials to be loyal and to act in the best interests of the government institution or agency that employs them. When bribes are accepted by such officials in exchange for some favorable treatment, there is a breach of loyalty. Similarly, the person offering the bribe is culpable of inducing someone to breach his or her duties.

The Foreign Corrupt Practices Act

Policy makers and political leaders in the United States were unimpressed by arguments that minimized the moral opprobrium of bribery. The anti-bribery forces won out in Washington, which decided to take a statutory approach to bribes in foreign markets. As a result of the Lockheed and Gulf Oil scandals along with many others of smaller scale, the Foreign Corrupt Practices Act (FCPA) was passed into law in 1977. The FCPA essentially outlaws the payment of bribes by "domestic concerns" to government officials and political parties, though the word *bribe* is never used in the statute. According to this law, these domestic concerns cannot "offer payment, promise to pay, or authorize the giving of anything of value to any foreign official for purposes of influencing any act or decision of such official in his official capacity . . . [or] inducing such foreign official to use his influence with a foreign government or instrumentality thereof to affect or influence any act or decision of such government . . . in order to assist such domestic concern in obtaining or retaining business."[18] Thus, to violate the FCPA, the bribery payment has to be made to a "foreign official" for the express purpose of getting or keeping business.

The FCPA uses morally neutral language such as "payments" and "gifts" or "offers" to avoid any confusion over the meaning of the word "bribe," which may vary from country to country. The law applies to any U.S. company, any company listed on the U.S. stock exchange, and any foreign firms operating on American territory. Enforcement was to be ensured by accounting requirements: companies were required to keep books reflecting their foreign transactions in "reasonable detail."[19]

Despite the new statute and its harsh penalties, many multinationals sought to sidestep the FCPA when they thought it was required by the economic urgency of a given situation. They believed the FCPA put them at a disadvantage for competing with their counterparts in other countries. In the airline industry, for example, there were credible allegations that the French multinational Airbus engaged in bribery before France's anti-bribery laws were enacted. American companies like Boeing were bound by the FCPA, but its competitors did not have this constraint. Airbus's first major sale in North America was a $1.5 billion deal to sell 34 aircraft to state-owned Air Canada. Was this sale expedited through the use of bribes? Airbus hired International Aircraft Leasing (IAL) to broker the deal, and records show that as Air Canada was taking delivery of their planes in the early 1990s, over $22 million was paid to IAL in commissions, some of which were allegedly paid to Canadian officials.[20]

Part of the problem with the FCPA has been many decades of haphazard enforcement. Bribery was not a priority for U.S. federal officials, who had bigger issues to contend with. As a result, the FCPA was not strongly enforced until the turn of the century, so the bribery scandals did not simply vanish. Many firms continued to engage in bribery, and some complained that it was the only way to get things done, especially in countries with dysfunctional governments where small-scale bribes were routine. Sometimes civil servants like customs workers are poorly compensated and seek to supplement their meager salaries through small payoffs.

With these factors in mind, a later amendment to the FCPA exempts "facilitation payments," that is, small payments made to expedite routine things such as clearing some goods through customs. The problem with this exception is that it's not always clear how facilitation payments differ from a bribe. Also, some critics say there is little distinction in practice between these payments and bribes, and that the facilitation payment is really the first move in a "chess game" that ultimately leads to full-blown bribery.[21]

For a long time, the United States was one of the very few countries with such a law, but eventually other countries followed suit. In 1997, the Organization for Economic Cooperation and Development (OECD) issued its Convention on Combating the Bribery of Public Officials in International Business Transactions. It strongly encouraged member countries to adopt this convention by adopting strict anti-bribery laws like the FCPA. That convention decrees that "enterprises should not, directly or indirectly, offer, promise, give, or demand a bribe or other undue advantage to obtain or retain business."[22] Many countries continued to resist legal measures to combat overseas bribery, but at the turn of the century, France enacted a strong set of anti-bribery laws in conformity with OECD convention.

Some years later the UK Parliament passed the Bribery Act of 2010, which is quite similar to the FCPA. Like the FCPA, the UK law also prohibits bribing of government officials in foreign countries. The crime of bribery is committed under this act if a person intends to influence a foreign public official in his or her capacity as such, and if he or she intends to obtain or retain business (or gain some advantage involving that business). However, the scope of the UK Bribery Act is broader than that of the FCPA. While the FCPA applies only to the corruption of foreign officials, the Bribery Act includes bribes offered or given to *any* person. Also, it is an offense under the UK law to request, agree to receive, or accept a bribe. The FCPA, on the other hand, applies only to persons giving or offering a bribe and not to those accepting one.[23]

Bribery Never Ends

Despite these bribery laws and renewed enforcement efforts, an OECD survey reports that 400 bribery cases closed between 1999 and 2014, most in industries like oil and construction. The OECD also reports that bribery techniques and methods have become much more opaque, making it difficult for regulators or prosecutors to conduct a proper investigation. Corporate structures are also more opaque and complex, and that makes it easier to conceal bribery.[24]

Thus, it is no surprise there are new bribery scandals all the time. Multinationals like Siemens, Lucent Technologies, Hewlett-Packard, BAE Systems, and Daimler-Benz have all been caught up in controversial bribery cases. Lucent provided funding for 1,000 Chinese officials, who were employed by Chinese telecom firms, so they could travel to Las Vegas and other destinations. In exchange, Lucent hoped to win lucrative telecom contracts. Siemens, Europe's largest engineering company, made bribery payments of $1.4 billion between 2001 and 2007 in order to win overseas contracts. In Argentina, the company allegedly paid a $40 million bribe to the country's president to win a billion-dollar contract for producing national identity cards. According to one investigator, "Bribery was Siemens' business model."[25]

Some regions of the world like Latin America have seen an endless stream of bribery scandals. In Peru, for example, there has been a web of bribery payments that have implicated the country's former president, Alejandro Toledo. He has denied charges that he received $20 million in bribes from the Brazilian construction firm Odebrecht that was wired to offshore accounts of businesses owned by one of his closest friends. In exchange for these payments, Odebrecht was awarded a big contract for building the Interoceanic Highway in Peru that cost $4.5 billion (four times over budget).[26]

Odebrecht has been at the center of a large network of graft that includes many other Latin American countries besides Peru. The firm has admitted to U.S. prosecutors that it paid $800 million in bribes throughout Latin America in order to win lucrative infrastructure contracts. Between 2001 and 2005, the company paid bribes on 100 projects in 12 countries and won contracts that netted Odebrecht $3.34 billion. In one case it purchased a local bank branch to conceal the transactions. Some of the money paid out took the form of contributions to political campaigns. Odebrecht allegedly donated $1 million to the president of Colombia's reelection campaign in exchange for contracts for projects, including a road that links the country's interior region to the Magdalena highway. The bribery scheme also created a political calamity in Brazil, which led to the impeachment of its former president, Dilma Rousseff. In 2016, Odebrecht settled with the United States, Brazil, and Switzerland for up to $4.5 billion. U.S. prosecutors pursued the construction company for violating the FCPA. These fines represent the largest anti-corruption settlement in history.[27]

Thus, despite comprehensive new laws and stricter enforcement of old ones, bribery, one of the oldest human offenses, remains rife throughout pockets of the global economy. Bribery truly is the worm that never dies. Bribes corrupt those who give and receive these illegal payments, while also diminishing economic efficiency and political legitimacy. Bribery in cases like Odebrecht is a betrayal of trust, and the social injury caused by breaches of trust takes a heavy toll on social harmony and on the integrity of free markets.[28]

CASE STUDY 14.1

GLAXOSMITHKLINE IN CHINA

Tucked away in a quiet part of the central city of Changsha, China, are the offices of the pharmaceutical giant GlaxoSmithKline (GSK). On June 27, 2013, those offices were raided by Chinese authorities. They seized documents, files, and laptop computers and interviewed numerous employees. They were looking for evidence to confirm their suspicion of "serious economic crimes." Those crimes included commercial bribery, tax evasion, and embezzlement. In Shanghai, four senior GSK executives, all Chinese nationals, were detained on that same day. The next day, GSK pledged to cooperate with Chinese authorities. The general manager of GSK China, Mark Reilly, had been out of the country at the time, but returned to assist in that investigation. GSK has deep roots in China, dating back to the opening of a factory there by Glaxo in the early 1990s. It also had successful business operations in many regions of China. But all of that was put in jeopardy by this sudden turn of events.

©iStockphoto.com/William Barton

GlaxoSmithKline

GlaxoSmithKline, sometimes referred to as GSK, is a British pharmaceutical company and one of Big Pharma's leading global enterprises. GSK is headquartered in Brentford, England, and operates around the world. The company was established in 2000 by the merger of Glaxo Wellcome and SmithKline Beecham. In 2016, GSK ranked as the world's sixth-largest pharmaceutical company, following Pfizer, Novartis, Merck, Hoffmann–La Roche, and Sanofi-Aventis. It employed over 100,000 people and had revenues approximating $40 billion.

The company's leading products include several well-known blockbuster drugs: the diabetes treatment Advair; its antinausea drug, Zofran; and two antidepressant drugs, Paxil and Wellbutrin. GSK also has one of the largest vaccine businesses in the world, distributing more than 1.1 billion doses of its vaccines to 173 countries. More recently, GSK received approval for the first new lupus treatment within the last 50 years. It also formed a partnership with Pfizer to create ViiV, a joint venture dedicated to fighting AIDS and helping destitute communities affected by HIV.

Glaxo Wellcome and SmithKline Beecham originated in the United States and England, respectively. Glaxo Wellcome was created in 1995 when Jason Nathan and Company (later Glaxo), which began in 1873, merged with Burroughs Wellcome and Company. The latter company was founded by Henry Wellcome and Silas Burroughs in 1880. John K. Smith and Mahlon Kline started their company in the 19th century. It expanded through the acquisition of vaccines business and, most notably, French Richards and Company, a well-respected drug wholesaler. Thomas Beecham started a small company called Beecham's Pills in England in 1842. Its business took off many decades later after the company's researchers discovered amoxicillin and sold the antibiotic as Amoxil in 1972. Beecham merged with Smith and Kline in 1989 to become SmithKline Beecham.

When GlaxoSmithKline was formed in 2001, the drug company was divided into three main segments—pharmaceuticals (treating cancer, heart disease, and HIV/AIDS), vaccines (treating hepatitis, polio, and typhoid), and consumer health care (treating oral and skin problems)—and has grown steadily, selling products in more than 170 countries. GSK had a strong presence in China and looked to increase revenues from developing countries to help deal with the patent cliff. This happens when branded, blockbuster drugs come off patent and must face the prospect of generic competition.[29]

GSK prided itself on its corporate philanthropy and its ethics code of conduct. According to the company, that code lays out "fundamental business conduct standards for all company staff. It brings together a number of policy principles, and provides a working guide for how employees should apply GSK's values of respect, transparency, integrity and patient focus to their everyday work." The GSK code of conduct also encourages employees to report fraud or other unethical activities without fear of retribution. This ethics code applies to the entire global workforce, within all sectors, regions, areas, and functions, and is subject to annual certification by all staff.[30]

GSK's operations in China predate the merger of Glaxo Wellcome and Smith Kline. Both companies began selling their drugs in China in the 1990s. After the merger, its Chinese presence expanded by acquisition of Nanjing MeiRui Pharma. This acquisition gave GSK access to MeiRui's urology and allergy drugs. GSK and other Big Pharma firms, which competed against many smaller Chinese drug companies, saw significant opportunities in China. The country's aging population, higher incomes, and rising need for health care meant more demand for pharmaceutical products. The market for drugs is now the second highest in the world at $108 billion.[31]

GSK had a large marketing and sales force in China geared to selling its products. Like its competitors, GSK compensated those employees through commissions and bonuses. Salespeople had ambitious targets that were based on the number of GSK drugs prescribed by doctors in their respective sales territories.[32] In addition, GSK insiders describe a "hard-selling culture" at GSK's Chinese offices, where "the mindset was more, more, more." There was also little oversight from corporate headquarters, consistent with GSK's decentralized management structure that encouraged autonomy for its country business units.[33]

China and Bribes to Chinese Doctors

After its transition to a market-oriented economy, many of China's politicians and government officials were not able to resist taking advantage of their positions. Consequently, corruption became a pervasive presence in Chinese corporate life. Many MNCs put local Chinese managers in charge of their China operations. They sometimes sensed shady dealings, but they did not want to upset Chinese cultural traditions such as *guanxi* (the importance of cultivating good connections), and so they just looked the other way.[34]

Hu Jintao, who led China from 2002 until 2012, warned party leaders and bureaucrats about the scale and ill effects of rampant corruption throughout the Chinese economic system but took little initiative to eradicate that corruption. In 2012, Transparency International ranked China 80th out of 176 countries in its corruption-perception index. When the charismatic Xi Jingping was chosen as Hu Jintao's replacement in 2012, he immediately signaled his commitment to rooting out corruption and reforming the economy. Xi has reinforced China's commitment to economic integration and free trade. But his presidency has also been shaped by a resolve to revive Chinese nationalism. During his first months in office, he pledged to restrict foreign companies' access to Chinese markets and to regulate multinationals more effectively. No longer would elite business and political leaders enjoy the fruits of corruption and payoffs.[35]

Prior to the Xi regime, China had been rather lax in rooting out corruption in industries like health care, which was especially susceptible to fraud and bribery. But everything changed abruptly in 2013. As a result, many companies such as GSK, which were complacent about corruption and illegal practices within their ranks, suddenly found themselves in the government's crosshairs.

After the June raids, on July 11, the Chinese Ministry of Public Security publicly accused GSK of paying millions of dollars in bribes to doctors, hospital officials, and health industry workers to increase the sale of its products. The ministry referred to this as a "huge scheme" to raise drug prices. The money to pay off doctors was allegedly funneled through travel agencies like China Comfort Travel or C.C.T., which falsified travel documentation. Some doctors were given money for going to fictitious conferences that never took place, while others received fees for speeches that were never given. Travel agencies, which created the receipts for these services never performed, cooperated with GSK in order to acquire its future business. In some cases, medical professionals received all-expense-paid vacation trips under the pretext of attending international conferences. A few doctors were even compensated with sexual favors instead of free trips or cash.[36]

Gao Feng, who was the head of China's fraud unit, claimed its investigation revealed a network of 700 middlemen and travel agencies, which facilitated the payment of these bribes to doctors who agreed to prescribe GSK drugs. The total amount spent on these bribes was estimated to be 3 billion yuan ($492 million). He also said these payments had been going on since 2007 and were a "core part" of GSK's business model in China. One executive who had been detained claimed the bribes increased consumer prices of GSK drugs by 30%.[37]

GSK first heard of the labyrinthine bribery scheme through a whistle-blower. In December 2011, that whistle-blower, a former GSK employee, sent a detailed email to Chinese regulators that explained GSK's fraudulent practices. In April 2012, GSK executives in China learned that this whistle-blower had sent these documents to Chinese officials. In January 2013, the whistle-blower sent a 5,200-word anonymous email to the GSK chairman, Andrew Witty, along with senior executives and the firm's external auditor, PricewaterhouseCoopers. Like the previous emails, this one described in some detail the extensive bribery scheme in China. The email was structured like a corporate memo. In the first section, titled "Conference Trip Vacations for Doctors," the whistle-blower explained how some doctors and medical professionals received fully paid vacations instead of cash for prescribing GSK drugs. GSK covered the costs of airfare, hotel rooms, meals, and sightseeing tours. Receipts were forged to make it appear the doctor attended a conference that never took place. In the next section, titled "GSK Falsified Its Books and Records to Conceal Its Illegal Marketing Practices in China," the email described how GSK marketed and sold drugs for unapproved purchases. The whistle-blower used the drug Lamictal as an example. It was promoted as a treatment for bipolar disorder, although it was approved in China only for epilepsy. Here is an excerpt from that email:

> [If] the Chinese regulatory authorities discovered that GSK had been knowingly marketing Lamictal for an unauthorized use and that this illegality almost killed a person, then the Chinese authorities could suspend GSK's operations throughout China, costing GSK much money.

A total of 17 emails were sent over a two-year period to Chinese regulators, GSK executives, and PricewaterhouseCoopers.[38]

At first, GSK refused to take the revelations in these emails seriously. The allegations were brusquely dismissed by GSK executives in London as a "smear campaign." Consequently, GSK did not order a full and thorough investigation of these serious accusations. The drug company did not fortify its internal controls in China, and it did not modify any of its marketing practices there. According to the *New York Times*, it even hired two private investigators to explore the whistle-blower's background, family life, and government connections in order to find material that might discredit her.[39]

But in early 2013, GSK realized these accusations would not just go away as they had hoped. Chinese authorities were beginning to ask questions and the whistle-blower kept sending her emails. The company finally set up a special "crisis management" team in China under the supervision of Mark Reilly. But that team began offering payoffs and gifts to Chinese regulators to persuade them to forestall their investigation. This was a common GSK strategy: placate officials and regulators with gifts and favors. One regulatory agency in China with several branches had received multiple emails from the whistle-blower. A GSK executive tried to ingratiate himself with an investigator from the Shanghai branch by giving him an iPad and taking him out for a lavish dinner. When that same executive asked for money to bribe a regulator at the Beijing branch, Mark Reilly gave the "go-ahead."[40]

Despite this trail of emails and behind-the-scenes drama, GSK's initial public response to the June raid was one of complete surprise. On July 15, 2013, the company declared it was "deeply concerned and disappointed by these serious allegations of fraudulent behavior and ethical misconduct." The statement went on to say that GSK had no evidence of wrongdoing in China, but it pledged full cooperation with the investigation. According to a confident GSK spokesperson, "We take all allegations of bribery and corruption seriously. We continuously monitor our businesses to ensure they meet our strict compliance procedures—we have done this in China and found no evidence of bribery or corruption of doctors or government officials."[41]

But Chinese investigators rapidly uncovered evidence to back up their allegations. They found significant discrepancies between bookings and revenue for travel agencies involved in the scandal. On July 16, 2013, one of the four detained executives confessed to the elaborate bribery scheme on state television. The testimony of Liang Hong was especially instructive for understanding the details of the company's methods. In late July, GSK finally admitted that some of the executives in its China branch offices had broken Chinese law by their involvement in making these illegal payments. There was sufficient evidence to prove these employees had bribed doctors and hospital medical staff with gifts, travel expenses, and cash payments in order to induce them to prescribe more of the company's drugs. There was also evidence that doctors had been compensated for attending conferences and professional events that never took place. In late July, 18 other employees were detained, and Mark Reilly was replaced as country manager by Herve Gisserot. GSK issued another statement to the press acknowledging that these four executives "acted outside of our process and controls which breaches Chinese law."[42] The company continued to insist, however, that corporate headquarters had had no knowledge about these illegal payments.[43]

The Relevant Laws

China has two major laws prohibiting bribery that impose both administrative and criminal penalties. The first statute is the PRC (People's Republic of China) Anti-Unfair Competition Law (AUCL), which was ratified by the Chinese government in 1993. This law forbids unfair competitive practices, including infringement of intellectual property rights, abuse of dominant economic power, and commercial bribery. No business operating in China can give bribes "in the form of property or other means for the purpose of selling and purchasing products and services." Those found guilty of violating this law could be fined, or they could be held criminally liable and subject to the PRC Criminal Law if the violation is serious enough. In 1996, China promulgated the Provisional Rules on Prohibition of Commercial Bribery, which reinforced the AUCL. It also clarified the definition of commercial bribery according to that statute and defined property "as any cash or non-cash payments, including, but not limited to, property disguised as marketing fees, consulting fees, as well as reimbursement of various expenses."[44]

Second, the PRC Criminal Law, which was enacted in 1979, outlaws and penalizes both public and commercial bribery for the purpose of securing certain "illegitimate benefits." This law, which makes bribery a criminal offense, was initially confined to the bribery of state officials. But a later amendment also bans bribes to nonstate officials or representatives of private corporations. Whether criminal bribery has been committed depends on the amount of money or property involved in the illicit payoffs along with the intentions of the briber.[45]

Also relevant, of course, were the U.S. Foreign Corrupt Practices Act, since GlaxoSmithKline did business in the United States, and the UK Bribery Act. The FCPA forbids the payment of bribes to any "foreign official" for the purpose of assisting a company's efforts to obtain or retain business in that country.[46] Doctors are not state officials in China, but the law defines "foreign officials" quite broadly so that it includes employees of foreign governments, governmental agencies, and public hospitals, where many of those doctors worked.

The UK Bribery Act, which took effect in July 2011, also prohibits all forms of bribery and all forms of "being bribed," not just bribery of foreign government officials. The UK statute includes both the bribee and the briber, and it also penalizes the failure of an organization or corporation to prevent bribery on its behalf. The UK Bribery Act has a broader scope than the FCPA, since it allows for prosecution of an individual or company with links to the United Kingdom, no matter where the bribery actually took place.[47]

China's Health Care System

Why were Chinese doctors and health care workers so susceptible to the bribes being offered by GSK and other drug companies? There are 2.3 million doctors in China, 90% of whom are trained in Western medicine (versus traditional Chinese medicine). The vast majority of these medical doctors are grossly underpaid, since many of their fees are set by law. A doctor's consulting fee, for example, is only $2. Oncologists and specialists operate under a state-set price structure that is quite low. Doctors are also prohibited from taking a second job. Chinese doctors "are chronically over-worked and under-paid."[48] These low salaries and restrictions have led to abuses and waste in the medical system.[49]

This system also created perverse incentives for doctors to supplement their salary with bribes and payoffs. Chinese citizens sometimes bribed doctors to ensure they received good care. Many doctors supplemented their income by ordering diagnostic tests, prescribing medicine, and performing procedures patients did not need. Sometimes a portion of the money paid by the patient for the medicine was kicked back to the physician. Also, doctors who were exposed for accepting bribes were rarely punished.[50]

Thus, doctors were easy prey for drug companies. They could easily be persuaded to write more prescriptions with tantalizing offers of cash, expensive gifts, or free vacations. Bribery and kickbacks became common practice among local Chinese drug companies, and these payments were even regarded as part of their marketing strategy. Like their Chinese counterparts, Big Pharma companies, including GSK, came to see bribery payments to doctors as a strategic necessity. GSK was not the only multinational involved in bribery. AstraZeneca was also under investigation by Chinese authorities. In addition, both Eli Lilly and Pfizer had already been implicated in bribing Chinese doctors, and both paid hefty fines to the U.S. government for violating the FCPA.[51]

There were also systemic problems with the health care and hospital system that magnified the potential for bribery and kickbacks. Over 90% of China's hospital beds are in public hospitals, which receive direct subsidies from the government. But those subsidies are inadequate, and many of these hospitals struggle to survive. Like doctors, hospital staff are also grossly underpaid. The system is designed to allow both public and private hospitals to make up their operating deficit by charging high fees for extra services. Public hospitals can mark up drug prices by as much as 15% to augment their revenues. However, this reliance on drug markups to fund their operations creates the wrong incentives for both doctors and hospitals. It encourages overprescription of drugs, since there is an incentive to prescribe medications patients do not really need. In addition, the system encourages the use of more expensive branded drugs (such as those marketed by GSK) rather than cheaper generic versions. There is also documented evidence that some hospitals have sold patients substandard or generic medications but charged the cost of the real, branded medicine and then pocketed the difference.[52] In the past, these pharmaceutical markups provided about 40% of public hospital revenues. Finally, underpaid hospital physicians and pharmacists have been susceptible to the sorts of bribes being offered by Big Pharma companies like GSK.[53]

In summary, both underfunded public hospitals and underpaid physicians could make more money from prescribing drugs and medical procedures patients did not need. Hospital officials and their staff along with doctors were an easy target for the alternative means of income proposed by GSK salespersons. They were incentivized to prescribe expensive drugs and further incentivized by their low pay to take kickbacks.[54] To some extent, GSK and other pharmaceutical companies were following local industry norms in China by participating in these bribery schemes.

GSK Convicted of Bribery

In September 2014, a Chinese court found GSK's China subsidiary guilty of bribery. It fined the British pharmaceutical company $500 million. This was the largest corporate fine ever imposed in China. Five of the company's top managers in China, including Mark Reilly, were also convicted of bribery charges and received suspended sentences for their crimes. Reilly was expelled from the country. The conviction was especially embarrassing for GSK, since it came just two years after the $3 billion U.S. fine for questionable practices in U.S markets. At that time, CEO Witty vowed, "We're determined that this is never going to happen again."[55] When the trial was over, GSK issued a special apology to the people of China: "GSK sincerely apologizes to Chinese patients, doctors, and hospitals and to the Chinese government and the Chinese people."[56]

After the conviction, GSK's business in China steadily evaporated as competitors poached its best salespeople. In 2014, China sales dropped by 30%. According to the *Wall Street Journal*, some GSK investors began to question Witty's leadership skills and wondered whether the China issues represented not an isolated incident but a more systemic problem for GSK. Earlier in 2014, another investigation into GSK began in Poland. Eleven doctors and a GSK general manager were charged with corruption as GSK was accused once again of paying doctors to promote their drugs. Meanwhile, sales have not yet rebounded in China.[57]

In September 2016, GSK reached an agreement with the Securities and Exchange Commission in the United States to pay a $20 million fine. By bribing foreign officials to increase its sales, GSK had violated the FCPA, and so it was subject to fines and other penalties. GSK also agreed to put in place anticorruption measures to prevent further incidents in its foreign markets. The company has yet to settle with the British government for violating the UK Bribery Act.[58]

EXHIBIT 14.1 ■ GSK Financial Data, 2012–2015 (in millions of GBP)				
	2012	**2013**	**2014**	**2015**
Revenues	26,431	26,505	23,006	23,923
Operating Income	7,300	7,310	3,597	11,165
Net Income	4,499	5,436	2,756	8,422

EXHIBIT 14.2 ■ Timeline of Events

December 2011: A GSK whistle blower sends emails to Chinese regulators alerting them to fraud and corruption at GSK China.

April 2012: GSK executives in China learn about the emails sent to Chinese officials.

June 28, 2013: Police in Changsa announce an investigation of GSK for economic crimes and detain four GSK executives.

July 11, 2013: The Public Security Ministry formally accuses GSK employees of bribing doctors.

July 16, 2013: One of four detained executives confesses to a bribery scheme on state TV.

July 23, 2013: GSK acknowledges that some Chinese employees acted outside of Chinese law.

February 2014: GSK announces that its sales of medicines fell 30% in China in the fourth quarter of 2013.

September 2014: GSK is fined $500 million after its employees are convicted of bribery in a Chinese court.

September 2016: GSK agrees to pay SEC $20 million for violating FCPA.

- Outline the economic and business issues in this case. How and why did the China health care system contribute to the problem?

- What are the moral and legal implications of giving these cash payments and other gifts to doctors and hospital officials so they will prescribe your drugs? How would you have acted as a GSK salesperson or sales manager under these circumstances?

- What do you think about the corporate culture at GSK? Why do they keep having to endure these bribery scandals? How can the company best address its systemic problems so this sort of scandal doesn't happen again? How can big corporations like GSK ensure that a "no bribery" policy is enforced across all of its markets?

CASE STUDY 14.2

SEEDS OF SCANDAL AT MONSANTO

Bribes and generous payments made to public officials have become a way of life in some countries. These payments are used by some companies to "buy" many things, such as government contracts or favorable treatment by regulators. In Indonesia, $700,000 in illicit payments was made to government officials and their families from 1997 to 2002. The ostensible aim of these payments was to win approval for the use of genetically modified cotton crops by Indonesian farmers. When an environmental impact study on those crops was ordered, Monsanto worried that its approval

might be in jeopardy. So it paid $50,000 to a senior official in the Indonesian Ministry of Environment as an inducement to repeal the requirement of an environmental assessment.

This case exposes the tangled web of politics and business in countries like Indonesia where corruption is rampant and the ethical risks of doing business can be quite high. The case also underscores the ambiguities involved in distinguishing bribes from a gift or a gratuity where there is no obligation of receiving something in return.

Monsanto's History

Monsanto traces its origins back to John Francisco Queeny, who founded the Monsanto Chemical Works in St. Louis, Missouri, in 1901. His first product was the artificial sweetener saccharin. He also produced staple products like vanilla and caffeine, and sales reached $1 million by 1915.[59]

After World War I, Monsanto evolved into a key supplier of chemicals, especially for the U.S. market. In the 1920s, Monsanto began a period of rapid growth as it expanded into basic industrial chemicals such as sulfuric acid, phosphorus, and PCBs. Monsanto began manufacturing DDT in 1944, along with some 15 other companies. This insecticide, critical to the fight against malaria, became a source of controversy when it was identified in Rachel Carson's book *Silent Spring* as a pesticide that killed birds and damaged the environment. DDT was banned in the United States in 1972. In 1977, Monsanto stopped producing PCBs, which were banned by Congress two years later. In the 1960s and 1970s, Monsanto was a major producer of Agent Orange for the U.S. government. This defoliant was widely used in Vietnam, and it was another source of controversy for Monsanto.

In 1985, Monsanto purchased G.D. Searle, the maker of NutraSweet, and in 1992, it acquired the Ortho lawn chemicals business from the oil giant Chevron. The company struggled in the decade of the 1990s with poor earnings and low-revenue growth. In 1997, Monsanto spun off its chemical business and began the process of reinventing itself. It spent over $1 billion to develop its biotech business, although biotech was regarded at the time as a "commercially unproven" market. It also sold off its sweetener business to a Boston investment group. Monsanto's new core businesses were pharmaceutical and agricultural products. One of its popular pharmaceutical products was the anti-inflammatory medicine known as Celebrex. In 1998, Monsanto purchased Cargill's international seed business, which gave it access to sales and distribution facilities in 51 countries. Under CEO Hugh Grant, who took over the company in 2003, Monsanto's strategic focus shifted from agrichemicals to both conventional and genetically modified seeds. With the help of more acquisitions, it developed and marketed genetically modified cotton and corn seed. After a merger with Pharmacia & Upjohn, the company renamed itself Pharmacia Corporation. The agricultural business became Monsanto Ag Company and was later renamed Monsanto Company. Pharmacia was acquired by Pfizer in 2003.

In 2005, Monsanto purchased the vegetable seed maker Seminis, whose 3,500 seed types have been distributed in 150 countries. With this and other acquisitions, Monsanto became a mammoth agricultural biotechnology corporation. Its headquarters remained in St. Louis, Missouri, and it employed about 12,600 workers, with annual sales in the $7 billion range. Monsanto still sells herbicides and other chemicals, such as the top herbicide brand called Roundup. It has become one of the leading producers of genetically engineered seed. It produces genetically modified corn, soybean, rice, potato, and cotton seed. In 2016, Monsanto accepted a purchase offer from Bayer for $66 billion.

Monsanto and GMOs

Thanks to advances in genetic technology, it is now possible to recombine DNA segments. This scientific breakthrough opened the way for genetically modified organisms (GMOs). According to the World Health Organization (WHO), genetically modified foods are foods designed from organisms whose genetic material or DNA has been altered in an unnatural way, usually by the introduction of genes from a different organism. Genetically modified foods currently are only plant foods, but in the future, foods derived from genetically modified animals are likely to be introduced in the market.[60]

Monsanto has been a pioneer in the production and distribution of seeds that produce genetically modified (GM) crops, which are more resistant to insects or plant disease and more tolerant of herbicides. The company has also developed drought-resistant crops. According to Monsanto, these GM crops have many benefits, including faster growth, higher yields, longer shelf life, and more nutritional value. The promise of higher yields has been a strong selling point for farmers in developing countries. Monsanto has used its expertise in genetics to breed hybrids at some of its acquisitions like Seminis. In affluent markets, Monsanto showcases its Vistive soybeans, whose oil does not need partial hydrogenization.[61]

As Monsanto built its seed business, GM food and crops became quite common in many countries. They gained rapid acceptance in the United States, Canada, Argentina, and China. By 2005, Monsanto's GM seeds had been sown on over 200 million acres. However, GM seeds were restricted in some countries in Southeast Asia and also in Europe. European scientists, concerned about the long-term health risks, convinced the European Union to limit the import and sale of GMOs through European Union countries. While there was little empirical evidence of health risks for food, these suspicions created a challenging environment for Monsanto.[62]

The Bribery Scandal

Indonesia has a long history of corruption and bribery. In the past, many of its leaders and politicians have been tainted by suspicions of corruption and graft. As a consequence, this country has earned a reputation as an environment where it is difficult to do business ethically. The problem is exacerbated by an ineffective court system. Things were especially bad under the regime of President Suharto. In the 1980s, the Suharto government had been accused of countless human rights abuses, and the country was sometimes described as a "human rights sinkhole." There has been improvement since the days of the Suharto regime, but Transparency International still ranks Indonesia 107th out of 175 countries in its index that measures the corruption level of countries' public sectors.[63]

In 1996, Monsanto began testing various strains of genetically modified cotton for cultivation in Indonesia, especially in the South Sulawesi region. Monsanto wanted to distribute its Bollgard or Bt cotton seed throughout Indonesia. According to Monsanto, the product was environmentally safe and less reliant on the need for pesticides. It also claimed this GM seed would produce 3 tons of cotton per hectare (about 2½ acres). The plans were opposed by some Indonesian farmers and environmental groups. The approval for use of these GM crops was put on hold until an environmental study could be conducted. However, in February 2001, the minister of agriculture, Bungaran Saragih, granted Monsanto limited approval to grow its genetically modified cotton in seven districts of South Sulawesi. In March 2001, 40 tons of GM cotton seed was flown into Makassar, the capital of South Sulawesi, and delivered to farmers.[64]

During this period (1997–2002), Monsanto, through its Indonesian subsidiary, PT Monagro, was giving "gifts" and gratuities to the right people in order to help ensure approval of its GM cotton crops. Over $700,000 in gifts and cash payments were made to at least 140 current and former Indonesian officials and their family members. In August 2001, for example, Monsanto paid for two government ministers to visit its corporate headquarters in St. Louis. Other gifts included cell phones, golf club memberships, and luxury travel; $8,100 was paid out to Ministry of Agriculture officials. Some of the more substantial payments included $29,500 in payoffs to officials at the agriculture ministry in South Sulawesi, where the initial shipment of Bollgard cotton was sent. The largest payment of $373,990 was made for the purchase of land and the design and construction of a house in the name of the wife of a senior official in the Ministry of Agriculture. Monsanto heavily lobbied that official to allow the cultivation of GM crops in Indonesia.[65]

But a few months after the planting of the first cotton seed crop, in September 2001, the Ministry of Environment issued the AMDAL environmental decree declaring that all biotechnology products, including the cotton seeds, would be subject to an environmental impact assessment before they could be grown. This decree came from the new environment minister, who was appointed earlier that year after a change in government. The decree was seen as an impediment to the success of Monsanto's Bollgard cotton project along with its ability to sell other GMO products in Indonesia and perhaps even elsewhere in the Asia Pacific region.[66]

The stakes were high and so Monsanto began a concerted lobbying effort to persuade the minister to abrogate the decree mandating the testing. In 1998, Monsanto had hired a local lobbying firm, PT Harvest International, to help it secure approval from the Indonesian government to sell its genetically modified seeds. PT Harvest lobbyists met on numerous occasions with the environment minister and his staff. However, despite their best efforts, the Ministry of Environment refused to reverse the decision. What could be done to incentivize these officials to repeal the decree requiring the environmental assessment?[67]

At this point, a desperate Monsanto reached the conclusion that it had to resort to bribery payments in order to get its way. In February 2002, a Monsanto senior manager, who was its government affairs officer, authorized and directed PT Harvest to make an illegal payment totaling $50,000 to a senior environment official as an incentive to help him change his mind. In February 2002, an employee of the consulting firm delivered the $50,000 in $100 U.S. bills to this official's home. The messenger explained that Monsanto wanted to do something for him in exchange for his effort to repeal the environmental impact study requirement. The senior official allegedly promised he would try to get the order repealed.[68]

However, the senior environment official kept the payment, but the AMDAL decree requiring the environmental impact study for Monsanto's products was never repealed. The limited approval of February 2001, which did not require environmental testing, ended in December 2002. New approvals for the GM crops would not be granted without the impact study. Monsanto did not conduct the necessary tests, and it did not seek a new permit for 2003.

Monsanto managers had to find a way to cover up the illicit $50,000 payment. They authorized the Indonesian consulting company to submit false invoices to Monsanto for "consultant fees" to obtain reimbursement for the bribe. Those invoices totaled $66,000 so that the amount paid by Monsanto would include funds necessary to cover the taxes associated with this consulting fee income. In March 2002, as promised, Monsanto paid the false invoices, thus reimbursing the consulting company for the $50,000 bribe. Monsanto's other payments were orchestrated through a scheme of bogus pesticide sales and overinvoicing, which financed an off-the-books slush fund.[69]

The corporate offices of Monsanto first became aware of financial irregularities within its Indonesian subsidiary in March 2001. The company initiated an internal investigation, which was extended at the request of the board of directors. The investigation uncovered many questionable payments, but it did not unearth the $50,000 payment that had been made to the environment ministry official. During this period from 1996 to 2002, Monsanto did not authorize any internal audits of its Indonesian subsidiary, PT Monagro Kimia. Statutory audits required by Indonesian law were also not conducted. Monsanto simply assumed the unaudited financial information it received was fully accurate. Monsanto management did not require the Indonesian subsidiary to substantiate any of the information in those financial statements. According to the Securities and Exchange Commission (SEC), "The absence of effective internal controls enabled the Indonesian management to conceal their illicit payment scheme."[70]

Aftermath

By February 2003, Indonesian farmers in South Sulawesi were no longer being supplied with Monsanto's Bt cotton seed. Many farmers had grown the cotton crop but had had poor crop yields. Over 70% of the Bt crop locations had not produced the promised yields. Despite Monsanto's assurances to the contrary, the crops had been attacked by many pests. Monsanto blamed "misplanting" for the disappointing yields, but scientists claim the wrong pests were targeted. By the end of 2003, Monsanto announced its decision to pull out of South Sulawesi.[71]

When Monsanto finished its internal investigations into these irregular payments, it informed the U.S. Department of Justice and the Securities and Exchange Commission. In January 2005, the SEC filed a complaint in the U.S. District Court for the District of Columbia charging Monsanto with direct violation of the Foreign Corrupt Practices Act.

A second claim charged Monsanto with failure to "devise and maintain" an adequate system of internal accounting controls.[72] In the court hearing, Monsanto admitted that its employees had made the illicit payments, including the $50,000 given to the senior environment minister in a bid to avoid the environmental impact assessment of its Bt cotton crop. Monsanto agreed to pay a $1.5 million fine for making that payment and for its other violations. The U.S. Justice Department did not pursue criminal charges against Monsanto or any of its employees.[73]

The bribery payments, which were made public in 2005, cast a shadow over Monsanto's genetically modified seed business. Critics wondered why the company would go to such lengths to avoid an environmental impact study when it had reassured the public that these crops were perfectly safe. Some wondered what Monsanto might have done in other countries using GM crops, where the stakes were far greater than in Indonesia.[74]

- Outline the payments made to Indonesian officials and their effect. What were the consequences of Monsanto's violation of the FCPA? Do you think the penalties imposed by the SEC were adequate? If not, what would you recommend?

- How would you assess Monsanto's actions from a moral point of view? (Keep in mind the course frameworks from Chapters 2 and 3.)

- How could Monsanto have avoided this scandal? Be as specific as possible.

- Is there anything wrong with some of the "gifts" proffered to Indonesian officials, such as a cell phone or country club membership? What about Monsanto's payment for two government officials to visit its St. Louis headquarters? Are these bribes or gratuities?

CASE STUDY 14.3

THE RESOURCE CURSE AND EQUATORIAL GUINEA

In 1995, a vast reservoir of oil was discovered in a remote region of Equatorial Guinea, and that small African country has never been the same. Equatorial Guinea is located on the west coast of Africa. It is composed of a mainland territory called Rio Muni and several islands, including Bioko, where the capital city of Malabo is located. The country is a former colony of Spain and has had a turbulent history since winning its independence in 1968. It was ruled for 11 years by the brutal dictator Francesca Micias Ngeuma. His long reign of terror forced a third of the popu-

AP Photo/Rebecca Blackwell

lation to flee their homeland. In 1979, Ngeuma was forced out in a coup by Teodoro Obiang Nguema Mbasgo. Obiang has also ruled the country as an intolerant and autocratic despot who uses brute force to retain his power.[75]

But thanks to the discovery of oil, Equatorial Guinea now enjoys almost unrivaled prosperity among African nations. Equatorial Guinea is the third-largest oil producer in sub-Saharan Africa. The country produces about 360,000 barrels of oil per day. Its GDP has grown from a paltry $130 million in 1991 to $2.5 billion in 2016. This is the highest GDP of any sub-Saharan African country. Yet this prosperity has not reached the citizens of Equatorial Guinea or improved their overall welfare. The vast majority of the population still lives in abject poverty. It ranks 138th out of 188 countries on the Human Development Index. The government invests only 2% to 3% of its budget in health and education. This is far less than in any other country in its high-income bracket. Its vaccination rate is the lowest in the world, and the infant mortality rate is exceptionally high. Most of the residents live in squalor, and only half the population has access to safe drinking water. There are few jobs outside the oil industry, and most people subsist on farming the land.[76]

Not only is there widespread poverty in this country, there are also systemic human rights abuses. Freedom of association and assembly are severely constrained. Reporters without Borders ranks Equatorial Guinea 158th worst out of 175 countries for freedom of the press. Local political activists who voice human rights concerns face intimidation and harassment. While Equatorial Guinea is nominally a democratic nation, in reality, Obiang's democratic party (PDGE) has a virtual monopoly over the country's political life. Opposition party members are routinely arrested and detained. They are frequently silenced by arbitrary arrests, criminal prosecution, and constant harassment.[77]

What has gone wrong for this obscure African country? Equatorial Guinea is a prime example of the "resource curse" at work. The combination of natural resources and foreign investment did not lift this country out of economic chaos and poverty, but only yielded conflict and political corruption.

The oil money has enriched the country's leader, President Obiang, along with his family and cronies, but it has not flowed to the people. While the people of Equatorial Guinea suffer in poverty, Obiang lives a lavish lifestyle. He owns several mansions, a yacht, sports cars, and a fleet of private jet planes. The family owns property in Malibu, the Potomac, and Paris. The president's indulgent playboy son, Teodorin, has been accused of money laundering in France and Switzerland. Teodorin Obiang spent almost $44 million on houses and luxury cars in the United States and Europe between 2004 and 2006, while the total educational budget of Equatorial Guinea in 2005 was only $43 million.[78] And the president sustains his power through force. According to Human Rights Watch, the "dictatorship under President Obiang has used an oil boom to entrench and enrich itself further at the expense of the country's people."[79] But is there a link between this government corruption and oil companies doing business in Equatorial Guinea?

ExxonMobil in Equatorial Guinea

In March 1995, Mobil (now ExxonMobil) struck oil in the 1.1-billion-barrel Zafiro field. By August 1996, production had reached 40,000 barrels of oil per day, and it surpassed 190,000 barrels in several years. This was a significant increase, since the country had only been producing 5,000 to 7,000 barrels per day of natural gas liquids in its Alba oil fields. For the first five years after production began in August 1996, the Zafiro field's oil capacity was significantly expanded. ExxonMobil holds a participating interest of 71.25% in Zafiro, GEPetrol has 23.75%, and the Equatorial Guinea government holds the remaining 5%. The accumulated oil production of the Zafiro field exceeded 1 billion barrels in 2015.[80]

In January 2015, Equatorial Guinea ratified a new deal with ExxonMobil for the exploration of one of its most oil-rich offshore fields. The oil field, titled Block EG-06, is located in Bioko Island, adjacent to the international border with Nigeria. The minister of mines, industry, and energy, Gabriel Mbaga Obiang Lima, said the ratification of the new Production Sharing Contract "signifies the start of a new adventure between old acquaintances and is expected to be as successful as the first one." He went on to say that this agreement with one of the oil industry's "supermajors" like ExxonMobil was a major vote of confidence in Equatorial Guinea, even as global commodity prices remain depressed. "This is added proof that offshore Equatorial Guinea continues to be an appealing jurisdiction for the exploration of hydrocarbons," he declared.[81]

ExxonMobil's commitment to Equatorial Guinea is not without controversy, thanks to Obiang's oppressive government with which it does business. Under the terms of the oil contract, the company keeps much of the oil it takes from Zafiro and pays the government royalties, bonuses, and taxes. That Zafiro oil is shipped primarily to the United States. ExxonMobil routinely deposits these royalty and tax payments in U.S. dollars in overseas banks. In 2004, a U.S. Senate investigation revealed that the Washington branch of the Riggs bank held payments from oil companies doing business in Equatorial Guinea, with the largest share coming from ExxonMobil. Hundreds of millions of dollars was deposited in 60 accounts for the government of Equatorial Guinea, top government officials, and their families. The bank also allowed millions of dollars from the government account to be wired into accounts of two companies owned by Obiang located in countries with bank secrecy laws.[82] According to a director at Human Rights Watch, Arvind Ganeson, "The government literally used the oil wealth of the country as a personal A.T.M." Mr. Ganeson contends the same kind of behavior still continues.[83]

There have also been allegations of questionable payments and business relationships on ExxonMobil's part. In 1998, ExxonMobil partnered with a company called Abayak, which is partially owned by Obiang and his wife. Abayak received a 15% share of ExxonMobil's profits in Equatorial Guinea. In addition, an ExxonMobil subsidiary leases office space in the Abayak office complex for $175,500 per year.[84] In the past, ExxonMobil, along with other oil companies, has made payments of over $4 million to support more than 100 students from Equatorial Guinea who are studying abroad. Most of these students were relatives of powerful families in the country with commercial ties to Obiang. Two companies, Amerada Hess and a subsidiary of ExxonMobil, paid $1 million for security services from a security firm owned by the president's brother, Armengol Ondo Nguema. In addition, through a subsidiary, a Hess-owned company, Triton Energy, transferred $250,000 to the Riggs bank account to send Ondo's children to school.[85]

But ExxonMobil is insistent that it has never bribed anyone in Equatorial Guinea or run afoul of the U.S. Foreign Corrupt Practices Act that forbids bribery payments to foreign officials. That may be true, but critics claim that such a close relationship with Obiang is problematic even if the law has not been broken. A spokesman for ExxonMobil defended the company by saying that when it deals with countries, it relies on laws (such as the FCPA) as a guide. According to Alan Jeffers, "We're a company that follows laws, [and] absent a law prohibiting something, we evaluate it on a business case basis."[86]

Oil companies like ExxonMobil have also been criticized for helping to sustain the Obiang regime, which continues to engage in vast corruption and human rights abuses. Oil revenues prop up this corrupt regime and help a despotic leader to stay in power. Human rights advocates such as Sarah Wykes observe that oil companies like ExxonMobil ignore all the "red flags" about how oil revenues or royalties are spent by the government. According to Wykes, "At the very least, there's an appearance of the complicity with corruption."[87] Another critic of ExxonMobil, Tutu Alicante, argues that by doing business in Equatorial Guinea under these conditions, oil companies reinforce the repressive power of Obiang. "Exxon definitely has enabled a government that once upon a time was very repressive but didn't have the resources to keep itself in power," Alicante has declared.[88]

Most corporations do not make any distinctions about their commercial engagements with resource-rich countries. If a country has strong institutions and good leadership, foreign investment can lead to more government spending in the social sector and a prosperous future for its citizens. But if there is an autocratic and incompetent regime along with weak institutions, that engagement can help the government carry out its repressive agenda. Despotic leadership and mineral wealth seem to be a lethal combination.[89]

Postscript

President Obiang once described his country's fortuitous discovery of oil as "manna from heaven." When he took office in 1979, the country had been ravaged by an 11-year dictatorship as it struggled to overcome centuries of colonialism that had stripped the country of its few natural resources. The discovery of oil had the potential to reverse the dismal fortunes of this struggling African nation, but regrettably that never happened.[90]

The country's elite have squandered its wealth. Equatorial Guinea abounds in oil, yet remains immersed in poverty because the people have been denied the tangible benefits of the revenues accruing from the country's oil. Also, resources deployed for extraction of oil draw capital away from other sectors of the economy like agriculture. And the large influx of foreign capital tends to inflate the country's exchange rate. The people of Equatorial Guinea suffer from this resource curse—extracting oil has fueled a fight for rents, inspired greater corruption, and damaged its already weak institutions. As Leif Wenar points out, "might makes right" in Equatorial Guinea and in many other oil-rich countries. Obiang's "coercive success" gives him the legal "right" to control oil extraction and exports in his country along with the revenue streams that come from that oil.[91]

EXHIBIT 14.3 ■ Key Facts about the Republic of Equatorial Guinea

Capital: Malabo

Population: 740,000

Area: 28,051 square kilometers (10,830 square miles)

Major languages: Spanish, French

Religion: Christianity

Life expectancy: 54 years (men), 57 years (women)

Currency: CFA (Communauté Financière Africaine) franc

- Should ExxonMobil be doing business in Equatorial Guinea under these conditions? Should it have signed the new deal to explore offshore oil?

- Was the company's arrangement with Abayak tantamount to a bribe (even if it did not technically violate the FCPA)? What about the tuition payments for some of the country's students studying abroad?

- Do you agree with ExxonMobil's principle as a reasonable guideline for doing business in corrupt countries: follow the law, and unless a law prohibits something, evaluate the situation on a business-case basis? If not, how might you modify this principle?

- What (if anything) should ExxonMobil do differently in Equatorial Guinea? For example, should it pressure the government to do more for its people?

CONCLUSION

The purpose of this chapter was to probe the nature and causes of bribery and corruption in foreign markets. Despite better enforcement of bribery laws such as the FCPA, bribery remains an insidious and intractable problem. Some have tried to defend bribery on utilitarian grounds, but most people find that defense unconvincing. Bribery is morally questionable because it represents unfair competition, tipping the market to one's advantage by paying someone off. As we saw in the bribery cases, there are no simple solutions. But every company that operates in emerging economies, including GSK and Monsanto, must implement effective internal controls and fortify its moral culture to combat the perennial temptation to bribe foreign officials in order to get new business or retain the business they already have.

The final case considered the related issues of corruption and the resource curse, and it questioned whether multinational oil companies should lend support in any way to corrupt regimes that amass oil rents for themselves while the people remain destitute.

Student Study Site

Visit **edge.sagepub.com/spinello.**

Key Terms

bribery   376

corruption   376

Review Question

1. What are the root causes of bribery and corruption? What impact does bribery have on a nation's economy and on society in general?

Discussion Questions

1. Why has bribery been such a persistent problem, and why has it taken countries so long to deal with the problem?

2. Do you agree with the moral arguments presented in this chapter against bribery? Which of those arguments is most convincing?

15

RESPONSIBLE OUTSOURCING

Fair Wages and Worker Safety

Even if I am on my death bed, they will ask me to make two more pieces before I die. We are nothing but machines to them.

—Bangladeshi garment worker[1]

We care about every worker in our worldwide supply chain.

—Tim Cook[2]

LEARNING OBJECTIVES

Upon completion of this chapter, you should be able to:

15.1 Discuss the moral and economic aspects of offshoring and outsourcing.

15.2 Demonstrate awareness of employee rights, including a just wage and acceptable working conditions.

15.3 Explain the issues of moral agency and complicity.

Within the most current phase of globalization, there has been a record level of "offshoring": the transfer of manufacturing jobs outside the home country of a corporation. Production takes place in the company's own factories located abroad, or it can be outsourced, which means it is done by outside contractors.[3] The prime motivation is usually to find low-cost countries where skilled or unskilled workers are much cheaper to hire. Offshore outsourcing has become the norm in some industries like toys, clothing, and electronics. Toy companies like Hasbro and Disney have most of their toys made by contractors in China, which is known as the world's "toy workshop."[4] Besides China, a considerable amount of routine, unskillful work has been moved to many other low-wage countries such as Mexico, Vietnam, India, and Taiwan. In 1991, 234 million people in developing countries worked in manufacturing, but that number increased to 304 million by 2014. Some companies such as Apple and ARM, the British chip company, own no factories of their own.[5]

Despite the public concerns over offshoring and outsourcing, the economic benefits have been immense. For workers in low-cost developing economies, it has meant factory jobs and a higher standard of living. For multinationals that outsource or invest abroad, these lower labor costs have increased profits and shareholder equity. Western consumers also benefit, with access to more products at lower prices.[6]

Nonetheless, some companies, under political pressure, have begun the task of "reshoring," bringing jobs back to their home countries and making more products in-house. They have realized that while there are still big gaps between wages in different countries, other factors such as quality and transportation costs offset them. Also, wages in some countries like China have skyrocketed over the years. However, many semiskilled manufacturing jobs are unlikely to return. They have been eliminated by productivity enhancements and disaggregated supply chains that magnify the distinction between routine labor and high-value-added activities. As the *Economist* points out, "There is no vice that can squeeze those genies back into their bottles."[7]

Although it pays big economic dividends, the strategy of offshore outsourcing poses numerous challenges. Companies must carefully consider where to produce their goods and what impact offshoring will have on the logistics of their supply chain. There are higher transaction costs because these companies do not control the operations that produce their products. Production makes a significant contribution to the success of research and development (R&D), and experience has demonstrated that innovation prospers when manufacturing and R&D are in the same location.[8]

There are also several ethical concerns that revolve around wages and working conditions. Should Western companies apply the lower standards of their host countries for workplace safety, or should they insist on the higher standards that are normative in their home countries? And should they intervene with their contractors to insist that workers making their products get at least a "living wage" and appropriate benefits? Richard De George has argued that every worker deserves "subsistence wages and as much above that as workers and their dependents need to live with reasonable dignity."[9] Critics of multinationals have focused on the low salaries paid in these international sweatshops and call for laws that mandate higher pay and minimum wages. They also demand improved working conditions, with more attention paid to worker health and safety.

But, as some economists point out, higher wages along with health and safety requirements increase labor costs, and these increased costs will lead to the employment of fewer sweatshop workers. As bad as sweatshop jobs are, they are better than the alternative. In most countries where there is a heavy concentration of sweatshops, the largest segment of the population works in agriculture. In Bangladesh, 85% of the population, most of which is employed in the agricultural industry, earns less than $2.00 a day. But workers in Bangladesh sweatshops earn more than $2.00 a day. Working in an average sweatshop in countries like Bangladesh, Vietnam, Cambodia, Honduras, and Nicaragua raises a worker's income above the average for that country. The fact that a sweatshop job is a worker's best option in these low-wage countries complicates the ethical debate over sweatshops and the economics of outsourcing.[10]

AN OVERVIEW OF THE CASES

The two cases in this chapter concentrate on the moral issues associated with offshoring and outsourcing. They fix our attention on how international corporations can source products from other countries in a socially responsible fashion. The first case focuses on Apple Inc. which outsources production of its core products such as the Macintosh and the iPhone to suppliers like Foxconn and Pegatron in China. Regrettably, there has been a history of worker abuses with Apple suppliers, which are detailed in this case. Like other manufacturers in the smartphone industry, Apple is motivated to reduce costs so it can appropriate as much value added as possible. Apple also keeps inventory supplies low and forces its suppliers to ramp up production quickly during periods of peak demand. But Apple's efficiency and low-cost goals lead to excessive overtime and unbearable pressure for many workers. Is Apple complicit in any of the workplace abuse going on at its major suppliers? How can Apple do a better job of attending to the welfare of its workers in its supply chain?

The second case reviews the issue of worker safety for offshore operations. It discusses two tragic incidents in Bangladesh, where many well-known retailers and clothing companies source their goods. The first event was a fire due to faulty electrical wiring that killed 112 workers, and the second was a building collapse at Rana Plaza that killed over 1,000 people. After these accidents, some Western companies, which were accused of pursuing profits at the cost of decent working conditions, vowed to take remedial action. But were the steps taken by these Western retailers adequate? Do corporations have a moral obligation to ensure there are safe working conditions within *every* factory of their global supply chain? Should they invest in a safer infrastructure for their suppliers, many of which cannot afford this investment? How far up the supply chain do these obligations extend?

One of the primary issues in both cases is the moral complicity of economic agents who may not directly cause any harm. Companies like Apple, Walmart, Disney, and many others are motivated to avert worker abuses by their suppliers to protect the integrity of their brand. But on moral grounds, shouldn't they avoid making any sort of causal contribution to the misdeeds of those suppliers? By refusing to take action to correct the deficient and unsafe working conditions in these low-wage factories, brand owners like Apple may be unjustly tolerating these practices from which they profit.[11]

CASE STUDY 15.1

WORKER ABUSES IN THE SUPPLY CHAIN: THE DISTURBING CASE OF APPLE IN CHINA

AP Photo/Bai kelin - Imaginechina

During the past two decades, Apple Inc. has introduced a series of remarkable new products and services that have opened new markets and transformed Apple into the most valuable publicly traded company. The iPod/iTunes, iPhone, and iPad were all introduced to captivated audiences by the charismatic Steve Jobs. Jobs was a risk taker who was willing to tolerate the chaos of being on the cutting edge, and his death in 2011 ended the company's historic run of innovation. Under Tim Cook, the company is more focused on profitability through scale and discipline. One key to its success is low-cost manufacturing, which is achieved through outsourcing to emerging economies with low wages.[12]

However, Apple has been beset by continuing scandals over the working conditions found in some of the factories in its Chinese supply chain. Worker mistreatment at Foxconn and also at Pegatron have been reported by the media and by nongovernment organizations (NGOs) like China Labor Watch. These abuses have been a source of great embarrassment for Apple executives. The company prides itself on its commitment to a strong social responsibility agenda and has defended its practices abroad on many occasions. A key ethical question in this case concerns Apple's accountability for the human rights violations in its supply chain, despite the fact that it does not own or directly control these operations. Also, are these ongoing labor abuses a foreseeable side effect of its aggressive manufacturing strategy built on low inventory levels and tight time frames for suppliers?

From Apple Computer to Apple Inc.

Apple was founded in 1976 by the creative genius Steve Jobs and his friend Steve Wozniak. Jobs sought to bring an easy-to-use personal computer to market, and he introduced the Apple II in 1978. That computer was replaced by the Macintosh in 1984, the first computer to rely on a mouse and graphical user interface. The Mac competed with the IBM PC and its clones made by companies like Dell and Hewlett-Packard. Unlike the Mac, these products ran on Microsoft's operating system (MS-DOS), which later became Windows. However, despite its stylishness and ease of use, the Mac did not fare so well. This was due to poor performance and the lack of application software. Computers running Windows had a much larger installed base of users, which attracted more independent software vendors. As a result, Jobs was forced out of the company he founded in 1985. But Apple continued to struggle under a succession of CEOs who tried different and often contradictory strategies that moved the company in different directions. Eventually Steve Jobs returned to Apple in August 1997. Jobs immediately introduced the colorful iMac, and in 1998 the company earned $309 million in profits after two years of financial losses. The successful iMac represented a revival for Apple and its demoralized employees. Jobs continued to improve the Mac over the years. It now runs on a superior microprocessor made by Intel and is the top-selling premium-brand computer. Yet the Mac remains a niche business, a very distant second to computers that run on Microsoft Windows.

Steve Jobs wasn't satisfied with revitalizing the Macintosh. He set out to broaden the Apple product line by introducing the iPod in 2001. The iPod quickly became the dominant portable music player in the world, and it was used to help launch the iTunes music store, a revolutionary system that led to the demise of many leading music retailers. With the iPod and its companion technology iTunes, Apple was on its way to becoming an electronics giant, not just a computer company.[13]

The popular iPod was followed by the iPhone, which was introduced in 2007. The groundbreaking iPhone was Apple's bold attempt to "reinvent the phone." Mobile phones produced by companies like Nokia and Motorola had become quite popular, but there was nothing like the new iPhone. Its touch screen, its capacity to run numerous apps, and many other features made this product a massive hit in the mobile-phone market. Compressed into a small device was a powerful networked computer, destined to alter consumer habits in areas like music and books.[14] The company launched its app store in 2008 to provide applications for its iPhone. Apple faced strong competition from products running Google's Android operating system, but its premium price allowed the company to generate handsome profits from its flagship product.

The next innovation of Jobs was a tablet known as the iPad, which was introduced to the market in 2011. This trendy product sold 300,000 copies on its first day of sale in the United States. While Jobs's iPhone shook up the mobile-phone world, the iPad became another essential electronic tool for its tech-savvy customers. Like the iPhone, the iPad depends on small applications or "apps," and Apple boasts over 1,500,000 apps in the Apple app store to satisfy the diverse needs of its users. All of these technologies constituted the expanding Apple ecosystem. Jobs also opened a chain of retail stores where Apple salespeople were quite adept at cross-selling its related products.

Despite the iPad's overnight success, the iPhone has become Apple's core business and the key driver of its sales and profits. In 2016, the iPhone has accounted for over 64% of Apple's revenues and 75% of its gross profit. Despite the intensifying competition in the smartphone industry, Apple still appropriates the lion's share of the industry's profits, with Samsung a distant second. The iPhone is one of the best-selling products in history, with 1.3 billion units sold since its product launch. But this success has also created certain challenges for Apple, raising the bar for innovation and transforming an underdog into a mammoth industry leader.[15]

The company changed its name from Apple Computer to Apple Inc., to reflect its diverse portfolio of products. By 2015, it had also added the Apple Watch, along with Apple Pay and its iCloud services, which further enhanced the ecosystem. The iCloud software, which allows users to store data on the Internet rather than on their devices, has built up switching costs for Apple's customers and helped insulate the company from its many agile and innovative competitors, such as Samsung Electronics. Apple's sustainable competitive position is helped by the strength of its brand and its reputation. In 2016, Apple was the most profitable U.S. company, with a net income of $45.7 billion (see Exhibit 15.1).

EXHIBIT 15.1 ■ Apple Financial Data (in millions)

	2013	2014	2015	2016
Revenues	$170,910	$182,795	$233,715	$215,639
Net Income	37,037	39,510	53,394	45,687
Total Cash and Marketable Securities	121,251	146,761	205,239	227,000

Tim Cook, Steve Jobs's successor, has not only introduced new products but also put more emphasis on enhancing Apple's reputation in the eyes of Apple customers and stakeholders. He has insisted that the company be guided by social values and be sincerely committed to corporate social responsibility. Cook has repeatedly articulated an obligation to all of Apple's stakeholders, including customers and employees, and not just its shareholders. In one speech, the Apple CEO was not reticent about stressing the company's commitment to moral values: "We believe that a company that has values and acts on them can really change the world. There is an opportunity to do work that is infused with moral purpose."[16] Cook has emphasized the centrality of social efforts such as philanthropy, corporate diversity, and renewable energy. According to one observer, Apple now has a more visible "internal social compass."[17]

In 2016, Apple introduced the new iPhone 7 Plus, which sold for $769. It included new features such as a two-camera system that could produce richer photos and videos along with more memory and a longer battery life. Despite Apple's success, it continues to face stiff competition from companies like Samsung. China has been a soft spot, and Apple has lost market share to less expensive smartphones from local rivals such as Huawei and Oppo Electronics. These smartphones along with those made by Samsung run on Google's Android. Unlike Apple's proprietary system, the Android is an open platform. Smartphone manufacturers can adopt this platform without paying Google a licensing fee, and they can adapt the underlying technology to customize Android. Whether the smartphone market in the long term can support these two diverse models is an open question. Apple's market share remains second to Samsung, but has dropped off in recent years to just about 14% of the market (see Exhibit 15.2).[18]

Under Cook, Apple has quadrupled R&D spending to $10 billion, but it has failed to come up with a new blockbuster product like the iPhone or the iPad. It continues to pin its hope for growth on the iPhone 7 Plus and its successors. Apple has reached the apex of its power, but without new disruptive innovations, it will face the prospect of stagnation and mediocre performance.[19]

EXHIBIT 15.2 ■ Smartphone Market Share, 2014–2016 (leading vendors)

Manufacturer	2014	2015	2016
Samsung	24.5%	24.0%	21.2%
Apple	14.8%	15.0%	14.6%
Huawei	5.7%	6.0%	9.5%

Manufacturer	2014	2015	2016
Lenovo	7.4%	5.1%	3.7%
LG	4.6%	4.0%	5.0%
Oppo	—	3.6%	7.3%

Production and Manufacturing

Apple directly employs over 80,000 U.S citizens and boasts handsome domestic facilities in Cupertino, California, and Austin, Texas. Over 6,000 people work in Apple's bright, new facilities in Austin. Dispersed throughout seven limestone-and-glass buildings, they handle technical support, update Maps software, and also help to run Apple's iTunes music and app stores. Experienced employees at the Austin complex earn on average $45,000 per year. They also receive generous benefits and small stock grants. The Austin campus has an elegant dining hall along with a full-service medical clinic. Apple also has 69 U.S. suppliers in 33 states that manufacture parts that go into its various products.[20]

For the last two decades, Apple has outsourced most of its production to a network of independent contractors. Instead of manufacturing, it has chosen to focus on high-value-added activities like product design, development, and marketing. The Mac was produced in the United States during the decade of the 1990s in plants like Elk Grove, which made computers for Apple's domestic market. Computers for the European market were produced in Cork, Ireland. But Apple gradually began selling off in-house manufacturing and shifting production to U.S. manufacturers. However, most of Apple's manufacturing now takes place abroad, where wages are much lower. This includes the production of its core products: the Mac computer and the iPhone. In 2004, Apple closed its last computer manufacturer at Elk Grove. Apple now relies most heavily on a number of outsourcing partners in China, such as Foxconn and Pegatron.[21]

Apple's strategy of extensive offshore manufacturing has sparked controversy and even became a polemical issue in the 2016 presidential campaign. President Trump asserted that he wanted Apple to begin making its iPhones in the United States so more citizens could be gainfully employed. "I'm going to get Apple to start making their computers and their iPhones on our land," said Trump, "not in China."[22] However, there are many advantages associated with manufacturing in China beyond low wages. There is a strong electronics supply chain throughout Asia, which makes it possible to ramp up production rapidly. Apple sources memory chips for its iPhones from Korean suppliers and displays from suppliers in Japan.

Thus, despite these political pressures, Apple is unlikely to reshore iPhone production, especially when competitors like Samsung make their products in low-cost countries such as China. Apple has over 200 foreign suppliers that make its different products along with the components of those products. According to Apple, "Substantially all of the company's hardware products are manufactured by outsourcing partners that are located primarily in Asia. A significant concentration of this manufacturing is currently performed by a small number of outsourcing partners, often in a single location."[23] Its biggest and most reliable supplier has been Foxconn, but after a series of scandals, Apple modified its contracts and now also relies heavily on Pegatron as an alternative supplier.

The operations of both of these suppliers have been configured to support Apple's manufacturing strategy. Apple eschews large stockpiles of inventory and strives for the lowest possible manufacturing cost structure. In one of its supplier reports, the company explained that it seeks to obtain products "within tight frameworks" and "at a cost that represents the best possible value."[24] Part of the reason for the quick turnaround demanded from suppliers is Apple's desire to keep new products a secret before they are introduced to the public and released. Thus, Apple suppliers must be flexible enough to accommodate peak demand periods where Apple will require them to ramp up production and rapidly increase product quantities. They must also be prepared to accept last-minute changes in product design. Steve Jobs, for example, decided to modify the screen to strengthen the glass on the iPhone four weeks before it was scheduled to be on store shelves. Sometimes tens of thousands of redesigned products must be produced each day on less than a week's notice. Since the Apple contract is so consequential to a supplier's revenues, they usually comply with Apple's excessive demands. The result for workers is obvious: psychological pressure along with excessive overtime at final assembly and supplier plants to meet high production quotas within a short time frame.[25]

Apple and Foxconn

Foxconn Technology, formerly known as Hon Hai Precision Industries, was founded in 1974 by Terry Gou. Foxconn is China's largest exporter and also one of its biggest employers. It has built massive factories in China with the help of government subsidies. Over 1.2 million employees work in its different manufacturing plants scattered around Taiwan and China. It has shifted some production operations elsewhere in Asia, including Vietnam and India, but about 95% of its employees work in China. Foxconn makes Kindles for Amazon and PlayStations for Sony, but one of its most loyal customers has been Apple Inc. When Apple began outsourcing production of computers along with its phones and tablets, it chose Foxconn because it had the scale, capabilities, and flexibility to produce adequate quantities of these products within short time frames. Also, the global supply chain for electronics remains firmly rooted in Asia.[26]

But demanding and unsafe working conditions at some of its plants thrust both Foxconn and Apple into the spotlight. Between January and November 2010, there were 13 suicides at the Foxconn factory in China making iPhones and iPads. Four other workers attempted suicide but were unsuccessful. The reasons seemed linked to the pressure of overtime along with harsh and isolating working conditions. One of the suicide survivors was Tian Yu, who worked 12-hour days. She felt estranged in this overwhelming plant where no conversations were allowed on the work floor. She had to adopt the required posture for production workers and keep her stool within clearly marked yellow and black lines. At the end of her first month, she received no pay due to a lost wage card. In desperation, with no money and no friends, she tried to kill herself. As the suicides and attempted suicides mounted, a Foxconn spokesperson defended the company by arguing that the rate of "self-killing" was not much higher than China's relatively high average. But Foxconn also responded with assurances that it would treat its workers better. The company increased wages and installed suicide prevention nets.[27]

A year later, however, Foxconn was making headlines again due to its unsafe working conditions. Within a seven-month period in 2011, there were two explosions at Foxconn factories making iPads. Four people were killed and 77 were injured. How did these explosions occur? In the Chengdu factory in China, scene of the first accident, shifts run 24 hours a day. A team of workers had been shining iPad cases with a sander, and this created hazardous aluminum dust throughout their work area. In China, iPad sales were rising swiftly, and Foxconn was being pressured to increase its supply. As a result, the Foxconn workers had been polishing more cases than usual. The cloud of aluminum dust became dangerously thick in this poorly ventilated facility, and the eventual result was a terrible explosion. Four people who had been doing the polishing were killed, and a number of others were severely injured. Apple (as well as Foxconn) had been informed just months earlier about this hazardous condition within the Chengdu plant, but it took no action. A defensive Foxconn insisted after the explosion that the factory was in complete compliance with local laws and regulations.[28]

After the Chengdu blast, Apple assembled a team of safety experts to make recommendations to other factories so this type of explosion would not recur. However, seven months later, in December 2011, the iPad factory in Shanghai was the scene of another devastating explosion, and once again the cause was excessive aluminum dust. While there were no fatalities this time, 59 workers were injured, 23 quite seriously. As safety experts have pointed out, the problem is relatively easy to solve. Adequate ventilation should virtually eliminate the risk of explosion from aluminum dust clouds within the plant.[29]

In 2016, there were two more deaths at the Foxconn plant in Zhengzhou. One man committed suicide after the night shift by jumping off the roof, and a woman was struck by a train when she climbed across the rails after flooding rains had blocked the safer path to her factory. Fellow workers said she was anxious because "Foxconn docks bonuses if you don't show up for work, even for bad weather." These two deaths once again shined a spotlight on the psychological effects of the harsh labor conditions at Foxconn, where low pay and 60-hour work weeks are the norm.[30]

Foxconn has a long history of many ongoing abuses, including excessive work hours (over 60 hours a week), paltry wages, and terrible living conditions in the dormitories it provides for its workers. At its Taiyuan and Longhua factories, where Apple products are made, the base wage is $320 per month, still low but a considerable improvement over the $152 base wage paid in 2010. However, at its Zhengzhou factory, the base wage in 2016 was $285 per month, which represents a mere $15 increase over the $270 base wage of 2013. Workers also receive a performance bonus of $30 per month, and Foxconn pays their social insurance. According to China Labor Watch, although the annual wage growth in China from 2011 to 2016 was 13%, Foxconn workers' wages hardly changed in some of its factories. These are below-subsistence-level wages for urban areas and must be supplemented with overtime pay so workers can make ends meet.[31]

Interviews with Foxconn workers and former workers suggest that its factories are still "labor camps," where workers are abused both physically and mentally. An interview by journalist Brian Merchant with a man known as Xu graphically exposed the working conditions at the Longhua factory. According to Xu, workers regularly log 12-hour shifts, and sometimes the work week exceeds the 60-hour-a-week standard set by Apple. Foxconn promises workers free housing but then charges exorbitantly high utility bills for electricity and water. Workers also reported they were required to perform a procedure or step in the mechanized manufacturing process within two or three seconds without making any unnecessary movements such as talking or walking around. At the end of the day, productive workers are praised by managers, but those who made mistakes are singled out and humiliated. Despite some improvements, Xu and others paint a bleak picture of a high-pressure work environment where suicides have become a normal event.[32]

Despite the publicity of the Foxconn suicides and Apple's efforts to address labor rights violations, the abuses at Foxconn factories continue. A 2017 China Labor Watch report confirms that the problem of excessive working hours has not been resolved. An undercover operation revealed that some workers accumulated 122 hours of overtime in a given month. Workers could choose not to work overtime. But if they refused overtime even once during the factory's busy periods, such as the months leading to a product launch, the assembly line supervisor would threaten to deprive them of any overtime for the entire month. Since the base wage is so low, most workers cannot survive without overtime, so they are forced into working all of these hours.[33]

Apple and Pegatron

Some of Apple's manufacturing was moved to Pegatron after the persistent problems at Foxconn factories were exposed. Pegatron Corp., a Taiwanese electronic company founded in 2008, describes itself as a "worldwide leader in electronics and DMS (Design and Manufacturing Services)." The company takes particular pride in its "flexible manufacturing capability." Pegatron employs 50,000 workers across China and Taiwan, and in 2016 reported annual revenues of $2.8 billion. Pegatron offered Apple the same flexible manufacturing services as Foxconn but with lower prices based on their low wage structure. This was an extra incentive to lure manufacturing away from Foxconn. Pegatron was chosen to produce the iPad mini and the iPhone version 6. It was later selected to produce version 7, which was introduced in 2016. With this move, Apple diversified its supply chain and expanded its output capacities.[34]

But, like Foxconn, Pegatron also has a history of poor working conditions in its factories. Serious abuses at several Pegatron facilities have been exposed by NGOs like China Labor Watch (CLW). In July 2013, CLW published an unflattering indictment of Apple called *Apple's Unkept Promises*. In that report, CLW presented evidence that many Pegatron employees making iPhones and iPads were working 100 to 120 hours of overtime per month. The report also highlighted low wages, environmental violations, and poor working conditions, including overcrowded dormitories.[35]

Despite Apple's repeated promises to address supply-chain labor issues, subsequent CLW reports issued in 2016 and 2017 suggest that things have not improved for Pegatron's workers. According to its close examination of pay stubs, over 60% of Pegatron employees producing Apple iPhones worked over 90 hours of overtime every month. This was a violation of Apple's explicit guidelines for its suppliers: "Except in emergency or unusual situations, Supplier shall limit the actual hours worked by each worker to no more than 60 hours per workweek."[36] Workers should also have at least one day off. Monthly overtime, therefore, should average about 80 to 82 hours. However, many Pegatron employees have been pressured into working "extreme overtime" of 109 hours per month beyond their regularly scheduled workdays. Pegatron insists overtime is "optional," but CLW reports that Apple's high production quotas lead to harsh management techniques and a denial of requests for time off. The low base wages are also an incentive for overtime as workers struggle to make ends meet.[37]

These very low wages paid by Pegatron were also a major focal point of the CLW report. Based on the pay stubs collected by CLW, most production line workers in Pegatron's Shanghai factory supplying Apple's iPhone 7 were being paid $304 per month, but in 2016, Pegatron bumped up the salary of these workers to $350. Pegatron workers who worked 80 hours of overtime (per month) earned $672, and those who worked 20 hours of overtime earned $407. These amounts include "compensation" and bonuses. In nonpeak production periods, overtime is scarce. But these low salaries are barely enough to survive on in the Shanghai area. They are well below the average monthly salary of Shanghai workers, which was $895 a month in 2016. The average consumption expenditures of urban residents of Shanghai were $464 a month. In addition, after Pegatron increased base salaries to $350, it no longer made the full payment for social insurance for their workers (about $50 per month). Without overtime, Pegatron workers making expensive Apple products could barely make ends meet living in Shanghai on their small base salaries.[38]

Workers at Pegatron must also endure dreadful work conditions. Those conditions were uncovered by an undercover CLW investigator, who took a job in the Shanghai factory as a production worker making parts for Apple computers. According to this report, almost every production worker toiled six days per week in 12-hour shifts. The overtime period ran from 5:30 p.m. until 8:00 p.m. But each day they were paid for only 10.5 hours because of unpaid meetings. After the long shift, workers took a 30-minute bus ride back to their dormitories, where 14 people were crammed together in one small room. In these ill-kept dorms, "mold grows pervasively along the walls; bed bugs have spread throughout the dormitory, and many workers are covered in red bug bites."[39]

Finally, China Labor Watch and other groups have accused Pegatron of abusive practices involving its interns. Chinese vocational schools require internships for students that can run from three months to a full year. There are roughly 8 million student interns a year throughout China. Many of these workers, who are often only 17 or 18 years old, work in coastal cities like Shenzhen and Shanghai, where the minimum wage is higher. Pegatron is a major employer of interns, who often perform monotonous tasks such as wiping down screens. According to Chinese law, interns cannot be asked to work overtime, but according to CLW and other sources, on average Pegatron interns work more overtime than full-time employees. A Fair Labor Association study also revealed that interns at Pegatron work longer hours than permitted by their young ages. In addition, students are not supposed to be working on production lines where the labor has nothing to do with their studies. Parents have complained that instead of allowing students to arrange internships related to their major, companies like Pegatron force them to work on assembly lines making smartphones or laptops.[40]

Apple has not ignored its supply chain problems and repeatedly reaffirmed the rights of those workers to a fair wage and decent working conditions. In 2015, Apple conducted 640 audits across its vast supply chain, many of them for the first time. Those audits revealed a moderate level of compliance with Apple's standards. For example, there was only 66% compliance with Apple's standard of "excellence" for "wages, benefits, and contracts." There were similar compliance rates for occupational health and safety standards and for hazard prevention.[41]

CLW investigations, however, have underscored the futility of Apple's audits. Through its undercover workers and other tactics, CLW has uncovered many instances of audit fraud. For example, it discovered that Foxconn workers would work for an entire morning or an entire afternoon without a break. When there were audits being conducted by Apple or other companies, workers were given a break for 10 minutes every two hours. The "rest policy" was effective only during the auditing period. Once the audit was finished, the 10-minute breaks were eliminated. Similarly, CLW provides evidence that raises suspicions about the results of Apple audits that show a high compliance rate with its overtime policy.[42]

Postscript

People do not associate the word *sweatshop* with sophisticated products like the iPhone or the iPad. What comes to mind are places like the Saipan islands where 34 garment factories employed immigrant labor who slaved to make apparel in facilities with appalling working conditions. The situation in China is not comparable to the egregious worker abuses that occurred in Saipan. But in the eyes of some NGOs and other critics, Foxconn and Pegatron qualify as sweatshops because of their callous labor practices. CLW argues that Apple "transfers social responsibilities to suppliers" and manipulates the competition among those suppliers to keep its labor costs as low as possible.[43] While Apple takes strong exception to these accusations, there is abundant evidence that conditions in the factories of both companies need significant improvement. At a minimum, Foxconn and Pegatron factories are correctly described as "labor camps," where there is still far too much abuse and psychological pressure.

Is Apple simply following the logic of capitalism in its relentless quest for low production costs and tight time frames to suit its well-orchestrated product launches? Or has something gone desperately wrong in the process of Apple's rise to preeminence in the world of high technology?

EXHIBIT 15.3 ■ Manufacturing Costs for the 32GB iPhone[44]
Retail Price: $649
Current Cost of Manufacturing: $224.80
Additional Cost (if made in the United States): $80–$90

EXHIBIT 15.4 ■ iPhone Sales, 2014–2016[45]			
	2014	2015	2016
Net Sales (in millions)	$101,991	$155,041	$137,700
Percentage of Total Sales	56%	66%	63%
Unit Sales (in thousands)	$169,216	$231,218	$211,884

EXHIBIT 15.5 ■ iPad Sales, 2014–2016[46]

	2014	2015	2016
Net Sales (in millions)	$130,287	$23,221	$20,628
Percentage of Total Sales	17%	10%	11%
Unit Sales (in thousands)	$67,997	$54,858	$45,590

- Outline the various allegations against Apple and the evidence to support those allegations. What are the most serious allegations?

- In your view, what is the root cause of the problem? Why has Apple had such a difficult time improving the working conditions of its suppliers?

- To what extent is Apple morally complicit in the abusive practices discussed in this case? What difference does it make that these individuals are not Apple employees but the employees of factories in Apple's complex and extensive supply chain?

CASE STUDY 15.2

SWEATSHOPS AND DEATHTRAPS: THE GARMENT INDUSTRY IN BANGLADESH

The Western media usually pay little attention to sweatshops and inferior working conditions in foreign countries. But two garment factory disasters in Bangladesh put the spotlight temporarily on the plight of workers in that destitute country. Both events sparked worldwide outrage. In November 2012, 112 employees were killed when the medium-sized Tazreen garment factory went up in flames. When the fire alarm went off, workers were told it was a false alarm and were ordered back to work. As the factory floor quickly filled with black smoke, some workers were able to break windows and jump to safety, but most of them perished in the overwhelming flames.[47] The devastating Tazreen factory fire was followed by a factory collapse in Rana Plaza just outside the capital city of Dhaka

Sipa USA via AP Photo/Sony Ramany

in April 2013 that killed 1,127 people. The sudden collapse of the eight-story Rana Plaza building that housed a number of clothing factories is one of the worst industrial disasters in history. Rana Plaza was built with substandard materials, and the owner was arrested for constructing the building without the required safety permits.

In this case, we consider the role of multinationals who sourced from these factories in Bangladesh. Do they bear any of the burden of responsibility for these two tragic and preventable accidents?

The Country and Economy of Bangladesh

Bangladesh, a delta of rivers that flow into the Bay of Bengal, is one of the world's most densely populated countries. Formerly known as East Pakistan, Bangladesh came into existence in 1971 when Pakistan split in two after a prolonged war that involved India. The country spent 15 years under military rule until democracy was restored in 1990. It has a population of 162 million people who speak Bengali.[48]

Bangladesh, which has a reputation for political corruption and cronyism, has been ruled since 2009 by Prime Minister Sheikh Hasina, who took over after the corrupt and incompetent rule of Khaleda Zia. During Hasina's regime, the country has improved relations with its neighbors, including India, China, and Japan. At the same time, the Hasina government has silenced media critics and tampered with the constitution to perpetuate its rule. To her credit, the prime minister has been successful in fortifying the Bangladeshi economy, which is now twice as big as it was under her predecessor. Growth in per-capita GDP has averaged about 4.4%. Under her leadership, poverty has fallen rapidly—since the turn of the century, the number of Bangladeshis living in poverty has dropped by more than 25%. However, one-third of the population is still below the poverty line.[49]

Much of this economic success comes from the explosive growth of the country's multibillion-dollar, labor-intensive garment industry. Despite its weak infrastructure, its lack of electricity, it's power shortages, its terrible roads and decrepit transportation system, and its political instability, the country's low wages give it an international trading advantage. Western retailers and brands have flocked to this once-obscure Asian country to benefit from those low wages. Bangladesh hopes to follow in the footsteps of Thailand and Sri Lanka, which used apparel manufacturing to build a more sophisticated and diversified economy.[50]

The ready-made garment industry in Bangladesh has over 5,000 factories and employs about 5 million people. By contrast, this number is far larger than the 2,500 factories in rival Indonesia and the 2,000 factories in Vietnam. Bangladesh has been an attractive investment target for clothing manufacturers and retailers that are looking for alternatives to China. Companies such as H&M, the Gap, and Walmart are major customers. With rising labor costs, China is losing its edge as a low-cost supplier to this industry. Bangladesh's garment exports total $23 billion, which represents 80% of the country's exports and 15% of GDP. Bangladesh is now the second-largest exporter of clothing after China, because its labor costs are less than that of any of its other Asian rivals. The minimum wage in Bangladesh is 32 cents an hour, or $68 a month. Another attraction of Bangladesh is that clothes produced there enjoy duty-free access to the European Union, but this isn't true for China and India.[51]

Working Conditions in the Clothing Industry

One setback for the Bangladeshi economy has been labor unrest. Workers are distraught over stagnant low wages in a country that has seen notable cost-of-living increases over the past several years. Wages have risen only twice in the last decade, even though inflation rose as much as 10% a year during that period. In December 2016, protests and demonstrations erupted at factories supplying clothing to several global fashion companies such as Inditex of Spain, owner of the Zara brand. Workers were protesting working conditions and low wages. Workers expected the government wage board that meets every three years to review wages, but when that did not happen, the protests began. Workers complain they cannot survive on $68 a month. The average cost of living in an urban area like Dhaka, Bangladesh, is $367 a month.[52]

Workers were also protesting other abuses, such as the denial of sick leave to garment workers. Under Bangladeshi law, all workers are entitled to 14 days of paid sick leave each year. This reform was implemented after a wave of protests shut down many factories in 2006. However, investigative reporters have revealed that many workers are routinely denied sick leave unless they are violently ill. Some workers have been told that if they take more than one sick day, they will be fired. One case that received national attention was Taslima Aktar, who worked for Windy Apparels. She had been suffering for two weeks with a fever and hacking cough but continued to work for fear of losing her job. Her supervisor refused repeated requests for sick leave because the company was rushing to fill a big order. She collapsed at her sewing machine and was rushed to the factory clinic. They sent her back to the factory floor, where she collapsed again, and this time she could not be revived. She died of cardiac failure due to "severe respiratory distress." Her employer left her uncovered body outside the factory gates until her husband came to pick it up several hours later.[53]

Labor reform is complicated by the close bonds between the Bangladeshi government and the garment industry. According to Transparency International, about 10% of Bangladeshi lawmakers are directly involved in the garment industry. Many of these legislators serve on key labor and commerce committees responsible for overseeing and regulating the industry. Many others have financial ties to the industry through relatives and intimate friends.[54]

The garment industry is represented by the powerful trade association, which lobbies on its behalf. The Bangladesh Garment Manufacturers and Exporters Association (BGMEA) has considerable political clout within the country. Siddiqur Rahman, president of the BGMEA, has indicated that factories would like to do something about wages and working conditions. But costs have risen 17.5% each year from 2014 to 2016, even as global clothing prices have decreased. After the turmoil of the strikes, both Gap and H&M indicated that they favored a wage review mechanism for the future.[55]

The Tazreen Factory Fire

In addition to below-subsistence-level wages and denial of sick leave, the two terrible accidents described above put considerable pressure on the Bangladesh government to address more comprehensively the issue of working conditions and safety standards. The first incident was the tragic fire that occurred at Tazreen Fashions Ltd., owned by

Tuba Group, one of the country's largest clothing manufacturers and exporters. The Tazreen factory, which opened its doors in 2007, was located just outside the city of Dhaka. It employed 1,500 workers and reported revenues of $35 million per year.[56]

In 2011, an inspection conducted for Walmart uncovered serious fire-safety violations. The inspections found that exits and stairwells were blocked and the factory lacked the necessary firefighting equipment. Tuba Group was informed of the violations, and it promised to make the necessary corrections by the end of June 2011. But those corrections were never made. A year and a half later, on November 24, 2012, the Tazreen factory went up in flames. One hundred twelve workers were killed in the conflagration. Some people jumped to their deaths from the upper floors because the stairwells were so engulfed in flames and thick black smoke. The fire escape was inside the building and led to the ground floor, where burning balls of yarn blocked the exit for many other workers. There were some reports that managers had routinely locked some of the doors every day in order to prevent workers from stealing garments.[57]

Fire safety has been a critical problem at Bangladeshi garment factories. Over 600 workers died in a series of factory fires from 2006 to 2012. A garment worker for Tazreen Fashions for two years said she never took part in fire-drill training while working at the factory.[58] Aside from poor safety precautions, the main cause of most of these fires, including Tazreen, has been subpar electrical wiring. According to one inspector, "The absolute root cause of fires in Bangladesh is the electrical situation." Fire-safety authorities have failed to maintain proper safety standards for electrical wiring for both old and new buildings. According to labor activists, prior to the Tazreen fire, factory owners had blocked efforts to improve electrical wiring standards.[59]

When Tazreen failed to correct its fire hazards and safety violations by the June 2011 deadline, it was denied a renewal of its safety certificate. But it continued to operate without that certificate. A follow-up investigation revealed that 25% of the factories operating in the industrial zone where Tazreen was located also lacked safety certificates because there were so many violations in their factories.[60]

A few weeks before the deadly Tazreen fire, the majority of the factory's assembly lines were set up for production for Walmart. Clothing for Sears Holding Company and 10 other brands was also made at the Tazreen factory. In May 2011, an inspection of Tazreen was carried out by NTD Apparel, Inc., which found many violations. When a follow-up inspection by an outside monitor revealed the problems had not been corrected, Walmart revoked the factory's authorization to make its products. So why was Tazreen Fashions still making clothing for Walmart? At the end of October 2012, Walmart stores placed an order with Simco Bangladesh Ltd. to produce 300,000 girls' shorts for shipment in early December. Due to capacity constraints, Simco subcontracted the order to the Tuba Group in early November without Walmart's authorization. Simco was familiar with Walmart's rules regarding unauthorized factories but believed the transfer was acceptable because some of Tuba Group's factories were approved for making clothing for Walmart. Tuba has a history of shifting orders between factories and passed the Simco order to Tazreen without Simco's knowledge.[61]

Most large retailers and apparel companies rely on outside monitors to inspect factories at least once a year. If they repeatedly discover problems and irregularities, orders are canceled. The monitors inspect both the direct suppliers—that is, the factories retailers have directly contracted to make their products—and the subcontractors—the factories used by these principal suppliers. Labor groups and worker advocates criticize this approach because they say it insulates retailers from direct responsibility for dealing with safety conditions in these factories, since they rarely publicly disclose when factories are substandard. These third-party monitors don't necessarily know if unauthorized subcontracting occurs with the factories they inspect. Moreover, by constantly shifting work to factories with marginally lower costs, retailers disincentivize factory owners from spending money on safety improvements. Walmart has said it's the responsibility of the suppliers to use factories approved by the company and warns suppliers that contracts will be canceled if they violate this policy.[62]

Walmart was dismayed by all this shifting of its orders, which underscores the lack of transparency in the supply chain. It learned that three of its other suppliers had worked with Tazreen during 2012. Jahangir Alam, an officer for ethical sourcing at Walmart, discussed the severe challenge of ensuring compliance with the company's standards: "With multiple subcontracts going on, it has become almost impossible for buyers to practice ethical sourcing in the true sense."[63]

The Rana Plaza Building Collapse

About six months after the Tazreen fire, a multistory building with garment factories collapsed in Dhaka, Bangladesh, killing 1,127 people. The Rana Plaza complex in Savor, a commercial center just north of the capital, collapsed at 9 a.m. after work had just begun in several factories. The eight-story complex housed 5,000 workers. The day before the building collapse, there was an evacuation when a large crack appeared on an exterior wall. Workers were sent home. Inspectors summoned by Rana Plaza's owner declared the building safe. The workers were instructed to return to work the next day—they were told the building would stand for another 100 years. Several companies within the Rana complex, such as Phantom Apparels, were rushing to complete orders for foreign buyers. They were behind schedule because of strikes called by the country's political parties. Workers were told that if they didn't work, they would lose a month's salary. But when they returned the following day and began to work, "everything went dark" as the factory shuddered and the concrete walls and floors gave way, trapping countless workers in a mass of concrete and debris. By nightfall, many of them had been rescued, but the death toll was still over 1,100 workers, mostly women.[64]

The construction of Rana Plaza reflects a trend in the Bangladesh garment industry toward factories operated by multiple tenants in buildings erected several stories high. As the city of Dhaka became more industrialized and populous, the price of land was driven up. The shortage and expense of land induced more and more factory owners to build up. But these multilevel factories operated by multiple owners tend to pose bigger risks than "low-slung" factories with a single tenant. Rana Plaza was built in 2007 by Mr. Rana, a local businessman, as a multiuse building for factories and shops. However, it had been built on the site of a filled-in pond without the appropriate safety precautions. An investigating committee also concluded that several large generators installed on the top floors caused vibrations that most likely aggravated the building's instability. The owner was arrested after the accident for constructing the building without safety permits. The mayor was also suspended for allegedly allowing the construction of Rana Plaza without those safety permits.[65]

Some retailers, including Walmart and Levi-Strauss, avoided multilevel factories because of the risks they posed. But the companies that occupied Rana Plaza had plenty of business. One garment factory, New Wave Style, moved to the sixth and seventh floors of Rana Plaza in 2010, where it had 40,000 square feet of space. It boasted a long list of clients like Benetton, the Italian fashion designer, for whom it had just completed an order for 185,000 cotton shirts.[66]

Initially, Benetton denied it had a commercial relationship with New Wave Style. With 700 suppliers, the company said it could not always keep track of those suppliers and their multiple subcontractors. Like other fashion companies, it relies on a large network of clothing manufacturers to provide "lightning-fast turnaround" in the "fast fashion" era where hit products need to be produced in a big hurry. This tangled web of middlemen, suppliers, and subcontractors makes it difficult to assess accountability when accidents happen. Benetton had placed an order with New Wave in September 2012. Benetton had been battling competitors like H&M and Zara, who were cutting costs thanks in part to sourcing from Bangladesh. Benetton decided to follow that same strategy by sourcing more goods from Bangladesh factories. In the summer of 2012, it undertook an assessment to ensure that New Wave could fulfill the order and deliver it on time. It is common for foreign retailers to order a separate third-party safety audit of a prospective manufacturer, but Benetton did not require such an audit. There is also a database of factory audits available to all retailers. Had Benetton checked the database, it would have found that in March 2012, New Wave had failed a safety audit due to many serious safety violations. However, once it determined that New Wave had the capacity to accommodate its requirements, Benetton put through this sizable order for the cotton shirts. The order was delivered at the end of March just before the building collapsed.[67]

Retailers and Clothing Companies Respond

Social and media pressure on these retailers and fashion houses began to intensify in the wake of the Tazreen factory fire and the building collapse in Dhaka. Benetton defended its use of these factories, observing that some of the multistory buildings conform to the proper specifications and are "perfectly safe."[68] After the accident, J.C. Penney and Sears followed Walmart's example and began phasing out the use of clothing manufacturers located in these buildings. Other companies like Disney, the world's largest licenser, ordered an abrupt termination to the outsourcing of any branded merchandise from Bangladesh. Disney's decision seemed motivated primarily by the impulse to protect its valuable brand and reputation rather than by any moral anxiety over sourcing from Bangladesh factories. According to Bob Chapek, president of Disney Consumer Products, "Disney is a publicly held company accountable to its shareholders, . . . and we felt this was the most responsible way to manage the challenges associated with our supply chain."[69]

In the aftermath of these tragedies in Bangladesh, apparel companies and retailers faced a painful dilemma. Should they follow the example of Disney and exit Bangladesh in order to protect their brands and reputations? A mass exodus, however, would be a major setback for Bangladesh and its people, who still need these jobs to escape from abject poverty. In this country, where some of the population still earns less than $2 per day, sweatshop jobs are the best option.[70] The other alternative is to stay and source from contractors operating safe facilities with decent working conditions. But how can companies be assured of safety in a corrupt economy where employee rights are not given a high priority?

Walmart at first took a unilateral approach to the problem. Unlike Disney, the giant retailer was committed to remaining in Bangladesh, but it refused to invest in safety remediation. After the fire, Walmart hired an experienced outside auditor, Bureau Veritas, to inspect all 257 factories where its goods are produced. Although the company refused to pay for any safety upgrades recommended by the inspectors, it conceded that the cost of those safety improvements could be factored into the cost of goods it purchases. Walmart's willingness to pay higher prices was intended to send a clear signal that factories should avoid frugality when safety is at stake. Walmart has also demanded that all of the factories making its products establish programs for fire-safety training.[71]

The dual tragedies also inspired other retailers to adopt a multilateral approach. Over 200 companies, primarily from Europe, have signed on to the Accord on Fire and Building Safety in Bangladesh. The accord requires the factories producing their clothes to undergo independent safety inspections and make upgrades to adhere to uniform safety standards when necessary. North American companies, including Walmart, Macy's, and Target, have forged a separate agreement known as the Alliance for Bangladesh Worker Safety. The alliance also requires factories making members' garments to undergo safety inspections and fix problems uncovered by safety inspectors. Companies that have signed on to either of these two agreements are expected to stop sourcing from factories that have failed to make the necessary safety improvements. By the end of 2016, 2,000 factories had been inspected, and many have begun the process of remediating their safety problems.[72]

According to factory owners, the big flaw in both agreements is that they represent an "unfunded mandate" to improve safety. While both accords require brands and retailers to pay for the inspections, neither one requires them to pay for the safety improvements themselves. The terms of the accord require brands and retailers to negotiate with suppliers to make it "financially feasible" for factories to be upgraded. Brands typically commit to maintaining their orders and may pay for some orders in advance, but they do not pay for the safety improvements. The alliance has set up a fund to provide low-cost loans for safety upgrades, but, like the accord, its factories must pay for their own safety remediation. Multinational apparel companies, which shift their business routinely between countries to find the lowest costs, are reluctant to invest in factories they do not own. According to the International Labor Organization, the total costs of the safety improvements could total over $1 billion.[73]

There is a certain rivalry between these two international consortiums. The alliance has claimed it is superior to the accord because it pays workers' salaries when factories are closed for mandated safety improvements. When the Softex factory was closed in March 2014, after accord inspectors found structural problems that needed immediate attention, 2,500 workers were temporarily out of work without pay. The accord claims that paying workers during closures for safety remediation was solely the factory owner's responsibility. On the other hand, the accord claims its inspections are more thorough. Within the first year of inspections, four factories were closed for fear of collapse. Despite the fact that 2,000 factories have been inspected by these two alliances, there are 3,000 other factories with worse conditions that have not been inspected. Thanks to opaque and tangled supply chains, it is still possible for middlemen or approved suppliers to send orders from Western brands and retailers to unapproved or uninspected factories.[74]

Postscript

Labor activists have insisted with some justification that a "race to the bottom" was the root cause of the appalling safety conditions in Bangladesh clothing factories. As long as retailers and fashion designers relentlessly pursue the lowest manufacturing costs, their goods will sometimes be made in factories that lack adequate safeguards and protection for employee rights. On the other hand, closing factories like those in Bangladesh that do not comply with common safety standards will only thrust workers into worse conditions elsewhere.[75]

Apparel retailers, apprehensive about damage to their reputation by being linked with these tragedies, have few other options. Clothing factories in most other low-wage countries such as Cambodia, Pakistan, and Indonesia have even greater safety risks than those found in the factories of Bangladesh. The drive to cut labor costs in these economies to satisfy customer demands creates the same incentive to compromise on safety. Yet multinationals are unlikely to abandon the quest for "sweatshop labor" and low-cost production. As a result, there will probably be many more fatal accidents in the future.[76]

- Discuss the economic factors behind these two tragedies of Tazreen and Rana Plaza. What parties are responsible for these disasters? Do you hold companies like Walmart and Benetton complicit in any way—should they be doing business with contractors that have such unsafe working conditions?

- How do you assess the accord and the alliance agreements? Should retailers and brands pay for some of the safety improvements? Should they pay for wages when factories are temporarily closed due to safety remediation?

- Have Western brands done enough to ensure safety and good working conditions in the factories they use in Bangladesh? Should they do something about the low wages?

CONCLUSION

This final chapter has followed up the theme of Chapter 12, which considered duties to the corporation's employees. Companies that engage in offshore outsourcing to achieve lower labor costs bear some degree of responsibility for the operations run by their contractors. In these cases, there are no direct employees involved, but arguably Apple and other companies have an obligation to ensure decent working conditions and a just wage for those who work for those contractors. Apple must find a more effective way to deal with the ongoing worker abuses at Pegatron and Foxconn. Similarly, a plausible case can be made that retailers like Walmart share in the responsibility to ensure the factories making their clothing in Bangladesh are reasonably safe. The thesis that companies have such obligations toward the employees of their contractors is subject to debate, but it is well grounded in certain ethical theories. The principal difficulty is monitoring what goes on within the walls of those foreign contractors.

Student Study Site

Visit **edge.sagepub.com/spinello.**

Review Question

1. Explain what is meant by offshoring and outsourcing. What is a just wage, and how would you characterize "acceptable" working conditions? Can a company say that it lacks the moral agency to deal with fair-wage or other employee issues of its suppliers?

Discussion Questions

1. Are sweatshops good for a developing country? Would a country be better off if it had no sweatshops?

2. What's the problem (if any) with letting the market set wages even if they are exceedingly low?

3. Is Apple an ethical company?

GLOSSARY

applications barrier to entry: A situation resulting from consumers' preference of operating systems for which a large number of applications have already been written and most software developers' preference to write software for systems with a large customer base

availability: The ability of employees and customers to use an information technology system without disruption

big-firm capitalism: A capitalist prototype in which corporation ownership is dispersed among investors representing millions of shareholders

bribery: One person's gain of something of value in exchange for providing a service

communications privacy: The extension of constitutional protections to oral, written, and electronic communications

confidentiality: The ability to keep valuable data private that are stored in an information technology system; this may be achieved by tools such as access controls and encryption software

consequentialism: The philosophy that one action with better consequences is preferable to another action whose consequences are not as good.

contextual integrity: A person's sense of privacy is disturbed when there are inappropriate flows of personal information

corporate insider: A person within a corporation with a fiduciary obligation to act in the best interests of the corporation and its shareholders

corporate mindset: Flows from a firm's norms and values, along with a discrete set of factual beliefs

corporate moral agency: The idea that a corporation has qualities similar to those of a person

corporate social responsibility (CSR): Commitment to a broad social agenda that includes philanthropic activities and contributions to the resolution of severe social problems.

corporation: A group, organized for a business purpose, that has been authorized by a sovereign state to act as a single entity and is recognized as such in law

corruption: The abuse of a public office for private gain

cultural distance: Dissimilarities in linguistic heritage, religious or philosophical beliefs, ethical standards, and social norms

cultural relativism: The claim that morality is relative to a given culture

data privacy: The protection of someone's personal data; also known as informational privacy

design patent: Protection of any new, original, and ornamental design for an article of manufacture

due process: An employer must meet reasonable standards in dealing with employees, and employees have the right to appeal, arbitration, or any other fair procedure relating to hiring

(DRJ) duties-rights-justice: A holistic approach to moral reasoning

duties: Voluntary and natural obligations along with obligations of solidarity.

economic distance: A different economic system or reliance on economic policies alien to those in an MNC's home country

employment-at-will: Any employee can quit or resign whenever he or she likes, but he or she can also be discharged or fired without notice

encryption: A means of securing or protecting data exchanges between two parties.

entrepreneurial capitalism: A capitalist prototype in which a corporation tries to create something radical or new

environmental ethics: Aspiring to a high level of environmental performance by competently managing risks and choosing strategies consistent with environmental sustainability

ethical risk: The risk that a company will violate its core values and participate in the deprivation of human rights or fail to protect those rights

evergreening: An attempt to "refresh" a patented product by making a modification to the drug's delivery mechanism, its dosage, or other characteristics

externality: An effect of one economic agent on another that is not taken into account by normal market behavior

fiduciary relationship: Whenever a certain party is entrusted with property, information, or power to make a decision that entails discretionary judgments for the benefit of someone other than this trusted party

fiduciary: The requirement of executives and managers to act in the best interests of the company an its shareholders.

flexicurity: A term coined to reference the creation of a more flexible economy without destabilizing the job security provided by the welfare state

globalization: The process of integrating economic activities across world cultures through international markets

informational privacy: The protection of someone's personal data; also known as data privacy

insider trading: Participation in trading in securities that are based on *material, nonpublic* information in violation of a fiduciary or similar duty to a corporation and its shareholders or to the source of the information.

integrity: The protection of information systems from being improperly altered or compromised

intellectual property: Any intangible objects or assets (such as software programs, music, or books)

justice: Performing actions without partiality

LIBOR: London Inter-Bank Offered Rate

market: The free choice of different parties to make certain exchanges

material information: Any information that if made public would have a significant effect on the market value of a corporation's securities

nonpublic information: Any information that has not yet been made available to the trading markets

normative ethics: A quest for the practical truth of how one's choices and actions will be good and worthwhile

oligarchic capitalism: A capitalist prototype in which the powers of the state are oriented toward the promotion of a small segment of the population (usually the dictator)

patent cliff: The expiration of patents on well-known blockbuster drugs

patent: A form of legal protection given to individuals who create an invention or process

political distance: An unfamiliar policy environment along with different regulatory processes

political risk: Refers to the possibility that political decisions or events in a particular country will cause foreign investors there to lose money or fail to capture their expected returns

positive competition: Competition without negativity that is based securely on the merits of one's products or services

process patent: Protection of a means of doing something

product patent: Protection of inventions or functional devices such as machines, articles of manufacture, or "compositions of matter"

property model: The shareholders' interests have primacy in all corporate affairs because they effectively "own" the corporate assets

property rights: Full proprietary control over tangible or intangible things

public goods: Any product or service that is nonrivalrous (someone's consumption of that good does not affect the consumption of others) and nonexclusive (it is difficult or even impossible to exclude or "fence out" people)

pure environmental goods: Any goods that do not bear on human welfare

right of ownership: A bundle of rights that are usually differentiated and defined in mature legal systems

rights: Owed to individuals by virtue of their rational personhood

sexual harassment: Any unwanted physical behavior and dialogue of a sexual nature, either overt or covert, that is exacerbated when the behavior is an abuse of workplace relationships

social entity model: The corporation exists not only to create shareholder wealth but also to satisfy the needs of customers, to provide jobs for employees, and to contribute to the vitality of the local community

state-guided capitalism: A capitalist prototype that tries to link the powers of state with the power of the free market

supplier opportunity cost: The least suppliers will accept for their inputs

temporary insiders: Persons such as accountants, lawyers, and investment bankers who become privy to inside information in the performance of their professional services

tippee: A person who receives information from a tipper (a corporate or temporary insider) also inherits a fiduciary duty to shareholders

utilitarianism: a philosophy focused on the effects individual actions will produce

utility patent: Protection of any new, useful, and nonobvious process, machine, or article of manufacture

vertically integrated: The structure of a company that performs all value chain activities in house, from research and development to manufacturing and marketing

willingness to pay: The most consumers will pay for a product, which usually corresponds to the price

NOTES

PREFACE

1. James S. H. Bossard and J. Frederick Dewhurst, *University Education for Business: A Study of Existing Needs and Practices* (Philadelphia: University of Pennsylvania Press, 1931), 410. See also Gabriel Abend, *The Moral Background: An Inquiry into the History of Business Ethics* (Princeton: Princeton University Press, 2014), 256–58.
2. Amy Zipkin, "Getting Religion on Corporate Ethics," *New York Times*, October 18, 2000, C1.
3. Lynn Sharp Paine, "Moral Thinking in Management: An Essential Capability," *Business Ethics Quarterly* 6, no. 4 (1996): 115.

CHAPTER 1

1. Vaclav Havel, *Summer Meditations* (New York: Random House, 1993), 49.
2. Irving Howe, "Images of Socialism," *Dissent* 1, no. 2 (1954): 122.
3. Bob Davis and John Lyons, "Globalization's Gains Come with a Price," *Wall Street Journal*, May 24, 2007, A1, A12. See also Clayton Rose, "Note on Comparative Capitalism" (Harvard Business School Press, Boston, MA, 2015), 1.
4. Robert Guth, "Bill Gates Issues Call for Kinder Capitalism," *Wall Street Journal*, January 24, 2008, A1, A15. See also Rose, "Note on Comparative Capitalism," 1.
5. Judy Shelton, "A Capitalist Manifesto," *Wall Street Journal*, October 13, 2008, A19.
6. Rebecca Henderson and Karthik Ramana, "Managers and Market Capitalism" (working paper, HBS Publications, Harvard Business School, Boston, MA, 2014).
7. Michael Novak, "The Future of Democratic Capitalism," *First Things*, June/July 2015, 33–38. See also David Bentley Hart, "Mammon Ascendant," *First Things*, June/July 2016, 33–37; Arthur Okun, *Equality and Efficiency* (Washington, DC: Brookings Institute, 1975), 9–10.
8. Henderson and Ramana, "Managers and Market Capitalism," 8–10.
9. Jerry Muller, *Adam Smith in His Time and Ours: Designing the Decent Society* (New York: Free Press, 1993), 60.
10. Charles Koch, *Good Profit* (New York: Crown Business Press, 2015), 25.
11. Aristotle, *Politics*, in *Complete Works of Aristotle*, ed. Richard McKeon (New York: Random House, 1941), 1263a25. See also Okun, *Equality and Efficiency*, 36.
12. Lawrence Becker, *Property Rights: Philosophic Foundations* (London: Routledge & Kegan Paul, 1977), 18–22. For a full specification of ownership rights, see A. M. Honore, "Ownership," in *Oxford Essays in Jurisprudence*, ed. A.G. Guest (Oxford: Clarendon Press, 1961), 107–47. See also Roger Scruton, *The Meaning of Conservatism* (South Bend, IN: St. Augustine's Press, 2002), 92–94.
13. Gerald Gaus, "The Idea and Ideal of Capitalism," in *The Oxford Handbook of Business Ethics*, ed. George Brenkert and Tom Beauchamp (Oxford: Oxford University Press, 2010), 73–99.
14. Ray Fisman and Tim Sullivan, *The Inner Lives of Markets* (New York: Public Affairs, 2016), 11–15. See also Okun, *Equality and Efficiency*, 50.
15. Michael Novak and Paul Adams, *Social Justice Isn't What You Think It Is* (New York: Encounter Books, 2015), 45. See also Fisman and Sullivan, *The Inner Lives of Markets*, 7–17.
16. Adam Smith, *An Inquiry into the Nature and Causes of the Wealth of Nations* (New York: Penguin, 1973), 162, emphasis added.
17. Smith, *Wealth of Nations*, 287.
18. John Tomasi, *Free Market Fairness* (Princeton: Princeton University Press, 2012), 6–8.
19. Shelton, "A Capitalist Manifesto."
20. Charles Taylor, *The Ethics of Authenticity* (Cambridge, MA: Harvard University Press, 1991), 110–11. See also Okun, *Equality and Efficiency*, 38; Tomasi, *Free Market Fairness*, 7.
21. William Baumol, Robert Litan, and Carl Schramm, *Good Capitalism, Bad Capitalism, and the Economics of Growth*

and Prosperity (New Haven, CN: Yale University Press, 2007), 60–62. See also Richard Spinello, *Global Capitalism, Culture, and Ethics* (New York: Routledge, 2014), 39–45.

22. Baumol et al., *Good Capitalism, Bad Capitalism*, 62–70. See also "The Visible Hand," *The Economist*, January 21, 2012, 3.

23. "What Kind of Capitalism?," *The Economist*, October 12, 2013, 20.

24. Baumol et al., *Good Capitalism, Bad Capitalism*, 71–79. See also Hernando de Soto, *The Mystery of Capital* (New York: Basic Books, 2000).

25. Leif Wenar, *Blood Oil: Tyrants, Violence and the Rules That Run the World* (Oxford: Oxford University Press, 2016), 57.

26. Martin Reeves, Knut Haanaes, and Janmejaya Sinha, *Your Strategy Needs a Strategy* (Boston: Harvard Business School, 2015), 27–29.

27. Alfred Chandler, "The Enduring Logic of Industrial Success," *Harvard Business Review*, March/April (1990): 33–41. See also Baumol et al., *Good Capitalism, Bad Capitalism*, 80–84.

28. John Kenneth Galbraith, *The New Industrial State* (New York: Signet Books, 1967), 202.

29. Reeves et al., *Your Strategy Needs a Strategy*, 89. See also "A Palette of Plans," *The Economist*, May 30, 2015, 66.

30. Scott Galloway, *The Four: The Hidden DNA of Amazon, Apple, Facebook, and Google* (New York: Penguin, 2017), 55.

31. "Growing the Polish Apple," *The Economist*, November 22, 2014, 62–63.

32. Baumol et al., *Good Capitalism, Bad Capitalism*, 90.

33. "The Visible Hand," 13–17.

34. "State Capitalism in the Dock," *The Economist*, November 22, 2014, 57-8.

35. "The Visible Hand," 18.

36. Okun, *Equality and Efficiency*, 49–52.

37. Paul Johnson, "The Capitalism and Morality Debate," *First Things*, March (1990), 32–36.

38. Andrei Shleifer, "Does Competition Destroy Ethical Behavior?," *American Economic Review* 94, no. 2 (2004): 414–18. See also Fisman and Sullivan, *The Inner Lives of Markets*, 180–81.

39. David Bentley Hart, "Mammon Ascendant," *First Things*, June/July 2016, 33–38.

40. Branko Milanovic, *Global Inequality: A New Approach for the Age of Globalization* (Cambridge, MA: Harvard University Press, 2016), 18–20.

41. See the review of this book by Brian Anderson, "Brothers in Marx," *Wall Street Journal*, October 8, 2009, A15.

42. Thomas Piketty, *Capitalism in the Twenty-First Century* (Cambridge, MA: Harvard University Press, 2014), 1–2.

43. Ibid., 26.

44. Robert M. Solow, "Thomas Piketty Is Right," in *After Piketty*, ed. Heather Boushey (Cambridge, MA: Harvard University Press, 2017), 50.

45. Ibid., 54–56.

46. Ibid., 58.

47. Piketty, *Capitalism in the Twenty-First Century*, 572.

48. See Wojciech Kopczuk and Allison Schrager, "The Inequality Illusion: Why a Wealth Tax Won't Work," *Foreign Affairs*, May 2014, 38–42.

49. Robert Arnott, William Bernstein, and Lillian Wu, "The Rich Get Poorer: The Myth of Dynastic Wealth," *Cato Journal* 35, no. 3 (2015): 72–95. See also Buttonwood, "RG-bargy," *The Economist*, June 20, 2015, 68.

50. Milanovic, *Global Inequality*, 192–93. See also Daniel Shuchman, "Beggar Thy Neighbor," *Wall Street Journal*, October 9, 2015, A11.

51. Piketty, *Capitalism in the Twenty-First Century*, 571.

52. Dominic Mele, "Leaving Behind the Model of Positivism and Utilitarianism for Economic Activity," in *Free Markets with Solidarity and Sustainability*, ed. M. Schlag and J. Mercado (Washington, DC: Catholic University of America Press, 2016), 32–33.

53. See Gregory Dees, "Responding to Market Failures" (Cambridge, MA: Harvard Business School, 1996), 2–4. See also John Roberts, *The Modern Firm* (Oxford: Oxford University Press, 2004), 78.

54. Joseph Stiglitz and Jay Rosengard, *Economics of the Public Sector*, 4th ed. (New York: W. W. Norton, 2015), 77–79.

55. Sherman Anti-Trust Act, Stat. 209 (1914), ch. 647, sec. 1.26.

56. Forest Reinhardt, "Conceptual Overview: Business and the Environment" (Boston: Harvard Business School, 1999), 9.

57. Roberts, *Modern Firm*, 82, which cites the research of Robert Spence, "Job Market Signaling," *Quarterly Journal of Economics* 87 (1973): 355–74. See also Dees, "Responding to Market Failures," 2.

58. Reinhardt, "Conceptual Overview," 3.

59. Ibid., 8.

60. Novak and Adams, *Social Justice*, 147–48.

61. David Schindler, "Does the Free Market Produce Free Persons?," in *Ordering Love: Liberal Societies*

and the Memory of God, ed. David Schindler (Grand Rapids, MI: Eerdmann's, 2012), 160.

62. Aristotle, *Nicomachean Ethics*, in *Complete Works of Aristotle*, ed. Richard McKeon (New York: Random House, 1941), 1095b4–5. See also Schindler, "Does the Free Market Produce Free Persons?," 158–61.

63. Jason Zwieg, "Ten Years On, Loss of Trust Still Hangs over Wall Street," *Wall Street Journal*, March 17, 2018, B1, B5.

64. Henderson and Ramana, "Managers and Market Capitalism," 10.

65. Alan Greenspan, "Dodd-Frank Fails to Meet Test of Our Times," *Financial Times*, March 29, 2011, 1. See also Frank Pasquale, *The Black Box Society* (Cambridge, MA: Harvard University Press, 2015), 2–3.

66. Michael Novak describes this system as "democratic capitalism." See Novak, "Future of Democratic Capitalism."

CHAPTER 2

1. Mark Achbar, Jennifer Abbott, and Joel Balkin, *The Corporation* (New York: Big Picture Media Corp., Zeitgeist Video, 2004), DVD, 116 minutes.

2. *The Oxford Dictionary of Quotations*, 2nd ed. (Oxford: Oxford University Press, 1966), 547.

3. Peter French, "The Diachronic Moral Responsibility of Firms," in *The Moral Responsibility of Firms*, ed. Eric Orts and Craig Smith (Oxford: Oxford University Press, 2017), 53–65.

4. "Peculiar People." *The Economist*, March 11, 2011, 78.

5. Schumpeter, "Why Do Firms Exist?," *The Economist*, December 18, 2010, 134.

6. *Principles of Corporate Governance: Analysis and Recommendations*, Section 2.01 (New York: American Law Institute, 1994), 53.

7. *Trustees of Dartmouth College v. Woodward*, 17 U.S. 518, 636 (1819).

8. Elizabeth Pollman, "Reconceiving Corporate Personhood," *Utah Law Review* 1629 (2011), 1636.

9. Ibid., 1637.

10. Adam Winkler, *We the Corporations* (New York: W. W. Norton, 2018), 85–87.

11. *Santa Clara v. Southern Pacific Railroad Company*, 117 U.S. 394 (1886).

12. Margaret M. Blair, "Corporate Personhood and the Corporate Persona," *University of Illinois Law Review* 785 (2013), 803.

13. *Hale v. Henkel*, 201 U.S. 43 (1906). See also Winkler, *We the Corporations*, 185–88.

14. *First National Bank of Boston v. Bellotti*, 435 U.S. 765 (1978). The dissenting justices argued that precisely because the corporation is an artificial entity dependent upon the state, the state can elect to constrain its political speech.

15. *Central Hudson Gas & Electric Company v. Public Service Corporation of New York*, 447 U.S. 557 (1980). In his dissent, Justice Rehnquist said, "I disagree with the Court's conclusion that the speech of a state-created monopoly . . . is entitled to protection under the First Amendment."

16. Winkler, *We the Corporations*, xx.

17. *Citizens United v. Federal Election Commission*, 130 U.S. 876 (2010).

18. Ibid., 950.

19. *Burwell v. Hobby Lobby Stores, Inc.*, 134 U.S. 2751 (2014).

20. Winkler, *We the Corporations*, 381–87.

21. *Federal Communications Commission v. AT&T Inc.*, 562 U.S. 1279 (2011).

22. John Finnis, *Natural Law and Natural Rights* (Oxford: Oxford University Press, 1980), 152–53.

23. Kendy Hess, "The Unrecognized Consensus about Firm Moral Responsibility," in *The Moral Responsibility of Firms*, 174–76.

24. Kenneth E. Goodpaster, *Conscience and Corporate Culture* (Oxford: Blackwell, 2007), 30–44. See also Hess, "Unrecognized Consensus," 183.

25. Hess, "Unrecognized Consensus," 183.

26. Karol Wojtyła, *The Acting Person*, trans. Andrezej Potocki (Dordrecht: D. Reidel, 1979), 277. See also John Finnis, *Intention and Identity* (Oxford: Oxford University Press, 2011), 86–91.

27. Thomas Donaldson, *Corporations and Morality* (Englewood Cliffs, NJ: Prentice Hall, 1982), 30. See also Hess, "Unrecognized Consensus," 184.

28. Hess, "Unrecognized Consensus," 183–84.

29. Goodpaster, *Conscience and Corporate Culture*, 20.

30. Richard Scragger and Micah Schwartzman, "Some Realism about Corporate Rights," in *The Rise of Corporate Religious Liberty*, ed. Micah Schwartzmann, Chad Flanders, and Zoe Robinson (Oxford: Oxford University Press, 2016), 345–71.

31. *Burwell v. Hobby Lobby*, 2797.

32. *Dodge v. Ford Motor Company*, 170 N.W. 668 (Mich. 1919).

33. William T. Allen, "Our Schizophrenic Conception of the Business Corporation," 14 *Cardozo Law Review* 261

(1992). See also William T. Allen, John Jacobs, and Leo Strine, "Management and Control of the Modern Business Corporation: The Great Takeover Debate: A Meditation on Bridging the Conceptual Divide," 69 *University of Chicago Law Review* 1067 (2002).

34. Allen, "Schizophrenic Conception of the Business Corporation," 270–72.

35. Charles Handy, "What's a Business For?" *Harvard Business Review*, 52 November/December 2002, 5.

36. Allen, "Schizophrenic Conception of the Business Corporation," 276.

37. Allen et al., "Management and Control," 1073–75. See also Kenneth Goodpaster, "Business Ethics and Stakeholder Analysis," *Business Ethics Quarterly* 1, no. 1 (1991): 61–62.

38. See, for example, Thomas Donaldson and Lee Preston, "The Stakeholder Theory of the Corporation: Concepts, Evidence, and Implications," *Academy of Management Review* 20 (1995): 65–91.

39. Allen et al., "Management and Control," 1089.

40. Goodpaster, "Business Ethics and Stakeholder Analysis," 61–63.

41. Germain Grisez, *Difficult Moral Questions* (Quincy, IL: Franciscan Press, 1997), 454.

42. Ibid., 455–59. See also Robert George, "Natural Law," 52 *American Journal of Jurisprudence* 55 (2007), 70.

43. Grisez, *Difficult Moral Questions*, 456–57.

44. Lynn Sharp Paine, "Guide to Leadership and Corporate Accountability" (Boston: Harvard Business School, 2007). See also Goodpaster, "Business Ethics and Stakeholder Analysis," 70, and Grisez, *Difficult Moral Questions*, 455.

45. Pankaj Ghemawat, *Strategy and the Business Landscape* (Reading, MA: Addison-Wesley, 1999), 58–60.

46. *Guth v. Loft, Inc.*, 23 Del. Sup. Ct., Ch. 255 A. 2d 503 (1939).

47. Lynn Sharp Paine, "The Fiduciary Relationship: A Legal Perspective" (Cambridge, MA: Harvard Business School, 2015), 1–4. See also Jason Zweig, "A Law Professor's Long, Relentless Drive for Trust," *Wall Street Journal*, December 2, 2017, B10.

48. Thomas Aquinas, *Summa Theologiae*, trans. Fathers of the English Dominican Province (New York: Benziger Bros., 1947–48), I–II, q. 90, a. 1. See also John Finnis, "Aquinas' Moral, Political, and Legal Philosophy," in *Stanford Encyclopedia of Philosophy* (Summer 2018 Edition), ed. Edward Zolta, 24–25, https://plato.stanford.edu/archive/sum2018/entries/Aquinas-moral-political.

49. James Boyd White, "What Can a Lawyer Learn from Literature?," 102 *Harvard Law Review* 2043 (1988).

50. Aquinas, *Summa Theologiae*, I–II, q. 90, a. 4. See also J. Budziszewski, *Commentary on Thomas Aquinas's Treatise on Law* (Cambridge, UK: Cambridge University Press, 2014), 36–37.

51. Albert Carr, "Is Business Bluffing Ethical?," *Harvard Business Review*, 18 January/February 1968, 66.

52. Christopher Stone, *Where the Law Ends: The Social Control of Corporate Behavior* (New York: Harper & Row, 1975), 93–100.

53. Aquinas, *Summa Theologiae*, I–II, q. 92, a.1, ad. 4.

54. Martin Luther King Jr., "Letter from a Birmingham City Jail," in *Moral Philosophy for Managers*, 5th ed., ed. R. Spinello (New York: McGraw-Hill, 2008), 191–96.

55. Lon Fuller, "Positivism and Fidelity to Law," 71 *Harvard Law Review* 630 (1958).

56. Milton Friedman, *Capitalism and Freedom*. See also Nien-he Hsieh, "Corporate Moral Agency, Positive Duties, and Purpose," in *The Moral Responsibility of Firms*, 188–205.

57. Grisez, *Difficult Moral Questions*, 454–57.

58. Kelega Sannah, "Everyone Hates Martin Shkreli; Everyone Is Missing the Point," *The New Yorker*, February 5, 2016, 34–37.

59. *Burwell v. Hobby Lobby*, 2766.

60. Joe Heschmeyer, "Martin Shkreli and the Crisis of Corporate Conscience," *First Things*, February 18, 2016, www.firstthings.com/blogs/firstthoughts/2016/02/martin-shkreli-and-the-crisis-of-corporate-conscience.

CHAPTER 3

1. Mary Midgley, *Heart and Mind* (New York: St. Martin's Press, 1981), 72, 75.

2. Peter Drucker, *The Practice of Management* (New York: Basic Books, 1955), 342.

3. David Oderberg, *Moral Theory: A Non-consequentialist Approach* (Oxford: Blackwell, 2000), 1.

4. Aristotle, *Nichomachean Ethics*, trans. Martin Oswald (Indianapolis: Bobbs-Merrill, 1962), bk. I, ch. 3, 1094b.

5. Oderberg, *Moral Theory*, 3–6.

6. John Finnis, *Aquinas* (Oxford: Oxford University Press, 1998), 129.

7. Thomas Aquinas, *Summa Theologiae*, trans. Fathers of the English Dominican Province (New York: Benziger Bros., 1947–48), I–II, q. 100, a. 3.

8. James Loughran, "Reasons for Being Just," in *The Value of Justice*, ed. Charles Kelbley (New York: Fordham University Press, 1979), 39–57.

9. Plato, *Gorgias*, trans. W. C. Helmbold (Indianapolis, IN: Bobbs-Merrill, 1952), 491e–492a.

10. Ibid., 506c.

11. Aquinas, *Summa Theologiae*, I–II, q. 58, a. 5. See also J. Budziszewski, *Commentary on Thomas Aquinas's Virtue Ethics* (Cambridge, UK: Cambridge University Press, 2017), 33–42.

12. Aristotle, *Nichomachean Ethics*, bk. II, ch. 1, 1103a.

13. Aquinas, *Summa Theologiae*, I–II, q. 55, a. 4. See also Budziszewski, *Commentary*, 17.

14. Oderberg, *Moral Theory*, 38.

15. Martha Nussbaum, "Virtue Ethics: A Misleading Category?," *Journal of Ethics* 3 (1999), 178. See also Jonathan Sanford, *Before Virtue: Assessing Contemporary Virtue Ethics* (Washington, DC: Catholic University of America Press, 2015), 101–3.

16. Rosalind Hursthouse and Pettigrove Glen, "Virtue Ethics," in *Stanford Encyclopedia of Philosophy*, ed. Edward Zalta (Winter 2016), https://plato.stanford.edu/archives/win2016/entries/ethics-virtue.

17. Daryl Koehn, "A Role for Virtue Ethics in the Analysis of Business," *Business Ethics Quarterly* 5, no. 3 (1995): 533–40.

18. G. E. M. Anscombe, "Modern Moral Philosophy," *Philosophy* 33 (1958), 11.

19. Martin Rhonheimer, *The Perspective of Morality* (Washington, DC: Catholic University of America Press, 2012), 397. See also Michael Sandel, *Justice* (New York: Farrar, Strauss & Giroux, 2011), 34–35.

20. G. E. Moore, *Principia Ethica*, 14th ed. (Cambridge, UK: Cambridge University Press, 1988), 146. See also Rhonheimer, *The Perspective of Morality*, 10–11, and Josef Seifert, *The Moral Action* (Irving, TX: International Academy of Philosophy Press, 2017), 34.

21. Lynn Sharp Paine, "Moral Thinking in Management: An Essential Capability," *Business Ethics Quarterly* 6, no. 4 (1996): 487. See also Moore, *Principia Ethica*, 149.

22. Sandel, *Justice*, 41.

23. Michael Slote, *Morals from Motives* (Oxford: Oxford University Press, 2001), 96.

24. Sandel, *Justice*, 225.

25. Ibid., 225–30.

26. Roger Scruton, *On Human Nature* (Princeton: Princeton University Press, 2017), 101–3.

27. Immanuel Kant, *Foundations of the Metaphysics of Morals* (New York: Macmillan, 1990), 68.

28. Immanuel Kant, *Critique of Practical Reason*, trans. Lewis Beck White (New York: Macmillan, 1993), 30.

29. Norman Bowie, *Business Ethics: A Kantian Perspective* (Oxford: Blackwell, 1996), 10–22.

30. Christine Korsgaard, *Creating the Kingdom of Ends* (Cambridge, UK: Cambridge University Press, 1996).

31. Ibid., 14.

32. Kant, *Foundations*, 41.

33. Ibid., 54.

34. Immanuel Kant, *Critique of Judgment*, trans. James Meredith (Oxford: Oxford University Press, 1952), 435–36.

35. This table is derived from Lynn Sharp Paine, Rohit Despande, and Joshua Margolis, "Up to Code: Does Your Company's Conduct Meet World-Class Standards?," *Harvard Business Review*, 55 November/December 2005, 31–39. See also Sandra Sucher and Nieh-He Hsieh, "A Framework for Ethical Reasoning" (Boston: Harvard Business School, 2011), 3, 9.

36. James Nickel, *Making Sense of Human Rights: Philosophical Reflections on the Universal Declaration of Human Rights* (Berkeley: University of California Press, 1987), 3.

37. Cass Sunstein, "Rightalk," *The New Republic*, September 2, 1991, 33–36.

38. Ronald Dworkin, *Taking Rights Seriously* (Cambridge, MA: Harvard University Press, 1977), xi.

39. Nickel, *Making Sense of Human Rights*, 16–7. See also John Finnis, *Human Rights and Common Good* (Oxford: Oxford University Press, 2011), 35

40. John Locke, *Two Treatises of Government*, ed. Peter Laslett (Cambridge, UK: Cambridge University Press, 1988), II, 44.

41. Ibid., II, 6. See also S. Adam Seagrave, *The Foundations of Natural Morality* (Chicago: University of Chicago Press, 2014), 52–55.

42. Aquinas, *Summa Theologiae*, II–II, q. 57, a.1c. See also Finnis, *Aquinas*, pp. 137–38, and Seagrave, *Foundations of Natural Morality*, 9.

43. Finnis, *Human Rights and Common Good*, 35.

44. John Finnis, *Natural Law and Natural Rights* (Oxford: Clarendon Press, 1980), 200–205.

45. Nickel, *Making Sense of Human Rights*, 35.

46. John Finnis, Joseph Boyle, and Germain Grisez, "A Sounder Theory of Morality," in *Nuclear Deterrence, Morality, and Freedom* (Oxford: Clarendon, 1987), 201–6. See also Robert George, "Natural Law," 52 *American Journal of Jurisprudence* 55 (2007).

47. Nickel, *Making Sense of Human Rights*, 107–13.

48. Ibid., 120.

49. Ibid., 14, 127.

50. Both Nickel and Thomas Donaldson propose many of these same rights, though in some cases I formulate them differently. See Donaldson, *The Ethics of International Business* (New York: Oxford University Press, 1989), 72–77.

51. Oderberg, *Moral Theory*, 76–85.

52. Finnis, *Natural Law and Natural Rights*, 225.

53. Henry Shue, *Basic Rights: Subsistence, Affluence, and U.S. Foreign Policy*, 2nd ed. (Princeton, NJ: Princeton University Press, 1996), 52–53. See also Donaldson, *Ethics of International Business*, 83–84.

54. Thomas Donaldson, "The Perils of Multinationals' Largess," *Business Ethics Quarterly* 4, no. 3 (1994): 367–71.

55. Seifert, *The Moral Action*, 81.

56. James Moor, "Just Consequentialism and Computing," in *Readings in Cyberethics*, ed. R. Spinello and H. Tavani (Sudbury, MA: Jones & Bartlett, 2001), 99–102.

57. Bernard Gert, *Morality: Its Nature and Justification* (New York: Oxford University Press, 1998), 152. See also Oderberg, *Moral Theory*, 79–80, and Moor, "Just Consequentialism," 101–2.

58. See, for example, Kevin Jackson, "Distributive Justice and the Corporate Duty to Aid," *Journal of Business Ethics* 12 (1993): 547–51.

59. "Just Good Business," A Special Report on Corporate Social Responsibility, *The Economist*, January 19, 2008, 6, 20.

60. Nathaniel Popper, "Did Goldman Make the Grade?," *New York Times*, November 4, 2015, B1.

61. Michael Porter and M. R. Kramer, "Creating Shared Value," *Harvard Business Review* 89 (January/February 2011): 64.

62. Eduardo Porter, "Corporate Action on Social Problems Has Limits," *The New York Times*, September 9, 2015, B1, B10.

63. Andrew Crane, Guido Palazzo, Laura J. Spence, and Dirk Matten, "Contesting the Value of 'Creating Shared Value,'" *California Management Review* 56, no. 2 (2014): 134–37.

64. *Dodge v. Ford Motor Company* 170 N.W. 668 (Mich. 1919), 697.

65. Milton Friedman, *Capitalism and Freedom* (Chicago: University of Chicago Press, 1962), 133. See also Friedman's celebrated article "The Social Responsibility of Business Is to Increase Its Profits," *New York Times Magazine*, September 13, 1970, 32–33, 122–26.

66. See "Six Sects of Shareholder Value," *The Economist*, January 21, 2017, 58.

67. Porter and Kramer, "Creating Shared Value," 66.

68. Kant, *Foundations*, 68.

69. Kathleen Bartlett, "Teaching Values: A Dilemma," 37 *American Journal of Legal Education* 519 (1987).

70. Niccolo Machiavelli, *The Prince*, trans. George Bull (New York: Penguin Books, 1975), ch. 15, 90–91.

CHAPTER 4

1. Karl Llewellyn, *The Bramble Bush: Classic Lectures on Law and the Law School* (Oxford: Oxford University Press, 2008), 16.

2. "Business Ethics Quotes/Responsibility Quotes," 12 Manage, accessed October 5, 2018, http://www.12manage.com/quotes_er.html.

3. Stuart P. Green, *Lying, Cheating and Stealing: A Moral Theory of White-Collar Crime* (Oxford: Oxford University Press, 2006), 193.

4. Aristotle, *Nicomachean Ethics*, trans. Martin Oswald (Indianapolis: Bobbs-Merrill, 1962), bk. III, ch. 1.

5. Ibid., bk. III, ch. 5.

6. Alasdair MacIntyre, *After Virtue* (Notre Dame, IN: Notre Dame University Press, 1984), 33.

7. I am indebted to Professor Ron Pawliczek of the Boston College Accounting Department for suggesting the idea behind this case study.

8. According to one study of Buddhism's ethical principles, "Buddhism believes in rebirth and teaches that individual human life begins at conception. Therefore, embryos should be respected equally with an adult life. Research involving the intentional destruction of human life, such as harvesting embryonic stem cells, is morally impermissible. Buddhism would see the moral issues raised by stem cell research as similar to those raised by IVF treatment involving the destruction of spare embryos and abortion." See "The Ethics of Stem Cell Research: Buddhist Views," accessed October 6,

2018, https//stemcellethics.weebly.com/buddhist-views.html.

9. The dilemma at the heart of this case was suggested by another short case study known as "Peter Green's First Day," in *Policies and Persons*, ed. John Matthews, Kenneth Goodpaster, and Laura Nash (New York: McGraw-Hill, 1985), 3–4.

10. I am indebted to Germain Grisez for the premise underlying this hypothetical case study. For a treatment of the problem discussed in this case, see Germain Grisez, *Difficult Ethical Questions* (Quincy, IL: Franciscan Press, 1993), 576–78.

11. Albert Z. Carr, "Is Business Bluffing Ethical?," in *Ethics in Practice: Managing the Moral Corporation*, ed. Kenneth R. Andrews (Boston: Harvard Business Review, 1989): 99–109. Carr's article originally appeared in the *Harvard Business Review* in 1968 (January/February).

12. Green, *Lying, Cheating and Stealing*, 76.

13. This case is loosely based on the safety problems that arose several decades ago with the McDonnell Douglas DC-10. See Douglas Birsch and John Fiedler, *The DC-10 Case: A Study in Applied Ethics, Technology and Society* (New York: SUNY Press, 1992).

14. I am indebted to Professor Daniel Coquillette, former dean of the Boston College Law School, for the basic idea behind this case.

15. According to Rule 1.6 of that code, "[a] lawyer shall not reveal information relating to representation of a client unless the client consents after consultation . . . except . . . to prevent the client from committing a criminal act that the lawyer believes is likely to result in imminent death or substantial bodily harm."

16. Carr, "Is Business Bluffing Ethical?," 102.

17. Niccolo Machiavelli, *The Prince*, trans. George Bull (New York: Penguin Books, 1961), ch. XV.

18. Michael Maccoby, "The Corporate Climber Has to Find His Heart," *Fortune*, December 1976, 100–104.

19. Aristotle, *Nicomachean Ethics*, bk. III, ch. 5.

20. See John Finnis, *Fundamentals of Ethics* (Washington, DC: Georgetown University Press, 1983), 139–40.

21. Richard Southern, *The Making of the Middle Ages* (New Haven, CT: Yale University Press, 1959), xi.

CHAPTER 5

1. *Western Tradition Partnership v. Bullock*, Montana Supreme Ct. DA-11-0081 (2011).

2. Richard Schragger and Micah Schwartzman, "Some Realism about Corporate Rights," *The Rise of Corporate Religious Liberty*, ed. Micah Schwartzman, Chad Flanders, and Zoe Robinson (New York: Oxford University Press, 2016), 351.

3. "Peculiar People," *The Economist*, March 26, 2011, 78.

4. Floyd Abrams, *The Soul of the First Amendment* (New Haven, CT: Yale University Press, 2017), 11.

5. James Bopp, Joseph La Rue, and Elizabeth Kosel, "The Game Changer: *Citizens United* Impact on Campaign Finance Law," 9 *First Amendment Law Review* 251 (2011).

6. *Burwell v. Hobby Lobby Stores, Inc.*, 134 U.S. 2751 (2014), 2787 (J. Ginsburg, dissenting).

7. Adam Winkler, *We the Corporations* (New York: W. W. Norton, 2018), xx.

8. Frederick Mark Gedicks and Andrew Koppleman, "Invisible Women: Why an Exemption for Hobby Lobby Would Violate the Establishment Clause," 67 *Vanderbilt Law Review* 51 (2014).

9. Germain Grisez, *Difficult Moral Questions* (Quincy, IL: Franciscan Press, 1997), 454–57.

10. *Citizens United v. Federal Election Commission*, 558 U.S. 310 (2010).

11. See "What Is Citizens United? An Introduction," Reclaim Democracy, accessed November 2018, www.reclaimdemocracy.org/who-are-citizens-united.

12. See 2 U.S.C. § 441b(b)(2) (2002).

13. Robert Ackerman and Lance Cole, "Making Corporate Law More Communitarian: A Proposed Response to the Roberts Court Personification of Corporations," 81 *Brooklyn Law Review* 895 (2016), 918–19. See also Jeffrey D. Clements, *Corporations Are Not People*, 2nd ed. (San Francisco: Berrett-Koehler, 2014), 11–15.

14. Winkler, *We the Corporations*, 325.

15. Transcript of oral argument, September 9, 2009, *Citizens United v. Federal Election Commission* (no. 08-205).

16. *Citizens United v. Federal Election Commission* (2010), 332.

17. Ibid., 340.

18. *First National Bank of Boston v. Bellotti*, 435 U.S. 765 (1978).

19. Ibid., 777.

20. Bopp et al., "The Game Changer," 255.

21. *Citizens United v. Federal Election Commission*, 359.

22. Ibid., 362.

23. Abrams, *Soul of the First Amendment*, 88–89.

24. Winkler, *We the Corporations*, 364.

25. *Citizens United v. Federal Election Commission*. See also Editorial, "The Rights of Corporations," *The New York Times*, September 21, 2009, A33.

26. *Citizens United v. Federal Election Commission*, 368. See also Winkler, *We the Corporations*, 364–45.

27. *Citizens United v. Federal Election Commission*, 394 (J. Stevens, dissenting). See also Ackerman and Cole, "Making Corporate Law More Communitarian," p. 919.

28. *Citizens United v. Federal Election Commission*, 390 (J. Stevens, dissenting). See also Clements, *Corporation Are Not People*, pp. 13–15.

29. Winkler, *We the Corporations*, 367.

30. Ibid., 370.

31. Congressman Alan Grayson (D–FL), "SCOTUS Decision Worst Since Dred Scott," *Politico*, January 21, 2010. The Dred Scott case held that people of African-American descent did not deserve the protection of the U.S. Constitution.

32. Bill Mears, "Supreme Court Erases Past on Corporate Campaign Spending," CNN Politics, January 21, 2010, www.cnn.com/2010/1-21-10/politics/campaign-finance-reform.

33. *Trustees of Dartmouth College v. Woodward*, 17 U.S. 518, 636 (1819).

34. Winkler, *We the Corporations*, 369.

35. People's Rights Amendment to the U.S. Constitution, reprinted in Clements, *Corporations Are Not People*, 195.

36. "Hobby Lobby Stores, Inc.: Revenue and Financial Data," 2016, www.hoovers.com/comany-information/cs/revenue-hobby_lobby_inc.

37. *Burwell v. Hobby Lobby*, 723 F. 3d 1114 (CA 10 2013).

38. John Riley, "Hobby Lobby Buys Ads Nationwide to Explain Easter," *Christian Post*, April 4, 2010, 6.

39. 26 U.S.C. § 5000A(f)(2); § 4980H(a)-(c)(2).

40. 42 U.S.C. § 300A(gg)(a)(4)-(13).

41. Women's Preventive Services: Required Health Plan Coverage Guidelines, 77 Federal Regulation (2012), 45 C.F.R. § 147.130 (a).

42. Women's Preventive Services, 45 CFR § 147.131(a).

43. Amy Sepinwall, "Conscience and Complicity: Assessing Pleas for Religious Exemptions in *Hobby Lobby*'s Wake," 82 *University of Chicago Law Review* 101 (2016), 140.

44. These included two emergency contraceptive (or so-called "morning after") pills, including Plan B (levonorgestrel) and ella, along with two

intrauterine devices (IUDs): ParaGard (copper IUD) and Skyla (levonorgestrel-releasing IUD).

45. According to most doctors and scientists, the morning-after pill may act by one or more of the following actions: delaying or preventing ovulation, blocking fertilization, or keeping a fertilized egg from implanting in the uterus. However, there is some evidence to suggest that levonorgestrel doesn't prevent a fertilized egg from implanting. It's not clear if the same is true for ella. For more about how the pill works, see https://www.mayoclinic.org/tests-procedures/morning-after-pill/pac-20394730. As for the status of the fertilized egg, modern embryology confirms that the human embryo from its inception is a complete and unified organism with the genetic structure proper to a human being. It also has the epigenetic primordia or first discernible traces of all its organs. See, for example, R. O'Rahilly and F. Mueller, *Human Embryology and Teratology*, 3rd ed. (New York: Wiley-Liss, 2000), pp. 15–16.

46. *Burwell v. Hobby Lobby Stores, Inc.*, 134 U.S. 2751 (2014), 2759. See also Sepinwall, "Conscience and Complicity," 116.

47. *Burwell v. Hobby Lobby Stores, Inc.*, 2778.

48. 42 U.S.C. § 2000B(bb)(a)(1).

49. See *Gonzales v. O Centro Espirita Beneficente Unido do Vegetal*, 546 U.S. 418 (2006).

50. *Conestoga Wood Specialties v. Secretary of U.S. Dept. of Health and Human Services*, 724 F.3d 377 (3d cir. 2013). See also Elizabeth Pollman, "Corporate Law and Theory in *Hobby Lobby*," in *The Rise of Corporate Religious Liberty*, 151–52.

51. *Hobby Lobby Stores, Inc. v. Sibelius*, 723 F. 3d 1114 (10th Cir. 2013).

52. *Burwell v. Hobby Lobby Stores, Inc.*, 2775. See also Sue Ganske, "*Burwell v. Hobby Lobby Stores Inc.*: The U.S. Supreme Court Holds That the Religious Freedom Restoration Act Trumps the Affordable Care Act," 31 *Journal of Contemporary Health Law & Policy* 1 (2015), 18.

53. Adam Liptak, "Supreme Court Rejects Contraceptives Mandate for Some Corporations: Justices Rule in Favor of Hobby," *New York Times*, June 30, 2014, A1.

54. *Burwell v. Hobby Lobby Stores, Inc.*, 2774. See also Liptak, "Supreme Court Rejects Contraceptives Mandate," A3.

55. *Burwell v. Hobby Lobby Stores, Inc.*, 2774.

56. Kent Greenawalt, "*Hobby Lobby*: Its Flawed Interpretive Techniques and Standards of Application," in *The Rise*

of Corporate Religious Liberty, 129. See also Pollman, "Corporate Law and Theory in *Hobby Lobby*," 168.

57. *Burwell v. Hobby Lobby Stores, Inc.*, 2765.

58. Greenawalt, "*Hobby Lobby*: Its Flawed Interpretive Techniques," 133–34.

59. *Burwell v. Hobby Lobby Stores, Inc.*, 2764–66.

60. Ibid., 2799 (Ginsburg, J., dissenting).

61. Greenawalt, "*Hobby Lobby*: Its Flawed Interpretive Techniques," 137–40.

62. Ibid., 142–43.

63. See Amy Sepinwall, "Corporate Piety and Impropriety: Hobby Lobby's Extension of RFRA Rights to the For-Profit Corporation," *Harvard Business Law Review* 5, no. 2 (2015), 175–76.

64. *Burwell v. Hobby Lobby Stores, Inc.*, 2761.

65. Winkler, *We the Corporations*, xx.

66. *Burwell v. Hobby Lobby Stores, Inc.*, 2812 (Ginsburg, J., dissenting).

67. Ibid., 2797 (Ginsburg, J., dissenting).

68. Ibid., 2813 (Ginsburg, J., dissenting).

69. Ibid., 2816 (Ginsburg, J., dissenting).

70. Ibid., 2815 (Ginsburg, J., dissenting). See also Sepinwall, "Corporate Piety and Impropriety," p. 180, and Pollman, "Corporate Law and Theory in *Hobby Lobby*," 160.

71. *Burwell v. Hobby Lobby Stores, Inc.*, 2751.

72. See Opposition to Plaintiff's Motion for Preliminary Injunction, *Hobby Lobby Inc. v. Sibelius*, 881 F. Supp. 2d 1287 (D. Colorado 2012): "By definition, a secular employer does not engage in any exercise of religion." See also Sepinwall, "Corporate Piety and Impropriety," 179–80.

73. *Burwell v. Hobby Lobby Stores, Inc.*, 2771.

74. Pollman, "Corporate Law and Theory in *Hobby Lobby*," 161.

75. "Could the Hobby Lobby Ruling Unleash a Parade of Horribles?" Knowledge@Wharton, Wharton School, July 2, 2014, knowledge.wharton.upenn.edu/article/hobby-lobby -case.

76. Binyamin Applebaum, "What the Hobby Lobby Ruling Means for America," *The New York Times Magazine*, July 22, 2014, 23–25.

77. Ackerman and Cole, "Making Corporate Law More Communitarian," 992.

78. Richard Garnett, "Accommodation, Establishment, and Freedom of Religion," 67 *Vanderbilt Law Review* 39 (2014), 41.

79. *Burwell v. Hobby Lobby Stores, Inc.*, 2766.

CHAPTER 6

1. Joseph French Johnson, *Business and the Man* (New York: Alexander Hamilton Institute, 1917), 124.

2. Jennifer Hughes, "Fooled Again," *Financial Times*, March 18, 2010, 7.

3. William D. Cohan, *Why Wall Street Matters* (New York: Random House, 2017), 22.

4. George Aragon, *Financial Ethics: A Positivist Analysis* (Oxford: Oxford University Press, 2011), 32–37.

5. Jason Zweig, "A Law Professor's Long Relentless Drive for Trust," *Wall Street Journal*, December 2, 2017, B10.

6. John Boatright, *Ethics in Finance* (Oxford: Blackwell Publishers, 1999), 16, 63–74. See also Stuart Green, *Lying, Cheating, and Stealing* (Oxford: Oxford University Press, 2006), 149.

7. Green, *Lying, Cheating, and Stealing*, 235.

8. David Enrich, *The Spider Network* (New York: HarperCollins, 2017), 6–24.

9. Eugene Soltes, *Why They Do It* (New York: Public Affairs, 2016), 124-25.

10. Yuling MaHuey-Lian Sun, "Where Should the Line Be Drawn on Insider Trading Ethics?," *Journal of Business Ethics* 17, no. 1 (1998), 67–68.

11. 15 USC §78(j)(b).

12. Lynn Sharp Paine and Christopher Bruner, "Note on Insider Trading Liability" (Boston: Harvard Business School, 2006), 1.

13. *In re Cady, Roberts & Co.*, 40 SEC 907 (1961), 912. See also Green, *Lying, Cheating, and Stealing*, 235–36.

14. Paine and Bruner, "Note on Insider Trading Liability," 2.

15. Boatright, *Ethics in Finance*, 134–35, and Green, *Lying, Cheating, and Stealing*, 237.

16. *Dirks v. SEC*, 463 U.S. 646 (1983). See also Patricia O'Hara and G. Robert Blakey, "Legal Aspects of Insider Trading," in *Ethics and the Investment Industry*, ed. Oliver Williams (Savage, MD: Rowman & Littlefield, 1989), 110.

17. *Dirks v. SEC*, 660.

18. Ibid., 664.

19. O'Hara and Blakey, "Legal Aspects of Insider Trading," 110. See also Paine and Bruner, "Note on Insider Trading Liability," 2.

20. *United States v. O'Hagan*, 521 U.S. 642 (1997). See also Green, *Lying, Cheating, and Stealing*, 238.

21. See Henry G. Manne, *Insider Trading and the Stock Market* (New York: Free Press, 1998). See also Green, *Lying, Cheating, and Stealing*, 236.

22. Kenneth Patrick, *Perpetual Jeopardy: The Texas Gulf Sulphur Affair* (New York: MacMillan, 1972), 1–27.

23. Ibid., 13–38.

24. John Brooks, "A Reasonable Amount of Time," in *Business Adventures*, ed. John Brooks (New York: Open Road, 2014), 140–41.

25. Ibid., 142.

26. Patrick, *Perpetual Jeopardy*, 44.

27. Ibid., 70–71. See also Brooks, "A Reasonable Amount of Time," 143.

28. *SEC v. Texas Gulf Sulphur*, 401 F. 2d 833 (2d Cir. 1968). See also Patrick, *Perpetual Jeopardy*, 71.

29. Patrick, *Perpetual Jeopardy*, 120.

30. *SEC v. Texas Gulf Sulphur*, 839. See also Brooks, "A Reasonable Amount of Time," 145.

31. *SEC v. Texas Gulf Sulphur*, 842.

32. Ibid., 840–41.

33. Patrick, *Perpetual Jeopardy*, 55–57.

34. Ibid.

35. Patrick, *Perpetual Jeopardy*, 56–57. See also Brooks, "A Reasonable Amount of Time," 155.

36. Patrick, *Perpetual Jeopardy*, 57. See also Brooks, "A Reasonable Amount of Time," 156.

37. *SEC v. Texas Gulf Sulphur*, 258 F. Supp 262 (SDNY 1966), 292–96.

38. Complaint, *United States v. Sean Stewart and Robert K. Stewart*, 15-CV-1634 (S.D.N.Y) (2015), 8–10.

39. *United States v. Sean Stewart and Robert K. Stewart*, 15–17.

40. Elkan Abramowitz and Jonathan Sacks, "Insider Trading Among Family Members," *New York Law Journal*, 256, no. 46 (2016), pp. 11–14.

41. Bob van Vanis and Christina Berthelsen, "Ex-Perella Banker Convicted of Tipping Dad on Health Mergers," Bloomberg.com, August 18, 2016, www.bloomberg.com/news/articles/2016-18-08/ex-perella-banker-convicted-ov-tipping-dad-on-health-mergers.

42. Peter Henning, "An Insider Trading Case That Pits Father Against Son," *New York Times*, August 23, 2016, B1, B4.

43. *United States v. Newman*, 773 F3d 438 (2d Cir. 2014) 442.

44. Abramowitz and Sacks, "Insider Trading Among Family Members," 12.

45. *United States v. Stewart*, 15-CR-00287 (S.D.N.Y.) Dkt. 174, 32 (2016).

46. Henning, "An Insider Trading Case That Pits Father Against Son," B4.

47. Christopher Matthews, "Son's Tips to Dad Lead to Conviction," *Wall Street Journal*, August 18, 2016, C1–C2.

48. John Riley, "Investment Banker Sean Stewart Gets Three Years in Insider Trading Case," *Newsday*, February 18, 2017, 1.

49. Quoted in Henning, "An Insider Trading Case That Pits Father Against Son," B4.

50. Barclays, "Barclays Business Structure," accessed May 2017, https://www.home.barclays/about-barclays/business-structure.html.

51. Barclays, "Barclays—A Quick History," accessed May 2017, https://www.archive.barclays.com/items/show/5819.

52. For mission statement and statement of values, see https://www.barclays.com/about/strategy, accessed May 2017.

53. Barclays 2017 Annual Report, https://www.home.barclays/annual-report-2017-html.

54. "Libor: What Is It and Why Does it Matter?," *BBC News*, August 3, 2015, www.bbc.com/business-1998765541. See also Frank Pasquale, *The Black-Box Society* (Cambridge, MA: Harvard University Press, 2015), 121, and David Hou and David Skeie, "LIBOR: Origins, Economics, Crisis, Scandal, and Reform," *Federal Reserve Bank of New York Staff Reports*, March 2014, 3.

55. House of Commons Treasury Committee, *Fixing LIBOR: Some Preliminary Findings* (London: House of Commons, 2012), 3–4.

56. British Banking Association, "LIBOR Information," July 2, 2012, 16. See also DealBook, "Behind the LIBOR Scandal," *New York Times*, July 10, 2012, and Hou and Skeie, "LIBOR: Origins, Economics, Crisis, Scandal, and Reform," 3.

57. "The LIBOR Scandal: The Rotten Heart of Finance," *The Economist*, July 7, 2012, 18–20.

58. House of Commons, *Fixing LIBOR*, 6.

59. Ibid., 16. See also "The LIBOR Scandal: The Rotten Heart of Finance," 19.

60. The federal funds rate represents how much banks charge each other to borrow money on deposit at the Federal Reserve, and it serves as the basis for interest rates for customer bank loans.

61. Enrich, *The Spider Network*, 34.

62. House of Commons, *Fixing LIBOR*, 15.

63. Ibid., 18.

64. Ibid., 21.

65. Ibid., 8–9.

66. Ibid., 6.

67. Mark Gilbert, "Barclays Takes a Money-Market Beating," *Bloomberg*, September 3, 2007; see also House of Commons, *Fixing LIBOR*, 24.

68. House of Commons, *Fixing LIBOR*, 23–24.

69. Gillian Tett, "LIBOR's Value Called into Question," *Financial Times*, September 25, 2007, 16.

70. Carrick Mollenkamp and Mark Whithouse, "Study Casts New Doubt on LIBOR," *Wall Street Journal*, May 29, 2008, C1, C4.

71. Federal Reserve Bank of New York, "New York Bank Responds to Congressional Request for Information on Barclays-LIBOR Matter," (New York: Federal Reserve Bank), July 13, 2012.

72. Ibid.

73. "The LIBOR Scandal: The Rotten Heart of Finance," 18–20.

74. David Enrich and Jean Eaglesham, "UBS Admits Rigging Rates in 'Epic' Plot," *Wall Street Journal*, December 20, 2012, A1, A14.

75. James McBride, "Understanding the LIBOR Scandal," CFR Backgrounder (New York: Council on Foreign Relations), October 12, 2016, http://www.cfr.org/united-kingdom/understanding-libor-scandal/p28729.

76. David Enrich, "U.K. Jury Acquits 6 in Libor Case," *Wall Street Journal*, January 28, 2016, C1–C2.

77. Kevin Dugan, "First US Trial over Libor Scandal Kicks Off," *New York Post*, October 14, 2015, 23.

78. "Calling to Accounts," *The Economist,* October 5, 2013, 80.

79. David Rhode, "The Libor Scandal and Capitalism's Moral Decay," *The Atlantic*, July 13, 2012, at www.theatlantic.com/businesses/archive/2012/07/the-libor-scandal-and-capitalisms-moral-decay/25981.

80. Louise Story and Gretchen Morgenson, "SEC Accuses Goldman of Fraud in Housing Deal," *New York Times*, April 16, 2010, A1, A16.

81. Gregory Zuckerman, Susanne Craig, and Serena Ng, "U.S. Charges Goldman Sachs with Fraud," *Wall Street Journal,* April 17, 2010, A1, A4.

82. Andrew Battle, "The Evolution of Goldman Sachs," Forbes.com, May 21, 2010, www.forbes.com/2010/05/21/goldman-sachs-fraud-case.

83. Ibid.

84. Ibid. See also Liz Hoffman, "Goldman Sachs Embraces Lending's Bland Side," *Wall Street Journal*, May 2, 2017, A1, A14.

85. Patrick Jenkins and Francesco Guerrera, "Goldman Versus the Regulators," *Financial Times*, April 19, 2010, p. 9.

86. "A Brief History of Goldman Sachs, the Most Hated Bank in the World," *Business Insider*, March 8, 2012, www.businessinsider.com/how-goldman-sachs-became-the-most-hated-bank-in-the-world.

87. Complaint, *Securities Exchange Commission v. Goldman Sachs & Co. and Fabrice Tourre*, 10-CV-23614 (S.D.N.Y) (2010), p. 5. See also Michael Lewis, *The Big Short: Inside the Doomsday Machine* (New York: W. W. Norton, 2010), 23, and "Crash Course," *The Economist*, September 7, 2013, 74.

88. Lewis, *The Big Short*, 29–31.

89. *Securities Exchange Commission v. Goldman Sachs & Co.*, 5. See also Lewis, *The Big Short*, 72–73, and "Crash Course."

90. *Securities Exchange Commission v. Goldman Sachs & Co.*, 6.

91. Ibid., 7. See also Jenkins and Guerrera, "Goldman Versus the Regulators."

92. *Securities Exchange Commission v. Goldman Sachs & Co.*, 10–11.

93. Zuckerman, Craig, and Ng, "U.S. Charges Goldman Sachs with Fraud," A1, A4.

94. Ibid., A4.

95. *Securities Exchange Commission v. Goldman Sachs & Co.*, 21.

96. Jenkins and Guerrera, "Goldman Versus the Regulators."

97. Francesco Guerrera, "Going for Goldman," *Financial Times*, April 24–25, 2010, 8.

98. Kate Kelly, "Trader Seized on Mortgage-Security Boom," *Wall Street Journal*, April 17–18, 2010, A5.

99. Scott Patterson, "Paulson, Wanting to Short Mortgages, Found a Partner," *Wall Street Journal*, April 17–18, 2010, A5.

100. Dealbook, "Goldman Settles with SEC for $550 Million," *New York Times*, July 16, 2010, B1–B2.

101. Goldman Sachs Financial Data, Yahoo Finance, accessed July 2017, www.financesyahoo.com/quote/GS/financials?p=GS.

102. Ibid.

103. Wells Fargo, "History of Wells Fargo," accessed July 2017, https://www.wellsfargo.com/about/company/history.

104. Ibid.

105. Robert Magnuson, "Former Bank Aide Admits Role in Embezzlement Plot," *Los Angeles Times*, August 11, 1981, pp. 1, 18.

106. Edward Iwata, "Bank Strife Likely to Spark Mergers, Asset Sales," *USA Today*, October 13, 2008, pp. 1, 16. See also Dealbook, "Wells Fargo to Acquire Wachovia in $15.1 Billion Deal," *New York Times*, October 3, 2008, B2.

107. John Carney, "John Stumpf's Crisis Cameo," *Wall Street Journal*, September 14, 2016, C1–C2.

108. Christina Rexrode and John Carney, "One of Banking Industry's Star Performers Stumbles," *Wall Street Journal*, October 13, 2016, A2.

109. Gretchen Morgenson, "Wells Fargo Board, Now in Spotlight, Recalls Its Role," *New York Times*, September 28, 2016, B1–2.

110. Ibid.

111. Mary Mack, "Community Banking," Wells Fargo & Company Community Banking Investor Day Presentation, May 11, 2017, https://www08.wellsfargomedia.com/assets/pdf/about/investor-relations/presentations/2017/community-banking-presentation.pdf.

112. Emily Glazer, "Wells Fargo Official in Eye of Storm," *Wall Street Journal*, September 20, 2016, C1–C2.

113. Andrew Ross Sorkin, "The Brazen Sham No One Noticed," *New York Times*, September 13, 2016, B1, B6.

114. Sheelah Kolhatkar, "Elizabeth Warren and the Wells Fargo Scandal," *New Yorker*, September 21, 2016, 14–16.

115. Emily Glazer, "Wells Fargo Tripped by Its Sales Culture," *Wall Street Journal*, September 17, 2016, A1, A8.

116. Morgenson, "Wells Fargo Board Recalls Its Role," pp. B1–B2. See also Glazer, "Wells Fargo Official in Eye of Storm," and Glazer, "Wells Fargo Tripped by Its Sales Culture."

117. The Bank Holding Act, which mandated the separation of banking and insurance, was repealed in 1999 and opened the door for the broad scope of cross-selling envisioned by these two companies.

118. Veronica Dagher, "Banks' Cross-Selling Can Help and Hurt," *Wall Street Journal*, September 17, 2016, B7. See also Aaron Back, "Wells's Questionable Cross-Sales," *Wall Street Journal*, September 10, 2016, B12.

119. Back, "Wells's Questionable Cross-Sales."

120. E. Scott Reckard, "Wells Fargo's Pressure-Cooker Sales Culture Comes at a Cost," *Los Angeles Times*, December 21, 2013, A1, A17. See also Aaron Back, "Wells Fargo Isn't Sorry Enough," *Wall Street Journal*, September, 14, 2016, C12.

121. Emily Glazer and Christina Rexrode, "Wells Fargo's Next Job: Fixing Its Mess," *Wall Street Journal*, December 28, 2016, A1, A8.

122. Matt Egan, "5,300 Wells Fargo Employees Fired over 2 Million Phony Accounts," CNN, September 9, 2016, http://money.cnn.com/2016/09/08/investing/wells-fargo-created-phony-accounts-bank-fees. See also Emily Glazer, "Wells Fargo Fined for Sales Scam," *Wall Street Journal*, September 9, 2016, A1, A6.

123. Glazer and Rexrode, "Wells Fargo's Next Job," A8.

124. Michael Corkery and Stacy Cowley, "Wells Fargo Moves to Smother Lawsuits over Sham Accounts," *New York Times*, December 7, 2016, A1, A3.

125. Anna Maria Andriotis and Emily Glazer, "Wells Pushed Overdraft Services," *Wall Street Journal*, October 11, 2016, C1–C2.

126. Emily Glazer, "Wells Branches Alerted on Monitors," *Wall Street Journal*, January 25, 2017, B2.

127. Stacy Cowley, "Fake Accounts at Wells Fargo Raised Alarms Starting in 2005," *New York Times*, October 12, 2016, B1, B3.

128. Michael Corkery and Stacy Cowley, "Well Fargo Warned Workers Against Sham Accounts but 'They Needed a Paycheck,'" *New York Times*, September 16, 2016, B1, B4.

129. Emily Glazer, "Wells Fires 4 Senior Managers over Sales Practices," *Wall Street Journal*, February 22, 2017, B1–B2. See also Emily Glazer, "How Wells Fargo's High-Pressure Sales Culture Spiraled Out of Control," *Wall Street Journal*, September 16, 2016, B1–B2.

130. Emily Glazer, "How the Scandal Unfolded," *Wall Street Journal*, October 14, 2016, A8.

131. Emily Glazer and Christina Rexrode, "Wells Boss Says Staff at Fault for Scams," *Wall Street Journal*, September 14, 2016, A1–A2.

132. Emily Glazer, "Wells Fargo's Botched Crisis Management," *Wall Street Journal*, October 14, 2016, A1, A8.

133. Michael Corkery, "Wells Fargo Chief Endures a Senate Committee's Bipartisan Wrath," *New York Times*, September 21, 2016, B1, B3.

134. Rachel Louise Ensign, "Wells CEO Is Placed on Hot Seat Again," *Wall Street Journal*, September 30, 2016, C3.

135. Michael Corkery and Stacy Cowley, "California Suspends Some Ties with Wells," *New York Times*, September 29, 2016.

136. Glazer, "Wells Fargo Official in Eye of Storm." See also Emily Glazer, "Wells Slams Former Bosses' High-Pressure Sales Tactics," *Wall Street Journal*, April 11, 2017, A1, A9.

137. Glazer, "Wells Slams Former Bosses," A9.

138. Emily Glazer, "New Wells Fargo CEO's First Task: Build Trust," *Wall Street Journal*, October 14, 2016, C1–C2. See also Aaron Back, "Wells Fargo Enters Realm of Uncertainty," *Wall Street Journal*, October 15–16, 2016, B12.

139. Emily Glazer, "A Year Later, Wells Fargo Woes Persist," *Wall Street Journal*, September 9, 2017, B10.

CHAPTER 7

1. See Matthew Perrone, "Lawmakers Blast Valeant for Price Gouging Tactics," *Daily Herald*, April 27, 2016, https://www.dailyherald.com/article/20160426/business/304269731.

2. Quoted in Marilyn Chase, "Burroughs Wellcome Reaps Profits, Outrage from Its AIDS Drug," *Wall Street Journal*, September 15, 1989, A1.

3. Robert Merges, *Justifying Intellectual Property* (Cambridge, MA: Harvard University Press, 2011), 5.

4. Wendy Gordon, "Asymmetric Market Failure and Prisoner's Dilemma in Intellectual Property," 17 *University of Dayton Law Review* 853 (1992).

5. *Brenner v. Manson*, 383 U.S. 519 (1966).

6. Richard A. Spinello and Maria Bottis, *A Defense of Intellectual Property Rights* (Cheltenham, UK: Edward Elgar, 2009), 52–58.

7. "A Patent Cure-All," *The Economist*, June 15, 1996, 75. See also F. S. Kieff, "Property Rights and Property Rules for Commercializing Inventions," 85 *Minnesota Law Review* 697 (2000).

8. Jorn Sonderholm, "Ethical Issues Surrounding Intellectual Property Rights," in *New Frontiers in the Philosophy of Intellectual Property*, ed. Annabelle

9. *Mazer v. Stein*, 347 U.S. 201, 219; reh'g denied, 347 U.S. 949 (1954). See also Alfred Yen, "Restoring the Natural Law: Copyright as Labor and Possession," 51 *Ohio State Law Journal* 517 (1990).

10. See Richard Brandt, *Ethical Theory: The Problems of Normative and Critical Ethics* (Oxford: Oxford University Press, 1959), 380.

11. Merges, *Justifying Intellectual Property*, 2. See also Yen, "Restoring the Natural Law," 518.

12. Kieff, "Property Rights," 705–10.

13. One study has found that intellectual property rights played a definite role in spurring innovation in the chemical and pharmaceutical industries. See Richard Levin, *Appropriating the Returns from Industrial Research and Development* (Washington, DC: Brookings Institute, 1987).

14. George Priest, "What Economists Can Tell Lawyers," 8 *Research in Law and Economics* 19 (1986).

15. Merges, *Justifying Intellectual Property*, 3–4.

16. John Locke, *Two Treatises of Government*, ed. Peter Laslett (Cambridge, UK: Cambridge University Press, 1988), II, §44. All subsequent references in the text are to this edition.

17. Merges, *Justifying Intellectual Property*, 35.

18. John Simmons, *The Lockean Theory of Rights* (Princeton, NJ: Princeton University Press, 1992), 273. See also Merges, *Justifying Intellectual Property*, 30–38.

19. Yochai Benkler, "Siren Songs and Amish Children: Autonomy, Information, and Law," 76 *New York University Law Review* 23 (2001).

20. David McGowan, "Copyright Nonconsequentialism," 69 *Missouri Law Review* 1 (2004).

21. Statista, "Major Global Pharmaceutical Companies Based on Pharma Revenue, 2017," accessed December 2016, www.statista.com/283061/major-global-pharmaceutical-companies-based-on-pharma-revenue-2017.

22. John LaMattina, "About Those Soaring Drug Profits," Forbes.com, January 23, 2018, www.forbes.com/sites/johnlamattina/2018-01-23/about-those-soaring-pharma-profits.

23. "Pharma Exec's Top 50 Companies 2017," Pharma. Exec.com, June 2017, www.pharma.exec.com/pharma-execs-top-50-companies-2017.

24. Alfred D. Chandler, *Shaping the Industrial Century: The Remarkable Story of the Evolution of the Modern*

Lever (Cambridge, UK: Cambridge University Press, 2012), 110–21.

Chemical and Pharmaceutical Industries (Cambridge, MA: Harvard University Press, 2005), 177–79.

25. Peter Temin, *Taking Your Medicine: Drug Regulation in the United States* (Cambridge, MA: Harvard University Press, 1980), 61–66. See also Bernard J. Stern, *American Medical Practice in the Perspective of a Century* (New York: Commonwealth Fund, 1945), 43.

26. Temin, *Taking Your Medicine*, 58.

27. Ibid., 58–68.

28. Meredith Wadman, "Medicine's Age of Wonders," *Wall Street Journal*, May 20, 2017, C6. See also Heinz Redwood, *The Pharmaceutical Industry: Trends, Problems, and Achievements* (Felixstone, UK: Oldwicks Press, 1987), 43, and Chandler, *Shaping the Industrial Century*, 179–80.

29. Temin, *Taking Your Medicine*, 79.

30. Peter Barton Hutt, "Drug Regulation in the United States," *International Journal of Technology Assessment in Health Care* 2 (1986): 620.

31. Food and Drug Administration, "The History of Drug Regulation in the United States" (brochure), accessed September 2016, www.fda.gov/AboutFDA/WhatWeDo/History, See also Willis Emmons, "Note on Pharmaceutical Industry Regulation" (Boston: Harvard Business School, 1994), 3.

32. U.S.C. 37 416 (1912).

33. Temin, *Taking Your Medicine*, 28–40. See also Emmons, "Note on Pharmaceutical Industry Regulation" 2–4.

34. Cynthia Crossen, "How Elixir Deaths Led U.S. to Require Proof of New Drugs' Safety," *Wall Street Journal*, March 11, 2007, B1.

35. Temin, *Taking Your Medicine*, 44. See also Hutt, "Drug Regulation in the United States," 621.

36. See *Rohm & Haas v. Roberts Chemical Company*, 245 F.2d 693 (4th Cir. 1957), which upheld a patent for the use of a well-known commercial product as a fungicide. See also Robert Merges, Peter Mennell, and Mark Lemley, *Intellectual Property in the New Technological Age*, 3rd ed. (New York: Aspen, 2003), 140–45, and Temin, *Taking Your Medicine*, 67.

37. Food and Drug Administration, "History of Drug Regulation."

38. Paul Howard, "Hail Mary Medicine," *Wall Street Journal*, November 13, 2015, A11.

39. Hutt, "Drug Regulation in the United States," 621.

40. Food and Drug Administration, "History of Drug Regulation." See also Hutt, "Drug Regulation in the United States," 621–22.

41. Branded drug companies typically run only one or two products on their production lines, but generic companies run 30 to 50 products. See Scott Gottlieb, "How Obama's FDA Keeps Generic Drugs Off the Market," *Wall Street Journal*, August 21, 2016, A20.

42. Hutt, "Drug Regulation in the United States," 622.

43. Darcy Olsen, "Wining the Right to Save Your Own Life," *Wall Street Journal*, November 27, 2015, A15.

44. Andrew Jack, "Perils for Pill Pushers," *Financial Times*, September 22, 2010, 9.

45. Temin, *Taking Your Medicine*, 128.

46. Ibid., 128–41. See also Emmons, "Note on Pharmaceutical Industry Regulation," 6 (along with notes accompanying this case). Robin Feldman and Evan Frondorf, *Drug Wars* (New York: Cambridge University Press, 2017), 22.

47. Darcy Olsen, *The Right to Try* (New York: Harper, 2016). See also Olsen, "Wining the Right to Save Your Own Life."

48. Chandler, *Shaping the Industrial Century*, 192–93.

49. Ibid., 198–99.

50. John Byrne, "The Miracle Company," *Businessweek*, October 18, 1987, 84–90. See also Chandler, *Shaping the Industrial Century*, 183–88.

51. William Rosen, *Miracle Cure* (New York: Viking, 2017), 224–29.

52. Edmund Pratt, *Pfizer: Bringing Science to Life* (Princeton, NJ: Princeton University Press, 1985), 7–20. See also Chandler, *Shaping the Industrial Century*, 188–92.

53. Chandler, *Shaping the Industrial Century*, 200–202.

54. Ravi Vij, "Pharma Merger and Acquisition Analysis: 1995–2015," accessed December 2016, www.revenuesandprofits.com/pharma-mergers-and-acquisitions-analysis-1995-2015.

55. Natasha Singer, "Merck to Buy Schering-Plough for $41.1 Billion," *New York Times*, March 9, 2009, D1.

56. Feldman and Frondorf, *Drug Wars*, 20.

57. Duff Wilson, "Facing Generic Lipitor Rivals, Pfizer Battles to Protect Its Cash Cow," *New York Times*, November 29, 2011, B1, B4.

58. Feldman and Frondorf, *Drug Wars*, 53–54.

59. Ibid., 69–70.

60. Stuart Eliott and Nat Ives, "Questions on the $3.8 Billion Drug Ad Business," *New York Times*, October 12, 2004, D1. See also Feldman and Frondorf, *Drug Wars*, 71–72.

61. "The Price of Failure," *The Economist*, November 29, 2014, 59.

62. Ed Silverman, "Can It Really Cost $2.6 Billion to Develop a Drug?," *Wall Street Journal*, November 21, 2014, B3.

63. Jonathan Rockoff, Jeanne Whalen, and Marta Falconi, "Global Drug Industry Does About-Face," *Wall Street Journal*, April 23, 2014, A1–A2.

64. Joseph Walker, "Eczema Drug Gets 'Responsible' Price," *Wall Street Journal*, March 29, 2017, B1, B4. See also "Regneron and Sanofi Announce FDA Approval of Dupixent," March 28, 2017, www.news.sanofi/2017-03-28/sanofi-and-regneron-announce-fda-aaproval- of-dupixent.

65. Jonathan Rockoff, "Drug Companies Keep Lid on Prices," *Wall Street Journal*, February 27, 2017, A1, A10. See also Joseph Walker, "Surging Drug Costs Inflict Pain," *Wall Street Journal*, May 30, 2017, B1.

66. Jeanne Whalen, "Doctors Attack Drug Prices," *Wall Street Journal*, July 23, 2015, B1–B2.

67. Jonathan Rockoff, "The Anatomy of a Drug Price," *Wall Street Journal*, December 9, 2015, A1, A12.

68. Michelle Boldrin and David Levine, *Against Intellectual Monopoly* (Cambridge, UK: Cambridge University Press, 2008), 238.

69. Patricia Werhane and Michael Gorman, "Intellectual Property Rights: Access to Life-Enhancing Drugs and Corporate Moral Responsibilities," in *Ethics and the Pharmaceutical Industry*, ed. Michael Santoro and Thomas Gorrie (New York: Cambridge University Press, 2005), 269–71.

70. Merges, *Justifying Intellectual Property*, 282.

71. Brian Zycher and John DiMasi, "The Truth about Drug Innovation," Manhattan Institute for Policy Research, April 2006, www.manhattan-institute.org/html/mpr_06.htm.

72. Stephen Witt, "Valeant Pharmaceutical's Novel Business Approach Made It a Wall Street Darling, Then a Pariah," *New York Magazine*, January 13, 2016, 31–37.

73. Witt, "Valeant Pharmaceutical's Novel Business Approach."

74. See the company website, www.valeant.com, for this and other background information about Valeant.

75. Jonathan Rockoff and Liz Hoffman, "Valeant Will Pay $10 Billion for Salix," *Wall Street Journal*, February 23, 2015, B1–B2.

76. Valeant, "Valeant's Mission and Values," accessed December 2016, https://www.valeant.com/about.

77. David Benoit and Jacquie McNish, "Architect of Valeant's Turnaround under Fire," *Wall Street Journal*, December 15, 2015, B1, B6.

78. Ibid., B6.

79. Andrew Pollack and Sabrina Tavernse, "A Drug Company's Price Tactics Pinch Insurers and Consumers," *New York Times*, October 5, 2015, A1, B2. See also Gretchen Morgenson, "A Top Investor Is Tripped Up by a Bold Bet," *New York Times*, March 20, 2017, A1, A9, and Stephanie Armour and Jonathan Rockoff, "Drug Firms Are Faulted on Price Increases," *Wall Street Journal*, February 3, 2016, B4.

80. Jonathan Rockoff and Ed Silverman, "Firms Buy Rival Drugs, Then Raise Their Prices," *Wall Street Journal*, April 27, 2015, A1–A2.

81. Ibid.

82. Ibid. See also Pollack and Tavernse, "A Drug Company's Price Tactics Pinch Insurers and Consumers."

83. Richard Blackwell, "Drugs Targeted in Valeant Pricing Controversy Acquired in February," *Globe and Mail*, September 29, 2015, 1, 16.

84. Andrew Pollack, "Drug Makers Sidestep Barriers on Pricing," *New York Times*, October 29, 2015, B1. See also Feldman and Frondorf, *Drug Wars*, 85–86.

85. Jonathan Rockoff and Jeanne Whalen, "Valeant's Ties to Pharmacy Scrutinized," *Wall Street Journal*, October 26, 2015, B1, B6. See also Matt Turner and Linette Lopez, "Leaked Documents Shed Light on the Defunct Pharmacy That Brought Valeant to Its Knees," *Business Insider*, November 8, 2016, www.businessinsider.com/leaked-valeant-documents-show-philidor-strategy-2016-11.

86. Caroline Chen, "Philidor Said to Modify Prescriptions to Boost Valeant Sales," Bloomberg.com, October 29, 2015, www.bloomberg.com/news/articles/2015-10-29/philidor-said-to-modify-prescriptions.

87. Andrew Pollack and David Jolly, "Valeant Drops Philidor Mail-Order Pharmacy," *New York Times*, October 30, 2015, B1.

88. Pollack and Tavernse, "A Drug Company's Price Tactics Pinch Insurers and Consumers," B2.

89. Ibid., B2.

90. Arlene Weintraub, "Gadfly Pharma Investor Shkreli Starts Anew after Ousting from Retrophin," Forbes.com, February 27, 2015, www.forbes.com/sites/arleneweintraub/2015/02/27/gadfly-pharma-investor-shkreli-starts-anew-after-ousting-from-retrophin.

91. Feldman and Frondorf, *Drug Wars*, 3, 10.

92. Joseph Walker, "Drug Makers Raise Prices Despite Protests," *Wall Street Journal*, July 15, 2016, B1–B2.

93. See Shkreli's interview with Forbes: "One-on-One with Pharma's Provocateur" (video), Forbes.com, December 8, 2016, https:// www.forbes.com/ video/4650565743001.

94. Jonathan Rockoff and Maureen Farrell, "Valeant Switches Strategy Amid Drug-Price Furor," *Wall Street Journal*, October 20, 2015, B3.

95. Perrone, "Senate Lawmakers Accused Embattled Drugmaker."

96. Katie Thomas, "Valeant Pharmaceuticals Picks Chief of Another Drug Maker," *New York Times*, April 26, 2016, B3. See also Jonathan Rockoff and Michael Rapoport, "Valeant Chief Vows 'New Chapter,'" *Wall Street Journal*, July 6, 2016, B1.

97. Jacquie McNish and Christopher Matthews, "Valeant Faces Criminal Probe," *Wall Street Journal*, August 11, 2016, B1, B6.

98. Dana Mattioli, David Benoit, and Jonathan Rockoff, "Valeant Sheds Assets to Pay Down Debt," *Wall Street Journal*, January 11, 2017, B1–B2.

99. Bruce Nussbaum, *Good Intentions: How Big Business and the Medical Establishment Are Corrupting the Fight against AIDS* (New York: Atlantic Monthly Press, 1990), 7–33.

100. Ibid., 44, 263–65. Nussbaum argues that AL 721 was especially promising but scientists and researchers at the NIH were prejudiced against this egg-based natural compound; FDA officials under political pressure to approve AZT did not give AL 721 a fair chance of success. "An open, fair drug approval system would have pushed AL 721 right to the top of any list of compounds to be tested" (264).

101. Nussbaum, *Good Intentions*, 331–32. See also Marilyn Chase, "Wellcome Unit's AZT Is Recommended as First Prescription Drug to Treat AIDS," *Wall Street Journal*, February 17, 1987, A11.

102. Michael Waldholz, "Drug Makers' Image Ills Are Self-Induced," *Wall Street Journal*, March 30, 1993, A14.

103. Philip Hilts, "U.S. Study of Drug Makers Criticizes Excess Profits," *New York Times*, February 26, 1993, D1–D2.

104. Marilyn Chase, "Bristol-Myers Guides AIDS Drug through a Marketing Minefield," *Wall Street Journal*, October 10, 1991, A1, A7.

105. World Health Organization, "Anti-viral Therapies," accessed December 2016, www.who.int/hiv/topics/treatment.en.

106. Sheryl Gay Stolberg, "Africa's AIDS War," *New York Times*, March 10, 2001, A1, A4.

107. World Bank, *Botswana: Selected Development Impact of HIV/AIDS* (Washington, DC: World Bank, 2001). See also Laura Alfaro and Deborah Spar, "Botswana: A Diamond in the Rough" (Boston: Harvard Business School, 2003), 11–12.

108. University of California at San Francisco, AIDS Policy Research Center, "HIV/AIDS in Zimbabwe," December 2003, accessed November 2016.

109. James Thuo Gathii, "Third World Perspectives on Global Pharmaceutical Access," in *Ethics and the Pharmaceutical Industry*, 344.

110. Gardiner Harris, "AIDS Gaffes in Africa Come Back to Haunt Drug Industry at Home," *Wall Street Journal*, April 23, 2001, A1, A6.

111. Sheryl Gay Stolberg, "Africa's AIDS War," *New York Times*, March 10, 2001, A1, A4.

112. Gathii, "Third World Perspectives on Global Pharmaceutical Access," 339.

113. Robert Block, "AIDS Activists Win Skirmish in South Africa," *New York Times*, May 7, 2001, A17.

114. Daniel Pearl and Alix Freedman, "Behind Cipla's Offer of Cheap AIDS Drugs: Potent Mix of Motives," *Wall Street Journal*, March 12, 2001, pp. A1, A8. Melody Petersen, "Lifting the Curtain on the Real Costs of Making AIDS Drugs," *New York Times*, April 24, 2001, C1, C10.

115. Werhane and Gorman, "Intellectual Property Rights," 272–75.

116. Mark Schoops and Michael Waldholz, "AIDS Drug Price War Breaks Out in Africa, Goaded by Generics," *Wall Street Journal*, March 7, 2001, A1, A14.

117. Daniel Jamison and R.G. Feachem, *Disease and Mortality in Sub-Saharan Africa*, 2nd ed. (Washington, DC: World Bank, 2006), 611–17.

118. See Jon Cohen, "South Africa's Bid to End AIDS," *Science*, June 29, 2016, www.sciencemag.org/news/2016/06/south-africa-s-bid-end-aids.

119. Ibid.

120. Geoffrey Carr, "Climbing the Helical Staircase," in "A Survey of Biotechnology," supplement to *The Economist*, March 29, 2003, 3.

121. "Forbes Best Small Companies: Myriad Genetics," Forbes.com, May 2017, www.forbes.com/companies/myriad-genetics.

122. Inside Myriad, "More Than 25 Years as a Leader in Molecular Diagnostics," accessed October 2018, www.myriad.com/about-myriad/inside-myriad/history.

123. Geoffrey Carr, "Special Report on the Human Genome," *The Economist*, June 19, 2010, 3–7.

124. C. Ben Mitchell, "The New Genetics and the Dignity of Humankind," in *Human Dignity in the Biotech Century*, ed. Charles Colson and Nigel S. Cameron (New York: Intervarsity Press, 2004), 60–74. See also *Association for Molecular Pathology v. Myriad Genetics*, 569 U.S. 1139 (2013).

125. Charles Zimmer, "Hope, Hype, and Genetic Breakthroughs," *Wall Street Journal*, March 11, 2011, C6.

126. Appellant brief, *Association for Molecular Pathology v. U.S. Patent Office and Myriad Genetics*, 653 F. 3d 1329, (2011), 41–42.

127. *Diamond v. Chakrabarty*, 447 U.S. 303 (1980).

128. *Association for Molecular Pathology v. U.S. Patent Office and Myriad Genetics*. See also *Diamond v. Chakrabarty*, 305.

129. David Resnik. "DNA Patents and Human Dignity," 29 *Journal of Legal and Medical Ethics* 52 (2001).

130. *Association for Molecular Pathology v. Myriad Genetics*, 569 U.S. 1139 (2013).

131. 35 U.S.C. §101.

132. *Diamond v. Diehr*, 450 U.S. 175, 185 (1981). See also *Diamond v. Chakrabarty* 447 U.S. 309 ("manifestations of nature [are] free to all men and reserved exclusively to none").

133. *Association for Molecular Pathology v. United States PTO*, 702 F. Supp. 2d 181 (U.S. Dist.) (2010); see also *Bilski v. Kappos*, 130 U.S. 1238 (2010).

134. *Association for Molecular Pathology v. United States PTO*, 653 F. 3d 1329 (U.S. App.) (2011).

135. *Diamond v. Chakrabarty*, 309.

136. *Association for* Molecular Pathology *v. United States PTO*, 1351.

137. Charles Harrison, "Neither Moore nor the Market: Alternative Models for Compensating Contributors of Human Tissue," 28 *American Journal of Law and Medicine* 77 (2002).

138. M. E. Horn, "DNA Patenting and Access to Healthcare: Achieving the Balance among Competing Interests," 50 *Cleveland State Law Review* 223 (2002).

139. Andrew Pollack, "U.S. Hopes to Stem Rush Toward Patenting Genes," *New York Times*, June 28, 2002, 18.

140. Chester Chuang and Denys Lau, "The Pros and Cons of Gene Patents," GGU Law Digital Commons, December 17, 2010, https://digitalcommons.law.ggu.edu/cgi/viewcontent.cgi?article=1171&context=pubs.

141. *Association for* Molecular Pathology *v. United States PTO*, 1355.

142. "Patenting Genes: Pros and Cons," Genetics Generation, accessed January 2017, www.knowgenetics.org/patenting-genes.

143. Kevin Kimberlin, "Gene Patents Drive Medical Innovation," *Wall Street Journal*, May 21, 2013, A15.

144. *Association for Molecular Pathology v. Myriad Genetics*, 569 U.S. 1139 (2013).

145. Ibid., 1153.

146. Ibid., 1168.

147. Jess Bravin and Brent Kendall, "Justices Strike Down Gene Patents," *Wall Street Journal*, June 14, 2013, B1–B2.

CHAPTER 8

1. J. Patrick Wright, *On a Clear Day You Can See General Motors: John Z. DeLorean's Look inside the Automotive Giant* (New York: Avon Books, 1980), 279.

2. Manuel Velasquez, *Business Ethics*, 4th ed. (Upper Saddle River, NJ: Prentice Hall, 1998), 322, 334–35.

3. Lena Goldberg, "Responsibilities to Customers" (Boston: Harvard Business School, 2014), 5–6.

4. Velasquez, *Business Ethics*, 346–49.

5. Richard Tennant, *The American Cigarette Industry* (New Haven, CT: Yale University Press, 1950), 4–28. See also Patrick Porter, "Origins of the American Tobacco Company," *Business History Review* (Spring 1969): 59–76.

6. "The American Tobacco Company," *Fortune*, December 1936, 97.

7. Robert Sobel, *They Satisfy: The Cigarette in American Life* (Garden City, NY: Anchor Books, 1978), 77–80.

8. Robert H. Miles, *Coffin Nails and Corporate Strategies* (Englewood Cliffs, NJ: Prentice Hall, 1982), 32–34. See also L. G. Tesler, "Advertising and Cigarettes," *Journal of Political Economy* 70, no. 2 (1962): 476.

9. "The American Tobacco Company," 100.

10. Allan M. Brandt, *The Cigarette Century: The Rise, Fall, and Deadly Persistence of the Product That Defined America* (New York: Basic Books, 2007), 264. See

also Brandt's entire discussion of this ad campaign, 261–65.

11. Gordon Fairclough, "Bold Promotions Land R. J. Reynolds in Controversies," *Wall Street Journal*, September 6, 2002, A1, A6.

12. Letter from E. Cuyler Hammond to Evarts Graham, March 26, 1954, quoted in Brandt, *The Cigarette Century*, 145, 153. See also E. Cuyler Hammond and Daniel Horn, "The Relationship between Human Smoking Habits and Death Rates," *Journal of the American Medical Association* 155, no. 15 (1954): 1316–428.

13. Public Health Service, *Smoking and Health: Report of the Advisory Committee to the Surgeon General of the Public Health Service* (Washington, DC: U.S. Department of Health, Education, and Welfare, 1964).

14. Robert H. Miller, "Government Action Relating to Smoking and Health, 1964–74," *Tobacco Situation* (June 1974): 33–38.

15. Miles, *Coffin Nails and Corporate Strategies*, 43

16. Ibid., 45–48.

17. Philip Boffey, "Health Groups Assail Cigarette Ads," *New York Times*, February 16, 1992, A16.

18. Richard Kluger, *Ashes to Ashes: America's Hundred Years Cigarette War, the Public Health, and the Unabashed Triumph of Philip Morris* (New York: Knopf, 1999), 445.

19. Angela B. Miller and Richard Miller, "Problems of Nicotine Addiction," *San Francisco Chronicle*, December 6, 1989, 9.

20. Tamar Lewin, "Harvard and CUNY Shedding Stocks in Tobacco," *New York Times*, May 24, 1990, C1.

21. Anthony Ramirez, "Reynolds Is Snuffing Five Cigarette Brands, Including Real, but Will Unveil New One," *Wall Street Journal*, June 24, 1980, 42, and Miles, *Coffin Nails and Corporate Strategies*, 93–94.

22. Anthony Ramirez, "A Cigarette Campaign under Fire," *New York Times*, January 12, 1990, D1, D5.

23. Michael Spencer, "Marketers Target Virile Females," Washington Post. February 17, 1990, 33. See also Anthony Ramirez, "New Cigarette Raising Issue of Target Market," *New York Times*, February 17, 1990, B6.

24. Ramirez, "New Cigarette Raising Issue of Target Market," B6.

25. Stuart Elliot, "Camel Cartoon Draws Buyers, Too," *New York Times*, December 12, 1991, D1, D17.

26. Kathleen Deveny, "Joe Camel Is Also a Pied Paper, Research Finds," *New York Times*, December 11, 1991, B1, B4.

27. David Adams and Edward Maine, *Business Ethics for the 21st Century* (Toronto: Mayfield Publishing Company, 1998), 408. See also Stuart Elliott, "Adoring or Abhoring [sic] the Camel," *New York Times*, July 29, 1992, D5.

28. Masayoshi Kanabayashi, "In 'Tobacco Smoker's Paradise' of Japan, U. S. Cigarettes Are Epitome of High Style," *Wall Street Journal*, September 23, 1991, B1, B6.

29. Janet Guyon, "Tobacco Companies Race for Advantage in Eastern Europe While Critics Fume," *Wall Street Journal*, December 28, 1992, B1, B8.

30. Vikrant Rana, "The Ambiguity Surrounding Tobacco Advertising in India," *Mondaq*, August 2, 2017, https://www.mondaq.com/india/x/616796/food+drugs+law/the-ambiguity-surrounding-tobacco-advertisingin-india.

31. Rupert Hargreaves, "Philip Morris Relies on Asia for Growth but One Region Is Out of Reach," *Motley Fool*, June 23, 2014, 12

32. Jennifer Maloney and Saabira Chaudhuri, "Tobacco's Surprise Rebound," *Wall Street Journal*, April 24, 2017, A1, A10.

33. Ibid.

34. Saabira Chaudhuri and Jennifer Maloney, "Deal Creates Tobacco Giant," *Wall Street Journal*, January 18, 2017, B1–B2.

35. Tripp Mickle and Jennifer Valentino-DeVries, "Marlboro Wins over Millennials," *Wall Street Journal*, November 29, 2016, B1–B2.

36. "Cigarette Companies: Plucky Strike," *The Economist*, January 21, 2017, 51–52.

37. "Tobacco on Trial," *The Economist*, May 11, 1996, 15–16.

38. Nate Hafez and P. M. Ling, "How Philip Morris Built Marlboro into a Global Brand for Young Adults: Implications for International Tobacco Control," *Tobacco Control* 14, no. 4 (2005): 262–71. See also Brandt, *The Cigarette Century*, 262.

39. Sarah Boseley, "Plain Cigarette Packaging Could Drive 300,000 Britons to Quit Smoking," *The Guardian*, April 26, 2017, 1, 17. See also Saabira Chaudhuri, "Big Tobacco Faces Fight in U.K.," *Wall Street Journal*, December 11, 2015, B6.

40. "BATA and the Australian Regulatory Landscape: Response to the Preventative Health Taskforce Technical Report 2," *Tobacco Control in Australia: Making Smoking History*, January 2009, 25–26.

41. Sarah Boseley, "Stricter Cigarette Packaging Comes into Force in UK," *The Guardian*, May 17, 2017, 1.

42. Chaudhuri, "Big Tobacco Faces Fight in U.K.," B6.

43. Chaudhuri, "Big Tobacco Faces Fight in U.K."

44. Wright, *On a Clear Day You Can See General Motors*, 220–24.

45. Micheline Maynard, "Chrysler: A Short History," *New York Times*, April 30, 2009, B1, B4.

46. David Halberstam, *The Reckoning* (New York: William Morrow, 1986), 479.

47. Wikipedia, "Automotive Industry in the United States," last modified October 31, 2018, https://en.wikipedia.org/wiki/Automotive_ industry_in_ the-United_States.

48. Eric Foner and John A. Garraty, *The Reader's Companion to American History* (New York: Houghton Mifflin Harcourt, 1991), 221–27.

49. Daniel Ikenson, "Hard Lessons from the Auto Bailout," *Cato Institute Policy Report*, November/ December 2009, https://www.cato.org/policy-report/novemberdecember2009/hard-lessons-auto-bailout.

50. See Marc Davis, "How The U.S. Automobile Industry Has Changed," Investopedia, accessed February 2017, http://www.investopedia.com/articles/pf/12/auto-industry.asp#ixzz4G6Us8v6K.

51. Michael R. Lemov, *Car Safety Wars: One Hundred Years of Technology, Politics, and Death* (Madison: Farleigh Dickinson University Press, 2015), 8–23. For a discussion of the second collision and recommended safety mechanisms, see Claire L. Straith, "Guest Passenger Injuries," *Journal of the American Medical Association*, May 22, 1948, 348.

52. Joel W. Eastman, *Styling Versus Safety: The American Automobile Industry and the Development of Automotive Safety 1900-1966* (Lanham, MD: University Press of America, 1984), xiii.

53. Quoted in John G. Graham, *Auto Safety: Assessing America's Performance* (Dover, MA: Auburn, 1989), 18.

54. Lemov, *Car Safety Wars*, 49–61. See also John H. Fielder, "The Ethics and Politics of Automobile Regulation," in *The Ford Pinto Case: A Study in Applied Ethics, Business, and Technology*, ed. Douglas Birsch and John H. Fielder (Albany, NY: SUNY Press, 1984), 285–301.

55. Interview with engineer Carl Nash, quoted in Lemov, *Car Safety Wars*, 67–68.

56. James Flink, *The Automobile Age* (Cambridge, MA: MIT Press, 1988), 292. See also Lemov, *Car Safety Wars*, 11.

57. Ralph Nader, *Unsafe at Any Speed: The Designed-In Dangers of the American Automobile* (New York: Bantam Books, 1972), 12.

58. For a discussion of the Corvair's flaws, see Dan Neil, "The 50 Worst Cars of All Time," *Time Magazine*, April 25, 2017, https://time.com/4723114/50-worst-cars-of-all-time.

59. Nader, *Unsafe at Any Speed*, 188.

60. Christopher Jenson, "50 Years Ago, *Unsafe at Any Speed* Shook the Auto World," *New York Times*, November 26, 2015, B1–B2.

61. Lemov, *Car Safety Wars*, 141.

62. Ibid., 145–56.

63. Peter Baker, "Human Error," *Wall Street Journal*, July 28, 2016, C1.

64. National Highway Transportation Safety Administration, "Investigative Report, Phase I: Alleged Fuel Tank and Filler Neck Damage in Rear-End Collision of Subcompact Passenger Cars," in *The Ford Pinto Case*, 91.

65. Lemov, *Car Safety Wars*, 187–95, 202–4.

66. Mike Spector, Jack Nicas, and Mike Ramsey, "Tesla's Autopilot Vexes Some Drivers," *Wall Street Journal*, July 7, 2016, A1, A8.

67. Ibid., A8. See also Christina Rogers and Leslie Scism, "Safe Cars Cost More to Insure," *Wall Street Journal*, April 4, 2017, B2.

68. Christina Rogers, "Ford Sets Plans for Cars without Steering Wheels," *Wall Street Journal*, August 17, 2016, B1–B2. See also Gordon Crovitz, "Humans: Unsafe at any Speed," *Wall Street Journal*, August 22, 2016, A11.

69. Rogers and Scism, "Safe Cars Cost More to Insure."

70. Peggy Lee, "Scranton Family Gets Victim Compensation for Deadly GM Crash," WNEP News (Scranton), October 1, 2014, wnep.com/2014/10/01/Scranton-family-gets-victim-compensation.

71. Neal Boudette, "Detroit Levels Productivity Playing Field," *Wall Street Journal*, June 6, 2008, B3. See also Randal Harris and W. Scott Sherman, "General Motors and the Chevy Cobalt Ignition Switch Crisis," *Case Research Journal* 37, no. 4 (Fall 2017), 4.

72. Jamie LaRear, "Chevrolet Counts on Cobalt to Be Big in Small Car Segment," *Automotive News*, January 3, 2005. See also Alex Damian, "Chevy Cobalt Is the Most 'Buzz-Worthy' Car for Gen Y Youth Market," *TopSpeed*, June 6, 2006, 8–9.

73. Wikicars, "GM Delta Platform," last modified May 25, 2010, www.wikicars.org/en/GM_Delta_Platform.

74. Jenner & Block, *Report to Board of Directors of General Motors Company Regarding Ignition Switch Recalls*, May 29, 2014, 20–22. (GM hired the law firm Jenner & Block to determine how and why it took so long to recall the Cobalt. Jenner was given access to witnesses and documents and provided GM with this final report.)

75. Business Day, "The Fault in the Cobalt Ignition Switch," *New York Times*, June 5, 2014, B6.

76. Jenner & Block, *Report to Board of Directors*, 34–36.

77. Business Day, "The Fault in the Cobalt Ignition Switch." See also Jenner & Block, *Report to Board of Directors*, 41–51.

78. Jenner & Block, *Report to Board of Directors*, 48.

79. Ibid., 58–59. See also Harris and Sherman, "General Motors and the Chevy Cobalt Ignition Switch Crisis," 6.

80. Ibid., 53–60.

81. Ibid., 60–65.

82. Ibid., 89.

83. Ibid., 70–89.

84. Ibid., 90–91. See also Harris and Sherman, "General Motors and the Chevy Cobalt Ignition Switch Crisis," 7.

85. Ibid., 9–10, 199. See also Harris and Sherman, "General Motors and the Chevy Cobalt Ignition Switch Crisis," 8.

86. Ibid., 102.

87. Max Blau, "No Accident: Inside GM's Deadly Ignition Switch Scandal," *Atlanta Magazine*, January 2016, 28–43.

88. Hilary Stout, Danielle Ivory, and Matthew Waldmarch, "Auto Regulators Dismissed Defect Tied to 13 Deaths," *New York Times*, March 8, 2014, B1–B2. See also Jenner & Block, *Report to Board of Directors*, 118–20.

89. Jenner & Block, *Report to Board of Directors*, 10–11. See also Harris and Sherman, "General Motors and the Chevy Cobalt Ignition Switch Crisis," 13.

90. Ibid., 206.

91. Ibid., 209.

92. Ibid., 211.

93. Ibid., 225–6.

94. Kristen Korosec, "Ten Times More Deaths Linked to Faulty Switches Than GM First Reported," Fortune.com, August 24, 2015, www.fortune.com/2015/08/24/feinberg-gm-faulty-igniton-switch.

95. Blau, "No Accident."

96. Takata, "Company History," accessed March 2017, www.takata.com/about/history_html.

97. Ibid.

98. Raphael Orlove, "The Complete Story of Takata's Airbags and the Biggest Recall in Auto History," *Jalopnik Review*, June 2, 2016, https://www.jalopnik.com/the-complete-story-of-takatas-airbags-and-the-biggest-re-1780143247.

99. Outsource Service, "Industry Report on Airbag Industry," 2011, www.outsource2india.com/pdf/airbag-industry-report.

100. Ibid.

101. Hiroko Tabuchi and Danielle Ivory, "Honda Drops Airbag Maker over Test Data," *New York Times*, November 4, 2015, A1, B9.

102. Hiroko Tabuchi and Christopher Jenkins, "Now the Air Bags Are Faulty, Too," *New York Times*, June 2014, B1, B4.

103. Robert Wright, "US Imposes Daily Fines on Takata in Deepening Airbag Crisis," *Financial Times*, February 20, 2015, 1.

104. Yoko Kubota and Mike Spector, "Honda Adds to Takata's Woes," *Wall Street Journal*, November 4, 2015, B1, B6. See also "Takata Airbag Recall: Everything You Need to Know," *Consumer Reports*, July 2016, 31-3

105. Hiroko Tabuchi, "Airbag Compound Has Vexed Takata for Years," *New York Times*, December 10, 2014, B1–B2. See also National Highway Traffic Safety Administration, "Report of TK Holdings, Inc.," June 30, 2016, 2–5.

106. Hiroko Tabuchi, "A Cheaper Airbag, and Takata's Road to a Deadly Crisis," *New York Times*, August 27, 2016, A1, B7. See also Hiroko Tabuchi, "Takata's Switch to Cheaper Airbag Propellant Is at Center of Crisis," *New York Times*, November 20, 2014, B2.

107. Tabuchi, "A Cheaper Airbag and Takata's Road to a Deadly Crisis."

108. Ibid. See also Tabuchi, "Takata's Switch to Cheaper Airbag Propellant Is at Center of Crisis."

109. Tabuchi and Ivory, "Honda Drops Airbag Maker over Test Data." See also NHTSA, "Report of TK Holdings, Inc.," 3.

110. Tabuchi and Ivory, "Honda Drops Airbag Maker over Test Data."

111. Hiroko Tabuchi, "Takata Airbag Defect Is Traced to Moisture and Temperature," *New York Times*, May 5, 2016, B1. See also Susan Berfield and Craig Trudell, "Sixty Million Car Bombs: Takata's Air Bag Crisis," Bloomberg.com, June 2, 2016, www.bloomberg.com/news/features/2017-06-14/sixty-million-car-bombs-inside-takatas-air-bag-crisis.

112. Tabuchi and Ivory, "Honda Drops Airbag Maker over Test Data," B9. See also Hiroko Tabuchi, "Takata Auto Recall Said to Grow by 35 Million," *New York Times*, May 3, 2016, B1.

113. Mike Spector, "Takata U.S. Staff Saw Problems in Air-Bag Tests," *Wall Street Journal*, November 25, 2015, B1, B6.

114. Danielle Ivory and Hiroko Tabuchi, "Takata Emails Show Brash Exchanges about Data Tampering," *New York Times*, January 4, 2016, B1.

115. Yoko Kubota, "Takata Chief to Resign," *Wall Street Journal*, January 29, 2016, B5.

116. Mike Spector, "Takata Pleads Guilty in Air-Bag Case," *Wall Street Journal*, February 28, 2017, B3.

117. Jonathan Cheng and Eun-Young Jeong, "Samsung Recall Takes Toll," *Wall Street Journal*, October 27, 2016, B1, B4.

118. Betsy Morris, "What the iPhone Wrought," *Wall Street Journal*, June 24, 2017, B3.

119. Jonathan Cheng and John McKinnon, "Samsung Recall's Fatal Flaw," *Wall Street Journal*, October 24, 2016, A1, A12. See also Timothy Martin, "Samsung's Latest Has Heavy Burden," *Wall Street Journal*, March 28, 2017, B4.

120. Evan Ramstad, "Samsung Presses Ahead with Android," *Wall Street Journal*, September 2, 2011, p. B6.

121. Dan Gallagher, "Google Feasts on Samsung's Woe," *Wall Street Journal*, October 12, 2016, C12.

122. Cheng and McKinnon, "Samsung Recall's Fatal Flaw."

123. Ibid.

124. George Wells, John D. McKinnon, and Yun Hee Kim, "Samsung Fumbles Smartphone Recall," *Wall Street Journal*, September 16, 2016, A1–A2. See also Cheng and McKinnon, "Samsung Recall's Fatal Flaw."

125. Wells, McKinnon, and Kim, "Samsung Fumbles Smartphone Recall."

126. Josh Beckerman and Georgia Wells, "Samsung Phone Recall Intensifies," *Wall Street Journal*, September 10, 2016, B1, B4. See also Wells, McKinnon, and Kim, "Samsung Fumbles Smartphone Recall."

127. Brian X. Chen and Choe Sang-Hun, "Samsung Junks Popular Phone Plagued by Fire," *New York Times*, October 12, 2016, A1, B5.

128. Sapna Maheshwari, "Samsung's Passive Response to Note 7's Risks Frustrates Carriers and Customers," *New York Times*, October 12, 2016, B5.

129. Jonathan Cheng, "Crisis Tests Samsung Heir Apparent," *Wall Street Journal*, October 12, 2016, B1, B5.

130. Ryan Knutson and Eun-Young Jeong, "Samsung Self-Tested Its Note 7 Batteries," *Wall Street Journal*, October 17, 2016, B3.

131. Geoffrey A. Fowler and Joanna Stern, "Samsung's Battery Fix Gets a C Grade, for Now," *Wall Street Journal*, January 23, 2017, B4.

132. Timothy Martin and Eun-Young Jeong, "Samsung Addresses Recall of Note 7," *Wall Street Journal*, January 23, 2017, B1, B4.

133. Timothy W. Martin and Eun-Young Jeong, "Eyes on Samsung Brand," *Wall Street Journal*, January 25, 2017, B4.

134. Eun-Young Jeong and Jonathan Cheng, "Samsung Looks for Reset for Its Phones," *Wall Street Journal*, February 11–12, 2017, B4.

135. Timothy Martin, "Battered Samsung Looks to Restore Trust," *Wall Street Journal*, March 30, 2017, B1, B4.

136. Song Jung-a, "Samsung Galaxy S8 Sales Highlight Speed of Recovery," *Financial Times*, May 29, 2017, 18.

137. See Emil Protelinski, "IDC: Smartphone Shipments Up 6.9% in Q. 4, 2016, Apple Overtakes Samsung for First Place," *Venture Beat*, February 1, 2017, https://venturebeat.com/2017/02/01/idc-smartphone-shipments-up-6-9-in-q4-2016-apple-overtakes-samsung-for-first-place/.

CHAPTER 9

1. Roger Scruton, *How to Think Seriously about the Planet: The Case for Environmental Conservativism* (Oxford: Oxford University Press, 2012), 18.

2. Ted Mann, "GE Nears End of Hudson Cleanup," *Wall Street Journal*, November 12, 2015, B3.

3. Rebecca Henderson, "Climate Change in 2018: Implications for Business" (Boston: Harvard Business School, 2018), 1–6.

4. Walter Nicholson, *Microeconomic Theory*, 3rd ed. (New York: Dryden Press, 1985), 756.

5. Scruton, *How to Think Seriously about the Planet*, 76, 182–83. See also Dale Jamieson, *Ethics and the Environment: An Introduction* (Cambridge, UK: Cambridge University Press, 2008), 9–20.

6. Jamieson, *Ethics and the Environment*, 10–12.

7. "Rescuing Environmentalism," *The Economist*, April 23, 2005, 11.

8. Forest Reinhardt, *Conceptual Overview: Business and the Environment* (Boston: Harvard Business School, 1999), 8–9.

9. Scruton, *How to Think Seriously about the Planet*, 31–32.

10. Films for Justice Institute, "Background on *Anderson v. W.R. Grace*, Seattle School of Law," accessed March 2017, https://www.seattleu.edu/centers-and-institutes/films-for-justice-institute/lessons-from-woburn.

11. Patrick Allitt, "Preexisting Condition," *Wall Street Journal*, June 22, 2016, A11.

12. David Germain, "There Is No Love Lost for Entrepreneur Who Envisioned Model City," *Los Angeles Times*, May 16, 1993, www.arti cles.latimes.com/1993-05-16/news-35999_1_love_canal.

13. Ibid.

14. Richard Newman, *Love Canal: A Toxic History from Colonial Times to the Present* (New York: Oxford University Press, 2016), 53.

15. Ibid., 66–67.

16. *United States v. Hooker Chemicals and Plastics Corp.*, 850 F. Supp. 993 (W.D.N.Y. 1994).

17. Ibid., 1007.

18. Ibid., 1007–8.

19. Ibid., 1009.

20. Ibid., 1014–16.

21. Ibid., 1020.

22. Newman, *Love Canal*, 88–89.

23. Tom Beauchamp, "Hooker Chemical and Love Canal," March 2013, 2, www.stephenhicks.org/wp-content/uploads/2013/03/Love-Canal-Hooker-Chemical.pdf. See also Newman, *Love Canal*, 99–108.

24. Allitt, "Preexisting Condition."

25. Beauchamp, "Hooker Chemical and Love Canal," 3, and Newman, *Love Canal*, 235–36.

26. Newman, *Love Canal*, 239.

27. *United States v. Hooker Chemicals*, 1057.

28. Beauchamp, "Hooker Chemical and Love Canal," 7.

29. Bruce Davis, quoted in "Landfill Use for Waste Is Not Our Problem," *Buffalo Courier Express*, August 8, 1978, 18. See also Newman, *Love Canal*, 185.

30. Newman, *Love Canal*, 184–86. See also Beauchamp, "Hooker Chemical and Love Canal," 5.

31. Newman, *Love Canal*, 265.

32. Erich Schwartzel and Sarah Kent, "'Deepwater' Reopens BP Drama," *Wall Street Journal*, October 1, 2016, B1.

33. Funding Universe, "The British Petroleum Company PLC History," www.fundinguniverse.com/company-histories/the-british-petroleum-company-plc-history.

34. Ibid.

35. Ibid.

36. Peter Elkind and David Whitford, "BP: An Accident Waiting to Happen," *Fortune*, January 24, 2011, https://features.blogs.fortune.com/ 2011/01/24/bp-an-accident-waiting-to-happen.

37. Brian Rogers and Paul Strobel, *British Petroleum: Defining a Strategic Vision* (Lausanne, Switzerland: IMD, 2011).

38. Tom Bergin, *Spills and Spin: The Inside Story of BP* (New York: Random House, 2011), 25.

39. Earl Boebert and James M. Blossom, *Deepwater Horizon: A Systems Analysis of the Macondo Disaster* (Cambridge, MA: Harvard University Press, 2016), 18–21.

40. Elkind and Whitford, "BP: An Accident Waiting to Happen."

41. Rogers and Strobel, *British Petroleum: Defining a Strategic Vision*, 2–4.

42. OSHA National News Release, "US Department of Labor's OSHA Issues Record Breaking Fines to BP," October 30, 2009, https:// www.osha.gov/news/news-releases/national/10302009.

43. Terry Macalister, "Hayward Outlines Restructuring to BP Staff," *The Guardian*, October 11, 2007, https://www.guardian.co.uk/busi ness/2007/oct/11/2. See also Rogers and Strobel, *British Petroleum: Defining a Strategic Vision*, B2, and Boebert and Blossom, *Deepwater Horizon*, 21.

44. National Commission on the BP Deepwater Horizon Oil Spill and Offshore Drilling, "Deepwater: The Gulf Oil Disaster and the Future of Offshore Drilling: Report to the President," January 11, 2011, 223 (hereafter National Commission report). See also Daniel Jacobs, *BP Blowout: Inside the Gulf Oil Disaster* (Washington, DC: Brookings Institute Press, 2016), 25–26. BP has now instituted this "stop work authority" practice.

45. Jacobs, *BP Blowout*, 151–53.

46. Boebert and Blossom, *Deepwater Horizon*, 36–39.

47. Ibid., 2.

48. National Commission report, 115. See also Russel Gold and Tom McGinty, "BP Relied on Cheaper Wells," *Wall Street Journal*, June 19, 2010, B1–B2.

49. Boebert and Blossom, *Deepwater Horizon*, 39–41. See also Karl Weick, "Review of *Deepwater Horizon: A Systems Analysis of the Macondo Disaster*," *Administrative Science Quarterly* 20 (2017): 322.

50. Ibid., 4.

51. Boebert and Blossom, *Deepwater Horizon*, 220.

52. Ed Crooks, "BP: The Inside Story," *Financial Times Magazine*, July 2, 2010, 18. See also Jacobs, *BP Blowout*, 22.

53. "BP Boss Admits Job on the Line over Gulf Oil Spill," *The Guardian*, May 13, 2010, 1.

54. Elkind and Whitford, "BP: An Accident Waiting to Happen."

55. Boebert and Blossom, *Deepwater Horizon*, 67.

56. See *In re: Oil Spill by the Oil Rig "Deepwater Horizon" in the Gulf of Mexico*, on April 20, 2010, Findings of Fact and Conclusions of Law, Phase One Trial, 21 F. Supp 3d 657 (E.D. La. 2014), at 674.

57. National Commission report, 99.

58. Ibid., 98–101.

59. Ibid., 4.

60. Ibid., 120. See also Boebert and Blossom, *Deepwater Horizon*, 2.

61. Jacobs, *BP Blowout*, 18.

62. *In re: Oil Spill by the Oil Rig "Deepwater Horizon" in the Gulf of Mexico*, 685. See also Jacobs, *BP Blowout*, p. 19.

63. Boebert and Blossom, *Deepwater Horizon*, 78.

64. Ibid., 2–6.

65. National Commission report, 209.

66. See National Wildlife Federation, "Five Years and Counting: Gulf Wildlife in the Aftermath of the Deepwater Horizon Disaster," March 30, 2015. See also National Resource Defense Counsel, "Summary of Information Concerning the Ecological and Environmental Impacts of the BP Deepwater Horizon Oil Spill," Issue Paper, June 2015, 4–6, www.nrdc.org/policy.

67. National Resource Defense Counsel, "Summary of Information," 6.

68. Debbie Elliott, "Five Years after BP Oil Spill, Effects Still Linger and Recovery Is Slow," National Public Radio, April 20, 2015, www.npr.org/2015/04/20/400374744/5-years-after-BP-oil-spill-effects-still-linger-and-recovery-is-slow.

69. National Resource Defense Counsel, "Summary of Information," 2.

70. Ibid., 6–7.

71. National Commission report, vii.

72. National Commission report, 223.

73. *United States v. BP Exploration and Production, Inc.*, Plea Agreement, No. 12-292 (E.D. La) (2013). See also Jacobs, *BP Blowout*, 75–76.

74. Post-Trial Brief of Defendants BP Exploration & Production Inc. et al., June 2013, 3.

75. Jacobs, *BP Blowout*, 12–13.

76. Michael Amon and Tapan Panchal, "BP's Gulf-Spill Tab Hits $62 Billion," *Wall Street Journal*, July 15, 2016, B3.

77. Graham Bowley and Melissa Eddy, "A Scandal Reverberates in a Company Town," *New York Times*, October 6, 2015, B1, B4.

78. Jack Ewing, *Faster, Higher, Farther: The Volkswagen Scandal* (New York: W. W. Norton, 2017), 1–9, 33.

79. Tim Bowler, "Volkswagen: From the Third Reich to Emissions Scandal," *BBC News*, October 1–2, 2015.

80. Ewing, *Faster, Higher, Farther*, 112.

81. Boston, "VW Probe Targets Engineers," *Wall Street Journal*, October 5, 2105, A1, A10.

82. Ibid., A10.

83. Marshall Brain, "How Diesel Engines Work," How Stuff Works, accessed June 2017, https://auto.howstuffworks.com/diesel.htm.

84. Environmental Protection Agency, "Effects of NO_2," accessed June 2017, https:// www.epa.gov/no2-pollution/basic-information -about-no2#Effect.

85. Jack Ewing, "Diesel Scandal at VW Spreads to Core Market," *New York Times*, September 23, 2015, A1, B8. See also Ewing, *Faster, Higher, Farther*, 113–15.

86. Boston, "VW Probe Targets Engineers," A10.

87. Jack Ewing, "VW Engine-Rigging Scheme Said to Have Begun in 2008," *New York Times*, October 5, 2015, B1, B10. See also Ewing, *Faster, Higher, Farther*, 115–17.

88. Ewing, *Faster, Higher, Farther*, 118–20.

89. Ewing, "VW Engine-Rigging Scheme Said to Have Begun in 2008."

90. Aruna Viswanatha and Christina Rogers, "VW Engineer Admits Diesel Scam," *Wall Street Journal*, September 10, 2016, A1, A10.

91. William Boston, Friedrich Geiger, and Mike Spector, "VW Crisis Spreads to Audi Engines," *Wall Street Journal*, November 27, 2015, B1–B2.

92. Patrick McGee, "How VW's Cheating on Emissions Was Exposed," *Financial Times*, January 11, 2017, https://www.ft.com/content/103dbe6a-d7a6-11a6-944b-c7eb37a6aaBe.

93. Ibid.

94. William Boston, "2014 VW Memo Warned of Probe," *Wall Street Journal*, February 16, 2016, B3.

95. William Boston and Mike Spector, "VW Draws Regulators' Ire," *Wall Street Journal*, November 19, 2015, B1–B2.

96. Jack Ewing, "Sarcasm and Doubt Precede VW's Update on Cheating Inquiry," *New York Times*, December 7, 2015, B1–B2.

97. Boston, "VW Probe Targets Engineers," A10.

98. William Boston, "VW Tries to Stem Growing Scandal," *Wall Street Journal*, September 24, 2015, A1, A12.

99. William Boston, "Sales Slide at VW Continues Globally," *Wall Street Journal*, January 9–10, 2016, B3.

100. William Boston, "VW Vows to Compensate Dealers," *Wall Street Journal*, July 18, 2016, B1–B2.

101. Aruna Viswanatha and Mike Spector, "States Say VW Scheme Ran Deep," *Wall Street Journal*, July 20, 2016, B1–B2.

102. Ewing, *Faster, Higher, Farther*, 89–92.

103. Jack Ewing, "VW Investigation Focus to Include Managers Who Turned a Blind Eye," *New York Times*, October 26, 2015, B3.

104. Andreas Cremer and Tom Bergin, "Fear and Respect: VW's Culture under Winterkorn," *Reuters*, October 10, 2015, www.reuters.com/article/us-volkswagen-emissions -culture/.

105. William Boston, Hendrik Varnholt, and Sarah Sloat, "VW Says 'Culture' Flaw Led to Crisis," *Wall Street Journal*, December 11, 2015, B1–B2.

106. Sonari Glinton, "'We Didn't Lie,' Volkswagen CEO Says of Emissions Scandal," National Public Radio, January 11, 2016, https://www.npr.org/sections/thetwo-way/2016/01/11/462682378/we-didnt-lie-volkswagen-ceo-says-of-emissions-scandal. See also Ewing, *Faster, Higher, Farther*, 228.

107. William Wilkes, "Volkswagen Adds to Scandal Cost," *Wall Street Journal*, February 2, 2017, B3.

108. William Boston and Mike Spector, "VW Set to Pay $4.3 Billion to U.S. in Emissions Cheat," *Wall Street Journal*, January 11, 2017, A1, A9.

109. Mike Spector and Mike Collas, "Volkswagen Faces Up to Penalties," *Wall Street Journal*, March 11–12, 2017, B1–B2. See also Samantha Masunaga and Del

Quentin Wilber, "VW Settles Emissions-Cheating Cases for $14.7 Billion and Agrees to Buy Back Cars," *Los Angeles Times*, June 29, 2016, A1, and Jan Schwartz, "VW's Dieselgate Bill Hits $30 Bn after Another Charge," Reuters, September 29, 2017, https://www.reuters.com/articles/legal-uk-volkswagen-emissions/vws-dieselgate-bill-hits-30-bln-after-another-charge.

110. Aruna Viswanatha, Mike Spector, and Mike Boston, "U.S. Indicts Six in VW Diesel Case," *Wall Street Journal*, January 12, 2017, B2.

111. Patrick McGee, "Volkswagen Emissions Scandal: 4 Questions," *Financial Times*, May 4, 2018, https://www.ft.com/content/82af7d02-4f83-11e8-9471-aG83a805aca7.

112. Alex Epstein, *The Moral Case for Fossil Fuels* (New York: Penguin, 2014), 71–72.

113. Texaco, "A Century of Performance," accessed July 2017, https://www.texaco.com/about/html.

114. William Langeweische, "Jungle Law," *Vanity Fair*, May 2007, https://www.vanityfair.com/news/2007/05/texaco200705.

115. Ibid. See also Texaco, "History of Texaco and Chevron in Ecuador," accessed August 2017, www.texaco.com/ecuador/en/history/chronology-of-events.aspx.

116. Paul Barrett, *Law of the Jungle* (New York: Broadway Books, 2014), 25.

117. Denis Arnold, "Texaco in the Ecuadorean Amazon," in *Case Studies in Business Ethics*, 5th ed., ed. Al Gini (Upper Saddle River, NJ: Prentice Hall, 2005), 113–15. See also Barrett, *Law of the Jungle*, 23.

118. Langeweische, "Jungle Law."

119. Ibid. See also Arnold, "Texaco in the Ecuadorean Amazon," 114.

120. Langeweische, "Jungle Law." See also Barrett, *Law of the Jungle*, 27.

121. Barrett, *Law of the Jungle*, 27.

122. Langeweische, "Jungle Law."

123. Eyal Press, "Texaco on Trial," *The Nation*, May 31, 1999, 22–25. See also Juan Forero, "In Ecuador, High Stakes against Chevron," *Washington Post*, April 28, 2009, A12; Barrett, *Law of the Jungle*, 29.

124. Forero, "In Ecuador, High Stakes against Chev ron." See also Langeweische, "Jungle Law."

125. Barrett, *Law of the Jungle*, 55–57.

126. Bret Stephens, "Anatomy of a Conspiracy," *Wall Street Journal*, October 29, 2014, A17.

127. Chevron, "Ecuador Lawsuit: Background," accessed August 2017, https://www.chevron.com/ecuador/background/#.

128. Robert Kennedy, "Preface" to Judith Kimerling, *Amazon Crude* (Washington, DC: National Resources Defense Counsel, 1991), xi–xii.

129. See *Aguinda v. Texaco, Inc.*, 142F. Supp. 2d 534 (S.D.N.Y.) (2001).

130. Marc Lifsher, "Chevron Would Face $5 Billion Tab for Amazon Cleanup, Expert Says," *Wall Street Journal*, October 20, 2003, A1.

131. Forero, "In Ecuador, High Stakes against Chevron."

132. "Oil in Ecuador: Murky Truth," *The Economist*, September 27, 2014, 86.

133. Jennifer Smith, "Judge Rips Lawyer, Boosting Chevron," *Wall Street Journal*, March 5, 2014, B1–B2. See also *Chevron Corp v. Donziger* 871 F. Supp. 2d (2014) (S.D.N.Y.) and "Oil in Ecuador: Murky Truth."

134. Nicole Hong, "Award against Chevron Blocked," *Wall Street Journal*, August 9, 2016, B2.

135. See Barrett, *Law of the Jungle*, 28.

CHAPTER 10

1. Steven Levy, *Crypto* (New York: Viking, 2001), 9.

2. See Susan Landau, *Surveillance or Security* (Cambridge, MA: MIT Press, 2011), 10–15.

3. Manuel Castells, *The Rise of the Network Society* (New York: Wiley-Blackwell, 1996), 17.

4. Julie E. Cohen, "Between Truth and Power," in *Information, Freedom and Property*, ed. Mireille Hidebrandt (New York: Routledge, 2016), 71.

5. Julie E. Cohen, "Information Rights and Intellectual Freedom," in *Ethics and the Internet* (Antwerp: Intersentia, 2001), 12.

6. Julie E. Cohen, "Between Truth and Power," 62.

7. Geoffrey Fowler, "You Are a Wide Open Book on the Web," *Wall Street Journal*, May 25, 2017, B1.

8. Judith Thompson, "The Right to Privacy," *Philosophy and Public Affairs* 4 (1975): 295.

9. *Charles Katz v. United States*, 389 U.S. 347 (1967). See also Landau, *Surveillance or Security*, 11.

10. Samuel Warren and Louis Brandeis, "The Right to Privacy," *Harvard Law Review* 4 (1890): 193.

11. Richard Posner, *The Economics of Justice* (Cambridge, MA: Harvard University Press, 1981), 272–73.

12. See Daniel Solove, *Understanding Privacy* (Cambridge, MA: Harvard University Press, 2008), 21–24.

13. Charles Fried, "Privacy: A Rational Context," in *Computers, Ethics, and Society*, ed. David Ermann (Oxford: Oxford University Press, 1990), 52.

14. Helen Nissenbaum, "Respect for Privacy as a Benchmark for Privacy Online," in *Privacy, Security and Accountability*, ed. Adam Moore (Lanham, MD: Rowman & Littlefield, 2016), 46–49.

15. Ibid., 48.

16. Jim Moor, "Towards a Theory of Privacy for the Information Age," *Computers and Society* 27, no. 3 (1997), 30. See also Jim Moor, "The Ethics of Privacy Protection," *Library Trends* 39, nos. 1–2: 76.

17. Herman Tavani, "Philosophical Theories of Privacy: Implications for an Adequate Online Privacy Policy," *Metaphilosophy* 38, no. 1 (2007): 10–11.

18. Julie Inness, *Privacy, Intimacy, and Isolation* (Oxford: Oxford University Press, 1992) 117.

19. Robert George, "Natural Law," 52 *American Journal of Jurisprudence* 55 (2007).

20. Martha Nussbaum, "Non-relative Virtues: An Aristotelian Approach," *Midwest Studies in Philosophy* 13, no. (1988): 48. See also Mark Murphy, *Natural Law and Practical Rationality* (Cambridge, UK: Cambridge University Press, 2001), 106.

21. Judith Wagner DeCew, *In Pursuit of Privacy: Law, Ethics, and the Rise of Technology* (Ithaca, NY: Cornell University Press, 1997), 64.

22. H. L. A. Hart, "Bentham on Legal Rights," in *Oxford Essays on Jurisprudence* (Oxford: Oxford University Press, 1961), 200–201.

23. James Nickel, *Making Sense of Human Rights* (Berkeley: University of California Press, 1987), 107–19.

24. Michael Katell and Adam Moore, "The Value of Privacy, Security and Accountability," in *Privacy, Security and Accountability*, 6.

25. Fowler, "You Are a Wide-Open Book," B4.

26. Katy Burne and Rosin Sidel, "Hackers Found Holes in Bank Network," *Wall Street Journal*, May 1, 2017, A1, A10. See also Katell and Moore, "The Value of Privacy, Security and Accountability," 6.

27. U.S. Homeland Security, "Cybersecurity Overview," accessed October 2017, https://www.dhs.gov/cybersecurityoverview.

28. P. W. Singer and Allan Friedman, *Cybersecurity and Cyberwar* (New York: Oxford University Press, 2014), 35–36. See also Richard A. Spinello, *Cyberethics:*

Morality and Law in Cyberspace, 6th ed. (Burlington, MA: Jones & Bartlett, 2017), 207–14.

29. Kenneth Himma, "Why Security Trumps Privacy," in *Privacy, Security and Accountability*, 146.

30. Katell and Moore, "The Value of Privacy, Security and Accountability," 6. See also Himma, "Why Security Trumps Privacy," 147.

31. David O'Brien, Ryan Budish, Rob Faris, Urs Gasser, and Tiffany Lin, "Privacy and Cybersecurity" (Harvard University, Berkman Klein Center for Internet and Society, 2016), 5–9.

32. Miguel Helf, "Yahoo's Chief Resigns and Company Founder Takes Over," *New York Times*, June 19, 2007, https://www.nytimes.com/2007/06/19/technology/19yahoo.html.

33. Yahoo Inc., "Yahoo: Our Beliefs as a Global Internet Company," February 2006, http://yahoo.client.hsreholder.com/press/relaesedetail.cfm?ReleaseID=187401.

34. Quoted in Sumner Lemon, "Yahoo Criticized for Curtailing Freedom Online," *PC World*, August 12, 2002, 16.

35. Jack Goldsmith and Tim Wu, *Who Controls the Internet* (Oxford: Oxford University Press, 2006), 9.

36. Eric Jackson, "A Yahoo Compare and Contrast: Carol Bartz and Marissa Mayer," Forbes.com, April 10, 2015, https://forbes.com/sites/ericjackson/2015/04/10/a-yahoo-compare-and-contrast-carol-bartz-and-marissamayer/#284alba830sb.

37. Brett Molina, "Long Troubled History of Yahoo's Top Execs," *USA Today*, July 25, 2016, 18. I am indebted to Molina's analysis for the account of the CEO tenures described in this case.

38. Douglas MacMillan, "Yahoo Board Is Under Pressure," *Wall Street Journal*, December 4, 2015, B4.

39. Todd C. Frankel, "Why Verizon Wants to Buy an Ailing Yahoo in $4.8 Billion Deal," *Washington Post*, July 25, 2016, C1.

40. Jack Schofield, "Google, Yahoo, Adobe, and Who," *The Guardian*, January 14, 2010, https://www.guardian.com/technology/2010/jan/14/google-yahoo-china-cyber-attack.

41. Ibid. See also Danny Yardon, "A Contrarian View on Data Breaches," *Wall Street Journal*, August 6, 2014, B1, B4.

42. Nicole Perlroth and Vindu Goel, "Hacker Threat Took Back Seat at Yahoo, Insiders Say," *New York Times*, September 29, 2016, B1, B4.

43. Ibid., B4.

44. Ibid., B4.

45. Robert McMillan, "Yahoo Data Breach Hits Millions," *Wall Street Journal*, September 23, 2016, A1–A2.

46. Ibid.

47. Nicole Perlroth, "Yahoo Says Hackers Stole Data on 500 Million Users in July 2014," *New York Times*, September 22, 2016, B1, B4.

48. Tracy Lien, "It's Strange Yahoo Took Two Years to Discover Data Breach, Security Experts Say," *Los Angeles Times*, September 23, 2016, 23–24.

49. Georgia Wells and Ryan Knutson, "Yahoo's Move May Put Deal at Risk," *Wall Street Journal*, December 16, 2016, B1, B4.

50. Robert McMillan, Ryan Knutson, and Deepa Seetharaman, "New Yahoo Breach Hits 1 Billion Users," *Wall Street Journal*, December 15, 2015, A1, A12.

51. Vindu Goel and Nicole Perlroth, "Yahoo Says 1 Billion User Accounts Are Hacked," *New York Times*, December 14, 2016, B1, B3. See also Wells and Knutson, "Yahoo's Move May Put Deal at Risk," B4.

52. Thomas Gryta and Deepa Seetharaman, "Verizon Puts Yahoo on Notice after Data Breach," *Wall Street Journal*, October 14, 2016, A1–A2.

53. Wells and Knutson, "Yahoo's Move May Put Deal at Risk," B4.

54. Robert McMillan and Deepa Seetharaman, "How Hackers Manipulated Yahoo's Systems," *Wall Street Journal*, March 17, 2017, B4.

55. Deepa Seetharaman and Robert McMillan, "Yahoo Probe Prompts Cut in CEO's Pay," *Wall Street Journal*, March 2, 2017, B4.

56. Ryan Knutson, "Verizon CEO Wrangles Lower Price for Yahoo," *Wall Street Journal*, February 22, 2017, A1–A2.

57. McMillan, Knutson, and Seetharaman, "New Yahoo Breach Hits 1 Billion Users."

58. Tamara Audi, Miriam Jordan, and Zusha Elinson, "California Shooters Leave Clues, but No Clear Motive," *Wall Street Journal*, December 4, 2015, A1, A8.

59. Katie Benner and Matt Apuzzo, "Narrow Focus May Aid FBI in Apple Case," *New York Times*, February 23, 2016, B1, B6.

60. Betsy Morris, "What the iPhone Wrought," *Wall Street Journal*, June 24, 2017, B3.

61. Tripp Mickle, "For Apple, There's a Silver Lining," *Wall Street Journal*, January 30, 2017, B1, B4.

62. Yukari Iwatani Kane and Jessica E. Vascellaro, "Tough to Follow: Apple after Jobs," *Wall Street Journal*, August 26, 2011, A1, A10.

63. Tim Cook, "Commencement Address at George Washington University," *Network World*, 4, May 18, 2015.

64. Jonathan Cheng, "Apple Squeezed by Android Phones," *Wall Street Journal*, July 29, 2016, B5.

65. Kevin Poulson, "Apple's iPhone Is a Godsend, Even If Cops Hate It," *Wired*, October 8, 2014, 10–11. See also Devlin Barrett and Danny Yardon, "Apple, Others Encrypt Phones, Fueling Government Standoff," *Wall Street Journal*, November 19, 2014, A1, A10.

66. Matt Olsen, Bruce Schneier, and Jonathan Zittrain, "Don't Panic: Making Progress in the 'Going Dark' Debate" (Cambridge, MA: Berkman Center for Internet & Society, 2016), 3–4.

67. Danielle Kehl, Andi Wilson, and Kevin Banston, "Doomed to Repeat History: Lessons from the Crypto Wars of the 1990's," Open Technology Institute, June 2015, 3.

68. "Cracked Credibility," *The Economist*, September 14, 2013, 65–67.

69. Olsen, Schneier, and Zittrain, "Don't Panic," 4.

70. Apple, "Privacy," 2015, http://www.apple.com./privacy/government-information-requests.

71. James Nicas and Robert McMillan, "Newer Phones Aren't Easy to Crack," *Wall Street Journal*, February 18, 2016, A6.

72. Ibid.

73. 28 U.S.C. § 1651.

74. Government's Motion, Order Compelling Apple Inc. to Assist Agents in Search, U.S. District Court for Central District of California, CM 16-10, February 16, 2016.

75. Kay Benner, "Narrow Focus May Aid FBI in Apple Case," B1, B6.

76. Danny Yardon, "Attacks Fan Encryption Debate," *Wall Street Journal*, November 20, 2016, B1, B6. See also Christopher Mims, "Apple CEO Cook's Risky Encryption Strategy," *Wall Street Journal*, February 18, 2016, B1.

77. Mark Scott, "Facebook Chief Sides with Apple against F.B.I. over Terrorist's iPhone," *New York Times*, February 23, 2016, B6.

78. Kay Benner, and Apuzzo, "Narrow Focus May Aid FBI in Apple Case," B6.

79. Olsen, Schneier, and Zittrain, "Don't Panic," 7.

80. James Comey, "Going Dark: Are Technology, Privacy and Public Safety on a Collision Course?," speech delivered at Brookings Institute, Washington, DC, October 2014, http://www.fbi.gov/news/speeches/going -dark.

81. Mims, "Apple CEO Cook's Risky Encryption Strategy."

82. Katie Benner and Matt Apuzzo, "U.S. Will Try to Open Phone without Apple," *New York Times*, March 22, 2016, A1, B3.

83. Cyrus Vance, Adrian Leppard, and Javier Zaragoza, "When Phone Encryption Blocks Justice," *New York Times*, August 11, 2015, A26.

84. Cindy Cohn, "The Debate over Encryption," *Wall Street Journal*, December 24, 2015, A11.

85. Alan Sorkin, "When the Moral High Ground Lacks Clear Boundaries," *New York Times*, February 23, 2016, B1, B6.

86. Zeke Turner, "Tunisian Man Arrested in Berlin Attack," *Wall Street Journal*, December 29, 2016, A16.

87. Securities and Exchange Commission, Apple Inc. 10-K Report, 2016.

CHAPTER 11

1. Thomas Hobbes, *Leviathan*, ed. Michael Oakeshott (New York: Collier Books, 1962), ch. 13, 98–99.

2. J. R. Lucas, "The Responsibilities of a Businessman," in *Ethics at Work*, ed. William Shaw (New York: Oxford University Press, 2003), 25–26.

3. Ibid., 26.

4. Arthur Murray, "For Policy Makers, Microsoft Suggests Need to Recast Models," *Wall Street Journal*, June 9, 2000, A1, A11.

5. "Internet Monopolies: Everybody Wants to Rule the World," *The Economist*, November 29, 2014, 19–22.

6. Greg Ip, "The Antitrust Case against America's Technology Behemoths," *Wall Street Journal*, January 17, 2018, A1, A10.

7. "Internet Monopolies," 20.

8. Ip, "The Antitrust Case against America's Technology Behemoths," A10. See also "Internet Monopolies," 20–21.

9. Lynn Sharp Paine, "Ideals of Competition and Today's Marketplace," in *Enriching Business Ethics*, ed. Clarence Walton (New York: Plenum Press, 1990), 91–112.

10. Clarence Walton, *Corporate Encounters: Ethics, Law, & the Business Environment* (Fort Worth, TX: Dryden Press, 1992), 18.

11. Robert Cooke, Review of *The Moral Manager* by Clarence Walton, *Business Ethics Quarterly* 3, no. 2 (1993): 307.

12. Michael Mandel, "Antitrust for the Digital Age," *Business Week*, May 15, 2000, 46.

13. Ip, "The Antitrust Case against America's Technology Behemoths," A10.

14. Daniel Lyons, "Slay Your Rivals," *Forbes*, December 14, 1998, 55.

15. Fred Moody, "Mr. Software," *New York Times Magazine*, August 26, 1991, 28.

16. Ibid., 26.

17. *United States v. Microsoft Corp.*, 253 F. 3d 34 D.C. Cir. (2001).

18. James Gleick, "Making Microsoft Safe for Capitalism," *New York Times Magazine*, November 5, 1995, 51.

19. Ibid., 52–55. See also John Heilemann, *Pride before the Fall* (New York: HarperCollins, 2001), 48.

20. Richard McKenzie, *Trust on Trial* (Cambridge: Perseus, 2000), 118.

21. Alison Sprout, "The Rise of Netscape," *Fortune*, July 10, 1995, 140. See also Julian Prokaza, "From Netscape to Internet Explorer: Do You Remember the Web Browser Wars?," BT.com, August 18, 2018, http://home.bt.com/tech-gadgets/internet/history-of-web-browser-microsoft-windows-95-mozilla-netscape-113639755314062.

22. Robert Guth, "In Secret Hideaway Bill Gates Ponders Microsoft's Future," *Wall Street Journal*, March 28, 2005, A1, A13.

23. Heilemann, *Pride before the Fall*, 64.

24. Prokaza, "From Netscape to Internet Explorer."

25. Ibid.

26. *United States v. Grinnell Corp.*, 384 U.S. 563, 570–71 (1966).

27. "Microsoft Accused," *The Economist*, May 23, 1998, 23. See also Heilemann, *Pride before the Fall*, 105.

28. Government's Complaint, *United States v. Microsoft Corp.*, 98-1232 D.D.C. May 18, 1998, 53. Case law has established that Section 1 of this act prohibits certain tying arrangements as a restraint of trade.

29. *United States v. Microsoft Corp.*, 2001, 258.

30. Ibid., 258.

31. Ibid., 260.

32. Ibid., 255.

33. This folder appears on the Windows desktop and contains the icons of proprietary client software of online service providers; clicking on one of these icons initiates the process of signing up for the OSP's services.

34. Heilemann, *Pride before the Fall*, 143. See also Findings of Fact, *United States v. Microsoft Corp.*, 87 F. Supp. 2d D.D.C. (1999), 289.

35. Ibid., 143.

36. *Eastman Kodak Co. v. Image Technical Services. Inc.*, 504 U.S. 451 (1992).

37. *Jefferson Parish Hospital District v. Hyde*, 466 U.S. 2 (1984), 21–22.

38. Heilemann, *Pride before the Fall*, 182.

39. "Microsoft Accused," 22.

40. Heilemann, *Pride before the Fall*, 133.

41. *United States v. Microsoft Corp.*, 2001, 277.

42. Microsoft Brief on Appeal, *United States v. Microsoft Corp.*, 1999 (hereafter Microsoft Brief).

43. Remedies Brief of Association for Competitive Technology and Computer Technology, re *United States v. Microsoft Corp.*, 97 F. Supp.2d 59 D.D.C. (2000), 122.

44. Microsoft Brief, 145.

45. Philip Areeda, *Antitrust Law* (New York: Aspen, 1991), 51–52.

46. *Northern Pacific Railway v. U.S.*, 356 U.S. 1 (1958).

47. Ibid., 5.

48. For the sake of simplicity, this case study has focused on only three violations of the Sherman Act. There were others, such as Microsoft's monopolization of the browser market, that were not considered and are not discussed in the case's outcome.

49. Paul Mozur, "Despite Censorship, China's Tech World Takes Cues from Silicon Valley," *New York Times*, December 5, 2106, B1, B4.

50. Natalia Drozdiak, "Google Faces New Charges," *Wall Street Journal*, July 11, 2016, B7.

51. Siva Vaidhyanathan, *The Googlization of Everything* (Berkeley: University of California Press, 2010), 41.

52. Ian Rogers, "The Google PageRank Algorithm and How It Works," IPR Computing Ltd., accessed July 2017, www.cs.princeton.edu/ ~chazelle/courses/BIB/pagerank.htm.

53. Scott Galloway, *The Four: The Hidden DNA of Amazon, Apple, Facebook, and Google* (New York: Penguin, 2017), 133.

54. "Google Core Values," accessed July 2017, www.scribd.com/doc/44700112/google-core-values.

55. Ben Elgin, "Why the World's Hottest Tech Company Will Struggle to Keep Its Edge," *Businessweek*, May 3, 2004, 82–90.

56. "Internet Monopolies," 19–22.

57. "Desktop Search Engine Market Share," May 2017, www.netmarketshare.com/search-en gine-market-share.aspx?.

58. "How Long Will Google's Magic Last?," *The Economist*, December 4, 2010, 77–79.

59. Securities and Exchange Commission, Alphabet Inc., 10-K Report, 2017, https://abc.xyz/pdf/20171231_alphabet_10k.pdf. See also Galloway, *The Four*, 136.

60. Jack Nicas, "Google Faces Challenge in Policing Content Across Its Vast Ad Network," *Wall Street Journal*, March 24, 2017, B4.

61. Jack Nicas, "How Search Giant's Ad Auctions Work," *Wall Street Journal*, January 20, 2017, B2. See also Galloway, *The Four*, 137.

62. Galloway, *The Four*, 131.

63. Daisuke Wakabayashi, "A Google Gold Mine below the Search Bar," *New York Times*, April 24, 2017, B1, B3.

64. Larry Page and Sergei Brin, "Google Founders' IPO Letter," April 2004, https://abc.xyz/investor/founder-letters/2004/ipo-letter.html.

65. Frank Pasquale, *The Black Box Society: The Secret Algorithms That Control Money and Information* (Cambridge, MA: Harvard University Press, 2015), 70. See also Danny Sullivan, "Once Deemed Evil, Google Now Embraces Paid Inclusion," *Marketing Land*, May 30, 2012, https://marketingland,com/once-deemed-evil-google-now-embraces-paid-inclu sion-13138.

66. Galloway, *The Four*, 152.

67. Brody Mullins, Rolfe Winkler, and Brent Kendall, "FTC Wanted to Sue Google,"*Wall Street Journal*, March 20, 2015, A1–A2.

68. Ibid., A2.

69. Quoted in Stefan Schultz, "How Anti-Competitive Is Google?," *Der Speigel* online, February 25, 2010, www .speigel.dr/international/business/eu-commission-inquiry/how-anti-competitive-is-google.

70. Natalia Drozdiak and Sam Schechner, "EU Slaps Google with Record Fine," *Wall Street Journal*, June 28, 2017, A1–A2.

71. Pasquale, *The Black Box Society*, 67–69.

72. Natalia Drozdiak and Sam Schechner, "Google Readies Europe Search Changes," *Wall Street Journal*, August 30, 2017, B4.

73. "Europe v. Google: Nothing to Stand On," *The Economist*, April 18, 2015, 55.

74. Natalia Drozdiak, "EU Presses Google Harder," *Wall Street Journal*, June 28, 2016, B4.

75. Rolfe Winkler, "Google Pushes Its Own Content," *Wall Street Journal*, August 19, 2014, B1, B5. See also Drozdiak and Schechner, "Google Readies Europe Search Changes."

76. Jack Nicas, "Google Searches Boost Its Own Products," *Wall Street Journal*, January 20, 2017, B1–B2.

77. Ibid., B2.

78. Drozdiak and Schechner, "EU Slaps Google with Record Fine," A2.

79. Shona Ghosh, "Why Google Just Got Fined €2.42 Billion for Google Shopping," *Business Insider*, June 27, 2017, www.businessinsider.com/why-google-just-got-fined-2.42- billion -for-google-shopping

80. Drozdiak and Schechner, "EU Slaps Google with Record Fine," A2.

81. Drozdiak and Schechner, "Google Readies Europe Search Changes."

82. Galloway, *The Four*, 131.

83. Sam Schechner, Natalie Drozdiak, and Alistair Barr, "Google Digs In for Protracted Antitrust Fight," *Wall Street Journal*, August 28, 2015, B1–B2. See also Natalie Drozdiak and Sam Schechner, "Google Feels Heat from EU Cases," *Wall Street Journal*, November 11, 2016, B2.

CHAPTER 12

1. Cathy Young, "Is Office Romance Still Allowed?," *Wall Street Journal*, December 2, 2017, C2.

2. Rick Wartzman, *The End of Loyalty* (New York: Public Affairs, 2017), 5.

3. Carol Hymowitz, Lukas Alpert, and Suzanne Vranica, "Harassment Scandals Prompt Rapid Workplace Changes," *Wall Street Journal*, November 11, 2017, A1, A9.

4. Lawrence E. Blades, "Employment at Will versus Individual Freedom: On Limiting the Abusive Exercise of Employer Power," 67 *Columbia Law Review* 1405 (1967), emphasis added. See also Patricia Werhane, "Individual Rights in Business," in *Just Business: New Introductory Essays in Business Ethics*, ed. Tom Regan (New York: Random House, 1984), 107.

5. Werhane, "Individual Rights in Business," 107–8.

6. Wartzman, *The End of Loyalty*, 148.

7. Ibid., 238–40.

8. Bryan Burrough, "In Good Company," *Wall Street Journal*, July 13, 2017, A13. See also Wartzman, *The End of Loyalty*, 6.

9. Nelson Schwartz and Michael Corkery, "In Its Heyday, Sears Spread the Wealth. Companies Today Don't," *New York Times*, October 24, 2018, A1, A17.

10. Lauren Weber, "The End of Employees," *Wall Street Journal*, February 3, 2017, A1, A10.

11. Sandra Sucher, Elena Green, and David Rosales, "Layoffs: Effects on Key Stakeholders" (Boston: Harvard Business School, 2014), 1–3.

12. *NLRB v. Jones & Laughlin Steel Co.*, 301 U.S. 1 (1937).

13. David Oderberg, *Moral Theory* (Oxford: Blackwell, 2000), 55–60. See also Robert George, "Natural Law," 52 *American Journal of Jurisprudence* 55 (2007).

14. Joseph DeJardins and Ronald Duska, "Drug Testing in Employment," in *Ethics at Work*, ed. William Shaw (New York: Oxford University Press, 2003), 101.

15. Werhane, "Individual Rights in Business," 108–10.

16. David Adams and Edward Maine, *Business Ethics for the 21st Century* (Mountain View, CA: Mayfield, 1998), 172–73.

17. Manuel Velasquez, *Business Ethics: Concepts and Cases*, 4th ed. (Upper Saddle River, NJ: Prentice Hall, 1998), 374.

18. DeJardins and Duska, "Drug Testing in Employment," 101.

19. Lauren Weber, "Tests Show More American Workers Using Drugs," *Wall Street Journal*, May 17, 2017, B1.

20. DeJardins and Duska, "Drug Testing in Employment," 102–6.

21. *Smyth v. Pillsbury Co.*, 914 F. Supp. 97 E.D. Pa (1996).

22. *Elgin v. St. Louis Coca-Cola Bottling Co.*, 4I05CV970-DJS (E.D. MI) (2005). See also Kamina Shaw, "GPS Tracking of Employee Devices—How Much Is Too Much," OnLabor blog, May 8, 2017, https://onlabor.org/gps-tracking-of-employee-devices-how-much-is-too-much/.

23. Shaw, "GPS Tracking of Employee Devices."

24. Germain Grisez, *Living a Christian Life* (Quincy, IL: Franciscan Press, 1993), 330, 763.

25. Greg Bensinger and Joann Lublin, "Uber Fires 20 in Wake of Probe," *Wall Street Journal*, June 7, 2017, B1.

26. Nathaniel Popper and Katie Benner, "Inside SoFi: 'A Frat House,'" *New York Times*, September 13, 2017, B1, B6.

27. Young, "Is Office Romance Still Allowed?" C1–C2.

28. Susan Dodds, Lucy Frost, Robert Pargetter, and Elizabeth Prior, "Sexual Harassment," *Social Theory and Practice* (Summer 1988), 111–30.

29. Ibid., 115–20.

30. Karol Wojtyła, *Love and Responsibility*, trans. Grzegorz Ignatik (Boston: Pauline Books & Media, 2013), 10.

31. Rob Copeland, Liz Hoffman, and Rachel Ensign, "Wall Street Evaded the #MeToo Spotlight," *Wall Street Journal*, January 20, 2018, B1, B10. See also John Crosby, *Personalist Papers* (Washington, DC: Catholic University of America Press, 2004), 246–50.

32. Although this is a real case, all the names, dates, places, and so forth have been altered to protect all the parties involved. Any resemblance to real people, institutions, or events is purely coincidental.

33. Sophie Sassard, Mark John, and Gilles Guillaume, "Peugeot: Decline of a Lion," *Reuters Special Report*, December 4, 2013, 6.

34. Ibid., 2.

35. "Peugeot Rallies," *The Economist*, August 11, 2016, 58. See also Sassard, John, and Guillaume, "Peugot: Decline of a Lion," 9–10.

36. For the history of PSA Group, see Groupe PSA, "Groupe PSA: 200 Years of Automotive and Industrial History," https://www.groupe-psa.com/groupe-psa-200-years-of-automotive-and-industrial-history.

37. Reuters Staff, "PSA Moves Swiftly to Stamp Authority on Opel/Vauxhall," August 1, 2017, https://www.reuters.com/articles/us-opel-m-a-psa-idUSKBNlAH39W.

38. "Opel Still Struggling after PSA Takeover," *DW*, March 1, 2018, https://www.dw.com/en/opel-still-struggling-after-psa-takeover/a-42778864.

39. Edward Taylor and Lawrence Frost, "PSA Union Solidarity Frays as Opel Workers Resist Cuts," Reuters, April 20, 2018, https://www.reuters.co.uk/article/psa-union-soliarity-frays-as-opel-workers-resist-cuts/idUSKBN1HR1GN.

40. Michael Stothard, "Peugeot-Owner PSA Report Historic Profit Margins," *Financial Times*, July 26, 2017, https://www.ft.com/content/60aefa0f0-71cd-11e7-aca6-c6bd07dfla3a.

41. Gilles Guillame, "PSA Plans 1,300 French Job Cuts under New Law, Union Says," *Automotive News*

Europe, January 9, 2018, https://www.europeanu-tonews.com/article/20180109/ANE/180109788/psa-plans-1300-frecn-job-cuts-under-new-law-union-says.

42. Liz Alderman, "Newfound Freedom . . . to Fire," *New York Times*, January 24, 2018, B1, B3. See also H. Jorgenson and P. K. Madesen, *Flexicurity and Beyond: Finding a New Agenda for the European Social Model* (Copenhagen: DJOF, 2007), along with Arthur Daemmrich and Benjamin Kramerz, "Denmark and the Welfare State" (Boston: Harvard Business School, 2012), 8–9.

43. "Global Niche Players," *The Economist*, February 2, 2013, 9–10.

44. Alderman, "Newfound Freedom," B3.

45. Brian Elluxson, "Sweeping Changes to French Labor Law Signal Employer Friendly Future," Fisher Phillips, https://www.fisherphillips.com/sweeping-changes-to-french-labor-law-signal-employer-friendly-future.

46. Alderman, "Newfound Freedom," B3.

47. The Local, "French Carmaker PSA Uses Macron Reforms for 1,300 Redundancies," January 9, 2018, https://www.thelocal.fr/20180109/french-carmaker-psa-uses-macron-refroms-for-1300-redundancies.

48. Eric Benziat, "La Rupture Conventionelle Collective Inquiète chez PSA," *Le Monde*, January 30, 2018, https://www.lemonde.fr/economie/article/2018/01/30/la-rupture-conventionelle-collective- inquiete-chez-psa_ 5248923_3234.html.

49. Alderman, "Newfound Freedom," B3.

50. "PSA Group Financials Summary," Pitchbook, https://www.pitchbook.com/profiles/company/43036-93.

51. *Cunningham v. New York State Dept. of Labor*, 2013 NY Slip Op 04838, decided June 27, 2013, Court of Appeals. Citations and footnotes within the case excerpts have been omitted along with ellipses or other indications that the content has been condensed for the sake of simplicity. The other material in this case study is largely drawn from the facts presented in the Court of Appeals opinion.

52. See *O'Connor v. Ortega*, 480 U.S. 709 (1987).

53. Rick Kaplan, "GPS Used to Track Fired State Worker Raises Privacy Issues," *Times Union*, September 16, 2011, https://www.timesunion.com/local/article/gps-used-to-track-fired-state-worker-raises-2172601.php.

CHAPTER 13

1. Anthony Giddens, "The Globalizing of Modernity," in *The Global Transformations Reader: An Introduction to the Globalization Debate*, 2nd ed., ed. David Held and Anthony McGrew (London: Wiley-Blackwell, 2003), 60.

2. Richard Barnett and Ronald Müller, *Global Reach: The Power of Multinational Corporations* (New York: Simon & Schuster, 1974), 45.

3. Daniel Litvin, *Empires of Profit* (New York: Texere, 2003), xiv–xv, 148.

4. B. Kogut, "Globalization," in M. Warner (ed.), *Concise International Encyclopedia of Business and Management* (London: Thomson Business Press, 1997), 99.

5. Gregory Ip, "We Are Not the World," *Wall Street Journal*, January 7–8, 2016, C1–C2.

6. Martin Wolf, *Why Globalization Works* (New Haven, CN: Yale University Press, 2004), 14.

7. See the discussion on the various forms of globalization in Lynn Hunt, *Writing History in the Global Era* (New York: W. W. Norton, 2014), 52–55.

8. Karl Marx and Friedrich Engels, *The Communist Manifesto* (New York: International Publishers, 1964), 61.

9. Hunt, *Writing History in the Global Era*, 55.

10. I am indebted to the extended discussion of this history divided into these four periods by Geoffrey Jones, *Multinationals and Global Capitalism*, (Oxford: Oxford University Press, 2005), 18–40.

11. Jagdish Bhagwati, *In Defense of Globalization* (Oxford: Oxford University Press, 2014), 11.

12. Stephen Broadberry and Kevin O'Rourke, *The Cambridge Economic History of Modern Europe* (Cambridge, UK: Cambridge University Press, 2010), 6–9.

13. "The World in 1913," *The Economist*, June 8, 2013, 86.

14. Jeffrey Frieden, *Global Capitalism: Its Rise and Fall in the Twentieth Century* (New York: W. W. Norton, 2005), 19.

15. Expropriation is defined as "an act whereby government takes into ownership, by compulsion if necessary, private property for a public use." See M. L. Williams, "The Extent and Significance of the Nationalism of Foreign-Owned Assets in Developing Countries," *Oxford Economic Papers* 27 (1975), 261.

16. Mira Wilkins, *The Maturing of Multinational Enterprise: American Business Abroad from 1914 to 1970* (Cambridge, MA: Harvard University Press, 1974), 23–26.

17. Frieden, *Global Capitalism*, 196–67. See also "The Depression Goes Global," *Wall Street Journal*, June 2, 2017, A13.

18. Frieden, *Global Capitalism*, 212–15.

19. Wilkins, *Maturing of Multinational Enterprise*, 350–55. See also Frieden, *Global Capitalism*, 293, 419–21.

20. Jones, *Multinationals and Global Capitalism*, 31.

21. Josef Joffe, "China's Coming Slowdown," *Wall Street Journal*, October 26, 2017, C1–C2.

22. Organization for Economic Community and Development, "FDI in Figures," April 2017, www.oecd.org/corporate/statistics/mn.

23. James Mackintosh, "Return of History Could Be at Hand," *Wall Street Journal*, May 26, 2017, B1–B2.

24. Bob Davis and Jon Hilsenrath, "Globalization Backers Face End of an Era," *Wall Street Journal*, March 30, 2017, A1, A12.

25. James Mackintosh, "Return of History Could Be at Hand," B1–B2. See also Schumpeter, "Beware of Sandstorms," *The Economist*, June 20, 2015, 66.

26. S. Zaheer, "Overcoming the Liability of Foreignness," *Academy of Management Journal* 38, no. 2 (1995): 341–63.

27. P. Ghemawat, "Distance Still Matters: The Hard Reality of Global Expansion," *Harvard Business Review*, September/October 2011: 138–52.

28. James Marson, "McDonald's Puts Down Stakes in Siberia," *Wall Street Journal*, January 24, 2017, B6.

29. Thomas Donaldson, *The Ethics of International Business* (Oxford: Oxford University Press, 1989), 14–19.

30. Aristotle, *Rhetoric*, in *The Basic Works of Aristotle*, ed. Richard McKeon (New York: Random House, 1941), 1373b5.

31. David Oderberg, *Moral Theory* (Oxford: Oxford University Press, 2000), 19–22. See also Donaldson, *Ethics of International Business*, 19.

32. Oderberg, *Moral Theory*, 22–23.

33. Thomas Donaldson and Thomas Dunfee, *The Ties That Bind: A Social Contract Approach to Business Ethics* (Boston: Harvard Business School Press, 1999), 43.

34. John Finnis, *Philosophy of Law* (Oxford: Oxford University Press, 2011), 115–17.

35. Heidi Deringer and Jennifer Wang, "Note on Political Risk Analysis" (Boston: Harvard Business School, 1991). See also Schumpeter, "Beyond Economics," *The Economist*, February 12, 2011, 75.

36. Schumpeter, "Beware of Sandstorms."

37. Schumpeter, "Beyond Economics."

38. Lawrence Norman, Benoît Faucon, and Alison Sider, "Firms Aren't Racing to Iran," *Wall Street Journal*, January 19, 2016, B4. See also Robert Wall, Asa Fitch, and Doug Cameron, "Boeing Homes In on Iran Orders Despite Static," *Wall Street Journal*, April 5, 2017, B1–B2.

39. Thomas Donaldson, *The Ethics of International Business* (Oxford: Oxford University Press, 1989), 131–35. I am indebted to Donaldson's entire discussion of disinvestment in Chapter 8 of his book, 129–44.

40. Litvin, *Empires of Profit*, 302.

41. Ibid., 155–57

42. ITT, "Our History: Nearly a Century of Value Creating Transformation," accessed June 2017, https://www.itt.com/about/history.

43. Richard Barnett and Ronald Müller, *Global Reach: The Power of Multinational Corporations* (New York: Simon & Schuster, 1974), 52–53.

44. ITT, "Company History."

45. "Conglomerates on Trial," *The Economist*, April 5, 1997, 55.

46. Schumpeter, "The Art of the Spin-Off," *The Economist*, May 4, 2013, 70.

47. Frieden, *Global Capitalism*, 293.

48. See an account of this in Antony C. Sutton, *Wall Street and the Rise of Hitler* (San Pedro, CA: GSG & Associates, 2002), 77–88. See also Charles Higham, *Trading with the Enemy* (London: Hale, 1983), ii–vi, and Barnett and Müller, *Global Reach*, 60–61.

49. Barnett and Müller, *Global Reach*, 61.

50. Sutton, *Wall Street and the Rise of Hitler*, 83–84.

51. Anthony Sampson, *The Sovereign State of ITT* (New York: Stein & Day, 1973), 40.

52. Ibid., 214. See also Barnett and Müller, *Global Reach*, 61.

53. The International Telephone and Telegraph Company and Chile, 1970–1971, *Report to the Committee on Foreign Relations, United States Senate, by the Subcommittee on Multinational Corporations*, June 21, 1973, 1–2 (hereafter *Report to the Committee on Foreign Relations*).

54. Ibid., 3–4.

55. "Covert Actions in Chile: 1963–73: Staff Report of the Select Committee to Study Government Operations with Respect to the Central Intelligence Agency," United States Senate, 1975, https://archive.org/

stream/covetactivitiesincile1963373/covet%20
action%20in%20Chile%201963-73_djvu,txt.

56. *Report to the Committee on Foreign Relations*, 6.

57. Ibid., 5–6.

58. Ibid., 4–5.

59. Ibid., 9.

60. Central Intelligence Agency, "CIA Activities in Chile," released September 18, 2000, www.cia.gov/library/reports/generalreports-1/chile. See also Maria Arana, "Story of a Death Foretold: The Coup against Salvador Allende," *Washington Post*, December 6, 2013, A32–A38.

61. *Report to the Committee on Foreign Relations*, 6–8.

62. Arana, "Story of a Death Foretold," A32.

63. Ibid., A33–A34.

64. *Report to the Committee on Foreign Relations*, 12–14.

65. Barnett and Müller, *Global Reach*, 85.

66. Paul Sigmund, *The Overthrow of Allende and the Politics of Chile* (Pittsburgh, PA: University of Pittsburgh Press, 1977), 193. See also Daniel Litvin, *Empires of Profit* (New York: Texere, 2003), 150.

67. Central Intelligence Agency, "CIA Activities in Chile," released September 18, 2000, www.cia.gov/library/reports/generalreports-1/chile.

68. Uri Friedman, "The Other 9/11: A CIA Agent Remembers Chile's Coup," *The Atlantic*, September, 11, 2014.

69. *Report to the Committee on Foreign Relations*, 16–17.

70. Ibid., 17.

71. Donald Sull, "The Dynamics of Standing Still: Firestone Tire & Rubber and the Radial Revolution," *Research and Ideas*, November 27, 2000, 18–25.

72. Ibid.

73. John Matthews et al., *Polices and Persons*, 2nd ed. (New York: McGraw-Hill, 1991), 368–76.

74. David Kiron, "Bridgestone Corp." (Boston: Harvard Business School, 2003), 8–9.

75. Fortune Global 500, "Bridgestone Financials," accessed September 2017, https://www.fortune.com/global500/bridgestone.

76. Morten Boas, "The Liberian Civil War: New War/Old War?," *Global Society* 19, no. 1 (2006), 75–77.

77. "Preliminary Report: Bridgestone/Firestone's Role in the Liberian Civil War," Corporate Campaigns/International Affairs Department, United Steelworkers of America, September 1996, 3.

78. R. J. Harrison Church, "The Firestone Rubber Plantations in Liberia," *Geography* 54, no. 4 (1969), 430–37.

79. "Rubber Production in Liberia: An Exploratory Assessment of Living and Working Conditions," *Verité*, 2012, 11–12.

80. Ibid., 12.

81. T. Christian Miller and Jonathan Jones, "Firestone and the Warlord: The Untold Story of Firestone, Charles Taylor, and the Tragedy of Liberia," *ProPublica*, November 21, 2014, www.propublica.org/firestone-and-the-warlord.

82. "Rubber Production in Liberia," Appendix 1, 43–44.

83. The Famous People, "Charles Taylor's Biography," www.thefamouspeople.com/charles/taylor, accessed September 2017.

84. "Preliminary Report," 5.

85. The Famous People, "Charles Taylor's Biography." See also "Liberia: First Civil War, 1989–1996," GlobalSecurity.org, accessed September 2017, www.globalsecurity.org/liberian-first-civil-war.

86. "Preliminary Report," 5.

87. "Plantation Boss Kept His Cool," *Akron Beacon Journal*, June 20, 1990, 1. See also "Preliminary Report," 7.

88. "Preliminary Report," 8. See also "Firestone and the Warlord," 24.

89. "Firestone and the Warlord," 26.

90. "Rubber Production in Liberia," 12–13.

91. A big percentage of the world's natural rubber supply comes from countries in Southeast Asia, including Thailand, Indonesia, Malaysia, and Vietnam. See "Rubber Production in Liberia," 12.

92. "Firestone and the Warlord," 26

93. "Preliminary Report," 10.

94. Ibid., 9. See also "Firestone and the Warlord," 33–35.

95. Timothy Newman, "Liberia Truth and Reconciliations Commission Highlights Firestone's Abuses," International Labor Rights Forum, December 3, 2014. See also "Firestone and the Warlord," 38.

96. "Firestone and the Warlord," 38–39.

97. Ibid., 45–46.

98. "Firestone and the Warlord," 39–40.

99. Human Rights Watch, "Lead Liberian Journalist Re-Arrested," July 4, 2002, https://www.hrw.org/news/2002/07/04/leading-liberian-journalist-re-arrested.

100. Marline Simons, "Ex-President of Liberia Aided War Crimes, Court Says," *New York Times*, April 26, 2012, A1, A12.

101. "Firestone and the Warlord," 58–59.

102. Simons, "Ex-President of Liberia Aided War Crimes," A12. See also "Ex-Liberia President Charles Taylor to Stay in UK Prison," BBC News, March 25, 2015, www.bbc.com/news/uk-32055482.

103. Erika Fry, "When Companies Do Business with Warlords," *Fortune*, November 19, 2014, http://fortune .com/2014/11/19/doing-buiness-with-warlords.

104. "Firestone Responds," PBS, November 18, 2014, http://www.pbs.org/wgbh/pages/for eign-affi-ars-defense/firestone-and-the-warlord/firestone-responds.

105. Ibid.

106. "Liberia Country Profile," BBC News, June 30, 2016, www.bbc.com/news/world-africa-13729504. See also "Rubber Production in Liberia," 6.

CHAPTER 14

1. Ngozi Okonjo-Iweala, *Reforming the Unreformable: Lessons from Nigeria* (Cambridge, MA: MIT Press, 2012), ix.

2. Scott Patterson and Rory Jones, "Israel Arrests Diamond Magnate," *Wall Street Journal*, December 20, 2016, B1–B2.

3. Dan Koeppel, *Banana: The Fate of the Fruit That Changed the World* (New York: Penguin Group, 2008), 169–75.

4. Leif Wenar, *Blood Oil* (Oxford: Oxford University Press, 2016), 58.

5. World Bank, "Corruption and Economic Development," 1, accessed January 2018, www.worldbank. org/publicsector/anticorrupt/corruptn/cor02.htm.

6. Ibid., 2. See also Dwight King, "Corruption in Indonesia: A Curable Cancer?" *Journal of International Affairs* 53, no. 2 (2000), 605.

7. Stuart P. Green, *Lying, Cheating, and Stealing* (Oxford: Oxford University Press, 2006), 194–200.

8. Ibid., 195–96.

9. "Bribery: The Worm That Never Dies," *The Economist*, March 2, 2002, 12.

10. "Graft Work," *The Economist*, December 6, 2014, 73.

11. Ibid.

12. 18 U.S.C. §201. See also Green, *Lying, Cheating, and Stealing*, 194.

13. Special Review Committee of the Board of Directors of Gulf Oil Corporation, reprinted as *The Great Oil Spill* (New York: Chelsea House, 1976), 101–3. See also John T.

Noonan, *Bribes: The Intellectual History of a Moral Idea* (Berkeley: University of California Press, 1987), *638*.

14. Edwin Reischauer, "The Lessons of the Lockheed Scandal," *Newsweek*, May 10, 1976, 20–21. For a more detailed account of this scandal, see David Boulton, *The Grease Machine* (New York: Harper & Row, 1978). See also Noonan, *Bribes*, 630–65.

15. Carl A. Kotchian, *Lockheed Sales Mission: 70 Days in Tokyo* (Berkeley: University of California Press, 1976), 230.

16. James Q. Wilson, "Corruption Is Not Always Scandalous," *New York Times Magazine*, April 28, 1968, 32–34. See also Noonan, *Bribes*, 547.

17. Norman Bowie, *Business Ethics: A Kantian Perspective* (Oxford: Blackwell, 1999), 26–27.

18. The Foreign Corrupt Practices Act, Pub. L. No. 95-213, 91 Stat. 1464 (1977), codified at 15 U.S.C. §78(m), (dd), (ff).

19. Noonan, *Bribes*, 678–79.

20. "Aircraft and Bribery: Airbus's Secret Past," *The Economist*, June 14, 2003, 55–58.

21. "Bribery: The Worm That Never Dies." See also "Bribery and Business: The Short Arm of the Law," *The Economist*, March 2, 2002, 63–65.

22. "Bribery and Business," 63.

23. Geoffrey Gauci and Jessica Fisher, "The UK Bribery Act and the US FCPA: Key Differences," Association of Corporate Counsel, June 2011, www.acc.com/legal/resources/quickcounsel/UKBAFCPA.cfm.

24. Laura French, "A History of Bribery," *World Finance*, March 8, 2015. See also "Graft Work."

25. Ibid., 3–6.

26. Ryan Dube, Luciana Magalhaes, and Rogerio Jelmayer, "Graft Probes Grow in Latin America," *Wall Street Journal*, March 9, 2017, A20.

27. Nicholas Casey and Andrea Zarate, "Brazilian Graft Scandals Echo Across Continent," *New York Times*, February 15, 2017, A3. See also Ryan Dube, "Brazilian Bribery Scandal Shakes Up Latin America," *Wall Street Journal*, December 23, 2016, B3.

28. World Bank, "Corruption and Economic Development," 5–6.

29. For the history of GSK, see the company website, www.gsk.com/history, and DrugWatch, "A History of GlaxoSmithKline," accessed June 2018, www.drug watch.com/manufacturer/glaxosmithkline.

30. GSK, "GSK Public Policy Positions," accessed June 2018, www.gsk.com/media/public-policy.

31. "The Pharma Business: A Better Pill from China," *The Economist*, March 18, 2017, 68.

32. French, "A History of Bribery," p. 8. See also Lina Salgol and John Aglionby, "Timeline: GSK's Mounting Woes in China," *Financial Times*, September 19, 2014, 18.

33. Andrew Ward and Patti Waldmeir, "GlaxoSmithKline Navigates Difficult Path in China after Scandal," *Financial Times*, November 26, 2015, 7.

34. "GlaxoSmithKline in China: Bitter Pill," *The Economist*, July 20, 2013, 56–57.

35. Jeremy Page, Bob Davis, and Tom Orlik, "China's New Boss," *Wall Street Journal*, November 10, 2013, C1–C2. See also Stephen Fidler and Te-Ping Chen, "China's Xi Preaches Merits of Globalization," *Wall Street Journal*, January 18, 2017, A1, A9.

36. Meredith Tracey, "A Full Timeline of the GSK Bribery Scandal," PM360, July 30, 2014, https://www.pm360online.com/a-full-timeline-of-the-gsk-bribery-scandal/.

37. Citizens Commission on Human Rights, "GlaxoSmithKline Bribes Chinese Doctors with Sexual Favors," 2015, www.cchrflorida.org/glaxosmithkline-bribes-chinese-doctors-with-sexual-favors.

38. David Barboza, "China Tightens Its Grip, and Glaxo Pays the Price," *New York Times*, November 2, 2016, A1, B8–B9.

39. Ibid., B8–B9.

40. Ibid., B8.

41. Laurie Burkitt, "China Accuses Glaxo of Bribes," *Wall Street Journal*, July 12, 2013, B5.

42. See Denise Roland, "Glaxo in China: History of a Crisis," *The Telegraph*, July 24, 2013, 1.

43. Tracey, "A Full Timeline of the GSK Bribery Scandal."

44. Martin Rogers, Bernard Chun Zhu, and Jerry Fang, "GSK: A Case Study," *China Law and Practice*, July/August 2014, 15.

45. Ibid., 15–16.

46. The Foreign Corrupt Practices Act, 15 U.S.C. §78 (m), (dd).

47. Rogers, Zhu, and Fang, "GSK: A Case Study," 17.

48. Benjamin Shobert, "Three Ways to Understand GSK's China Scandal," *Forbes*, September 4, 2013, 55.

49. "GSK Scandal and Bribery in China Explained," Internships China, July 15, 2016, www.internships-china.com/gsk-scandal-bribery-china-explained.

50. Connor Lee, "China and Corruption: The Case of GlaxoSmithKline," Seven Pillars Institute, July 13, 2015, http://www.sevenpillarsinstitute.org/news/china-and-corruption--the-case-of-glaxosmithkline.

51. "GlaxoSmithKline in China." See also "GSK Scandal and Bribery in China Explained."

52. Lee, "China and Corruption."

53. Claudia Süssmuth-Dyckerhouse and Jim Wang, "China's Health Care Reform," *Health International* 10 (2010), https://www.mckinsey.com/~/media/mckinsey/dotcom/client_service/healthcare%20systems%20and%20services/health%20international/hi10_china_healthcare_reform.ashx.

54. "GlaxoSmithKline in China."

55. Citizens Commission on Human Rights, "GlaxoSmithKline Bribes Chinese Doctors with Sexual Favors."

56. Hester Plumridge and Laurie Burkitt, "GlaxoSmithKline Found Guilty of Bribery in China," *Wall Street Journal*, September 19, 2014, A1, B5.

57. Ibid., B5. See also Tracey, "A Full Timeline of the GSK Bribery Scandal."

58. Matt Robinson, "Glaxo to Pay $20Million SEC Fine over Bribery in China," Bloomberg.com, September 30, 2016, www.bloomberg.com/news/articles/2016-09-30/glaxo-to-pay-20-million-sec-fine-over-bribery-in-china.

59. The Monsanto Company, Encyclopedia.com, www.encyclopedia.com/businesses/monsanto-company. I have drawn from this article to discuss the various details of Monsanto's complicated history.

60. World Health Organization, "Health Topic: Genetically Modified Food," www.who.int/topics/food-genetically-modified/en.

61. The Monsanto Company.

62. Wendell Wallach, *A Dangerous Master: How to Keep Technology from Slipping beyond Our Control* (New York: Basic Books, 2015), 102–4.

63. "Corruption in Indonesia: A Damnable Scourge," *The Economist*, June 4, 2015, 33–34.

64. Derek Tuck, "Genetic Engineering and the Privatization of Seeds in Indonesia," History Commons, https://www.historycommons.org/timeline.jsp?timelien=seeds_tmin&seeds_cases_studies-gm_crops=seeds_indonesia.

65. *United States SEC v. Monsanto Company*, Civ. Act No. 23-7043, January 2005.

66. Ibid.

67. Peter Fritsch and Timothy Mapes, "In Indonesia, a Tangle of Bribes Creates Trouble for Monsanto," *Wall Street Journal*, April 5, 2005, A1, A6.

68. *United States SEC v. Monsanto Company.*

69. Ibid.

70. Ibid.

71. Antje Lorch, "Monsanto Bribes in Indonesia," Northwest Resistance Against Genetic Engineering, February 2005, www.nwrage.org/content/extensie-article-monsanto-bribes-indonesia

72. *United States SEC v. Monsanto Company.*

73. "Monsanto Fined $1.5 Million for Bribery," BBC News, January 7, 2005, news.bbc.co.uk//2/hi/business/4153635.stm.

74. Lorch, "Monsanto Bribes in Indonesia."

75. "Equatorial Guinea Country Profile," BBC News, August 5, 2016, www.bbc.com/news/world-africa-13317174.

76. Sarah Saradoun, "Ill-Gotten Gains: Equatorial Guinea Is a Case Study in Self-Dealing," Human Rights Watch, June 20, 2017, https://www.hrw.org/2017/06/20/ill-gotten-gains-equatorial-guinea-case-study-self-dealing.

77. "Equatorial Guinea: Events of 2009," Human Rights Watch, World Report 2010, accessed June 2018, www.hrw.org/world-report/2010/country-chapters/equatorial-guinea.

78. Wenar, *Blood Oil*, 70.

79. "Equatorial Guinea: Account for Oil Wealth," Human Rights Watch, July, 9, 2009, www.hrw.org/news/2009/07/09/equatorial-guinea-account-oil-wealth.

80. "Zafiro and Exxon Mobil: Ongoing Commitment to Equatorial Guinea," *The Oil and Gas Year*, April 3, 2015, https://www.theoilandgasyear.com/articles/zafiro-exxonmobil-ongoing-commitment-to-equatorial-guinea.

81. Onyedimmakachukwu Obinkwu, "Equatorial Guinea Ratifies Exploration Deal with ExxonMobil for Offshore Oil Block," *Ventures Africa*, April 2, 2015, www.venturesafrica.com/equatorial-guinea-ratifies-exploration- deal-with-exxonmobil-for-offshore-oil-block.

82. Justin Blum, "U.S. Oil Firms Entwined in Equatorial Guinea Deals," *Washington Post*, September 7, 2004, E1–E2. See also Tutu Alicante, "How Our Incoming Secretary of State Helped to Enrich Africa's Nastiest Dictatorship," *Washington Post*, February 1, 2017, A15.

83. Ben Hubbard, Dionne Searcey, and Nicholas Casey, "Under Rex Tillerson, Exxon Mobil Forged Its Own Path Abroad," *New York Times*, December 13, 2016, A1, A16.

84. Alicante, "How Our Incoming Secretary of State Helped to Enrich Africa's Nastiest Dictatorship."

85. Blum, "U.S. Oil Firms Entwined in Equatorial Guinea Deals."

86. Hubbard, Searcey, and Casey, "Exxon Mobil Forged Its Own Path Abroad."

87. Blum, "U.S. Oil Firms Entwined in Equatorial Guinea Deals."

88. Hubbard, Searcey, and Casey, "Exxon Mobil Forged Its Own Path Abroad."

89. Wenar, *Blood Oil*, 77.

90. "Manna from Heaven?" Human Rights Watch, June 15, 2017, www.hrw.org/2017/06/15/manna-from-heaven.

91. Wenar, *Blood Oil*, 41, 71–77.

CHAPTER 15

1. Quoted in Anjali Kamat, "Bangladesh's Factories Still Have Appalling Working Conditions," *Slate*, December 15, 2016, www.slate.com/articles/business/the_grind/2016/12/15/bangladesh_factories_still_have_appalling_working_conditions.

2. Quoted in Jack Schofield, "Pegatron Is Exploiting Workers Making Apple iPhone in China," ZDNET.com, August 28, 2016, www.zdnet.com/article/pegatron-is-exploiting-workers-making-apple-iphone.

3. "Special Report: Outsourcing and Offshoring," *The Economist*, January 19, 2013, 1–2.

4. Raymond Zhong, "India Has Designs on Toy Manufacturing," *Wall Street Journal*, January 7, 2016, A7.

5. "Manufacturing: They Don't Make 'Em Like That Any More," *The Economist*, January 14, 2017, 18–20.

6. "Special Report: Outsourcing and Offshoring," 5.

7. "Manufacturing," 19. See also "Special Report: Outsourcing and Offshoring," 1.

8. "Special Report: Outsourcing and Offshoring," 12–13.

9. Richard De George, *Competing with Integrity in International Business* (New York: Oxford University Press, 1993), 356–357.

10. Benjamin Powell, *Out of Poverty: Sweatshops in the Global Economy* (New York: Cambridge University Press, 2014), 23–47.

11. Albino Barrera, *Market Complicity and Christian Ethics* (New York: Cambridge University Press, 2014), 121–30.

12. Scott Galloway, *The Four: The Hidden DNA of Amazon, Apple, Facebook, and Google* (New York: Penguin, 2017), 67–69.

13. Yukari Iwatani Kane and Jessica Vascellaro, "Tough to Follow: Apple after Jobs," *Wall Street Journal*, August 26, 2011, A1, A10.

14. Betsy Morris, "What the iPhone Wrought," *Wall Street Journal*, June 24, 2017, B3.

15. Tripp Mickle, "How iPhone Decade Reshaped Apple," *Wall Street Journal*, June 21, 2017, B1, B8.

16. Tim Cook, "Commencement Address at George Washington University," *Network World*, May 18, 2015, 24.

17. Seth Fiegerman, "Apple under Tim Cook: More Socially Responsible, Less Visionary," *CNN Technology*, August 24, 2106, www.money.ccom/2016/08/24/technology/apple-tim-cook-five-years.

18. Tripp Mickle, "For Apple, There's a Silver Lining," *Wall Street Journal*, January 30, 2017, B1, B4. See also Tripp Mickle, "Apple Breaks Losing Streak, as Sales of iPhone Shine," *Wall Street Journal*, February 1, 2017, A1, A10.

19. Tripp Mickle, "Apple Performance Slips, CEO's Pay Cut," *Wall Street Journal*, January 7, 2017, A1, A7.

20. Vindu Goel, "How Apple Empowers, and Employs, the American Working Class," *New York Times*, November 21, 2016, B1, B4.

21. Jenny Chan, Ngai Pun, and Mark Selden, "The Politics of Global Production: Apple, Foxconn, and China's New Working Class," *New Technology, Work and Employment* 28, no. 2 (2013), 100–15.

22. Chan, Pun, and Selden, "The Politics of Global Production," 105–10.

23. Apple Inc., "Annual Report for the Fiscal Year Ended September 29, 2012," 7, http://investor.apple.com/secfiling.cfm?filingID=1193125-12-444068&CIK=320193. See also Chan et al., "The Politics of Global Production," 105.

24. Apple Inc., "Apple and Procurement," 2013 www.apple.com/procurement.

25. Chan et al., "The Politics of Global Production," 106–7. See also Connor Myers, "Corporate Social Responsibility in the Consumer Electronics Industry: A Case Study of Apple Inc.," selected papers published by Georgetown University, Edmund A. Walsh School of Foreign Service.

26. David Barboza, "A Manufacturing Model Tough to Export," *New York Times*, September 20, 2017, B1, B3.

27. Jay Greene, "Riots, Suicides, and Other Issues in Foxconn's iPhone Factories," CNET, September 25, 2012, https://www.cnet.com/news/riots-suicides-and-other-issues-in-foxconns-iphone-factories.

28. Charles Duhigg and David Barboza, "In China, Human Costs Are Built into an iPad," *New York Times*, January 25, 2012, B1, B3.

29. Ibid.

30. Ben Sin, "Latest Foxconn Worker Deaths Build Case for Apple to Move Operations from China," Forbes, August 22, 2016, https://www.forbes.com/ben-sin/2016/08/22/the-real-cost-of-the-iphone-7-more-foxconn-worker-deaths/#28f497cd61b7.

31. China Labor Watch, "Analyzing Labor Conditions of Pegatron and Foxconn," February 2015, 6, www.chinalaborwatch.org/report/73. See also China Labor Watch, "A Year of Regression in Apple's Supply Chain," May 3, 2017, 11, www.chinalaborwatch.org/report/82.

32. Brian Merchant, *The One Device: The Secret History of the iPhone* (New York: Little Brown, 2017), 269–73. See also Myers, "Corporate Social Responsibility in the Consumer Electronics Industry," 10.

33. China Labor Watch, "A Year of Regression in Apple's Supply Chain," 3.

34. See company website: www.pegatron.com/company.

35. China Labor Watch, "Apple's Unkept Promises: Investigation of Three Pegatron Group Factories Supplying Apple," July 29, 2013, www.chinalaborwatch.org/report/68.

36. Apple Inc., "Supplier Responsibility Standards," quoted in China Labor Watch, "Analyzing Labor Conditions of Pegatron and Foxconn," 12.

37. China Labor Watch, "Apple Making Big Profits but Chinese Workers' Wage on the Slide," August 24, 2016, www.chinalaborwatch.org/report/77. See also Nicki Lisa Cole, "iPhone or iExploit? Rampant Labor Violations in Apple's Supply Chain," Truthout, August 25, 2016, www.truthout.org/news/item/37363.

38. Schofield, "Pegatron Is Exploiting Workers Making Apple iPhone in China." See also China Labor Watch, "Apple Making Big Profits," 10.

39. Asian Century Institute, "Working for Apple in China," July 10, 2016, www.asiacenturyinsti tute/development/1191-working-for-apple-in-china.

40. Eva Dou, "China Fills Tech Factories with Student Labor," *Wall Street Journal*, September 25, 2014, B1–B2. See also Schofield, "Pegatron Is Exploiting Workers Making Apple iPhone in China."

41. See Asian Century Institute, "Working for Apple in China."

42. China Labor Watch, "A Year of Regression in Apple's Supply Chain," 16–17.

43. Ibid., 17.

44. Kathy Chu and Juru Osawa, "Trump's Made in U.S.A. Snag: Asia," *Wall Street Journal*, November 17, 2016, B1–B2.

45. Securities and Exchange Commission, Apple Inc., 10-K Report, 2016.

46. Ibid.

47. Syed Zain Al-Mahmood, Kathy Chu, and Tripti Lahiri, "After Fire, Pressure on Bangladesh," *Wall Street Journal*, December 15, 2012, B1, B4.

48. "Bangladesh Country Profile," BBC News, March 2, 2017, https://www.bbc.com/news/world-south-asia-12650940.

49. "Politics in Bangladesh: One and only One," *The Economist*, September 20, 2014, 35–36. See also Gordon Fairclough, "Factory Paychecks Trump Danger, Long Days for Bangladesh Women," *Wall Street Journal*, June 22–23, 2013, A1, A11.

50. Fairclough, "Factory Paychecks Trump Danger," A11.

51. Rachel Abrams and Maher Sattab, "Turmoil in a Global Apparel Hub," *New York Times*, January 23, 2017, B1, B4. See also "Bursting at the Seams," *The Economist*, October 26, 2013, 75.

52. Abrams and Sattab, "Turmoil in a Global Apparel Hub."

53. Kamat, "Bangladesh's Factories Still Have Appalling Working Conditions."

54. Ibid.

55. Abrams and Sattab, "Turmoil in a Global Apparel Hub."

56. V. Bajaj, "Fatal Fire Highlights the Dangers Facing Garment Workers," *New York Times*, November 25, 2012, B1.

57. Syed Zain Al-Mahmood and Tripti Lahiri, "Fire Warnings Went Unheard," *Wall Street Journal*, December 11, 2012, B1, B9.

58. Tripti Lahiri and Syed Zain Al-Mahmood, "Bangladesh: How Rules Went Astray," *Wall Street Journal*, December 6, 2012, B4.

59. Syed Zain Al-Mahmood and Kathy Chu, "After Fire, Pressure on Bangladesh," *Wall Street Journal*, December 15, 2012, B1, B4.

60. Steven Greenhouse, "Factory in Bangladesh Lost Fire Clearance before Blaze," *New York Times*, December 7, 2012, B1. See also Powell, *Out of Poverty*, 63.

61. Lahiri and Al-Mahmood, "Bangladesh: How Rules Went Astray," B1, B4.

62. Miguel Bustillo, Tom Wright, and Shelly Banjo, "Tough Questions in Fire's Ashes," *Wall Street Journal*, November 30, 2012, B1, B6.

63. Al-Mahmood and Lahiri, "Fire Warnings Went Unheard."

64. Syed Zain Al-Mahmood and Shelly Banjo, "Deadly Collapse," *Wall Street Journal*, April 25, 2013, A1, A10. See also Fairclough, "Factory Paychecks Trump Danger," A1, A11.

65. Syed Zain Al-Mahmood, Christina Passariello, and Preetika Rana, "The Global Garment Trail: From Bangladesh to a Mall Near You," *Wall Street Journal*, May 4–5, 2013, A1, A11. See also Suzanne Kapner and Shelly Banjo, "Before Dhaka Collapse, Some Firms Fled Risk," *Wall Street Journal*, May 3, 2013, A7.

66. Al-Mahmood et al., "The Global Garment Trail."

67. Ibid.

68. Kapner and Banjo, "Before Dhaka Collapse, Some Firms Fled Risk," A7.

69. Steven Greenhouse, "Some Retailers Rethink Roles in Bangladesh," *New York Times*, May 2, 2013, A1, A4.

70. Powell, *Out of Poverty*, 56.

71. Shelly Banjo and Suzanne Kapner, "Wal-Mart Crafts Own Bangladesh Safety Plan," *Wall Street Journal*, May 15, 2013, B1–B2.

72. Kamat, "Bangladesh's Factories Still Have Appalling Working Conditions."

73. Syed Zain Al-Mahmood, "Alliance to Help Bangladeshi Plants," *Wall Street Journal*, December 8, 2014, B3. See also Kamat, "Bangladesh's Factories Still Have Appalling Working Conditions."

74. Steven Greenhouse and Elizabeth Harris, "Battling for a Safer Bangladesh," *New York Times*, April 22, 2014, B1, B8.

75. Powell, *Out of Poverty*, 64.

76. Kathy Chu, "Tough Options for Apparel Retailers," *Wall Street Journal*, May 8, 2013, B1.

SELECTED BIBLIOGRAPHY

Abrams, Floyd. *The Soul of the First Amendment*. New Haven, CT: Yale University Press, 2017.

Allen, William T. "Our Schizophrenic Conception of the Business Corporation," *14 Cardozo Law Review* 261 (1992).

Andrews, Kenneth, ed. *Ethics in Practice: Managing the Moral Corporation*. Boston: Harvard Business Review Press, 1989.

Aquinas, St. Thomas. *Summa Theologiae* (Summary of Theology). 3 volumes. Translated by the Fathers of the English Dominican Province. New York: Benziger Bros., 1947–1948.

Aragon, George A. *Financial Ethics: A Positivist Analysis*. Oxford: Oxford University Press, 2010.

Aristotle. *Nichomachean Ethics*. In *The Complete Works of Aristotle*. 2 volumes. Edited by Jonathan Barnes. Princeton: Princeton University Press, 1984.

Barnet, Richard, and Ronald Muller. *Global Reach: The Power of Multinational Corporations*. New York: Simon & Schuster, 1974.

Barrera, Albino. *Market Complicity and Christian Ethics*. New York: Cambridge University Press, 2014.

Barrett, Paul. *Law of the Jungle*. New York: Broadway Books, 2014.

Baumol, William, Robert Litan, and Carl Schramm. *Good Capitalism, Bad Capitalism, and the Economics of Growth and Prosperity*. New Haven, CT: Yale University Press, 2007.

Bentham, Jeremy. *Introduction to the Principles of Morals and Legislation*. Oxford: Oxford University Press, 1907.

Bergin, Tom. *Spills and Spin: The Inside Story of BP*. New York: Random House, 2011.

Blair, Margaret, M. "Corporate Personhood and the Corporate Persona." 2013 *University of Illinois Law Review* 785 (2013).

Boatright, John. *Ethics in Finance*. Oxford: Blackwell, 1999.

Boebert, Earl, and James M. Blossom. *Deepwater Horizon: A Systems Analysis of the Macondo Disaster*. Cambridge, MA: Harvard University Press, 2016.

Bopp, James, Joseph LaRue, and Elizabeth Kosel. "The Game Changer: Citizens United's Impact on Campaign Finance Law." *9 First Amendment Law Review* 251 (2011).

Borgmann, Albert. *Crossing the Postmodern Divide*. Chicago: University of Chicago Press, 1983.

Bourdieu, Pierre. *Practical Reason: On the Theory of Action*. Stanford, CA: Stanford University Press, 1998.

Bowie, Norman. *Business Ethics: A Kantian Perspective*. Oxford: Blackwell, 1999.

Brandt, Allan M. *The Cigarette Century: The Rise, Fall, and Deadly Persistence of the Product that Defined America*. New York: Basic Books, 2007.

Brenkert, George, and Tom Beauchamp, eds. *The Oxford Handbook of Business Ethics*. Oxford: Oxford University Press, 2010.

Brinkley, Douglas. *Wheels for the World: Henry Ford, His Company, and a Century of Progress*. New York: Penguin Books, 2004.

Broadberry, Steven, and Kevin O'Rourke. *The Cambridge Economic History of Modern Europe*. Cambridge, UK: Cambridge University Press, 2010.

Budziszewski, J. *Commentary on Thomas Aquinas's Treatise on Law*. Cambridge, UK: Cambridge University Press, 2014.

Chan, Jenny, Ngai Pun, and Mark Selden, "The Politics of Global Production: Apple, Foxconn, and China's New Working Class." *New Technology, Work and Employment* 28, no. 2 (2013), 100–11.

Chandler, Alfred D. *Shaping the Industrial Century: The Remarkable Story of the Evolution of the Modern Chemical and Pharmaceutical Industries*. Cambridge, MA: Harvard University Press, 2005.

China Labor Watch. *Apple's Unkept Promises: Investigation of Three Pegatron Group Factories Supplying Apple*. Available at www.chinalaborwatch .org/report/68.

Clements, Jeffrey D. *Corporations are not People*, 2nd ed. San Francisco: Berrett-Koehler, 2014.

Cohan, William. *Why Wall Street Matters*. New York: Random House, 2017.

Cohen, Julie. "Between Truth and Power." In *Information, Freedom and Property*, edited by Mireille Hildebrandt, 57–80. New York: Routledge, 2016.

Colson, Charles, and N. Cameron, eds. *Human Dignity in the Biotech Century*. New York: Intervarsity Press, 2004.

Cullen, Francis T., William Maakestad, and Gray Cavender. *Corporate Crime under Attack*. Cincinnati: Anderson, 1987.

Dam, Kenneth. "The Economic Underpinnings of Patent Law," 241 *Journal of Legal Studies*, 23 (1994).

DeCew, Judith. *In Pursuit of Privacy: Law, Ethics, and the Rise of Technology*. Ithaca, NY: Cornell University Press, 1997.

DeGeorge, Richard. "Intellectual Property and Pharmaceutical Drugs: An Ethical Analysis," *Business Ethics Quarterly 15* (2005): 549–76.

DeGeorge, Richard. *Competing with Integrity in International Business*. New York: Oxford University Press, 1993.

De Soto, Hernando. *The Mystery of Capital*. New York: Basic Books, 2000.

Dodds, Susan, Lucy Frost, Robert Pargetter, and Elizabeth Prior. "Sexual Harassment." *Social Theory and Practice* (Summer 1988): 111–30.

Donaldson, Thomas. *The Ethics of International Business*. New York: Oxford University Press, 1989.

Donaldson, Thomas, and Thomas Dunfee. *Ties that Bind: A Social Contract Approach to Business Ethics*. Boston: Harvard Business School Press, 1999.

Dworkin, Ronald. *Taking Rights Seriously*. Cambridge, MA: Harvard University Press, 1977.

Eastman, Joel, W. *Styling Versus Safety: The American Automobile Industry and the Development of Automotive Safety 1900–1966*. Lanham, MD: University Press of America, 1984.

Enrich, David. *The Spider Network*. New York: Harper Collins, 2017.

Ewing, David. *Faster, Higher, Farther: The Volkswagen Scandal*. New York: W. W. Norton, 2017.

Feldman, Robin, and Evan Frondorf. *Drug Wars*. New York: Cambridge University Press, 2017.

Finnis, John. *Human Rights and the Common Good*. Oxford: Oxford University Press, 2011.

Finnis, John. *Natural Law and Natural Rights*. Oxford: Oxford University Press, 1980.

Finnis, John. *Reason in Action*. Oxford: Oxford University Press, 2011.

Fisman, Ray, and Tim Sullivan. *The Inner Lives of Markets*. New York: Public Affairs, 2016.

Food and Drug Administration. *Brochure: The History of Drug Regulation in the United States*. Available at http:// www.fda.gov/AboutFDA/WhatWeDo/History.

Frederick, Robert, and W. Michael Hoffman, "Environmental Risk Problems and the Language of Ethics." *Business Ethics Quarterly 5* (1995): 699–711.

Freeman, Edward, ed. *Business Ethics: State of the Art*. Oxford: Oxford University Press, 1991.

Freeman, Michael. *Human Rights*. Cambridge, UK: Polity Press, 2011.

Fried, Charles. "Privacy." 475 *Yale Law Journal* 77 (1968).

Frieden, Jeffrey. *Global Capitalism*. New York: W. W. Norton, 2005.

Friedman, Milton. *Capitalism and Freedom*. Chicago: University of Chicago Press, 1962.

Friedman, Milton. "The Social Responsibility of Business Is to Increase Its Profits." *New York Times Magazine*, September 13, 1970, 32–33, 122–26.

Galbraith, John Kenneth. *The New Industrial State*. New York: Signet Books, 1967, 1984.

Galloway, Scott. *The Four: The Hidden DNA of Amazon, Apple, Facebook, and Google*. New York: Penguin, 2017.

George, Robert. "Natural Law." 52 *American Journal of Jurisprudence 55* (2007).

Gert, Bernard. *Morality: Its Nature and Justification*. New York: Oxford University Press, 1998.

Ghemawat, Pankaj. "Distance Still Matters: The Hard Reality of Global Expansion." *Harvard Business Review*, September/October 2001, 138–52.

Giddens, Anthony. "The Globalizing of Modernity," in *The Global Transformations Reader: An Introduction to the Globalization Debate*, 2nd ed., edited by David Held and Anthony McGrew, 58–69. London: Wiley-Blackwell, 2003.

Goldberg, Lena. "Responsibilities to Customers." Boston: Harvard Business School, 2014.

Goldsmith, Jack, and Tim Wu. *Who Controls the Internet?* Oxford: Oxford University Press, 2006.

Goodpaster, Kenneth E. *Conscience and Corporate Culture*. Oxford: Blackwell, 2007.

Goodpaster, Kenneth E. "Business Ethics and Stakeholder Analysis." *Business Ethics Quarterly* 1, no. 1 (1991), 53–73.

Green, Stuart P. *Lying, Cheating and Stealing: A Moral Theory of White-Collar Crime*. Oxford: Oxford University Press, 2006.

Grisez, Germain. *Living a Christian Life*. Quincy, IL: Franciscan Press, 1993.

Grisez, Germain. *Difficult Moral Questions*. Quincy, IL: Franciscan Press, 1997.

Halberstam, David. *The Reckoning*. New York: William Morrow, 1986.

Handy, Charles. "What's a Business For?" *Harvard Business Review*, November/December 2002, 3–8.

Hart, H. L. "Bentham on Legal Rights." In *Oxford Essays in Jurisprudence: Second Series*, edited by A. Simpson, 211–39. Oxford: Oxford University Press, 1971.

Hart, H. L. "The Separation of Law and Morals," 71 *Harvard Law Review* 593 (1958).

Hayek, Friedrich. *The Road to Serfdom*. Chicago: University of Chicago Press, 2007.

"Here, There, and Everywhere: Outsourcing and Offshoring." *The Economist*, January 19, 2013, Special Report.

Heilemann, John. *Pride before the Fall*. New York: Harper Collins, 2001.

Henderson, Rebecca, and Karthik Ramana. "Managers and Market Capitalism." Boston: Harvard Business School, 2014.

Hobbes, Thomas. *Leviathan*, edited by Michael Oakeshott. New York: Collier Books, 1962.

House of Commons Treasury Committee. *Fixing LIBOR: Some Preliminary Findings*. London: House of Commons, 2012.

Hunt, Lynn. *Writing History in the Global Era*. New York: W. W. Norton, 2014.

Hutt, Peter Barton. "Drug Regulation in the United States." *International Journal of Technology Assessment in Health Care* 2 (1986): 619–28.

"Internet Monopolies: Everybody Wants to Rule the World." *The Economist*, November 29, 2014, 19–22.

Jackson, Kevin. "Distributive Justice and the Corporate Duty to Aid." *Journal of Business Ethics* 12 (1993): 547–51.

Jacobs, Daniel. *BP Blowout: Inside the Gulf Oil Disaster*. Washington, DC: Brookings Institute Press, 2016.

Jamieson, Dale. *Ethics and the Environment: An Introduction*. Cambridge, UK: Cambridge University Press, 2008.

Jenner & Block. *Report to Board of Directors of General Motors Company Regarding Ignition Switch Recalls*. Detroit: General Motors, 2014.

Johnson, Paul. "The Capitalism and Morality Debate." *First Things*, March 1990, 32–36.

Jones, Geoffrey. *Multinationals and Global Capitalism*. Oxford: Oxford University Press, 2005.

Kant, Immanuel. *Foundations of the Metaphysics of Morals*. New York: MacMillan, 1990.

Kao, Grace. *Grounding Human Rights in a Pluralist World*. Washington, DC: Georgetown University Press, 2011.

Kimberling, Judith. *Amazon Crude*. Washington, DC: National Resources Defense Council, 1991.

Kline, John. *Ethics for International Business*, 2nd ed. New York: Routledge, 2010.

Kluger, Richard. *Ashes to Ashes: America's Hundred Years Cigarette War, the Public Health, and the Unabashed Triumph of Philip Morris*. New York: Knopf, 2008.

Koeppel, Dan. *Banana: The Fate of the Fruit That Changed the World*. New York: Penguin Group, 2008.

Korsgaard, Christine. *Creating the Kingdom of Ends*. Cambridge, UK: Cambridge University Press, 1996.

Ladd, John. *Ethical Relativism*. New York: Wadsworth, 1973.

Landau, Susan. *Surveillance or Security*. Cambridge, MA: MIT Press, 2011.

Lemov, Michael R. *Car Safety Wars: One Hundred Years of Technology, Politics, and Death*. Madison: Farleigh Dickinson University Press, 2015.

Lever, Annabelle, ed. *New Frontiers in the Philosophy of Intellectual Property*. Cambridge, UK: Cambridge University Press, 2012.

Levine, Adeline. *Love Canal: Science, Politics and People*. Lexington, MA: D. C. Heath, 1982.

Levy, Steven. *Crypto*. New York: Viking, 2001.

Lewis, Michael. *The Big Short: Inside the Doomsday Machine*. New York: W. W. Norton, 2010.

Litvin, Daniel. *Empires of Profit*. New York: Texere, 2003.

Llewellyn, Karl. *The Bramble Bush: Classic Lectures on Law and the Law School*. Oxford: Oxford University Press, 2008.

Locke, John. *Two Treatises of Government* edited by Peter Laslett. Cambridge, UK: Cambridge University Press, 1988.

Maccoby, Michael. "The Corporate Climber Has to Find His Heart." *Fortune*, December 1976, 100–104.

Machiavelli, Niccolo. *The Prince*. Translated by George Bull. New York: Penguin Books, 1975.

MacIntyre, Alsadair. *After Virtue*. Notre Dame, IN: Notre Dame University Press, 1984.

Maddison, Angus. *The World Economy: A Millennial Perspective*. Paris: Development Center of the Organization for Economic Cooperation and Development, 2001.

Manne, Henry. *Insider Trading and the Stock Market*. New York: Free Press, 1998.

Mayer, Carl, J. "Personalizing the Impersonal: Corporations and the Bill of Rights," 41 *Hastings Law Journal* 577 (1990).

Mayer, Colin. *Firm Commitment*. Oxford: Oxford University Press, 2013.

McGowan, David. "Copyright Nonconsequentialism." 69 *Missouri Law Review* 1, 2004.

McKenzie, Richard. *Trust on Trial*. Cambridge, MA: Perseus, 2000.

Merchant, Brian. *The One Device: The Secret History of the iPhone*. New York: Little, Brown, 2017.

Merges, Robert. *Justifying Intellectual Property*. Cambridge, MA: Harvard University Press, 2011.

Midgley, Mary. *Heart and Mind*. New York: St. Martin's Press, 1981.

Milanovic, Branko. *Global Inequality: A New Approach for the Age of Globalization*. Cambridge, MA: Harvard University Press, 2016.

Miles, Robert H. *Coffin Nails and Corporate Strategies*. Englewood Cliffs, NJ: Prentice Hall, 1982.

Miller, T. Christian, and Jonathan Jones, "Firestone and the Warlord: The Untold Story of Firestone, Charles Taylor, and the Tragedy of Liberia." *ProPublica*, November 2014. Available at http://www.propublica.org/firestone-and-the-warlord.

Moor, James. "Just Consequentialism and Computing." In *Readings in Cyberethics*, edited by Richard Spinello and Herman Tavani, 98–104. Sudbury, MA: Jones & Bartlett, 2001.

Moor, James. "Towards a Theory of Privacy in the Information Age." *Computers and Society*, *27* (1997): 27–32.

Muchlinski, Peter. *Multinational Enterprises and the Law*. Oxford: Oxford University Press, 1995.

Nader, Ralph. *Unsafe at Any Speed: The Designed-In Dangers of the American Automobile*. New York: Bantam Books, 1972.

Newman, Richard. *Love Canal: A Toxic History from Colonial Times to the Present*. Oxford: Oxford University Press, 2016.

Newman, Richard, and Daniel Payne, eds. *Palgrave Environmental Reader*. New York: Palgrave MacMillan, 2005.

Nickel, James. *Making Sense of Human Rights: Philosophical Reflections on the Universal Declaration of Human Rights*. Berkeley: University of California Press, 1987.

Nissenbaum, Helen. *Privacy in Context*. Stanford, CA: Stanford University Press, 2010.

Nissenbaum, Helen. "Respect for Privacy as a Benchmark for Privacy Online." In *Privacy, Security and Accountability*, edited by Adam Moore, 39–62. Lanham, MD: Rowman & Littlefield, 2016.

Noonan, John T. *Bribes: The Intellectual History of a Moral Idea*. Berkeley: University of California Press, 1987.

Novak, Michal, and Paul Adams. *Social Justice Isn't What You Think It Is*. New York: Encounter Books, 2015.

Nussbaum, Bruce. *Good Intentions: How Big Business and the Medical Establishment Are Corrupting the Fight against AIDS*. New York: Atlantic Monthly Press, 1990.

O'Brien, David. "Privacy and Cybersecurity." Cambridge, MA: Berkman Center for Internet and Society, Harvard University, 2016.

Oderberg, David. *Moral Theory*. Oxford: Blackwell, 2000.

Okun, Arthur. *Equality and Efficiency*. Washington, DC: Brookings Institute, 1975.

Olsen, Darcy. *The Right to Try*. New York: Harper, 2016.

Olsen, Matt, Bruce Schneir, and Jonathan Zittrain. *Don't Panic. Making Progress in the "Going Dark" Debate*. Cambridge, MA: Berkman Center for Internet and Society, Harvard University, 2016.

Orts, Eric, and N. Craig Smith, eds. *The Moral Responsibility of Firms*. Oxford: Oxford University Press, 2017.

Paine, Lynn Sharp. "Ideals of Competition and Today's Marketplace." In *Enriching Business Ethics*, edited by Clarence Walton, 91–112. New York: Plenum Press, 1990.

Paine, Lynn Sharp. "Managing for Organizational Integrity." *Harvard Business Review*, March/April 1994, 106–17.

Paine, Lynn Sharp. "Moral Thinking in Management: An Essential Capability." *Business Ethics Quarterly* 6 (1996): 477–92.

Paine, Lynn Sharp. *Value Shift*. New York: McGraw-Hill, 2003.

Paine, Lynn Sharp, Rohit Deshpandé, and Joshua Margolis. "Up to Code: Does Your Company's Conduct Meet World-Class Standards?" *Harvard Business Review*, November/December 2005, 31–39.

Pasquale, Frank. *The Black Box Society: The Secret Algorithms That Control Money and Information*. Cambridge, MA: Harvard University Press, 2015.

Patrick, Kenneth. *Perpetual Jeopardy: The Texas Gulf Sulphur Affair*. New York: Macmillan, 1972.

Piketty, Thomas. *Capital in the Twenty-First Century*. Cambridge, MA: Harvard University Press, 2014.

Pollman, Elizabeth. "Reconceiving Corporate Personhood," 28 *Utah Law Review* 1629 (2011).

Porter, Michael, and M. R. Kramer. "Creating Shared Value." *Harvard Business Review*, January/February 2011, 59–68.

Powell, Benjamin. *Out of Poverty: Sweatshops in the Global Economy*. New York: Cambridge University Press, 2014.

Rawls John. *A Theory of Justice*. Cambridge, MA: Harvard University Press, 1971.

Rawls, John. *The Law of Peoples.* Cambridge, MA: Harvard University Press, 1999.

Redwood, Heinz. *The Pharmaceutical Industry: Trends, Problems, and Achievements.* Felixstone, UK: Oldwicks Press, 1987.

Regan, Tom, ed. *Just Business: New Introductory Essays in Business Ethics.* New York: Random House, 1984.

Richards, Jay. *Environmental Stewardship.* Grand Rapids, MI: Acton Institute, 2007.

Roberts, John. *The Modern Firm.* Oxford: Oxford University Press, 2004.

Rosen, William. *Miracle Cure.* New York: Viking, 2017.

Sampson, Anthony. *The Sovereign State of ITT.* New York: Stein & Day, 1973.

Sandel, Michael. *Justice.* New York: Farrar, Straus, and Giroux, 2009.

Sanford, Jonathan. *Before Virtue: Assessing Contemporary Virtue Ethics.* Washington, DC: Catholic University of America Press, 2015.

Santoro, Michael, and Thomas Gorrie, eds. *Ethics and the Pharmaceutical Industry.* New York: Cambridge University Press, 2005.

Schartzman, Micah, ed. *The Rise of Corporate Religious Liberty.* Oxford: Oxford University Press, 2016.

Scruton, Roger. "Corporate Persons." *Proceedings of the Aristotelian Society* Supplement 63 (1989): 239–66.

Scruton, Roger. *How to Think Seriously about the Planet: The Case for Environmental Conservatism.* Oxford: Oxford University Press, 2012.

Seagrave, S. Adam. *The Foundations of Natural Morality.* Chicago: University of Chicago Press, 2014.

Sepinwall, Amy. "Conscience and Complicity: Assessing Pleas for Religious Exemptions in *Hobby Lobby*'s Wake." 82 *University of Chicago Law Review* 101 (2016).

Shaw, William, ed. *Ethics at Work.* New York: Oxford University Press, 2012.

Shue, Henry. *Basic Rights: Subsistence, Affluence, and U.S. Foreign Policy*, 2nd ed. Princeton, NJ: Princeton University Press, 1996.

Sigmund, Paul. *The Overthrow of Allende and the Politics of Chile.* Pittsburgh, PA: University of Pittsburgh Press, 1977.

Singer, P. W., and Allan Friedman. *Cybersecurity and Cyberwar.* New York: Oxford University Press, 2014.

Slote, Michael. *Morals from Motives.* Oxford: Oxford University Press, 2001.

Smith, Adam. *An Inquiry into the Nature and Causes of the Wealth of Nations.* Oxford: Oxford University Press, 1976.

Sobel, Robert. *They Satisfy: The Cigarette in American Life.* Garden City, NY: Anchor Books, 1978.

Solove, Daniel. *Understanding Privacy.* Cambridge, MA: Harvard University Press, 2008.

Soltes, Eugene. *Why They Do It.* New York: Public Affairs, 2016.

Spar, Deborah. "The Spotlight Effect and the Bottom Line." *Foreign Affairs* 77 (1998): 7–12.

Spinello, Richard. *Cyberethics: Morality and Law in Cyberspace.* 6th ed. Sudbury, MA: Jones & Bartlett, 2017.

Spinello, Richard. *Global Capitalism, Culture and Ethics.* New York: Routledge, 2013.

Spinello, Richard, and Maria Bottis. *A Defense of Intellectual Property Rights.* Cheltenham, UK: Edward Elgar, 2009.

Stone, Christopher. *Where the Law Ends: The Social Control of Corporate Behavior.* New York: Harper & Row, 1975.

Strauss, Leo. *Natural Right and History.* Chicago: University of Chicago Press, 1950.

Sucher, Sandra, Elena Green, and David Rosales. "Layoffs: Effects on Key Stakeholders." Boston: Harvard Business School, 2014.

Sutton, Anthony C. *Wall Street and the Rise of Hitler.* San Pedro, CA: GSG & Associates, 2002.

Talbot, William. *Which Rights Should Be Universal?* New York: Oxford University Press, 2005.

Tavani, Herman. "Philosophical Theories of Privacy: Implications for an Adequate Online Privacy Policy." *Metaphilosophy* 38 (2007): 9–22.

Tavani, Herman, and Jim Moor. "Privacy Protection, Control of Information, and Privacy-Enhancing Technologies." *Computers and Society* 31 (2001): 6–11.

Temin, Peter. *Taking Your Medicine: Drug Regulation in the United States*. Cambridge, MA: Harvard University Press, 1980.

Tennant, Richard. *The American Cigarette Industry*. New Haven, CT: Yale University Press, 1950.

Thompson, Judith. "The Right to Privacy." *Philosophy and Public Affairs 4* (1975): 281–95.

Tomasi, John. *Free Market Fairness*. Princeton, NJ: Princeton University Press, 2012.

United Nations Charter. "The Universal Declaration of Human Rights." In *Moral Philosophy for Managers*, 5th ed., edited by Richard Spinello, 293–97. New York: McGraw-Hill, 2008.

United States Senate Subcommittee on Multinational Corporations. *The International Telephone and Telegraph Company and Chile, 1970–1971, Report to the Committee on Foreign Relations*. Washington, DC: U.S. Senate, June 21, 1973.

Vaidhyanathan, Sethi. *The Googlization of Everything*. Berkeley: University of California Press, 2010.

Velasquez, Manuel. "Debunking Corporate Moral Responsibility." *Business Ethics Quarterly* 13 (2003): 531–62.

Vincent, R. J. *Human Rights and International Relations*. New York: Cambridge University Press, 1998.

Vogel, David. *The Market for Virtue: The Potential and Limits of Corporate Social Responsibility*. Washington, DC: Brookings Institute, 2005.

Wallach, Wendell. *A Dangerous Master: How to Keep Technology from Slipping beyond Our Control*. New York: Basic Books, 2015.

Walton, Clarence. *Corporate Encounters: Ethics, Law, & the Business Environment*. Fort Worth, TX: Dryden Press, 1992.

Wartick, Steven, and Donna Woods. *International Business and Society*. Oxford: Blackwell, 1998.

Wartzman, Rick. *The End of Loyalty*. New York: Public Affairs, 2017.

Wenar, Leif. *Blood Oil: Tyrants, Violence and the Rules That Run the World*. Oxford: Oxford University Press, 2016.

Werhane, Patricia H. *Persons, Rights, and Corporations*. Englewood Cliffs, NJ: Prentice Hall, 1985.

Werhane, Patricia H., and Michael Gorman. "Intellectual Property Rights, Moral Imagination, and Access to Life-Enhancing Drugs." *Business Ethics Quarterly* 15 (2005): 604–15.

Westin, Alan. *Privacy and Freedom*. New York: Atheneum, 1967.

Wilkins, Mira. *The Maturing of Multinational Enterprise: American Business Abroad from 1914 to 1970*. Cambridge, MA: Harvard University Press, 1974.

Williams, Oliver, ed. *Ethics and the Investment Industry*. Savage, MD: Rowman & Littlefield, 1989.

Winkler, Adam. *We the Corporations*. New York: W. W. Norton, 2018.

Winner, Langdon. *Autonomous Technology: Technics Out-of-Control as a Theme in Political Thought*. Cambridge, MA: MIT Press, 1978.

Wolf, Martin. *Why Globalization Works*. New Haven, CT: Yale University Press, 2004.

Wright, J. Patrick. *On a Clear Day You Can See General Motors: John Z. DeLorean's Look inside the Automotive Giant*. New York: Avon Books, 1980.

Zaheer, S. "Overcoming the Liability of Foreignness." *Academy of Management Journal* 38 (1995): 341–63.

Zeadally, Sherali, and Mohamad Badra, eds. *Privacy in a Digital, Networked World*. Dordrecht, Netherlands: Springer, 2015.

Zycher, B., and DiMasi, J. "The Truth about Drug Innovation." New York: Manhattan Institute for Policy Research, 2006. Available at http://www.manhattan-institute-org/htm/mpr_06.

INDEX

NOTE: Page references with exhibits, figures, and tables are marked as (exhibit), (fig.), and (table), respectively.